THE BRITISH
WOOL MANUAL

MICROGRAPHS OF

WOOL STRUCTURES

ILLUSTRATIONS OF

WOOL TEXTILE
MACHINERY

The transverse section of lamb's wool shown in Plate I was treated with 2 per cent phosphotungstic acid in 50 per cent aqueous ethanol at pH3 for two hours. The magnification is 4200 diameters reduced to 2400 diameters in reproduction.

The transverse section of a Lincoln wool fibre shown in Plate 2 was set in water and reduced with thioglycollate and then treated with OsO_4. The magnification of 120,000 diameters has been reduced to 60,000 diameters in reproduction.

The transverse section of $\propto$-keratin shown in Plate 3 was reduced with thioglycollate and treated with OsO_4. The magnification (820,000 diameters) has been reduced to 550,000 diameters in reproduction.

The protofibrils of merino wool shown in Plate 4 had an original magnification of 400,000 diameters, reduced to 200,000 in reproduction.

THE BRITISH
WOOL MANUAL

Edited by

H. SPIBEY,

C.B.E., M.SC.TECH.

formerly H.M. Staff Inspector (Textiles)
Department of Education and Science, London
Honorary Fellow University of Leeds,
Member of the Platt Mission to report on
Productivity in the American Textile Industry

COLUMBINE PRESS

FOREWORD

The British Wool Manual was first published in 1952 with the object of providing an authoritative work on the wool textile industry which would serve the dual function of a text book for students and a work of reference for those actively engaged in the industry. Since that time, however, the industry, faced with the ubiquitous demand for increased productivity and the added necessity of adapting itself to meet the specialized requirements imposed by the ever-increasing use of man-made fibres, has undergone many changes. Traditional processes have had to be modified, new materials and techniques introduced and advantage taken of developments in the design, lay-out and control of plant and equipment.

The industry's post-war development has been reflected in the extensive revision necessary to bring the British Wool Manual up to date. In fact, this Second Edition is virtually a new book. No less than nine of the thirteen sections comprising the subject matter—including those chapters relating to woollen and worsted yarn manufacture and the dyeing of wool and wool unions—have been largely rewritten, while the remaining four have been subject to considerable revision and the addition of new matter.

The whole of the work has been undertaken by a team of specialists, each a recognized authority in his respective subject, and it is important that due acknowledgement should be made here to the contributions of, and the valuable co-operation which the Editor has received from, the following well known textile technologists.

J. W. Bell, PH.D., F.T.I., University of Leeds.
C. L. Bird, M.SC., F.R.I.C., F.S.D.C., University of Leeds.
J. C. H. Hurd, F.T.I., formerly Leicester Regional College of Technology.
J. B. Lancashire, F.T.I., formerly Leicester Regional College of Technology.
H. Lemon, formerly Wool Industries Research Association.
G. Marshall, F.T.I., formerly Carding Specialists Co. Ltd.
E. Oxtoby, M.SC., F.T.I., Leicester Regional College of Technology.
Professor A. Robson, PH.D., A.R.I.C., F.T.I., University of Leeds.
C. B. Stevens, PH.D., F.S.D.C., University of Leeds
P. P. Townend, PH.D., F.T.I., University of Leeds.
G. Waggett, M.SC., A.T.I., Courtaulds Ltd.
Professor C. S. Whewell, PH.D., F.R.I.C., F.T.I., F.S.D.C., University of Leeds.

In addition, acknowledgement must be made to the generous assistance rendered by numerous firms in loaning the drawings and photographs which have made adequate illustration of the book possible.

A new and larger format has been adopted and within the five-hundred or so pages which the book contains every effort has been made to provide adequate coverage of the many phases of this diverse and complicated industry. In this respect it should serve as a useful technical background against which to study and assess the recommendations of the recently issued H.M.S.O. report on "The Strategic Future of the Wool Textile Industry", as well as fulfil the requirements of a text book and work of reference.

It is confidently hoped therefore that, at least for several years to come, this Second Edition of "The British Wool Manual" will maintain the tradition set by its predecessor and again be recognized as a concise, up-to-date and authoritative work on the wool textile industry.

HORACE SPIBEY,
Editor.

August, 1969.

CONTENTS

CONTENTS

LIST OF PLATES

SECTION ONE

SHEEP AND THEIR WOOL

IT IS GENERALLY BELIEVED that the origin of all existing breeds of domestic sheep is to be found in three main types of wild sheep[1], namely, the Mouflon (*ovis musimon*), the Argali (*ovis ammon*) and the Urial (*ovis vignei* or *orientalis*). Another type of wild sheep is the Bighorn (*ovis canadensis*), the wild sheep of the Rocky Mountains, but it is doubtful whether this animal has any connection with domestic breeds.

The Mouflon once ranged over South-Eastern Europe, North Africa and Mesopotamia, and still exists in the Mediterranean area. The ram has long curving horns, somewhat similar to those of the ibex, but the ewe may be hornless or have small upright horns. The Argali is still to be found in Asia, from Bokhara in the west to Kamchatka in the east. It was also known to the Ancient Egyptians. Its horns curve backwards and then down and forwards like those seen in representations of the sheep-headed god Ammon. Marco Polo met one type of Argali high in the Pamir plains on his journey to the court of Kublai Khan, and it was named after him, *ovis poli*. The Urial was the wild sheep of Persia, Afghanistan, India and Tibet, and it still lives in that area, being found at various altitudes from about 14,000 ft. in Tibet to a few hundred feet in the Punjab. The horns are similar to those of the Mouflon.

Fat-tailed and Long-tailed Sheep: In the wild state these sheep are essentially of the mountain type, in that their fleeces consist of a fine soft inner coat protected by a coarse hairy outer coat. In domestication the fleeces have become modified in various ways. In the main these modifications have been brought about by man, but, in addition, some natural developments have resulted from changes of environment.

The Asiatic fat-rumped sheep, and the fat-tailed sheep originally to be found in the Gobi Desert and which migrated to Arabia and Africa, exemplify a natural modification which has been accentuated by some breeders. The fat rump or tail provides a reserve of fat without which the animal could not exist in desert regions.

A broad-tailed sheep which is still of some importance is the Karakul, bred in South-West Africa and California. This ancient Persian breed was referred to a thousand years ago by an Arab geographer as "the Black Roses of Bokhara". Persian lamb skin, so called, is produced from Karakul lambs, which have to be killed when they are only two or three days old, before the tightly-curled black or grey ringlets of wool begin to open out.

EARLY BRITISH SHEEP

European domestic breeds are believed to have descended mostly from the wild Mouflon, but it is possible that they also owe something to the Urial. Fortunately there still exists a breed which is thought to be similar to the sheep which neolithic farmers brought to Britain in about 3,000–2,500 B.C. This breed, the Soay – sometimes known as Viking Sheep – lives in a perfectly wild state on the St. Kilda group of islands, forty miles west of the Outer Hebrides, where it has remained as a pure breed for many hundreds of years, probably having been brought there originally by the Vikings.

Soay sheep are of a chocolate colour, with some cream on the belly and face; the wool is mostly short and hairy, but there are some fine fibres. The rams have horns sweeping back like those of the Mouflon, while those of the ewes are shorter. Evidence for prehistoric sheep in Britain having been of the Soay type is given by skeletal remains at archeological sites. Similar evidence, and examination of parchments made from sheep skin, indicate that this type of sheep was still common in Britain in the Middle Ages[2].

The Romans during their occupation of Britain no doubt brought some of their own sheep to improve the native stock, but there is very little definite information about the types of sheep and qualities of wool grown in Britain during this period, the Middle Ages, and indeed for some time after. It was not until the last part of the 18th century that agricultural writers began to give useful information about the different breeds of sheep and their wool; and by that time breeding developments had resulted in many changes.

During the Middle Ages the sheep farmers in Britain were mainly the Cistercian monks and other large land owners, but there were also many small tenant farmers. There would seem to have been two main types of sheep at that time – small mountain sheep which thrived on hills and moorlands, and a larger type which was more suited to the richer grasslands[3].

The former was the 'heath' type, the black-faced breed generally considered to be the ancestor of the Scottish Blackface, the Rough Fell, the Swaledale and similar breeds. Typical of the larger, lowland sheep were the Lincoln, Leicester and Cotswold.

There is much conflicting evidence regarding the length and fineness of medieval wools. In the early Middle Ages the majority of the wool grown in Britain was probably short and fine. Then, as suggested by Bowden[4] in "The Wool Trade in Tudor and Stuart England", the increase of enclosed pasture farming which took place from the mid-15th century onwards provided improved grassland feeding for sheep, and the predominantly short and fine medieval wool was gradually replaced by a longer and coarser staple.

The small, hill sheep produced short wool suitable for carding, and the larger sheep longer wool suitable for combing. The Ryeland was famed for its short fine wool ('Lemster Ore') and yet it was a hill type. Nevertheless, the bulk of the so-called 'long, fine wool' exported during the Middle Ages came from the Cotswold and Lincoln breeds. It should be borne in mind, however, that the Lincoln of those times undoubtedly had shorter and finer wool than it has today. Moreover, it should also be remembered that in those days combing was done by hand, and the wool had to be longer than the short-stapled fine wool used for machine combing today. Such wools as Lincoln and Cotswold were long enough for hand combing, and yet reasonably fine, and thus suitable for processing into light worsteds.

The 18th century was a period of progress in sheep breeding, though the aim was often to improve the mutton rather than the wool. Robert Bakewell showed how an improvement could result from the mating of closely related animals and he was instrumental in establishing the new Leicester breed of long-wool sheep. John Ellman will always be remembered for his work on the Southdown breed.

By 1800 there were about twenty different sheep breeds in Britain which had gradually evolved in different environments and as a result of cross-breeding. These sheep can be grouped into four main types, namely (i) the black-faced, horned, hill type descended from the 'heath', (ii) the white-faced, horned, hill type such as the Shetland, Cheviot, Welsh Mountain, Exmoor Horn and Dorset Horn, (iii) the lustre long-wool breeds such as the Lincoln, Leicester and Cotswold, and (iv) the fine, short-wool breeds, — the Ryeland in the marches of Wales, and the Southdown on the Sussex Downs. Many of the other Down breeds are of comparatively recent origin, and at some stage of their development Southdown blood has been introduced.

At the present time there are between thirty and forty recognized sheep breeds in Great Britain, some of which are used as foundation stock all over the world.

BRITISH SHEEP AND THEIR WOOL

THE MAGNITUDE of the British sheep and wool growing industry and its value to this country are not always appreciated. Some revealing figures will be found in the results of the Twentieth Wool Questionnaire for 1965/66, prepared by the Commodities Division of the Commonwealth Secretariat, the International Wool Textile Organisation and the International Wool Study Group. The provisional estimated figures for 'woolled sheep population', in millions, are 157·6 for Australia, which of course is the world's largest sheep and wool producer, 57·3 for New Zealand, and 30·0 for the United Kingdom[5]. This figure of 30·0 is in fact not far short of that for South Africa (38·0) which is recognized as an important wool producing country. Raw wool production figures (from the same source) for 1966/67 for the above countries are (million lb. greasy basis): Australia 1,712; New Zealand 715; South Africa 308; and the United Kingdom 129.

CLASSIFICATION OF BRITISH SHEEP AND WOOL

The large number of quite distinct breeds of sheep in the British Isles is explained partly by the large variety of types of country, soil and grazing. Before any breeding policies were undertaken, these factors had already led to the development of many local types of sheep. It is possible to classify these sheep [6,7,8] in several different ways, but in the wool textile industry their wools are grouped under four headings: (*i*) Lustre (or Long); (*ii*) Demi-lustre; (*iii*) Down; and (*iv*) Mountain. This classification is arbitrary and differences of opinion may be held regarding certain sheep and their wool. For example, both Border Leicester and Romney Marsh may be classed as Lustre or Demi-lustre, while the Shetland is usually classed as a mountain breed although it bears the finest wool grown in the British Isles.

Apart from the above classification, wool is grouped internationally into three types in terms of Bradford quality. A widely accepted division, published by the Commonwealth Economic Committee in 1965, is: Merino – 60s and upwards; Crossbred – 46s to 58s, and Carpet – Up to 44s.

The British clip is also divided into three categories according to the age of the animal:

Lamb – Shorn from the lamb.

Hog (or *Teg*) – Wool from a yearling that was not shorn as a lamb (there is a tendency to use teg for the finer wools).

Wether (or *Ewe*) – Wool from second and subsequent shearings. (Note: a wether is a castrated male.)

Reference has been made above to the grouping of wools by the wool textile industry into four main classes and a few notes regarding these specific types may be useful.

LUSTRE WOOL

Most of the long-wool British sheep probably owe something in their development to the Lincoln, which is a very old breed. Many British half-breds have been produced by means of the Lincoln ram, which was also used in establishing the Corriedale in New Zealand and the Polwarth in Australia. The Leicester was bred from the old type of Leicester by Robert Bakewell in about 1755-1760, and was sometimes known as the Dishley. It has been used to improve many British breeds, and also to develop some of the cross-breeds in the Dominions. Another interesting long-wool breed is the Wensleydale, which was developed about a hundred years ago by crossing ewes of the ancient Teeswater breed with a Leicester ram. The Wensleydale is now used for crossing with the Scottish Blackface to produce the Masham ('Massam'), a useful breeding ewe.

The chief attributes of lustre wools are their length, strength and lustre. They are used for furnishings, linings, bunting, bootlaces, mechanical cloths and roller lappings. Further details are given in Table 1.1.

TABLE 1.1. LUSTRE WOOL — AVERAGE QUALITY OF FLEECE 36-44s

Breed	Wool	Particular Uses
Lincoln	Longest lustre wool. Staple slightly wavy. Very heavy fleece.	Bunting, bootlaces, linings, roller lappings.
Leicester ('Lester')	Less lustrous and not so long as Lincoln; slightly finer.	Braids, bunting, linings, serges.
Devon Longwool	Hangs in long curly locks. Firm handle; hard wearing.	Carpet blends, bunting, linings, mechanical cloths.
Wensleydale	Long ringlet staple resembling mohair. Very lustrous. (Known as 'Ripon Wool').	Linings, lustre yarns, tweeds.

DEMI-LUSTRE WOOL

The ram of the Border Leicester is important for cross-breeding. Crossed with the Cheviot it produces the Half-bred; crossed with the Scottish Blackface it produces the Greyface. The Romney Marsh, a very old breed, was improved by crossing with the (New) Leicester. It grazes on the rich pastures of the marshes all the year round, and is noted for its resistance to foot rot and liver fluke. It has become acclimatized to many parts of the world: New Zealand, Australia, South America, the Falkland Islands, East Africa, Russia and other countries. The Romney Marsh breed of sheep is, in fact, an important British export.

Demi-lustre wools are lustrous but not as long as the Lustres, and they have a somewhat crisp handle. Further details are given in Table 1.2.

TABLE 1.2. DEMI-LUSTRE WOOL—AVERAGE QUALITY OF FLEECE 46-50s

Breed	Wool	Particular Uses
Border Leicester	Finer and shorter than Leicester.	Moquettes.
Romney Marsh	Quality fine for length. Somewhat similar to Leicester.	Hosiery, knitting yarns, moquettes, papermakers' felts.

DOWN WOOL

The Southdown is a very pure breed, having been developed by means of selection within the breed rather than by cross-breeding. It has been used extensively in the evolution of other Down breeds. The Shropshire Down is essentially a dual-purpose breed, but it produces a heavy clip of fine wool having a good yield; it is not so fine as Southdown but is longer. It has been exported to many parts of the world, and thrives in remarkably diverse climates and conditions. The Suffolk Down is now widely dispersed throughout England and Scotland. It is first and foremost a mutton breed, and is used for crossing with the Scottish half-bred and others to produce fat lamb. Suffolk is nevertheless a good hosiery wool. The Hampshire Down has also made itself at home all over the world, being able to adapt itself to very variable condition and climates.

Down wools are used mainly for hosiery, knitting yarns, fine woollens, papermakers' felts, tweeds and blankets. Further details are given in Table 1.3.

TABLE 1.3. DOWN WOOL—AVERAGE QUALITY OF FLEECE 48-56s

Breed	Wool	Particular Uses
Southdown	Finest English wool.	Speciality felts, fine woollens, hosiery, flannels, soft handling tweeds.
Dorset Down	Fine quality.	Papermakers' felts, tweeds.
Suffolk Down	Crisp soft handle and curly staple. Some dark fibres.	Hosiery, knitting yarns, tweeds.
Hampshire Down	Moderate length. Fine.	Hosiery, tweeds.
Oxford Down	Longer than other Downs. More open fleece.	Hosiery, knitting yarns, tweeds.
Shropshire Down	Good yield. Regular in quality.	Hosiery, knitting yarns, papermakers' felts, tweeds.
Dorset Horn	Very white and free from dark fibres. Crisper than Dorset Down.	Hosiery, knitting yarns, papermakers' felts, piano felts, tweeds.
Ryeland	Very soft handle. Dense. Very uniform in quality. Free from dark fibres.	Hosiery, knitting yarns, felts.
Kerry Hill	Firm and springy. Even growth. Very white. Free from dark fibres.	Hosiery, knitting yarns.
Clun Forest	Short. Often fine.	Hosiery, knitting yarns, felts.
Devon Closewool	Fair length. Medium lustre. Good handle. Regular in quality.	Hosiery.
Radnor	Some kemp and dark fibres.	Hosiery, knitting yarns.

MOUNTAIN WOOL

The mountain breeds are the greatest numerically in the United Kingdom, and are extremely important as the basis of healthy crossing stock for fat lambs. The hill farmer tends to breed a sheep with the right type of fleece for withstanding local weather conditions. Thus, in a particularly rainy district the emphasis will be on a fleece that sheds rain well. Although the value of the fleece to the wool industry is not overlooked, this certainly takes second place to its value as a protective coat for the living animal. Unlike many other British sheep, the mountain types have not been acclimatized very successfully to conditions abroad, even in hilly districts. A brief classification of mountain breeds, their wool and its uses is given below.

TABLE 1.4. MOUNTAIN WOOL—AVERAGE QUALITY OF FLEECE 28-40s

Breed	Wool	Particular Uses
Scottish Blackface	Coarse, long, often kempy.	Mattresses, carpets, tweeds.
Lonk	Various. Very white. Good handle.	Carpets, tweeds, hosiery, knitting yarns.
Swaledale	Finer and shorter than Blackface.	Carpets, tweeds, knitting yarns.
Rough Fell	Rather shorter than Swaledale.	Carpets.
Gritstone	Finer than Lonk. Springy handle.	Hosiery.
Herdwick	Coarse, open. Kempy. Some dark fibres.	Carpets, linings.
Welsh Mountain	Variable but often fine.	Flannels, blankets, tweeds, hosiery, knitting yarns, carpets.
Black Welsh Mountain	Black or dark brown. Often fine.	Flannel.
Exmoor Horn	Strong and fairly soft. Good colour and handle.	Tweeds, papermakers' felts, hosiery.
Dartmoor	Good length. Free from kemp. Coarse, but some classed as demi-lustre.	Bunting, mechanical cloths, blankets, serges.
Cheviot	Fine and white. Crisp handle. Free from dark fibres.	Tweeds, rugs, hosiery, carpets.
Shetland	Fine and soft inner coat. Hairy outer coat. White, black, grey, and reddish brown.	Shawls, scarves, hand-knitted wear, knitting yarns.

The Scottish Blackface has a strong, hairy outer coat and an inner one of shorter and finer fibres. In addition, there are some *heterotypes*, which are coarse and hairy at the outer end and finer and softer towards the root. A great variety of wool is obtained from the Blackface, variations occurring between districts and within individual flocks. As a general rule the longer and stronger wool is used for mattresses, the medium grades (having some springiness) for carpets, and the shorter, finer wool for tweeds of the Harris type. Large quantities are exported, to Italy for mattresses and to the U.S.A. for carpets. Other similar mountain breeds are the Lonk, the largest of the mountain breeds, to be found in the hills of Yorkshire, Lancashire and Derbyshire; the Greyface, already mentioned as a Border Leicester – Scottish Blackface cross; and the Swaledale, a breed which was obtained by crossing Wensleydale rams with Scottish Blackface ewes.

The Herdwick is a very pure breed, having been restricted to the fells of Cumberland and Westmorland for many hundreds of years. Each flock grazes its own part of the fell generation after generation, and the animals have no tendency to stray. Herdwicks change hands with the farm; they would soon find their way back if they were taken to another district. A large proportion of the clip is exported to the U.S.A. where the wool is used for the manufacture of carpets.

The Cheviot is widely spread in Scotland, and there are also flocks in Northumberland and Ulster. It is exported to Argentina, New Zealand and the Falkland Islands.

Shetlands are classed as a mountain breed, but their inner coat produces the finest wool in the British Isles. Colours are white, grey, black, and 'moorit', a reddish-brown shade. Owing to cross-breeding there are also other shades such as 'shaila' (greyish-black) and 'cat mougat' (mainly light, but belly dark). 'Rooing', or pulling, is still practised by some crofters when the wool tends to shed easily, but clipping is becoming more common because of its greater speed.

THE BRITISH WOOL MARKETING BOARD

The British Wool Marketing Board came into being in October 1950, with five main objectives[9]: (*i*) to stabilize returns to growers through standard prices and a stabilization fund; (*ii*) to achieve maximum prices for British wool by presenting it in ways which meet users' needs – e.g. national grades, offerings spread throughout the year by quantity and type; (*iii*) to reduce or minimize costs within the marketing channel; (*iv*) to improve the physical condition of the British wool clip by price incentives and grower education; and (*v*) to promote consumer demand for articles made from British wool.

The Board consists of twelve members elected by the producers (one from each of ten regions and two special members) and three members appointed by the Government – fifteen members in all. The Board is responsible for marketing virtually all fleece wool produced in the United Kingdom. At the same time, it maintains liaison with the producers through regional committees, and with the wool textile industry through advisory committees on which the various trade organizations are represented. With few exceptions, all producers send their wool to the Board's agents, who grade it and pack it into convenient lots for sale.

Each year, after consultations with the farmers' unions, the Government fixes an average guaranteed price for wool, and this is announced a month or two before the start of the shearing season. The Board, after deducting its estimated marketing costs for the coming year, is then able to prepare a schedule of prices covering every grade of British wool – nearly 350 grades. These grades come under such headings as (to quote from the 1965 Wool Price Schedule): (*a*) Down wools, (*b*) Fine wools, (*c*) Medium wools, (*d*) Masham, Cross and Leicester, (*e*) Lustre wools, (*f*) Cheviot, Radnor and Welsh (this included Shetland), (*g*) Swaledale, Blackface and Herdwick, (*h*) Lamb wools, and (*i*) Oddments and Daggings.

One of the objects of the scheme is to improve the condition, and thus the value of the British clip. Price reductions are therefore made for fleeces which have been artificially stained for show purposes, branded with tar or paint, tied with baler twine, and for one or two other defects. Auction sales are conducted on behalf of the British Wool Marketing Board by the Committee of London Wool Brokers. The sales, which are held at Bradford, London, Leicester, Exeter, Edinburgh and Belfast, are spread throughout the year, a procedure of great convenience to the textile industry. If the Board makes a surplus on its operations during any year, the amount is placed in a reserve fund to meet deficiencies which might occur in other years. If reserves cannot meet a deficiency, an advance is made by the Treasury, any such advance being repayable from future surpluses.

MERINOS AND CROSSBREDS

CREDIT for the early development of the ancestors of the Merino may be due to, or shared by, the Ancient Greeks and Romans, the Venetians and Carthaginians. There is no doubt, however, that fine-woolled sheep were developed in Spain at an early period, and that the Moors who occupied Spain for some 700 years, played an important part in establishing what was to become known as the Spanish Merino breed.

There were two main types of sheep in Spain at that period, the Transhumantes which were migratory, spending the summer in the northern mountains and the winter in the south, and the Estantes which remained in one district. The fine-woolled Merinos of different types owe their origin to the Transhumantes, which were bred almost entirely for wool. The Estantes had larger bodies and coarser wool.

During and before the 18th century, Merinos were not allowed to be exported from Spain, but this embargo was evaded from time to time. In 1765 Saxony obtained some of the Escurial type, which grew the finest wool. Subsequently, the Spanish Merino was introduced into France (1776), Prussia (1786), South Africa (1789), Australia (1797 – from South Africa), the U.S.A. (1798), and later to many countries. Space permits only a brief glance at the Merino in some of these countries.

John Macarthur obtained four ewes and two rams when the first Merinos (or Spanish fine-woolled sheep) arrived in Australia, and from these and subsequent importations he developed a strain of pure-bred Australian Merinos. Samuel Marsden also obtained some of the 1797 lot and he became a pioneer of cross-breeding. During the 19th century, Merinos were brought into Australia from England (from George III's flock), Spain, France, Saxony, Silesia, and lastly from the U.S.A. As sheep breeding spread inland from the coast, various types of sheep and fleece became established, and fleeces became heavier and wool quality finer.

Australian Merino wools [10,11] are generally known at the present time by trade names related to the particular district from which the wool is derived. Thus the wool from New South Wales is known as 'Sydney', from Victoria as 'Port Phillip', 'Melbourne' or 'Geelong', from South Australia as 'Adelaide', from Queensland as 'Brisbane', from Western Australia as 'Perth' or 'Fremantle' and from Tasmania as 'Tasmanian'.

The term 'Crossbred', although loosely used to describe any type of sheep obtained by crossing a long-woolled sheep with a Merino, is well understood in Australia, and by wool men generally, to refer to a wool of quality from 58s downwards. Crossbred wools are obtained from sheep that have been bred by crossing a British Lustre or Down ram with a Merino ewe. The resultant half-bred may be crossed back again with Merino to produce a 'quarter-bred' which, if crossed again with Merino, results in an animal giving a wool known as Comeback. This is of a quality almost as fine as pure Merino, and is also long, soft, and has a pronounced crimp. The Corriedale, famous in New Zealand (see below), is bred in this way from Lincoln, Leicester or Border Leicester rams. The Polwarth is bred in Australia in a similar way from a Lincoln ram.

The Merino did not thrive in New Zealand when it was first taken there from Australia in about 1840, mainly due to the wetter climate. During the middle part of the century, therefore, several English breeds were imported, notably Romneys (now New Zealand's most popular breed), Lincolns, Leicesters, Border Leicesters and Southdowns. In the 1870's the crossing of Merinos with Lincolns and Leicesters, and subsequent selective breeding, produced the Corriedale, which was named after the property where James Little began his breeding experiments. It is now recognized as a pure breed. Corriedale wool has much of the fineness and density of Merino combined with greater length. The quality averages 56s and goes up to 60s.

New Zealand has now become the world's largest producer of crossbred wool, there having been in recent years a marked increase in both the number of sheep and in wool production in that country. This is partly accounted for by the development of aerial topdressing, about a million tons of fertilizer now being spread from the air each year. The heavier feeding, however, is resulting in a gradual coarsening of the clip[12], as is shown by the significant figures in Table 1.5, taken from the *World Wool Digest* (quoting F. S. Arthur of the New Zealand Wool Commission).

TABLE 1.5 COARSENING OF THE NEW ZEALAND CLIP.

Year	Percentage of Each Quality in Total Clip				
	60/58s	56s–58/60s	50–50/56s	46/50s	46/48s and 48/50s and coarser
1954/55	2·7	14·0	30·2	42·9	10·2
1964/65	1·9	10·0	18·2	38·5	31·4

The Merino in South Africa has been developed from various types, but owes more to the Australian Merino than to any other breed. There are about 34 million wool-bearing sheep in South Africa, and most of these are Merino, grazing the Karroo plains. About 90 per cent of the clip is Merino wool. It is of fine quality, the bulk being 64s to 70s, with some 80s, but the length depends on the period between shearing which is sometimes done twice a year. The South African wool clip is sold almost entirely by public auction in Port Elizabeth, East London, Cape Town and Durban, the sales taking place from September to May.

The Spanish Merino was introduced into the U.S.A. in 1798, and was followed by the Rambouillet or French Merino, which proved to be very successful. The Vermont type was evolved in the New England state of that name, its most distinctive feature being a very wrinkled or folded fleece. This led to some irregularity in fibre length and fineness owing to the growing conditions varying in different parts of the folds, and to difficulties in shearing. The Delaine was evolved in Ohio from the Rambouillet and is almost completely free from folds.

At one time it was the custom in the U.S.A. to divide Merinos into three classes according to the extent of folding of the skin: viz, type A, the Vermont variety which was heavily folded; type B with folds almost entirely restricted to the neck; and type C the Delaine, entirely free from folds. Type A has now practically disappeared, the fleeces of American Merinos and Rambouillets being of type C. A new fine-wool breed, the Debouillet, has been produced by crossing Delaine rams with Rambouillet ewes, and this breed has been established by interbreeding[13]. Examples of crossbreds in the U.S.A. are the Columbia and Panama from Lincoln rams and Rambouillet ewes, and the Romeldale from Romney rams and Rambouillet ewes. Today the entire U.S.A. clip goes to its home industry.

South America has become one of the important wool producing areas of the world. In 1965-66 there were in Argentina, Uruguay, Brazil, Peru and Chile, about 116 million sheep, compared with 157.6 million in Australia. For the same five countries the estimated production of raw wool (greasy) was 770 million lb compared with 1,712 million lb. for Australia[14]. The above figures are provisional.

TABLE 1.6.   SOUTH AMERICAN WOOLS

Marketing Centre	Wool Production Area	Remarks
Buenos Aires (BA)	Argentina	Merino and Crossbred. Some 6-months' clip, known as 'Second Clip BA'. Small amount of carpet type.
Montevideo (MV)	Uruguay and Brazil	Mostly medium Crossbred; used for hosiery.
Punta Arenas (PA)	Chile, Patagonia and Tierra del Fuego	Chile – fine Crossbred, soft handling. Patagonian Merinos are finest in South America.

Merino sheep were first taken to Argentina in 1794. Today the Rambouillet type is found to be most suited to the climatic and other conditions, but other popular breeds are the Corriedale, Romney Marsh, Cheviot and Lincoln. Most of the wool now produced is crossbred, the remainder being Merino – except for a very small amount of carpet wool. The marketing centres for South American wools are given in Table 1.6 on page 11.

The first sheep in the Falkland Islands were Cheviots, but the predominant breeds now are Corriedale and Romney. The quality of the wool is mostly fine Crossbred. It is lofty, resilient and springy, which makes the finer types attractive for hosiery and knitting yarns. The medium types are blended with New Zealand and other Crossbreds in topmaking.

SHEARING AND CLASSING

METHODS OF SHEARING vary in different countries and may be carried out either by hand or machinery (driven by electricity, or by an oil or steam engine, through overhead shafting). In Australia, and other countries where large numbers of sheep have to be shorn, blade shearing (hand) is only used when for some reason machinery is not available, or only a small batch of sheep is to be shorn. Stud animals are sometimes shorn by hand, particularly when conditions are such that they would benefit by the additional length of fleece that can be left on them when hand shearing is employed.

Before shearing proper is started, the wool is cut from the lower parts of the legs and from round about the head, and these parts of the fleece, together with any small pieces which may fall to the floor at a later stage, are placed on one side and classed as *locks*. The wool is also cut off the belly and kept separately as *bellies*.

Some remarkable feats of shearing have been recorded. Over 320 Merinos have been shorn by hand by one man in under eight hours; and in 1965 Kevin Sarre, the Australian shearing champion and Australian Wool Board's instructor, set up a world record by shearing 346 Merinos in 7 hours 48 minutes, using the Board's new 'Tally-Hi' method[15].

The technique of shearing, and of handling the animal, so that the main part of the fleece comes away neatly and easily in one piece, varies with the district and the individual, and also depends on whether blade or machine shearing is being used. The method used by the famous New Zealand exponent of the craft, Godfrey Bowen, is described in detail in his book, *Wool Away*[16]. This book covers the subject thoroughly, and in addition gives much useful information on the Merino, Corriedale, Half-bred, and British breeds in New Zealand.

The next operation, known as *skirting*, consists in removing all parts of the fleece that would be objectionable in any way. The amount taken off depends upon the individual fleece, its general attributes in relation to the remainder of the clip, and the class to which it is judged to belong. The aim is to produce a fleece with as high a degree of uniformity as is compatible with the number of classes into which the clip is being divided. A good Merino fleece might be skirted fairly heavily in order to bring it into the highest class of the clip. A poorer fleece, on the other hand, would be treated more lightly and relegated to a lower standard. Seeds and burrs are taken into account because a high quality fleece should be relatively free from these. Skirtings are sorted into grades, large intact portions being known as *pieces*. Locks and bellies are also sorted, this operation being known as *picking*.

After skirting, the fleece is rolled, the usual procedure being to fold it lengthways from each side so that the opposite edges meet, and then roll it, starting at the britch end so that the shoulder wool – which is often the best part of the fleece – is left visible on the outside.

Advice on shearing, and the general presentation of the British clip, is given by the British Wool Marketing Board in such publications as *Wool on the Farm* and their yearly *Wool Price Schedule and Notes for Wool Growers*.

GRADES AND QUALITIES

The number of grades into which the classer divides the clip depends both on the size of the flock and on the average characteristics of the fleeces in it. He must take into account primarily the regularity of quality and fibre length, soundness, yield, colour, and also that somewhat indefinable attribute known as *style*, covering such features as handle, lustre and crimp[17].

Quality is mostly a matter of fineness, which is one of the main factors determining the length of yarn per unit weight that can be spun from it. Length of staple largely determines the use to which the wool is suited – in particular for worsted or woollen processing. Combing wools are classed as Noble or French, with such extra terms as Extra Super, Super, Warp Length (3 inches and more), Half Warp (2 to 3 inches). Soundness (tensile strength) is important for combing wools. Tender wools should not therefore be included with a combing type or the whole lot will be depreciated. Yield is the percentage of clean wool that will remain after all the impurities, such as grease, suint (sweat), sand and dirt, have been extracted. This has traditionally been a matter of judgment, but modern methods of assessment have been developed. The colour of 'white' wool varies considerably. Some Down wools tend to be chalky white, Merinos have a pearly whiteness, Lustres can have an almost golden tint. In addition, there are such natural colour faults as 'urine-stained', 'yolk-stained' and 'dust-stained'.

In dealing with a whole flock, the classer will probably have one particular standard in view, say in the case of Merinos, 70s and 64s (classed together) or 64s alone; any fleece not coming up to the required standard will be graded into a lower class. Merino fleeces below 60s quality are usually classed as Crossbred.

An important type of wool, particularly from New Zealand, is 'Slipes' or skin wool, taken from the skin of animals that have been slaughtered for mutton. Wool taken from animals that have died from natural causes is known as 'Dead Wool'. When lime is used for removing the wool, difficulties may arise in scouring but slipes nevertheless have certain advantages, one example being the absence of very short lengths of fibre such as are caused by the shearer cutting over the same part of the fleece twice.

In Great Britain fleeces are normally classed according to breed type, as has been previously explained.

OTHER ANIMAL FIBRES

THE PRINCIPAL ANIMAL FIBRES, other than wool[7,13,18], which are employed in the textile industry and usually known as speciality hair fibres, are mohair, cashmere, alpaca (and llama, vicuna and guanaco), camel and Angora rabbit, A few notes on these individual fibres are given below.

MOHAIR

Mohair is the hairy coat of the Angora goat (*capra hircus aegagrus*), which has been bred in Asia Minor for 2,000 years or more. This goat is now bred also in the U.S.A. (chiefly Texas), South Africa and Basutoland *. In addition, mohair production is just beginning in Australia. Figures issued by the Commonwealth Economic Committee in 1966 give the number of Angora goats in 1964 as 5.6m. in Turkey, 4.6m. (clipped) in the U.S.A., 1.7m. in South Africa and 0.7m. in Basutoland. Mohair producttion in million lb. is given as Turkey 18.7, U.S.A. 29.8, South Africa 12.5 and Basutoland 2.1.

The long fibres (6 to 12 inches) are strong, durable and highly lustrous; they are the most 'glassy' of the animal fibres. The normal colour is white, but some fleeces are yellowish, and there is a reddish-ginger shade known as 'Gingerline'. Fibre diameter varies from about 25μ (0.025 mm.) in the finest kid grade to about 55 μ (0.055 mm.) in the coarsest grades. The fibres are regular in thickness along the length, and they have a tightly closed scale formation which accounts for the lustre effect. As dust does not readily adhere to this smooth scale structure, mohair is particularly suitable for furnishing fabrics.

The main uses for mohair are pile fabrics, hood fabrics for cars and prams (with cotton warp), tropical suitings (sometimes blended with

* Now Lesotho

Lustre or New Zealand wools), imitation furs and rugs. Mohair is not used as much as it used to be for upholstery and linings.

CASHMERE

The Cashmere goat (*capra hircus laniger*) is to be found in Tibet, Iran, Iraq, Kashmir and Mongolia. It has a coarse outer coat of long, straight hair up to five inches long, protecting a fine inner coat of soft down, which for fineness is excelled only by vicuna. This fine cashmere was renowned many hundreds of years ago for the beautiful shawls made from it in Kashmir. The largest quantities and finest qualities of cashmere come from North-West China.

The fleece is obtained by means of hand combing the animal when it is moulting, and the separation of the fine undergrowth from the long coarse hairs is done in the factory. The fine hairs are one to three inches long, very nearly circular in cross-section, and finely tapered at the tip end. There is commonly a blunter tapering at the root end due to the shape of the root itself which often comes away in the combing. Cashmere fibres are mainly greyish-white, fawn and grey, but some from Iran are ginger and black.

The fine downy fibres in the form of noil are used in the production of woollen yarns for dress materials, rugs, knitwear, stoles, scarves and other soft luxury articles. They are also blended with wool for dressing gown, waistcoat and overcoating materials. The coarse hairs are often used in the country of origin for making bags, while in England they are employed for mechanical cloths.

THE LLAMA GROUP

The llama genus, which belongs to the camel family, consists of four main varieties: alpaca, llama, vicuna and guanaco (huanaco). Cross-breeding of the alpaca and llama has also led to the production of two hybrids, the huarizo resulting from a llama father and alpaca mother, and the misti from an alpaca father and llama mother. All of the llama group inhabit the heights of the Andes in South America. The llama and alpaca have been domesticated since pre-Inca times, but the vicuna and guanaco have never readily submitted to domestication.

Attempts to acclimatize the llama group elsewhere than in South America have not met with much success.

Alpaca: There are two types of alpaca (*llama glama pacos*), namely the huacaya, which resembles the llama, and the suri, which has a thicker and more lustrous fleece than the huacaya. Despite this, the huacaya is the more numerous of the two, probably because, as Wildman suggests, the native breeders have not taken advantage of the conditions which favour the production of increased numbers of suri.

The alpaca is reared primarily for its fleece, which consists of long lustrous fibres ranging from the coarseness of the llama almost to the fineness of the vicuna. The fleece is more uniform than those of the the other llamas and the colours are of great natural beauty, fawns, browns, black and white. The best alpaca fleeces come from the Arequipa district in the south of Peru, and are shipped from the nearby port of Mollendo. Alpaca is a better heat insulator and is stronger than wool, and yet is very soft. According to quality it is used for high-class hosiery, coatings (with laid pile), linings, tropical suitings, furnishings, beltings and press cloths. Most of the alpaca hair is exported to the U.S.A. and the United Kingdom.

Llama: Since the time of the Ancient Peruvians the llama (*llama glama glama*), the largest of the group, has been kept for meat and as a beast of burden. The male works as a pack animal in the high Andes at altitudes and in conditions inimical to the horse and the mule, while the female is used for breeding and for fibre production, the fleece of the male (which serves as padding for the pack) usually being taken only when the animal dies. The fleece is generally much coarser than that of the alpaca, but there is an inner coat of finer fibres. As a rule, however, the coat is rather mixed, and the fine fibres are not easy to sort from the coarse. The fleeces are of mixed colours – brown, white, black, speckled and fawn – and are not usually classed in separate shades as are the better types of alpaca fleece.

Vicuna: The vicuna (*llama vicuna*), the smallest of the llama group, is timid and graceful, with a gazelle-like head. It can be domesticated only when born in captivity or when captured very young. At one time it was hunted and shot, and was in danger of becoming extinct until protected by decree of the Peruvian government. The vicuna lives wild, in small flocks, at a high altitude in Peru and Bolivia. The fleece of the vicuna, which is a cinnamon shade, is about two inches in length, has a very soft handle, and is the finest animal fibre used in textile manufacture. It is available only in very small quantities, and is used for fine qualities of knitwear, shawls and scarves, and sometimes for dressing gowns and overcoats.

Guanaco: The guanaco (*llama glama huanaca*) is very wild, and has tended to move southward away from the areas where others of the llama group are to be found. The fleece is therefore not of much commercial importance; it is a mixture of shaggy hairs and soft down, the colouring being somewhat similar to vicuna, but more of a dark chestnut brown. The Patagonian Indians use the complete pelt as a cloak.

CAMEL HAIR

Camel hair for use in the textile industry is collected from the bactrian or two-humped camel (*camelus bactrianus*), the dromedary, with only one hump, being the animal used in such countries as Egypt, Syria and Arabia as a beast of burden and for riding. Its hair is generally coarser than that of the bactrian camel but it is suitable for some textile purposes. The modern bactrian has been developed from crossing between the old pure bactrian and the dromedary. It has an outer coat of coarse hairs up to 15 inches long and an inner coat of soft down varying in length between one and five inches.

Up to the end of the second world war camel hair production was mainly confined to Outer Mongolia and North-West China, although the animal inhabits practically all parts of Asia. Now, however, camel hair is also obtained from Afghanistan, Iran, Iraq, Syria and Pakistan, Nevertheless, the finest camel hair still comes from Sinkiang in North-East China, most of the Chinese production being exported from Shanghai and Tientsin, the principal markets being London and the U.S.A.

Bactrians are not shorn or plucked, the hair being collected as it moults or is rubbed off. When received by the textile industry it is combed to separate the long coarse hair from the valuable soft noils. The raw material is graded into fine, medium and coarse types. The colour deteriorates as the quality becomes lower. The fine fibres (noil) are used for dressing gowns, and ladies' and men's overcoats. The long coarse hairs are used for inter-linings, belting and mechanical fabrics. From time immemorial the coarse hairs have been used in China and other countries of origin for making ropes.

RABBIT HAIR

The rabbit is a fur-bearing animal and so its coat consists of outer guard hairs and shorter soft fur fibres. The fur of the Angora rabbit (*lepus caniculus*) is used in the textile industry, and the animal is now bred on a large scale for this purpose in France, Czechoslovakia and Japan; it is also bred to a lesser extent in many other European countries and in the U.S.A. The coat, which is combed, plucked or shorn once or more during the year, consists of mostly white, very attractive silky fibres. They are used alone, or blended with wool, for luxury fabrics and for spinning into lofty, soft hand-knitting yarns. They are also spun with a nylon core.

HORSE AND COW HAIR

For use in the textile industry, horse hair is divided into tail hair and mane hair, the tail hairs being longer, harder and more bristly. According to quality they are used for various hair cloths and stiffening fabrics. The shorter hairs are used in the upholstery trade for stuffing. Cow hair, often blended with wool, is used for carpets, underfelts, horse blankets, and insulating cords for steam pipes.

REFERENCES

1. Lydekker, R., *The Sheep and its Cousins*, George Allen, 1912.
2. Ryder, M. L., *Sheep Breeds in History*, National Sheep Breeders Association, Year Book, 1960.
3. Power, Eileen, *The Wool Trade in English Medieval History*, Oxford University Press, 1941.
4. Bowden, Peter, J., *The Wool Trade in Tudor and Stuart England*, Macmillan, 1962.
5. World Wool Digest, published by International Wool Secretariat and Wool Bureau Inc., 22nd June, 1967.
6. Haigh, H. and Newton, B.A., *The Wools of Britain*, Pitman, 1952.
7. Onions, W. J., *Wool: An Introduction to its Properties, Varieties, Production and Uses*, Benn, 1962.
8. *British Pure Bred Sheep*, National Sheep Breeders Association, 1952 (a new edition is being prepared).
9. *The British Wool Marketing Board – Its Organization and Operations*. Brochure published by the B.W.M.B.
10. Cox, E. W., *The Evolution of the Australian Merino*, Angus and Robertson, Sydney, 1936.
11. Ponting, K. G., *The Wool Trade Past and Present*, Columbine Press, 1961.
12. World Wool Digest, 4th Aug. 1966 (quoting F. S. Arthur of the New Zealand Wool Commission).
13. Bergen, W. von, (Ed.), *Wool Handbook*, Vol. 1, 3rd ed., John Wiley, New York. 1963.
14. World Wool Digest, 22nd June 1967.
15. World Wool Digest, 25th Nov. 1965.
16. Bowen, Godfrey, *Wool Away – The Technique and Art of Shearing*, Whitcombe and Tombs, New Zealand, 1955.
17. Cowley, Clarence, E., *Classing the Clip*, Angus and Robertson, Sydney, 4th ed., 1944.
18. Haigh, H. Stansfield, Speciality Fibres, *J. Text. Inst.*, *40*, No. 8, Aug. 1949, P749–813.

STRUCTURE AND PROPERTIES OF THE WOOL FIBRE

THE CONSUMER APPEAL of wool textiles derives partly from their appearance and construction and partly from the structure and properties of the wool fibres themselves. It follows therefore that a clear understanding of the latter should help in the selection of wools for a variety of end uses and also indicate, in cases where no suitable wool is available, how the characteristics of wool may be modified to suit. At present this desirable aim is not entirely realizable, in that the complexities of the chemical and physical properties of wool fibres are imperfectly understood. Nevertheless, in an increasingly sophisticated industry the ability of wool to compete with other textile fibres must depend to a large extent on the skill with which information already gleaned is applied.

THE STRUCTURE OF WOOL

THE MANY QUALITIES of wool used in the textile industry vary according to the breeds of sheep from which they are taken. Their fibres range in diameter from 18μ (0.018 mm.) for fine wools to about 40μ (0.040 mm.) for coarser varieties, while staple lengths vary from 4 cm. to 35 cm. Their morphological structures have both common and distinguishing features, emphasizing that there is no unique assembly of components, be they molecules or multi-molecular aggregates, which constitutes the structure of wool. Moreover this is not only true of the morphological structure but also of the chemical structure.

MORPHOLOGICAL AND MOLECULAR STRUCTURE

An impression of a fine, non-medullated, wool fibre can be gained from the drawing reproduced in Fig 2.1. The sheath of the fibre is composed of flattened cells, the scales, each consisting of endocuticle, exocuticle and 'a' layer, which overlap and interlock in such a way that about one-third of each scale is covered by its neighbour [1,2]. A membrane, about 100 Å thick, is thought to cover the entire length of these scales; this is the epicuticle[3]. The whole structural unit constitutes the cuticle, and represents about 10 per cent of the weight of the fibre. The remaining 90 per cent or so is the cellular material which comprises the cortex. In crimped wool fibres this cortex has two segments, the orthocortex and the paracortex, differentiated by their structures and their reactions with chemical agents[4,5]. (Plate 1). The cortical cells of both segments are of comparable size, and are enclosed by membranes of at least three distinct layers. Each cell is comprised of macrofibrils. The macrofibrils of the orthocortex are comparatively small and uniform with well-defined boundaries, with the remnants of cell nuclei and non-keratinous materials distributed evenly within them, whereas the macrofibrils of the paracortex are larger and more irregular in shape, with ill-defined boundaries, outside which nuclear debris and other cell detritus are concentrated in much larger aggregates (Plate 2). The orthocortex is on the outside of the crimp wave.

At higher magnifications of the electron microscope the macrofibrils of both types of cell are seen to be composed of microfibrils set in a matrix of less-ordered material[1]. The microfibrils appear to be of a uniform diameter of 75Å , but the pattern of their packing to form the macrofibrils is not the same in the two types of cell. The paracortex seems to have more matrix protein.

Even when the limit of resolution of the electron microscope is approached the substructure of the microfibrils is barely perceptible[6]. It is most probable, however, that the images obtained at such magnifications are artefacts, because the phase-contrast mechanism of image formation gives images that vary with the setting of the objective lens, the semi-angular condenser and the wavelength associated with the electron beam[7]. (Plate 3). Nevertheless there is a substructure in the microfibrils, which is believed to consist of protofibrils, formed from two or three coiled protein chains, with their long axes parallel to the main axis of the microfibril, and surrounded by disordered protein. More reliable evidence for the existence of protofibrils comes from electron microscope examination of microfibrils disintegrated by ultrasonic irradiation into finer filaments with diameters of about 20Å (Plate 4.)[8].

This account of the architecture of the wool fibre refers to the finer types of fibre, such as Merino, which have been the most intensively studied. Coarser types usually have an additional central core called the medulla, formed from axial cells which do not fill with the proteins of keratin, but consist largely of vacuoles. These structural features have been revealed by light and electron microscopy, and encompass a wide range of dimensions from 200,000 Å to 20 Å, but for finer structural detail x-ray diffraction techniques must be used.

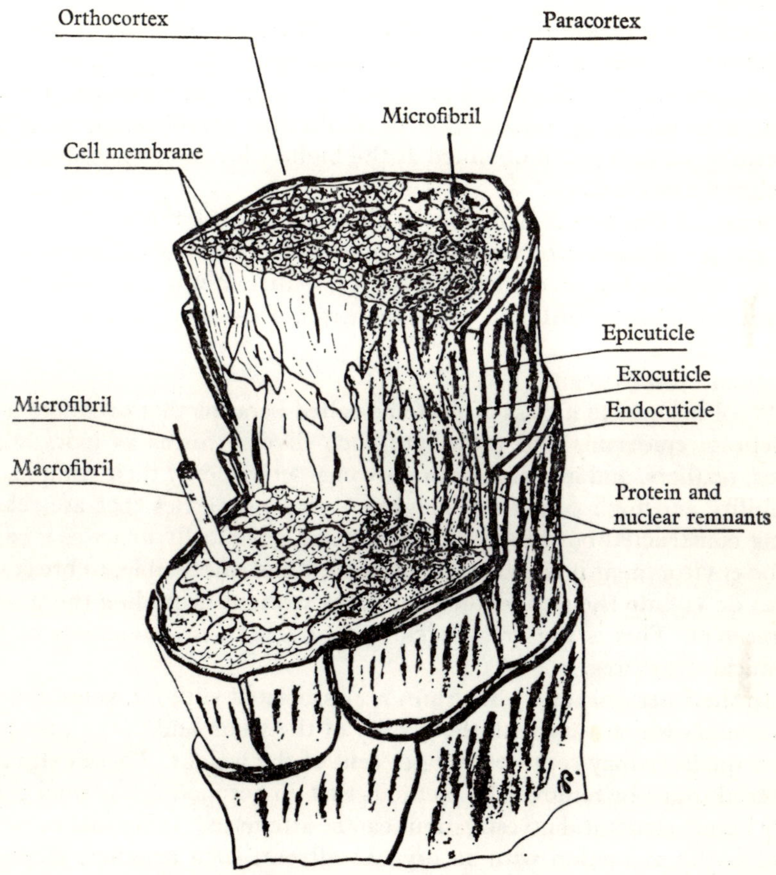

FIG. 2. 1. STEREOGRAM OF A FINE WOOL FIBRE

Reproduced from a drawing by Dr. J. Sikorski

One of the most outstanding achievements in the investigation of wool structure was the demonstration that the x-ray pattern exhibited by the native fibre, the ∝-pattern, changes to a completely new pattern, the ß-pattern, when the wool fibre is stretched in steam[9]. The molecular structure which conforms best with the x-ray data is that of a rope made of two or three protein chains, each of which is coiled helically, with the pitch of the helices corresponding to 3.6 amino-acid residues[10]. Such a rope has a diameter of about 20 Å and is the protofibril revealed by electron microscopy. The ß-pattern indicates complete extension of the $\propto$-helix.

On releasing the stress the wool fibre returns to its original length, and again shows the $\propto$-pattern by x-ray diffraction. This reversible $\propto$-ß transformation thus affords an explanation in molecular terms for the elasticity of the fibre.

Careful examination of other features of the x-ray data shows that there is a structural unit in the fibre with a diameter of about 75 Å, and this is almost certainly the microfibril revealed by electron microscopy. Thus, in addition to providing information on molecular organization, x-ray data confirm structural detail obtained at the highest levels of magnification of the electron microscope.

Some of the key dimensions in the structure of the wool fibre are: 200,000 Å – diameter of wool fibre; 20,000Å – diameter of cortical cell; 100 Å – spacing between microfibrils; 75Å – diameter of microfibril; 20 Å – diameter of protofibril; and 11Å – diameter of $\propto$-helical protein chain.

CHEMICAL STRUCTURE

Wool belongs to a class of proteins called keratins that originate in the vertebrate epidermis and grow into such diverse forms as hairs, claws, horns, feathers, and hoofs. Keratins are characterized by their complete insolubility and high content of sulphur – two properties that are related. Being constructed both morphologically and chemically to act as a barrier to the environment it is extremely difficult, if not impossible, to break wool fibres down into their constituent proteins without degrading the proteins themselves. This is the greatest single obstacle to investigations of their chemical structures.

In their natural state wool fibres are associated with fat, suint and dirt, in amounts which vary with the quality of the wool, and in the case of the finest qualities may represent 37 per cent of the weight. These extraneous materials must be removed by methods that do not modify the wool chemically before structural investigations can be attempted. It is usual to remove wool fat by extraction with an organic solvent, such as ether, ethanol or azeotropic benzene-methanol. Suint can then be dissolved in water, and particulate dirt released by agitation under water. The dry weights of all these impurities can be easily determined after removal of the solvents used. Burrs, and other adhering vegetable matter, if present, can be removed by hand.

The sulphur and nitrogen contents of a representative range of wools and allied fibres are given in Table 2.1. Here the differences in sulphur content are much more striking than those in nitrogen content, because the substitution of a non-sulphur-containing amino acid for one containing sulphur will make an appreciable change in sulphur content but a barely perceptible change in nitrogen content. The sulphur content of a wool fibre varies along its major axis from root to tip, and along its minor axis from cuticle to medulla[11]. Indeed, the medullary cells are almost free of sulphur.

TABLE 2.1. NITROGEN AND SULPHUR CONTENTS OF WOOL

Fibre	Nitrogen Content (% on dry weight)	Sulphur Content (% on dry weight)
Alpaca (black)	15·85	3·90
Alpaca (brown)	16·66	4·35
Alpaca (white)	17·00	3·93
Dog wool	16·44	5·07
Rabbit wool	16·72	4·30 − 4·14
Australian merino lamb	16·73	—
Australian merino wool (ram)	—	3·88
Australian merino wool (ewe)	—	3·91
Welsh Mountain wool	—	4·00
Scotch Blackface (fine)	—	3·82
Scotch Blackface (medullated)	—	3·33
Scotch Blackface (kemps)	—	3·24
Mohair (fine)	16·83	3·36
Mohair (coarse)	16·70	3·03

Hydrolysates of wool obtained by boiling in 50 per cent hydrochloric acid consist almost wholly of amino acids, and the degradation products of amino acids. A small amount of mineral matter is also present, but although other possible organic constituents, such as carbohydrates, have been sought, none has been found. Wool fibres are almost entirely protein.

The nineteen amino acids listed in Table 2.2 are present in virgin wools.

The observed variations in sulphur and nitrogen contents among different types of fibres, and types of wool cells, reflect corresponding variations in amino-acid compositions. Thus the amino-acid compositions of wools depend on the strain, breed, species and nutrition of the sheep from which they are taken, and the duration and severity of the weathering to which the fleeces have been exposed[12, 13]. Cuticular, cortical and medullary cells also show differences in amino-acid composition, but these are slight in comparison with the quite distinctive composition of the epicuticle[14,15,16]. Typical analyses of some of these materials are presented in Table 2.3, where the amino-acid compositions are expressed as the number of residues of each amino acid present in every thousand residues.

When comparing amino-acid analyses of wools and their histological components care should be exercised in accepting the published data. Their reliability should be assessed after careful consideration of the procedures used for the isolation, purification, and hydrolysis of the materials examined, and of the methods of amino-acid analysis. The most reliable methods, most carefully applied, will only assay to within 3 per cent of the true amino-acid content. Moreover, during hydrolysis tryptophan is destroyed

TABLE 2.2.   AMINO-ACID COMPOSITION OF WOOL

The general formula for α-amino acids is $\genfrac{}{}{0pt}{}{NH_2}{COOH}\!\!\!\!\diagdown\!\!\!\!\diagup\, CH - R.$

In the column headed 'Structural formula' only –R groups are given except for the *imino acid*, proline, which is given in full.

Amino Acid	Structural Formula (R groups)	Weight (in g.) in hydrolysate of 100 g. of dry wool[25,26]
Alanine	$-CH_3$	4·3
Arginine	$-CH_2-CH_2-CH_2-NH-C\genfrac{}{}{0pt}{}{NH_2}{NH}$	10·1
Aspartic Acid	$-CH_2-COOH$	6·8
Cysteine	$-CH_2-SH$	0·36
Cystine	$-CH_2-S-S-CH_2-$	12·5
Glutamic acid	$-CH_2-CH_2-COOH$	14·5
Glycine	$-H$	5·5
Histidine	$-CH_2-C=CH$ (imidazole ring: N, NH, CH)	1·2
Isoleucine	$-CH\genfrac{}{}{0pt}{}{CH_2-CH_3}{CH_3}$	3·7
Leucine	$-CH_2-CH\genfrac{}{}{0pt}{}{CH_3}{CH_3}$	8·9
Lysine	$-CH_2-CH_2-CH_2-CH_2-NH_2$	3·3
Methionine	$-CH_2-CH_2-S-CH_3$	0·56
Phenylalanine	$-CH_2-$ (phenyl ring)	4·0
Proline	CH_2-CH_2 / CH_2 $CH-COOH$ / NH (pyrrolidine ring)	6·8
Serine	$-CH_2-OH$	10·6
Threonine	$-CH\genfrac{}{}{0pt}{}{CH_3}{OH}$	7·0
Tryptophan	$-CH_2-$ (indole ring: NH)	0·94
Tyrosine	$-CH_2-$ (phenyl ring) $-OH$	5·7
Valine	$-CH\genfrac{}{}{0pt}{}{CH_3}{CH_3}$	5·7

completely and the amounts of serine, threonine, tyrosine and cystine are reduced according to the severity of hydrolytic conditions. Other amino acids, valine and isoleucine, are difficult to release from peptide linkage. Thus an acid hydrolysate of a wool sample is not a true reflection of its amino-acid composition, and since most analyses are carried out on hydrolysates, and are not corrected for the changes described, they must be accepted with reservation. In addition, it is not unusual for the chemical procedures used to isolate the various cellular components of wool fibres to modify the protein constituents. With these considerations in mind it is probable that variations of up to 10 per cent in the amino-acid compositions of different wools may be due either to methodical errors in assay, or to differences in protein composition, or to both. Variations above 10 per cent, however, most probably reflect differences in protein content.

TABLE 2.3.   AMINO-ACID COMPOSITIONS OF CELLULAR COMPONENTS OF WOOL
(Amino-acid residues per 1000)

Amino-acid Residues	Cuticle	Cellular Components		
		Ortho-cortex	Para-cortex	64s Merino Wool
Glutamic acid	92	115	118	114
Cystine/2	114	109	136	113
Serine	137	118	111	111
Glycine	96	82	77	83
Leucine	62	80	69	74
Proline	90	95	88	67
Arginine	49	60	72	67
Threonine	50	60	74	66
Aspartic acid	42	60	55	61
Valine	65	48	47	55
Alanine	57	50	47	53
Tyrosine	29	37	27	39
Isoleucine	25	29	28	31
Phenylalanine	19	22	29	27
Lysine	29	26	14	26
Histidine	9	7	7	7
Methionine	4	n.d.	n.d.	5

n.d. = not determined.

Many of the chemical properties of the wool fibre, such as the equilibria attained in aqueous solutions of acids and bases, and the uptake of dyes, may be largely explained in terms of its amino-acid composition. Other types of chemical reactivity, however, such as changes in cystine content and the introduction of cross-linking molecules, produce changes in the conformation of the protein constituents with concomitant changes in mechanical properties. Their complete understanding requires a sound knowledge of the tertiary and quaternary structures of the proteins in wool. Most of what is known about these comes from the electron microscope and x-ray diffraction studies previously described. Unfortunately, these in-

TABLE 2.4. AMINO-ACID COMPOSITIONS OF HIGH AND LOW SULPHUR PROTEIN FRACTIONS FROM WOOL
(Amino-acid residues per 1000).

Amino-acid Residues	Low-Sulphur Proteins			64s Merino Wool	High-Sulphur Proteins		
	SCMKA	α-Keratose	U.S.3		γ-Keratose	SCMKB1	SCMKB2
Glutamic acid	140	154	142	114	77	98	114
Cystine 1/2	67	52	72	113	191	233	218
Serine	79	104	99	111	141	150	152
Glycine	87	73	65	83	65	63	88
Leucine	101	103	93	74	34	18	19
Proline	42	38	46	67	130	123	107
Arginine	72	73	74	67	63	52	31
Threonine	47	53	66	66	107	118	114
Aspartic acid	80	88	82	61	24	8	10
Valine	59	56	58	55	55	42	40
Alanine	63	68	65	53	34	30	34
Tyrosine	42	34	32	39	18	21	19
Isoleucine	36	35	36	31	28	27	41
Phenylalanine	30	27	26	27	15	7	13
Lysine	40	32	36	26	7	5	0
Histidine	6	6	7	7	7	6	0
Methionine	5	n.d.	n.d.	5	n.d.	0	0

n.d. = not determined.

vestigations, while they clearly indicate that the wool fibre has at least two distinct phases, give little or no information on the types and numbers of proteins involved. They emphasize, however, two salient features of the proteins present in the microfibrillar and matrix phases. The x-ray evidence requires that proteins of the protofibrils, and hence of the microfibrils, contain substantial stretches of $\propto$-helix in their chains. The electron microscope evidence reveals a greater uptake of metal in the reduced proteins of the matrix than in the corresponding proteins of the microfibrils, which implies that the former have the higher cystine content.

Over the past decade extensive studies on the chemical degradation of wool by a variety of procedures have shown that two main groups of protein fractions, high-sulphur and low-sulphur fractions, may be isolated. For example, when the cystine residues of wool are oxidized to cysteic acid residues, by performic or peracetic acids, 90 per cent of the oxidized fibre dissolves in dilute alkali[17,18]. On adjusting the resultant solution to pH 4.7, 55 per cent of the weight of the fibre precipitates in the form of $\propto$-keratose, leaving about 36 per cent in solution as γ-keratose. In like manner wool may be reduced by thioglycollate in alkaline solution, and the thiol groups blocked with iodoacetate[19,20]. The S-carboxymethylkerateine (SCMK) thus formed is almost entirely soluble at pH 11, and subsequent adjustment to pH 4.5 precipitates the protein fraction SCMKA, leaving SCMKB in solution. Both $\propto$-keratose and SCMKA are heterogeneous, low-sulphur, protein fractions of identical amino-acid composition, while SCMKB and γ-keratose are heterogeneous, high-sulphur, protein fractions of like amino-acid composition. The compositions of these fractions immediately suggest that they may be responsible for the microfibrillar and matrix phases. This point of view is supported by the findings that the cystine residues of the low- and high-sulphur regions of the wool protein structure may be incorporated at different times, and that the feeding of sheep abomasally on high-protein and sulphur-rich diets affects the proportions of the high-sulphur and low-sulphur proteins present in the keratinized fibre[21,22,23].

The consensus on the ultrastructure of the wool fibre supports the view that the microfibrillar phase consists mainly of low-sulphur protein(s), whose amino-acid compositions favour α-helical chains, whereas the matrix is composed of protein(s) with high-proline and high-cystine contents that preclude $\propto$-helix formation[24]. It should be stated, however, that while this interpretation is reasonably consistent with the experimental evidence, it is not wholly satisfactory, and alternative points of view have been expressed. For example, the results of amino-acid sequence studies on the peptides produced by enzymic digestion of another protein fraction from oxidized wool, U.S.3, obtained by dissolution in urea buffered at pH 5.6, suggest that the greater part of the wool fibre consists of a single protein or protein unit. This protein may be modified structurally by the addition of high-sulphur peptides during keratinization, and the modified material constitutes the matrix phase of the fibre cortex[26a].

Whatever their true origins may be, there seems little reason to doubt that the microfibrillar and matrix phases differ in both their amino-acid compositions and the conformations of their proteins. Our knowledge of the primary, secondary and tertiary structures of these is sparse, and much more must be known before changes in mechanical and physical properties of wool resulting from chemical changes can be properly understood.

The primary structure of a wool protein is simply the sequence of its amino-acid residues; it is specific, and is determined by a corresponding gene in the nucleus of a cell. The important chemical bond in the primary structure is the peptide bond formed by condensation between the amino group of an amino acid and the carboxyl group of another, thus:

$$NH_2 - CHR' - COOH \; + \; NH_2 - CHR'' - COOH$$

$$\downarrow \; [-H_2O]$$

$$NH_2 - CHR' - CO - NH - CHR'' - COOH$$

Further condensations extend the chain, until the amino-acid sequence determined by the coding gene is complete. The primary structure, together with the environment of the protein, governs the secondary and tertiary structures. The chemical bonds which stabilize these structures are (i) disulphide bonds, (ii) hydrogen bonds, (iii) ionic bonds and (iv) hydrophobic bonds.

Disulphide bonds: These bonds form by oxidation between two cysteine residues, which may be in the same protein chain, when the bond is termed *intra-chain*, or in different protein chains, when it is termed *inter-chain*.

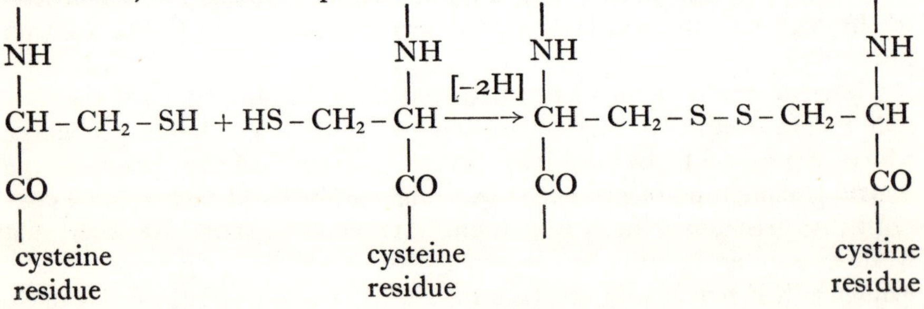

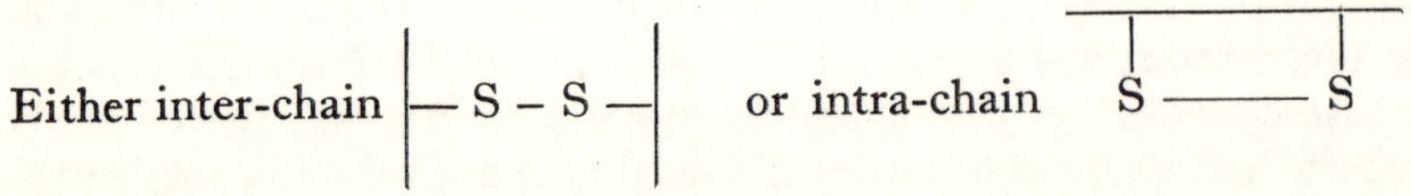

$$
\begin{array}{llll}
| & | & | & | \\
NH & NH & NH & NH \\
| & | & \;\;\;[-2H] \;| & | \\
CH-CH_2-SH \; + \; HS-CH_2-CH & \longrightarrow & CH-CH_2-S-S-CH_2-CH \\
| & | & | & | \\
CO & CO & CO & CO \\
| & | & | & | \\
\text{cysteine} & \text{cysteine} & & \text{cystine} \\
\text{residue} & \text{residue} & & \text{residue}
\end{array}
$$

Either inter-chain $\;\; | - S - S - | \;\;$ or intra-chain $\;\; S \longrightarrow S$

In the wool fibre there is one disulphide bond for every 18 amino-acid residues but, as has been shown, these are not evenly distributed, and in the low-sulphur proteins which predominate in the microfibrils, the disulphide-bond density is only one per 33 amino-acid residues, whereas in the high-sulphur proteins of the matrix it is one disulphide bond per nine amino-acid residues. There is good reason to believe that the density is even greater in certain regions of these protein chains. It is probable that both inter-chain and intra-chain disulphide bonds are present, but until the primary structures are known their relative proportions will remain unknown.

Hydrogen bonds: There are numerous possiblities for the formation of hydrogen bonds, both intra-chain types which stabilize the secondary structure of an individual protein chain, and inter-chain types which help to stabilize tertiary structures.

(a)   Hydrogen bond between peptide groups.

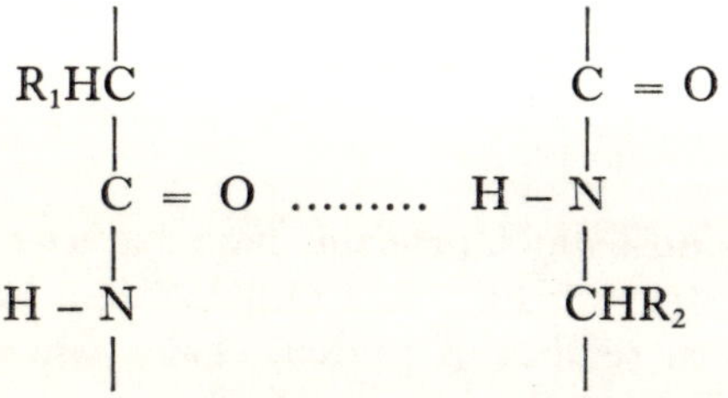

(b)   Hydrogen bonds between neutral groups in side chains of amino-acid residues.

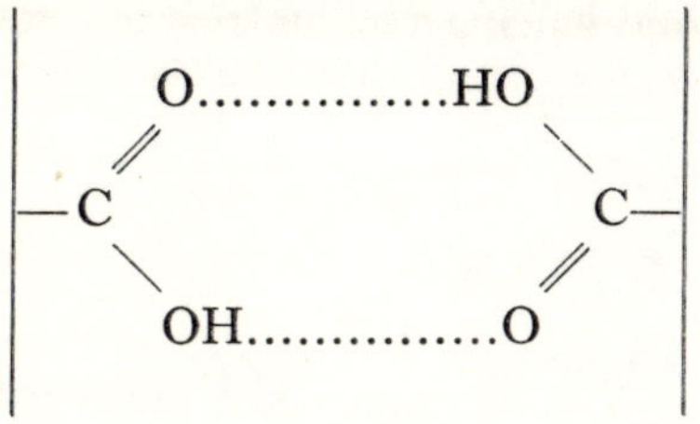

(c)   Hydrogen bonds between neutral and charged groups in side chains of amino-acid residues.

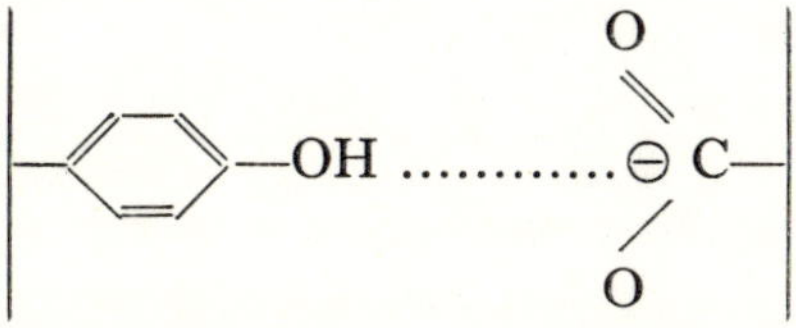

Hydrogen bonds of type 'a' are of prime importance in stabilizing α-helical sequences in protein chains, and these sequences form a large part of the proteins of the microfibrils. Although the bond-energy of the hydrogen bond is much less than that of the peptide and disulphide covalent bonds, the large numbers of such bonds make a substantial contribution to the overall inter-chain and intra-chain bonding energy.

Ionic bonds: These bonds form between oppositely-charged groups on adjacent protein chains, as indicated below:

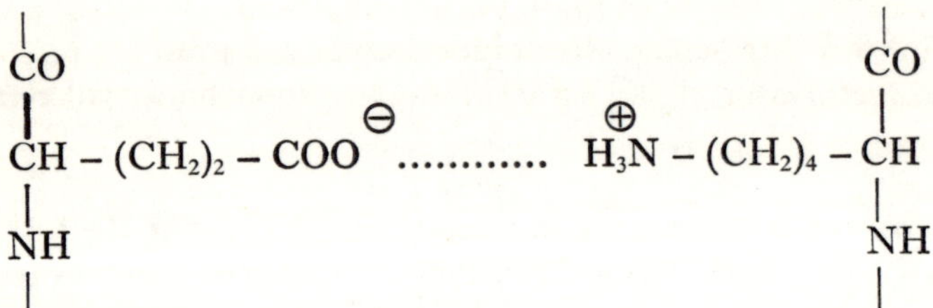

$$CO \qquad\qquad\qquad\qquad\qquad\qquad CO$$
$$CH - (CH_2)_2 - COO^{\ominus} \cdots\cdots\cdots H_3\overset{\oplus}{N} - (CH_2)_4 - CH$$
$$NH \qquad\qquad\qquad\qquad\qquad\qquad NH$$

Glutamic acid residue   Lysine residue

Ionic bonds are important in wool proteins, especially in the low-sulphur proteins, which contain a high proportion of acidic and basic amino-acid residues.

Hydrophobic bonds: These bonds, which probably have a greater part to play in stabilizing the tertiary structures of wool proteins than has been supposed hitherto, form between regions of protein chains where polar groups are either absent or few. A typical example, which may occur in the low-sulphur proteins containing one leucine residue per ten amino-acid residues, is shown below:

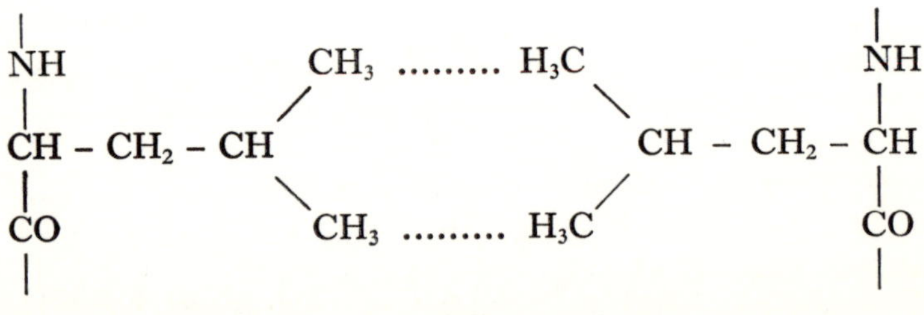

$$NH \qquad\qquad CH_3 \cdots\cdots H_3C \qquad\qquad NH$$
$$CH - CH_2 - CH \overset{\diagup}{\underset{\diagdown}{}} \qquad\qquad \overset{\diagup}{\underset{\diagdown}{}} CH - CH_2 - CH$$
$$CO \qquad\qquad CH_3 \cdots\cdots H_3C \qquad\qquad CO$$

Hydrophobic bond between two leucine residues.

With so many and varied types of chemical bond involved in the structures of wool proteins, it will be appreciated that the interpretation of the mechanical changes which occur following a chemical or environmental change of wool proteins, where several types of bond may be involved, is a hazardous undertaking.

PHYSICAL PROPERTIES OF WOOL

OF THE VARIOUS PHYSICAL PROPERTIES possessed by the wool fibre, perhaps the most important from the point of view of its use as a textile fibre are its hygroscopicity, elasticity and rigidity.

HYGROSCOPICITY

In common with other textile fibres, wool adsorbs water from moist atmospheres. Consequently, for commercial purposes standards of moisture content or regain (see Table 2.5) have been adopted for wool in its various forms.

TABLE 2.5. MOISTURE CONTENT OF WOOL

Material	Moisture Regain
Scoured wools	16 per cent
Noils	14 per cent
Tops combed with oil	19 per cnet
Tops combed without oil	18¼ per cent
Worsted yarn	18¼ per cent
Woollen yarn	17 per cent

The amount of moisture adsorbed at equilibrium, however, is a function of the relative humidity of the atmosphere, as shown by the figures[27] in Table 2.6 and there is pronounced hysteresis between adsorption and desorption.

TABLE 2.6. WATER ADSORPTION AND DESORPTION

Relative Humidity (per cent)	Adsorption (per cent on dry weight)	Desorption (per cent on dry weight)
7·0	3·40	4·77
25·0	6·96	—
34·2	8·41	10·57
49·8	11·22	13·36
63·3	13·97	16·12
75·0	16·69	18·69
92·5	23·81	24·70
100	33·3	33·3

Since water is adsorbed with evolution of heat, it is to be expected that the amount of adsorption would decrease with rising temperature, but at temperatures above 55 °C., the issue is complicated by degradation of the wool[28]. When wool is dried from regains below saturation, its adsorptive power decreases with increasing temperature of drying. Acetylation and deamination also cause a slight reduction in water adsorption.

ELASTIC PROPERTIES

The load-extension curve obtained when wool fibres are stretched consists of three parts, one in which the extension is small and proportional to the load, a second in which comparatively small increases in load produce large changes in extension, and a third in which the extension increases less rapidly with increasing load[29]. These features of the curve are clearly shown in Fig. 2.2, which also shows that there is a marked hysteresis between extension on loading and that recorded when the load is removed.

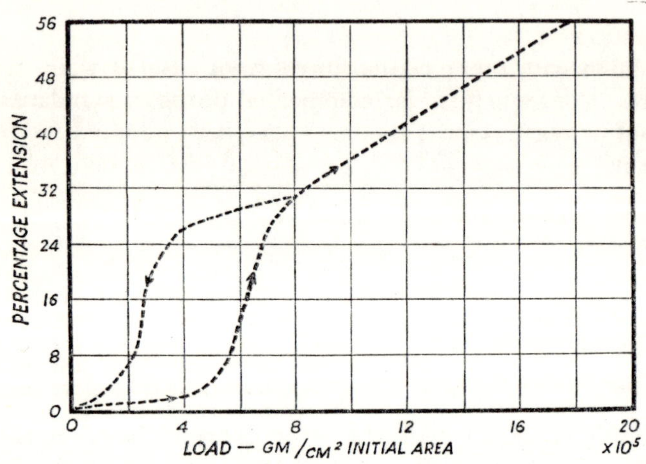

FIG. 2.2. LOAD-EXTENSION CURVE FOR WOOL

The ease of stretching fibres is affected by the nature of the medium in which the stretching takes place and by the rate of loading. For example, Young's modulus and breaking load both decrease with increasing relative humidity[27], as shown in Table 2.7, while similar changes produce an increase in extensibility.

TABLE 2.7.   EFFECT OF HUMIDITY ON STRENGTH OF WOOL

Relative Humidity (per cent)	Breaking load (gm/cm²–initial area)	Young's Modulus (dynes/cm²)
0·0	$22·1 \times 10^5$	$4·76 \times 10^{10}$
8·3	$21·6 \times 10^5$	$4·80 \times 10^{10}$
34·2	$19·4 \times 10^5$	$4·19 \times 10^{10}$
49·8	$16·8 \times 10^5$	$3·84 \times 10^{10}$
65·0	$16·1 \times 10^5$	$3·55 \times 10^{10}$
75·0	$15·4 \times 10^5$	$3·28 \times 10^{10}$
100·0	$14·9 \times 10^5$	$1·81 \times 10^{10}$

With increasing rates of loading – except where the latter is very small – the breaking load increases and the extension at break decreases, while at a constant relative humidity, the resistance of fibres to extension increases with rising temperature[29].

When a fibre is stretched rapidly in water to about 30 per cent of its original length and then allowed to relax in water for 24 hours, its original load-extension curve may be reproduced but, if the fibre is stretched slowly or held under tension for a time, it does not return to its original length when the stretching force is removed[30]. There is also a decay of tension in a fibre which is held extended, the rate of decay being least in acid, and greatest in solutions of alkalis, sulphites and bisulphites[31].

At 25 °C., when stretched fibres are released in atmospheres not saturated with water vapour, the rate and extent of recovery increase with increasing relative humidity but all fibres regain their original dimensions when placed in water. When the temperature of stretching is raised, however, the fibres fail to return to their original dimensions in water unless they are heated to a temperature a few degrees higher than that at which they were originally held stretched. Thus, fibres held stretched in steam for 30 minutes do not return to their original length when boiled for one hour in water after relaxation. This extension, permanent to boiling in water for one hour, is usually referred to as "permanent set." By examining[9] the effect of time of steaming upon the amount of set produced it was found that, if the time of steaming was two minutes only, the stretched fibre, after relaxation and boiling in water for one hour, contracted to an equilibrium length about 30 per cent smaller than its original length. This shrinkage has been termed "supercontraction". At times of steaming between two minutes and 30 minutes, various degrees of supercontraction and of set are realized. Fibres also supercontract when they are boiled in a relaxed state in aqueous solutions of sodium bisulphite or silver sulphate[32]and, consequently, it has been suggested that the phenomenon of supercontraction is associated with fission of -S-S-linkages.

Further work[33] has shown that fibres also contract when heated in phenol or formamide and, in these cases, it is probable that the supercontraction arises primarily from the splitting of hydrogen bonds in the fibre. It has also been shown that when fibres are placed in solutions of cuprammonium hydroxide and then washed in distilled water, they contract by about 28 per cent and contain adsorbed copper[34]. On removing the copper by treatment with dilute sulphuric acid, the fibres return to their original length.

Since deaminated fibres do not take a permanent set under conditions which are favourable for setting untreated fibres, and the ability of fibres to take a set is directly proportional to their sulphur content, it has been postulated[35] that the mechanism of setting involves both -S-S- and salt linkages.

Since setting requires initial breakdown of protein structure, followed by rebuilding in a new extended conformation, hydrogen bonds will also be broken and re-formed. So far as the disulphide bonds are concerned the first step is believed to be hydrolytic fission according to the equation given on the following page.

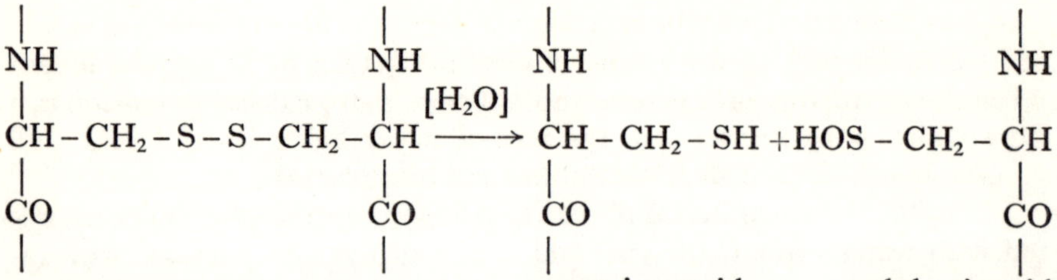

$$\begin{array}{c} | \\ NH \\ | \\ CH-CH_2-S-S-CH_2-CH \\ | \\ CO \\ | \end{array} \xrightarrow{[H_2O]} \begin{array}{c} | \\ NH \\ | \\ CH-CH_2-SH +HOS-CH_2-CH \\ | \\ CO \\ | \end{array}$$

cysteine residue   sulphenic acid residue

The sulphenic acid residue has never been detected, and is probably extremely unstable, decomposing by β-elimination to give a dehydroalanine residue and releasing H_2O and S, according to:

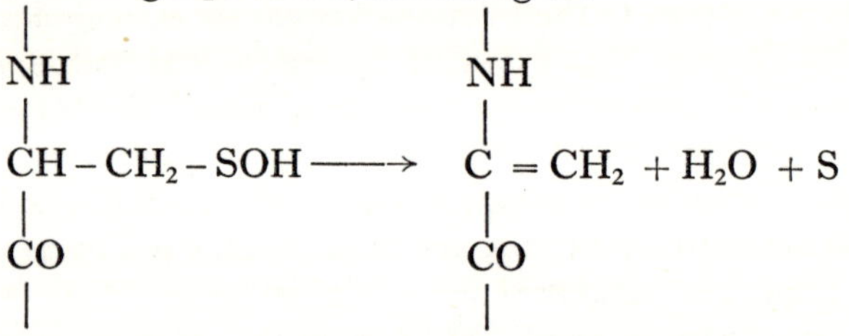

$$\begin{array}{c} | \\ NH \\ | \\ CH-CH_2-SOH \\ | \\ CO \\ | \end{array} \longrightarrow \begin{array}{c} | \\ NH \\ | \\ C = CH_2 + H_2O + S \\ | \\ CO \\ | \end{array}$$

An early explanation of the linkage rebuilding that occurred was that the sulphenic acid residue condensed with a lysine residue[32].

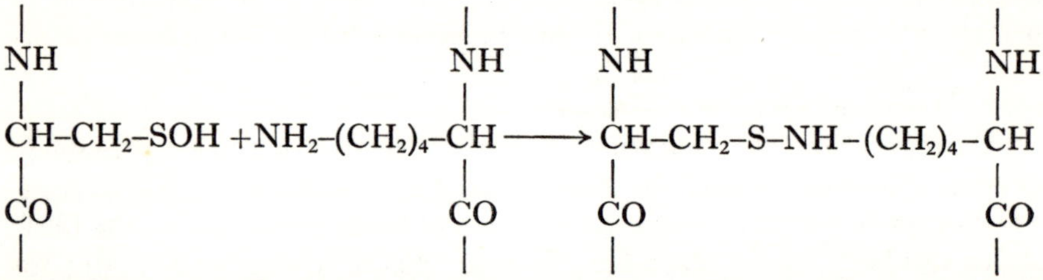

$$\begin{array}{c} | \\ NH \\ | \\ CH-CH_2-SOH +NH_2-(CH_2)_4-CH \\ | \\ CO \\ | \end{array} \longrightarrow \begin{array}{c} | \\ NH \\ | \\ CH-CH_2-S-NH-(CH_2)_4-CH \\ | \\ CO \\ | \end{array}$$

The sulphenamide supposedly formed, however, has never been detected, whereas the amino acids lanthionine and lysinoalanine have both been isolated from hydrolysates of steamed wools[36, 37]. Lanthionine almost certainly forms by addition of a cysteine residue and a dehydroalanine residue, and lysinoalanine by addition of a lysine residue to a dehydroalanine. Thus:

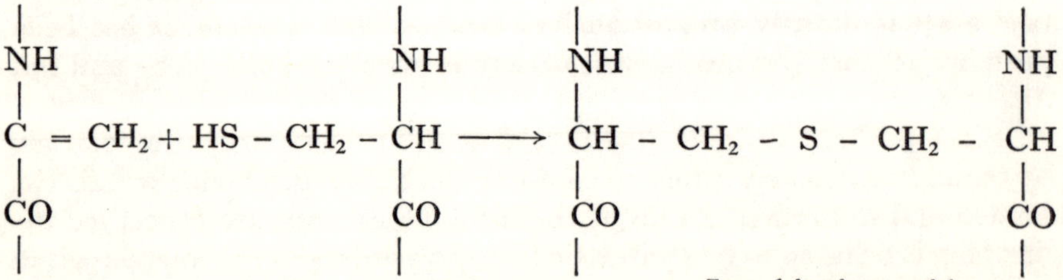

$$\begin{array}{c} | \\ NH \\ | \\ C = CH_2 + HS-CH_2-CH \\ | \\ CO \\ | \end{array} \longrightarrow \begin{array}{c} | \\ NH \\ | \\ CH-CH_2-S-CH_2-CH \\ | \\ CO \\ | \end{array}$$

Lanthionine residue

$$
\begin{array}{c}
| \\
\mathrm{NH} \\
| \\
\mathrm{C}=\mathrm{CH_2} + \mathrm{H_2N} - (\mathrm{CH_2})_4 - \mathrm{CH} \longrightarrow \mathrm{CH} - \mathrm{CH_2} - \mathrm{NH} - (\mathrm{CH_2})_4 - \mathrm{CH} \\
| \\
\mathrm{CO} \\
|
\end{array}
$$

Lysinoalanine residue

It seems probable, therefore, that the sulphenamide does not exist.

The ease with which fibres can be set varies with the pH of the medium, and it has been demonstrated that the optimum pH for setting is 9.2. At this pH lysinoalanine and lanthionine cross-linkages are formed, increasing in amount with the severity of treatment, but setting is accompanied by hydrolytic damage. If this is to be restricted to a minimum, setting should not be carried out at pHs greater than 7.

RIGIDITY

The torsional rigidity of wool fibres is extremely sensitive to changes in relative humidity, this being shown by the values[38] given in Table 2.8.

TABLE 2.8. EFFECTS OF HUMIDITY ON RIGIDITY OF WOOL

Relative Humidity (per cent)	Relative Rigidity*	Relative Humidity (per cent)	Relative Rigidity*
0·0	1·000	64·5	0·584
10·0	0·974	74·5	0·459
25·0	0·920	89·7	0·204
34·7	0·852	100	0·068
49·5	0·732		

(*Rigidity compared with that of a dry fibre)

SURFACE PROPERTIES

THE SURFACE PROPERTIES of textile fibres are complicated by the ease with which fibres are deformed and by the irregular contour of the fibre surface. In the case of wool, the coefficient of friction is dependent on the direction of motion and although this variation may be associated with the particular chemical composition of the surface layers[39], it is probable that the existence of two coefficients is due to the presence of surface scales on the fibre, particularly as the two values μ_2 and μ_1 apply respectively to motions opposed and not opposed by the surface scales.

The presence of scales on the surface of wool gives rise to the ability of wool fibres to felt and to move when rubbed between two reciprocating surfaces, e.g., when rubbed between the finger and thumb, the movement being parallel to the length of the fibre, always in the direction of the root end. Several attempts have been made to express this uni-directional property, termed the "Directional Frictional Effect (D.F.E.)" in terms of the two coefficients of friction and the following are considered satisfactory by the authors who developed them:

$$\mu_2 - \mu_1 \;:\; \frac{\mu_2 - \mu_1}{\mu_1} \;:\; \frac{\mu_2 - \mu_1}{\mu_2 + \mu_1} \;:\; \frac{1}{\mu_1} - \frac{1}{\mu_2}$$

where μ_2 is the frictional coefficient operating when the fibre tip moves first and μ_1 the frictional coefficient when the fibre moves root first.

It is clear that in all cases the difference between the coefficients is important. An alternative method of measuring the unidirectional surface property which does not involve determination of μ_1 and μ_2 has been developed[40]. In this method a fibre is rubbed lengthways between two reciprocating surfaces and the maximum tension developed when the fibre is held at the tip and is then rubbed is recorded. The instrument used is known as a lepidometer.

Values of μ_1 and μ_2 and of D.F.E. vary from wool to wool and are affected by the conditions under which the determination is made. Moreover, chemical treatment of wool may seriously alter these characteristics. The D.F.E. expressed as $\mu_2 - \mu_1 / \mu_1$ is greater for fine wools than for coarse[41], and experiments have indicated a positive correlation between fibre fineness and the coefficients of friction[42]. The coefficients of friction for wet fibres are greater than those for dry. Frictional properties are also slightly affected by the pH value of the medium; it was found that μ_1, μ_2 and $(\mu_2 - \mu_1)/(\mu_2 + \mu_1)$ were all greater at pH4 and pH7 than at pH1 or pH11[43], while $\mu_2 - \mu_1$ was greatest at pH1 and least at pH5[44].

Chemical treatment of wool may cause changes in surface properties. Chlorination, while increasing the values of μ_1 and μ_2, causes considerable reduction in the value of the D.F.E., and the creeping power of the fibres as measured on the lepidometer is also reduced. Treatment of wool with proteolytic enzymes also reduces the D.F.E.; μ_2 is not seriously altered but μ_1 is increased[42].

CHEMICAL PROPERTIES

REFERENCE has been made in a previous paragraph to the effect which chemical treatments can have on the surface properties of wool. Important though this undoubtedly is, it nevertheless represents only one of a range of effects which chemical modification of the wool fibre can produce and which vary with the modifying agent employed. In this connection it is appropriate to consider separately the effects produced by water and steam, acids, alkalis and other reagents.

EFFECT OF WATER AND STEAM

Although water at room temperature has no permanent effect on the properties of wool, it modifies the fibre at temperatures above approximately 50 °C by hydrolytic fission of the disulphide bonds, as follows:

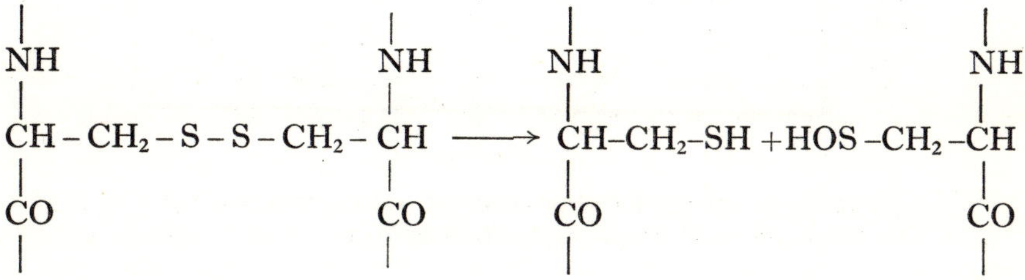

$$\begin{array}{ccc}
\mid & \mid & \mid \qquad\qquad\qquad \mid \\
NH & NH & NH \qquad\qquad\qquad NH \\
\mid & \mid & \mid \qquad\qquad\qquad\quad \mid \\
CH-CH_2-S-S-CH_2-CH & \longrightarrow & CH-CH_2-SH + HOS-CH_2-CH \\
\mid & \mid & \mid \qquad\qquad\qquad\quad \mid \\
CO & CO & CO \qquad\qquad\qquad\ CO \\
\mid & \mid & \mid \qquad\qquad\qquad\quad \mid
\end{array}$$

Following the fission some hydrogen sulphide is evolved, possibly according to the equation[45]:

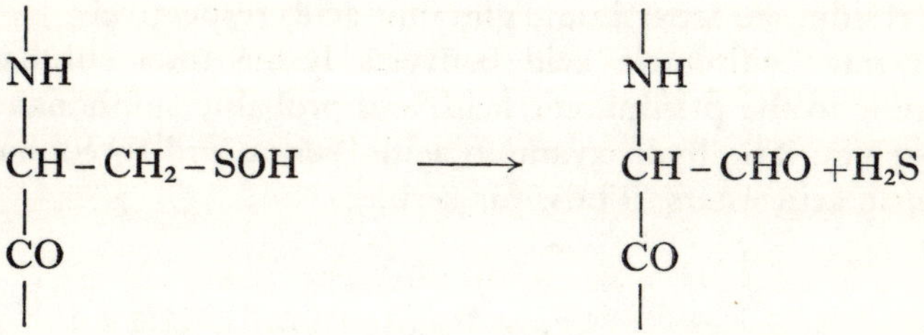

$$\begin{array}{ccc}
\mid & & \mid \\
NH & & NH \\
\mid & & \mid \\
CH-CH_2-SOH & \longrightarrow & CH-CHO + H_2S \\
\mid & & \mid \\
CO & & CO \\
\mid & & \mid
\end{array}$$

In steam, however, dehydroalanine residues form as previously described, and result in the formation of lanthionine and lysinoalanine cross-linkages. Quantitative analyses of these, and of the unaffected disulphide bonds, show that there is a reduction in the total number of cross-linkages originally present as disulphide.

EFFECT OF ACIDS

When wool is boiled in 6N solutions of hydrochloric or sulphuric acids it dissolves, yielding first peptides and ultimately a mixture of amino acids. The amounts and types of amino acid present in these hydrolysates are not the same as the amounts of the corresponding amino-acid residues in the wool proteins. For example, tryptophan is totally destroyed, serine and threonine are reduced in amount, and the cystine is partly converted to bis (2-amino-2-carboxyethyl) trisulphide, and partly to the corresponding tetrasulphide, bis (2-amino-2-carboxyethyl) tetrasulphide[46]. The amounts of

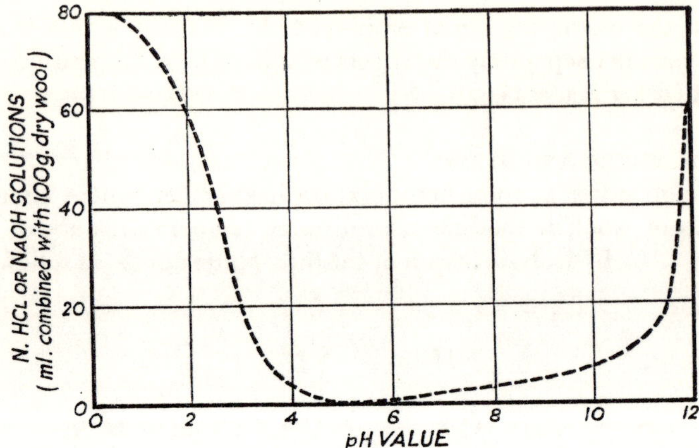

FIG. 2.3. ADSORPTION OF MINERAL ACID AND ALKALI
BY WOOL FROM AQUEOUS SOLUTIONS OF VARYING pH VALUE

these, and other unidentified decomposition products of cystine, increase
with increasing time of hydrolysis, and may account for as much as 20 per
cent of the original cystine. Acid hydrolysis also converts asparagine and
glutamine residues to aspartic and glutamic acids respectively.

Concentrated sulphuric acid converts lysine to a sulphamic acid,
phenylalanine to the p-sulphonic acid, and probably sulphonates tyrosine
and tryptophan. The hydroxyamino acids, serine and threonine, become
the sulphuric acid esters. Thus, for serine:

$$\begin{array}{ccc}
| & & | \\
NH & & NH \\
| & & | \\
CH-CH_2-OH +H_2SO_4 & \longrightarrow & CH-CH_2-O-SO_2-OH +H_2O \\
| & & | \\
CO & & CO \\
| & & |
\end{array}$$

Nitric acid rapidly yellows wool, and ultimately decomposes it. The
yellowing is due to the nitroderivatives of the aromatic amino acids,
tyrosine, phenylalanine and tryptophan.

Dilute acid solutions produce comparatively little permanent damage.
Wool adsorbs a considerable amount of mineral acid from dilute aqueous
solutions, the exact quantity depending upon the pH value of the medium[47],
(as shown in Fig. 2.3). The extent of combination is small between pH6
and 4, but gradually rises to a maximum at pH1 when 80 ml. of normal
acid per 100g. of dry wool are combined. A similarly-shaped curve (Fig.

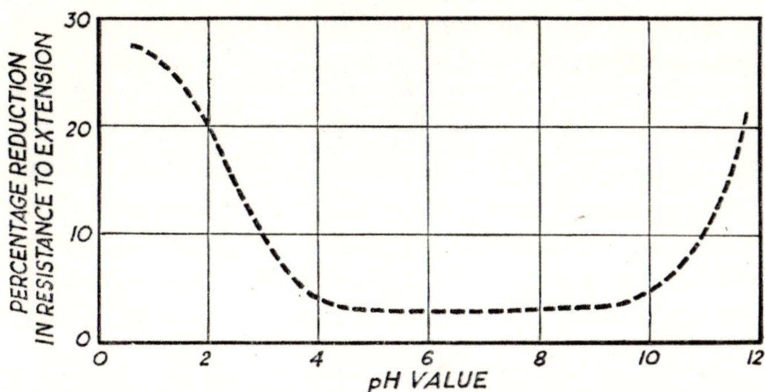

FIG. 2.4. CURVE SHOWING INCREASED EXTENSIBILITY OF
WOOL AFTER IMMERSION IN ACID OR ALKALI SOLUTIONS

2.4) is obtained[48] when the extensibility – the percentage reduction in work required to stretch the fibre 30 per cent in acid solutions of various concentrations – is plotted against the pH value of the liquor. Fibre extensibility increases with fall in pH, and there is a linear relation between the amount of acid bound at different pH values and the percentage reduction in work to stretch 30 per cent. Union between strong acids and wool is believed to take place through the salt linkage as follows:

$$
\begin{array}{ccc}
| & & | \\
NH & & NH \\
| & \ominus \qquad \oplus & | \\
CH-(CH_2)_2-COO \cdots\cdots\cdots H_3N-(CH_2)_4-CH \\
| & & | \\
CO & & CO \\
| & & |
\end{array}
$$

$$\downarrow \ [HCl]$$

$$
\begin{array}{ccc}
| & & | \\
NH & & NH \\
| & \oplus & | \\
CH-(CH_2)_2-COOH \quad + \quad H_3N-(CH_2)_4-CH \\
| & \ominus & | \\
CO & Cl & CO \\
| & & |
\end{array}
$$

Since the -COOH group is only weakly acidic, it remains unionized and the electrical charges which constituted the linkage are eliminated. The lower the pH value of the medium, the greater is the number of salt linkages broken, and the easier it is to stretch the fibre, until at pH1, all the salt linkages disappear and the limiting reduction in work to stretch is realised. The acid is completely removed by prolonged washing in distilled water, and the salt linkages are restored.

Evidence supporting this mechanism of acid adsorption is provided by the reduction in resistance to extension which takes place when wool is treated with nitrous acid[49]. The reaction involved is shown in the following equation; the percentage reduction in work to stretch 30 per cent in water following complete deamination is equal to that produced by stretching an untreated fibre in acid at pH1 . Deaminated fibres show equal resistance to extension whether stretched in solutions of pH1 or of pH5, due to the removal of salt linkages.

$$\begin{array}{ccc}
\mid & & \mid \\
NH & & NH \\
\mid & [HNO_2] & \mid \\
CH-(CH_2)_4-NH_2 & \longrightarrow & CH-(CH_2)_4-OH+N_2+H_2O \\
\mid & & \mid \\
CO & & CO \\
\mid & & \mid
\end{array}$$

Although the mechanochemical work supports the view that ionic bonds play a major role in the cross-linking of protein chains, another school of thought believes that their presence in hydrated wool has not been established[50].

Weak acids such as acetic and chloracetic behave differently[51], for at the same pH values the amount of weak acid combined is in excess of the amount of strong acid. Similarly, at the same pH value, fibres are more easily stretched in solutions of weak acids, and the swelling and heat of reaction are greater than the corresponding values for fibres in strong acids. These phenomena may be accounted for in terms of the Donnan membrane hypothesis coupled with the possibility of additional active groups in the peptide chains being available as points of combination for molecules of weak acids, The anions of acids also combine with wool and the affinities of various anions for wool vary; in general, the higher the molecular weight the greater is the affinity[52].

EFFECT OF ALKALIS

In strongly alkaline solutions, especially at high temperatures, wool dissolves rapidly by hydrolysis, and concomitantly cystine, serine, arginine and histidine are destroyed. Tryptophan, completley destroyed during acid hydrolysis, is only partially decomposed. The solubility of wool in dilute (0.1 N) caustic soda increases with increasing degradation of the fibre, and is thus used as a test for fibre damage.

The action of dilute alkali, or alkaline buffers, is to convert part of the disulphide to lanthionine and lysinoalanine and there is some indication that other amino-acid residues, probably serine, are converted to dehydro-alanine[53].

The formation of lanthionine and lysinoalanine cross-linkages during the alkali-treatment of wool increases the stability of the fibre, reducing its solubility in urea-bisulphite and phenol-thioglycollate solutions.

EFFECT OF REDUCING AGENTS

Reducing agents, such as thiols, thioglycollic acid, etc., reduce disulphide bonds to thiol groups. The latter can easily be re-oxidized to disulphide by hydrogen peroxide. This process of reduction followed by oxidation forms the basis of the permanent waving of hair. Re-oxidation of the thiol groups can be prevented by blocking with monofunctional reagents, thus:

$$
\begin{array}{ccc}
| & & | \\
NH & & NH \\
| & & | \\
CH-CH_2-SH \; +ICH_2COOH \longrightarrow & CH-CH_2-S-CH_2-COOH \; +HI \\
| & & | \\
CO & & CO \\
| & & | \\
\text{cysteine} \quad \text{iodoacetic acid} & \quad \text{S}-\text{carboxymethylcysteine} \\
\text{residue} & \text{residue}
\end{array}
$$

If bifunctional reagents are used new cross-linkages are introduced, as in the following example:

$$
\begin{array}{ccc}
| & & | \\
NH & & NH \\
| & & | \\
CH-CH_2-SH \; +Br-(CH_2)n-Br \; +HS-CH_2-CH \longrightarrow \\
| & & | \\
CO & & CO \\
| & & | \\
\text{cysteine} \quad \text{dibromo alkyl} \\
\text{residue} \quad\;\; \text{compound}
\end{array}
$$

$$
\begin{array}{cc}
| & | \\
NH & NH \\
| & | \\
CH-CH_2-S-(CH_2)n-S-CH_2-CH \; +2HBr \\
| & | \\
CO & CO \\
| & |
\end{array}
$$

EFFECT OF OXIDIZING AGENTS

Prolonged reaction of wool with oxidizing agents such as hydrogen peroxide, peracetic acid and performic acid, causes fission of the disulphide bonds of cystine residues to yield cysteic acid residues.

$$
\begin{array}{ccc}
| & | & | \\
NH & NH & NH \\
| & | \quad [5O] & | \\
CH-CH_2-S-S-CH_2-CH & \xrightarrow[\ [H_2O]\ ]{} & 2\ CH-CH_2-SO_3H \\
| & | & | \\
CO & CO & CO \\
| & | & |
\end{array}
$$

When the reaction is not carried to completion not all the disulphide bonds are broken, but oxidation products intermediate between cysteic acid and cystine are formed. If, for convenience, the abbreviation 'Cy' is used to represent $NH_2 -(COOH) - CH - CH_2 -$, these oxidation products are $Cy - SO - S - Cy$, $Cy - SO_2 - S - Cy$, $Cy - SO - SO - Cy$, $Cy - SO_2 - SO - Cy$, $Cy - SO_2 - SO_2 - Cy$, $CySO_2H$ and $CySOH$[54]. Although many of them have been separated from wool hydrolysates by high-voltage electrophoresis on paper, they have not been unequivocally identified.

Cystine, tryptophan, tyrosine and methionine residues are also attacked when wool is treated with other oxidizing agents such as permanganate, chlorine and chlorine peroxide. The oxidation products are complex.

SULPHITOLYSIS OF WOOL

At pH 5.5 sulphitolysis of the disulphide bonds of the cystine residues in wool occurs according to the equation:

$$
\begin{array}{cccc}
| & | \quad\quad | & & | \\
NH & NH \ \ominus\ NH & & NH \\
| & |\ HSO_3\ | & \ominus & | \\
CH-CH_2-S-S-CH_2-CH & \longrightarrow CH-CH_2-SH & +O_3S-S-CH_2-CH & \\
| & |\quad\quad | & & | \\
CO & CO \quad CO & & CO \\
| & |\quad\quad | & &
\end{array}
$$

cysteine S – cysteine sulphon-
residue ate residue

Approximately 50 per cent of the bonds are broken. On washing with water partial reversal of the reaction occurs and about half of the severed bonds re-form[55].

When sulphitolysis is carried out at alkaline pHs in the presence of cupric ion, iodosobenzoate or tetrathionate, the disulphide bonds of the cystine residues of wool are quantitatively converted to cysteinyl sulphonate residues.

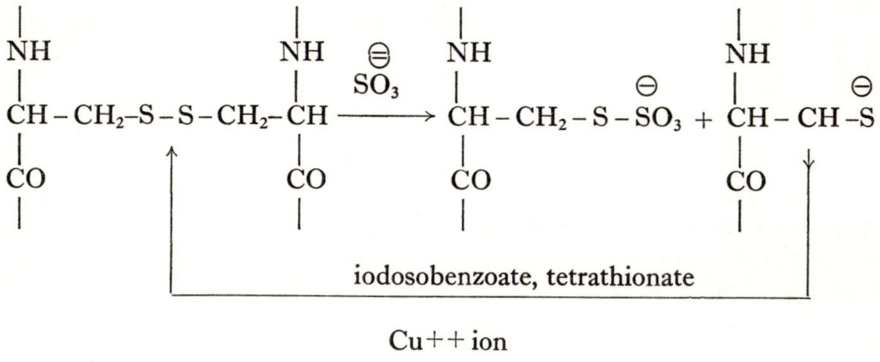

$$
\begin{array}{llll}
| & | & | & | \\
NH & NH & NH & NH \\
| & | \quad \overset{\ominus}{SO_3} & | & | \\
CH-CH_2-S-S-CH_2-CH & \longrightarrow & CH-CH_2-S-SO_3^{\ominus} + CH-CH-S^{\ominus} \\
| & | & | & | \\
CO & CO & CO & CO \\
| & | & | & |
\end{array}
$$

iodosobenzoate, tetrathionate

$Cu++$ ion

EFFECTS OF MISCELLANEOUS REAGENTS

Fluorine reacts rapidly with wool to give a limited amount of cysteic acid, but the evolution of gaseous fluorides of sulphur indicates that cystine residues are being decomposed. Chlorine has been widely used in shrinkage-resistance treatments on wool. The extent of its reaction depends on the conditions; free chlorine converts most of the cystine residues to cysteic acid, whereas the hypochlorite ion only oxidizes about 25 per cent. Almost quantitative conversion of cystine residues to cysteic acid residues occurs in bromine water. At the same time tyrosine is converted to its dibromo derivative.

In aqueous media iodine reacts slowly with wool. The cystine residues are not affected, but small amounts of tyrosine residues are iodinated to monoiodo- and diiodo-tyrosine residues. The reaction with iodine in alcoholic solution, however, is much more vigorous and tyrosine residues are almost quantitatively converted to diiodotyrosine residues:

$$
\begin{array}{c}
| \\
NH \\
| \\
CH-CH_2-\langle\bigcirc\rangle-OH \quad \xrightarrow{[I_2]} \quad CH-CH_2-\langle\bigcirc\rangle\overset{I}{\underset{I}{OH}} \\
| \\
CO \\
|
\end{array}
$$

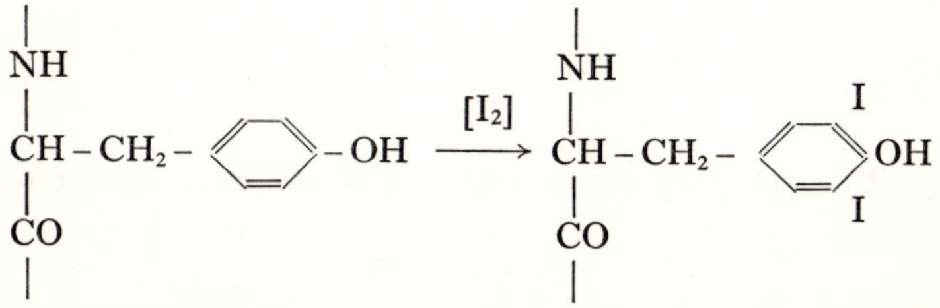

Treatment of wool with 0.1N KCN at 56°C for 24 hours converts the cystine residues of wool to lanthionine residues.

$$
\begin{array}{c}
| \\
NH \\
| \\
CH - CH_2 - S - S - CH_2 - CH \\
| \\
CO \\
|
\end{array}
\quad
\xrightarrow{[KCN]}
\quad
\begin{array}{c}
| \qquad | \\
NH \quad NH \\
| \qquad | \\
CH - CH_2 - S - CH_2 - CH \quad +KCNS \\
| \qquad | \\
CO \quad CO \\
| \qquad |
\end{array}
$$

When wool is treated with formaldehyde it acquires an increased resistance to extension and a reduced affinity for dyes. These phenomena imply formation of new cross-linkages and various possibilities have been suggested. One of these is:

$$
\begin{array}{c}
| \\
NH \\
| \\
CH - CH_2 - CO - NH_2 + CH_2O + NH_2 - (CH_2)_4 - CH \\
| \qquad\qquad\qquad\qquad\qquad\qquad\qquad | \\
CO \qquad\qquad\qquad\qquad\qquad\qquad\qquad CO \\
| \qquad\qquad\qquad\qquad\qquad\qquad\qquad |
\end{array}
\longrightarrow
$$

$$
\begin{array}{c}
| \\
NH \\
| \\
CH - CH_2 - CO - NH - CH_2 - NH - (CH_2)_4 - CH \\
| \qquad\qquad\qquad\qquad\qquad\qquad\qquad\qquad\qquad | \\
CO \qquad\qquad\qquad\qquad\qquad\qquad\qquad\qquad\qquad CO \\
| \qquad\qquad\qquad\qquad\qquad\qquad\qquad\qquad\qquad |
\end{array}
$$

With reduced or sulphited wools formaldehyde reacts with cystine residues to give thiazolidine-4-carboxylic acid residues or djenkolic acid residues as indicated below and on the opposite page.

$$
\begin{array}{c}
| \\
NH \\
| \\
CH-CH_2-SH + CH_2O + SH-CH_2-CH \\
| \\
CO \\
|
\end{array}
\longrightarrow
\begin{array}{c}
| \qquad | \\
NH \quad NH \\
| \qquad | \\
CH-CH_2-S-CH_2-S-CH_2-CH- \\
| \qquad | \\
CO \quad CO \\
| \qquad |
\end{array}
$$

Djenkolic acid
residue

$$
\begin{array}{ccc}
\overset{\displaystyle |}{NH} & & \overset{\displaystyle |}{N} \!\!-\!\! CH_2 \\[4pt]
| & & | \qquad\quad \diagdown \\[2pt]
& & \qquad\qquad S + H_2O \\[2pt]
& & \qquad\quad \diagup \\[2pt]
CH\!-\!CH_2\!-\!SH \; + \; CH_2O \;\longrightarrow\; CH\!-\!CH_2 & & \\[4pt]
| & & | \\[2pt]
CO & & CO \\[2pt]
| & & |
\end{array}
$$

Thiazolidine-4-carboxylic acid
residue

REFERENCES

1. Birbeck and Mercer, *J. Biophys. Biochem. Cytol.*, 1957, **3**, 203.
2. Simpson and Sikorski, *J. Roy. Micr. Soc.*, 1959, **78**, 35.
3. Lindberg, *Text. Res. J.*, 1949, **19**, 43.
4. Horio and Kondo, *Text. Res. J.*, 1953, **23**, 137.
5. Rogers and Filshie, in 'Ultrastructure of Protein Fibres', R. Borasky, Ed., p.123, Academic Press, New York, 1963.
6. Filshie and Rogers, *J. Mol. Biol.*, 1961, **3**, 784.
7. Johnson and Sikorski, *Nature*, 1962, **194**, 31.
8. Dobb, *J. Mol. Biol.*, 1964, **10**, 156.
9. Astbury and Woods, *Phil. Trans. Roy. Soc.*, 1933, A **232**, 333.
10. Pauling and Corey, *Proc. Natl. Acad. Sci. Washington*, 1951, **37**, 261.
11. Bonsma, *J. Text. Inst.*, 1931, **22**, T305.
12. Simmonds, *Aust. J. Biol. Sci.*, 1955, **8**, 537.
13. Simmonds, *Proc. Inst. Wool Text. Res. Conf.*, Australia, 1955, C, 65.
14. Golden, Whitwell and Mercer, *Text. Res. J.*, 1955, **25**, 334.
15. Leveau, *Bull. Inst. Text. France*, 1959, **85**, 57.
16. Bradbury, Chapman and King, *Aust. J. Biol. Sci.*, 1965, **18**, 353.
17. Alexander and Hudson, In '*Wool: its Chemistry and Physics*' p.354, Chapman and Hall, London, 1954.
18. Corfield, Robson and Skinner, *Biochem. J.*, 1958, **68**, 348.
19. Gillespie and Lennox, *Biochem, Biophys. Acta.*, 1953, **12**, 481.
20. Thompson and O'Donnell, *Aust. J. Biol. Sci.*, 1964, **17**, 277.
21. Reis and Schinckel, *Aust. J. Biol. Sci.*, 1963, **16**, 218.
22. Gillespie, Reis and Schinckel, *Aust. J. Biol. Sci.*, 1964, **17**, 548.
23. Downes, Sharry and Rogers, *Nature*, 1963, **199**, 1059.
24. Robson, *Text. Inst. Industr.*, 1966, **4**, 37.
25. Corfield and Robson, *Biochem. J.*, 1955, **59**, 62.
26. Fletcher and Robson, *Biochem. J.*, 1962, **84**, 439.
26a. Corfield, Fletcher and Robson, *Biochem. J.*, 1967, **102**, 801.
27. Speakman, J. B., *J. Soc. Chem. Industr.*, 1930, **49**, 209T.
28. Speakman, J. B. and Cooper, *J. Text. Inst.*, 1936, **27**, T183.
29. Speakman, J. B., *J. Text. Inst.*, 1926, **17**, T475.
30. Speakman, J. B., *Proc. Roy. Soc.*, 1928, B**103**, 377.
31. Speakman, J. B. and Shah, *J. Soc. Dyers and Col.*, 1941, **57**, 108.
32. Speakman, J. B., *Nature*, 1933, **132**, 930.
33. Elod, Nowotony and Zahn, *Textilber.*, 1944, **25**, 73.
34. Whewell and Woods, *Nature*, 1944, **154**, 546.
35. Speakman, J. B., *J. Soc. Dyers and Col.*, 1936, **52**, 335.
36. Speakman, J. B. and Whewell, *J. Soc. Dyers and Col.*, 1936, **52**, 380.
37. Ziegler, Troisième Congrés Int. Recherche Textile Lainière, 1965, **2**, 403.

38. Speakman, J. B., *Trans. Faraday Soc.*, 1929, **25**, 92.
39. Martin, *J. Soc. Dyers and Col.*, 1944, 60. 325.
40. Speakman, J. B. and Chamberlain, *J. Text. Inst.*, 1945, **36**, 791.
41. Speakman, J. B. and Stott. *J. Text. Inst.*, 1931, **22**, T339.
42. Martin and Mittelman, *J. Text. Inst.*, 1947, **38**, T269.
43. Mercer, *J. Text. Inst.*, 1947, **38**, T227
44. Bohm, *J. Soc. Dyers and Col.*, 1945, **61**, 278.
45. Schoberl, *Angen. Chem.*, 1940, **53**, 227.
46. Fletcher and Robson, *Biochem. J.*, 1963, **87**, 553.
47. Speakman, J. B. and Stott, *Trans. Faraday Soc.*, 1934, **30**, 539.
48. Speakman, J. B. and Hirst, *Trans. Faraday Soc.*, 1933, **29**, 148.
49. Speakman, J. B. and Stott, *Nature*, 1938, **141**, 414.
50. Crewther, Fraser, Lennox and Lindley, *Adv. Protein Chem.*, 1965, **20**, 191.
51. Speakman, J. B. and Stott, *Trans. Faraday Soc.*, 1935, **31**, 1425.
52. Steinbardt, Fugitt and Harris, *Amer. Dyestuff Rep.*, 1942, **31**. 77.
53. Corfield, Wood, Robson, Williams and Woodhouse, *Biochem. J.*, 1967 **103**, 15c.
54. Savige and Maclaren, In 'Organic Sulphur Compounds' (N. Kharasch Ed.) Vol. 2. Pergamon Press, New York, 1964.
55. Phillips, *Symp. Fibrous Proteins*, 1946, p.39. Published by Society of Dyers and Colourists.

REVIEWS

'Levels of Molecular Organisation in $\propto$-Keratins' by H. P. Lundgren and W. H. Ward. *Arch. Biochem. Biophys.* 1962, Supplement *1*, 78.
'The Chemistry of Keratins' by W. E. Crewther, R.B.D. Fraser, F. G. Lennox and H. Lindley. *Advance Protein Chem.* ,1965, *20*, 191.
Wool Science Reviews, Nos. 21, 22, 23 and 24.

BOOKS

'Wool: Its Chemistry and Physics' by P. Alexander and R. F. Hudson. Revised by C. Earland. Chapman and Hall, 1963, 2nd Edition.
'Physics of Fibres' by H. J. Woods. Institute of Physics, 1955.

PRELIMINARY PROCESSING

THE WOOLLEN AND WORSTED INDUSTRIES originated as processors of wool, and at present this is still the most important, and greatest by weight, of the fibres used in these sections of the textile trade. In addition, other animal, vegetable, and man-made fibres are used.

WOOL

Wool which has not previously been used is called virgin wool. For trade purposes this is sub-divided into combing and clothing wools:

Combing wools: These are regarded as suitable for processing on a worsted system and in general have a maximum fibre length not less than $1\frac{1}{2}$ to 2 inches. Wools with a maximum fibre length of about 4 inches or more are processed on the Bradford or Pin-drafting systems, whereas the shorter wools are processed on the Continental system.

Clothing wools: These are processed on the woollen system, and are usually less than $1\frac{1}{2}$ to 2 inches maximum fibre length. Longer wools are also processed on the woollen system, including wools heavily contaminated with burr, and also carpet wools which may be coarse and long.

Apart from the above division which is based mainly on fibre length, there is a general classification of wools into qualities regardless of length. It has already been pointed out in Section 1 that there is a tremendous variety of wools available from different breeds of sheep reared in widely different habitats. The wool quality number is said to have originally been based on the finest count of yarn which could be spun from the wool on the worsted system. This is no longer the case, although there is a relationship between limit count and wool quality number[1,2], due to the close correlation between fibre diameter and quality number[3,4]. The present trend is for wool quality to be described in terms of fibre diameter, although other features are also important. After diameter, length is important, as it influences yarn strength, spinning twist required, and finishing properties, as well as having a slight influence on the spinning count limit[5,2] and yarn regularity[6]. Other features of some importance include strength, crimp, elasticity, colour, lustre, and freedom from vegetable matter[7-12]. A survey of the features of the chief wools of the world has been made and is published in the literature [13].

A broad division of wools, based on quality numbers, is given below:

Merino: This is generally accepted to include all qualities of 60s and higher, i.e. with a mean fibre diameter of about 24 microns or less.

Crossbred: This group is sub-divided into three categories, viz. (*a*) Fine crossbred 58s – 56s qualities (about 26 – 29 microns inclusive); (*b*) Medium crossbred 54s – 48s qualities (about 30 – 35 microns inclusive); and (*c*) Coarse crossbred 44s – 36s qualities (about 38 – 52 microns inclusive). It should be pointed out, however, that the description of crossbred given to a wool does not necessarily mean that the sheep of origin is a crossbred sheep; many 'crossbred' wools are obtained from pedigree English mutton breeds.

Carpet: This group includes all coarse hairy wools not included in the apparel category given above.

ANIMAL HAIR

Animal fibres other than wool which are used for textiles have been described in some detail in Section 1 and it will suffice here to reiterate that the chief hairs used in the textile industry are, in order of importance, mohair, cashmere, alpaca, camel and vicuna. The coats of most of these animals consist of a long outer coarse fibre called guard hair, and a short inner coat which is often fine and soft. The two lots of fibre may be separated, the longer fibres often being processed on the worsted system, and the shorter on the woollen system.

MAN-MADE FIBRES

Fibre in staple form accounts for more than 10 per cent of the total weight of fibres of all types processed on the woollen and worsted systems. The fibres commonly used include viscose and modified viscose rayons, acetate, triacetate, acrylics, nylons, polyesters and polypropylenes, while recently elastomerics have been used as a core for stretch yarns (in filament form). The reasons for blending man-made fibres with wool include, in some cases, cheapness. In addition they may be used to impart technical advantages to the blend, such as strength and hard wearing properties, crease resistance or retention, improved draping properties, differential shrinkage rates to confer bulk in finishing and facilities for cross-dyed effects. Man-made fibres are usually provided in approximately the same dimensions as the fibres with which they are to be blended, as this facilitates processing [14,15].

ADDITIONAL RAW MATERIALS FOR THE WOOLLEN INDUSTRY

In addition to the natural and man-made fibres referred to above, the woollen industry also uses noils, waste fibres and remanufactured fibres.

Noils: These are the fibres rejected by the worsted comb as too short for worsted processing; this by-product of the worsted section of the trade forms a large and useful proportion of the raw material used in woollen yarn manufacture. Noils are available in standard qualities, depending on the wool originally combed, and there is a consistent supply of them. The best noils are double-combed white noils. Other double-combed noils will be coloured and, apart from black, may be only available in relatively small quantities. Single-combed noils will normally be white, but shorter in length, and more burry. It is usual for noils to be carbonized to remove the vegetable matter present.

Wastes: Processing wastes from the worsted section of the trade form a useful raw material for woollens. The best of these are clean and free of twist, and include drawing wastes, laps and broken tops. Hard waste is the name used for waste which contains twist, and includes waste from spinning and twisting operations. In addition there is brush and fly waste which, although twistless, is frequently dirty. Most wastes need to be sorted for shade and quality, and some may need garnetting to disentangle the fibres.

Remanufactured fibres: Shoddy is produced by pulling rags made from yarns which contain little twist, and from loosely constructed fabrics such as knitwear. Mungo is pulled from rags which have a more solid structure; the yarns may contain more twist, or the fabrics may be heavily milled and felted. Mungo yields a shorter fibre length than shoddy[16]. The classifying of rags has become much more complex in recent years due to the large amounts of wool/man-made fibre mixture fabrics now produced, and the difficulty of identifying some of the fibres. Work is progressing to separate wool/man-made fibre blends mechanically. Rags are broadly classified into new and old, and each division is sorted according to fibre content. Stocks are built up in various colours and this may mean holding some rags in stock for a considerable period of time.

Cotton and waste cotton: These are used in the low woollen industry to improve the spin. Peruvian cotton is preferred, being coarse and rough handling.

WOOL CLASSING, SORTING AND BLENDING

IMMEDIATELY after the wool is sheared, the fleece is classed. First the edges of the fleece may be removed, the small portions of discarded fleece, which are called 'skirtings' often being burry, dirty, and irregular. These skirtings may be sub-divided into pieces, belly wool, crutchings, locks, and, possibly into even further sub-divisions. The remaining fleece is then classed according to its best quality of wool, which is on the shoulders. In this way, the clip is broadly divided into the different grades of wool produced. This helps the producer to realize a better price and the user to obtain more constant standards of supply.

WOOL SORTING

On arrival at the mill the fleeces may be broken up into sections according to the qualities of wool present. This operation is called wool sorting. The sorter, aided by experience, sight, and touch, selects the different matchings. The subjective assessment of quality in wool tops has been investigated, and has some bearing on the problems of the wool sorter[17].

A general idea of the wide range covered in different types of wools, and the variety of qualities which may be found on an individual fleece is given by Fig. 3.1, while Table 3.1, compiled by Capt. R. P. Pitcher, of Airedale Combing Co. Ltd., shows the various amounts of each sort obtained from various wool classes. Details of the sorts obtained from British wools have also been published[13,18].

TABLE 3.1.   FLEECE CLASSIFICATIONS

Classed Fleece Grades		*Sorted Matchings*								
		70s	64s	60s	58s	56s	50s	48s	46s	44s & *Various*
		%	%	%	%	%	%	%	%	%
Australian Wool	70s	90	8	2	—	—	—	—	—	—
	64s	15	78	7	—	—	—	—	—	—
	60s	—	10	70	15	5	—	—	—	—
	58s	—	—	25	40	25	5	5	—	—
	56s	—	—	—	30	30	30	10	—	—
New Zealand Wool	58s	—	—	5	75	20	—	—	—	—
	56s	—	—	—	20	66	8	6	—	—
	50s	—	—	—	—	5	80	10	5	—
	48s	—	—	—	—	—	10	75	10	5

Sorting is a valuable process, its value being reflected in the better prices obtained for the finer qualities. Processing is also improved by sorting, in that better fibre control may be exercised by the spinner when fibre variations are minimized.

At this point, some reference should be made to anthrax, a fatal disease commonly affecting animals in Asiatic countries, and which can be passed on to man by skin infection or by inhalation of germs present in dust, excrement, or skin particles from infected animals. The Factories Acts now enforce certain regulations which aim at the prevention of the disease.

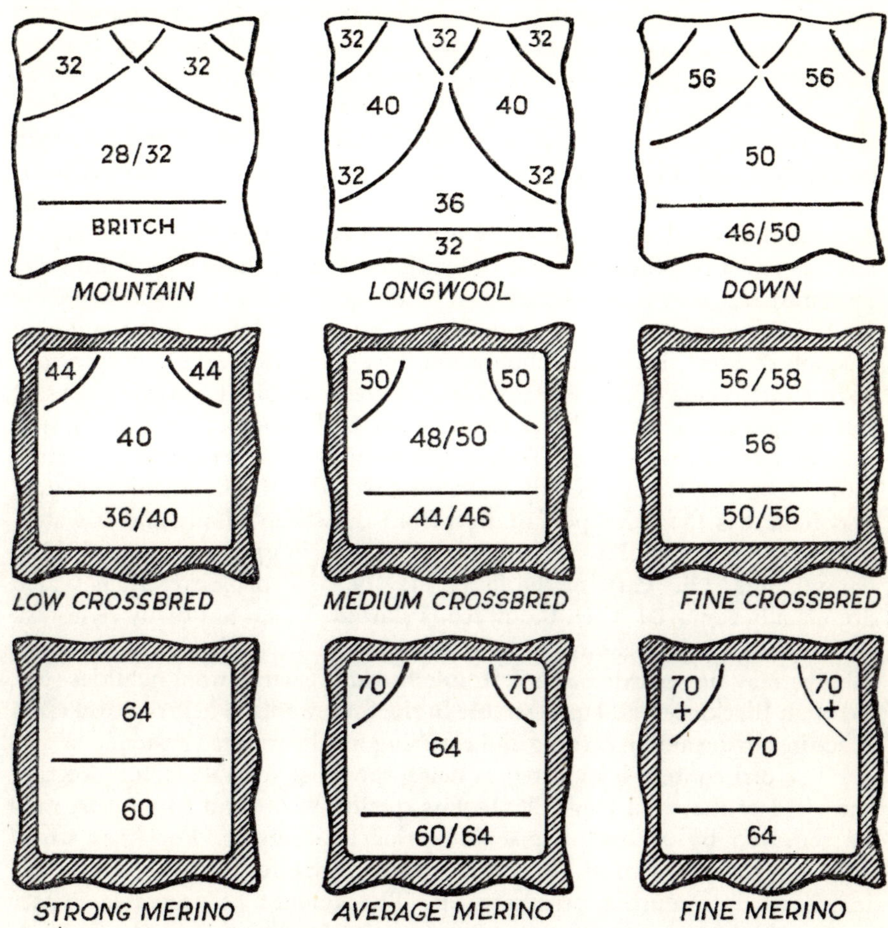

FIG 3.1. GENERAL DIVISIONS OF FLEECES IN WOOL SORTING

The upper end of each fleece is the neck end and the lower end the britch. The shaded areas are removed as skirtings when classing takes place prior to woolsorting. The numbers indicate the approximate qualities which may be sorted from each fleece.

WOOL BLENDING

Wool blending is frequently carried out in order to obtain certain blend properties from wools of similar qualities, but from different sources. It also helps to stabilize the blend characteristics from one season to another. In the woollen system, blending is a very important subject, price frequently being the most important factor.

WOOL CLEANSING

Raw wool contains impurities which may conveniently be grouped into three categories, viz., natural, acquired and applied impurities. Natural impurities may be secretions (wool grease and suint, collectively called 'yolk'), excretions (dung and urine) or accretions (kemps – coarse fibres shed from the follicle). Acquired impurities include those of mineral origin (sand, dust and soil), vegetable matter (burrs, seed, etc.) and animal parasites such as ticks and lice. Applied impurities are mainly marking materials, dipping fluids, salves and possibly lime. To enable the fibres to be separated, to assist in processing and to facilitate dyeing, these impurities must be removed.

Wool grease may be regarded as a mixture of free and combined alcohols (waxes), including cholesterol, together with varying proportions of free fatty acids[19,21]. It is insoluble in water, soluble in organic solvents, but is unsaponifiable. It has a melting point of about 100°F (38°C), and may be emulsified by soap/alkali solutions above this temperature. Alternatively, it may be removed by being dissolved directly in organic solvents. Wool suint is the dried perspiration from the sheep's body and is water-soluble. It is a complex mixture of fatty acids, inorganic salts, and other components [20-24]. Parts of the fleece may be stained by excretions which are usually removed when the fleece is skirted. When not easily removed, these stained portions have to be cut away, usually in the sorting process. Kemps may be regarded as a desirable feature in some wool qualities (e.g. Scottish Blackface), and undesirable in the finer wools. Their removal takes place in sorting and in carding and combing for the worsted system.

The dirt content is reported as being the most variable factor affecting the yield of the wool clip[25, 26]. In low quality wools and hairs, dust may be removed by a shaking machine prior to scouring. For finer wools vigorous treatment must be avoided to minimize felting; the dirt is released in the scouring process itself. The amount of vegetable matter varies, depending on the vegetation in the locality where the wool is grown[29]. About 10 per cent of the Australian wool clip is heavily contaminated with burr; most of this wool will enter the woollen trade. Removal of vegetable matter is effected either chemically, by subjecting it to an acid treatment, known as carbonizing, or by mechanical methods of crushing, burr beating, or combing.

The presence of lime impedes scouring by the formation of lime soaps, which are non-detergent in property. Lime may be present due to the sheep grazing on grassland where the mineral is present or to its application for removal of the wool from the pelt of slaughtered sheep. As much as possible should be removed by shaking before scouring commences. Parasites which survive up to the scouring process will perish due to the heat and chemical composition of the scouring solutions. Brand marks should nowadays consist of approved fluids which are based on lanolin[27] and which are removed without any additional treatment.

Impurities vary considerably in amount on different parts of the fleece[21, 28], and also between fleeces in the same bale[30]. Care must be taken in scouring not to under-scour or over-scour local parts of the fleeces.

There are several methods of scouring, the most common being the emulsion system, in which the principal agents are soap and alkali in water. If preliminary rinsing with water takes place, the process is sometimes called 'desuintage scouring'. In another system—the solvent system—an organic solvent is used to dissolve the wool grease. The use of ultra-high frequency sound waves has also been suggested as a possible method[31] but this system has not yet been adopted, probably due to the high power consumption involved.

EMULSION SCOURING

Emulsion scouring is the oldest and yet the most widely used method. The scouring agents used are water, soap, (or some synthetic detergent) alkali, heat, agitation and time. These may be varied in amounts depending on the types and proportions of impurities present in the wool to be scoured.

Water provides the basis of the necessary solutions in each bowl, and it dissolves the suint in the wool. It also forms a means of transport for the material in the conventional system, and a medium through which heat may be applied. Water may be classed as hard or soft, depending on its ability to form a lather with a detergent soap. Hard water requires the addition of more soap to form a lather than does a soft water, due to the presence of calcium or magnesium salts which combine with the soap to form non-detergent soaps. Sufficient detergent soap must be added to neutralize these salts before the task of forming a lather can commence and thus there is a waste of soap. For this reason, hard water must be softened before being used for wool scouring. A further point is that the non-detergent soaps form a sticky film on the fibres, making processing difficult, attracting dirt, and interfering with subsequent dyeing.

Usually sodium or potassium soaps are used, the former being more commonly used in the form of hard soap because of its cheapness, and also, possibly, because it can be more easily and more thoroughly rinsed off the fibre afterwards. The functions of the soap are to assist in wetting out the greasy wool (by reducing the surface tension), to emulsify the grease and maintain a stable emulsion, and to help retain the dirt in suspension. This is possible due to the unique behaviour of the soap molecule in water. Soaps have the general formula R.COOM, where R is a long chain hydrocarbon, and M is sodium, potassium, or ammonium[32]. In water, the soap is ionized, and one of the ions is "amphipathic", *i.e.*, one end of the ion has affinity for water, while the other end is attracted to grease, but repelled by water. Such ions will be attracted to the grease-water interface, and will surround grease droplets so that the ends attracted to water are on the outside. In this way the droplets will be held in suspension and prevented from amalgamating into larger units of grease. Synthetic detergents—for example, 'Lissapol' and 'Nonidet'—act in a similar way[33].

These synthetic detergents are capable of scouring in neutral conditions, minimizing the possibility of alkali damage to the wool. They are effective in the presence of lime (present on some skin wools) and they may also be used to advantage when processing burry wools where the presence of alkali could cause staining from the burr. The recovery of the grease from waste liquors containing synthetic detergents is more difficult than from liquors used in soap scouring and for the time being Bradford Sewage Works has agreed only to accept a restricted quantity of detergent being used on a trial basis while the effect on the works processes is observed[34]. This affects mainly the worsted section of the wool scouring industry.

The alkaline agent used in scouring is usually sodium carbonate, the object being to maintain a pH of about 10 in the main emulsifying bowl, although later in the set a pH of about 9 is more suitable[35]. Alkali used at normal concentrations and temperatures causes little damage to the wool, although excessive heat or concentrations may result in extensive fibre damage[36, 37]. The purpose of the alkali is to maintain conditions under which the soap may function more efficiently. As wool has an affinity for alkali, compensation has to be made for loss from the bowls due to this reaction. In addition, it is likely that a small amount of fatty matter in the wool grease is saponified by the alkali. Howitt observed[38] that of 3.5 per cent residual fatty matter in wool emerging from the first bowl, 1.5 per cent was wool grease, and 2.0 per cent soap, the latter presumably being formed by saponification of free fatty acid in the wool grease.

The function of the heat applied in scouring is to melt the wool grease and so assist in the formation of an emulsion. As wool grease melts at about 100°F (38°C), temperatures in excess of this have to be used. Usually the first bowl has a temperature of 130°F (55°C), while following bowls have their temperatures reduced by 5°F to 10°F (about 3°C to 5.5°C). Slightly lower temperatures may be used for crossbred wools, and when lustre wools and hairs are scoured the maximum temperature may be limited to about 100°F (38°C) to prevent damage to the fibre surface. When alkali is present excessive temperatures may cause discolouration and weakening of the fibre[39].

Some form of agitation is necessary to bring about relative motion between the wool and the liquor. This may involve propelling the wool through the liquor, or the liquor through the wool. Conventional scouring machinery uses a fork mechanism which dips down into the liquor and moves the wool forward about 12 inches before withdrawing and moving back to the original position ready to repeat the operation. The harrow fork mechanism does this in a relatively gentle manner and is preferred for the processing of fine wools, whereas the rake mechanism is much more vigorous and is preferred for lower quality wools and hairs where there is little danger of felting. On reaching the end of the bowl, the wool is carried by an auxiliary fork, up an inclined plate from where the liquor carries the fibres down to the nip of heavily loaded squeeze rollers. These squeeze rollers contribute to the agitation required for cleansing the wool by causing the liquor to move through the fibres at high velocity, carrying away dirt at the same time. The subject of agitation is worthy of more than passing consideration by wool scourers as efficient use of soap and alkali depends largely on the speeds of the fork mechanism and of the squeeze rollers. In one investigation it was shown that detergent consumption decreased when squeeze roller speed was increased, whereas the detergent consumption was increased when the speed of the fork mechanism was increased[40].

Time may be regarded as the 'balancing agent'; if other agents are active, less time is needed, and vice-versa. The length of time during which the material is immersed throughout the whole process varies from about four to nine minutes, depending on the number of scouring bowls and on the fork and squeeze roller speeds. According to Howitt[33] prolonged immersion of greasy wool at pH 11 has no significant effect on the chemical and physical properties of the fibre.

PRELIMINARY SHAKING AND STEEPING

Wools containing considerable amounts of sand or lime may have their scouring performance improved by shaking them in a simple type of two-cylinder machine prior to scouring. This makes possible longer scouring runs with smaller additions of soap and alkali. However, the process is not used for fine wools where any increased entanglement can result in excessive felting in the scouring bowl.

Occasionally the scouring set is preceded by a scouring bowl which contains only warm water; an alternative is to use machines specially designed to spray the wool and squeeze it before it enters the normal first scouring bowl. This practice, which is usually restricted to Merino wool, is known as desuintage scouring. Its object is to remove some of the mineral impurities, and also the water-soluble suint which may be recovered separately from the wool grease if desired. It also serves thoroughly to soften the grease and to wet out the wool before it enters the bowl containing soap and alkali. The formation of 'secondary droplets' of water inside the emulsified grease globules is minimized by a pre-liminary hot water steep[38]. It has been calculated that more soap may be used up inside the grease globules which contain secondary water droplets than is used around the droplets to maintain the emulsion.

CONVENTIONAL EMULSION SCOURING

In conventional emulsion scouring the wool is fed automatically by a hopper to the first scouring bowl, the purpose of this mechanism being to give a continuous and regular supply of material and thus enable the wool to be subjected to uniform treatment. Provision is made in the mechanism for changes in the rate of feed. Until recently, the hopper capacity ranged from 300 lb. to 600 lb., but some firms have now installed very large hopper bins with a capacity of about 10,000 lb. As the wool enters the first bowl it is sprayed by jets of scouring liquor, and positively pushed underneath the surface of the scouring liquor by the immersing box, a perforated metal plate mounted full width across the machine, and attached to the fork mechanism in a horizontal position. The wool is then propelled by the forks, allowing grease and dirt to be removed as it passes along.

On arriving at the far end of the scouring bowl, the wool passes through the squeeze rollers. The bottom roller is covered with brass or nickel, while the top roller has an outer covering of roller-lapping top or synthetic rubber. The bottom roller is positively driven, while the top roller revolves by surface contact under normal running conditions. If, however, a blockage occurs, the top roller takes up a positive drive until the blockage is cleared. The squeeze rollers aid in the cleansing action by causing liquor to flow through the fibres as they enter the roller nip. The liquor extracted is returned to the bowl after filtering, thus contributing to the efficient use of solutions, and the material is delivered from the last bowl with a moisture content of about 40 per cent. A lattice conveys the wool from the squeeze rollers of one bowl to the entry point of the next bowl in the set.

Washbowl Cross-sections: Cross-sectional views of two types of wash-bowl are illustrated in Fig. 3. 2, an ordinary type of scouring bowl being shown in part *A*. The actual scouring section, along which the wool passes, is supported by a perforated grid *C*, through which mineral im-purities can pass to settle at the bottom of the main part of the bowl at *E*. Mounted over the grid is the fork mechanism *D*.

The cross-section of a self-cleansing bowl is shown in part *B* of Fig. 3. 2. In this design the impurities falling through the grid are directed by the sloping sides of the bowl to a semi-circular depression *G* which runs longitudinally along the full length of the bowl. In the depression is mounted a scroll shaft *H* which has one half left-hand thread, and the other half right-hand thread. As the dirt falls, it is conveyed by the scroll to a central point where it is ejected from the bowl by intermittent flow of liquor through an outlet valve. Provision is made to alter the

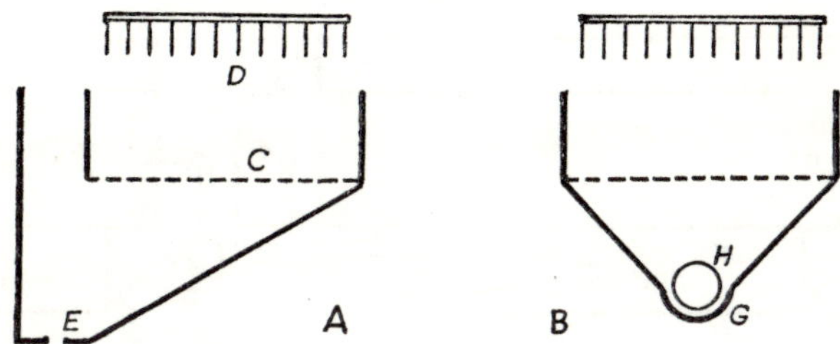

FIG 3.2.   CROSS-SECTIONS OF (A) AN ORDINARY AND (B)
A SELF-CLEANSING SCOURING BOWL

C—Perforated grid;   *D*—Washbowl forks;   *E*—Base of main bowl where mineral impurities accumulate; *G*—Semi-circular depression into which mineral impurities fall; *H*—Scroll shaft which conveys impurities to the outlet.

frequency and duration of the flushing action according to the impurities being removed from the wool. The self-cleansing bowl is normally used as the first bowl in a set, where the majority of mineral impurity is removed. By this means longer runs are possible before it is necessary to stop scouring and clean out the polluted liquor.

LIQUOR CIRCULATION IN CONVENTIONAL SCOURING

The circulation in a conventional scouring set may be sub-divided into three parts: viz. (i) internal circulation of each separate bowl; (ii) feed back circulation to maintain liquor levels; and (iii) blow-back after emptying the exhausted liquor. To assist in the description of these forms of circulation, a plan view of the first bowl in a scouring set, together with part of the second bowl, is given in Fig 3.3.

Internal Circulation of Each Bowl: Liquor from the squeeze rollers *A* passes to the settling tank (which may be alongside or underneath, the scouring bowl), any fibre present being caught in the screen *B*. The settling tank, as its name suggests, provides undisturbed conditions for the liquor to "settle" into various layers. The greasy layer floats to the top and is constantly decanted by the overflow pipe *C*; the dirt settles at the bottom of the tank, leaving a relatively clear layer of liquor which is withdrawn by a centrifugal pump P_1 through a pipe D which is raised from the bottom of the settling tank. A hand-operated valve V_1 is set so that the flow of liquor re-entering the bowl via the jets E is equal in volume to that being removed at the squeeze roller end of the bowl. In this way, the level of liquor in the bowl is kept constant. The steady flow of liquor from E to A in the main bowl, resulting from this circulation, helps to convey the material being scoured.

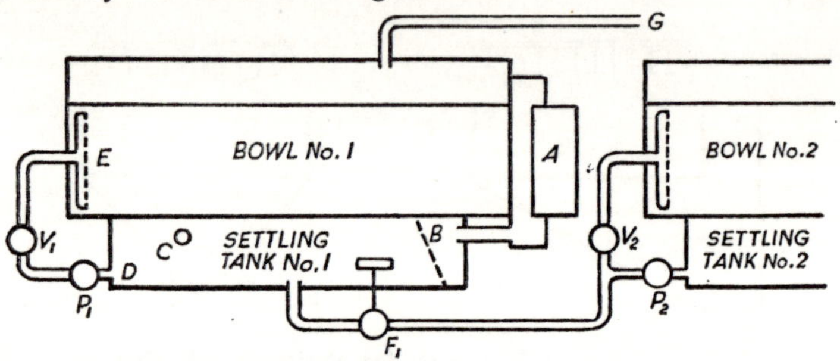

FIG. 3.3. DIAGRAMMATIC PLAN ILLUSTRATING
WASHBOWL CIRCULATION

A—Squeeze rollers; *B*—Filter; *C*—Overflow pipe;
D—Pipe outlet from side of settling tank; *E*—Immersing jets;
F—Float-operated valve; *G*—Blowback pipe; *P*—Centrifugal
pump; *V*—Hand-operated valve.

Due to the fact that the squeeze rollers do not remove all the liquor from the wool as it leaves the first bowl, a certain amount is carried into the second bowl and this constitutes a constant loss for which compensation must be made. For example, if it be assumed that the raw wool input is 1,000 lb. per hour, made up of 900 lb. of wool and dirt, and 100 lb. of moisture, and the amount leaving bowl 1 is also 1,000 lb. per hour, but this time made up of 600 lb. wool plus dirt, and 400 lb. of moisture then it follows that not only are 300 lb. of impurity removed every hour, but also that 300 lb. of liquor are carried through the squeeze rollers by the delivered wool in that time. This constitutes an hourly loss of 30 gallons of liquor. Moreover, if the first bowl is of the self-cleansing type, there will be additional loss due to the automatic flushing mechanism. As the hand-operated valve V_1 is set to maintain a constant level in the scouring bowl, it follows that the level of the liquor in the first settling tank will be lowered. To make up for this liquor loss from bowl 1, the second form of liquor circulation described in the following paragraph is employed.

Feed-back Circulation to maintain Liquor Levels: When the level of liquor in settling-tank 1 is lowered, the float-operated valve F_1 opens, allowing liquor from the settling tank of bowl 2 to feed back via the pump P_2, and thus restore the liquor in settling tank 1 to its original level. This feed-back obviously causes a lowering of the level of liquor in settling-tank 2 and this has to be compensated for by a similar feed-back from the settling-tank of bowl 3. This procedure is followed throughout the range, the liquor level of the settling-tank of the last bowl in the set being maintained by a feed from the clean water supply.

This method of feed-back helps to maintain the cleanliness of the liquors throughout the scouring set, and prolongs the length of time during which scouring may continue. Eventually, however, the liquor in the main scouring bowl becomes too heavily laden with grease and dirt for scouring to continue successfully. There is also a danger under such circumstances that grease may be re-deposited on to the fibres, particularly when the liquor grease level rises to about 4 per cent. In consequence the third form of liquor circulation is employed.

Blow-back: When the condition described above is reached, the grease-laden liquor of the main scouring bowl is run to the grease recovery plant (or sewers) along with the liquor in the settling tank of bowl 1, and the bowl and tank are cleaned out by hose and brush. A steam jet is then used to drive liquor from bowl 2 via pipe G into bowl 1. Similar pipes are used to feed liquor from each of the succeeding bowls, and the final bowl is replenished from the clean water supply. In this way, cleanliness of the liquors is restored, enabling scouring to continue, while at the same time maximum economy in the use of soap, alkali, heat, and water is obtained. Moreover, the efficiency of the last bowl in the set is ensured by providing it with clean rinse water at a low pH.

SCOURING PRACTICE

Such a wide variation in emulsion scouring practice exists that it is not practicable to give detailed examples of scouring sets representative of current practice and a general outline, with only such details as the number of bowls, and solution strengths (see Table 3.2), must suffice.

TABLE 3.2. RELATIVE SOLUTION STRENGTHS FOR DIFFERENT CLASSES OF WOOL

Relative Solution Strengths

Class of Wool	*Bowl 1*	*Bowl 2*	*Bowl 3*	*Bowl 4*	*Bowl 5*
Longwools, Crossbred and Hairs	Very strong	Weak	Rinse	—	—
Fine Crossbred, Merino	Strong	Medium	Weak	Rinse	—
Fine Merino	Steep	Fairly Strong	Medium	Weak	Rinse

Even with such a broad generalization as this, there must be exceptions, due to the wide range of raw materials and the amounts of impurities present. Similarly there is no standard solution strength for a given quality and thus Table 3·3 can serve only as an approximate guide.

TABLE 3.3.　COMPOSITION OF SCOURING SOLUTIONS

Percentage Solution Strength

Constituent	*Bowl 1*	*Bowl 2*	*Bowl 3*	*Bowl 4*
Soap	0·5	0·5	0·2	—
Alkali	0·2	0·1	—	—

The usual practice is to boil up the soap and alkali in separate tanks to produce 5 per cent stock solutions or alternatively to purchase the solutions ready made. In either case they are then used for making additions to the scouring liquors. When commencing with fresh solutions after 'blow-back', the necessary amounts of soap and alkali are added to the settling tank, and the liquor is then circulated before scouring commences. As scouring proceeds, further additions will be required and these may be made by a drip feed into the main tank. This addition can be made continuously under meter control, but in practice, correct solution strengths are frequently determined by observation of the scouring set. For example, if a foam persists along about one-third of the length of the scouring bowl and settling tank from the point of entry of the liquor, sufficient soap is present. Again, persistent sticking of the wool to the squeeze rollers indicates that it is not sufficiently scoured, and that the wool will not be as 'lofty' as it should be. In addition, the smell of the wool will indicate the presence of too much grease. A well scoured wool will have a lofty (springy or bulky) handle, and a good colour; its residual grease content should be about 0.5 to 0.75 per cent.

As may be expected, there are modern scientific aids to wool scouring control and tests suggested[41] include measurement of (*a*) the residual grease content of the washed wool; (*b*) the residual alkali content of the washed wool; (*c*) the residual soap content of the washed wool; (*d*) the grease content of the effluent; and (*e*) the water content of the centrifuged grease. In addition, measurements of pH, liquor solution strengths and temperatures should be available.

Dimensions of Scouring Bowls: The bowls in any set are of the same width, but they may vary from 3 ft. to 6 ft. wide from set to set. The lengths of the bowls in a set vary, however, so that a greater liquor volume may be available for the dirtiest wool. As the amount of dirt is reduced, the bowl capacity is reduced. The capacities of different makes of machinery vary slightly, and there is usually less capacity in a self-cleansing scouring bowl of given dimensions than in an ordinary bowl of similar size, the self-cleansing capacity being about 85 per cent of the ordinary bowl capacity. Table 3.4 gives approximate bowl sizes related to capacity for bowls 4 ft. wide; other widths of bowl have a capacity in direct proportion to width.

TABLE 3.4. CAPACITY OF SCOURING BOWLS
(Width of bowl 4 ft.)

Length of bowl (ft.):	30	24	21	18
Capacity (gallons):	1800	1500	1250	1000

Production Rate: Due to the wide range of impurities found in any given wool quality, it is not possible to give exact production rates. Generally, lower qualities have a smaller amount of impurity and may be treated more vigorously. With such qualities, it is therefore possible to have a higher input rate than that necessary for higher grades of wool. Table 3.5 will serve as a guide to maximum production rates which may be attained with bowls 4 ft. in width[42].

TABLE 3.5. SCOURING RATES WITH 4FT. WIDE BOWLS

	Approx. Greasy Input
Greasy Merino (Yield 50 – 60%)	2,000 lb. per hour
Medium Crossbred (Yield 60 – 70%)	2,200 lb. per hour
Low Crossbred (Yield 70 – 80%)	2,400 lb. per hour
Some Carpet Wools	2,700 lb. per hour

Rinsing: A steady inflow of clean water is essential to minimize soap deposition on the fibres and to keep the pH of the wool as low as possible. A high residual soap content increases fibre entanglement and nep formation in carding [43]. If soft soap, which contains unsaturated fatty acids, is not thoroughly rinsed off the fibres, the film of soap remaining on the fibre will undergo oxidation, cause yellowing of the fibre and interfere with sub-sequent dyeing. An efficient squeeze roller action at the bowl preceding the rinse will minimize the amount of soap and alkali carried into the last bowl. If the rinse liquor has a pH of 8.5 – 9.0, rinsing is proceeding satisfactorily. In some worsted firms it is the practice to add anti-static agents and/or combing oil (about 1 per cent) after drying to improve carding.

MODERN EMULSION SCOURING MACHINERY

It has long been realized that conventional emulsion scouring leaves much to be desired as regards control of fibre movement; a small degree of felting takes place which leads to the formation of entanglements and to fibre breakage in carding[43]. In consequence, machines have been developed in which fibre movement is restricted while scouring takes place. At the present time there are three such types of machine, all based on the principle

of jetting the wool with scouring liquor, while at the same time restricting
fibre movement. One of the new systems, based on research by the Commonwealth Scientific and Industrial Research Organisation (C.S.I.R.O.) at
Geelong, Australia, was originally intended to operate with solvents, but
has been adapted to use soap and alkali solutions[44]. This system is now
manufactured commercially in this country[42] in an improved and modified
form, as shown in Fig. 3.4 which illustrates a four-unit aqueous jet scouring machine of approximately half the length of an equivalent conventional harrow-type wool washer.

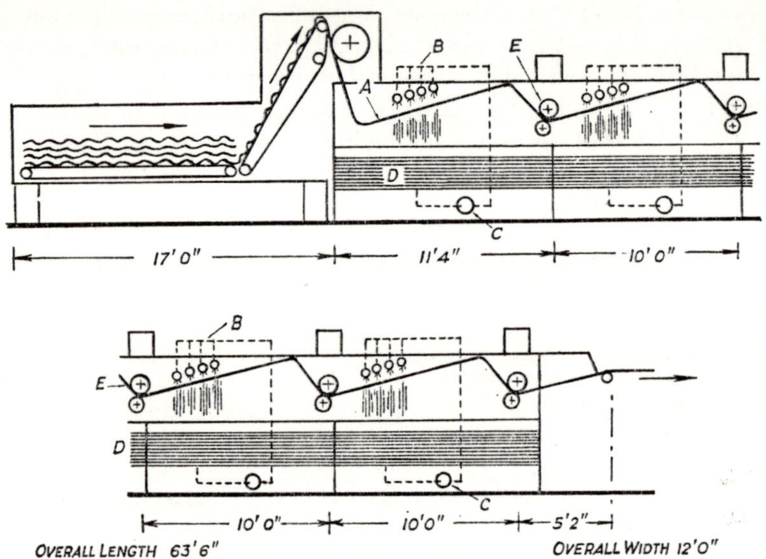

FIG 3.4   FOUR-UNIT AQUEOUS JET SCOURING MACHINE

A—Self-cleaning permeable conveyor; B—Jet headers and nozzles; C—Pump;
D—Liquid container; E—Air-loaded squeeze rollers.

(By courtesy of Petrie & McNaught Ltd.)

In each unit of the machine illustrated above the wool is carried on a
positively driven permeable conveyor at A which is designed to be self-
cleaning and over which are mounted four independently controlled jet
headers B, each having eighteen nozzles providing a line of overlapping
jets. The filtered liquor is pumped (by pump C) to the jets from a container D which may be located at any convenient point according to the
circumstances of the installation. Compressed air cylinders are used directly to load the squeeze rollers E which are automatically lifted out of
contact when the air supply is cut-off. Commercial operation of this
machine has indicated that less than half-a-gallon of water is used per
pound of wool scoured, compared with 1-$1\frac{1}{2}$ gallons when using conven-

tional machinery, and that the delivered wool is lofty, open and free from entanglement, with the original lock formation of the greasy wool still preserved.

The second method using jets was introduced under the name of 'Aqueous compression jet scouring'. This system[45] was developed at the University of New South Wales, Australia. The wool is confined between a perforated drum and an open belt while it is subjected to jets within the scouring liquor. Two jets pass from the inside to the outside of the perforated drum, and two jets pass in the opposite direction.

The third method uses two endless belts to sandwich the greasy wool while it is carried through the liquor[46]. During its submerged passage, the wool is subjected to several air jets and squeeze rollers which brings about the necessary agitation.

All these new systems are claimed to subject the wool to minimum disturbance, and so to reduce fibre entanglement in carding, thus making a higher production rate possible without detriment to quality. Due to the reduced breakage, a better tearage and yield from the comb is to be expected, with fewer neps in the final top.

SOLVENT SYSTEMS OF SCOURING WOOL

Two systems of solvent scouring had been operated before the Second World War. One, the Burnell system, was a Belgian development in which benzene was used as the solvent. The process was continuous, treatment of the wool with solvent being followed by one in which hot water was employed. The Maerton system was first announced in 1898, and was used at the Arlington Mills, U.S.A. for 35 years before being discarded. This was a batch process in which 5,000 lb. of wool contained in each of two large kiers were processed at a time using naphtha as the solvent.

Post-war interest in solvent scouring was revived by the development of two systems, one in Australia[47], the other in Sweden[48]. The Australian system used white spirit in the first two stages, followed by water treatment in the second and third stages. Lack of interest in this system led to its adaptation (referred to in the section dealing with modern emulsion scouring machinery) for use with soap and soda solutions. The Swedish system was unlike any of the other systems of solvent scouring in that the solvent dissolved the suint as well as the grease. The solvent was stated to be a 'petroleum fraction similar to kerosene'. In this system the scouring took place in an open bowl and, after centrifuging, the wool still contained about 10 per cent of solvent, the recovery of which was not attempted.

Many advantages have been claimed for solvent scouring systems. These include the fact that no harmful agents are used, there is little agitation, no formation of lime-soaps and no soap residues left on the wool. The scoured top is delivered at pH7 or less (an advantage in melange top printing as the unprinted part of the fibre does not yellow when steamed) and higher production rates are possible in carding where nep formation and fibre breakage are almost eliminated. Combing tear is increased, the mean fibre length of the top is as good as with conventional scouring, and there is a higher yield of top and noil. Finally, there is high effluent recovery and the scouring agent is recovered and re-used.

In view of such a formidable list of advantages, it is surprising that one or more of these systems has not been enthusiastically adopted by the trade. Presumably the reason for this is to be found in the disadvantages, which include a higher level of risk to personnel and plant due to fire, explosion and toxic fumes, and the need for a higher operative skill, the plant being more complicated. Capital and running costs are no lower than with emulsion scouring, and operation of the system necessitates close control. Moreover, the recovered grease is sometimes polluted by colloidal clay; and the wool must be dry for successful degreasing to take place.

EFFLUENT TREATMENT

Wool scouring effluents contain detergents such as soap and alkali, wool grease in emulsion, particles of sand, excrement, fine clay particles, soluble salts from the suint, vegetable fibres, and burrs. The treatment and recovery of the valuable grease and potash salts is quite a problem, particularly as one mill alone may have to dispose of one third of a million gallons of effluent a day[49]. Some firms recover the grease at the scouring mill, while others discharge the grease laden-effluent into the sewers. In Bradford this happens on a large scale, but the problem has been turned to advantage. The average flow of sewage into the municipal sewage works is about 23m. gallons a day[50], and from this, about 750 tons of sludge per day is removed and treated for removal of the wool grease, which yields a range of about twenty products which are marketed along with the annual output of 16,000 tons of organic fertilizer. Incidentally these sales greatly assist the finances of running the sewage department.

The recovery of wool grease may be accomplished in various ways; namely, (*i*) by acid cracking, (*ii*) by centrifuging (*iii*) by aeration, and (*iv*) by the use of solvents. In the United Kingdom effluents discharged into rivers must be acidic and therefore the method most commonly used in this country is the acid cracking system.

Acid Cracking: This process consists of breaking down the soap-stabilized emulsion by lowering the pH down to about 3.5. Three layers form; the centre layer of clear aqueous solution is drawn off, and the other two layers are combined to form 'Magma' (grease, dirt, and water). This is put into a steam-heated press, and the water and as much grease as possible are forced out. The remaining 'press-cake' is a valuable source of fertilizer after the grease content has been further reduced. About 50 per cent of the grease in the original liquor is recovered by the acid cracking process. For every ton of grease produced, about 15 to 30 cwt of commercial concentrated sulphuric acid is used. This system of recovery is not successful, however, when synthetic detergent effluents are to be treated.

Centrifuging: This method of grease recovery was first successful in 1928 with the development of the Adams centrifuge. The liquor is allowed to settle, heated in a tank after being filtered, and then passed to a centrifuge running at about 6,000 r.p.m. for removal of the mud. A second centrifuge running at about 16,000 r.p.m. is then used to extract concentrated grease. This method is often used at the scouring mill, being simple to operate, and requiring very little labour for its supervision. The product is neutral wool grease, and commands a high price. The effluent passed into the sewers must be acid cracked to satisfy the river board requirements.

Aeration: The principle of the aeration system is to apply agitation so that a froth is formed. This froth has a disproportionately high grease content, and may be removed. There are three versions of this system: (*i*) Battage (using hand-paddles); (*ii*) Barber jet (using compressed air); and (*iii*) Mertens process (using high-speed electrified beaters). As grease recovery is only from 25 to 50 per cent, it is necessary when the method is used in this country for the process to be followed by acid cracking.

Use of Solvents: This method refers to the system of grease recovery used in conjunction with solvent scouring. The solvent is passed through one or two centrifugal separators to remove the mineral impurities, and then through a distillation plant which separates the solvent from the grease. Any residual solvent in the mineral sludge from the centrifuges is removed by a water treatment.

WOOL DRYING

WOOL leaving the squeeze rollers of a scouring machine may have a moisture content of about 40 per cent. It is, however, essential that wool to be blended (woollen system), and carded or prepared (worsted system), should have a uniform moisture content so that uniformity of shade or sliver weight may be maintained. The amount of moisture required depends on the method of processing to be used, and on whether the wool is to be stored in the scoured state. For fine wools which are to be carded on the Bradford worsted card a moisture content of 20 to 25 per cent is required, but a lower level is satisfactory for coarser wool qualities. Long preparing wools should have a moisture content of about 16 per cent, the same as that required for woollen carding and continental worsted carding. Too high a level of moisture may cause rusting of machinery, and in carding may contribute to excessive nep formation[43]. Where wool is to be stored in the scoured state (woollen and continental worsted) a high moisture content may result in mildew or in spontaneous combustion.

Before further processing takes place, it is necessary to reduce the moisture content from that in the wool as delivered by the scouring bowl squeeze rollers. This may be done in two ways, either by the use of mechanical methods or by hot air drying. In the mechanical method, besides using squeeze rollers, a centrifugal hydroextractor may be employed, but neither of these methods will reduce the moisture content to that required for further processing. Although mechanical extraction of water may serve to save heat in the following process, the economics of the method will depend on the relative costs of labour and power.

HOT AIR DRYING

Air has a capacity to hold moisture which increases with increase of temperature, as shown in Table 3.6 (extracted from the tables of the Institute of Heating and Ventilating Engineers), and it is this property which is employed as the basis for the hot air drying of wool.

TABLE 3.6.　Moisture Carrying Capacity of Air

Air temperature		Moisture (grains/lb dry air)	Volume of 1 lb dry air
°F	°C	to produce saturation	(cu. ft.)
30	−1	24·4	12·59
60	15	78·4	13·53
90	32	220·0	14·77
120	49	576·0	16·79
150	65	1480·0	20·50
180	82	4584·0	32·90

In the first place it should be noted that the moisture carrying capacity of air is not directly proportional to the temperature but increases at a much faster rate. Theoretically, therefore, the higher the temperature the more efficient the drying. Nevertheless, dryers are normally operated at about 180°F. (82°C.) as this gives good drying, and a safe margin of error. It has also been shown that heating wool up to 212°F. (100°C.) reduces its capacity to adsorb moisture[52,53]. However, if the wool is in a wet state, although the air temperature may be too high, the heat loss by evaporation will keep the wool temperature at a lower level. Heat is an expensive item, and must be kept to a minimum compatible with good drying.

Other factors which govern the rate of evaporation of water from the wool are (*i*) the effective velocity of the air over the wool, usually measured by stating the volume of air circulation in cu. ft. per minute, (*ii*) the state of the material to be dried (thickness of layer, quality, packing density), (*iii*) the length of time during which the wool is exposed to the drying air, and (*iv*) the direction of the air currents.

The earlier types of continuous dryer were made to convey the wool by lattices (or some alternative device) placed one above the other, and arranged so that the wool, which was either carried mechanically or blown by a blast of hot air to the top tier of the machine, was carried along each tier and dropped on to the one below. In dropping from one tier to the next, the wool was disarranged, enabling the hot air currents to meet a larger surface. Only one fan and one heater were provided for heating and circulating the air, and under these conditions, there are three possible ways in which the air may be used.

In the first method, the wool is subjected to air at a constant temperature as it passes through the dryer. In the second method, conditions are such that the wool, as it passes through the dryer, comes into contact with the hotter air. This is achieved by arranging the direction of air circulation in opposition to the general movement of the wool. The result is that the hottest (and driest) air is brought into contact with the driest wool, and consequently there is a danger of scorching. This type of dryer is still popular for carbonizing, where an increasing temperature in drying is an advantage. In the third method, the wool experiences a lowering of air temperature as it passes through the dryer, the direction of air circulation being the same as the general movement of the wool through the dryer. In this way, the coolest (and wettest) air is brought into contact with the driest wool, but there is a danger here of moisture condensing back on to the wool.

IMPROVEMENTS IN MODERN DRYERS

Modern dryers have been made more efficient and their rate of output increased by attention to the following points: (*i*) By the provision of more than one heating unit, the temperature of the air can be increased as it approaches saturation point, thus increasing its moisture-carrying capacity. (*ii*) By recirculating the air in a controlled manner, the maximum amount of moisture can be absorbed before the air is finally exhausted from the machine. (*iii*) By the provision of more than one fan, a boost can be given to the circulation when otherwise it would become sluggish. In this connection, it should be remembered that the air expands as its temperature increases (see Table 3.6), and accordingly its velocity must also be increased. (*iv*) By drawing air from the atmosphere into the machine through the hot wool being delivered, the air is pre-heated, and the wool pre-cooled, thus improving the thermal efficiency of the plant. (*v*) Effective insulation minimizes heat losses through the casing of the machine. (*vi*) By constructing the machine in sections any required length may be supplied from standard parts. Moreover, a longer machine may have the wool fed through at an increased speed, giving a higher production rate. (*vii*) The adoption of a design which causes minimum disturbance of the fibres which are nevertheless subjected to air currents in alternate directions.

BASIC TYPES OF WOOL DRYER

There are two basic types of wool dryer, the lattice dryer and the suction drum dryer. In the former type (shown in Fig. 3.5) there is a single lattice conveyor *L* which carries the wool from one end of the machine to the other while the hot air currents are directed alternately from above and below. The basic unit consists of two compartments, each with its fan *F* and heater *H* mounted alongside the main compartment. The air spirals through the wool more than once in each compartment, before passing to the next compartment, and spiralling in the opposite direction. A full dryer may be made up of any number of basic units to give the required produc-

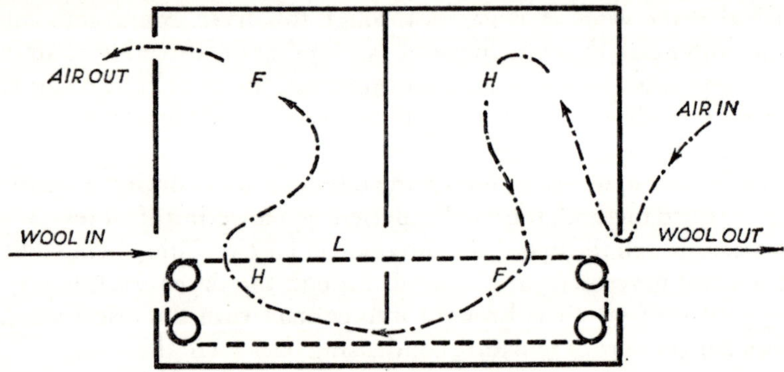

FIG. 3.5. MODERN LATTICE-CONVEYOR DRYER

F—Fan;   *H*—Heater;   *L*—Lattice-conveyor

tion capacity. Another model of the lattice conveyor type of dryer has a basic unit consisting of three compartments, but additions may be made in units of two compartments. In both these dryers the counterflow principle is used, i.e. the general direction of air flow is in the opposite direction to that of the wool.

The other type of modern dryer, the suction drum dryer, is now being manufactured with various refinements. This type of machine is based on an entirely new principle (see Fig. 3.6); instead of blowing the air through the dryer, suction is used. This makes it possible to use a higher rate of air flow without causing the fibre disturbance which would be associated with such a rate of air flow in other type dryers. The basic unit consists of two perforated drums into which the air is drawn continuously, a stationary baffle *A* inside each drum blocking part of the circumference to the entrance of air and thus controlling its direction. As the material enters the machine from the feed sheet, it is sucked onto the surface of the first drum and carried on the outside of that drum until it is transferred to the second drum. The transfer is brought about automatically by the suction of one drum terminating at the point where that of the second drum commences, the point being determined by the stationary baffles, to which reference has already been made. In this way, the layer of wool is 'turned over' without fibre disturbance being caused. The air is re-circulated through the dryer a number of times before it is finally exhausted at *B*. Heating and re-heating

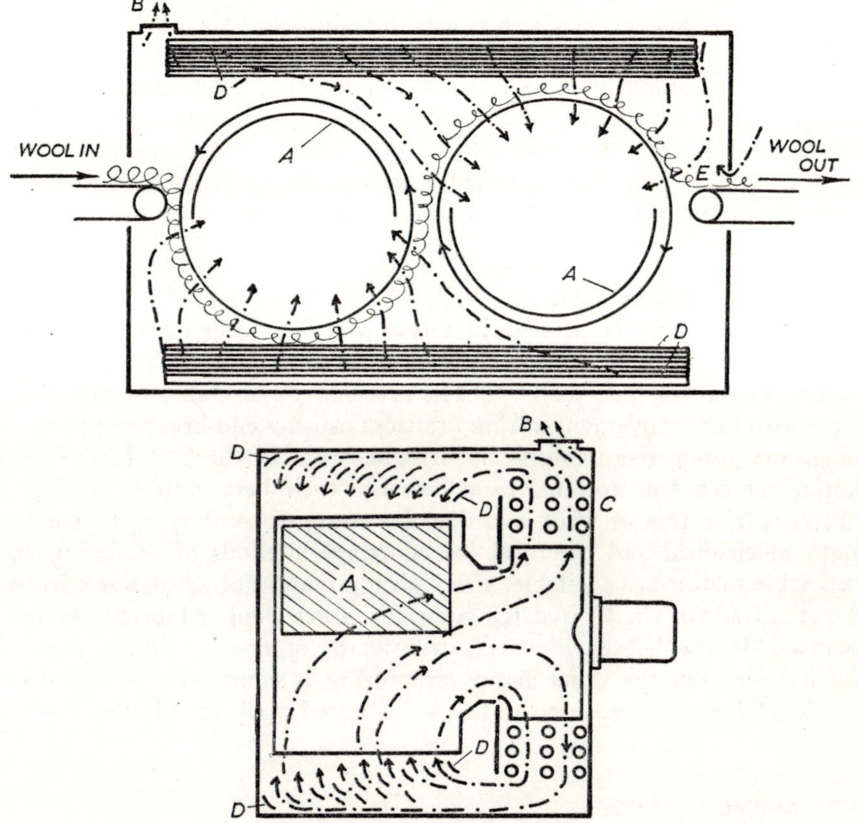

FIG. 3.6. LONGITUDINAL AND CROSS-SECTIONAL VIEWS OF A MODERN SUCTION DRUM DRYER

A—Stationary baffle; *B*—Exhaust air; *C*—Heating pipes; *D*—Baffles to distribute air evenly across the width of the dryer; *E*—Air intake.

of the air is by a battery of steam pipes at *C*, and even distribution of the warm air across the width of the drums is ensured by the baffles *D*. The air intake is through the wool at the point of delivery *E*.

This type of machine is versatile and it may be used for loose scoured wool, slivers after backwashing, knitted fabrics and yarn hanks, synthetic staple and tow. It has been widely adopted for backwashing and hank-scouring, but has not been so enthusiastically received for the drying of loose wool. It is stated in the industry that the suction dryer leaves the wool less lofty than does the lattice-type dryer, and that this is the reason for the latter being preferred for the drying of loose stock.

Advantages claimed for the suction dryer are: (*i*) a minimum of fibre disturbance, making it suitable for continental backwashing after combing; (*ii*) very little fibre migration, making it suitable for drying coloured slivers after dyeing; (*iii*) the machine is self-threading and therefore useful for slivers after backwashing; and (*iv*) it has a high production for a small amount of occupied floorspace. In this connection a two-drum machine occupies 11 ft. x 7 ft. (approx.) and produces 500 lb. per hour, while a three-drum machine occupies 18 ft. x 7 ft. (approx.) and produces 1,000 lb. per hour. In addition, there is the technical advantage that reversal of air flow (through the material) takes place in this type of machine.

REMOVAL OF VEGETABLE MATTER

VEGETABLE MATTER is present in virgin wool in several forms, for example as burr, seed, and straw, the type and quantity differing with the pasture and habits of the sheep[54-57]. The presence of vegetable matter interferes with fibre movement during drafting, causing end breakages in spinning, and giving rise to slubs and irregularities. In the final fabric these impurities can lead to speckiness, because their behaviour in dyeing is different from that of wool, and they can cause discomfort to the wearer. Both mechanical and chemical (carbonizing) methods of removing the vegetable matter are available, although it is not a normal practice in the worsted trade of the United Kingdom for either wool or fabric to be carbonized. In the U.S.A. however, carbonizing of worsted fabrics may be carried out. On the other hand carbonizing is commonly practised on woollen fabrics and on some of the loose scoured wools used in the woollen trade.

MECHANICAL METHODS

Mechanical methods of treatment may be sub-divided into those using special machines designed to give a preliminary treatment before processing proper commences, and special treatments applied during the normal sequence of processing. This latter group may be further sub-divided into (*i*) treatment at the card, (*ii*) treatment at the card followed by final removal of vegetable matter at the comb – a method which applies to the worsted trade only, and (*iii*) the removal of vegetable matter from fabric by burling irons before the final finishing treatment and a 'picking-over' by burling irons after finishing.

Fleece Deburring Machines: These machines may only be used on complete fleeces and their use is therefore restricted to the fellmongering industry. The burry skins are gripped by rollers while pinned deburring rollers are drawn through the wool fibres, removing a large proportion of the burrs, together with certain other foreign matter.

Wool Deburring Machines: These machines are used for some very burry virgin wools. The wool is subjected to a series of pin and beater treatments which knock the burrs out while the wool is retained in the pins.

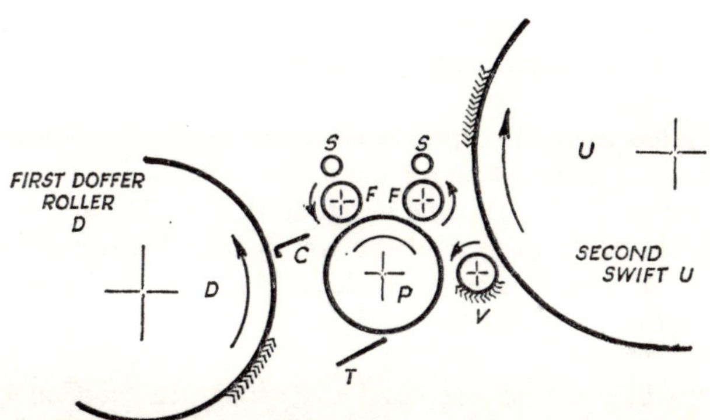

FIG. 3.7. DRAWING ILLUSTRATING THE PRINCIPLE OF
THE HARMEL BURR CRUSHER

D—Normal card first doffer roller; *U*—Second swift; *C*—Doffing comb; *P*—Plain-surfaced roller; *F*—Fluted rollers; *S*—Cleaning rollers; *T*—Scraper blade; *V*—Angle stripper

Burr Beaters: With these devices the object is to remove as much burr as possible in the early stages of carding while the burrs are still balled-up and bulky; later in carding the burrs become opened out and burr beaters are then ineffective. The burr beater is equipped with radial blades (often 32 in number) and has a diameter of 5 inches. It runs at a high surface speed (e.g. 16,000 in. per minute) with the surface moving in the opposite direction to that of the wire-clad roller beneath it. Frequently the card roller under the burr beater is clothed with Morel wire, the effect of which is to make the burrs protrude from the card wire while the wool fibres sink down between the card teeth. In this way the burrs are flicked off by the blades into a tray which is set close to the beating point to minimize fibre loss. The burrs which collect in the tray are automatically conveyed to the side of the machine, and deposited in cans.

The Harmel Burr Crusher: The principle on which this device operates is illustrated by Fig. 3.7 in which *P* represents an accurately surfaced plain roller over which the material passes after being removed from the first doffer D by a doffing comb C. The thin web of material is subjected to a high pressure by two fluted rollers F, one of which has 124 flutes and the other 210 flutes, the idea being that what is not crushed by the first flutes will be crushed by the second series. The flutes of the two rollers are cleaned by brass rollers S which traverse from side to side and engage with the flutes of the rollers, while the plain-surfaced roller is cleaned by a scraper blade T. The web of material is passed on to the second swift U via the angle-stripper V, and the normal carding which follows allows some of the crushed material to fall out. The remaining vegetable matter is subsequently removed in combing, giving a very burry noil.

Most worsted cards incorporate the Morel roller/burr-beater arrangement (the most common place for the Morel roller being the third licker), while some also have the Harmel crushing device. The former's function is to remove the hard burrs and the trefoil burr (before it becomes unrolled), while the latter is used to crush the grass and seeds, as well as burrs which escape the action of the burr-beaters.

Peralta Rollers: These are used extensively in woollen carding. In this case the thin carded web delivered by the scribbler doffer is passed through a pair of heavily weighted plain steel rollers which crush the vegetable matter present in the blend, and in addition break up any thready matter present. This is then dropped from the blend as it passes through the carder section of the machine. Scrapers are used to keep the Peralta rollers clean.

CHEMICAL METHODS

The use of carbonizing is common in the woollen trade. For treating virgin wools or noils, wet carbonizing is used, but for treating rags, dry carbonizing is favoured. In both cases the cellulosic impurity to be removed is converted to a brittle hydrocellulose by the action of certain mineral acids or their salts. The hydrocellulose can then be removed by mechanical treatment.

Wet Carbonizing: This method[60-62] is usually carried out on wool previously scoured. The wool is passed through a long stainless steel-lined bowl containing sulphuric acid with a specific gravity at room temperature of 1.02 to 1.04. Alternatively, two acidizing tanks may be used, the first containing acid with a specific gravity of 1.04 and the second acid with a gravity of 1.02. The acidified wool is then dried. The drying process consists of two stages, the first being a thermo-physical action (the drying of the wool) and the second, a thermo-chemical action in which the cellulose is converted to hydrocellulose.

It has been shown[58] that the use of two dryers is better than one, the first being operated at about 160°F (71°C.) to dry the wool, while the second at about 200°F. (93°C.) bakes the acidified cellulose. In practice, however, it is usual to use a single dryer of the increasing temperature type. After drying, the wool is passed through pairs of crushing rollers and a shaking machine to remove the hydrocellulose. The wool is then passed through scouring bowls which contain sodium carbonate to neutralize the acid before the wool is rinsed and dried. The addition of a small amount of soap to the rinse water is quite common, the object being to use the soap as a "feeder" and improve the handle of the wool.

In the conventional process outlined above, it has been found that up to 8 per cent of the wool is lost, and the rest weakened. Recent research[59] indicates that if ½lb. of Lissapol NX is added to each 100 gallons of acidizing solution, damage is reduced, enabling an additional 5 per cent of processed wool to be recovered. Moreover, the yarn is stronger than is conventionally carbonized yarn. There is also published information demonstrating how the strength of carbonized wool can be retained while the vegetable matter is completely removed[62].

Dry Carbonizing: This method[63] is used for the carbonizing of rags which are to be used as a source of fibre for woollen blending. The rags are first heated and then thrown into a large, slowly rotating drum. A perforated pipe passes through the centre of this box to introduce the gas which is formed in a retort outside the chamber by dripping liquid hydrochloric acid on to a hot plate. The temperature of the chamber is kept fairly high, the whole box being enclosed in an outer chamber, between which the flue gases pass. As the box rotates, the rags are raised by hooks and allowed to fall through the gas to become uniformly saturated. The period of time required depends on the thickness and construction of the rags, and on the proportion of cotton they contain, an approximate time being about three hours. The treated rags are then removed from the chamber, allowed to cool for about a half-hour, and shaken. Whether the process is followed by neutralization depends on the processing which is to be used subsequently; if the rags are to be dyed, neutralizing is not necessary, but it is necessary if rag pulling is directly to follow.

REFERENCES

1. Stanbury and Byerley, *J. Text. Inst.*, 1934, **25**, T295.
2. Bastawisy, Onions and Townend, *J. Text. Inst.*, 1961, **50**, T1.
3. Barker and Winson, *J. Text. Inst.*, 1931, **22**, T314.
4. Wool Research 1918-48, Vol. 6. p.225, W.I.R.A.
5. Galceran-Escabat, *Bull. Inst. Text.*, France, 1952, **30**, 213.
6. Monford, *Wool Science Review*, 1954, **12** and **13**.

7. Lang, *J. Text. Inst.*, 1947, **38**, T257.
8. Duerden, *J. Text. Inst.*, 1929, **20**, T93.
9. Lang, *J. Text. Inst.*, 1957, **48**, T495.
10. Barker, 'Wool Quality' Pub. by H.M.S.O., 1931.
11. Matthews, 'Textile Fibres'. Pub. by John Willey & Son. Inc., 1913.
12. Barker and Priestley, 'Wool Carding and Combing' Pub. by Cassel & Co. 1912.
13. Onions, 'Wool', Pub. by Interscience Publishers, 1962
14. Hamilton and Cooper. *J. Text. Inst.*, 1958, **49**, T687.
15. Townend and Dewhirst, *J. Text. Inst.*, 1964, **55**, T485.
16. Gee, N. C., *Text. Mfr.*, 1942, **68**; 1943, **69**; 1944, **70**.
17. Harper, McKennell and Onions, *J. Text. Inst.*, 1958, **49**, P126.
18. Barker, *J. Roy. Agric. Soc. of England*, 1924, **85**, 32.
19. Drummond and Baker, *J. Soc. Chem. Ind.*, 1929, **48**, 232T.
20. Green and Preston, *J. Text. Inst.*, 1959, **50**, T497.
21. Truter, 'Wool Wax', Pub. by Cleaver Hume Press, London, 1956, 66.
22. Howitt and Preston, *J. Text. Inst.*, 1960, **51**, T841.
23. Farnworth, *Aust. J. App. Sci.*, 1956, **7**, 233.
24. Deane and Truter, *J. Chem. Soc.*, 1959, 2746.
25. Sweeten, *J. Text. Inst.*, 1949, **40**, T727.
26. Lipson and Black, *J. Roy. Soc. New S. Wales*, 1945, 76.
27. Lipson, *Proc. Int. Wool Text. Res. Conf.*, Australia, 1955, E 376.
28. Lang, Aust. J. Agric. Sci., 1955, **21**, 103.
29. *Wool Science Review*, Vol. 8, p.31.
30. Woollner and Tanner, *Ind. Eng. Chem (Anal. Edn.)*, 1941, **13**, 883.
31. Acoustics Associates Inc., Long Island, New York.
32. Whewell, *Text. Rec.*, 1942, May, 33.
33. Shell Chemical Co., Information sheet DET/IS/11 and I.C.I. Technical Inf. Leaflet (Dyehouse) No. 880.
34. Private Communication, City of Bradford Sewage Dept., July 1966.
35. Phillips, *J. Text. Inst.*, 1936, **27**, P 208.
36. Whewell, *Text. Rec.*, 1941, Nov. 29.
37. Barmore, *Amer. Dyestuff Rep.*, 1931, **20**, 743.
38. Howitt, *Proc. Int. Wool Text. Res. Conf.*, Australia, 1955, E 315. Anderson, *ibid*, E363
39. Townend and Tweddie, *J. Text. Inst.*, 1949, **40**, T389.
40. Grové, *J. Text. Inst.*, 1963, **54**, T259, T385.
41. Veldsman and Palmer, *Proc. Inst. Wool. Text. Res. Conf.*, Australia, 1955.
42. Petrie & McNaught Ltd., Rochdale, England.
43. Townend and Spiegel, *J. Text. Inst.*, 1944, **35**, T21.
44. Anderson, C. A., and Poulter, *Text. Res. J.*, 1962, **32**, 387.
    Anderson, C. A., Lipson and Wood, *J. Text. Inst.*, 1964, **55**, T576.
45. Chaikin and Samson. *Text. Res. J.*, 1962, **32**, 871.
    Text. Rec., 1962, Nov., 137.
46. Ateliers, Charpentier & Cie, Veiviers.
47. Sinclair, *Proc. Int. Wool Text. Res. Conf.*, *Australia*, 1955, E 347.
48. Lindberg and Ekegren, *ibid*, E 342.
49. *The Dyer*, 1948, **99**, 513, 581.
50. *Telegraph & Argus*, Bradford, March 2, 1962.
51. *Wool Science Review*, Vol. 12, p.29.
52. Woodmansey, *J. Soc. Dyers & Col.*, 1918, **34**, 227.
53. Speakman, Cooper and Stott, *J. Text. Inst.*, 1936, **27**, T183.
54. Wig, *Amer. Dyestuff Rep.*, 1935, **24**, 270.
55. Woollner, Tanner and Michelson, *ibid*, 1944, **33**, 375.
56. Lipson, *ibid*, 1945, June, 18.
57. Milthorpe, 'Vegetable Matter in the N.S.W. Wool Clip', Australian Central Wool Committee Testing House, 1943.
58. Harrison, *J. Soc. Chem. Ind.*, 1918, **37**, 264 A.
59. Mizell, Davis and Oliva, *Text. Res. J.*, 1962, **32**, 497.
60. Simmonds, 'Carbonizing Investigations I', Wool Textile Research Lab. C.S.I.R.O. Technical paper No. 2.
61. Pressley, 'Carbonizing Investigations, II', *Proc. Inst. Wool Text. Res. Conf.*, Australia, 1955, E389.
62. Crowther, 'Carbonizing Investigations III', *ibid*, E408.
63. Gee, N. C., '*Shoddy and Mungo Manufacture*', Pub. by Emmott, 1950.

WORSTED YARN MANUFACTURE

THE WORSTED INDUSTRY in the United Kingdom is arranged on a system of horizontal integration, although in recent years there has been a tendency for mills to be combined into large organizations. In this respect it differs from the woollen industry which is largely based on a vertical system in which numerous small family businesses carry out the complete processing procedure from raw wool to finished cloth. In the worsted section of the trade it is the exception rather than the rule for a weaver to own his own worsted spinning plant. Thus the worsted industry is mainly divided into definite sections, viz., topmaking; drawing, spinning and twisting; weaving; dyeing and finishing. Such an arrangement is more suited to the adoption of mass-production methods than is that of the woollen industry which has to cope with more variable raw materials and, in many cases, smaller lots of material.

Originally it could be clearly stated that all worsted yarns were made from combed wool, the only exceptions being a small percentage used for the carpet trade and some hosiery yarns. Due to the increased use of man-made fibres, however, this is no longer true, and today more than 20 per cent of all fibres processed on worsted drawing and spinning machinery in this country are man-made, being processed either into blends with wool or into 100 per cent man-made fibre yarns. Thus the term 'worsted' has now come to be accepted as meaning a method of processing rather than the name for a particular type of fibre, and a 'worsted-spun' yarn may possibly contain no wool. However, the term 'worsted yarn' is still reserved for 100 per cent wool yarns.

In considering the influence which increasing use of man-made fibres in the worsted trade has had, and will probably have, on the methods and processes used, it should be borne in mind that, when man-made fibres first made their appearance, they were a relatively unimportant raw material, entering an industry which had developed specifically to process wool during the previous 150 years or so. The very term 'artificial silk' indicated the general attitude towards these new fibres and, when used in the industry, they had to fit, as best they could, into the existing pattern of production, being carded, combed, etc., whether such processing was or was not strictly necessary. Later, when the new fibres increased both in importance and quantity, it became possible to devise processes specifically to meet their requirements. This trend will presumably continue in the future. Accordingly, in the following description of worsted yarn manufacture some consideration has been given to the influence of man-made fibres on processing procedure, to the modification, where necessary, of wool processing machinery and, where appropriate, to the use of new machines. Nevertheless, it must be borne in mind that at present wool is still the most important fibre entering the worsted industry.

PREPARATORY PROCESSING

AFTER THE WOOL has been scoured and dried, as described in Section 3, there are two principal methods available to prepare the wool for combing, the chief factor determining which method is to be used being fibre length. The first method, known as 'Longwool Preparing', is used for long wools (maximum fibre length not less than about eight inches), lustre wools, mohair, alpaca, and other hair fibres. This group includes the coarser qualities, and 50s wool quality is about the finest processed by the longwool preparing system. Whenever the material is short enough, the second method, 'Carding', is employed as this system is more productive and requires far less labour. On the other hand, the initial cost of a card is much greater than that of a set of preparing boxes. Both methods are described in the following paragraphs.

LONGWOOL PREPARING

The objects of this process are: (*i*) to disentangle the matted staples of fibres with as little breakage as possible; (*ii*) to straighten the fibres and orientate them in more-or-less parallel array; (*iii*) to form a continuous sliver for convenience in processing and handling, ready for combing; and (*iv*) to promote maximum regularity of sliver thickness and fibre distribution.

A preparing set usually consists of six machines or gill boxes, although for mohair and similar fibres seven machines (the first three being sheeters) are used. The usual set for wool consists of two sheeter boxes, the rest being can boxes. The sheeter preparer delivers the material on to a felt apron, in the form of a lap which has to be broken when removed and fed to the following machine. The can type preparer, as its name suggests, delivers a continuous sliver into a can. Essentially, all the machines are alike in that they consist of back rollers, fallers, and front rollers, but the machine parts become finer as the wool passes down the set[1]. In this way there is a gradual increase in mechanical treatment as the wool becomes more open, without any increase in severity. The principles of gilling are dealt with later in the section dealing with gill boxes in drawing.

An example of a possible arrangement ot drafts and doublings, along with the sliver weights delivered, is given in Table 4.1. In this arrangement the first three processes are concerned with converting the loose wool into a continuous form, and the last three with improving levelness.

TABLE 4.1. DRAFTS, DOUBLINGS AND SLIVER WEIGHTS IN LONGWOOL PREPARING

| Machine | Draft | | | Doublings | App. Wt. Delivered | |
	Back	Front	Total		oz./5 yd.	ktex
First sheeter	6	7	42	—	lap*	
Second sheeter	6	6	36	3 laps thick*	lap*	
First can	5	5	25	3 laps thick*	32*	198
Second can	4	5	20	10	16	99
Third can	3	4·5	13·5	10	12	74
Fourth can	2·5	4	10	10	12	74

*It is not customary to state sliver weights for these items because of the type of feed and the irregularity of the product at this stage.

The back draft used in these machines is high in comparison with the drafts used in drawing because of the good opening effect which is produced, the pins being drawn through the wool as it is slowly fed forward by the back rollers. In consequence, the tips of the fibres are 'combed through' first, and the length of fibre subjected to this action is gradually increased. This action is severe, causing fibre breakage, and for this reason back draft has to be kept to a minimum compatible with good opening and gradually reduced throughout the set as opening of the material proceeds. With front draft, the action is rather different, the material being drawn through the pins, producing a good straightening effect which is less severe than the effect of back draft. In the case of cotted or matted fleeces the wool may be passed through a cott box prior to scouring. This machine is similar in principle to the preparer but is more sturdily built.

In processing mohair and similar fibres, the material – after passing through the first three machines (sheeter boxes) – is given a preliminary rough combing, followed by four can preparers and a second combing. For very long fibres a double-screw preparer (called the Clough and Kelly gill box) may be used for the first two operations. This machine has two sets of fallers, the second set travelling faster than the first. Thus a draft is produced between the two sets of fallers in addition to the normal front and back draft.

Intersecting preparer gill boxes may be used for the can preparers, the main advantage being that with these machines lower back drafts may be used, and fibre breakage thereby minimized. Backwashing may be carried out as part of the fourth or fifth preparer stage, or it may be added as an additional process. It is not common to backwash prepared wools.

Preparer gill boxes should be well maintained if maximum fibre length and combing tear are to be obtained. This applies particularly to the faller pins and the leather aprons. The front ratch at the first machine is usually about one-quarter of the maximum fibre length, and this ratio is reduced to about one-fifth of the maximum fibre length at the last machine. Too long a front ratch gives insufficient parallelization of the fibres, whereas too close a front ratch causes increased fibre breakage.

WORSTED CARDING

The objects of this process are the same as those outlined in the previous section for longwool preparing but, in addition, carding has the further purpose of removing vegetable matter, or of preparing for its removal by the comb. The card has been used traditionally for wools shorter than about eight inches. The main reasons for this are (*i*) finer wools tend to be more entangled than long wools after scouring and drying; (*ii*) the shorter and finer wools often contain burrs and other vegetable matter which are regarded as best dealt with by the card; and (*iii*) wools longer than about eight inches are difficult to process on a card which is equipped with standard sized rollers.

The worsted carding process, unlike woollen carding, is followed by many other processes before the material is spun into a yarn. Nevertheless, it is important that optimum carding conditions should be attained; for example, the amount of noil formed in combing is greatly influenced by the standard of carding. The basic purpose of worsted carding, like that of woollen carding, is to disentangle and mix the fibres. The main differences between the two types of card are that the worsted card has no condenser delivery and no cross-fibre intermediate feeds. In consequence of the latter omission, the worsted card probably gives a more orientated fibre array in the delivered card sliver than does the woollen card. It is sometimes argued that the card does not parallelize the fibres and this is probably true in the sense that the fibres are frequently hooked when leaving the card. On the other hand, if comparison is made between the general orientation of the fibres before and after carding, it cannot be denied that the card does contribute to parallelization, although this is far from being completed by the card alone.

Worsted carding has two main divisions: (*i*) the Bradford system, used for wools with a maximum fibre length of more than about four inches, and (*ii*) the Continental system, used for the shorter and more burry merino wools, and for crossbred wools up to about six inches maximum fibre length. The roller arrangement of the standard Bradford card forepart is shown in Fig. 4.1, and that of the Continental worsted card in Fig. 4.2.

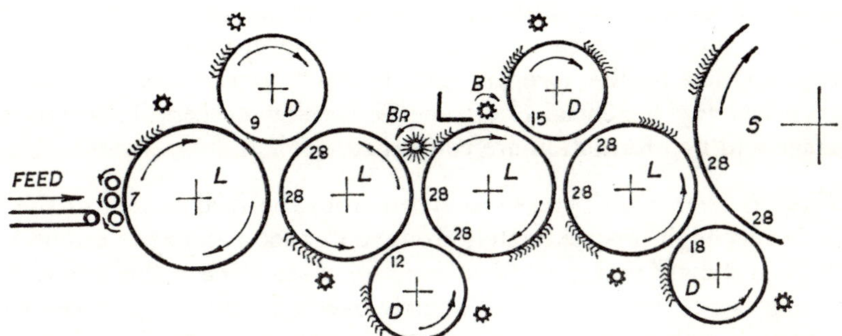

FIG. 4.1. STANDARD BASIC FOREPART FOR BRADFORD WORSTED CARD
L—Licker rollers; *D*—Divider rollers; *B*—Burr beater; *BR*—Brush; *S*—Swift. Numbers indicate typical settings for 64s wool.

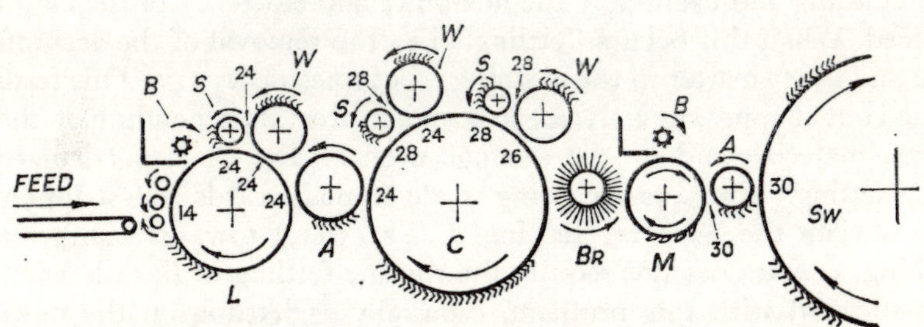

FIG. 4.2. BASIC FOREPART FOR CONTINENTAL WORSTED CARD
A—Angle stripper; *B*—Burr beater; *BR*—Brush; *M*—Morel clothed roller; *S*—Strippers; *W*—Workers; *SW*—Swift; *L*—Licker; *C*—Breast roller.

There is a trend to move away from the Bradford type forepart to the Continental forepart and to make the machines wider. At one time machines 60 inches wide were common, but new machines are being made with widths up to about 96 inches, giving a corresponding increase in production. For a 72-inch wide card, production of low crossbred is from 85 lb. to 140 lb. per hour, and for merino wools from 60 lb. to 110 lb. per hour.

The Continental card frequently has metallic clothing throughout, whereas the Bradford card usually has flexible wire clothing, except for the first three lickers and two or three dividers. The swift section of the card is similar to that of the woollen card, having pairs of workers and strippers and a fancy roller. The Bradford card usually has only three pairs (12 in. workers, 5 in. strippers, 16 in. fancy), while the Continental card frequently has four pairs (8 in. workers, 4 in. strippers, 10 in. fancy). Usually the full card has two swifts linked by an angle stripper or by a burr crushing device.

An automatic feed is used similar to the one employed in woollen carding, but in worsted carding, due to the many subsequent processes, accuracy is not as critically important. The Bradford card may have steam heating applied to the forepart, but tests[2, 3] do not indicate that this practice has any beneficial effect on the carding process insofar as fibre breakage and nep formation are concerned.

Feed Rollers: The increase in speed from the feed rollers to the first licker is very high (approximately from 20 to 1000 inches per minute) and it has been shown[4] that most fibre breakage takes place at this point. It has been suggested[3] that this may be partly overcome by using three or four lines of feed rollers, each having a greater surface speed than that of the preceding line. Another alternative would be to use a small diameter licker before the existing first licker, operating at an intermediate speed.

Fettling: As carding proceeds, some fibres become embedded in the card clothing and eventually the flexibility and efficiency of the clothing is reduced. When this occurs, fettling – i.e., the removal of the accumulated fibre and other matter in the clothing – becomes necessary. This fettling is carried out at approximately 40- to 60-hour intervals depending on the type of raw material, and on the settings used on the card, particularly the fancy setting. Attempts are being made to make cards self-stripping and thus obviate the need for fettling[5-9]. The trend towards using metallic clothing, which does not require the routine fettling of flexible wire, may be associated with this problem, especially as fettling on the new wide cards is more difficult. It may be that these developments will be more readily accepted for woollen carding, but looking ahead, it seems that worsted carding must also eliminate fettling, if this is possible, in order to increase production, the loss caused by fettling being approximately 2 to 3 per cent.

Grinding: After processing upwards of 10,000 lb. of wool, the surfaces of the card wire tips are worn smooth. The wire on the rollers is therefore lightly ground by being rotated in contact with a rotating emery roller. In this way, the points of the clothing are restored with a rough surface and the rollers made truly circular, ready for setting.

Grinding is important, contributing to better fibre disentanglement, and less nep formation[2,3].

Setting: After grinding, the rollers must be replaced at the correct distance apart. This process is called card setting. The only rollers which touch each other are the fancy and the swift, all the other rollers being set with a small clearance which depends on (*i*) the wool fibre diameter, finer wool requiring closer settings, (*ii*) the action between the rollers, stripping usually requiring a close setting (28s–30s gauge) unless the material actually passes between the rollers (e.g. Bradford card – first divider/second licker), in which case an additional allowance may be necessary, depending on the state of the material, and (*iii*) the position on the card, working actions usually being set progressively closer as the material becomes more open in the course of its passage through the card.

It has been shown[2] that too open a setting of the card rollers results in the formation of more neps. Typical settings for 64s wool are indicated in Figs. 4.1 and 4.2. The setting gauge used is closely related to the following S.W.G. scale, equivalent thicknesses in thousandths of an inch being given in parenthesis: 14 (83), 16 (64), 18 (48), 20 (36), 22 (28), 24 (22), 26 (18), 28 (14·8), 30 (12·4), 32 (10).

Card delivery: A recent development is to group about eight cards into a battery feeding an autolevelling gill box[10]. Previously, coiler can delivery was favoured on the Bradford system for each individual card, whereas the Continental system had a battery of cards feeding to a common balling head.

FAULTS IN CARDING

The chief faults in worsted carding are a cloudy sliver, neps, and fibre breakage. A cloudy sliver may be due to irregular feeding, inefficient setting or wrong speeds, clothing in poor condition, or too high a production. Nep formation may be due to entanglements formed in scouring and to small particles of impurities remaining in the wool[2], other contributory factors being the regain, cleanliness and oil content of the feed wool, swift speed, production, settings, feed roller/licker speed ratio, divider actions, fancy speed, and grinding. The opening power of the card is largely related to the efficiency of the worker rollers[11]. Fibre breakage is largely related to the entangled state of the material being processed[12], and it would seem that the chances of a fibre being broken are proportional to its length[13], although all fibres present may be subject to being broken near the weathered tip of the fibre[14].

CARDING OF MAN-MADE FIBRES

Originally all man-made fibres entering the worsted trade as staple fibre were carded, the processing being basically similar to that employed for wool. Nep formation and fibre breakage occur in carding these fibres but the formation of fly waste is a bigger problem, due to the influence of static electricity. Unlike wool, the addition of water to these fibres is not possible because of their low regains. The problems caused by static electricity in carding, however, have been reduced by modern developments in fibre dressings applied by the manufacturer and difficulties may be further limited by avoiding excessive roller speeds, and by humidifying the atmosphere in the card room. Man-made fibres do not require the same amount of opening as wool, and for this reason it is usual to use a single swift card with only two lickers and dividers in the forepart. Nep formation should be avoided, particularly with strong fibres such as nylon and Terylene, as once formed, the neps are difficult to remove.

TOW TO TOP CONVERTERS

As man-made fibre output increased, it became economically possible to develop and introduce machines specially designed to process these fibres. Various machines have been made to cut or break continuous filament and to form it into a continuous sliver ready for further processing on the worsted system[15, 16]. The machines used for this purpose have certain features in common; namely (*i*) a creel, incorporating knot detectors, to feed and tension the incoming tow; (*ii*) a heater unit through which the fibres may be passed and stretched, fibres so stretched being later relaxed if necessary, to confer bulk to the blend being processed; (*iii*) a cutting or breaking unit which converts the continuous staple to the required fibre length, with the required distribution of fibre length; and (*iv*) a sliver-forming section which suitably distributes the fibres, crimps them (if required), and delivers the sliver into a suitable package form.

The input to this type of machine may be as much as 2,000,000 denier (220 ktex), giving a delivery of about 100,000 denier (approximately 230 drams per 40 yards or 11·1 ktex) at a production rate of about 100 to 130 pounds per hour.

After the first 'teething' troubles were overcome, tow to top converters have been highly successful; so much so, in fact, that they have almost completely eclipsed the original carding process. For certain purposes combing may also be dispensed with, but for coating yarns after dyeing and blending with wool, recombing usually takes place.

THE GEELONG CONVERTER FOR WOOL

For wools shorter than about eight inches, which conventionally would be carded, the Geelong Converter is proposed as an alternative process[17-19]. Although the system is reminiscent of longwool preparing, it differs from it in several important respects. The proposed apparatus consists of three intersector gill boxes arranged in tandem. Between each of these machines (called converters) are transfer mechanisms which break the sliver, and feed sections which overlap each other (in effect forming doublings) on to the feed sheet of the following machine[20]. The first converter is fed by a weighing type hopper and a high back draft is used (about four or five), the back ratch being set shorter than the mean fibre length of the wool being processed, while the front draft is about two, giving a total draft of about eight to ten. Roller diameters are small so that close ratches may be used. On the following machines, back draft is reduced and front draft increased to give total drafts of about 12 to 16. Production of the converter set is about 180 pounds per hour, compared with a rate of 60 to 110 pounds per hour from the conventional card, and it is thought that improvements could be made to give an industrial production rate of about 200 pounds per hour. It may be thought that departure from the conventional carding process would introduce difficulties when burry wools have to be processed, but experiments[19] indicate that by using a coarse preliminary rectilinear combing, followed by the normal combing, satisfactory results may be obtained. If this system proves satisfactory on a large commercial scale it should result in considerable economies. In this connection it should be pointed out that one converter only occupies 170 sq. ft., compared with 1700 sq. ft. for the same carding productive capacity. Again, maintenance costs are lower, fettling and grinding are not required, and less skill is necessary to obtain optimum conditions. Finally, the slivers produced should give a greater top yield, less nep, and no more vegetable particles than those produced by conventional means[19].

BACKWASHING AND WOOL OILING

FOR SHORT WOOL PROCESSING, backwashing follows carding in the English method, but follows combing in the Continental system. In a longwool preparing set, backwashing may be included at the fourth or fifth stage, although it is frequently omitted from longwool preparing. The first, and perhaps main, object of backwashing is to remove any grease and dirt persisting in the wool after scouring, along with emery dust and fibre dust from the card, and any soap and alkali remaining from the scouring process. There is, however, also the question of colour improvement. Natural wool has a slightly yellow appearance, and by using a dye it may be made to look whiter. The normal practice is to drip-feed a blue or violet dye into the rinse water or to use a peroxide bleach. The newer type of fluorescent dyewares (optical bleaches) have been tried, but as these were found to interfere with colour matching in subsequent processing, they are no longer used for this purpose. The addition of oil (for oil combing on the English system), and the addition of moisture are other objects of back-washing.

The conventional backwash machine consists of three parts, the scouring and rinsing section, the drying section, and the gilling and oiling section. One bowl, containing a soap solution of approximately 0·5 per cent, is used for scouring and one or two bowls, with a drip-feed of the blueing agent, are used for rinsing. If the wool has been previously scoured with a synthetic detergent without the addition of alkali, soap will not perform satisfactorily at the backwash due to the affinity of the wool for the alkali present in the soap. In this case a synthetic detergent will also have to be used for backwashing. The scouring bowl temperature is usually about 110°F. (43°C.), and that of the rinse about 95°F. (35°C.), but if backwashing is being used after top-dyeing, lower temperatures may be employed. The conventional backwash is usually made double width and each side is fed with 20 to 30 slivers which are guided through the bowls, being squeezed while immersed and also after each stage to remove surplus liquor.

For the English method the conventional backwash dryer employs a hot-air system, but a contact drying system is preferred for the Continental method of processing. The hot-air type consists of a series of perforated cylinders around which the slivers are threaded and through which the warm air is blown, passing through the wool. The contact dryer, used after combing with a rectilinear comb, consists of a large number of small-diameter rollers (about 40 rollers of five inches diameter) arranged in a semi-circle round a large cylinder. The slivers are passed round the series of rollers which dry the wool by contact with the hot cylinder surface. This method is claimed to have an ironing effect on the fibres, leaving them straighter. Both the above types of dryer have now been superseded by the suction drum dryer (*see* page 68) which, because of its high productive capacity, makes it more economical to deliver the sliver into cans after drying. In this way, two backwash units will balance the production of three sets of intermediate gilling.

The last section of the conventional backwash consists of the gill box which, although attached to the other sections, is a complete machine in itself. Before the material enters the back rollers, oil is added. On the Bradford system 3 per cent of class A combing oil is usually employed, but on the Continent 0·5 per cent of mineral-based oil and an anti-static agent is usual. The conventional backwash has a double-head delivery, producing two balls.

Care must be taken in backwashing to ensure that rinsing is thorough and followed by efficient squeeze rollers and drying. Excessive temperatures and prolonged stoppages must be avoided, otherwise the tear and mean fibre length of the top will be adversely affected[21].

THE ADDITION OF OIL

The object of adding oil in the English method of processing is to provide a lubricant in combing, to minimize fibre breakage and to increase cohesion between the fibres during drawing and spinning, while at the same time reducing the effects of static electricity which is generated when the fibres are drawn over each other in the dry state[22]. In recent years considerable research and development work has been carried out on the subject of wool oils and spinning assistants, ranging from oils to be added after drying to aid carding, to anti-static agents to be added in drawing to assist in spinning[23-27]. These fall into three main classes: (*a*) scourless lubricants, (*b*) anti-static agents, and (*c*) silica additives. The first two have similar bases, are water soluble and easily removed in scouring. They also attract moisture from the atmosphere during processing, thereby minimizing the effects of static electricity. The third group increases inter-fibre friction and improves drafting control and yarn strength. At present, however, woolcombers in this country continue to add class A combing oil.

The requirements of a good combing oil are given by Garner[28] as: (*i*) freedom from oxidation, (*ii*) ease of scouring, even after long storage, (*iii*) no tendency to smell or to become rancid, (*iv*) suitable viscosity, (*v*) pale colour, (*vi*) satisfactory as regards insurance companies' requirements, (*vii*) steady price, (*viii*) regular quality, and (*ix*) abundant source of supply.

Prior to the second world war, olive oil was used almost exclusively as a lubricant in the worsted industry even though it had definite limitations[29]. The main faults were that it varied in quality, and also caused tops which had been stored for a long period to become so sticky with oxidized oil that they were almost unworkable. However, a slight degree of oxidation, such as that produced by a storage period of three to six months, gave a slight increase in drag during drafting and this was generally regarded as desirable. Due to a shortage of supplies during the civil war in Spain and in the second world war, a series of standardized combing oils was recommended to the trade by the Combing Oil Association, and since 1949 class A combing oil – a blend of sperm oil and castor oil, with an anti-oxidant (naphthol) – has become standard.

The oil is usually added during the backwashing process between the slivers emerging from the drying section and entering the gill section. Spinning tests show that there is a definite relationship between the quantity and quality of the added oil and the spinning performance[29,30,71].

INTERMEDIATE GILLING

THE OBJECTS of these processes are to improve the parallelization of the fibres ready for combing, to produce a homogeneous mixture of fibres, and to deliver a sliver of uniform weight distribution. It is important that there should be an even number of operations between carding and combing so that the fibres enter the comb in the opposite direction to that being travelled as they leave the card[72]. This is because most of the fibres have the trailing end hooked as they leave the card; by entering the comb in the opposite direction, these hooked ends are fed into the comb as leading hooks. This results in a greater mean fibre length in the final top. The action of drafting and doubling used in intermediate gilling helps to remove the hooks from some of the fibres before combing takes place.

GILL BOX CONSTRUCTION AND DRIVE

Basically, the gill box consists of a pair of fluted back rollers which feed the slivers forward to a set of fallers. The fallers carry the fibres forward to another pair of fluted rollers, called the front rollers, which grip the fibres and draw them out of the fallers. The sliver is then either wound on to a ball or fed into a can. There are three basic forms of gill box: an open gill, an O.P.S. gill, and an intersecting gill.

The open gill box has a single set of fallers, with the pins pointing upwards, penetrating the fibres as they pass from the back to the front rollers. It is necessary to run the fallers at a higher speed than the back roller surface speed in order to tension the fibres, and to ensure pin penetration; this is called back draft, and is usually kept to a minimum which will give good pin penetration. The fallers are supported at each end by a metal 'saddle', and are driven forward by a rotating screw at each end. As each faller approaches the front roller, it is knocked down by cams on the ends of the screws, whence it becomes supported by a lower saddle. It is then driven backwards by return screws situated underneath the fallers which are carrying the material forward.

When a faller is knocked down, the pin control which it was exercising is abruptly terminated, and this results in an uneven flow of fibres into the front rollers[31]. In the open gill box, two rows of pins are removed from the material simultaneously, making the formation of 'faller marks' (intermittent patches of short fibres in the sliver) more pronounced. The amplitude of these faller marks depends on the draft, and on the distance from the front roller nip to the nearest row of faller pins (front ratch) – an increase of either of these causes an increase in faller marking. The minimum setting of the front ratch depends on the diameter of the front rollers, and on the pitch of the screw which drives the fallers. In the Bradford-type gill box, using front roller diameters of 2–2½ inch, the front ratch cannot be less than 1⅞ inch. This is satisfactory for Bradford-quality tops which have a mean fibre length of about 7 cm. (2·8 inch), with 50 per cent coefficient of variation, but a smaller front ratch is necessary when the shorter rectilinear combed materials are to be processed. This may be achieved by using small rollers of about one-inch diameter, as in the O.P.S. (Offerman-Prince-Smith) type of open gill box, or the Continental type of intersecting gill box.

The O.P.S. machine (no longer manufactured) was an open gill box, but one in which the front row of pins in the fallers were short and round, and the back row long and flat. By means of an auxiliary cam and an intermediate saddle the faller was only lowered sufficiently to remove the short row of pins first, the last row of long flat pins being left in the material until the faller came even closer to the front roller and was finally knocked down on to the return screw.

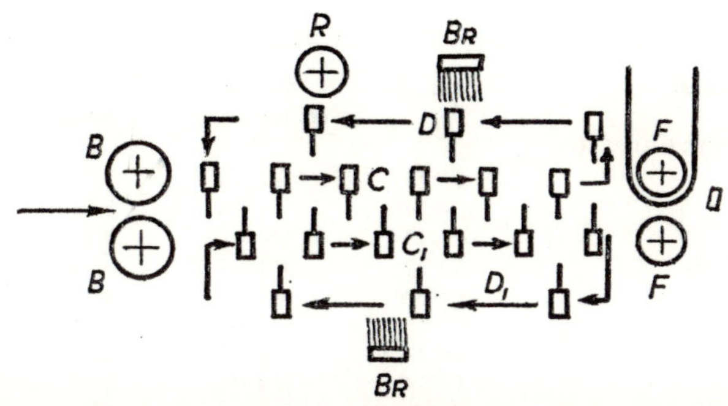

FIG. 4.3. SIMPLIFIED SIDE VIEW OF AN INTERSECTING GILL BOX

B—Back (feed) rollers: BR—Faller cleaning brushes: R—Felt covered roller: F—Front (drafting) rollers: C—Upper fallers in forward screw; C_1—Lower fallers in forward screw: D—Upper fallers in return screw: D_1—Lower fallers in return screws.

The intersecting gill box has two sets of fallers; each faller has only one row of pins, and in consequence is narrower. The lower set of fallers (C_1 and D_1 in Fig. 4.3) occupies the same position as do the fallers in an open gill box, while the upper set of fallers (C and D in Fig. 4.3) have the pins pointing downwards, penetrating between each row of pins in the lower set. The fallers are withdrawn from the material near the front rollers alternately, one from each set in turn. This type of gill box has the advantage that no back draft is necessary, as the fibres are bound to be penetrated by the intersecting faller pins. Also, it is possible to have a heavier feed sliver weight and thus a higher production rate, because the material cannot over-ride the pins. (This cannot be exploited where sliver weights are limited, as for example in second finisher gill boxes after combing.) Better control of the short fibres is also possible when a heavier feed is used.

The intersecting gill box is made in two versions. The Bradford version has rollers and ratch dimensions similar to those in the open Bradford gill box. The Continental version has small diameter front rollers (about one inch), and a short front ratch (about $\frac{7}{8}$ inch) – similar to the O.P.S. dimensions.

In recent years an alternative to the screw drive to the fallers has been developed in the H.M.G. gill box[32]. This uses a chain-drive system, giving a faller speed equivalent to 4000–6000 drops per minute, compared with about 650 drops for the conventional Bradford gill box, or 1500 to 1800 for the modern high-speed gill boxes which use screw-type faller propulsion. The use of the H.M.G. gill box in top finishing and intermediate gilling has been recommended[10].

TABLE 4.2 MAIN GILL BOX DIMENSIONS AND FALLER SPEEDS

Process		Quality	Low Front Roller Dia.	Screw Pitch	Pins per in.
A.	**INTERMEDIATE GILLING**				
	Backwash	56/70	3 in.	$\frac{1}{2}$ in.	10
		50/54	3 in.	$\frac{5}{8}$ in.	8
		46/48	3 in.	$\frac{5}{8}$ in.	5
	First gill box.	56/70	$2\frac{1}{2}$ in.	$\frac{7}{16}$ in.	10
		50/54	$2\frac{1}{2}$ in.	$\frac{1}{2}$ in.	9
		46/48	3 in.	$\frac{5}{8}$ in.	8
	Second gill box.	56/70	$2\frac{1}{2}$ in.	$\frac{7}{16}$ in.	12
		50/54	$2\frac{1}{2}$ in.	$\frac{1}{2}$ in.	10
		46/48	$2\frac{1}{2}$ in.	$\frac{5}{8}$ in.	10
B.	**COMB FINISHER GILLING**				
	First finisher	56/70	2 in.	$\frac{3}{8}$ in.	12
		50/54	$2\frac{1}{2}$ in.	$\frac{7}{16}$ in.	10
		46/48	$2\frac{1}{2}$ in.	$\frac{1}{2}$ in.	9
		40P/46P	$2\frac{1}{2}$ in.	$\frac{5}{8}$ in.	8
	Second finisher	56/70	2 in.	$\frac{3}{8}$ in.	14
		50/54	$2\frac{1}{2}$ in.	$\frac{7}{16}$ in.	12
		46/48	$2\frac{1}{2}$ in.	$\frac{1}{2}$ in.	11
		40P/46P	$2\frac{1}{2}$ in.	$\frac{5}{8}$ in.	10
C.	**OPEN DRAWING**				
		60/80	1 in.	$\frac{3}{8}$ in.	15/18
		50/58	$2\frac{1}{2}$ in.	$\frac{3}{8}$ in.	12/14
		46/48	$2\frac{1}{2}$ in.	$\frac{7}{16}$ in.	10/12
		Mohair	$2\frac{1}{2}$ in.	$\frac{1}{2}$ in.	10/12
		Longwools	3 in.	$\frac{5}{8}$ in.	8/10
D.	**CONTINENTAL DRAWING**				
		60/80	1 in.	$\frac{5}{16}$ in.	16/18

E. HIGH-SPEED GILL BOXES (PIN DRAFTERS)—1500–1800 faller drops/minute.

$\frac{7}{8}$ in. $\frac{5}{16}$ in.   29 (max)

F. H.M.G. (Chain faller drive—equivalent to 6,000 drops/minute).

$\frac{7}{8}$ in. $\frac{3}{8}$ in.

RECOMMENDED MAXIMUM FALLER SPEEDS for A, B, C & D*

Pitch of screw	$\frac{3}{8}$ in.	$\frac{7}{16}$ in.	$\frac{1}{2}$ in.	$\frac{5}{8}$ in.
Faller drops per minute	600	550	500	400

*Some firms exceed these speeds by about 15 per cent.

Conventional gill boxes have a leather apron passing round one of the front rollers. The purpose of this is to provide a resilient nip point, so that heavy pressure may be applied without the fibres being damaged. Unfortunately, as the leather becomes worn and thinner, it beds down into the flutes of the rollers, giving an apparent increase in draft. When a new leather is put on, there is an abrupt decrease in draft which must be allowed for by changing the draft wheel. A further disadvantage of the leather is the joint; each time it passes round, it may cause a periodic draft change. Periodicity may also be caused by the deeply fluted rollers, which tend to grip the fibres in bunches.

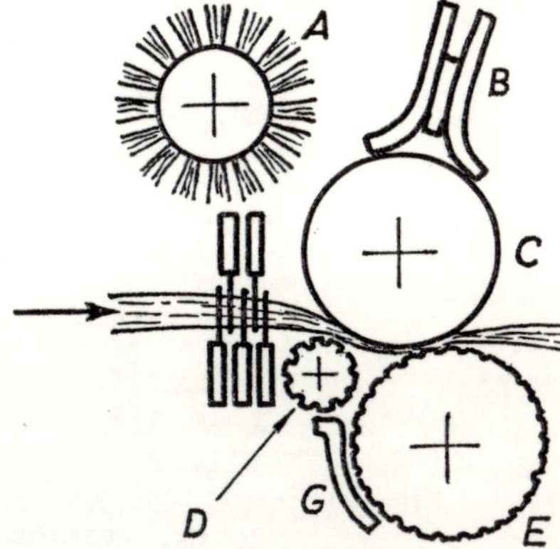

FIG. 4.4.   THREE-LINE ROLLER ASSEMBLY AS USED ON AMERICAN PIN DRAFTERS

A—Brush; *B*—Felt roller cleaner; *C*—Upper press roller with synthetic covering; *D*—Inner nip roller · *E*—Outer nip roller : *G*—Felt roller cleaner for both nip rollers.

A post-war development is the three-line roller assembly, illustrated in Fig. 4.4. This allows a short front ratch of $\frac{7}{8}$ inch, while the scratch-fluted rollers do not cause periodicity. Unfortunately, the processing of oil-combed material is not successful on this arrangement, as the material tends to lap round the rollers. As an alternative to the synthetic-covered press roller *C*, a synthetic apron (jointless) has been tried in an attempt to overcome this tendency to lap, but even this is not completely successful. This form of roller arrangement is, therefore, mainly restricted to use on the American (pin drafting) and Continental systems of drawing.

DRAFT IN GILLING

The amount of draft used in gilling depends largely on: (*i*) the mean fibre length of the material, (*ii*) the variation in fibre length, (*iii*) the state of the material and the degree of parallelization of the fibres, this being different in longwool preparing, intermediate gilling, and drawing, (*iv*) the thickness of the fibre assembly being processed, (*v*) the front ratch (i.e. the distance from the front roller nip to the nearest row of faller pins immediately after a faller has been knocked into the return screw) and (*vi*) the type of fibre. In this last mentioned respect, Terylene, for example, needs more *calculated* draft than all-wool to obtain the same *actual* draft.

Draft may take place between the back rollers and fallers (back draft), and between the fallers and front rollers (front draft). Apart from longwool preparing gill boxes, and the Geelong converter, back draft is usually kept to the minimum necessary to tension the slivers sufficiently to permit pin penetration. The front draft is the major draft, and is the one usually

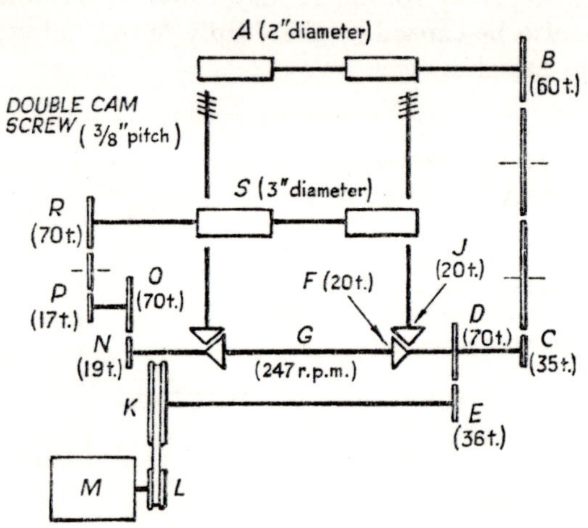

FIG 4.5. PLAN OF THE GEARING DRIVE OF A
CONVENTIONAL BRADFORD GILL BOX

A—Lower front (drafting) roller;　*B*—Front roller wheel;　*C*—Draft change wheel; *D*—Driven speed wheel;　*E*—Driving speed wheel;　*F*—Shaft driving bevel;　*G*—Upper back shaft;　*J*—Driven screw bevel;　*K*—Pulley on lower back shaft;　*L*—Motor pulley; *M*—Motor;　*N*—Upper back shaft wheel;　*O*—Large double stud wheel;　*P*—Small double stud wheel;　*R*—Back roller wheel;　*S*—Back (feed) roller.

altered when a change of draft becomes necessary. The total draft is the product of the back draft and front draft. An approximate guide is to add one to the maximum fibre length (measured in inches) to determine how much draft may be applied.

DRAFT CALCULATIONS

The gearing drive of a conventional gill box is represented diagrammatically in Fig. 4.5, which assumes a front roller *A* with a diameter of two inches, a front roller wheel *B* with 60 teeth, a draft change wheel *C* with 35 teeth and an upper back shaft *G* with a speed of 247 r.p.m. On this basis the front roller surface speed can be determined as shown below. Similarly, the back roller surface speed and the faller surface speed can be calculated from the appropriate roller and wheel dimensions in Fig. 4.5:

$$\text{Front roller surface speed} = \frac{247 \times 35 \times 2\pi}{60}$$

$$= 905 \text{ in. per minute.}$$

$$\text{Back roller surface speed} = \frac{247 \times 19 \times 17 \times 3\pi}{70 \times 70}$$

$$= 153{\cdot}5 \text{ in. per minute.}$$

$$\text{Faller surface speed} = \frac{247 \times 20 \times 0{\cdot}75}{20}$$

$$= 185 \text{ in. per minute.}$$

In the above calculation for faller surface speed, the figure of 0·75 is the *lead* of the faller screw, i.e. the distance travelled by a faller per *one* revolution of the screw. The screw pitch (i.e. the distance between adjacent grooves in the screw) is $\frac{3}{8}$ inch, but the screw is double-cut. As there are therefore two grooves (or threads) running alternately around the screw, the distance from the shoulder of a groove, to the nearest shoulder of the same groove further along the screw is twice the pitch. The lead is, in fact, the product of the pitch and the number of cuts (or number of cams).

Once the surface speeds have been determined, it is possible to calculate the various drafts on the gill box:

$$\text{Back draft} = \frac{\text{Faller surface speed}}{\text{Back roller surface speed}} = \frac{185}{153{\cdot}5} = 1{\cdot}21$$

$$\text{Front draft} = \frac{\text{Front roller surface speed}}{\text{Faller surface speed}} = \frac{905}{185} = 4{\cdot}9$$

$$\text{Total draft} = \frac{\text{Front roller surface speed}}{\text{Back roller surface speed}} = \frac{905}{153{\cdot}5} = 5{\cdot}9$$

$$\text{Front draft} \times \text{Back draft} = 4{\cdot}9 \times 1{\cdot}21 = 5{\cdot}9.$$

If the surface speeds are not already known, and are not particularly required, it is simpler to calculate the drafts directly:

$$\text{Back draft} = \frac{{\cdot}75 \times 20 \times 70 \times 70}{20 \times 19 \times 17 \times 3\pi} = 1{\cdot}21$$

$$\text{Front draft} = \frac{2\pi \times 35 \times 20}{60 \times 20 \times {\cdot}75} = 4{\cdot}9$$

$$\text{Total draft} = \frac{2\pi \times 35 \times 70 \times 70}{60 \times 19 \times 17 \times 3\pi} = 5{\cdot}9$$

Machine Gaugepoint: It will be noted that the above calculation, insofar as it relates to a specific machine, incorporates only one variable, viz. the size of the change wheel (35 in the above example). It follows, therefore, that if this is omitted from the calculation, a constant for the machine is obtained. This value (0·1685 in the example) is known as the 'draft gaugepoint' and, once determined, serves as a rapid basis for the calculation of the draft produced by incorporating a specific change wheel. Thus in the example given, the total draft is 0·1685 × 35 or 5·9. Conversely if a particular draft is required, and the gaugepoint is known, the size of the necessary changewheel can easily be calculated. For example, supposing a draft of 6·4 to be required, then the necessary changewheel would have 6·4/0·1685 or 38 teeth.

Ratch: In machines not using pin control, the ratch is the distance from the front roller nip to the back roller nip. In the case of a gill box, however, a different type of fibre control is employed and, in consequence, a different description of ratch has been adopted. Thus, front ratch is understood to mean the distance from the front roller nip to the nearest row of faller pins *immediately after a faller has been transferred to the return screw*. Normally, front ratch is set at, or near to, the physical minimum possible when the machine is erected, and it usually remains unaltered. Back ratch is the distance from the back roller nip to *halfway* along the fallers. This distance should be set slightly longer than the longest fibre being processed. Where long and short wools are blended in gilling, the general rule is to ratch for the long fibres, and draft for the short.

DIRECTION OF DRAFTING

Slivers should not be drafted twice in the same direction consecutively[73]. By reversing the direction of drafting at alternate processes, any groups of fibres which were fed by the fallers to the front rollers with the leading ends approximately aligned will tend to be separated at the next operation due to the variation in fibre lengths.

DOUBLINGS

This term refers to the practice of feeding more than one end into a drafting unit; thus several are combined together in the single end delivered. The use of doublings brings about a certain degree of mixing and it helps to reduce irregularity both across and along the sliver.

WOOLCOMBING

WOOLCOMBING is a basic operation in the preparation of a worsted yarn made from 100 per cent wool. It has three objects: namely, (*i*) removal of short fibres from the carded or prepared sliver; (*ii*) parallelization of the fibres – combing is the most effective single operation; and (*iii*) removal of blemishes such as vegetable matter, neps, and slubs.

All the methods of combing at present in use are based on the same principle, namely, the holding of the uncombed fibres over a portion of their length by some device while the remainder of the fibres is combed by pins. Any fibre not held will be combed away as short fibre, whereas entangled fibres will either be straightened or broken, short pieces from broken fibres once again being combed out. The combed portion of the fibres remaining is then held while the remaining length is combed, resulting in the further removal of fibres. This completes the combing process, and the tufts of fibres are re-joined to form an endless sliver.

Before describing the process and the machinery employed, it may be useful to give a brief definition of some of the terms commonly used in woolcombing:

Noil consists of the short fibres, slubs, neps, etc., which have been rejected by the comb as unsuitable for worsted processing but which can be used in the woollen industry.

Comb sliver is the continuous assembly of parallel fibres delivered by the comb for use in the worsted spinning industry. The fibres in a comb sliver are not evenly distributed.

Top sliver is produced by passing comb slivers through finisher gill boxes, so that the drafting and doubling used will evenly distribute the various fibres both along and across the sliver produced.

Tear is the ratio of the weight of comb sliver to the weight of noil, the term being used to indicate the amount of noil removed in the combing process.

Noil percentage is the ratio of the weight of noil to the combined weight of noil and comb sliver, expressed as a percentage. It is sometimes used (especially in recombing) as an alternative to tear to describe the amount of noil removed.

The success of the combing operation depends to a very large extent on the efficiency of the scouring, drying, carding, and gilling processes which precede it. This cannot be over-emphasized, particularly with regard to the scouring operation, which is probably the most important of all.

There are three types of combing machine currently manufactured, the choice depending on the length of the wool being combed, on the degree of vegetable matter in the wool, and on the quality of top desired. The combs may be classified against fibre length as follows:

> Short, medium and long wools – the Noble comb.
> Short and very short wools – the rectilinear comb.
> Long and very long wools – the Lister comb.

Each of the combs is capable of combing wools which cannot be successfully combed on the other two machines, and this accounts for the continued survival of the three separate types. The Holden comb, which is no longer made, although being technically excellent, was at an economic disadvantage as regards production rate, and could only deal with medium and short wools which could also be combed on other machines.

THE NOBLE COMB

This is the most popular comb in the English system of combing because of its simplicity, low cost of upkeep, adaptability over a wide range of fibres, and its high productive capacity. In this last mentioned respect, however, the Noble comb is in danger of being overtaken by the rectilinear comb if recent developments to increase the productivity of the latter continue. Because of the adaptability of the Noble comb, in that the circles and drawing-off rollers can be changed to suit different diameters and lengths of fibres, it can comb any fibre with a maximum fibre length of not less than about four inches. It is therefore used in the combing of long prepared wools, mohair, alpaca, camel hair, coarse hair of all kinds, carpet wools, coarse, medium and fine crossbreds, merinos, man-made staple fibres, and in the recombing of dyed merino tops.

Due to the design of the comb, it is first necessary to wind four slivers alongside each other to form a compact ball weighing from 15 to 30 lb, depending on the quality. The machine used to do this operation is called the 'Punch', and the product 'punch balls'. These balls are then placed on the comb creel. The regain of the material at this stage has considerable influence over the combing performance; it is usual for the wool entering the comb to have a regain of 19 to 21 per cent. Higher regains than normal cause a decrease in noil percentage, nep content, and mean fibre length of top[33]. An example of this is given in Table 4.3.

TABLE 4.3. EFFECT OF COMBING REGAIN ON NEP CONTENT AND MEAN FIBRE LENGTH

Combing Regain (per cent)	Neps per gramme	Mean Fibre Length (cm.)
42·5	3·5	6·1
10·2	11·9	6·7

The basic design of the Noble comb is shown in the diagrammatic plan given in Fig. 4.6. It consists principally of three circles – a large one B of

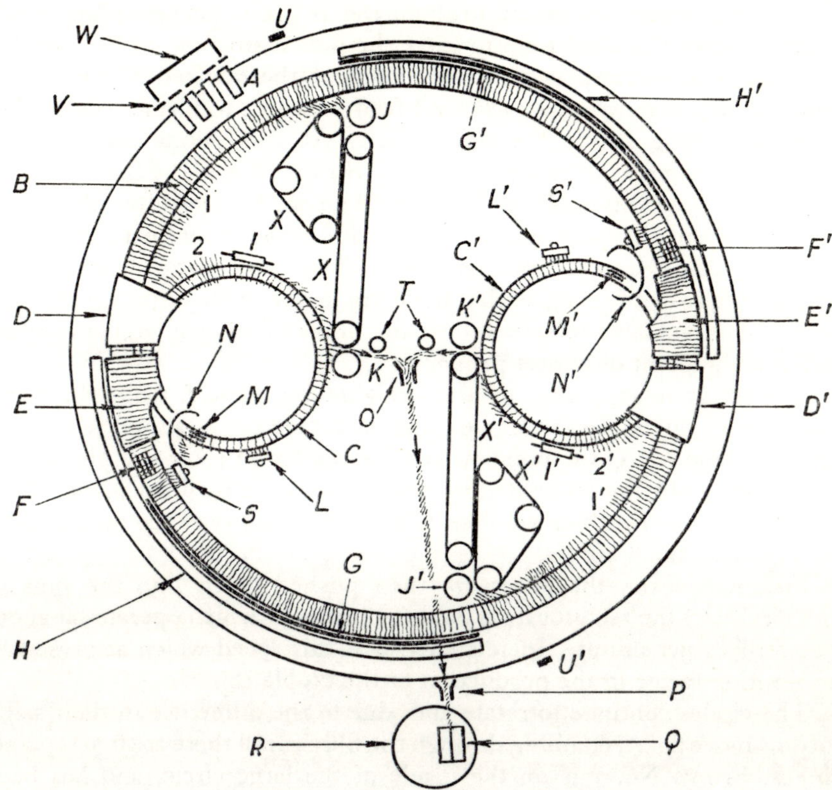

FIG. 4.6. SIMPLIFIED PLAN VIEW OF THE NOBLE COMB

A—Feed boxes; *B*—Large circle: *C*—Small circle; *D*—Dabbing brush; *E*—Straightening plate; *F*—Plough knives: *G*—Feed knife: *H*—Inclined plane: *I*—Air current directed at fringe of fibres held in small circle: *J*—Outside drawing-off rollers: *K*—Inside drawing-off rollers: *L*—Noil brush: *M*—Noil knives: *N*—Noil tin: *O*—Centre funnel: *P*—Coiler funnel: *Q*—Calender rollers: *R*—Coiler can: *S*—Large circle clearing brush: *T*—End detector stop motion: *U*—Creel feed cam: *V*—Sliver guide plate: *W*—Punch ball: *K*—Leather aprons: **1** and **2**—Fibre fringes: Note—The R.H. side of the machine is an inverted duplicate of the L.H. side and combing takes place at both sides of the comb concurrently.

approximately 43 inches inside diameter, and two small ones *C* and *C*¹ of approximately 16 inches outside diameter. The large circle is mounted on a carriage which also supports the creel carrying the 18 punch balls *W*, sliver guide plates *V*, and feed boxes *A* (only one of the 18 parts *W*, *V* and *A*, are shown in the diagram). All three circles rotate in a clockwise direction with approximately the same surface speed (about 500 inches per minute) at the face row of pins. Each circle is covered with several rows of vertically set pins; on the large circle the inside row (called the face row) is the finest, while the position is reversed on the small circle.

The brass circles are heated to about 180°F. (82°C.), a procedure which is said to allow the oiled wool to leave the pins easily, and to heat-set the fibres while the crimp is removed. Each of the 72 feed slivers is fed intermittently through guides V, and feed boxes A, to form a continuous fringe projecting inside the large circle. At two points diametrically opposite, the slivers are drawn in through the feed box A, by the combined action of the feed knives G and the inclined planes H. Soon after, the slivers are raised from the pins of the large circle by the combined action of a rotating brush S and the plough knives F (sloping plates, curved to fit between the rows of pins), so that the extra length of sliver drawn through the feed boxes is able to spread over the pins of both the large and small circles at the point of closest proximity.

The fringe is supported by the straightening plate E while the fibres straighten out over the two circles, and each feed box is supported by the inclined plane H. At the point where the wool is to enter the pins of the two circles, both the straightening plate E and the inclined plane H are terminated, and the fibres are then left unsupported over the pins of both the large and small circles.

Instantaneously, the fibres are then pushed down into the pins of both circles by the reciprocating dabbing brush D, which operates at about 1000 strokes per minute. Incidentally, it is this speed which at present is the limiting factor in the production of the Noble comb.

The circles continue to rotate and, due to the difference in their sizes, the pins move apart, combing through the fibres until there are two separate fringes. Fringe No. 1 is on the inside of the large circle, and has been combed through by the small circle pins, while fringe No. 2 is on the outside of the small circle having been combed by the large circle pins. The ends of the fibres still held in the circle pins remain uncombed at this stage.

Final combing takes place when the fringe of projecting fibres is removed from the pins by drawing-off rollers. The large circle fringe No. 1 is drawn off by the outside drawing-off rollers J, while the small circle fringe No. 2 is drawn off by the inside drawing-off rollers K. A similar action takes place at the other side of the comb, where rollers J' draw off fringe No. 1', and rollers K' draw off fringe No. 2'. The fibres from the large circle are conveyed between leather aprons X, to be united with the small circle fringe at K. Thus the fibres passing through K include both fringe No. 1 and fringe No. 2. Similarly, the fibres passing through K' include fringes Nos. 1' and 2', and all these slivers are united as they pass through a rotating funnel O. The combined sliver is conveyed to a coiler can R via a second funnel P, and calender rollers Q.

Any fibres which are too short to protrude from the small circle are raised from the pins by a rotating noil brush L and noil knives M, and along with neps, slubs, and vegetable matter, are deposited into the noil

tins N, or conveyed pneumatically direct to bags being packed with noil.
Short fibres in the large circle pins will be prevented from being drawn-off
at J by the density of the face-row pinning of the large circle, and so will be
fed over into the pins of the small circle at the next dabbing operation.
Some details of recommended pinning for the Noble combing of different
qualities of wool are given in Table 4.4.

TABLE 4.4. RECOMMENDED PINNING FOR THE NOBLE COMBING OF
DIFFERENT WOOL QUALITIES

| Material | Large Circle | | Small Circle | |
	No. of Rows	Pins/inch (face row)	No. of Rows	Pins/inch (face row)
Merino wools	11	42	7	46
56s/58s short staple	11	36	7	40
56s/58s long carding	10	36	6	40
44s/52s prepared or long carding	10	28	6	32
38s/46s long prepared	9	22	5	24
FOR RECOMBING				
Merino wools	11	38	7	40
Fine crossbred wools	9	32	6	36

The diameter of the outside drawing-off rollers J varies from three
inches for coarse long material, to $1\frac{1}{4}$ inches for fine merino; the inside
drawing-off rollers K are usually smaller than the outside ones because
they have to draw-off shorter fibres; they vary from two inches to $1\frac{1}{8}$ inches.

Sliver weights fed into the comb, production, and tear vary considerably, but an approximate guide is given in Table 4.5.

TABLE 4.5. INPUT SLIVER WEIGHTS, TEAR AND RECOMMENDED
PRODUCTION RATES FOR NOBLE COMBING

| Materials | Input Sliver Weight | | Tear | Rec. Prodn* |
	(oz./10 yd.)	(ktex)		(lb./hr.)
Goathair	28-32	87-99	3:1-10:1	55
40s Prepared	24-28	75-87	12:1	90
44s Prepared	24-28	75-87	12:1	78
48s Prepared	24-28	75-87	12:1	70
56s Carded	16-20	50-62	14:1	55
60s Carded	15-17	46·5-53	8:1-11:1	45
Merino wool	14-16	43·5-50	8:1	40
Recombing	18-20	56-62	19:1-32:1	65

*Production rates from 10-20 per cent higher than those tabulated may be
obtained, probably at the expense of noil and quality.

One of the chief weaknesses of the Noble comb lies in the fact that the
large and small circles do not touch each other, with the result that there is
always a small portion of uncombed wool. The subject of feeding problems
has been investigated[34], and a comb control unit has been described[35]. This

unit controls the feed throwover (the length of fringe over the small circle) to within 0·012 in., as compared with variations from 0·030 to 0·085 in. by an overlooker. It follows, therefore, that the control unit should give a more uniform top, with a more constant noil extraction rate.

It has been known for a long time that the comb 'makes its own noil', i.e. it breaks some of the fibres which are ultimately removed as noil. This question of fibre breakage has been the subject of considerable research effort[36, 37], and formulae have been advanced which enable the breakage rate to be predicted with some degree of accuracy.

Further disadvantages of the Noble comb include the rapid wear of the dabbing brush which occurs where the circle pins are densely concentrated at the tangent point, the wear of the drawing-off leathers, and the fact that heating of the comb makes working conditions unpleasant. It has been shown that if the small circles are tilted and a simpler type of brush is used, wear of the dabbing brush can be reduced[38], but this idea has not been adopted.

The main control over the amount of noil extracted is the setting of the feed knife (or comb control unit), which determines the length of feed over the small circle. Other factors which influence the tear ratio are: (*i*) the diameter and setting of the drawing-off rollers to the circles; (*ii*) the fibre length distribution in the uncombed material; (*iii*) the efficiency of the previous processes (scouring, carding, and gilling); (*iv*) the thickness of the feed slivers; and (*v*) the depth of dabbing, and pinning used. If the comb is functioning under normal conditions, the condition of the sliver has a far greater effect on tear than has normal mechanical adjustment[39].

THE RECTILINEAR COMB

This machine (also known as the 'French', 'Heilmann' or 'Schlumberger' comb) is used in the worsted industry for combing wools which are too short or too burry for the Noble comb, i.e. wools with a maximum fibre length less than about four inches, but it can also be used for longer wools. Unlike the Noble comb, the rectilinear comb is not heated, and oil is not added to the material. The product is processed on the Continental systems of drawing, to be made into 'dry-spun' yarns. The machine is also used for the re-combing of neppy tops, and of tops after dyeing, the fine pinning ensuring the removal of faults without removing much noil.

The chief advantages of this comb are that the whole length of the fibre is combed, that it produces the clearest top, and that there is greater control over tear; almost any desired tear ratio is possible within reasonable limits. The fact that the comb is not heated makes it pleasanter for the operative, and no special feed arrangements are necessary, the feed being from cans or balls. Although less noil may be extracted than with the Noble comb, as might be expected, this is reflected in the character of the top produced, the rectilinear combed top being more lofty, presumably due to the inclusion of more short fibres.

A disadvantage is the lower production rates on similar qualities, although models introduced in the post-war years have almost doubled the output. A further advance of this nature will seriously threaten the position of the Noble comb, which has remained unchanged as regards production due to the limitation of dabber speed. The rectilinear comb is mechanically more complex than the Noble comb, most of the parts having a reciprocating motion which is controlled from a common camshaft, and the timing of the various movements is critically important for first-class combing.

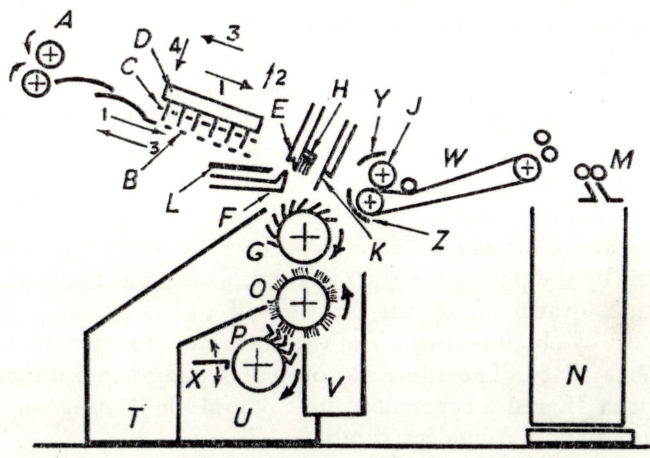

FIG. 4.7. DIAGRAMMATIC SIDE ELEVATION OF A RECTILINEAR COMB

A—Feed rollers: *B*—Feed box: *C*—Feed gill clearer plate: *D*—Feed gill; *E*—Upper nip jaw; *F*—Lower nip jaw: *G*—Porcupine roller: *H*—Nip brush: *J*—Drawing-off rollers: *K*—Intersector comb: *L*—Shovel plate: *M*—Coiler head: *N*—Coiler can; *O*—Porcupine clearing brush; *P*—Card-clothed roller: *T*—Second noil tin: *U*—First noil tin: *V*—Dust box: *W*—Leather apron: *X*—Doffing comb: *Y*—Sword: *Z*—Counter sword.

A simplified side-elevation of the rectilinear comb is shown diagrammatically in Fig. 4.7. About 24 slivers are fed from balls or cans via an overhead creel, through the feed rollers *A*, which have an intermittent rotary movement in the direction shown. It is important that the slivers feeding the comb should be of uniform thickness and evenly distributed across the width of the machine, otherwise there will be difficulty in gripping the fibres firmly in the nipper jaws. The slivers then pass through the feed unit which consists of three plates *B*, *C* and *D* working together in a fourfold movement. The lower feed box *B* and the middle clearer plate *C*, grooved and slotted respectively, support the slivers while a series of pins projecting downwards from the upper plate (feed gill *D*) pass through the slots in clearer plate C to penetrate the slivers and move them towards the open nipper jaws E and F in movement No. 1. When the nipper jaws have closed on the fringe of fibres, the feed box B and clearer plate C move back to their former position in movement No. 3, and at the same time the feed gill D follows movements Nos. 2, 3, and 4, so that the feed unit is ready to repeat the action.

When the nipper jaws close, they are lowered so that the fringe of fibres is initially combed by the rows of pins of the porcupine roller G. This action is assisted by the presence of a brush H, attached to the upper nipper jaw, ensuring that the fibres are depressed into the porcupine pins. The porcupine pins remove the short fibres not gripped by the nipper jaws, along with neps, slubs, and vegetable matter.

When the last row of porcupine pins has passed through the fringe, the nipper jaws are raised and opened to present the fringe to the spirally fluted drawing-off rollers J which move towards the nipper jaws, and commence to rotate to withdraw the fibres. At the same time the inter-sector comb K descends and pierces the fringe, which is supported by the shovel-plate L projecting through the nipper jaws. Thus as drawing-off takes place, any short fibres etc. are held back by the intersector comb, to be removed by the porcupine at its next cycle of initial combing.

The tufts drawn off by the drawing-off rollers are lapped over the previous tuft by about two-thirds of the maximum fibre length, so forming a continuous sliver. The sliver so formed is passed intermittently via a leather apron W and a coiler head unit M, into a rotating can N (36 in. high, 24 in. diam., on modern combs).

The noil left behind in the porcupine pins G is removed by a brush roller O, which runs at a higher surface speed, and is then deposited on the pins of a slowly rotating card-clothed roller P before being finally deposited in the first noil box U. Some short fibres which fail to cling to the brush collect in the second noil tin T, while fibre dust from the doffing action between O and P collects in the dust box V. Later models now use suction devices for noil removal.

The parts which require maximum maintenance are the drawing-off leather, and the porcupine pins. The life of a leather varies considerably, depending on the class of work being done. Thus, it may only last a fortnight when peroxide bleached wool is being combed; alternatively, it may last up to about nine months under more favourable conditions. The porcupine segments require re-pinning, on average, every four weeks or so, but individual segments may last from only one day to up nine months.

The chief factors governing the tear in a rectilinear comb are the length characteristics of the wool being combed and the type of top required. The condition of the sliver prior to combing has an effect on the result, the more parallel the fibres the less noil being produced. The main means of exercising control over the noil percentage are (*i*) by increasing the distance between the drawing-off rollers and the nipper jaws, a procedure which increases the amount of noil removed, and (*ii*) by increasing the length of tuft per combing cycle to increase the amount of noil. Other factors which exert less influence are the timing of the descent of the nipper jaws relative to the first row of pins of the porcupine, the density of pinning of the porcupine and the depth of penetration of the intersector comb. Some of these factors have been the subject of a preliminary investigation into rectilinear combing[40].

The production of the comb is dependent on four main items: (*i*) the number of cycles per minute (on modern combs this is about 170); (*ii*) the amount of feed per cycle (usually from three to ten millimetres); (*iii*) the thickness of the feed slivers (about $1\frac{1}{2}$ oz. per five yards, or 9 ktex, on older models and about $4\frac{1}{2}$ oz. per five yards, or 28 ktex, on newer models); and (*iv*) the number of slivers fed into the machine (frequently 24 slivers on older models, but only about 12 slivers on newer models).

THE LISTER COMB

This machine has a very limited use, being confined almost exclusively to the combing of long wools and hairs. Due to its excellence for this purpose, it is not likely to be displaced by the other two combs already described. There are approximately 60 combs of this type in use throughout the world[41].

The machine consists of a feeding unit which is similar to an ordinary gill box, except that it contains curved fallers and nipper jaws instead of front rollers, and a carrier comb which conveys the tufts of fibres from the nipper jaws to the third part of the machine – a comb circle. Horizontal drawing-off rollers withdraw the fibres from the circle pins in such a way that the sliver formed has long fibres at one side, graduating to the shortest fibres at the other side. This is called a 'hen-wing sliver'. The comb circle rotates at about one revolution per minute, giving a production of approximately 65 pounds per hour.

TOP FINISHING

The objects of the top finishing processes are (*i*) thoroughly to mix the fibres of the combed sliver (both along and across the sliver); (*ii*) to obtain sliver regularity (of thickness and weight); (*iii*) to produce a certain sliver weight, according to the wool quality (lower qualities require thicker slivers to give the necessary cohesion); (*iv*) to retain the parallel state of the fibres; (*v*) to add moisture, if necessary, so that the product is at standard regain when delivered; and (*vi*) to wrap the sliver so that it forms a suitable package (bumped top or ball) for subsequent transport. Hitherto the top contained a standard length of sliver, depending on the wool quality and type of top. The length is frequently 256 yards, producing a top which weighs approximately seven pounds but there is a welcome trend to make tops with longer sliver lengths and weighing about ten pounds in ball form or 20 to 50 pounds in bumped form.

Recently the Worsted Spinners' Federation, the British Wool Federation, the Woolcombing Employers' Federation and the Dyers' and Finishers' Association have jointly agreed that it is in the interests of all section of the industry that, over a period, standardization of the characteristics of undyed combed and converted packages should be established on the following basis:

1. A coiled pressed bump of 22 kg. (about 48½ lb.) having a diameter of not more than 28 in. for all undyed combed and converted packages (including man-made fibres but excluding hairs and speciality fibres).

2. A standard sliver weight for all combed/converted packages, irrespective of quality, of 20g. per metre (3·25 ounces per five yards), giving a standard sliver length of 1100 metres (1200 yards).

3. A total fatty matter content for undyed tops, sold in the following states, is given below:

	Conventional Continental	Conventional Bradford	
Oil Content	*18¼% regain*	*19% regain*	
Nil	0·634%	0·5%	Dry spinning systems.
1·5%	1·634%	1·5%	Pin drafting systems.
3·5%	3·634%	3·5%	Conventional Bradford systems.

The method of test to be a gross scour loss test.

The objectives enumerated above are usually achieved by using at least two gilling operations with drafts, doublings, and pin control. The first finisher gill box is fed with a large number of comb slivers – usually between 20 and 30 – and the sliver delivered from the gill box front rollers passes over a moistened roller so that the required amount of moisture is added. An autoleveller gill box may be used for the first finisher, in which case there is little variation in weight between the packages produced. If an ordinary gill box is used, the packages from the first finisher are weighed and heavy packages are paired with light packages, so that the feed to the second finisher is of standard weight. The second finisher may be fed with two or three slivers, and the draft is arranged so that the sliver weight delivered is correct. Some details of first and second finisher gill boxes are given in Table 4.2 on page 88.

The tops finally produced are usually weighed as a check on the processing. If the weight of a top differs from the standard weight required by more than a given amount, the top is rejected and fed into the first finisher gill box in place of some of the comb slivers. The permitted weight tolerance on which acceptance or rejection is based varies from firm to firm, but it may be in the region of four per cent. After leaving the second finisher, tops are usually stored for a time before going to the drawing process. This allows the moisture to become evenly distributed throughout the top, and provides an opportunity for static charges and fibre tensions built up in processing to be dissipated before further processing takes place.

RECOMBING

Recombing is used after top dyeing in the coloured worsted trade on 58s quality and finer. For 56s quality and lower, regilling is usually considered sufficient, although there may be exceptions to the 56/58 change-over point. In the finer qualities the warm wet treatment of dyeing causes the fibres to felt slightly and if regilling were used, the product would tend to be neppy and perhaps slubby. Recombing is also used on undyed material where a particularly fine quality yarn is required, and on some hair fibres to remove the longer and coarser fibres.

At one time it was common practice to dye top slivers in hank form, a procedure known as 'slubbing dyeing', but the modern approach is to dye the complete top. When slubbing dyeing is employed, the wool is dried in hank form, after which the hanks must be unwound before further processing can be carried out. The machine used for this purpose is known as a 'tin hat winder'. In the case of top dyeing it is usual to unwind the tops as they are passed through a suction drum dryer after dyeing, and to regill the slivers, winding them into top form.

Usually three processes of gilling are employed to prepare wool for recombing and, as heavy sliver weights are involved, intersector gill boxes are useful at this stage.

Recombing may be done on either the rectilinear comb or the Noble comb. The latter is more popular in this country, one of the advantages claimed for it being its good mixing power, as the Noble comb is fed from 72 slivers.

Where large lots of coloured materials are to be blended, the usual practice is to divide the material into small batches called 'setts', weighing up to about 150 lb per sett. Each sett contains the specified proportions of component, and one sett is fed into the gilling before the next sett is used. This eliminates the danger of long-term shade-variations arising.

It is usual for three per cent of noil to be extracted from up to 60s quality, four per cent from higher qualities, and up to five per cent from melanges. The recombing process removes about 80 per cent of the neps present in the original tops, and reduces the variation in fibre length slightly, while hardly altering the mean fibre length.

Top finishing follows the actual combing operation in the same way as in single combing.

Blending of wool and man-made fibre is often carried out in recombing. The slivers are weighed out into setts in the required blend proportions and gilled together before the actual recombing process. In some cases the Noble comb has to be run cooler than for 100 per cent wool, and at a slower speed, with coarser circle pinning. In making up the sett proportions, allowance has to be made for the preferential rate of noil removal which is likely to occur, depending on the relative strengths of the blend components. If such an allowance is not made, the result may be not only wrong proportions in the final product, but also an off-shade.

STANDARD TYPES OF TOPS

Over a period of time the wide range of different wools available has become categorized into groups related to spinning performance. These groups are known as wool qualities, and are perpetuated by reference to standard samples. It is said that the quality number originally indicated the finest worsted count which could be spun; but this relationship is no longer maintained. The finest count which can be spun from a given material under commercial conditions is hard to define. It depends for example on the type of spinning machinery used, package size, spindle speed, twist being inserted, and not least, on the end breakage rate accepted as tolerable.

100s *Quality:* Very limited in amount; made from the very finest parts of best merino fleeces; exceedingly white and soft handling, and by suitable noil extraction is made uniform in length; used by only one or two firms for the production of very fine yarns.

90s *Quality:* Very fine wool, picked and specially sorted; usually Victorian merino; very white, soft handle; length should be uniform.

80s *Quality:* Also specially sorted from fine merino fleeces; very white, soft handle.

70s *Quality:* This quality is far more common than those referred to above, being used by many worsted spinners as their finest quality. Obtained from the fore-part of fine merino sheep from all parts of Australia and the South African Cape area.

64s *Quality:* A very common quality, forming the basic material for many worsted spinners. Made from Australian, Cape, and South American merino.

60s *Quality:* Made from the back and haunches of merino fleeces, this is the lowest quality normally described as merino. It is not as soft in handle as those mentioned previously, but is very serviceable; known as super, ordinary, and weft qualities.

All the merino qualities are used for ladies' dress goods, coatings, and hosiery.

58s Quality: This is called a fine crossbred quality, although the wool used for its manufacture may be from comeback and strong merino as well as from fine crossbred sheep. It is a popular quality for making 2/1/fold and 2/2/fold frescoe yarns.

56s Quality: This is also called fine crossbred. The sources of wool used are crossbred and down. The latter is finer in appearance and more resilient, and is used for hosiery purposes; the former, longer and harsher in handle, is used for fine serges and medium coatings.

50s Quality: The finest of the group of qualities known as medium crossbred, it is distinctly different from 56s in that the fibres are longer, thicker, less wavy, and poorer in colour. Several sources of wool are used: English long wool, made from specially sorted hog fleeces, is the finest lustre wool, and is used for cloths requiring lustre and strength. English down is largely used for hosiery purposes, while crossbred may be used as an imitation of the former for medium serges.

48s P Quality: English wool quality, usually termed 'pick hog', used for serges. (N.B. The suffix 'P' denotes longwool prepared.)

46s C Quality: This is the coarsest of the medium crossbred group of top qualities, which may be made from either crossbred or down wools processed separately. Used for medium serges and hosiery. (N.B. The suffix 'C' denotes that the wool has been carded in preparation for combing, as opposed to longwool preparing.)

44s P Quality: This, and lower qualities, are known as coarse cross-breds. For this quality very long wool (14–15 in.) is used. The wool is used for serges, Sicilians, etc.

44s C Quality: Largely crossbred wool, yellow in colour. Used for serges and low hosiery yarns.

40s Quality: English and crossbred wools, the former being used for lustre yarns for linings, Sicilians, etc., and the latter for serges and linings.

36s Quality: English and crossbred wools. Used for bunting yarns, low serges, cheap hosiery yarns.

32s Quality: Mainly English wools, although overseas crossbreds are also used. The wool is used for cheap serges.

28s Quality: Lowest class of wool tops; contains strong fibres and kemp. Used for braid yarns, backing yarns and press filter cloths.

The practical count limits currently used by many spinners, along with the mean fibre diameters encountered for Bradford-type tops in the more common quality range, are shown in Table 4.6.

TABLE 4.6. MEAN FIBRE DIAMETER AND APPROXIMATE SPINNING
COUNT LIMITS FOR BRADFORD TOPS

Quality		70s	66s	64s	60s	58s	56s
Mean Fibre Diameter							
(*Microns*)	..	20·5	21·5	22·5	24·0	26·5	28·5
Count Limit (*Worsted*)	..	60	50	48	40	32	29
(*Tex*)	..	15	18	18·5	22	28	30·5

SPECIAL TOPS

Roller Lappings: Made from long lustre wool of selected lengths and fineness, and combed specially to produce a top for wrapping top squeeze rollers in wool scouring bowls.

Devon Tops: Devon wool is worth more than wools of similar quality by reason of its strength, and because it requires less twist; for this reason it may be processed separately. Suitable for bunting cloth.

Puntas: Used as a substitute for down top because of its spongy handle.

Mohair, Alpaca, etc.: These are largely combed by firms who also draw and spin them. The tops may not therefore be marketed as commonly as wool tops.

Hair and Low Wools: These are largely produced by spinners. Tops made for sale are disposed of privately.

TOP TESTING

A considerable amount of testing of tops is carried out by various conditioning houses. The amount of moisture present is most important commercially and, along with oil content, is probably the most commonly required test. More reliance is being placed on the routine testing of fibre diameter by the airflow method[42], and of fibre length by the W.I.R.A. Fibre Diagram machine[43]. Other tests required may include oil analyses, pH determinations and tests for residual soap, nep, dark fibres and vegetable matter.

Traditional methods of visual examination are still used, but more reliance is being placed on the objective tests now available. This is particularly noticeable in the case of fibre diameter, where there is a tendency for some customers to specify fibre diameter when ordering tops.

THE PRINCIPLES OF WORSTED DRAWING

THE FUNCTION of the drawing set is to convert the top sliver into a fault-free roving from which a yarn can be spun in a single operation, using a suitable draft. The manner in which this is achieved and the effectiveness of the process depends, not only on the following of certain basic principles, but on a variety of factors which have to be taken into consideration.

In the first place, the roving required for spinning is thinner than the top sliver, and therefore some method of reduction must be employed. In practice, this is achieved by the application of draft, the amount applied depending on the machinery installed, the material being processed, and the ultimate use of the material. Unfortunately, the drafting operation introduces irregularity, the effects of which, however, can be minimized by the use of 'doublings', a term used to describe the practice of feeding more than one end into a single drafting zone so that they will be combined into one single end when delivered by the front rollers after drafting.

The use of doublings not only serves to minimize irregularities but to promote blending. Insofar as the former purpose is concerned, it must be appreciated that the possibility of a thin (or thick) place in one doubling coinciding with a thin (or thick) place in another doubling is remote and that, in consequence, the irregularity in the combined fibre assembly will be lower than that of its individual components. With regard to blending there is no doubt that doublings assist in the formation of a more homogeneous fibre mixture. Once this object has been achieved, however, no further improvement in the intimacy of the blend can be obtained by their further use.

An important factor in drawing is the ratch, i.e., the distance between the back and front rollers of a drafting unit. The actual ratch is determined by the length of fibres being processed and by the thickness of the fibre assembly.

When the material is thicker the effect of the roller nip extends further through the material, and so a longer ratch must be allowed. Normally ratch is arranged so that the longest fibres are *not* subjected to the grip of the back and front rollers simultaneously. An exception to this rule is where the material has a small proportion of very long fibres, in which case the ratch may be set deliberately to break them. This sacrifice is considered worthwhile in order to exert a greater control over the bulk of the shorter fibres.

It is difficult to generalize in the matter of ratch settings. In fact, the only definite statement which can be made is that too short a ratch will lead to fibre breakage and a 'cockly' yarn, due to the fibres being stretched during drafting. Ratching is probably more critical in the processing of long wools and hairs than in the treatment of short and medium wools. It appears that the ratch setting is by no means as important as the setting of the devices used between the back and front rollers to obtain fibre control.

The only fibres under positive control are those held in either the front or back roller nips, the former moving at front roller surface speed and the latter at back roller surface speed. When a normal Bradford 64s A quality top is being drafted with a ratch slightly longer than the longest fibre, only about 40 per cent of the fibres fall into this category of 'fully controlled' fibres. The remaining 60 per cent or so are dependent on their chance contacts with other fibres to obtain their movement. These 'floating fibres', as they are called, may accelerate and decelerate more than once while passing from the back to the front rollers, and they may reach any speed from back to front roller surface speed, although it is improbable that they achieve front roller speed, except possibly near the front roller nip[31]. In any drafting zone, it is necessary to try to obtain a balance between the influence of the fibres moving at back roller surface speed ('back beard'), and the smaller number moving at front roller surface speed ('front beard'). This is done by applying pressure to the assembly of fibres. The various ways of achieving this are described later.

If a sliver of perfect uniformity (of weight per unit length) were to be made, it would be necessary every time a fibre terminated, for it to be followed by another fibre of the same weight per unit length, or by two or more fibres which together gave the same total weight per unit length. It is perhaps worth mentioning that, if such a product were made, it would probably not look perfectly uniform in thickness, due to differences in fibre density, etc. To produce 'perfect uniformity', absolute control would have to be exercised over each individual fibre, and as this cannot be achieved under present conditions, the best fibre arrangement which can be hoped for is a random fibre distribution. It has been shown[44] that with a random fibre distribution, there is a certain amount of irregularity which is inevitable. This has been calculated:

$$\text{Percentage Coefficient of Variation} \simeq 112/\sqrt{n}$$

where n is the number of fibres in the cross-section of the fibre assembly. In addition to this basic irregulatiry, irregularities due to imperfections in the drafting unit[45, 46] must also be taken into consideration.

At any one operation there are three possible ways of combining drafts and doublings: they may be equal to each other, or either one may exceed the other. If draft is equal to the number of doublings, then the material delivered will be the same weight per unit length as *one* of the doublings. If the draft is increased, the material will be thinner, and if the draft is decreased, the material delivered will be thicker than one of the doublings. In a drawing set all three combinations may be used to varying degrees. Where doublings equal or exceed draft, the main achievement is blending since there is no reduction in weight. Where draft is greater than the number of doublings, the material is reduced in thickness, the reduction depending on the draft-doublings ratio. Usually this ratio is increased as the material progresses through a drawing set by slight increases in draft, combined with fewer doublings. The result therefore is increasing attenuation, but less blending, as the material passes through the drawing set.

The following conclusions regarding the influence on roving levelness of drafts, doublings, and number of operations in conventional Bradford drawing have been made[47]:

> In performing a given amount of reduction, if the number of drawing operations is reduced by increasing the individual drafts and keeping the number of doublings per stage constant, the irregularity of the final roving increases.

> If the number of operations is kept constant and the number of ends per operation is increased by increasing the draft at each operation, any benefit obtained by increasing the number of doublings is more than offset by the detrimental effect of increasing the individual drafts.

> In performing a given amount of reduction, provided that a certain minimum amount of doubling is done, the factor which governs roving irregularity is the draft used, high drafts being injurious.

> Given a particular material and a particular form of fibre control, there is an *optimum* draft. Increasing draft up to this point makes little difference to roving irregularity. Increasing beyond this point increases roving irregularity.

It will be clear from the above that it is unwise, in an attempt to reduce the number of processes, to increase drafts beyond the optimum, while nothing is to be gained by using excessive doublings. In fact, one may conclude that if the operations are to be reduced without ill effects, the number of doublings should be kept to a safe minimum.

Although the above conclusions were arrived at before the advent of high-draft spinning and autolevelling, they nevertheless remain substantially correct, not only for the conventional Bradford system, but for all the other systems, old and new.

Before discussing autolevelling, reference should be made to another factor in the technique of drawing, namely the reversal of draft direction which results from the fact that the first end of a sliver produced is placed at the bottom of a can or on the inside of a bobbin. Thus, when the material is withdrawn at the following process, this is the last end to be processed. This is a fortunate coincidence, because fibres which in one process have been drafted forward as a bunch will be presented to the next process in the opposite direction. Provided the fibres are not all of the same length, the leading fibre ends of the reversed tuft will not be in line with each other, and there will be a tendency for the fibres to be drafted separately, so breaking up the original fibre bunch. This is the reason why it is important for the stronger man-made staple fibres to be made with variable fibre lengths; with square-cut staple, reversal of draft direction does not break up the fibre bunches, and roving irregularity may be twice that of a variable cut staple. This was clearly demonstrated in an experiment concerned with the gilling of fibres[48].

Finally, reference should be made to the fact that the material delivered by the drafting rollers must be capable of withstanding handling between one process and the next. How this requirement is satisfied by container design is described in some detail later.

AUTOLEVELLING

Autolevelling may be described as the automatic and continuous adjustment of draft in accordance with changes in the thickness of the incoming material. In this way thick places are given more draft and thin places less draft, the result being that the material delivered is more regular than a fixed draft could produce. Autolevelling also reduces the need for doublings, but some doublings are still required for the purpose of blending.

The Raper Autoleveller was introduced to the trade in 1953, since when it has been widely adopted. Other autolevellers have also been introduced but while these differ in certain details of design, they all operate on the same basic principles. For convenience, therefore, specific references in this description have been restricted to the Raper unit which consists of four basic parts, a measuring unit, a relay, a transmitter and a variable-speed unit.

The Measuring Unit: To measure the variations in sliver thickness, the incoming material is passed between tongued and grooved rollers under considerable compression. As the top roller is fulcrummed, its height varies in direct proportion to changes in thickness of the material between the rollers. Thus, the roller system acts as a sensing mechanism, the information provided by the top roller movement serving as the basis of draft control.

There are three points worthy of mention with regard to this system of measurement. Firstly, variations in moisture content hardly influence the measurement. Secondly, different materials have different compressibilities. Allowance for this is easily achieved by a suitable choice of draft change wheel and it is not a serious drawback to the system of measurement. Thirdly, care must be taken to ensure that material does not lap round one of the measuring rollers, as this would obviously affect the measurement and cause the wrong draft to be applied.

The Relay: After the measuring rollers have measured a thick (or thin) place, it is necessary to delay the change in draft until that particular place reaches the drafting zone. This is achieved by a relay unit which is in effect a device for temporarily recording the changes in thickness until the draft change has to be made at a distance approximately equal to half the mean fibre length from the front roller nip.

The Transmitter: This is a means of converting the temporary thickness record into a control movement which may then be passed to the variable speed unit.

The Variable Speed Unit: In the Raper Autoleveller this consists of a pair of cones, arranged with parallel axes but lying in opposite directions and linked by a belt. The lower cone is driven at a constant speed, while that of the top cone depends on the position of the belt. It is sometimes argued that this form of cone control is the weakest part of the Raper Autoleveller, as any sticking of the belt as it traverses across the cones will influence the standard of autolevelling. It is counter-argued that the performance of the belt can easily be maintained by routine inspection which only takes a minute or so to perform. In practice, provided regular attention is given to this point, no trouble is encountered. This form of drive is much cheaper and simpler than some of the alternatives offered on other machines and which include P.I.V. gears, hydraulic differentials and electrical variable speed drives.

The Raper Autoleveller is available in several versions of gill box both for drawing and for combing first finishers, and in several versions of draw-box for use in shortened drawing sets.

In considering the capabilities of the autoleveller, it is important to remember that it only corrects long-term variations; and that the drafting zone of the unit will still allow short-term irregularities to be formed. Input variations up to plus or minus 25 per cent are within the range of the draw-box and the latest versions of the gill box; these variations are reduced to about plus or minus one per cent in the output. The efficiency of this performance has been reported elsewhere[50, 51].

There is no doubt that autolevelling is one of the greatest recent advances in worsted processing. The principles of autolevelling have been applied to all systems of drawing, and it is inconceivable that any new system could be developed without it. It is for this reason that it has been included here as one of the basic principles of drawing.

METHODS OF FIBRE CONTROL

Reference has been made previously to the principles involved in the control of fibres in the drafting zone. The different methods of control available may be classified according to whether they are based on pin control, the applications of direct pressure, the use of twist, or the combined application of twist and direct pressure. These various methods are considered separately below.

Pin Control: This method of control is based on the fact that, if pins penetrate through a bundle of fibres which are already held under tension, the pressure between the fibres will be increased; this method is only suitable for material in a twistless state. The amount of inter-fibre pressure obtained may be controlled by selection of appropriate pin length, thickness and density. Machines which use this form of control include gill boxes (previously described), porcupine drawing boxes and machines which are, in effect, a cross between the two (e.g. the Whitin 'Roto-drafter'). The porcupine drawing box will be briefly described later in the section dealing with conventional French drawing.

With the development of precision-built, high-speed gill boxes the trend has been to use these machines to a greater extent than was previously the case, a development which has been most marked in the modern Continental and American (pin-drafting) drawing sets.

Direct Pressure: This method of control consists of applying lateral pressure to a twistless fibre assembly. There are several ways in which this can be done, as the following paragraphs will show.

In one method, illustrated at A in Fig. 4.8, a set of positively driven rollers $\mathcal{J}$, called carriers, support the fibres, while a set of tumbler rollers K rest on the material, which is thus compressed between the carriers and the tumblers. The tumbler weight and/or the distance between the carriers and the front and back rollers may be adjusted to obtain the necessary control. In a variation of this method, shown at B in Fig. 4.8, a continuous and positively driven apron L is used instead of separate carriers to support the material, which is pressed down against the apron by the tumblers K. As these tumblers are fitted into slots, it is a simple matter to alter the distance between a tumbler and the front roller. In a further variation, shown at C in Fig. 4.8, the material is compressed between two positively driven aprons L. With this arrangement, both speed and pressure are adjustable, while a close setting to the front rollers is possible, as the aprons can be guided round small rollers or stationary metal bars without the danger of lapping.

Another type of direct pressure control is employed in the pressure drafter, two types of which are in use on Raper Autoleveller draw boxes. The original version, shown at D in Fig. 4.8, is known as the two-point pressure drafter. It consists essentially of a rectangular-sectioned channel through which the material passes between the back and front rollers. The height of the bottom of the channel can be adjusted at two points (1 and 2) from two dials marked from 0 to 20. These numbers are purely arbitrary, and are merely provided to enable repetitive settings to be obtained. The two points are adjusted so that the required balance of fibre control is obtained. The later version, shown at E in Fig. 4.8, is fitted with a continuous base plate N, over which are mounted three adjustable presser feet M. The principle of operation is the same as that of the two-point version, but better fibre control can be obtained when material with an irregular fibre length distribution is being processed, while closer settings to the front roller nip are also possible.

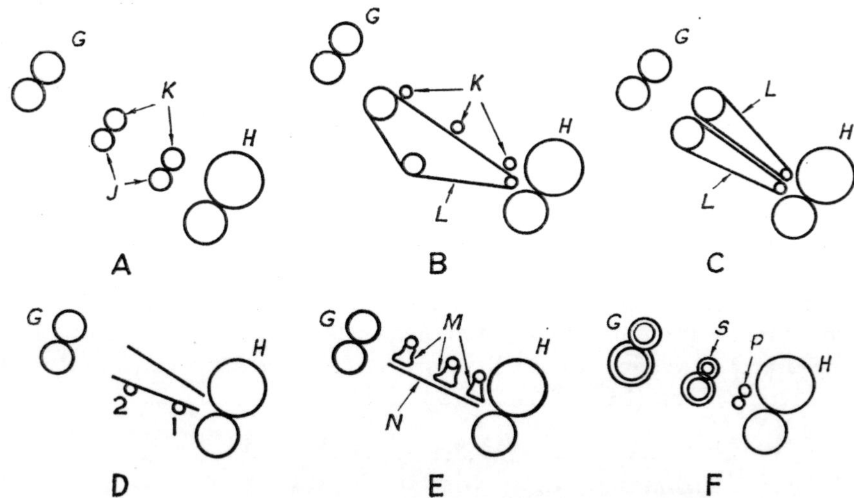

FIG.4.8. METHODS OF OBTAINING FIBRE CONTROL IN THE DRAFTING ZONE BY THE APPLICATION OF DIRECT PRESSURE

A—Carriers and tumblers: B—Apron and tumblers: C—Double aprons: D—Two-point pressure drafter: E—Three-point pressure drafter: F—Ambler draft unit. G—Back (feed) rollers: H—Front (drafting) rollers: J—Carriers: K—Tumblers: L—Aprons: M—Pressure drafter adjustable feet: N—Pressure drafter plate: S—Tongued and grooved tension rollers: P—Small tension rollers: 1 and 2—Adjustment controls for positioning lower plate of two-point pressure drafter.

The Amblerdraft unit was developed as an alternative to the pressure drafter, particularly for short material; it is extremely versatile, being suitable for botany, crossbred, man-made fibres and blends, oil-combed or dry. Basically it consists of two pairs of rollers S and P, as shown at F in Fig. 4.8, set at a fixed distance apart (two inches), but the unit as a whole may be moved so that the distance from the front roller nip to the small (half-inch) diameter tension rollers P can be varied from $1\frac{1}{2}$ to $3\frac{1}{2}$ inches. The back scratch-fluted tension rollers S are tongued and grooved so that the material is compressed into a rectangular cross-section. The load applied to the front tension rollers P is from $\frac{3}{4}$ to $1\frac{1}{2}$ pounds. Minimum load should be applied if fibres extend from the front roller nip to beyond the front tension rollers, but for very short fibres which do not extend so far, the maximum load should be applied. The load on the back tension rollers S may be up to 12 pounds. When short fibres are being processed, these act as back rollers, and a load of eight to 12 pounds should be used. If, however, the fibres held by the front rollers extend beyond the back tension roller nip S, the pressure should then only be one to three pounds. All four rollers are positively driven at a surface speed higher than that of the back roller G.

Twist Control: This method of fibre control is based on the principle that, if to a twisted fibre assembly longitudinal tension is applied (as in a drafting zone), inward radial pressures will be exerted. To control the distribution of twist between the back and front rollers, carriers and lightweight tumblers are used. Strictly speaking, therefore, some direct pressure is applied, but as this is only sufficient to prevent the slubbing from rotating and redistributing the twist, it can be ignored. The main fibre control is from the controlled twist present in the material. This method which, in appearance is similar to that shown at A in Fig. 4.8, is only suitable for the longer-fibred materials used in the Bradford and cone-drawing systems. In the Bradford system, the approximate value of twist required may be calculated from the following formulae[52]:

$$\frac{5 \cdot 8}{\sqrt[1 \cdot 5]{\text{drams}/40 \text{ yd.}}} = \text{t.p.i., or } \frac{3040}{\sqrt[1 \cdot 5]{\text{tex}}} = \text{t.p.metre.}$$

These may be reduced by about 20 to 30 per cent for cone drawing.

Combined Twist and Direct Pressure: In this, the fourth method of fibre control, a reduced amount of twist is used, but the pressure applied is more than would be strictly required to prevent the slubbing from rotating. Carriers and tumblers, or apron arrangements, similar in diagrammatic appearance to those shown at A, B, and C in Fig. 4.8 may be used. The most sophisticated form of control of this type is the Ambler Superdraft system (and its Uniflex descendant). This enables spinning drafts of about 140 to be used under commercial conditions on wool which previously would have only had a draft of about six on conventional machinery.

The unit arrangement, which is shown in Fig. 4.9, consists of a guide A which condenses the material before it passes between the tension rollers B. The bottom tension roller is grooved, and the top tension roller tongued to fit the grooves of the bottom roller. Pressure is applied to the top tension roller directly by weights which may be adjusted. The material then passes through the flume C, a narrow channel which gently presses against the sides of the fibre assembly and helps to prevent redistribution of twist if this is present in the material. It is possible to set the front end of the flume very close to the front roller nip (minimum 0·5–0·3 inch, depending on front-roller diameter), and this accounts for the high degree

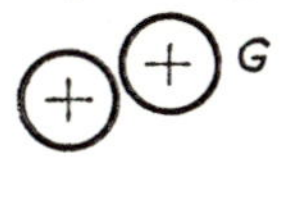

of fibre control which enables such high drafts to be used. The Uniflex version is capable of processing material with, or without, twist in it, and the system could, therefore, have been described with the others employing direct pressure. When twistless material is processed, an additional carrier *J* and tumbler *K* are used.

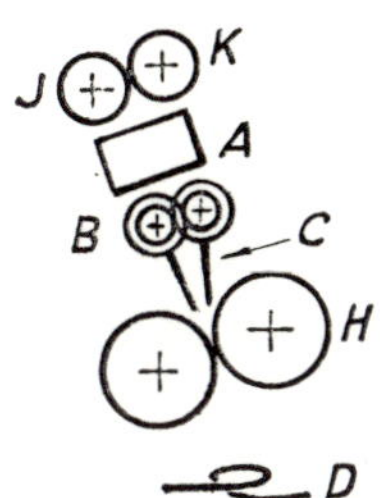

FIG. 4.9. SIMPLIFIED SIDE VIEW OF AMBLER SUPERDRAFT AND UNIFLEX DRAFTING ZONES

G—Back rollers: *J*—Carrier roller: *K*—Tumbler roller: *A*—Sliver guide: *B*—Tension rollers: *C*—Flume: *H*—Front rollers: *D*—Yarn guide lappet.

METHODS OF FORMING A SUITABLE PACKAGE

The material must be delivered into or onto a package which will protect it during transfer from one process to another. Even the slightest mechanical fibre disturbance may cause the formation of slubs. A further essential requirement is that the material can be removed from the package satisfactorily without drafting of the fibres or other disturbance. In addition, it may be necessary to insert twist into the material as it is wound on to the package.

Can Delivery: This method is used for gill boxes, where relatively thick slivers are to be delivered. The simplest form is a stationary can, but this allows the entering material to pile up, and then to fall down, trapping the fibres against the can side. Slight improvements are made by having a simple reciprocating can motion, or better still, a rotating can motion, but even these are not capable of packing the maximum amount of material into the can. Undoubtedly the best can arrangement is the coiler can delivery. In this system, the material is delivered down a funnel which, at its lower end, follows a circular path. Beneath is mounted a slowly rotating can, the centre of which is outside the circular path of the funnel. With this arrangement, the circular coils from the funnel are distributed around the can. A similar arrangement is used where two slivers are to be delivered together into one can, but in this case the can is made to rotate a full revolution in alternate directions so that the slivers are not twisted together; this arrangement is called 'bicoiler' can delivery.

Balling Head Delivery: In this arrangement, the material delivered from the front rollers is cross-wound on to a rotating bobbin. This method may be used where no twist is required, and where the material is too thin to be delivered into a can. The slivers must be consolidated by rubbing between reciprocating rubbing leathers, or by passing them through a rotating funnel, before being wound on to the bobbin; otherwise difficulty will be encountered when the material is unwound.

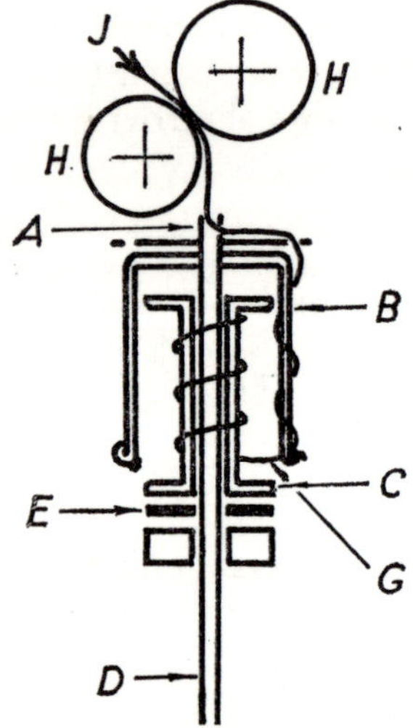

FIG. 4.10. DRAWING ILLUSTRATING THE BRADFORD DRAWING BOX FLYER DELIVERY (FLYER LEAD)

A—Hollow top of spindle: *B*—Flyer leg: *C*—Bobbin: *D*—Spindle: *E*—Drag washer: *G*—Slubbing: *H*—Front (drafting) rollers: *J*—Slubbing after being drafted.

Bradford Drawing Box Delivery: This method is used where, in addition to package formation, twist insertion is required. It is only suitable for the relatively long-fibred materials processed on Bradford drawing systems. It will be seen from Fig. 4.10 that material *J* from front rollers *H* is inserted through the hollow spindle top *A* before beng passed down the flyer leg *B*, and onto the bobbin *C*. The flyer is attached to the spindle *D* and is positively driven. The bobbin fits loosely outside the spindle, rests on a felt drag washer *E* and is free to rotate at a different speed from that of spindle and flyer. As the flyer rotates twist is inserted, one turn for each spindle revolution; at the same time the bobbin is dragged round against the friction of the drag washer by the slubbing at *G*. Due to the material winding onto the bobbin, the speed of the latter is lower than that of the spindle and depends, in fact, on spindle speed, front roller delivery rate, and bobbin circumference. In general terms:

$$\text{Bobbin speed (r.p.m.)} = \text{Spindle speed (r.p.m.)} - \frac{\text{Front roller surface speed}}{\text{Bobbin circumference}}$$

It will be seen from the above that, as the diameter of the material on the bobbin increases, so also will the bobbin speed.

Control of tension on the slubbing during winding-on is achieved in two ways. The total drag is dependent on the diameter of the drag washer *E*, a large diameter drag washer offering more resistance to bobbin rotation and applying more tension to the material. This control determines the density of the package; a soft, spongy bobbin requires a larger diameter washer to make it firmer. The increased tension applied by a larger diameter drag washer is not due to its increased surface area but to the increased torque effect, as is indicated in the following formula where μ is the coefficient of friction, N is the normal pressure, R is the major diameter of the washer and r the diameter of the washer hole:

$$\text{Torque} = \mu N \left(\frac{R + r}{2} \right)$$

It may be that the tension required to build a firm package is too much for the material between the front roller nip and the top of the spindle; at this point the material is almost without twist and is at its weakest. To reduce the tension on the material here it is wrapped once or twice round the flyer leg at B, the point being that the greater the number of wraps round the flyer leg, the greater will be the tension 'used up' in pulling the material down the leg, and the less the tension remaining at the top where the material is weakest. As the bobbin diameter and weight increase, the pressure on the drag washer also increases, with consequent increase in frictional resistance. Fortunately, at the same time there is also an increase in the leverage used to pull the bobbin round (i.e. the bobbin diameter), with the result that the tension on the slubbing at G is apparently no greater when the bobbin is full than when it is empty.

Cone Drawing Box Delivery: This system was originally developed for cotton, a short fibre which could not satisfactorily pull the bobbin round. The system has been adapted to the processing of short length wools where similar conditions apply. No tension is applied in winding-on, both the flyer and the bobbin being positively driven. Usually the bobbin is arranged to rotate at a higher speed than the flyer in order to wind on the material delivered by the front rollers; such an arrangement is called 'bobbin lead'. Incidentally, the bobbin rotates at its fastest when empty, its speed gradually reducing as the bobbin fills.

Three arguments are raised in favour of bobbin lead for cone drawing. Firstly, the power requirements of the machine are evened out (as the bobbin weight increases, its speed decreases). Secondly, if the belt used in the drive to the bobbim slips when the machine is started, it will *reduce* tension on the material between the front roller nip and the flyer top. Thirdly, if an end should break between the front roller nip and the flyer top, it will not result in the material on the bobbin unwinding itself, as the outer end is a trailing end when bobbin lead is used.

Positive control of the bobbin speed necessitates a complex arrangement of mechanisms, making the machine more expensive than the Bradford-type drawing box, and more complicated from the setting and maintenance point of view. This is why the cone box is only used instead of the Bradford type where there is a distinct advantage to be gained by not having winding-on drag, i.e. where short fibred material, thin rovings, or low twisted rovings are needed.

Ring Spindle Delivery: At one time there was a production advantage in using a ring spindle delivery for the last drawing operation (roving) instead of the flyer method. This advantage has been removed by the introduction of the 'Eclipse' spindle (a patent of Prince-Smith & Stells Ltd.). Ring-processed rovings tended to be less smooth than flyer rovings, and more twist had to be inserted to withstand ballooning of the thread.

DRAWING SYSTEMS

DRAWING SYSTEMS may be broadly divided into three groups, viz., draft-against-twist systems, twistless systems and systems using twist in the later stages only. In the first of these – the draft-against-twist systems – twist is relied on as a major form of fibre control in most of the operations. This group includes cone drawing and conventional Bradford drawing (collectively called 'open' drawing systems), and also the New Bradford system. The materials are usually oil-combed, and of good fibre length. Moderately short material may, however, be processed on cone. The twistless systems use pin control or direct pressure fibre control. Conventional Continental and New Continental systems, which process dry-combed tops, frequently of short fibre length, are included in this group. Systems which use twist in the later stages only are, in effect, a combination of the first two systems. Most of the operations use twistless processing, followed by a small number of processes using a reduced amount of twist control. This group includes the pin-drafter systems developed in the United States and designed to process material with an oil content intermediate between oiled and dry, and preferably with a square staple diagram. Also included in this group is the Anglo-Continental system which, although no longer manufactured, is still in use in a few mills and was designed to process mixtures of good length oil-combed tops with short dry-combed material.

CONVENTIONAL BRADFORD DRAWING

This system, which evolved over a long period of years during the industrial revolution, can process a wide range of wool qualities and man-made fibre blends. Developments in autolevellers have limited the use of the full conventional Bradford set, although there are many sets still in use. It is impossible to describe any particular set as being 'standard' because of the range of variations which exist in the number of processes, doublings, and drafts used. However, all Bradford sets have the same basic layout, as indicated in Table 4.7.

For undyed long wools only five processes may be required, whereas undyed merino and fine crossbred may have eight or nine operations. In both cases there may be only one can gill process, but where colours are to be blended in the drawing set, up to four gillings may be used before the spindle gill. This latter has a gill box drafting zone, followed by a Bradford drawing box type delivery. There is invariably only one process of spindle gill in a Bradford drawing set, converting the material from slivers (twistless) to slubbing (twisted). The drawing boxes use twist control and the Bradford drawing box delivery. The drawing boxes become progressively finer in build, delivering onto smaller bobbins at higher spindle speeds, and applying increasing drafts with a reduced number of doublings. One of the middle drawing boxes performs the additional function of a 'weigh-box' and is set to deliver a known length of slubbing onto bobbins of known weight ('tared' bobbins). Each full bobbin delivered is weighed, and 'paired off' against another set of bobbins so that the total gross weight being fed to each spindle of the subsequent machine remains the same, even though there may be variations in individual bobbin weights. The object of this is to minimize very long-term count variations.

TABLE 4.7. BASIC FEATURES OF A CONVENTIONAL BRADFORD DRAWING SET

Type of Machine	No. of Processes	Feed	Delivery	Function
Can Gill Box	1-4	Twistless	Twistless	Blending
Spindle Gill Box	1	Twistless	Twisted	Blending and twist insertion. Slight reduction
Bradford Drawing Box	3-9	Twisted	Twisted	Blending at a decreased rate combined with reduction at an increasing rate

One example of a conventional Bradford drawing set is given in Table 4.8. Due to the fine roving being produced, the production of this set would be limited to only 70 pounds per hour, even though the operations before roving are capable of a higher output. If the same doublings were used, but the drafts altered to give a roving weight of three drams per 40 yards (146 tex), the production would be raised to 120 pounds per hour. In this case each operation would be capable of producing the same amount; i.e. there would be a 'balance of production' contributing to maximum productive efficiency. If drafts were altered further, to produce a still heavier roving, the later operations would be capable of producing more than 120 pounds per hour, but production would be limited by the capacity of the earlier stages.

CONVENTIONAL CONE DRAWING

As there is no advantage to be gained by using the cone-type delivery on the thicker slubbings in the earlier stages of a drawing set, the cone drawing box is normally only employed for the last three operations indicated in Table 4.8. The drafts and doublings are the same as for Bradford drawing, and the cone drawing box uses the same form of fibre control during drafting; only the winding-on is different. Due to the machine design, a cone drawing set usually has twice the capacity of a Bradford set, but comparing sets of similar capacity, the cone set occupies a smaller floorspace and requires fewer operatives and less power. Other advantages include lower twisted rovings and longer lengths of slubbing wound on a bobbin per doff. The main disadvantages are that it is more complicated and, due to the machine size, it is only suitable for large lots. For this reason its use is mainly restricted to the production of fine rovings, and to the processing of shorter length wools.

TABLE 4.8. CONVENTIONAL BRADFORD DRAWING SET FOR MERINO WOOL TOPS WEIGHING 272 DRAMS PER 40 YARDS (13·2 KTEX) TO PRODUCE 2 DRAMS PER 40 YARDS ROVING FOR FINE COUNT SPINNING

Operation	Doublings	Draft	Delivery		Ratch in.	Bobbin size in.	Deliveries per machine	Machines	Operatives
			drams/40 yd.	ktex					
1. Doublehead Can Gill Box	5	5.7	238	11.5	—	—	2	1	
2. Spindle Gill Box	5	5.8	206	10.0	—	14×9	2	2	1
3. Weigh Box	4	6.0	137	6.65	6.5	14×9	4	1	
4. Draw Box	4	6.1	90	4.35	6.25	14×7	6	1	1
5. First Finisher	3	6.2	43.5	2.10	6.0	12×6	8	2	
6. Second Finisher	3	6.3	20.8	1.01	5.75	9×5	12	2	1
7. Reducer	2	6.4	6.5	0.32	5.5	8×4	32	3	1
8. Rover	2	6.5	2.0	0.097	5.25	6×3	30	12	3

NEW BRADFORD SYSTEM

This system is based on the use of the Raper Autoleveller (both gill box and draw box), and the use of Ambler Superdraft (or Uniflex) spinning. A typical arrangement is shown in Table 4.9.

TABLE 4.9. NEW BRADFORD DRAWING SET PRODUCING "ROVINGS" TO BE SPUN ON SUPERDRAFT TO ANY COUNT

Operation	Doublings	Draft	Delivery		Bobbin size in.	Deliveries per machine	Machines	Operatives
			drams/40 yd.	ktex				
1. Autoleveller Gill Box	12	6	540	26·2	—	1	1	
2. Autoleveller Draw Box	1	6	90	4·35	14×7	10	1	1
3. Bradford-type Finisher	3	6	45	2·18	10×5	10	2	1

Advantages of the system include less waste, fewer operatives, reduced floorspace, less power, fewer chances of faults being made (if correctly maintained), a yarn levelness as good as that of conventional processed yarn, less wheel-changing, and a higher productive efficiency. Against these is the fact that a higher standard of maintenance is required, and there is insufficient mixing to blend colours or qualities satisfactorily. If blending is required, then additional gilling must precede the drawing set, or alternatively (and better) tops blended in recombing may be used where possible. A further disadvantage of this very short process is that certain speciality colour effect yarns (such as marls) cannot be satisfactorily produced. For this reason it may be preferable to use conventional low-draft spinning.

HEAVY ROVING UNIFLEX SYSTEM

Further modifications to the drafting zone of the Uniflex spinning frame have been developed by Prince-Smith & Stells Ltd. The main features of these modifications include a considerable increase in the tension roller weighting and an increase of tension roller width from the standard size of 2 mm. to a width of 6 mm. in order to accommodate a roving input of 7 ktex (approximately 140 drams per 40 yards). Using drafts from less than 100 up to about 200, yarns from 1/3s to 1/24s worsted (300 to 37 tex) may be spun. It is largely the influence of twist in the thick roving which enables such high drafts to be used; to obtain drafts exceeding 30 without the presence of twist would require a very complicated drafting zone.

It is difficult to envisage a much simpler drawing set than the one required for the new Heavy Roving Uniflex spinning frame, details of which are given in Table 4.10.

TABLE 4.10. DRAWING SET PRODUCING 'ROVINGS' TO BE SPUN TO MEDIUM COUNTS ON THE HEAVY ROVING UNIFLEX SPINNING FRAME

Operation	Doublings	Draft	Delivery		Bobbins size in	Deliveries per machine	Machines	Operatives
			drams/ 40 yd	ktex				
1. Raper Autoleveller Gill Box	14	6	840	42	—	1	1	
2. Autoleveller Draw Box	1	6	140	7	14 x 7	14	1	1

It is anticipated at the time of writing that a further model of the Uniflex spinning frame may become available to cover a finer count range. This will have a tension roller width of 4 mm. to accommodate a 4·5 ktex roving (approximately 90 drams per 40 yards) and will permit yarns from 1/12s to 1/40s worsted (74 to 22 tex) to be spun with drafts up to about 200.

AUTOLEVELLER DRAWING FOR LOW-DRAFT SPINNING

Originally the system which was recommended included single-end feed processing at the reducer. This arrangement, however, has not proved to be popular with many firms, and an alternative arrangement has been used, as shown in Table 4.11. As in the New Bradford system, the autoleveller draw box has a Bradford-type delivery spindle, and the drafting zone is either a pressure drafter or an Amblerdraft unit.

TABLE 4.11. AUTOLEVELLER DRAWING SET PRODUCING
ROVINGS FOR CONVENTIONAL LOW-DRAFT SPINNING

Operation	Doublings	Draft	Delivery		Bobbin Size in.	Deliveries per machine	Machines	Operatives
			drams/ 40 yd.	ktex				
1. Autoleveller Can Gill Box	12	7	470	22·8	—	1	1 ⎫	
2. Autoleveller Draw Box	1	7·7	61	2·96	14 × 7	14	1 ⎬	1
3. Finisher	3	6·4	28·5	1·38	10 × 5	12	2	1
4. Reducer	2	6·6	8·7	0·42	8 × 4	32	3	1
5. Rover	2	6·9	2·5	0·12	6 × 3	30	12	3

Autoleveller drawing sets of this type are more common at the present time than is the New Bradford system, probably due to the high capital cost of installing new spinning machinery. As spinning machinery is replaced, it is likely that more New Bradford or Uniflex sets will be used.

CONVENTIONAL FRENCH DRAWING

This system was developed to process short dry-combed wools into worsted yarns. Pin control was used throughout, and the resultant yarn was bulky and particularly suitable for knitting. For the first three operations Continental intersecting gill boxes were used, and these were followed by six or seven operations on French porcupine drawing boxes, the number depending on the thickness of roving required. The fibre control of a porcupine box is not particularly good, and the highest draft giving a reasonable product is about four. For this reason alternative drawing sets have been devised, although the porcupine drawing box may still be used for the roving operation. This type of drafting zone is shown in Fig. 4.11 which gives a simplified elevation of a French drawing box.

MODERN CONTINENTAL DRAWING SETS

Although a few slightly differing versions of this type of set are available, the arrangement given in Table 4.12 may be taken as being reasonably representative of the trend being developed. The high-draft finisher is similar to the porcupine drawing box, but uses a double-apron control instead of the porcupine. As alternatives to this type of finisher there are

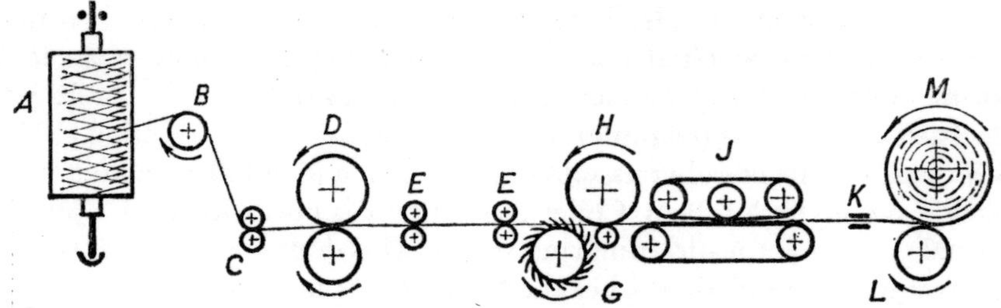

FIG. 4.11. SIMPLIFIED SIDE ELEVATION OF A FRENCH DRAWING BOX

A—Supply package supported by boxwood peg mounted in a porcelain footstep:
B—Positively driven creel roller: *C*—Traversing guide: *D*—Back (feed) rollers:
E—Carriers and tumblers: *G*—Porcupine roller: *H*—Front (drafting rollers): *J*—Rub-
bing leathers: *K*—Guide: *L*—Balling head roller: *M*—Package.

machines which use faller control, and some firms still use the conventional
porcupine machine. If these latter machines are used at least one additional
process will be required, due to the lower draft which must be employed.

TABLE 4.12. MODERN CONTINENTAL DRAWING SET PRODUCING
ROVINGS TO BE SPUN UP TO 1/48s WORSTED (18·5 TEX)

Operation	Doublings	Draft	Delivery drams/ 40 yd.	ktex
1. Autoleveller Intersecting Gill Box	12	10	495	24·0
2. Intersecting Gill Box ..	5	10	248	12·0
3. Intersecting Gill Box ..	4	8	124	6·0
4. High Draft Finisher ..	1	18	6·9	0·34

ANGLO-CONTINENTAL SYSTEM

This system was specifically designed for processing blends of long-
fibred oil-combed tops with short dry-combed tops to produce a roving
which could be spun on the existing conventional low-draft Bradford
cap-spinning frame. The system was generally similar to the conventional
French drawing set, the principal difference being in the last three processes. Thus, an Anglo-Continental cone finisher – a cone drawing box
with a porcupine drafting zone – was used to convert slivers to slubbings,
while the last two processes were carried out by ordinary cone drawing
boxes with carrier and tumbler control.

The Anglo-Continental system is now seldom used, and is no longer
manufactured, having been designed because of economic considerations
which do not apply today.

AMERICAN WORSTED DRAWING SETS

Various systems were developed, originating from modified cotton
machinery, and adapted first to process the longer man-made fibres, and

then medium-length wools. Later the machine makers reverted to more conventional type worsted machinery, and the systems now seem to be settling down to a fairly standard arrangement, as indicated in Table 4.13. The basis of this set is the pin drafter, a precision-built intersecting gill box with three-line front-roller assembly (Fig. 4.4), a long faller bed (about $7\frac{3}{4}$ inches), and no back rollers. Coiler can delivery is normally used. Spinning is usually on an apron-drafting ring frame, with drafts up to about twenty. The feature which distinguishes the 'American' pin-drafting systems from the modern Continental systems is the use of twisted roving.

TABLE 4.13.   MODERN AMERICAN WORSTED DRAWING SET
PRODUCING ROVINGS FOR MEDIUM COUNT YARNS

Operation		Doublings	Draft	Delivery drams/ 40 yd.	ktex
1. Single Head Pin Drafter*	..	10	7·6	460	22·3
2. Dual Head Pin Drafter	..	4	7·6	242	11·7
3. Quad Head Pin Drafter	..	3	7·5	97	4·7
4. Apron/Cone Rover..	..	1	12·1	8	0·39

*May be autolevelling

Where possible, thick counts are spun (1/20 to 1/40 worsted, 44–22 tex), as this gives high production and avoids spinning to count limit. Frequently weft yarns are single; this permits spinning counts twice as thick as would be required for equivalent two-fold yarns, giving approximately three times the spinning production, and eliminating the twisting operation. The raw material must have a square fibre diagram, which is a limitation, but on the other hand, the system handles synthetics well. If colours or qualities are to be blended, two additional pin-drafting operations are needed. Oil content must not exceed $1\frac{1}{2}$ per cent and about 75 per cent relative humidity is needed (this latter condition also applies to the Continental systems).

ENGLISH 'NEW CONTINENTAL' SYSTEMS

Although these systems, introduced by Prince-Smith & Stells Ltd., were described by the company as 'New Continental', they do use twist in the later stages. It is now generally accepted that the difference between the Continental and American systems is that the Continental is completely without twist, whereas the American system uses a reduced amount of twist in the later stages. In this respect the 'New Continental' systems are similar to the American systems, but pin-drafters are not used so extensively. The constitution of the original 'New Continental' system is given in Table 4.14. The third operation is very similar to the fourth operation in Table 4.13; similarly, the spinning frame to follow is an apron-drafting ring frame.

Later, Prince-Smith & Stells Ltd. introduced a further 'New Continental' system, its purpose being to enable Ambler Superdraft spinning to be used on Continental materials. The first two operations were as shown in Table 4.14, but the third operation employed a Bradford-type delivery finisher with an Amblerdraft unit in the drafting zone. The latest system to be introduced, again by the same company, is the Uniflex system. The Uniflex spinning frame is designed to process oil-combed or dry-combed materials with or without twist, although it would appear that the best arrangement probably uses a small amount of twist in the final stage before spinning. The Uniflex spinning frame may be used for high-draft spinning (from 20 dram roving), or for superdraft (from 40 dram roving) for rovings produced on existing Bradford or Continental drawing sets. If a new drawing set is to be installed to supply rovings for Uniflex frames, the most versatile arrangement is to have the first two operations as shown in Table 4.14 and to follow by cone roving with Amblerdraft fibre control. This set can produce either 20 or 40 dram rovings for high-draft or super-draft spinning, respectively.

TABLE 4.14. ENGLISH-MADE "NEW CONTINENTAL" SYSTEM DRAWING SET USING RAPER AUTOLEVELLERS

Operation	Doublings	Draft	Delivery drams/ 40 yd.	ktex
1. Autoleveller Gill Box ..	12	8·0	620	30·0
2. Autoleveller Bi-coiler Draw-Box (Amblerdraft drafting zone)	1	7·5	82	4·0
3. Cone/Apron Reducer ..	1	12·0	6·9	0·33

It will be clear from this brief outline of drawing sets, that the machinery makers have been very active in recent years. At the moment there is a bewildering range of choice for the worsted spinner; no doubt, natural selection will eliminate one or more of the existing systems in the years to come. It would seem that high-draft spinning, using drafts of about twenty to thirty will probably prove to be the most popular choice for the future.

YARN COUNTING SYSTEMS FOR WORSTED SPINNING

SPINNING consists of a single operation in which the roving is drafted to give the correct yarn thickness and then sufficient twist inserted to prevent further drafting of the fibres in later processes, the yarn so formed being subsequently wound onto a suitable container.

It will be apparent from this brief definition that thickness and twist are important parameters, the description and measurement of which warrant explanation before proceeding to a detailed survey of spinning methods and machines.

In the first place, it is necessary that the thickness of yarns should be describable in a way which is simple, accurate and repeatable. The method adopted is to take a long length of yarn which has been accurately measured and to weigh it. The results obtained may be expressed in two different ways, weight per unit length or length per unit weight. The former is called the direct method and includes the Tex system, recommended by the International Standards Organisation to be used for *all* types of yarn. The latter is called the indirect method and includes the English Worsted and Metric systems.

ENGLISH WORSTED COUNTING SYSTEM

At present the English worsted system is most commonly used in worsted spinning mills in this country. It is based on a hank length of 560 yards, the count number being the number of hanks of this length which weigh one pound. Thus the English worsted count number multiplied by 560 will give the number of yards of yarn per pound.

English Spinning Conversion Gaugepoint: The English worsted spinner measures the thickness of slivers and slubbings throughout drawing in drams per 40 yards. At the spinning frame the *input* to the drafting zone is measured in this way, but the *delivery* is measured in count units. It is, therefore, necessary to be able to convert from drams per 40 yards, to English worsted counts. The conversion factor or gaugepoint which enables this calculation to be made is $(40 \times 256)/560$ or $18 \cdot 3$.

This will best be understood by the following simple calculation. Suppose a 36s worsted yarn is to be spun from a $3 \cdot 5$ dram roving, then the yards per pound in the yarn will be 36×560 and the yards per pound in the roving will be $(256 \times 40)/3 \cdot 5$. The draft in spinning will be the ratio of these two, namely $(36 \times 560 \times 3 \cdot 5)/(256 \times 40)$. In this calculation, the numbers 560, 256 and 40 are constants and $560/(256 \times 40)$ equals $1/18 \cdot 3$. Thus it will be seen that the draft in spinning equals the required worsted yarn count multiplied by the roving weight (drams per 40 yards) and divided by $18 \cdot 3$.

As an example the draft required to spin 1/48s English worsted from a $2 \cdot 5$ dram roving will be $(48 \times 2 \cdot 5)/18 \cdot 3$, or $6 \cdot 6$.

Similarly, if the count to be spun and the draft to be used in spinning is known, then the roving weight can easily be calculated. For example, to spin a 36s worsted yarn with a draft of 7 the required roving weight will be $(7 \times 18 \cdot 3)/36$, or $3 \cdot 6$ drams per 40 yards.

Spinning Frame Gaugepoint: Once the draft gaugepoint of a spinning frame is known, the draft change wheel for any particular draft is easily calculated by dividing the gaugepoint by the draft required. Thus, assuming a particular spinning frame has a draft gaugepoint of 362 and the draft required is 6·6 (as in the previous example), then the draft change-wheel must have 362/6·6, or 55 teeth.

Use of a Compound Gaugepoint: Instead of carrying out separate calculations with two distinct gaugepoints as shown above, it is often more convenient to use a compound gaugepoint which is the product of the conversion gaugepoint and the frame gaugepoint. Thus, in the example above, the compound gaugepoint would be 362 × 18·3, or 6625. This enables the draft wheel required to be calculated in one step:

$$\text{Draft wheel} = \frac{\text{Compound gaugepoint}}{\text{Roving weight (dr./40 yd.)} \times \text{Required count number}}.$$

Thus the draft change-wheel required to spin 1/48s English worsted on the frame quoted from a 2·5 dram roving must have 6625/(48×2·5), or 55 teeth. It must, of course, be understood that this particular compound gaugepoint (6625) only relates to a spinning frame with a draft gaugepoint of 362.

METRIC COUNTING SYSTEM

This system is based on a hank length of one kilometre, the count number being the number of hanks of this length which weigh one kilogramme. The system therefore differs from the English worsted system only insofar as metric units are employed and, provided this is taken into account, all the calculations referred to above apply. To convert from the English to the metric system, all that is necessary is to multiply the former by 1·129. Similarly, the metric count divided by 1·129 will give the English worsted count number.

THE TEX SYSTEM

This internationally recommended system is based on the weight in grams of one kilometre of yarn. In effect, therefore it is the reciprocal of the metric count, multiplied by 1000, i.e., tex = 1000/metric count. Similarly, tex = 885·8/English worsted count.

The examples given below show the relationship between the English worsted count and tex systems and also the method of denoting two-fold and three-fold yarns in the tex system (R represents 'resultant' and the number after the 'dash' the number of components):

1/36s English worsted = 24·5 tex.
2/36s English worsted = R49 tex/2.
3/36s English worsted = R74 tex/3. (approx.).

For fibres where the tex number would be less than unity, the millitex unit is recommended, this being the weight in milligrammes per kilometre.

For cords and heavy slivers where very high tex numbers would be involved, the kilotex unit is recommended, this being the weight in kilogrammes per kilometre.

Thus the tex system, with its multiple and sub-multiple, covers the whole range of yarns in all the existing count systems.

CHECKING COUNTS

In the spinning room the $12\frac{1}{2}$-grain weight is frequently used as a basis for count testing. This is based on the fact that one yard of 1s count weighs $12\frac{1}{2}$-grains, as also do two yards of 2s count, and so on. In general terms, x yards of xs count weigh $12\frac{1}{2}$ grains.

Frequently the overlooker uses a 50-grain weight, and takes the test yarn from four spinning bobbins. For example, if 30 yards is taken from each of four bobbins (i.e. a total of 120 yards) and this is found to weigh 50 grains, then the count will be 30s English worsted. This method is not particularly accurate due to the small sample size, but it does indicate if a large change is needed in the draft change-wheel.

A more accurate form of test to be carried out in the laboratory is to take a much larger yardage (e.g., 280 yards is common), obtain the weight after drying and then calculate the count at standard regain. This gives a result which is unaffected by the atmospheric conditions, whereas the overlooker normally spins to a count which is about 5 per cent light, to allow for the dryness of the yarn as spun.

SPINNING TWIST

The twist inserted during spinning must be sufficient to prevent fibre slippage when tension is applied to the yarn. Spinning frames are normally run at maximum spindle speed for the material being processed, an increase in twist causing a reduction in output. For this reason it is usual to spin with the minimum twist which will give reasonable spinning conditions. Not more than five end-breakages per 100 spindle-hours is often regarded as acceptable.

Various empirical formulae for determining twist have been advanced from time to time and these may be summarized as follows:

$$1. \qquad \frac{\text{English worsted count no.}}{x} + y = \text{t.p.i.}$$

where x and y are constant values[53, 54]. For example, assuming x and y to be 3 and 2, respectively, then a 1/48s worsted (18·5 tex) would require (48/3) + 2, or 18 turns per inch. This formula gives a straight-line relationship between count and twist which only applies over a very limited range of count numbers.

2.
$$\frac{\text{English worsted count no.}}{x} = \text{t.p.i.}$$

where the value of x is specified. With this formula[55], again taking the specified value of x to be 3, then a 1/48s worsted (18·5 tex) would require 48/3 or 16 t.p.i. The same comment applies to this formula as to the one above, namely that it gives a straight-line relationship between count and twist which only applies over a very limited range of count numbers.

3.
$$K \sqrt{\text{English worsted count no.}} = \text{t.p.i.}$$

where the value of K is specified. With this formula[56-60], assuming the value of K to be 2·5, then a 1/48s worsted would require $2\cdot5\sqrt{48}$, or 17·3 t.p.i.

This formula does not give a straight-line relationship between count and twist, but it is intended to give the same 'angle of twist' in a series of yarns of different count. In practice it is found that the same angle is not required; a higher value of K is needed for higher English worsted count numbers. Over a small range of counts this relationship is satisfactory, but when large count differences are considered, the discrepancies from practical requirements are too large.

4.
$$1\cdot2 \times {}^{1\cdot5}\sqrt{\text{English worsted count no.}} = \text{t.p.i.}$$

With this formula[61], a 1/48s worsted (18·5 tex) would require $1\cdot2 \times {}^{1\cdot5}\sqrt{48}$, or 16·0 t.p.i.

This formula again is purely empirical, being based on observations of the actual twists used by many worsted spinners in the United Kingdom. It applies over a very wide range of counts, having been used from 1/4s to 1/140s English worsted (222 tex to 6·35 tex) in qualities from 56s to 100s inclusive.

The same relationship ${}^{1\cdot5}\sqrt{}$ also applies to drawing twists for slubbings and it has been used up to 200 drams per 40 yards (9·7 ktex). For drawing, the twist is about 16 to 20 per cent less than for spinning. (The drawing twist formula was given on page 114).

CLASSIFICATION OF SPINNING MACHINES

WORSTED SPINNING MACHINES may be considered as falling into two main groups, according to whether they operate on an intermittent or continuous basis. Representatives of the intermittent group are the mule and centrifugal spinning machines, while flyer, cap and ring spinning frames represent the group of continuously operating machines.

THE WORSTED MULE

At one time, the worsted mule was used extensively for the spinning of twistless rovings produced on Continental drawing system machinery from dry-combed tops, and from the technical viewpoint it is still the finest machine for producing very fine counts with low twist content, as the tension applied to the yarn during spinning is capable of being controlled to a fine degree. On the other hand, the worsted mule is a complex machine, occupies a large amount of floorspace and has a low rate of production due to its intermittent operation. In recent years it has been almost completely replaced by the ring spinning frame.

The worsted mule follows the general lines of the woollen mule and as this is described in detail in Section 5 (see pages 174–176), it will suffice here to point out certain essential differences, the chief of which are as follows:

A. Instead of a single set of delivery rollers, there is a full worsted drafting zone, with back rollers, carriers and tumblers, and front rollers. The rollers are small in diameter to deal with the short fibre length, and drafts of about 10 are usual with this machine.

B. Spindle drafting is not used on the worsted mule to any great extent; there may be a slight 'gain' of one or two inches per carriage draw over the front roller delivery speed.

C. The spindle tip is more pointed than that of the woollen mule.

THE CENTRIFUGAL SPINNING FRAME

The P.S.C. machine was introduced by Prince-Smith & Stells Ltd., after the second world war as a revolutionary method of spinning at spindle speeds of up to 18,000 r.p.m. and twisting at about 14,000 r.p.m. Thus, although an intermittent spinning frame, the machine had an output which compared favourably with that of a more conventional frame running at about 7,000 r.p.m. In the P.S.C. machine, twist is inserted in the material being delivered from the front rollers by passing it down a hollow tube which traverses up and down inside a vertical rotating canister and deposits the yarn onto the inside of the canister. Centrifugal force presses the yarn firmly outwards against the sides of the canister, and provides the tension required to draw the yarn down the guide tube. When a sufficient length of yarn has been delivered, spinning is stopped by terminating the front roller delivery. At the same time, winding-on commences by the empty bobbin being raised inside the canister (which continues to rotate). The yarn inside the canister is transferred onto the bobbin in about two minutes.

When all the yarn in the canister has been transferred onto the bobbin, the full bobbins are lowered, front roller delivery is resumed, and the next cycle of spinning commences. Full bobbins may then be removed and replaced by empty bobbins while spinning is in progress. The P.S.C. spinning frame bobbin holds eight ounces of yarn while twisting bobbins hold one pound. The full cycle of operation is automatic, except for the removal of the full bobbins, and their replacement by empty bobbins.

Unfortunately, the yarn produced when 100 per cent wool is being processed is somewhat rough and hairy. Power consumption is also high and there is a danger of yarn wastage in the event of a power failure. P.S.C. frames are no longer manufactured and it is doubtful whether many frames are still operating in the United Kingdom. A Japanese company, however, has recently introduced a machine operating on the centrifugal principle intended for fine count yarns.

FLYER SPINNING

The spindle arrangement of a flyer spinning frame is the same in principle as that shown in Fig. 4.10, and described under the heading "Bradford Drawing Box Delivery" on page 116. Bobbin capacity is about two to three ounces and spindle speeds are about 2500–3500 r.p.m. This relatively low speed constitutes the main reason why the system has largely been abandoned in favour of ring spinning whenever this is possible, but flyer spinning is still considered necessary for the production of coarse-fibred materials which do not spin satisfactorily on the ring system.

Two types of mechanically assisted doffing frames have been produced. In one type the flyer is driven by a wharle mounted above, and separate from, the spindle peg which supports the bobbin, while there are two interchangeable spindle peg rails for doffing purposes. With this arrangement it is possible for one person to doff one side of a frame in about 30 seconds, but it is only suitable for counts thicker than about 1/18s English worsted (49 tex). The other type also has the wharle mounted above the flyer, but the flyer is still attached to the spindle; this gives less drag on the bobbin, allowing up to 1/28s worsted (32 tex) to be spun for hosiery type yarns, and up to 1/40s mohair (worsted count), (22 tex). The operation of doffing is rather more involved, the spindle having to be swung forward at the lower end to allow full bobbins to slide down on to a row of pegs, and empty bobbins to slide up from a further row of pegs. This means that doffing takes slightly longer – about one minute.

It would seem that flyer spinning, although producing a smooth and full-handling yarn, will decrease – except for the spinning of a few materials difficult to process by other methods – unless new and radical developments can be applied to the system.

CAP SPINNING

This system has been widely popular in the United Kingdom for the spinning of fine count, oil-combed yarns for coatings, but in recent years it has been losing ground to the ring spinning system which can produce a larger package size and a smoother yarn[62].

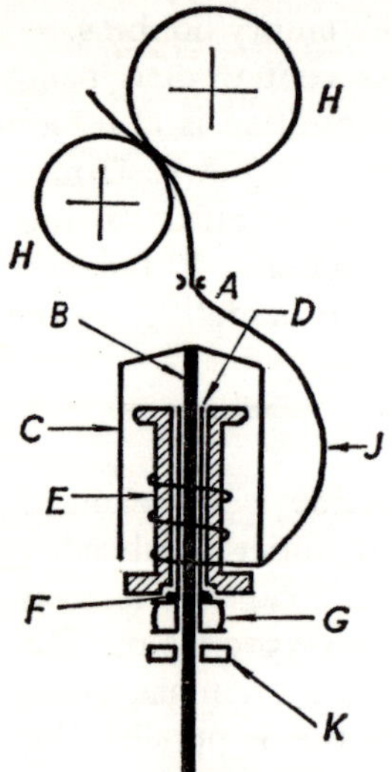

FIG. 4.12. SIDE ELEVATION OF A
CAP SPINNING FRAME

A—Porcelain thread guide; *B*—Spindle; *C*—Cap; *D*—Rotating tube; *E*—Bobbin; *F*—Bobbin driving pegs; *G*—Spindle wharle; *H*—Front (drafting) rollers; *J*—Balloon; *K*—Lifter rail.

A simplified side-elevation of a cap spinning machine is given in Fig. 4.12. The spindle *B* supports the cap *C*, both of which remain stationary. Mounted on the spindle is a tube *D*, which rotates due to the tape drive to the spindle wharle *G*. The bobbin *E* has two slots in its lower flange which locate on the driving pegs *F*. Twist is inserted by the bobbin rotating on its own axis while one end of the yarn is held between the delivery rollers *H*. Centrifugal force throws the yarn outwards to form a balloon *J* which is retarded by air drag and the friction between the yarn and the lower edge of the cap. The yarn is distributed along the length of the bobbin due to the upward and downward movement of the lifter rail *K*.

The tension applied to the yarn can be adjusted to allow a wide range of counts to be spun. To some extent tension is self-adjusting, as a finer yarn will meet less air resistance and create less centrifugal force. If, however, a large change in yarn count is to be made, it may be necessary to make one or more adjustments. Thus to reduce the spinning tension: (*i*) the spindle speed may be reduced; (*ii*) the balloon length may be shortened by raising the spindle height; (*iii*) smaller diameter caps may be used to narrow the balloon and to reduce the distance between the edge of the cap and the bobbin barrel; and/or (*iv*) the latter effect may be achieved by using a larger diameter bobbin.

There is a fundamental difference between the flyer system, which gives a constant twist insertion, and the cap system, in which the twist varies as the bobbin diameter increases. With the flyer system the balloon of material is driven at constant speed, while the bobbin speed varies. On the cap frame the situation is reversed; the bobbin is driven at a constant speed and the balloon speed increases as bobbin diameter increases. For each revolution of the balloon, one turn of twist is inserted; it follows, therefore, that the twist insertion will increase as the bobbin fills.

The conventional cap spinning frame may have a spindle speed as low as 4500 r.p.m. for thick counts in the region of 1/18s worsted (49 tex), but speeds of 6000 to 7000 r.p.m. are more commonly used for the medium and fine count range. Package sizes vary from less than an ounce for very fine count frames with small diameter caps, to the more usual $1\frac{1}{2}$ to $2\frac{1}{2}$ oz. capacity.

A mechanically assisted doffing device has been introduced for cap spinning, but as it was mechanically complex, it never proved particularly popular.

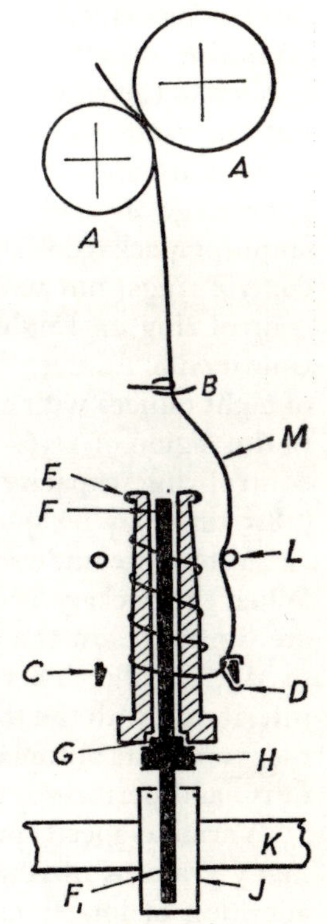

FIG. 4.13. SIDE ELEVATION OF A
RING SPINNING FRAME

A—Front (drafting) rollers; *B*—Yarn guide lappet; *C*—Ring (cross-section); *D*—Traveller; *E*—Bobbin; *F*—Spindle; F_1—Spindle bearing extension; *G*—Bobbin driving pegs; *H*—Spindle wharle; *J*—Spindle bearing assembly; *K*—Stationary spindle rail; *L*—Balloon control ring; *M*—Balloon.

RING SPINNING

Ring spinning appears to be the system with the brightest future for most sections of the trade, large package sizes and prospects of automatic doffing offering advantages which at the moment seem to put the system ahead of the others. As in cap spinning the bobbin is driven at a constant speed and the balloon speed varies, giving slightly less twist on an empty bobbin than when the bobbin is full.

A simplified diagram illustrating the arrangement of a ring frame is given in Fig. 4.13. The bobbin *E* receives its drive in a manner similar to that in cap spinning, namely via the locating pegs *G*, which in this case are part of the actual spindle *F*. The drive to the spindle is usually by tape or belt to the wharle *H*, and the spindle extension F_1 is mounted in the bearing assembly *J*, which is supported in the stationary spindle rail *K*.

On leaving the front rollers A the yarn passes through a lappet B before being threaded through the traveller D, which is free to slide around the package, and is supported by the ring C. Twist is inserted by the bobbin rotating on its own axis while one end of the yarn is held between the delivery rollers A. Centrifugal force throws the yarn outwards to form a balloon M, which is retarded by air drag and the friction of the traveller D. The diameter of the balloon is usually restricted on modern ring frames by one (or sometimes two) balloon control rings L. This creates the effect of an apparently smaller balloon, allowing higher spindle speeds, and larger packages than would otherwise be possible[63].

The yarn is distributed along the length of the package by the upward and downward movement of the ring rail, which is accompanied by a similar movement of the lappet B and the balloon control ring L to minimize variations in tension in the ballooning yarn. The tension applied to the yarn can be adjusted by altering the weight of the traveller D, but the range of counts covered by one ring size is not as great as that covered by one cap size on the cap frame. Smaller ring diameter allows a finer range of yarns to be spun, but package capacity is reduced. Where the spinning package is shorter than 11 inches, it is unusual to employ balloon control rings, but with packages above that length it is usual to have one control ring on English machines, while two rings may be used on some Continental frames. With a nine-inch tube, and no control ring, a capacity of eight ounces with a $2\frac{1}{4}$-inch ring is obtained with a spinning count limit in the region of 1/36s worsted (24 tex). By using an 11-inch package with a control ring, capacity is raised to 10 ounces and counts up to about 1/48s (18·5 tex) may be spun.

Automatic underwinding has been developed as an aid to hand doffing. When the package is full, the ring rail is lowered so that a few coils of yarn are wound below the package container (usually a paper or plastic tube) on to the spindle. This enables the full packages to be removed without interfering with the threading of the yarn in the traveller. Modern developments include automatic doffing devices which relieve the operative of this duty, and perform it at a higher speed[64-68].

Variable-speed spinning, which has been in use in Continental mills for many years, is increasing in popularity in the United Kingdom with the adoption of longer machines. Variable-speed motors are more expensive than those of the constant speed types and their use on short spinning frames is uneconomic. On frames with about 200 spindles per side, however, the variable-speed motor becomes an economic proposition due to the increased output obtained, an increase of about 15 per cent in production being not unusual. Spindle speeds may range from about 4000 r.p.m. to 12,000 r.p.m., giving traveller speeds up to a maximum of about 120 feet per second. The spindle speed is only reduced while spinning conditions are at their worst, namely when the ring rail is lowered and when the package diameter is at a minimum. An alternative arrangement is to use two constant-speed motors with different sized pulleys, each being used alternately. When variable-speed spinning is employed, the lifter motions at both sides of the frame must be united so that the same speed variations are provided for both sides at the same time.

Drafting zones in use on ring frames include apron drafting (popular in U.S.A. and on the Continent), roller drafting using small diameter rollers to allow 'middle drafting' up to about twenty, and the new Uniflex drafting zone which allows spinning from 20 or 40 drams per 40 yards (0·97 to 1·94 kilotex). The Uniflex frame can be used for twisted or twistless, oil-combed or dry, wool or man-made fibres and blends. The drafting zone is illustrated in simplified form in Fig. 4.9. If short untwisted dry-combed rovings are being processed, a steel tumbler K and carrier J are used between the back rollers G and the unit condensing guide A, while the front bottom roller has a diameter of two inches, allowing flume settings of as little as 0·3 inch minimum.

Spindle drives on the newer ring frames include the conventional tape drive, redesigned so that reverse spindle rotation may be obtained without re-threading all the tapes, and using ball-bearings and balanced pulleys. A snake belt drive is also used by some manufacturers, this being a leather (reinforced) continuous belt used to drive all the spindles on one side of the frame. With this form of drive the pressure of the belt against individual spindle wharles must be adjusted to give the correct spindle speeds. The chief advantage of the snake belt drive is the ease with which a narrow frame may be constructed. Some Continental frames use a positive helical gear drive, which also permits of a narrow frame construction and gives as near a perfect spindle drive as one could reasonably expect. Care has to be taken, however, in the maintenance of the drive shafts as it is possible for wear to develop in the bearings, causing twist variation.

Rings and travellers have received some attention in recent years. The steel traveller is still the cheapest and most commonly used in worsted spinning, but it is possible, where conditions permit and at only a moderate increase in cost, to obtain increased spindle speeds by using travellers coated with molybdenum disulphide. Conical rings have been widely applied to worsted spinning, and for light pastel shades, the porous sintered metal (P.S.M.) ring gives clean running combined with good lubrication. Care must be taken to avoid damage to the ring when changing travellers, as P.S.M. rings are very brittle. Another development is the introduction of the matt-finish rings; these are exactly the same as other rings, except that polishing has been omitted in the final stages of manufacture. This reduces the price by about 10 to 15 per cent, and simplifies the 'running-in' procedure when the rings first come into use. Matt rings become polished in use, and are probably no better than polished rings, except that the dimensions are possibly more accurate.

It would seem that the greatest limitation of the ring spinning frame for worsteds, lies not in the frame but in wool quality. Below 50s quality, difficulties arise due to the fibres catching in the traveller and causing end-breakages.

GENERAL FEATURES OF SPINNING FRAME CONSTRUCTION

In addition to the developments in specific methods of spinning described in the foregoing paragraphs, there have been many improvements in all types of spinning frame, in consequence of developments in engineering materials and techniques and the application of electrical devices and control systems. These improvements include:

1. More liberal use of ball-bearings, needle-bearings and roller-bearings.

2. Piped centralized lubrication systems using transparent polythene piping, and pressure-gun application.

3. Electrical guard interlock switches, preventing accidental running of machines with the guards open.

4. Electrical yardage stop-motions to give the required number of yards per doff without involved calculations and gearwheel changing.

5. Combined length and shift counters for one, two, or three-shift working; usually these are only fitted as extras.

6. Tachometers giving direct indication of front roller delivery and direct indication of spindle speed.

7. Automatic underwinding on ring frames to assist manual doffing.

8. Provision of lappets instead of a thread board with porcelain eyes, giving better balloon control, and minimizing the effects of fly-waste[49].

9. Suction underclearing to collect broken ends and to prevent the formation of laps on rollers and the formation of spinning double. Such underclearing is more effective with dry-combed than with oil-combed material.

10. Thread illuminating lamps which in many cases may be fitted as an optional extra but which, unfortunately, are not particularly effective with some shades in coloured spinning.

11. Screw ratch adjustment which enables adjustment of each line of rollers (or units) from the front roller while the machine is running, the setting distance being automatically indicated on a dial. For this form of adjustment the lines of rollers are mounted on collars each supported on a screwthread parallel to the drafting zone. The adjustment consists of rotating the collars so that they ride up or down the screwthread supports. As the collars are rotated by one control (for one set of rollers), the rollers automatically maintain alignment.

12. Central support and spring-loading of pressure rollers. This arrangement, combined with suction underclearers, simplifies the piecing technique and permits higher front-roller delivery speeds.

13. Automatic snarl elimination is provided on some ring spinning frames. This consists of a slight time delay on the delivery rollers when the machine is started-up, thus allowing the balloon tension to build up, and snarls to be removed before delivery recommences.

14. Electrical control of spindle speed, enabling a suitable spindle speed to be selected while the machine is running, instead of having to change pulleys or sprockets.

15. Variable-speed spinning, automatically controlled from the lifter motion, has been a standard arrangement on Continental ring frames for many years.

16. Simplified lifter motions are provided instead of the Scaife lifter motion, it no longer being considered necessary to have a lifter which will provide three different types of motion. With the advent of automatic single yarn winding and clearing, the spinning frame can be used with a standard package designed to give maximum spinning efficiency.

YARN TWISTING

MOST WORSTED YARNS are twisted (or folded) together to form a compound thread composed of two or more singles. This is achieved by using the twisting operation one or more times. When single yarns are combined together, they lose their individual identities, and become merely a component part of the final thread. This applies more in the case of solid and mixture yarns than for colour effects. The result is that a greater degree of levelness is produced, the levelness of the compound thread being inversely proportional to the square root of the number of component threads. In addition, there is an increase of yarn strength, and a reduction in the strength variation.

The above remarks apply to ordinary folded yarns, the majority of which are two-fold, but there is, in addition, a further group of yarns of considerable commercial value. This group includes novelty (or fancy) yarns in which the novelty effects may be produced in one or more of the following ways:

1. By the combination of different types of fibres to give a distinctive appearance or behaviour to the yarn, an example being the combining of fibres of different shrinkage rates to produce a bulky yarn.

2. By the combination of different colours, a procedure which is very common in the speciality coloured worsted trade.

3. By the combination of different thicknesses of yarns to produce spiral yarns.

4. By the combination of different lengths of component threads to produce knops, spirals, and bouclé yarns.

5. By the use of unusual amounts of twist to produce special effects, such as, for example, frescoes, and crepes.

For the classification of the bulk of two-fold worsted folding twists, it is convenient to state the folding twist to be used as a proportion of the single-yarn spinning twist. Normally in worsted spinning, spindle direction is clockwise, producing 'Z' twist single yarn. Most two-fold yarns have the folding twist in the opposite direction to the spinning twist, i.e., folding twist is usually 'S' twist. The examples given below are based on 1/48s worsted (18·5 tex) spun with 16 turns Z twist.

The three types of two-fold yarns most commonly produced are hosiery yarns, coating or suiting yarns and yarns with contrasting colours.

Hosiery Yarns: For these yarns, the folding twist is half the spinning twist. Thus it may be assumed that of the original 16 turns Z spinning twist for a 1/48s English worsted (18·5 tex), approximately eight will be removed in twisting by using a folding twist of 8S. In each of the singles, therefore, there will be approximately 8Z residual spinning twist. This gives a bulky yarn with good extension, suitable for knitting. When this type of yarn is twisted, it becomes slightly longer and this must be allowed for in the spun count. It is usual to spin about 3·5 per cent light to allow for this fact and for regain (+5 per cent for regain − 1·5 per cent for extension), i.e., about 49·6s worsted count (17·9 tex) for a 100 per cent wool yarn to produce 2/48s worsted (R37 tex/2) at standard regain.

Coating (or Suiting) Yarns: For these yarns folding twist equals spinning twist and it may therefore be assumed that all the 16Z spinning twist will be removed by the 16S used in twisting and that there will be no residual spinning twist remaining in the single component threads. The yarn produced is strong and elastic enough for weaving purposes, and gives a compact appearance. The length after twisting is the same as before, and so an allowance of 5 per cent for regain only is required in spinning. Thus if a yarn is spun about 5 per cent light, i.e., 50·4s worsted (17·6 tex), it will be approximately at the correct count of 2/48s worsted (R37 tex/2) at standard regain.

Colour Twists: For yarns with colour-twist, folding twist equals spinning twist multiplied by 1·5. This type of twist is used for folding yarns which have component threads of contrasting colours, and for marls, half marls, etc. The reason for this is to obtain a small unit of colour in the yarn. Failure to do this may result in the formation of a peculiar streaky effect, due to the coincidence, or near coincidence, of the number of spots of colour per inch, showing in the yarn with the number of ends or picks used when weaving the cloth. This twist combination means, in approximate terms, that not only is the original 16Z spinning twist removed but that it is replaced by 8S in the single components, due to using 24S in the folding operation. In this type of yarn, there is contraction in length during twisting, and so the spun count must be $8\frac{1}{2}$ per cent to 10 per cent light to allow for this fact and for regain (5 per cent for regain $+ 3\frac{1}{2}$ to 5 per cent for contraction in length). Thus a 100 per cent wool yarn would be spun to about 53·0 worsted (16·7 tex) to give a final folded yarn of 2/48s worsted (R37 tex/2) at standard regain.

In addition to the three most commonly used twists outlined above, there are variations which some spinners employ. Of these, reference may be made to the following:

Balanced Twist: This form of twist is theoretically supposed to give the most stable yarn possible, completely free from the tendency to snarl which is common in many yarns produced. This non-torque requirement is particularly important for certain applications in the knitwear industry. The intention is to make the residual twist of the single component threads equal, in total, to the folding twist, and opposite in direction. In theory, therefore, the torque effect of the folding twist will just be cancelled out by the combined effect of the single twists. To produce this effect the folding twist should equal the spinning twist multiplied by $N/(N + 1)$, where N is the number of component singles. Thus for a 2/48s worsted, produced from singles with 16 t.p.i. Z twist, $10\frac{2}{3}$ t.p.i. S folding twist will be required. Of the original 16 t.p.i. Z twist, $5\frac{1}{3}$ t.p.i. Z twist will remain in each of the singles, giving a *total* residual twist equal and opposite to the folding twist.

Warp Twist: For this the folding twist should equal the spinning twist minus one. In theory this results in one turn of the original Z spinning twist remaining in each component thread, giving a compact thread with a soft handle in the cloth.

Gaberdine Twist: To produce this, the folding twist should equal the spinning twist plus one. In theory, this results in the removal of all the single twist and the insertion of one turn in the single components in the S direction, giving a compact round yarn with little surface fibre, combined with increased strength and good elasticity.

In addition to yarns having folding twists opposite to spinning twists, there are many yarns made with other arrangements, such as twist-on-twist, i.e., with both spinning and folding twists in the same direction. In such a case it may be assumed that all the folding twist is additive to spinning twist, giving a compact, solid yarn, suitable for crepe yarns and bold striping threads. To prevent snarling, the yarns must be steam-set, preferably in a vacuum steaming oven.

TWISTING MACHINERY

TWISTING MACHINERY requirements depend on the type of yarn which is to be produced. From this point of view, the yarns may be broadly grouped into three categories, viz., two-fold yarns, multi-fold yarns, and fancy yarns.

TWO-FOLD YARN TWISTING

There are two basic approaches to two-fold yarn twisting, one being to twist direct from the spinning package, and the other to assembly-wind the two components together before twisting. The former method necessitates a detector/stop motion on each spindle so that if a supply package breaks or runs out, the delivery of the other component will stop at the same time as the spindle.

The simplest form of two-fold twister, which has been used for many years, is the dolly trap twister. This mechanism is only suitable where folding twist is opposite to spinning twist and approximately equal in amount. When one supply thread breaks or runs out, the remaining thread has its twist removed and is unable to hold down the detector motion which then stops the delivery of the remaining thread. The spindle, however, continues to rotate. This machine is not suitable for multi-fold yarns or twist-on-twist yarns. A further disadvantage is that all knots must be two-fold. Some modern large-package twisters are made with a similar limitation, the only difference being that each thread passes through a detector and, when a thread breaks, a cutter severs the remaining thread. Other modern ring twisters have individual end-detectors which operate both a yarn delivery stop-motion and a spindle stop-motion.

An entirely different approach to the twisting process is 'two-stage' twisting, which, as the name implies, consists of two operations. The first employs a ring twister which only inserts about a half-turn of twist per inch. This machine is fitted with end detectors which operate delivery and spindle stop-motions. The package produced by this machine is designed to fit into the container of the second twisting machine. When handling the packages between operations care must be exercised, as the slightest disturbance of the layers of yarn is likely to cause difficulty in the second twisting operation. This second operation is performed on a form of up-twister. The package from the first operation is placed in an enclosed container which has an outlet hole at the top through which the yarn passes. The container is made to rotate at about 9500 r.p.m. and, as the yarns are already pre-twisted slightly and tension limited by the smooth-sided container preventing a large balloon from forming, no end-breakages are likely to occur. In consequence, the machine can be left to run for about 36 hours without attention on a count like 2/48s worsted (R37 tex/2), giving a productive output when other types of machine would be idle, such as, for example, at weekends. The package produced weighs about two pounds, contains only single knots and is in cone form. The main attractions of this type of twisting are the low tensions developed at such high spindle-speeds and the absence of fibre migration from one spindle to the next. This allows different shades of yarn to be twisted on adjacent spindles.

The 'two-for-one' or 'double-twist' spindle has now found a place for itself in the twisting of thick and medium worsted yarns from 6s to 48s worsted (14·8 to 18·5 tex). Spindle speeds of up to about 8000 r.p.m. may be employed, and as two turns are inserted for each revolution, this means a twist insertion rate of 16,000 turns per minute. The spindle pitch is wide (9¾ inches) but this disadvantage has been overcome by producing a double-deck twister.

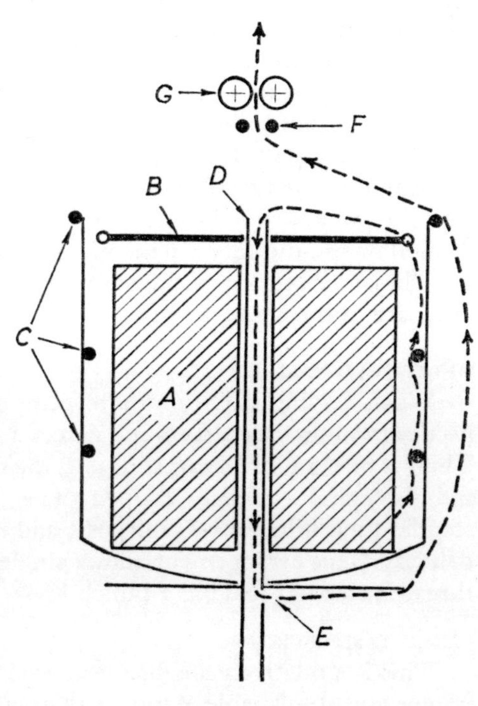

FIG. 4.14. DRAWING ILLUSTRATING THE DOUBLE TWIST (TWO-FOR-ONE) SPINDLE.

A—Assembly-wound supply package; *B*—Freely rotating flyer arm guide; *C*—Balloon control rings; *D*—Hollow rotating spindle; *E*—Outlet hole; *F*—Yarn guide; *G*—Yarn feed wheels.

The general principle of this form of spindle construction is indicated in Fig. 4.14. The supply yarns are previously assembly-wound onto a package *A* which is held, so as not to rotate, by means of a magnetic stabilizer. The threads (shown as dotted lines) are withdrawn from the package, and pass through a flyer eye on *B* which is able to rotate freely under the influence of the rotating yarn. Tension is applied at this point by a ball-drag arrangement in the flyer mounting; this incorporates a ball which rotates in a nylon seating. From this point the yarn, which has its balloon size restricted by balloon control rings *C*, passes down through *D* at the top of the hollow rotating spindle, to an outlet hole *E*, a nylon tube being used to prevent the yarn from nicking the outlet hole *E*. The yarn then passes through a self-threading yarn guide *F* before reaching the positively driven yarn feed wheels *G*. The purpose of these wheels, which consist of a pair of discs mounted on a positively driven shaft, is to assist in providing a more constant twist in the yarn. As the discs rotate, although they do not positively grip the yarn, they help to stabilize tension and yarn delivery rate and give a more regularly distributed twist. The speed of the discs is adjustable so that the best results may be achieved with various yarns which may have different frictional properties. From this point the yarn is taken to the winding head which produces a cone package, or a parallel cheese, as required. The upper and lower decks may be run at different spindle speeds and in opposite directions of rotation, and each side of each deck may be run to insert different twists.

The principle of the double-twist spindle is as follows: Each full revolution of the twister tube inserts one turn of twist into two sections of yarn, i.e., one turn is inserted into the yarn which lies down the centre of the hollow spindle between the points *D* and *E*, and one turn is also inserted into the outer section of the yarn between the points *E* and *F*. These two turns are in the same direction in the yarn, and are, therefore, additive.

MULTI-FOLD YARN TWISTING

When folding three or more components in a single operation it is necessary to provide a feed-end detector for each individual supply thread. Thus, if one end breaks or runs out, the delivery of supply yarns is stopped and the spindle is also stopped. The 'Universal' twisting frame is the standard machine for this purpose, and it is usually made with a ring-type delivery. This arrangement allows single knots to be tied in the individual thread instead of making a bunch knot.

FANCY YARN TWISTING

This is a relatively small, specialized branch of the trade. The twisting frames must be capable of giving a fluctuating or intermittent yarn delivery for one or more components, with provision for controlling the variations in feed as required.

TWISTING FAULTS

The twisting operation gives rise to a number of yarn faults of which the following are fairly common:

Slack Twist: This means a lower amount of twist than that intended. It may be due to a variety of causes, but basically the causes are either too fast a delivery of the supply yarn or too slow a spindle speed (or the unlikely combination of both). These are usually caused by incorrect threading of supply yarns, slippage of supply yarn round the delivery roller, slippage in the spindle drive, or accumulated waste.

Hard Twist: In this case more twist is present in the yarn than was intended. The basic causes are either a supply yarn delivery which is too slow, or a spindle rotation which is too fast. The latter, however, is extremely unlikely, although it is not impossible; a spindle wharle of the wrong size could account for such a fault. Slow delivery of supply yarn is most likely to be due to the accumulation of waste on the creel pegs, although a slipping twist-change wheel, a wrong sized delivery roller or an incorrectly set dolly trap motion could account for this type of fault.

Wrong Number of Component Threads: This may be due to threads passing down to an adjacent spindle, or to one or more component threads missing. In either case the fault is basically due to the detector motion being ineffective.

Wrong Direction of Twist: This fault is less common, and is only likely to be caused by the incorrect threading of a spindle tape.

Tensioning Faults: These faults may give rise to a spiral yarn appearance in the final thread due to one component thread being under a greater or lesser tension than the other. This variation in tension may be due to the presence of waste on the creel pegs, or to incorrect threading of one component. It is important that all the single component threads should be treated in an exactly similar manner. In the case of contrasting coloured components, all component threads of one shade should be placed on the back creel pegs.

TYPES OF YARN

THE USE OF COLOUR in worsted yarn manufacture gives rise to a wide range of yarns, the names of which are often confused. Some of the most common types are described below. ('Black' and 'white' are included in the term 'colour'.)

Solid Shades: This term applies to yarns in which all the fibres are intended to be the same colour. These will include hank-dyed or package-dyed materials. A similar effect is obtained by piece-dyeing fabrics containing only one type of fibre.

Mixture Shades: This term applies to those cases where the individual fibres composing a yarn are of different colours. The fibres are therefore dyed first and then mixed together later. A similar effect is obtained by piece-dyeing fabric composed of a fibre mixture, i.e., by cross-dyeing.

Melange (or Vigoureux): In this yarn each individual fibre contains more than one colour. This is brought about by printing bands of colour across sliver before drawing and spinning. The effect is similar to a colour mixture but the shade produced by melanging is much more uniform.

Colour Twist: A two-fold yarn in which the single components are of different colours, either solid or mixture. Usually the singles are the same count and quality.

Single Mottle: A single yarn made from two half-weight rovings of different colours spun together. The colours are clearly distinct at the point where they meet. This is rarely produced commercially due to the low roving production entailed, this being only about one-third of the normal-weight roving production.

Single Marl: A single yarn produced from a roving which has been made from two differently coloured reducers. The colour distinction is not as clear as a mottle, but the roving production is normal.

Marl: A two-fold yarn made of two identical single marls. This gives less colour distinction than does a single marl due to the partial release of single twist, but there is a good distribution of each colour, giving a speckled effect.

Double Marl: A two-fold yarn made from two single marls of different colours, giving four colours in the final two-fold. The effect is an evenly distributed multi-colour effect.

Half Marl: A two-fold yarn combining a single marl with a solid or mixture shade single yarn. Usually the solid or mixture is the same shade as the dark component of the single marl. The effect is a speckled one, with a small proportion of the light shade.

Hosiery Marl: A multi-ply yarn, each single component being an identical single marl. The colour components are usually independent mixtures which give a colourful folded yarn. The marled appearance is obvious, giving less contrast than different coloured solid or mixture singles would give due to the mingling of colours in the marls.

Mock Marl: Hosiery yarns composed of different coloured solid or mixture singles giving an imitation marl effect. Usually it is a three-fold yarn, and the components are assembly wound to give even tensions and single knots. If more than three components are used, the component threads may change their positions, breaking the regularity of colour distribution.

Splash Yarns: These yarns are spun from a printed roving prepared from a bleached top. Two or more colours are applied two to four inches wide at intervals, leaving two to four inches of undyed roving between the colours. The roving is steamed to set the colours, rinsed and dried. The coloured and white fibres become intermingled where they meet during drafting, giving a gradual shading of colour. Variations in splash yarns may be introduced by variations in colour and in the width of spacings, by variations in roving weights and spinning drafts to alter the repeat distance in the yarn, by spinning two half-weight rovings into one single yarn (combination of 'splash' and 'mottle') to give more colour combinations and by folding single splash yarns with different coloured single yarns.

In addition to the effects which are dependent on colour, there is a wide range of fancy yarns which depend on special fancy twisting machinery for their production. Some of these fancy yarns as follows:

Cloud Yarn: This yarn is made from two threads of different colours which are made alternately to form the base and cover. Two pairs of delivery rollers with fluctuating speeds are required.

Spiral Yarn: A plied yarn in which one component smoothly spirals round the other. It may be made by combining 'S' and 'Z' singles, different lengths, or different counts.

Gimp Yarn: A compound yarn containing a twisted core with semi-circular loops emerging from it. It is made by combining a spiral (made from different lengths) with a thread in the opposite direction to the initial spiralling twist.

Eccentric Yarn: This is an undulating gimp yarn, usually produced by binding an irregular yarn, such as a stripe or slub, in reverse direction to the initial stage, to create graduated half-circular loops along the compound yarn.

Knop Yarn: A yarn containing prominent bunches of one or more of its components at regular or irregular intervals.

Loop Yarn: A compound yarn which has circular loops projecting from the core. Frequently mohair is used to form the loops.

Slub Yarn: A yarn in which slubs are deliberately made. The slubs may be formed by an intermittent roller action on the spinning frame, or they may be inserted between foundation threads on the twisting frame.

Snarl Yarn: A compound yarn with snarls of highly twisted yarn projecting from the core.

Stripe Yarn: A yarn containing elongated knops.

For fuller information on coloured yarns and definitions, the reader's attention is directed elsewhere[69, 70].

REELING

BASICALLY, the reeling process consists of winding yarns from bobbins, cops, or cheeses, onto a swift from which the yarn may be removed in hank form. The process may be used for yarns which are to be bleached, dyed, scoured, or steamed, for some handknitting yarns, and for yarns which are to be exported with minimum volume and tare weight.

Where wet processing is to be used on the hanks, cross-reeling is used. In this case the yarn traverses the full width of the hank at every traverse, crossing the previous traverse at an angle. Thus no two consecutive revolutions of the swift lay the yarn in adjacent coils and, as the threads are not parallel, there is less entanglement of the threads. For use where wet treatment is not involved normal, or lea reeling, is used the hanks being built up in sections. The threads are only traversed intermittently in one direction as they are wound onto the swift, to form a series of parallel-wound sub-hanks. By moving the guide rod at intervals in this way, thread build-up at any one point is avoided, and there is a minimum variation of length of each thread forming the hank.

Swifts are made telescopic so that different girths of hank may be reeled, and also to facilitate removal of the hanks. The strength of the reel arms is of importance, for if the reel is too long, there is a possibility of the arms warping, with the result that different hanks may vary in length. This is particularly important where synthetic crimped yarns are to be processed. For the same reason, the length of a reel is limited to a maximum of about 40 spindles of four-inch pitch. English machines are usually made with a multiple of 12 spindles for working in dozens, whereas Continental machines have multiples of 10 for the metric system. Modern swift speeds range from about 250 to 550 r.p.m.

There are two types of modern reeling machine available, depending on the running time. Where this is more than five minutes, interchangeable swifts are recommended. Here a two-swift machine is employed with the swifts supported in a single pivoted frame. Each swift may be brought into the running and doffing positions by disconnecting and pivoting the frame. Thus, while hanks are being wound almost without interruption on one side of the machine, tying and doffing can proceed simultaneously at the other side. Where running time is less than five minutes, double reeling machines are recommended. This type of machine is provided with two swifts which are supported in cantilever fashion on both sides of the machine headstock. The swifts have independent drives, control, and measuring equipment, and doffing is by sliding the hanks over the free ends of the swifts. In this machine, the swifts are usually only half the length of those on the change reeling machine.

Conditioning motions may be fitted to the reeling machines if required.

REFERENCES

1. 'Longwool Preparing Catalogue', Prince-Smith & Stells Ltd., Keighley.
2. Townend and Spiegel, *J. Text. Inst.*, 1944, **35,** T 21.
3. Townend and Spiegel, *J. Text. Inst.*, 1946, **37,** T 58.
4. Townend, P. P., Ph.D. Thesis, University of Leeds.
5. Bottini, B.P. 893, 421 (April, 1958).
6. Wright Hargeaves Engineering Co. Ltd., B.P. 921,361 (June, 1958).
7. *Wool Record*, 1963, 104.
8. Windisch, Reiterer and Nifenecker, B.P. 909,830 (Nov., 1957).
9. T.M.M. Research Ltd., B.P. 933,834 (March, 1961).
10. Grignet and Monfort, *J. Text. Inst.*, 1960, **51,** T 1058.
11. Townend, *J. Text. Inst.*, 1948, **39,** T 385.
12. Townend and Spiegel, *J. Text Inst.*, 1946, **37,** T 58.
13. Anderson S. L., *Ann. Sci. Text. Belges*, 1963, **1,** 30.
14. Walls, *J. Text. Inst.*, 1963, **54,** T 79.
15. Hardaker, *Text. Recorder*, Jan., 1959.
16. Kirk, *Text. Inst. and Ind.*, May, 1964.
17. Walls and Taylor, *J. Text. Inst.*, 1960, **51,** T 986.
18. C.S.I.R.O., B.P. 886,103 (Jan., 1958).
19. Morgan, Taylor and Walls, *J. Text. Inst.*, 1962, **53,** P 512.
20. C.S.I.R.O., B.P. 886,102 (Jan., 1957).
21. Townend and Pitcher, *J. Text. Inst.*, 1956, **47,** T 611.
22. Speakman and Greenwood, *J. Text. Inst.*, 1935, **26,** P 271.
23. Buck, *J. Text. Inst.*, 1961, **52,** P 119.
24. Schönfeldt, *J. Text. Inst.*, 1963, **54,** T 301.
25. Wegener and Röhrig, *Textil Praxis*, 1963, **18,** 551.
26. Wegener and Topf, *ibid*, 1963, **18,** 327,417.
27. Shell International Research, B.P. 930,336 (March, 1961).
28. Garner, *J. Text. Inst.*, 1937, **28,** P 57.
29. Barritt, *J. Text. Inst.*, 1938, **29,** P 47.
30. Parkin, W., F.T.I. Thesis, the Textile Institute.
31. Taylor, *J. Text. Inst.*, 1955, **46,** T 284.
32. *Text. Recorder*, 1961, **78,** Sept., 87.
33. Taylor and Walls, *J. Text. Inst.*, 1963, **54,** T 183.
34. Taylor and Walls, *J, Text. Inst.*, **1960, 51,** T 1002.
35. Taylor, *J. Text. Inst.*, 1958, **49,** T 532.
36. Dyson & Happey, *J. Text. Inst.*, 1960, **51,** T 1016.
37. Bownass, *J. Text. Inst.*, 1960, **51,** T 1035.
38. Griffin, *J. Text. Inst.*, 1947, **38,** P 91, P 166.
39. Townend, *Text. Recorder*, 1948, **65,** Jan, 49, March, 50, April, 47.
40. Belin and Walls, *J. Text. Inst.*, 1963, **54,** T 171.
41. *Wool Textile Industry*, June, 1965, 14.
42. B.S. Handbook, No. 11, 1963, p. 51.
43. *W.I.R.A. Bulletin*, Vol. 21, No. 2, (April 1959).
44. *Wool Research*, 1918-48 (W.I.R.A.) Vol. 6, p. 51.
45. Martindale, *J. Text. Inst.*, 1942, **33,** p. 9.
46. Martindale, *J. Text. Inst.*, 1945, **36,** T 213.
47. *Wool Research*, 1918-48 (W.I.R.A.), Vol. 6, p. 115.
48. Townend and Grffiin, *J. Text. Inst.*, 1957, **48,** T 153.
49. Oxtoby, *J. Text. Inst.*, 1963, **54,** T 501.
50. Brearley and Oxtoby, *Text. Recorder*, May, 1962, 66.
51. Brearley and Oxtoby, *Ibid*, Aug., 1962, 47.
52. Oxtoby, *Ibid*, Sept., 1963, 92.
53. Brierley S, Unpublished work.

54. Beevers, "Practical Spinning on the Bradford System", p. 30, published by National Trade Press.
55. Buckley, Unpublished work.
56. Ashenhurst, "Textile Calculations and the Structure of Fabrics", p. 47.
57. Herzfeld, "Technical Testing of Yarn and Textile Fabrics", p. 91.
58. Armitage, *Journ. Huddersfield Text. Soc.*, 1904-5, 37.
59. Bannister, "Relationship between Twist, Counts and Diameters of Single Yarn" (prize essay), *ibid*, 1908-9, 77.
60. Barker, "Woollen and Worsted Spinning", p. 238.
61. Oxtoby, *Text. Recorder*, Dec., 1963, 50.
62. Boswell and Townend, *J. Text. Inst.*, 1957, **48,** T 135.
63. Bracewell and Greenhalgh, *J. Text. Inst.*, 1954, **45,** T 730.
64. S.A.C.M., Societe Alsacienne de Constructions Mecanique, Mulhouse, France.
65. Deutscher Spinnereimaschinenbau Ingolstadt, Ingolstadt, Germany.
66. Saco-Lowell Shops, Greenville, U.S.A.
67. Platt Bros. (Sales) Ltd., Oldham, England.
68. Whitin International Ltd., Whitinsville, U.S.A.
69. 'Textile Terms and Definitions', the Textile Institute.
70. Beevers, *J. Text. Inst.*, 1954, **45,** P 462.
71. Townend and Mayerson, *J. Text. Inst.*, 1965, **56,** T 581.
72. Townend and Judson, *Proc. Inst. Wool Textile Research Conf.*, 1955, E 181.
73. Papp and Townend, *J. Text. Inst.*, 1958, **49,** P. 47.

WOOLLEN YARN MANUFACTURE

Yarns spun on the woollen system may be produced from virgin wool, from wool mixed or blended with man-made fibres, with cotton or various forms of waste, or they may be produced entirely from man-made fibres or from waste materials. The woollen process lends itself to the use of mixtures which could not be spun on the worsted system where a greater degree of fibre uniformity is necessary and where much higher drafts are used than is possible on the woollen system.

Man-made fibres of the cellulosic type are blended with wool to produce cheaper yarns and they have largely replaced the use of cotton for this purpose. The acrylic fibres are used for both hosiery and dress and coating yarns. Courtelle is generally preferred for hosiery yarns because of the full, soft handling properties imparted to knitted outerwear, while for yarns for the dress and coating trades, Acrilan is widely used. Nylon in the form of staple fibre and also nylon wastes are used extensively, either blended with wool or alone. It has a very wide application, being used in the manufacture of hosiery, coating and carpet yarns all of high quality, and additionally for any yarns where outstanding strength is required. Polyester fibres are blended with wool to produce yarns of increased strength and also to impart special properties to fabrics manufactured from these blended yarns.

USE OF WASTES IN WOOLLEN YARN PRODUCTION

The various forms of waste used in woollen yarn production can be classified under three main headings, namely, (*i*) soft wastes, (*ii*) hard wastes, and (*iii*) fabric wastes. While many are used for producing cheaper yarns, some better qualities of soft wastes (e.g., drawing laps and some qualities of noils) have all the qualities of virgin wool, except that the laps do not contain short fibres, which makes them particularly valuable for some high-class yarns, while the noils, of course, consist entirely of short fibres.

Soft and Hard Wastes: The principal soft wastes are obtained from worsted processing, e.g. noils from combing, laps from drawing, and card waste. Additionally there are small quantities of brush waste from combing and drawing, waste from the side settling tanks of wool scouring machinery, woollen card waste (used in blends of lower quality) and flocks from cloth finishing processes. Hard wastes comprise, in the main, waste yarns from the spinning, winding, twisting and warping departments, and thrums from weaving.

Fabric Wastes: Fabric wastes comprise pieces of cloth, such as tailors' clippings, patterns, or discarded garments, the two former being known as new, and the latter as old rags. These wastes may be all-wool, or they may contain any of the wide range of fibres in use today. Again, they may be all-white or coloured, and accordingly a sorting process is necessary before they can be re-used. The complexity of this process depends on the wastes concerned, but it is obvious that the sorting of rags, particularly old ones, is quite complicated because of their unknown history. Sorting has to be performed by hand and the constituents of the waste assessed by handle and appearance. This process creates serious problems as it is impossible, simply by hand sorting to differentiate between the various fibres present in fabrics, and which, if re-processed indiscriminately, would lead to many troubles, particularly in finishing and dyeing.

TREATMENT OF SOFT AND HARD WASTES.

Soft wastes are usually classified according to type, quality and colour. Sorting is simple as the different types and qualities are usually collected separately during processing. In the case of card and combing wastes special treatments such as carbonizing and shaking may be necessary, but, otherwise, this class of waste, if clean, does not require any special treatment other than that normally given to a blend prior to carding. In general, the characteristics of soft wastes resemble more closely than those of any other type the characteristics of the original fibres, as these have not, in the main, been subjected to a great deal of processing.

After sorting into like qualities, hard wastes are subjected to processes designed to transform them to a fibrous form. The advantages of steeping twisted wool wastes in warm water prior to processing cannot be over estimated, as such a process allows the fibres to swell, softens the yarns and enables the machines to produce a longer fibred waste.

The two chief machines used for the treatment of wastes are the knot breaker and the garnett machine, the former being used for the first treatment of thrums after which the material is passed to the garnett machine.

The chief feature of a garnett machine is the special type of metallic wire used for covering the rollers. This is rigid, extremely strong and sharp-pointed and is most effective in disentangling yarns to their fibrous form. A garnett machine may consist of one, two, three or four swifts and may carry from six to eleven workers over each swift. Machines are made 36, 48 or 60 inches wide, but production varies considerably according to the type of waste being processed.

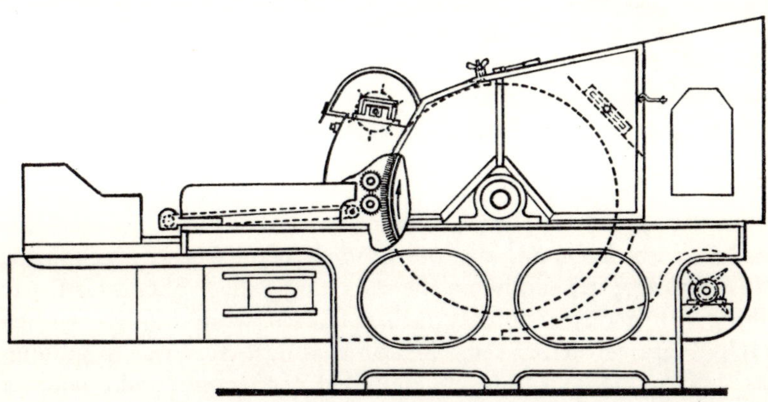

FIG. 5.1. MACHINE FOR THE TREATMENT OF FABRIC WASTE
By courtesy of Walker and Smith (Batley) Ltd.

TREATMENT OF FABRIC WASTES.

Old rags are usually shaken to remove surplus dust, it being recognized that the removal of dust and dirt not only renders subsequent working conditions more congenial but leads to the production of a cleaner shoddy, enabling machines to operate for longer periods without stoppages for cleaning. On this account, rags might be subjected to a washing process, the extra expense being amply repaid by increased efficiency. Old rags may need seaming, i.e., a process in which the sewing seams, button holes, metal hooks, etc., are cut away. The removal of cotton by this method cuts out carbonizing, provided there is no other cellulosic material in the rags themselves. If this is not the case, the process is necessary unless the shoddy is to go forward as an angola waste. The removal of metal hooks and eyes, buttons, etc., is extremely important and cannot be over emphasized. Their presence may result in the kindling of a spark in the rag-pulling or carding processes which might lead to fires.

On account of the many classes involved, the sorting of rags into various categories is a highly skilled occupation. Broadly speaking, however, rags can be subdivided into two chief classes, new and old, each of which can be further divided into two classes, viz., all-wool and wool plus other fibres. The all-wool rags may be further subdivided into knit goods, worsteds and woollens according to their origin. Knit goods may comprise Berlins, medium, coarse and very coarse qualities. Worsted rags may comprise the fine, medium and coarse qualities (quality referring to the fineness of the fibre going to make up the rag), and flannels, which again are subdivided into fine, medium and coarse qualities. Woollen rags are also subdivided into the classes of fine, medium and coarse and flannels. Again it must be remembered that most of these rags will be dyed, and thus further subdivision is possible and often made on a colour basis.

The "wool and other fibres" class may either be carbonized or go straight forward; in the latter case they are known as angola wastes. In either case the same state of subdivision is made as with the all-wool rags.

RAG PULLING

After sorting, the various kinds of rags are taken to the rag machine and reduced to a fibrous condition, the product being known, technically, as shoddy or mungo, depending on the rag being pulled. Shoddy is the result of pulling knit goods or loosely milled fabrics, while mungo is obtained from felted fabrics such as felts, melton coatings, etc. Prior to pulling, the rags are laid on the floor in layers and oiled, the amount and quality of the oil varying with the rag being pulled, the function being to reduce the fibre breakage which is necessarily involved in the process.

The function of the rag machine is to reduce the rags to a fibrous form. This is accomplished by feeding them forward between slowly moving, heavily weighted feed rollers to the action of a toothed swift revolving at a high speed, the shoddy or mungo being blown into a shoddy house at the back of the machine. Any rags which are not broken down to the desired degree are either deflected on to the feed sheet to be passed forward again by the bit roller or deflected into the bit box by the bit knife, and again fed to the machine.

Machine details vary according to the class of rags being pulled. Swifts are usually 18 inches wide and 40 inch diameter for pulling mungo rags, and 28 inch diameter for stockings and lighter rags. The tempered steel teeth may be inserted into wooden lags or into a steel swift, and the actual pinning may vary from 128 teeth to 500 teeth per lag, depending on the type of rag, there being 48 lags on a 40 inch diameter swift.

The efficiency of the rag pulling process is governed by the relative surface speeds of feed roller and swift, the distance between these components, the density of pinning of the swift, and the type and condition of the swift teeth. The product is judged by the absence of rag bits in the pulled product, by its condition (burst or stringy), by the fibre length and, by its resilience.

Recent improvements are (*i*) wider machines, (*ii*) the adoption of a variable speed drive, (*iii*) spring loaded feed rollers, (*iv*) variable speed drives to the feed rollers including a reversing mechanism, and (*v*) a top roller drive. The swift speed varies from, say 400 r.p.m. for coarse knit goods to 700 r.p.m. for felts, the production being about ten cwt. and four cwt. of pulled material per ten-hour day, respectively.

Identification of shoddy or mungo in a blend of fibres is extremely difficult and calls for much practice before it can be said, with any certainty, that such fibres are mixed with virgin ones.

WOOL BLENDING AND OILING

A YARN, like a cloth, is designed to possess special properties, such as, for example, strength, elasticity, milling power, bulkiness, colour, novelty, etc., and a blender must therefore possess a sound knowledge of the raw materials involved if full advantage is to be taken of their individual and distinctive characteristics. In addition, the blender is very much concerned with the production of a yarn not only with the requisite characteristics, but at a price consistent with the use to which it is to be put.

The actual process of blending is concerned primarily with the efficient mixing of the various lots which go to make a yarn, and it is of the utmost importance that the different lots used should be mixed as intimately as possible so that the resultant yarn may react uniformly to every subsequent process. Ideally, every fibre of a blend should be of the same length and diameter, but the variable nature of animal fibres will always preclude the possibility of such an ideal being attained. However, it is generally believed that the nearer the fibres approach to this state of affairs the more uniform will be the subsequent yarn.

Secondary objects of this process of blending are (*i*) the cleaning of the fibres by a dusting process as they pass through the machinery, although it is better to dust each lot prior to the blending process, (*ii*) a partial opening of the fibres by the fearnought to assist the card in the subsequent mixing process and to lengthen the life of the card clothing, and (*iii*) the application of a lubricant to minimize fibre breakage in carding and to assist fibre movement in spinning.

Alternative systems of blending, such as the continuous method and the batch system, are available, the first being more suitable for large blends and particularly for the blending of coarse fibres for blanket, carpet and rug-wool yarns. The second is a safer system where the mixing of colours and/or qualities is important. In general, the machinery used in a blending room consists of a teaser and a fearnought, though some mills prefer a wool plucker to the teaser.

BATCH BLENDING

In batch blending the materials comprising the blend are weighed into bales which are grouped round a suction trap in a duct which is coupled to a special fan designed to handle fibrous material without clogging. Materials are fed into the trap in proportion to the weights of materials in the blend. The usual method is to adopt a double-handful as the unit. Thus for a blend made up of 1,500 lb. of white wool, 1,000 lb., of dyed wool and 500 lb. of nylon, three double-handfuls of the white wool would be followed by two of the dyed wool and one of the nylon, the sequence being continued until all the material had been fed into the trap. By means of ducting the material is fed to a teaser, or wool plucker, which opens the material to some extent, removes loose dust and dirt, and performs a small amount of mixing. From the machine used, a second fan blows the material along further ducting to a blending bin. This bin is fitted with a rotary spreader, operated by the flow of air from the conveyor fan, and in consequence, the material is spread evenly over the floor of the bin.

After all the blend has been fed into the bin an operative enters, opens a trap-door at the bottom of the bin and, striking down the pile vertically, pushes the material into the ducting, through which it is conveyed either to a second bin to give a further degree of mixing or, if this is not required, to a fearnought which further opens the material. From this machine the material passes through an oiling chamber where atomized oil is applied under pressure to the air-borne fibres, and then either to a sheeting-up machine or to bins in the card room for storage. As the blend is pulled down other traps are opened so as to avoid the need for moving the material across the floor.

If the materials to be used in making up a blend contain a large amount of dust, sand or lime, they should be given a dusting prior to blending by passing them through an opening machine fitted with a cyclone dust extractor. Where it is necessary to mix a very small proportion of one colour with a large proportion of another, as, for example, when $2\frac{1}{2}$ per cent of white is to be mixed with $97\frac{1}{2}$ per cent of black, then a preliminary mixing or 'melling' should be made, using all the white with 20 per cent of the black and then using this mixture as one constituent of the blend.

Compared with the old system of blending when no blending bins or oiling machines were available, the present method has the advantage of giving a much higher rate of production with a smaller number of operatives and a reduction in the manual labour involved. Another advantage is that the oil is only applied after the material has passed through the opening machines, and these therefore remain clean, while the fact that the fibres are not oiled at an early stage enables dust to be removed much more freely throughout the process. In consequence, less fettling of the cards is required. The oil is also applied to the fibres more evenly and economically.

WOOL OILING

Reference has been made in preceding paragraphs to the addition of oil at some stage of the blending process. The object of oiling is to minimize fibre breakage, to reduce fly in carding, and to assist the spinning process by providing a lubricant to facilitate fibre movement. Originally oil was added by hand as the pile was being built up, usually by means of a large can with a T-shaped spout. Alternatively, mechanical means could be applied, one method being to employ a spray to add oil to the pile at six-inch intervals, as when using the oil-can, or a spraying mechanism could be placed over the feed-sheet of the fearnought. The most modern method, now widely used, is to pass the opened and dusted wool through a spray of oils as in the Spenstead-Vortex wool oiling system.

Textile oils may be classified under such headings as (*i*) fatty oils (e.g. olive oil and arachis oil) (*ii*) oleines (i.e. fatty acids), (*iii*) blends of fatty oils and oleines, known commercially as blended oils, (*iv*) modified mineral oils, and (*v*) recovered oils.

Oleines are widely used for oiling wool to be processed on the woollen system. For the best quality materials the oleine consists almost entirely of free fatty acids but in the lower trades wool oleines often contain considerable amounts of mineral oil. Recovered oils which contain considerable amounts of mineral oil are used primarily to facilitate rag pulling, but they also find application in oiling low woollen blends of recovered fibres. It is, however, false economy to use very low-grade oils as they give rise to difficulties in the finishing processes.

The widespread use of man-made fibres has increased the demand for special lubricants and there are available today both oilless lubricants and antistatic substances for incorporation in the oils used. There has also been considerable development in the production of detergents and this has made possible a wider use of mineral oils.

Oilless lubricants such as 'Frescolene' are synthetically produced liquids with lubricating properties. They are soluble in water and therefore provide economies in scouring. However, while the lubricant may be removed by water alone, or in a dyebath, it is usually found advisable to give a very mild scour to remove any soiling which has occurred during processing. These lubricants have been found to be particularly suitable for use with acrylic fibres, and they are used extensively by carpet yarn spinners on blends of synthetic or regenerated fibres. In this case the amount of lubricant is much less than would be used with a normal wool-oil, e.g. two to four per cent on the weight of the blend.

Oil may be applied directly to the wool, this being known as 'dry or straight oiling', or it may be applied as an emulsion, the oil being mixed with water in the presence of some substance capable of maintaining a stable emulsion, usually an ammonium salt. Oleine is now provided by the different makers as "emulsifiable oleine", which forms a perfectly stable emulsion or wool cream on the addition of water. The advantages of emulsion oiling lie in the fact that the same amount of oil is spread over twice the area (in the case of a 50/50 emulsion), while the yarn produced by this method is stronger than that produced by the straight method. Finally, the use of emulsions is particularly suited to modern methods of quick processing. The chief points to note when considering the suitability of an oil are as follows:

Viscosity: The oil must be thick enough to coat the fibres and yet not too thick or it will assume the condition of a grease; on the other hand, too thin an oil will run from the blend during storage.

Oxidation: Most animal and vegetable oils oxidize, some at a greater rate than others. If the oil is an unsaturated compound, it will take up oxygen at a greater rate than if it were more saturated. Oils are on this account termed drying, semi-drying and non-drying oils, examples of these types being linseed oil, cotton seed oil, and olive oil, respectively. Only the non-drying oils should be used, as oils with any tendency to oxidize are apt to produce a film-like skin on the fibres which resists removal and discolours the wool. In addition, they may cause difficulties in carding and spinning, and increase the fire risk.

Ease of Removal: It is essential that the added oil be easily removable from the yarn or cloth. Oleines with a high percentage of free fatty acids are converted into a soap by the addition of an alkali and so scour themselves from the cloth. Consequently the use of these is widespread. The use of mineral oils which possess the properties required in a wool lubricant has become a practical proposition in recent years, owing to the development of detergents capable of removing them satisfactorily, but careful control is required.

Flash Point: Insurance companies require a minimum flash point of 340°F. (open test).

Effect on Metals: Oleine has little effect on iron which is the chief metal with which the oil will come in contact in the carding and spinning processes. The corrosive action of fatty acids decreases rapidly when these are mixed with neutral oils.

The amounts of oil or emulsion added to different types of blend vary. A general figure for the pure wool trade is about 8-10 per cent oil or 16-20 per cent emulsion (50/50 oil and water). This has been shown to give stronger yarns and less fibre breakage than other quantities[1]. It has been stated that 36 per cent of a 50/50 emulsion is used for the shorter wools on the Continent. As much as 25 per cent of a recovered oil may be added in the pulling of rags.

WOOLLEN CARDING

WOOLLEN CARDING might be defined as an opening or disentangling and mixing process, insofar as the fibres forming the locks or pieces of waste making up the blend must be separated fibre from fibre in order that they may be intimately mixed. The blended fibres emerge from the machine as a thin web equal in width to that of the machine. This web is then divided into a series of narrow strips, which are passed through a pair of reciprocating aprons, made either of leather or some synthetic material, which convert them into round twistless slubbings, known as condensed slubbings. It is of the utmost importance that the web, before being split up, should be as uniform as possible with regard to the disposition of the fibres and the weight both across and along the web. The former requirement ensures uniform appearance and behaviour of the spun yarn, and the latter, uniform count.

It will be apparent from the above that woollen carding is an operation of primary importance, not only because it is responsible for the change-over from a discontinuous lock order to continuous slubbings, but because, any fault or irregularity in the condensed slubbing will persist into the spun yarn, and may even cause serious visible defects in many types of fabric subsequently produced from such yarns.

A carding machine consists of a number of units or swift parts, each consisting of a series of rollers, viz; swift, doffer, fancy, angle stripper and a number of pairs of workers and strippers, the number varying from three to seven pairs according to the class of trade in which the machine is engaged. Each roller is covered with card clothing and the action between any two rollers is dependent on the direction in which the card teeth point, the direction of rotation, and the relative surface speeds of the rollers. The number of swift parts going to make up a machine and the manner in which they are arranged, i.e. whether the machine is of two or three parts, is dependent on the type of machine and on the class of trade for which it was intended when installed.

To ensure better mixing and to produce a more uniform web, the card is always divided into at least two and sometimes into three parts. In a two-part machine these are the scribbler and the carder, while in a three-part machine, there is an intermediate between the scribbler and the carder. Some idea of the units used in the various trades may be gained from Table

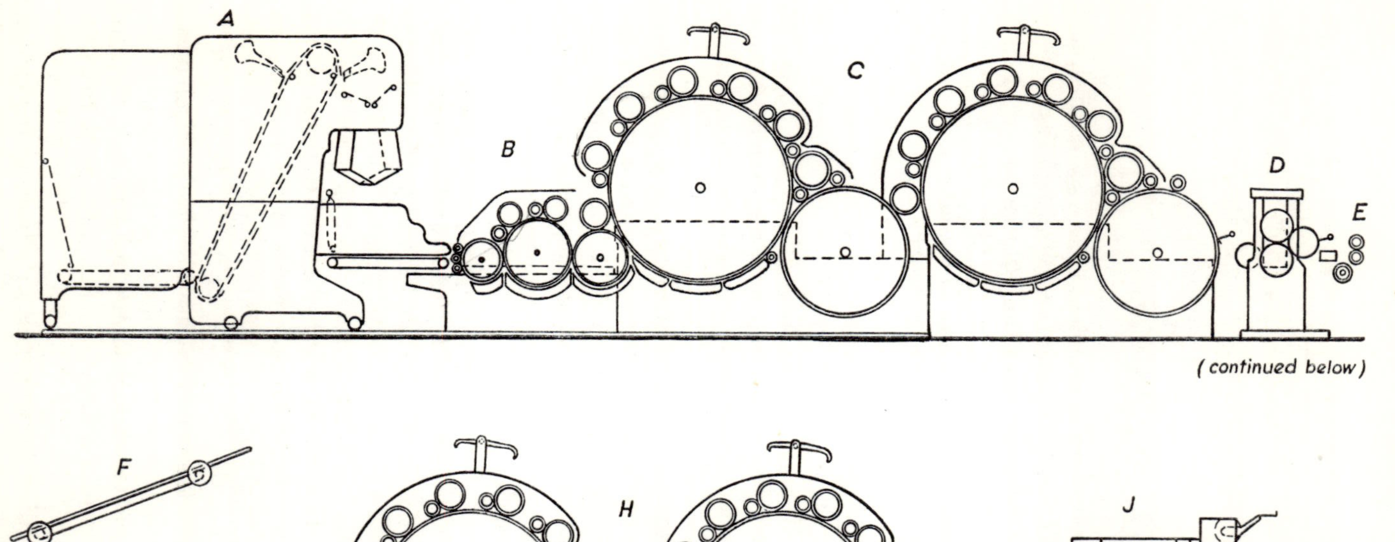

FIG. 5.2.   TATHAM SEMI-CONTINENTAL CARD SET

A—Single automatic hopper feed: *B*—Breast section: *C*—Two-part breaker or scribbler card: *D*—Crosrol web purifier: *E*—Centre draw: *F*—Overhead conveying lattices: *G*—Scotch feed: *H*—Two-part finisher or carder part: and *J*—Four-height tape condenser.

By courtesy of William Tatham Ltd., Rochdale

5.1. The first unit in any set is preceded by an automatic feeding arrangement together with feed rollers and licker-in, the latter roller passing the material forward to the swift through the action of the angle stripper, while the last doffer of the carder is always followed by a condenser to divide up the web.

TABLE 5.1. CARDING UNITS FOR VARIOUS TRADES.

Class of Trade	Scribbler	Intermediate	Carder	Con-denser
Blanket and carpet yarns	3 swifts. 4 workers per swift	—	2 swifts. 4 workers per swift	Double doffer or tape
Scotch tweed	Breast and 2 swifts. 4 workers per swift	1 swift. 4 workers per swift	2 swifts. 4 workers per swift	Tape
Flannels and medium tweeds	3 swifts. 4 workers per swift	—	2 swifts. 4 workers per swift	Tape
Mungo and shoddy	4 swifts. 4 workers per swift	—	2 swifts. 4 workers per swift	Tape
Fine and medium wools (British system)	Breast and 2 swifts. 4 workers per swift	1 swift. 4 workers per swift	2 swifts. 4 workers per swift	Tape
Fine and medium wools (Continental system)	Breast and 1 swift. 6 workers per swift	1 swift. 6 workers per swift	1 swift. 6 workers per swift	Tape
Fine and medium wools (American system)	Breast and 2 swifts. 7 workers per swift	—	2 swifts. 7 workers per swift	Tape

The modern trend is to install the semi-Continental type of set which consists of a scribbler containing a garnett breast and two swift parts, an intermediate feed, and a two-part carder followed by a tape condenser (see Fig. 5.2).

INCLINATION OF CARD TEETH

The direction of inclination of the card teeth of the various rollers is shown in Fig. 5.3. The carding actions can be summarized under three headings: (a) working or point-to-point action as between swift and worker; (b) stripping or point-to-back action as between stripper and worker and swift and stripper; and (c) raising or back-to-back action as between fancy and swift. The relative direction of the teeth, combined with the surface speed of the rollers at their points of action, the space between the rollers and the condition of the teeth largely determine the efficiency of carding.

The separation of locks of wool or other fibre agglomerations into individual fibres is effected as they are split up at the worker-swift area of co-operation. As a lock approaches the first worker, the leading end of the top portion of the lock is arrested by the teeth of the worker; the remainder of the lock is then carried forward by the high speed swift through the setting gap, until the back end is carried forward to become the leading end. Fibres which have become firmly hooked on to the teeth of the worker are combed by the action of the teeth of the swift while any loose fibres are drawn back on to the swift. The lower portion of the lock which does not become held

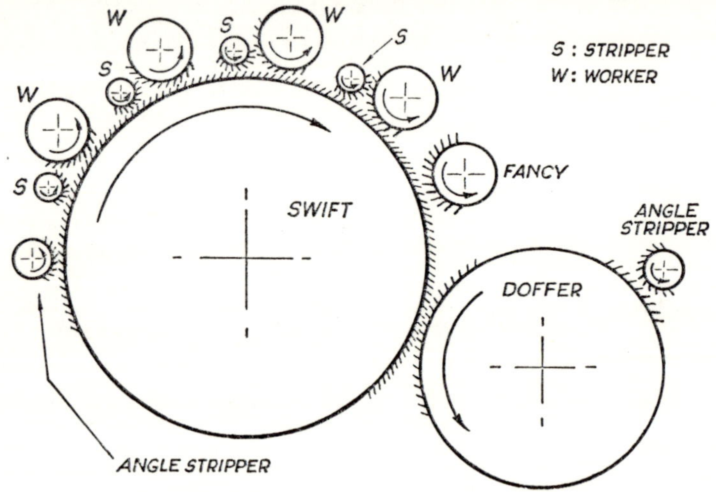

FIG 5.3. DRAWING ILLUSTRATING THE INCLINATION
OF TEETH ON THE VARIOUS CARDING ROLLERS

by the worker tends to be forced down into the teeth of the swift, and does not receive any further treatment until it has been raised to the surface by the action of the fancy. The portion retained by the worker is eventually replaced on the swift to be mixed with new material being brought forward. This splitting of the locks and the combing action is the most essential action in carding, for until the locks are separated into fibres, mixing to the required degree is impossible.

Mixing also results from the placing of the material from the swift on to the doffer. According to the speed of the swift and the lower speed of the doffer, material from 10 to 30 inches of swift may be placed on to one inch of doffer surface.

CARD CLOTHING

Card clothing is the covering with which the various rollers are wrapped. There are two classes, sheet and fillet. The former has a leather foundation and is made in sheets about five inches deep, its width corresponding to that of the roller to be covered. These sheets are nailed around the surface of the roller. Fillet consists of an endless length of cotton webbing, varying in width from half-inch to three inches, depending on the diameter of the roller to be covered, and is wrapped in spiral form around the roller. The webbing is made up by cementing several (usually three to seven) layers of cloth together, while the top of the cloth is often covered by a layer of vulcanized rubber to prevent the oil added to woollen blends acting as a solvent on the rubber solution used to cement the various layers together.

Other types of fillet have a thin or thick layer of felt, or a rubber composition, on top of the cloth to give more support to the teeth; these types are commonly used on semi-Continental and Continental types of machines. Although sheet cards had certain advantages over fillet, their use is gradually declining and even the blanket and carpet trades are now going over extensively to the use of fillet.

Card teeth are made in the form of staples, each carrying two points. They are inserted from the back of the card at a definite angle of back-prick and then, after insertion in the foundation, are given a definite angle of forward inclination, thus forming the knee of the tooth. The angles of back prick and bend are varied according to the function of the roller for which the fillet is intended and its position in the machine. The length of cut of the wire, i.e. the total length of the staple, varies in like manner.

The card teeth are arranged in the foundation in various orders; plain, double rib, treble rib and twill. The plain order is used almost exclusively for sheets and the rib setting for fillet, while double rib is used for coarse cards, and treble for fine. Twill setting in various forms is generally used for the fancy rollers, the setting being such as to minimize marking or uneven wear of the teeth on the swifts.

Card clothing dimensions are given by the count, crown and gauge of wire. The count is the number of staples in any one line of five inches down the length of the fillet or down the sheet card. Crown is the number of staples measured across the card or fillet in one inch in one repeat of the design. Gauge is the thickness of the wire by the Imperial standard wire gauge. The points per square inch of a card can be obtained by multiplying one-fifth the counts by double the crown, e.g. the number of points per square inch in a 100/10 card would be 20 x 20, i.e. 400. Typical card clothing dimensions for processing fine and coarse wools are given in Table 5.2.

Card teeth are made from hardened and tempered steel wire. Tinned wire is commonly used in worsted carding where the wool is carded damp, but not in woollen carding.

For the breast part of Continental and semi-Continental machines, where the usual arrangement is a breast cylinder 24 inches in diameter, two pairs of workers and strippers, and a transfer roller to carry the material

TABLE 5.2. CARD CLOTHING DIMENSIONS FOR FINE AND COARSE WOOLS.

	Fine Wool				Coarse Wool		
	Count	Crown	Gauge	..	Count	Crown	Gauge
SCRIBBLER:							
Feed Rollers	Garnett				12's needle point		
Licker	,,			..	,,		
Angle Stripper	60	6	24	..	40	4	20
Breast	80	8	27	..	50	5	22
,, Workers	85	8	27	..	55	5	24
,, Strippers	70	6	26	..	40	4	22
,, Fancy	60	6	27	..	40	4	22
Fancy Stripper	110	10	33	..	—	—	—
Breast Doffer	80	8	27	..	55	5	24
Angle Stripper	70	6	26	..	40	4	22
First Swift	110	10	31	..	80	8	26
,, ,, Workers	115	11	30	..	85	8	28
,, ,, Strippers	80	8	28	..	60	6	26
,, ,, Fancy	65	6	29	..	50	5	26
,, ,, Doffer	115	$10\frac{1}{2}$	30	..	85	8	28
Fancy Stripper	110	10	33	..	—	—	—
Angle Stripper	80	8	28	..	60	6	26
Second Swift	120	10	32	..	110	10	32
,, ,, Workers	125	10	31	..	115	11	33
,, ,, Strippers	90	9	31	..	80	8	30
,, ,, Fancy	70	7	32	..	60	6	30
,, ,, Doffer	110	$10\frac{1}{2}$	32	..	115	10	32
Fancy Stripper	110	10	33	..	—	—	—
INTERMEDIATE							
Feed Rollers	18's needle point						
Licker	12 x 24 Diamond wire						
Angle Stripper	80	8	28				
Swift	125	10	32				
,, Workers	130	11	31				
,, Strippers	90	9	31				
,, Fancy	80	8	34				
,, Doffers	130	$10\frac{1}{2}$	32				
Fancy Stripper	110	10	33				
CARDER							
Feed Rollers	Garnett.			..	14's needle point		
Licker	,,			..	,,		
Tummer	80	8	20	..	70	7	26
,, Worker	100	9	32	..	90	9	28
First Swift	130	11	34	..	110	10	32
,, ,, Workers	135	12	35	..	115	11	33
,, ,, Strippers	100	9	32	..	80	8	30
,, ,, Fancy	80	8	34	..	60	6	30
,, ,, Doffer	130	$10\frac{1}{2}$	32	..	115	10	32
Fancy Stripper	110	10	33	..	110	10	32
Angle Stripper	95	9	33	..	80	8	30
Second Swift	140	12	34	..	120	10	32
,, ,, Workers	145	12	35	..	125	11	33
, ,, Strippers	110	9	32	..	85	8	30
,, ,, Fancy	80	8	34	..	70	7	32
,, ,, Doffer (Tape)	140	12	34	..	—	—	—
Fancy Stripper	110	10	33	..	110	10	32
Stripping Motion	120	10	32	..	80	8	30
Top Ring Doffer (Rings $\frac{7}{8}$ inch wide)	..	..	..	..	120	11	33
Bottom Ring Doffer (Rings 1 inch wide)	..	..	..	..	120	11	33

from the breast to the following cylinder, metallic wire is frequently used. This form of wire has no separate foundation, the teeth being cut or punched from a strip of steel to give the required shape and size. Its advantages lie in its rigidity and the sharpness of its points. Disadvantages are that on woollen blends it tends to grease up rather quickly and is more difficult to fettle than fillet clothing.

On the English type of card in which the breast cylinder is usually 50-54 inches in diameter, the breast part is commonly clothed with diamond point wire. This wire has a specially hardened point and the teeth are cut to the required shape and not ground. To give this type of clothing sufficient strength to withstand the strains imposed on it by the relatively unopened material the wire is of much heavier gauge from front to back than from side to side, thus making it possible to have a very firm card which is not too full of wire.

During the past two or three years considerable developments have been made in the production of both flexible and metallic wire, in the former type by the extended use of glass-hardened points and in the latter by making teeth with much narrower tolerances and with more highly hardened points. From experience in cotton carding, where metallic wire is almost completely replacing flexible wire, it would appear that there is room for a larger application of the former in the woollen trade.

SETTING THE CARDS

Setting, i.e. the adjustment of the rollers to each other, is extremely important and must be carried out meticulously, if the best carding results are to be obtained. It has a threefold object: firstly, to ensure that the machine cards the material as efficiently as possible; secondly, to distribute the wool over the whole width of the machine[2]; and thirdly, to keep a sharp point on the teeth of the swift, doffer and worker, and, at the same time, to retain a smooth surface on the rollers. All these objectives are equally important. It is essential that the rollers be true, or close setting becomes impractical and does more harm than good, in that it removes the point from the card teeth. For this reason, practically all new machines now have iron swifts and doffers and aluminium workers.

Setting is accomplished with the aid of steel gauges, about a foot in length, two inches broad, and varying in thickness with the gauge number (the imperial standard wire gauge) the ones used normally being from 20 to 36 gauge. The actual setting of any roller is determined by (a) the type of material being carded, the general rule being that fine short materials require closer setting than do longer and coarser fibres, (b) the condition of the card wire, for where this has a really good point it is not necessary to set as close as that required where the point is not so good, and (c) the function of the roller and its position in the machine, setting being progressive through the machine. Thus, while a worker on the breast part may be set with a 24 or 26 gauge, one on the last part of the carder, working on the same material, would probably be set with a 30 or 32 gauge.

Progressive setting on the same swift part may also be practised to try to distribute the work of carding uniformly over all the workers. The practice of using the same gauge and setting 'easy', 'medium', and 'tight' is not to be recommended; the only correct setting between two rollers is when there is just the thickness of the gauge between them. The card wires being flexible, setting needs to be done very carefully. The gauge must be moved both across the machine and against the points of both rollers. This will enable any tendency for the teeth to rise in working to be detected. Rollers are rarely, if ever, perfectly true and setting must therefore always be carried out at the point where the rollers being set are closest to each other.

All rollers, with the exception of the fancy, are set to the swift to a gauge. The fancy has to be so set that its teeth enter those of the swift, so that in combination with its higher surface speed the fibres embedded in the swift teeth are raised to the surface. It is also common practice in some districts for the workers to be set to touch the strippers, the setting being made by ear. The advantage of this is that not only are the workers kept clean for a longer period, but the point is kept on the teeth with no necessity for regular regrinding.

In setting it is important that the bearings of the workers and strippers are free from fly and dirt. Although modern sleeve bearings obviate this difficulty, this factor should nevertheless be stressed, for it is obviously futile to set two rollers with a 30's gauge, (i.e. one-eightieth of an inch) if there is a layer of fly between the shaft and the bearing. The stripper belt should always be kept on the pulleys when the strippers are being set. Finally, the settings must be checked at both sides of the machine and, when the machine is started, both ears and eyes must be used to check that no worker, stripper or doffer is touching the swift.

CARDING SPEEDS

Speed in carding is always referred to that of the main cylinder of the machine. Table 5.3 lists the swift speeds commonly found in the various classes of trade, but swift speed is meaningless unless it is related to the diameter of the roller, or expressed as a surface speed.

Although the speeds given in Table 5.3 are those which are commonly used, many variations are possible. The speed at which the swifts run is, in fact, determined by two factors, namely the type of material to be processed, and the type of machine employed. High surface speeds are an advantage in that the layer of fibres on the swifts is kept thin, and the carding action in more intense, but while these factors have an effect on the rate of production which it is possible to obtain, they are not the most important. The speed at which the doffers are run can have a far greater effect in this respect.

TABLE 5.3.

SWIFT DIAMETERS AND SPEEDS FOR VARIOUS SECTIONS OF THE WOOLLEN INDUSTRY

| | Swift | |
Class of Trade	Diameter	Speed
Blanket and carpet yarns	54 in. ..	70 r.p.m.
Scotch tweeds and hosiery yarns	50 in. ..	80 r.p.m.
Flannels, medium tweeds	50 in. ..	70-75 r.p.m.
Low woollens	50 in. ..	65-75 r.p.m.
Fine and medium wools (semi-Continental) ..	50 in. ..	80-120 r.p.m.
Fine and medium wools (Continental)	50 in. ..	100-140 r.p.m.
Short and medium wools (U.S.A.)	50 in. ..	65 r.p.m.

As a general rule, Continental and semi-Continental types of machine which have covers over the fancies, side plates to cover the ends of the rollers, and which may be fitted with undergrids, are run at higher speeds than are the older type of set which has neither covers nor undergrids. For materials, however, which are difficult to control, which tend to fly excessively, or which are likely to drop out under the card, a relatively low swift speed is generally used. Long-fibred coarse wools, smooth man-made fibres and some of the exceedingly short-fibred recovered wastes fall into the above category. It must be observed that high swift speeds do not necessarily cause more fibre breakage than low ones[3].

All other rollers are driven directly or indirectly from the swifts. On any one machine the speed of the strippers and angle-strippers is constant while the speed of the workers, doffers and fancies can be varied to suit the needs of different materials and rates of production. While the range of speeds of the workers and doffers may vary in different classes of trade, a range giving speeds of from 3 r.p.m. to 12 r.p.m. is common. The surface speed of the fancy must be higher than that of the swift or the fibres will not be raised to the surface, the doffer will be unable to receive them, the swift wires will become choked, and carding becomes impossible. It should be possible to have a fancy surface speed from 5 per cent to 40 per cent higher than that of the swift, the usual range employed being between 15 and 30 per cent.

On modern cards the workers are driven from the swifts instead of from the doffers so that their speed, and even their direction of rotation may be varied independently of the doffer. Similarly, the fancy is driven from the swift usually by a combination of chain and gears and not, as on older machines by a belt which also drives the strippers. This makes it possible to run the strippers at a lower speed, approximately at 200 r.p.m. instead of 300 r.p.m.

Speed cannot be isolated from setting, but there is no doubt that the speeds of the various rollers influence the efficiency of the machine as a whole. At one time it was thought that low worker and doffer speeds were essential in order to give the maximum difference in speed between themselves and the swift and thereby maximum working power. It is now generally accepted, however, that higher speeds give better results, more free teeth being presented to the swift[4] to give better mixing in the case of the worker, and better clearance of the swift in the case of the doffer.

AUTOMATIC FEEDING

All carding machines are fed with the aid of an automatic feed. This consists of a hopper, i.e. a receptacle for the wool, in which an endless spiked apron grasps the staples and carries them over the top, where they are stripped from the apron and allowed to drop into a scale pan, and weighed. As soon as the required weight is in the pan the apron is automatically stopped. A timing mechanism operates at fixed intervals to release the wool on to the scribbler feed sheet on which it passes forward to the feed rollers.

The chief requirements of any automatic feed are (*i*) that it shall distribute the wool uniformly over the breadth of the feed sheet, (*ii*) that there shall be no variation between any two weighs, (*iii*) that there shall be no sorting of the fibres of the blend in the hopper, (*iv*) that it shall be capable of repeating the same performance under like conditions, and (*v*) that it shall be as simple, mechanically, as possible.

The chief problem arising in automatic feeding is that of obtaining identical successive weighs, the difficulty being due to the fibrous nature of the wool and the time lag which occurs between the pan getting the weigh and the trap door, which prevents any further entry of the wool, being closed. The entry must be fairly wide because of the bulky nature of the wool and the time factor involved between successive tipples. Other problems are the uniform distribution of the wool across the pan, this being dependent on the setting of the beater comb in the hopper, and the difficulty in ensuring that the hopper is always filled to the same level.

The problem of the hopper continually emptying is an ever-present one. A certain minimum amount of wool must be present in the hopper if the pan is to receive its weigh in the appointed time determined by the tippling gear. However, the weight of material fed into the scale pan can vary considerably according to the amount in the hopper. The most accurate weigh is obtained when there is just sufficient material present to allow the weigh to be obtained in time. When the hopper is full, more material is carried by the spiked lattice and however carefully the beater comb and the weighing mechanism are set, heavier weighs will be obtained.

This serious problem can now be avoided by the use of the double-hopper. Material is fed into the first of the two hoppers in the normal manner either by hand, or automatically where this system operates, but instead of feeding to a scale pan this first hopper feeds into the second one which conveys the material to the weigh pan in the normal manner. Accurate weighing is maintained because the mechanism is so arranged that the amount of material in the second hopper is kept constant. Although this type of hopper was introduced in the first place for machines working on materials for carpet yarns, it is proving an advantage in the processing of all types of materials.

It is also important that each weigh be laid over the same area of the sheet and that the wool on the sheet shall be uniformly spread over the whole area. From this, it follows that each new weigh shall join up with the previous one.

There are three methods in common use of depositing the wool on the feed sheet; one uses a revolving scale pan, another has a pan which revolves through a half turn and then reverts to its original position, while in the third the bottom of the pan is released to allow the material to drop on to the sheet.

In recent years all carding machine makers have paid considerable attention to improving the sensitivity of the hopper, and this along with the introduction of the double-hopper, has been responsible for a marked improvement in the accuracy with which wool is fed to the card.

Improvements to the scale-pan mechanism include an electrical control system whereby the slightest downward movement of the pan completes a circuit which stops the apron and beater. The pan bottom has been divorced from the sides and ends so that the actual scale is much lighter and therefore more sensitive. Self-centring pans are now used which ensures that the weight of the pan and the wool shall always be acting at the same distance from the fulcrum.

However accurate the mechanism, there are certain points which must be observed if accurate weighing is to be maintained. For example, it is important that the material being fed should have a constant oil and moisture content, otherwise variations will inevitably occur in the condensed slubbing. The beater comb and stripping brush must be accurately set, and care must be taken to see that all knife edges supporting the scale pan are kept clean and in good condition. If a double-hopper is not being used, every effort must be made to keep the amount of material in the hopper as near constant as possible by feeding regularly in small amounts at a time.

INTERMEDIATE FEEDS

The intermediate feed is a mechanism for transporting the material from one section of the machine to the next, e.g. scribbler to intermediate or carder. The mechanism is introduced into the carding machine (*a*) to ensure a level feed to the following part of the machine by reducing any irregularities brought about either by the hopper or by the card itself, *e.g.*, draughts at the fancies, and (*b*) to increase the mixing power of the card. In this respect it should be pointed out that, without such an arrangement there would be no mixing across the card and any unevenenss in shade or quality present after blending would be carried through to the slubbing. The use of an intermediate feed also enables an inspection of the sliver to be made at a stage where it is possible to assess the efficiency of the scribbler. The ideal intermediate feed should have both a high mixing and high levelling capacity, continuity, be simple mechanically, occupy a small amount of floor space and make as little waste as possible.

Feeds may be classified as cross or straight fibre, according to the direction in which they lay the fibres on the feed of the following part of the machine, cross-fibre feeds being those which lay the fibres pointing across the machine, while straight-fibre feeds lay them pointing in the lengthwise direction. This question of direction is not a matter for serious concern, as the action between the first worker of the carder or intermediate is to lay the fibres once again in the direction of the length of the machine.

Types of intermediate feed available include (*i*) the Scotch feed with either side or centre draw arrangement, (*ii*) the continuous parallel-fibre feed, (*iii*) the ball and bank, (*iv*) the Blamire, and (*v*) lap drum and lap former types.

The Scotch feed is the most widely used type in this country. It is simple and adaptable but is somewhat deficient in mixing and doubling power. Therefore, for the shorter Continental and semi-Continental types of machine the straight-fibre continuous-feed is sometimes preferred. This feed has considerable mixing and doubling capacity, but is much more complicated than the Scotch feed and, therefore, requires more maintenance. The ball and bank feed is still widely used in the tweed trade in Scotland though it is rarely made today. This feed has excellent mixing and doubling powers, but must never be used as the only intermediate feed on a machine. The most usual arrangement is to have this type between scribbler and intermediate, and a Scotch feed between intermediate and carder, though in some instances two ball and bank feeds are used, in which case the number of balls in the bank equals the number of rings on the single ring doffer.

The Blamire feed was formerly used in the low woollen trade, particularly in the Morley district, where it was difficult, with the very short fibres employed, to make a cohesive sliver for the Scotch feed which would be able to withstand the strains involved in travelling from the calender rolls to the overhead lattice. Today this feed is used principally in the making of laps on cards used in the manufacture of pressed felts and has been superseded in the low woollen trade by Scotch feeds of improved design and construction.

The lap drum and lap former types of feed are used mainly on the Continent. With the former the sliver from the scribbler back doffer is gathered round a drum which extends the full width of the machine and which has a circumference equal to the width of the intermediate part. When a predetermined number of revolutions of the drum have been made, the lap is broken and laid across the feed of the intermediate at right angles to the direction in which it left the scribbler. A number of laps may be used on top of each other. The lap former is used on the intermediate part of the machine, and with this, the sliver, instead of being wrapped round a roller, is carried round a 36-foot length of felt carried on suitably mounted rollers. When a predetermined number of layers have been obtained, the lap is wound on to a roller and placed on the feed of the carder. These feeds have very good mixing and levelling powers, but as they require more labour than the continuous types, their use is declining.

CONDENSING

The purpose of the condenser is to convert the web of fibres lying on the back swift of the carder into a series of soft twistless threads or slubbings suitably wound on to condenser bobbins for the spinning process. Condensers can be divided into two classes, ring and tape, the former including single and double-ring doffers, while the latter includes the series, endless or single tape condensers. A third type, the Bolette steel tape may still be found on old machines on the Continent, particularly in Belgium.

In most classes of trade, tape condensers have now replaced the ring doffer type, largely because of their greater versatility, and productive capacity. Exceptions to this are found where freedom from excessive variation in count of the slubbing and yarn is imperative as in the production of single hosiery yarns. In such cases the single-ring doffer is preferred, while certain carpet yarn spinners still use the double doffer although the general preference now is for the tape condenser. With the single-ring doffer every slubbing receives exactly the same treatment. The division of the web by means of rings on the doffer involves no cutting or tearing of the web, and therefore the slubbings produced are as uniform as can be produced from the web presented to the doffer.

While the modern tape condenser is a far better machine than earlier models and produces more regular slubbings, there is still more risk of count variation than with the single-ring doffer because of the difficulty of maintaining absolutely uniform tension between the different tapes. A tight tape always tends to take more material than an adjacent slack one, and so produces a heavier count. With modern condensers this risk has been reduced, because the tapes are driven so that their tight side is employed to split the web whereas formerly the division was made by the slack side. If on the series type a uniform tension is not maintained between the different banks of tapes there will be a variation between the different condenser bobbins. While it is generally claimed that the endless or single-tape machine produces more uniform slubbings than does the series type, improvements effected in the latter have considerably reduced this difference in uniformity. In considering the use of the endless type, account should be taken of the length of tape employed – up to 1,100 feet – and of the greater difficulty in rethreading which this presents.

The tape condenser has many advantages over the single-ring doffer. For example, because it is possible to use narrow tapes and to take as many as 180 threads from a 60-inch wide machine, finer counts can be produced. Also, the much greater rubbing power permits of a much higher rate of production. Today, the tape condenser is by far the commonest type in use. The four-height machine, usually producing about 100 good threads is the general utility machine of the trade, being able to deal with a wider range of material and counts than can either of the ring types of condenser. For fine counts, the most suitable condenser is a six-height machine producing from 150 to 180 threads, according to the width of card and the counts to be produced. The single-ring doffer is the most suitable condenser for a limited type of yarn and a limited range of counts but it is lacking in rubbing power and cannot process long fibres very successfully. The double doffer has the disadvantage that the top doffer tends to take more than its share of the longer fibres in the blend and, when this machine is used in the low woollen trade, the bobbins produced from the two doffers are always spun separately.

IRREGULARITIES IN CONDENSED SLUBBINGS

All woollen slubbings, and therefore yarns, vary in count to some degree, the degree of irregularity which can be tolerated depending on the use for which the yarn is intended [5,6]. In attempting to minimize this irregularity, it is first necessary to determine the type of variation, *e.g.*, does it occur across the card or along the length of the slubbing. Variations across the card may be caused by (*i*) draughts which displace fibres, particularly those connected with the fancy, and also to some extent the swift, (*ii*) irregular distribution of the wool by the intermediate feed, (*iii*) the irregular setting of one roller to another, particularly the back doffer of the carder, (*iv*) variation of tension in the tapes of a tape condenser; and finally, (*v*) badly clothed rollers. Variations along the length of the slubbings may be due to (*i*) irregular weighings by the hoppers (*ii*) variations in moisture content of the blend, (*iii*) irregular distribution of fibres on the feed sheet of either scribbler or carder, (*iv*) slipping of driving belts or to incorrectly set gears, (*v*) badly clothed rollers: or to, (*vi*) incorrect speeding of rollers, especially in the case of workers having a jerky movement, or strippers having too great a surface speed. Another variation is where one bank of bobbins is heavier than another due to a whole bank of tapes being tighter than another.

DEVELOPMENTS IN CONDENSERS

Among improvement made to condensers which will lead to increased production is the rubber drive capable of imparting up to 600 rubs per minute[7]. This is a particularly desirable feature at the present time when many fibres other than wool have to be processed. Other advances have been effected with the object of increasing the weight which can be wound on to a condenser bobbin, either by setting the surface drums out of centre[8] or by traversing the surface drums instead of the raddle. The most recent development, however, is one made necessary by the increased use of the spinning frame which requires larger cheeses to accommodate the wider pitch of the spindles. This has been brought about by the use of the traversing creel whereby the whole front of the condenser is made to traverse.

CRUSHING MECHANISMS

Most woollen cards are now equipped with either Peralta rollers or the Crosrol Web Purifier [9,10], the purpose of these mechanisms being to crush any vegetable impurities or pieces of skin present in wool, or hard threads in blends containing recovered materials. This is achieved by passing the web between metal rollers, chilled iron in the case of the Peralta and hardened steel with the Crosrol. The rollers of the Peralta are 12 inches in diameter, while those of the Crosrol are either 10 inches in the heavy model or six inches in the standard one, for it has been found that perfect contact between the rollers is more important than heavy pressure. Nevertheless, the larger rollers are still necessary where very large impurities are present in the wool and their use is recommended for blanket and carpet wools. Both mechanisms work on the principle that, as the impurities present in the web of material are thicker than the thin film of fibres forming the web, all the pressure of the rollers – applied to the top roller by a hydraulic system – will be exerted on the impurities, while the fibres are undamaged. To obtain the necessary conditions, the web must be kept as thin as possible, i.e. the doffer preceding the apparatus must run at the highest speed at which a satisfactory web can be produced. It is also essential that the material to be treated should have been thoroughly opened so that a uniform web is obtained. The most usual place, therefore, to apply the mechanism is at the end of the scribbler following the last doffer.

With these mechanisms skin and vegetable matter and hard cotton threads are disintegrated and all the skin bits and hard thread extracted in the further carding process. Most of the vegetable matter, burr, shive or seed, is also removed, but, though the substance of these is destroyed, it is impossible to guarantee their complete removal because of their nature. Worsted threads are softer than cotton threads and are not destroyed but flattened, and are teased out in the carder part of the machine. The use of these mechanisms therefore allows finer and stronger yarns to be produced.

There is also a marked improvement in processing, the number of broken ends in spinning, winding and weaving is substantially reduced and there is also a considerable saving in mending and burling (picking) costs. For many types of fabric the use of these mechanisms enables carbonizing to be completely eliminated, while very burry wools can be satisfactorily processed without carbonizing, if a light carbonizing is subsequently given to the cloth to remove any small remaining particles of vegetable matter.

PRODUCTION IN CARDING

Owing to the extensive range of materials processed on the woollen system and to the wide variety of yarns produced, production rates in carding vary considerably and it is therefore impossible to provide a table of production figures which would be applicable to the trade as a whole.

Because cards vary in width, the present trend being to make them wider than formerly, particularly for the coarse fibre section of the trade, production is now sometimes given in terms of pounds per inch width of card. While this may be useful to, say, the spinner of carpet yarns as a basis of comparison, it cannot be used as an indication as to what the production of a card should be, without very clear reference to the type of material being processed and the count of slubbing produced.

In the production of carpet and similar yarns production rates are high and it is claimed that new cards 100 inches in width, with double doffers either throughout the machine or to the last part of the carder, are capable of production rates of from 200 to 300 pounds per hour, or from two to three pounds per inch of width per hour. For yarns for suitings or for knitted fabrics, production per inch width rarely reaches $1\frac{1}{2}$ pounds per hour, and may, on certain types of machines be as low as 0.2 pounds per hour. An example of this is to be found in the production of a high-quality single hosiery yarn on a 60 inch card equipped with a single-ring doffer condenser, where the weight produced may be only 12 pounds per hour or 0.2 pounds per inch of width per hour.

In general, a card fitted with a four-height tape condenser producing slubbings between 10 and 20 Yorkshire skeins (195 to 96 tex) would have the nine-inch diameter surface drums revolving between 15 and 30 r.p.m. or in exceptional cases up to 40 r.p.m. At this latter speed the production rate for a 10-skein slubbing would be 1.26 pounds per inch width of the card per hour, while for the production of a 20-skein slubbing, it would only be 0.63 pounds per inch of width per hour.

In processing for medium and fine yarns, production rates in carding are governed by the types of materials from which the yarns are to be made, by the amount of carding and the degree of mixing necessary, and by the quality which is required, and this, of course, will vary according to the end-use of the yarn or the type of cloth to be made. With coarse fibre yarns for carpets and similar uses, the limiting factor is usually the rubbing capacity of the condenser.

To obtain maximum production irrespective of the type of blend, the following points must be observed: (*i*) The carding machine must be of a type suitable for the class of work: (*ii*) The card clothing must be of suitable type and density and maintained in first-class condition: (*iii*) The speeds of the various rollers, swifts, workers, doffers and fancies, and particularly the two latter rollers, must be correct; (*iv*) Settings must be made accurately to the appropriate gauge, and (*v*) the card must be maintained in good condition.

If a wide variety of materials are to be processed on the same card owing to trade or seasonal changes in demand, the modern system of driving the card by means of variable speed motors has an advantage in that the speed of the machine may be readily adjusted to that most suitable for the particular material being processed at any one time.

SEMI-WORSTED YARNS

A system of producing semi-worsted yarns has been adopted by a number of woollen spinners producing yarns for the carpet trade and particularly for the tufted carpet section. The process finds its widest use where man-made fibres are employed, although it is possible to use it for the production of yarns from wool. The system differs considerably from the traditional woollen process, for although a card is used, this is usually of the flax-card type, though in some cases a card similar to a worsted card is employed. Following carding, the system is, in principle, that of the worsted process, and in reality the yarns produced are coarse worsted yarns, despite the absence of a combing operation.

The advantage of the system lies in the high rate of production from the card – 200 to 300 pounds per hour. There is no condenser, the product of the card being a thick sliver.

From the point of view of a woollen spinner, the disadvantage is that the system can only deal with a limited range of materials, and produce a restricted range of counts. For the carpet yarn spinner, however, it has a serious application. Although, as stated above, wool can be processed on this system, it involves certain limitations. For example, the amount of grease left in the wool must be carefully controlled, for if this exceeds 0.5 per cent, trouble will be experienced in gilling and spinning. Again, the elimination of foreign matter cannot equal that of cards on which it is possible to use mechanisms of the Peralta type.

WOOLLEN SPINNING

THE PURPOSE of the spinning process is to convert the condenser slubbing into a yarn which will satisfy the requirements of such subsequent operations as winding, warping, weaving or knitting. These requirements vary with the different conditions encountered in manufacturing, but all demand certain standards of strength, elasticity, and uniformity in count, twist and appearance.

The conversion from condensed slubbing to spun yarn is accomplished by the application of draft and twist. Draft implies the drawing out of the slubbing to a longer length, through the slippage of the fibres one over the other, while twist is the action of turning the yarn on its axis with one end held fast. This latter action binds the fibres together, so that slippage becomes increasingly difficult and eventually impossible, and gives strength to the yarn. There are, however, limits to the amount of draft and twist which can be inserted into any yarn. While the draft employed in woollen spinning rarely exceeds two, it is known that a stronger and more level yarn results from the imposition of as high a draft as possible[17].

The amount of draft which can be employed in woollen spinning is dependent primarily on the quality, length and uniformity of the fibres in the blend. In drafting, the fibre movement is controlled by twist actually applied in the spinning process and, for successful operation, a correct balance between the twist inserted and the amount of draft and the speed at which it is carried out is essential.

The amount of twist to be imparted to the yarn is governed by the use for which the yarn is intended and by the economic factor. Hosiery yarns which require to be full and soft-handling are given little twist and, in many instances, weft yarns are spun with less twist than are warp yarns. In all cases, however, the type of cloth ultimately to be produced and the finish it must receive have to be taken into consideration.

There are two methods of spinning woollen yarns, namely, on the mule and on the ring frame.

MULE SPINNING

Mule spinning utilizes the principle of spindle draft as distinct from the roller draft used in worsted spinning. The spindle acts as the drafting agent in that it is responsible for drawing out the condensed slubbing during the outward run of the carriage. It is also responsible for the insertion of twist, by means of which fibre control is achieved during the operation.

The mule cycle consists of five phases, viz: (a) the delivery of the condensed slubbing, (b) the drafting period, (c) the insertion of the required amount of twist, (d) backing-off, and (e) winding-on. The time taken by each of the first three operations may vary widely according to the type of material being spun, but the last two are constant on any one mule.

Delivery is achieved through the motion of the delivery rollers during the first part of the outward run of the carriage. At a predetermined point, according to the amount of draft required, the delivery rollers stop while the carriage continues to run out. During both these stages the spindles run at slow speed, to insert the required amount of twist, but during the drafting period the speed of the carriage is gradually reduced so that the correct balance of draft and twist may be obtained. The insertion of the remainder of the twist needed to impart strength to the yarn is accomplished while the carriage is halted as the end of the outward run, with the spindles revolving at high speed. During this operation the carriage may make a slight inward movement to compensate for the take-up in the yarn due to the twist insertion. This is known as 'jacking-up'. A reversal of the direction of motion of the spindles is then necessary to unwind the yarn wrapped round them from the nose of the cops to the spindle tip in preparation for winding: this is known as 'backing-off'. During this action the winding and counter fallers are brought into position to wind and tension the yarn, respectively, during the inward run of the carriage. The carriage is then run back to the rollers and, in doing so, the spun yarn is wound on to the cop. During winding the necessary variations in spindle speed are obtained from the action of the quadrant mechanism, while the position of the winding faller is controlled by the shaping mechanism.

It will be seen from the above that the first three parts of the cycle of movements are those concerned with the construction of the yarn, and it is therefore in these movements that the chief spinning problems arise. This is not to imply, however, that 'backing-off' and 'winding-on' are unimportant. On the contrary, these operations are responsible for the production of a yarn package which will work satisfactorily in subsequent processing.

The success of woollen mule spinning depends, firstly, on the realization that a woollen slubbing consists of a series of non-uniform fibres arranged in an unparalleled order – though the majority of the fibres tend to lay in the direction of the length of the slubbing – and, secondly, on the maintenance of an ease of fibre movement during the drafting period essential to the production of a uniform yarn. Operational factors in spinning are (i) the linear speed of the rollers, (ii) the linear speed of the carriage and therefore of the spindles, and (iii) the speed of rotation of the spindles. Successful spinning depends on the achievement of a correct balance between these factors.

During the delivery period all the above factors are in operation at the same time. For the majority of yarns, the linear speed of both rollers and carriage should be approximately the same, though exceptions to this rule are necessary for material in which the fibres tend to 'set-up' quickly and

for fibres which are difficult to draft. For such fibres it may be necessary
to run the carriage slightly faster than the rollers, using what is known as
'carriage-drag', but incorrect use of this is liable to cause 'twitty' or uneven and weak yarns. The amount of twist which must be inserted at this
stage is critical; too much will create difficulties in that ease of drafting in
the next stage will be impossible, while too small an amount will not give
sufficient control of fibre movement. As drafting proceeds, gradually more
twist is required and this can only be obtained by a gradual reduction in
carriage speed. To achieve this, the carriage is driven by means of a scroll.

It will be apparent that mule spinning is a complex operation, calling
for a sympathetic understanding of what is happening during the various
stages of the spinning cycle. At the same time, the mule is highly adaptable
and can be used to spin almost any type of fibre. Change points are provided for the following effects. A gear, generally known as the pinion
wheel, is used for altering the speed of the rollers and the carriage, a second
gear (the drag wheel) serves only to affect the speed of the carriage, while
a rope pulley (the small rim-wheel) drives the spindles during delivery
and drafting. Different types of scroll are available, so that the amount of
draft may be selected to suit the particular material being processed and
the type of yarn being spun. A final adjustment to the speed of the carriage
during drafting can be made by altering the position of the scroll so as to
use more or less of the 'nose', the smallest portion used at the end of the
outward run. The jacking-up motion used to move the carriage slightly inwards during the twisting phase can also be varied in speed and amount
of movement.

The principal advantage of the mule lies undoubtedly in its adaptability and in the fact that fine adjustments can be made to enable difficult
materials to be 'humoured' and spun successfully. On the other hand, the
mule as a spinning machine has certain disadvantages, the chief being (*i*)
its intermittent operation, (*ii*) its low production, (*iii*) its complex mechanism, (*iv*) the limited size of package obtainable, (*v*) the large floor space
occupied, and (*vi*) the fact that it does not lend itself to automatic doffing.

Developments in mule mechanisms have been designed chiefly with
the object of increasing its production and, in this connection, it is now
possible to change over the spindle speed during the outward run of the
carriage, either to the spindle speed employed on the older type of mule
for twisting at the head, or to a speed intermediate between that employed
during delivery and that for twisting at the head. The modern mule may
also incorporate the Rabbeth type of spindle which can be run at 5,000 to
6,000 r.p.m., while another improvement is that of reversing the direction
of rotation of the spindles by simple mechanical means in the carriage
square when it is required to change from S to Z or Z to S twist instead of,
as previously, reversing the direction of every spindle band.

RING-FRAME SPINNING

Ring-frame spinning of woollen yarns originated in the early part of the present century, but despite all its apparent advantages—continuous spinning, high production, large packages and a comparatively simple mechanism occupying a relatively small floor space—it is only recently, say since 1960, that the ring frame has become a viable proposition in the woollen industry. The present trend in the use of the ring frame in this country is shown statistically by the figures reproduced in Table 5.4[11], and similar trends exist in other countries.

TABLE 5.4.

MULE AND RING-FRAME SPINDLES IN THE UNITED KINGDOM WOOLLEN INDUSTRY

Year							Mule		Ring Frame
1963	..	..	..	..	..	..	1,750,000	..	100,000
1965	..	..	..	..	..	..	1,411,228	..	136,428
1967	..	..	..	..	..	..	1,244,164	..	133,999

The ring frame can be used to spin a wide variety of blends from all-wool and wool wastes to mixtures of wool and man-made fibres and 100 per cent man-made fibre blends, and at the present time it is fast replacing the mule in the carpet industry. It can also be used to spin mixtures of wool and cotton and cotton wastes produced on the condenser system.

In the ring frame, spinning proceeds continuously. The bobbins of condensed slubbing are mounted in a creel, from which the slubbing is delivered by means of a surface drum down to a pair of back rollers. These pass the slubbing forward to the front rollers, some 10 inches to 20 inches away, and as these have a greater surface speed than that of the back rollers, a drafting action occurs. To draft a woollen slubbing some means of fibre control is necessary and this is achieved by passing the slubbing through a rotating false-twist tube placed as close to the front rollers as possible. In this way sufficient twist is inserted between the back and front rollers to allow drafting to take place. On leaving the nip of the front rollers, the slubbing is wound onto a bobbin by a conventional spinning technique in which a lappet eye, ring and traveller are responsible for inserting the required twist in the yarn and for winding the yarn onto the bobbin.

It will be apparent from the above brief outline that the ring spinning process involves two distinct operations, drafting and spinning, which in view of their importance warrant separate and detailed consideration.

THE DRAFTING ZONE IN RING SPINNING

Before describing the actual drafting zone[12,13], it should be stressed that no drafting action should take place during delivery of the slubbings to the back rollers from the surface drums on which the condenser bobbins from the cards are mounted and which operate by frictional contact. These back rollers mark the start of the drafting zone and their purpose is to grip the slubbing and to prevent it being pulled apart while it remains in its untwisted state. To this end the upper back roller serves merely as a weighted delivery roller, only the bottom back roller being positively driven.

Drafting takes place between the back and front rollers due to the latter having a higher surface speed than that of the former. In practice, the draft in woollen ring frames is about 1·3 to 1·4, (i.e., a 10s Y.S.W. slubbing, 195 tex, would be spun to a 13s to 14s Y.S.W. yarn 150-140 tex). Although it is possible to attain a draft of 1·8, this is exceptional.

Several factors limit the draft attainable, namely the wide divergence of fibre lengths in the slubbings, the fact that the fibres are not parallel— indeed, cohesion has been brought about by simply rubbing the rectangular slubbing—and in many cases the fibres are hooked at one or both ends. Moreover, the problem of drafting is further complicated by the high short-term variation in weight and fibre number along the length of the slubbing. Even with the low drafts referred to above, it is necessary to control fibre movement to ensure that regular drafting takes place.

Control of fibre movement during drafting is achieved by means of a false-twist tube—a short tube about two inches long with a small bore through which the slubbing passes on its way from the back to the front rollers. Let into the conical mouth of the tube are two or four small pegs with hemispherical tops, while the other end of the tube is equipped with a pair of jaws, one fixed and one hinged, which grip the slubbing and turn it on its axis as the tube rotates. The grip must not, of course, be so firm as to prevent the front rollers pulling the slubbing through the tube. The jaws of the tube are placed as close to the nip of the front rollers as is possible and the twist in the slubbing imparted by the rotating jaws runs up the tube and is distributed by the notches on the top. Experiments have demonstrated that the twist, say two to four turns per inch, is densest in the tube just about the jaws and is gradually reduced to zero at the back rollers. Drafting therefore takes place just inside the back rollers, say within three to four inches of the nip, where the twist in the slubbing is at a minimum. Incidentally, the distance over which drafting takes place can be increased or reduced by reducing or increasing, respectively, the speed of the false-twist tube.

It will be appreciated that the twist is 'false' in the sense that the slubbing is effectively prevented from rotating by the nips of both the front and back rollers. Thus, once the frame is running, the slubbing emerges from the front rollers in a twistless state. It is also interesting to note that there is no false twist in the slubbing between the jaws of the tube and the front rollers. This is presumably because the S-twist above the jaws rides down on the end and cancels out the Z-twist which is formed below the jaws.

Contact of the slubbing with the notches can be increased or decreased by lowering or raising a rod which is placed just above the tube and over which the end rides. It is said that the jerky movement imparted to the slubbing by the rotating notches tends to give a fuller and bulkier yarn, but in the light of other frame arrangements where the path of the slubbing from the back to the front rollers takes a straight line and where the tubes used contain no notches, it would appear to be doubtful whether these latter do other than distribute twist.

In other forms of tube used in the production of yarn for coarse blankets or carpets, the jaws are replaced by a thin steel finger projecting downwards from the inner surface of the tube near its lower end. Apparently the slubbing wraps itself round this finger and so produces the drafting twist before the material enters the front rollers. In another method, used on the Continent, the finger is replaced by a series of intersecting needles which are directed downward and inward to form a revolving 'basket', past which the slubbing is drawn.

Many attempts have been made to do away with this type of twister tube because of the difficulty of threading the slubbing, involving the use of felt-covered wire, and a device known as a false-twist spiral is now in use. This consists of a small spiral of wire which is introduced into the path of the slubbing between the back and front rollers. Although this offers advantages in simplifying threading and in the abolition of a moving part, it cannot be adjusted to vary the amount of false twist. It has therefore proved most useful in the spinning of coarse counts where few alterations are necessary.

Another modification in the drafting zone is the replacement of the two-roller, front roller nip by three rollers, two of which are positively driven, while the third is a press roller on the outside of the machine. This arrangement, it is claimed, gives better drafting and, at modern production rates, is probably necessary.

THE SPINNING ZONE IN RING SPINNING

On leaving the front rollers the slubbing enters the spinning zone[14]. First, it is deflected outwards by a porcelain ring, after which it passes under the traveller rotating round the steel spinning ring and thence onto the package carried on the positively driven spindle.

Twist is inserted into the slubbing by the action of the traveller as it is pulled round the ring by the spindle, the number of turns inserted into the yarn being equal to the number of revolutions of the traveller round the ring. In woollen yarn spinning, however, the turns per inch

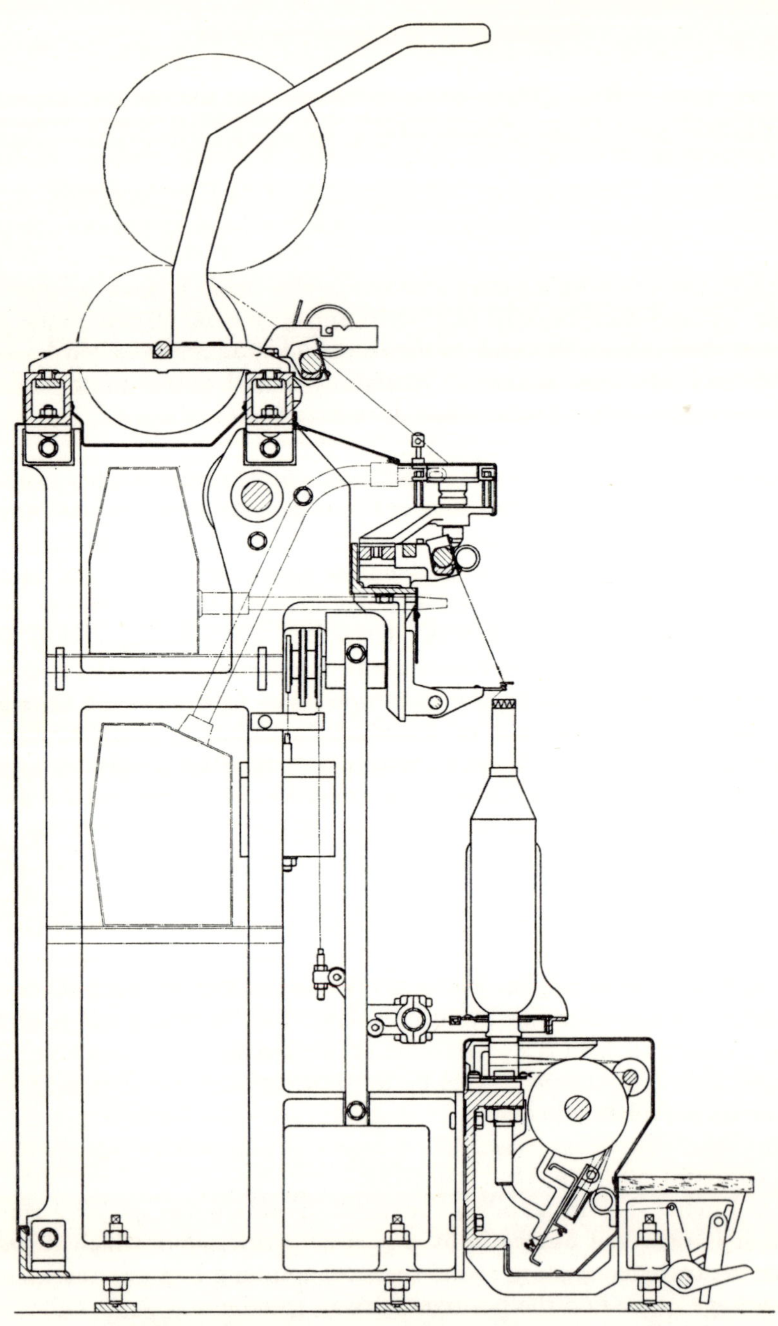

FIG. 5.4. SECTIONAL ELEVATION OF SINGLE-SIDED WOOLLEN
RING FRAME (822) FOR MEDIUM AND FINE COUNT YARNS.

By courtesy of Prince-Smith & Stells Ltd.

approximate to the number of spindle revolutions per minute divided by the surface speed of the front rollers in inches per minute.

In addition to inserting twist, the traveller also has a second function, namely to wind the yarn on to the package, this being achieved by the traveller lagging behind the spindle. This lag is brought about by the frictional forces between traveller and ring and by the air drag on the yarn as it balloons round the spindle. Winding onto the package is achieved, either by reciprocating the ring rail—which carries all the rings—in a manner determined by a cam system, or by moving the spindle rail up and down in the same manner. The former method is the simpler and the more common, since it involves only the raising and lowering of a constant weight of ring rail and obviously avoids the raising and lowering of rotating spindles with the attendant problem of spindle drive. On the other hand, the reciprocating ring rail does involve a variable size balloon which is avoided where the reciprocating spindle rail is employed. Nevertheless, it is doubtful whether the advantages of the latter method, namely a constant balloon and less variation in the tension on the yarn, outweigh its disadvantages.

During spinning the yarn is subjected to varying tensions in its passage from the nip of the front rollers to the package, e.g., that occurring between the front-roller nip and the thread guide, the tension in the yarn balloon and the winding tension between the traveller and the package. A yarn will break in any of these zones whenever the instantaneous tension at some point of the yarn path exceeds the yarn strength at that particular point.

Although winding tension is some 10 to 50 per cent greater than the balloon tension which, in turn, is slightly higher than that between the front rollers and the guide, the majority of breakages in conventional spinning occur near the front rollers. This is because at this position the slubbing emerges from the rollers in a twistless state and the yarn, not being twisted completely, is relatively weak. Furthermore, since the yarn is being wound onto a package of varying diameter, the yarn tension has a strong cyclic variation, being at a maximum when winding onto the smaller diameter, the nose of the cop, and at a minimum when winding onto the shoulder.

In the past, the deficiency of strength in the yarn as it emerges from the front rollers has limited both spinning speed and package diameter. However, the development of the Pross Spindle by Houget Duesberg-Bosson and other spindle-top attachments, such as the thistle and crown tops by other machine makers, has revolutionized the applicability of the spinning frame. In the Pross spindle specially shaped wires, fixed to the top of the spindle, hold the yarn and cause it to wrap round the spindle, thus collapsing or suppressing the balloon. In this way, yarn tension above

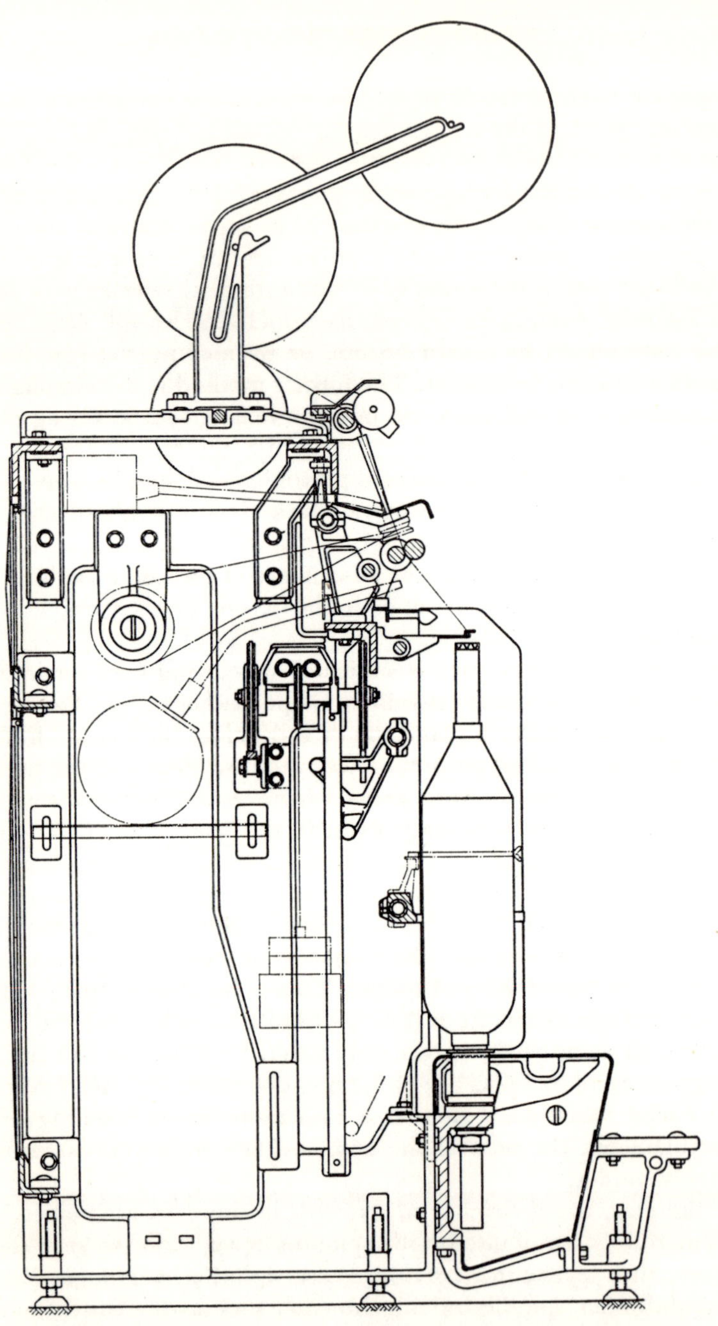

FIG. 5.5. SECTIONAL ELEVATION OF SINGLE-SIDED WOOLLEN RING FRAME (823) FOR COARSE COUNT, LARGE PACKAGE SPINNING.

By courtesy of Prince-Smith & Stells Ltd.

the thread guide is reduced and the traveller with the collapsed balloon system only winds on the yarn. Restriction of balloon size also results in the battering action of the balloon, which increases in diameter with spindle speed, being almost eliminated and much higher spindle speeds are therefore possible. This advantage is also due in part to the fact that the spindle top is acting as a twist inserter. As this twist is pushed up to the front-roller nip, the yarn between the nip and the thread guide, which was previously in a very weak state, is greatly strengthened. With this device, the setting of the thread guide relative to the top of the spindle is particularly critical, but in practice a satisfactory spin is easily achieved.

The positive advantages accruing from the adoption of the spindle-top attachment are obviously higher speeds and larger packages, but these in turn have necessitated the use of suction devices, the redesign of roller stands, balloon control rings, developments in traveller and ring design, and the employment of more powerful motors.

In high-speed ring spinning where front-roller speeds can be of the order of 32 yards per minute with a small diameter front-roller of $1\frac{1}{4}$ inches rendered necessary because of the uncontrolled distance between the end of the twister tube and the roller nip, some form of suction device, to collect broken ends until they can be pieced, is essential.

Roller stands have had to be redesigned to enable the operative to place a broken end, either at the creel or from the package, behind the top roller to facilitate piecing. Balloon control rings and separators are also necessary in high-speed spinning.

High-speed spinning has also affected the design of traveller and ring. There would appear to be an upper limit to the speed at which a traveller can revolve, this being of the order of 120 feet per second. Thus the larger the ring, the lower will be the maximum possible speed. For example, while it is possible to run a traveller at 7,000 r.p.m. on a $3\frac{1}{2}$ inch diameter ring, the peripheral speed being 107 feet per second, a ring size of 5 inch diameter will necessitate a maximum speed of 5,000 r.p.m., if the peripheral speed of the traveller is to be maintained at the above figure. The traveller may be made of steel or nylon, the former being the more conventional although nylon travellers do permit of higher speeds. The latter, however, tend to be cut by animal fibres and accordingly may have a restricted life, but in any case the life of a traveller depends on many factors and in practice may vary from 40 hours to 400 hours running time. Recent developments in this field have led to the use of nylon travellers with metal inserts.

Automatic lubrication of rings is most important and has been greatly assisted by the development of forced lubrication systems. Frames with this type of lubrication are now being made with 5 inch diameter rings, running at spindle speeds of 7,500 r.p.m., producing a package two pounds in weight and suitable for use over a wide range of counts. It must be realized, however, that high spindle-speeds are very costly in power.

Modern ring-spinning frames[15] require motors of high horse-power, say 25 h.p. per 120 spindles per side. Usually these are of the variable speed type, enabling the speed to be varied throughout the build of the package—low during the formation of the cop, then high during the building of the major part of the bobbin and slightly lower at the bobbin top. With large rings, say of 7 inch diameter for a $5\frac{1}{2}$ inch diameter package, it is well worth introducing a variable-speed drive to give a maximum speed on the cop shoulder and a minimum on the nose.

COMPARISON OF MULE AND RING-FRAME

It is difficult to compare the techniques and products of mule and ring-frame spinning and to assess their relative merits in that so much depends on such non-comparable factors as the blend being processed or even the handle required in the ultimate cloth. Nevertheless, attention may usefully be drawn to a number of essential differences.

One of the main differences is in the power required to drive the two types of machine, the mule having a much lower power consumption. Thus, to quote an example, a mule equipped with Rabbeth spindles will require about two horse-power per 120 spindles. Against this, a ring frame will require about 25 horse-power for the same number of spindles.

Where package size is the criterion, the ring frame is outstanding. On the mule the largest package obtainable weighs about four ounces. On the other hand, a ring frame using an 18 inch lift and a seven inch diameter ring, can spin a package of 54 ounces. It is, in fact, this ability to spin, and thus twist, large packages with few or no knots which constitutes one of the main advantages of the frame, especially for the production of thick yarns and in the carpet manufacturing industry. As regards production—in pounds per hour—the ring frame also has the advantage, a variable-speed frame producing three to four times that of the mule, the finer the count, the less being the difference.

The labour requirements of the two types of machine may be exemplified by the following figures of the labour force required for the same production in the carpet trade:

Mule Spinning—14 mules (370 spindles each).
  One overlooker, seven spinners (male), seven piecers and one weighman: Total, sixteen.
Ring Spinning—Four large-package ring frames (240 spindles each).
  One overlooker, eight spinners (female—120 spindles each), a setting-in and doffing team of two, and one weighman: Total, twelve.

While the space occupied by mules for the same production is far greater

—three times as much—that that taken up by frames, the space occupied per machine does not differ greatly with the two types, modern ring frames being much wider than the older models.

One advantage of the mule is its ability to achieve a higher draft than the ring frame when spinning fine material and blends containing re-manufactured wastes, although it is doubtful whether this is the case where coarser fibres, such as are used in the carpet trades, are concerned. This ability to draft more on the mule, due to its greater number of change points and its increased flexibility compared with the frame, influences the type of material used in the blend which, in consequence, may probably be cheaper for the mule than for the frame. Further, in frame spinning, the quality of carding is more important than in processing for the mule, demanding a higher standard of levelness and a greater removal of faults. It is also necessary to condense finer in the card for frame spinning where the draft is, say, 1·4 as compared with the 1·8 imposed in the mule. It should also be remembered that, other things being equal, the greater the draft in spinning, the stronger is the yarn[16].

With regard to end breaks, one would expect these to be less in mule spinning, although suppressed balloon spinning has reduced the incidence of end breaks to about ten per hundred spindle-hours for 6s Y.S.W. yarns (320 tex). At one time piecing was a problem on the frame and it was said that frame piecings were weaker than mule piecings. However, actual tests on piecings have not shown this to be true.

A COMPARISON OF YARNS AND FABRICS

At least two surveys have been made with the object of comparing the properties of mule-spun and frame-spun yarns and of cloths subsequently produced from these yarns[17]. It would seem from these that there need be little or no difference between the strength, regularity of weight per unit length, or of the optically measured diameter of yarns spun on the ring frame and those spun on the mule, provided these were prepared from the same blend and on the same card. Insofar as distribution of twist was concerned, the surveys showed no differences between the two sets of yarns and technicians failed to distinguish between them by visual examination. It should perhaps be pointed out, however, that a periodic variation in twist does occur in mule spinning with a wave length equal to the mule draw and that this effect does not arise in frame spinning. There may also be a coarsening of the yarn towards the top of the mule cop due to 'sloughing off' and this also does not occur in frame spinning.

From examination of cloths woven from comparable yarns, it was evident that, at least for the particular structure chosen, the method of spinning had comparatively little effect. Differences in the dimensional changes occurring during scouring were also very small. However, there were differences between cloths made from mule-spun and ring-spun yarns insofar as milling shrinkage and increase in thickness were concerned, but even these were not really important.

REFERENCES

1   Townend, *J. Text. Inst.*, 1940, **31**, T31.
2   Townend, *J. Text. Inst.*, 1948, **39**, T385.
3   Townend and Spiegel, *J. Text. Inst.*, 1946, **37**, T58.
4   Martindale, *J. Text. Inst.*, 1945, **36**, T 213.
5   Thorndike, *J. Text. Inst.*, 1949, **40**, No. 2.
6   Townend, *J. Text., Inst.*, 1949, **40**, No. 2.
7   "Woollen Machinery, English, Scotch and American Carding Systems" by Platt Bros. (Sales) Ltd., Oldham.
8   B.P. 570, 129.
9   Townend, *Text. Mfr.*, 1943, **69**, 333.
10   Marshall, *Text. Mfr.*, 1948, **74**, 520.
11   "Wool Industry Bureau of Statistics", published by the Wool Textile Delegation.
12   Townend and Jowett, *J. Text. Inst.*, 1951, **42**, 997.
13   *Wool Science Review*, 1957, **17**, 3.
14   Greenwood, F. A., *Textile Recorder*, 1961, Sept., 67.
15   Firth, L., *Text. Mfr.*, 1961, Sept., 356.
16   Townend, *J. Text. Inst.*, 1946, **37**, 490.
17   Townend and Whewell, *J. Text. Inst.*, 1951, **42**, 239.

YARN PREPARATION FOR WEAVING

THE PROCESS OF WEAVING requires two sets of yarns, weft and warp. For the former, woollen and worsted yarns are often spun or twisted directly on to tubes or cops of a size and shape suitable for the loom shuttles. The present tendency when using orthodox looms, however, is to spin and twist on to larger containers and to rewind on to smaller ones. This rewinding of the weft yarn allows of more economical spinning conditions, permits of the discovery and removal of faults prior to weaving and provides a more uniformly wound weft package. In the case of shuttleless weaving or where loom winders are used, the weft is usually cleared and presented as a cone or cheese. The warp consists of a wide sheet of ends laid side by side and wound under uniform tension on to large diameter weaver's beams. Except for making short warps, as is the practice in certain sections of the woollen trade and for handlooms, it is not economical to warp directly from spinning tubes or bobbins, owing to the short length of yarn which such packages contain and which would involve excessive stopping of the warping machine in order to tie-in new ends. To overcome this difficulty, the warps are wound from larger packages—bobbins, cheeses or cones—which have been prepared from the spinning tubes or bobbins at a separate rewinding operation.

The process of weft winding and warp winding constitute the first sections of this chapter and these are followed by descriptions of warp making and warp sizing. These operations, together with looming or drawing-in, as described in Section 7, comprise the main pre-weaving processes[1-6].

WEFT WINDING

SOME OF THE WEFT used in the woollen and worsted industry is still spun directly on to packages suitable for weaving, such as cops, spools or tubes. Such yarn contains spinners' piecings, and such faults as slubs and thick ends which are normally removed when rewinding is carried out. Again, many packages from the spinner are not full-size or are badly shaped due to end breakages and other spinning faults. Moreover, it is usual for such packages to be passed through conditioning machines to allow a small amount of moisture to be absorbed to replace that lost during spinning, a process which is not always beneficial in that the yarn on the outside of the package usually absorbs much more moisture than that on the inside. Altogether, therefore, there is a good case for the rewinding of weft.

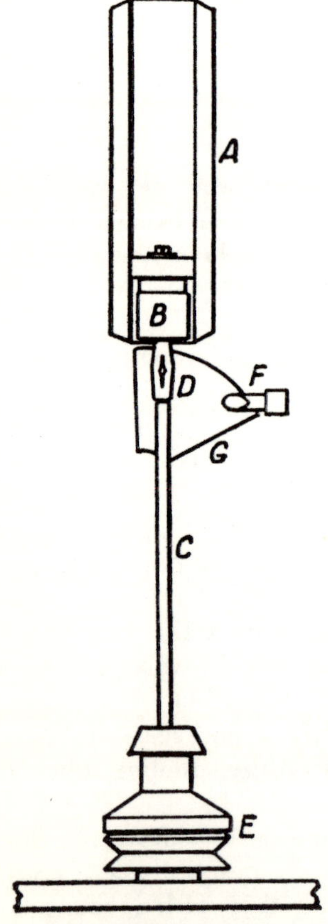

FIG. 6.1. ONE SPINDLE OF A VERTICAL TUBE WINDER

THE VERTICAL TUBE WINDER

Much of the twofold worsted weft yarn, such as that required for coating fabrics, was twisted onto normal double-ended twisting bobbins and rewound on to pirns as a separate operation. A typical machine for this purpose, still occasionally used, is the vertical tube winder, one spindle of which is illustrated in Fig. 6.1, where A is a grooved metal slide in which the head B is free to move in a vertical plane. Freely supported at the lower end of B is a spindle C over which the empty tube is placed and positioned by the spring clip D. The lower end of the spindle fits into a groove in the wharle E and the whole spindle blade is of such a length that when the head B is at the top of the slide, the tip of the spindle is just clear of the wharle and ceases to be driven by it. By means of a porcelain guide F, oscillated in a short arc by a central cam, the yarn is guided onto the tube. The shape of the tube is governed by the cone block G, this being adjustable and fixed in such a way that it causes the running tube to push itself and consequently the spindle and head B upwards. When the tube is full the spindle slips from the wharle and the whole unit falls forward ready for doffing.

NON-AUTOMATIC WEFT WINDING MACHINES

The development of automatic looms gave rise to a need for standardized weft packages to suit the type of magazine and shuttle being used. The feeler motion on such looms for indicating an empty pirn usually operates through the medium of a metal rib or band which is uncovered by the last coils of weft and, accordingly, a special type of pirn has had to be developed. Moreover, a length of yarn is required at the bottom of the pirn to act as a reserve supply until the change has been effected. These developments have necessitated special weft winding machinery and standard empty pirns, which will produce weft packages uniform in diameter and length, holding the maximum length of yarn, built with a motion designed to give an even winding-off tension and having an accurately placed reserve or bunch of yarn, adjustable in length. Such machines also offer facilities for the removal of spinning faults.

The advantages of rewinding weft yarn have proved so great that a considerable proportion of weft for all types of loom is now rewound from spinners' bobbins. This also allows larger spinning bobbins to be used, necessitating fewer doffings and allows longer lengths of yarn, free from faults, to be placed on each weft package. The modern tendency is for the spinner to provide cleared weft yarns to the weaver on cones to be used directly on certain types of loom or to be rewound on the particular type of pirn required for the orthodox looms installed.

There are many types of non-automatic weft winder but all incorporate the following features. The feeding bobbins or cones are placed in a creel and the ends passed individually through a suitable tensioning device, usually discs or grates, to a spooling mechanism. Each spooling unit has a horizontal spindle and alongside it a traverse bar. A group of spindles is usually driven by a long flat belt. The yarn is led on to the rotating spindle by a guide which is reciprocated on the guide bar by means of a cam. At the same time, the guide is gradually pushed along the length of the bar, usually by causing the chase of the spool to rotate a disc on the guide bar which is threaded to advance the guide. Auxiliary motions such as that to stop the spindle when the spool is full and the provision of a bunching mechanism to provide the small reserve supply of weft, are usually incorporated.

The speed of the spindles has to be varied to suit the count, quality and type of yarn being wound, while means are also available on these machines for modifying the taper of the pirn, its diameter, rate of traverse and the length of the bunch. A declutching mechanism allows each spindle to be stopped for doffing and for repairing broken ends. Most modern winders have a magazine creel, i.e., one in which two cones are used for each winding unit, the end of the second cone being tied to the bunch on the running cone, so providing a continuous source of yarn supply.

These types of winder are built in units, usually singly but sometimes in twos or fours. A number of these are arranged side by side to form one machine. There are many minor modifications of the above, introduced by individual makers. For instance, some provide a means of decreasing the diameter of the tube from bottom to tip, with the view of allowing for bent shuttle pegs, while in other machines the feeler disc is moved independently of the traverse rod. A cone former is occasionally provided which allows pirns to be made without the initial chase on the empty pirn.

AUTOMATIC WEFT WINDING MACHINES

There are two distinct parts to automatic weft winding machines, the pirn winder proper which is essentially as described above, and the changing mechanism, this being a means of replacing a full pirn by an empty one without the intervention of the operative. In these cases, the operative is responsible only for creeling, keeping filled the magazine of empty pirns and repairing any broken ends, though the latest winders usually incorporate means for conveying empty pirns from a hopper to the reserve position at each of the winding heads and for removing full pirns for stacking in boxes, pin boards or other devices. Travelling blowers are usually used in one form or another to keep cones and yarn paths clean. There are many different methods employed to effect the automatic replacement of full pirns by empty ones, but the usual method is to support the pirn tubes in chucks which allow for their quick release.

Although most modern winders are straight machines built-up in sections, single or double sided, the following description of the Abbott travelling winder will exemplify the principles of operation. In this machine the winding heads, each complete in itself with supply cone, tension discs and spooling mechanism, travel slowly along two sides and round the ends of the machine. At one side of the machine is the stationary automatic head which effects the changing of the pirn. The driving chuck which holds the head of the pirn, is at the end of the armature shaft of a motor and just before reaching the automatic head, the supply to the motor is cut off and the pirn becomes stationary. The yarn is slackened, the guide pushed back to the bottom of the pirn and the outer chuck, normally pressed against the tip of the pirn, is moved outwards. This allows the full pirn to drop from its winding position on to a tray below. Empty pirns are stored in a large hopper, from which they pass forward, one at a time in a vertical position. A second slide causes the pirns to fall into two pairs of fingers which grip them in a horizontal plane at the same height as the chucks. When the travelling head reaches this point the outer chuck moves inwards to secure the pirn which is released by the fingers. The new pirn catches the yarn, the connection with the full pirn is severed, the bunch is made and the driving chuck restarted at full speed for winding the body of the pirn. On this machine, the reciprocating builder rod is controlled by a cam driven from a worm on the motor shaft. The thread guides are advanced along a rack by a feeler which is moved forwards by the chase of the pirn.

LOOM WINDERS

Under certain conditions, pirns can be wound on the loom itself[4,7], the best known means being the Leesona 'Unifil' Loom Winder illustrated by Plate 27. With this machine[8], which can be applied to most pirn changing looms, an automatic pirn winding spindle with bunch builder produces pirns from a cone supply at a rate slightly greater than is required by the loom. These pirns are then transferred to a pirn magazine where they are stored until required by the loom, the change mechanism of which is not altered in any way. On a weft change taking place, the spent pirn is rejected from the shuttle and passed to a stripper, from which it is automatically conveyed to the empty pirn magazine, correctly aligned for feeding to the winding spindle.

WARP WINDING

THE NECESSITY for rewinding warp yarns from spinners' packages on to bobbins or in the form of cones or cheeses containing comparatively long lengths of yarn has already been outlined in the introduction to this chapter. For this work, various types of machine have been developed, of which reference may be made to the following.

THE BOBBIN WINDING MACHINE

This is probably the oldest type of machine for winding yarn and though technically obsolete, it is still occasionally seen in the woollen and worsted trades. Its essential details are shown at Fig. 6.2, where A is one of a series of vertical spindles driven individually by bands from a common tin cylinder B. The warping bobbins, wooden barrels with a flange at each end, rest on collars fixed to these spindles and draw yarn on to themselves. The yarn is guided on to the bobbins by a rising and falling traverse rail C controlled by a cam or mangle wheel. The serious disadvantage of increasing yarn speed on tension as the bobbins fill can be overcome by driving the bobbins at constant surface speed by frictional contact with a line of bosses.

THE SPLIT DRUM WINDER

One of the early successors to the above machine was the split drum winder which is still used though gradually being superseded by more modern versions. The essential parts of this machine are illustrated at

Fig. 6.3. The drum *A* is hollow and made in two parts, the split between the two parts acting as a guide for the yarn. The slit is in the form of two curved diagonals across the width of the drum; yarn is threaded through

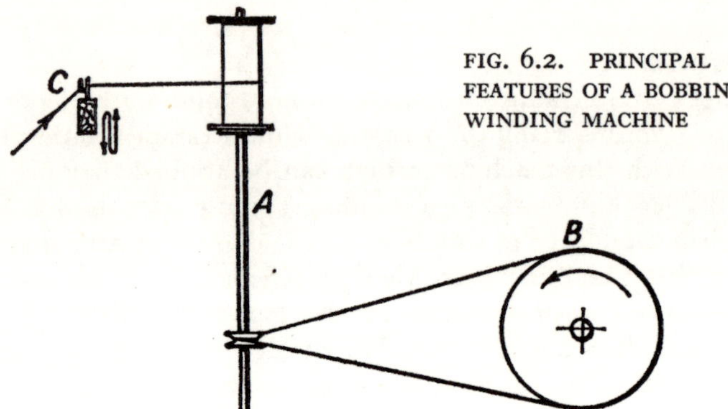

FIG. 6.2.   PRINCIPAL FEATURES OF A BOBBIN WINDING MACHINE

the slit at the bottom of the drum and emerges through the slit at the top where it is wound by friction on to a paper tube held by the arm *B*. Each drum is driven separately by a rope *C* from a central pulley shaft *D*, the

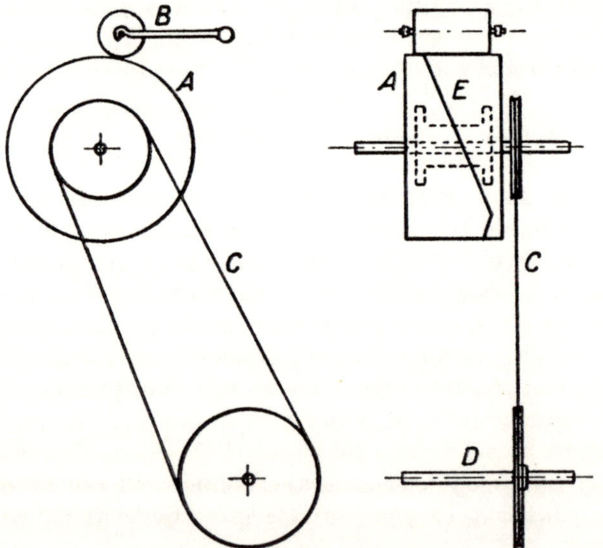

FIG. 6.3.   THE SPLIT DRUM WINDER

guard *E* being employed to prevent a broken end from being wrapped round the spindle of the drum. Cones or cheeses can be made at will by altering the relative position of the two arms holding the spindle and the paper or wood cone. Yarn is usually taken over-end from the feeding bobbin, passed through disc clearers and often over the surface of a conditioning roller, a hollow brass roller rotating in a trough of water or dilute oil emulsion. The speed of this roller can be altered to modify, within limits, the amount of moisture taken up by the yarns. Besides its low production, there is a chafing of the yarn at the split; later winding machines have been designed to overcome these two drawbacks.

RECIPROCATING THREAD GUIDE WINDERS

Early developments from the above were to use small, plain, positively driven drums in front of which yarn guides were reciprocated to give the necessary traverse. Speeds were low in the early models due to the mech-

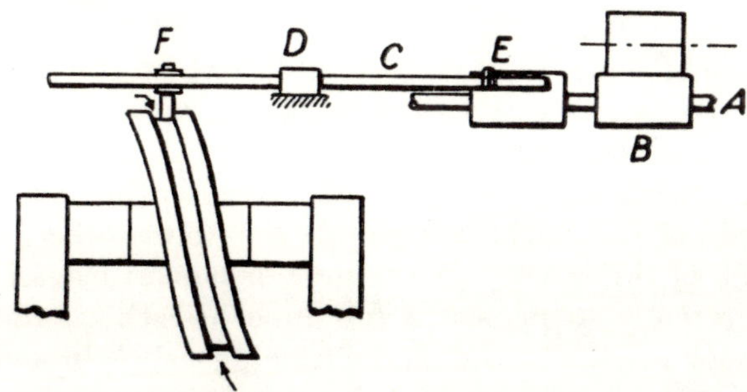

FIG. 6.4. RECIPROCATING THREAD GUIDE MOTION

anical difficulty of controlling the long heavy traversing bars with quick return action at the ends. The traverse bar was made as light as possible and the reciprocating motion was obtained by a large cam situated either at the outer end of the machine or in the middle.

One example, typical of this type of machine, is shown in Fig. 6.4. This machine has a shaft A, running the length of the machine and on to which is keyed a number of small diameter, smooth-surfaced drums B. A traverse rod C, connected to a cross-head at one end of the machine, moves to-and-fro in a suitable guide D immediately in front of the drums, the traverse of the rod being slightly less than the width of the drums. Yarn guides E are attached to the traverse rod, one to each drum, and control the wind of the yarn as it is taken up by the cone or cheese rotating on the drums. In this example, the cross-head F has a pin which works in the groove of a cam, the cam being positively driven and running in a bath of oil.

Although these types of machine are still successfully used commercially, their obvious weakness lies in the mechanical upkeep of the comparatively heavy and cumbersome guide bars and the large cams; there is also a limitation on winding speeds. These disadvantages have been overcome in later machines in two ways; firstly, by having a separate cam and guide bar to each drum and, secondly, by using drums with a grooved surface, the ends being guided by the helices on the drum much in the same way as in the split drum winder.

TRAVELLING PACKAGE WINDERS

This type of machine employs an individual traverse motion for each winding unit. The system, developed from the original Abbott machine, is now semi-automatic in the sense that running ends are automatically found and tied to the free ends once per cycle. The operator's duties are thus restricted to keeping a magazine full of supply bobbins and to doffing the full cheeses or cones.

The Abbott machine is double-sided; on each side is a single, small-diameter driving drum extending almost the full length of the machine. The winding units, each consisting of a short spindle to carry the feeding tube, a tensioning device, an oscillating guide and means of supporting one end of the running cone, are moved slowly along each side of the machine, a mechanism being provided to allow the units to be carried round each end of the machine from one side to the other.

At one end of the machine is the tube or bobbin magazine which revolves intermittently to present a full tube to each winding unit as it reaches the tying head. The end on the running cone is brought to the end of the feeding tube by suction and the two ends are tied together automatically, the tube or bobbin being automatically transferred to the peg on the winding unit at the same time. The cone is turned slowly round to take up the slack yarn and when the unit reaches the winding drum or roll, the cone is lowered on to it. Winding then commences and continues until the farther end of the machine is reached, when the cone is again lifted from the roll, the unit carried round the outer end of the machine and the cone lowered on to the second roll for winding to re-continue.

The length of the machine and the speed of winding are designed to allow the feeding tubes to be run out during one complete circuit of the machine. A lamp indicator denotes when the cones are full-size, after which they are doffed by hand at either end of the machine. An empty cone is substituted and a short length of yarn run on for the purpose of attaching the new supply at the tying head.

Pattern breakers are now incorporated to prevent ribbing on the cone surfaces, while bobbin breakers are employed to reduce yarn tension variations during the unwinding of each tube.

ROTARY TRAVERSE WINDERS

The main feature of these machines is a rotating metal or plastic drum or roll provided for each spindle and having helical grooves cut round its periphery, the grooves being so designed that an even traverse of the yarn is obtained. The yarn is taken overend from the feeding tubes or bobbins, passed through suitable clearers, a tensioning device and guide before being led through the grooves on to the cheese or cone rotated by frictional contact with the drum. The yarn rides in the grooves formed in the face of the drum and travels with it until taken up by the cheese or cone. In this way, the abrading action of the split drum winder or of the guides is avoided while the lack of reciprocating parts allows very high yarn speeds to be obtained, up to 900 yards per minute being achieved with good yarns. The 'Roto-coner' is an excellent example of a winder working on this principle.

The same principle has been adopted in the 'Auto-spooler' for making large diameter short traverse cheeses. It has a long frame with a large number of separate winding units arranged on each side. A travelling head is mounted on top of the machine and moves slowly round it, its function being to change the feed bobbins, tie the new ends on to the cheeses and start each cheese again in turn round the frame. It is timed to make a complete circuit of the machine in approximately the same time as it takes a bobbin to run off. The operative has to follow the traveller to supply reserve bobbins to the bobbin holder and to replace full cheeses by 'starters'. The travelling head can only tie the new end to one already present on the cheese so an auxiliary winding machine has to be used to wind a short length of yarn on to the 3-inch diameter hollow cylinders used as cores for the cheeses. The traverse of the roll is small, giving a cheese $2\frac{1}{2}$ inches wide but the diameter of the cheeses can be up to 12 inches. They are subsequently unwound over-end in a specially designed creel.

YARN CLEARING

Originally the larger imperfections in the yarn were removed during cheese or cone winding by causing the yarn to pass between two fixed plates, the gap being set just to prevent the passage of those slubs which were required to be removed. Too tight a setting resulted in scraped yarns and reduced winding efficiency. Mechanical clearers have been developed in many ways, with particular attention given to the shape of the gap and the alignment of the blades relative to the yarn path, to provide greater ease and accuracy of setting as well as more efficient clearing. In addition, locking devices have been developed to prevent tampering by operatives. More recently, a range of electronic clearers has been introduced, using either photo-electric or capacitance principles. While more costly than mechanical clearers, these electronic devices are more sensitive, do not scrape the yarn and have characteristics which make them particularly suitable for certain applications.[9]

GENERAL REMARKS ON WARP WINDING

The marked general development in warp winding machinery[10-13], particularly, in respect of higher speeds and in the adoption of certain automatic operations, which has taken place in recent years has been aimed largely at the cotton trade. But some of the methods—and automatic operations now include knotting of broken ends, replacement of empty tubes and, to a degree, the creeling of tubes from ancillary supply—modified to suit the different yarn characteristics are gradually being incorporated into the woollen and worsted industries.

The success of high-speed warp winding machinery depends not only on its mechanical construction but also on the nature of the yarns to be wound. In the woollen and worsted trade, it is not considered possible to standardize yarns and cloths to the extent possible in the cotton industry. A large portion of it is a high-class trade where the correct construction of the yarns and cloths is most important and where, in general, any particular fabric is made in relatively short lengths. For such work, slower winding speeds and maximum personal supervision are obvious requirements. There are, however, certain sections of the woollen and worsted trade where some standardization may with advantage be effected, such as, for example, in the manufacture of serges and fabrics where sufficiently long lengths are made to warrant a modified mass production method being adopted. It should also be remembered that the average counts of worsted and woollen yarns are usually heavier than those of cotton yarns, and this together with a difference in structure, necessitates lower winding speeds than can be employed for cotton yarns. Again, the magazines on modern winding machines do not normally accommodate small cap bobbins, while oiled yarns are not always readily acceptable.

The development of modern high speed warping machinery has largely depended on the use of conical packages or cones from which the yarn can be drawn over-end, the cone itself remaining stationary. Cones for warping creels, as distinct from those for knitting, have a taper of about 5° (as against approximately 10°) and are usually built up with a uniform traverse. They weigh up to four pounds and contain sufficient yarn to make several warps. The steeper slope of the cones is needed to allow higher yarn speeds to be obtained during unwinding without danger of sloughing.

WARPING

IN THE WARPING PROCESS the various warp ends are unwound from the bobbins, cones or cheeses, arranged side by side in correct order and the correct length wound under uniform tension on to a weaver's beam. Several methods of warping have been evolved to suit various requirements and trades but all embody (*a*) a creel to contain the cheeses or cones representing all or part of the number of ends required in the warp, (*b*) a reed for spacing the ends in proper order, (*c*) a stop motion to stop the machine when an end breaks, (*d*) a tensioning device to take up the slack from the cheeses on stopping and to prevent jerking on starting, (*e*) a measuring device to allow cut marks to be made and the correct length of warp to be obtained, and (*f*) a beam on to which the ends are wound under constant tension. Owing to the large number of ends in a normal warp it is customary to use a relatively small number of cheeses or cones in the creel and to make several separate sections which are afterwards run together on to a weaver's beam.

As the hand warping method admirably illustrates the principle of warping and as it is still used for much pattern work, a brief outline of this process may be useful before proceeding to the description of typical warping machines.

HAND WARPING

This method is used for making warps for hand looms, still often employed for initial pattern production and also for short pattern warps for power looms, due to its adaptability for pattern change and for complicated warping plans. The usual system of hand warping is to use two vertical rows of stout pegs fixed to a board on a wall. A small number of ends is drawn from bobbins in a small creel, leased, and attached to one of the top pegs. The tow or rope of ends is then passed across from one vertical row to the other, moving down one peg at each change until the required length of yarn has been obtained. A second lease is made, the ends cut and the process repeated until the total number of ends needed in the warp has been obtained. The large rope of ends is then removed for dressing on to a weaver's beam. One of the difficulties with this procedure is to maintain an even tension from one section to another and within each section. To minimize this difficulty, the size of the sections is restricted to a relatively small number of ends, often of the order of fifty.

THE BRADFORD UPRIGHT WARPING MILL

The hand warping method has been mechanized in many ways, one of the earliest and simplest machines being the Bradford upright mill. This is still used to a small extent, especially for making short ball warps or warps with complicated patterns, but for general production purposes it has now been superseded by other types. The machine consists of a large reel, usually 15 to 18 yards in circumference with 10 foot ribs, mounted with its central shaft supported vertically in a footstep bearing. The reel is rotated slowly and winds on to itself a small rope of ends drawn from bobbins arranged in a small creel. The ends from the creel are passed through a coarse reed which, starting at the lower end of the mill is raised slowly during the warping of each section so as to cause the ends to be wound spirally up the reel. Foot and head leases are made for each section and when the required number of sections has been combined, the complete warp is drawn off the mill in the form of a large tow of ends which can be balled or chained ready for dyeing or transport, or for immediate dressing on to a weaver's beam. Smaller 5-yard circumference reels are occasionally used for making very short pattern warps.

The calculations involved in this system of warping are elementary. If a warp is to have 4,000 ends and the creel holds 200 bobbins, 4,000 divided by 200 or 20 sections would be needed. If the length of the warp is to be 360 yards and the circumference of the mill is 15 yards, the number of revolutions it must make to complete each section will be 360 divided by 15, equalling 24. It is advisable after making each section to return the 'beck' or reed to the bottom for the next section to avoid the possibility of section marking or stripiness due to the different directions of surface fibre which would result from alternating the direction of sections.

SECTION WARPING MACHINES

This method of warping, still used by a few firms in the worsted industry, prepares each section of the warp separately on narrow-width flanged beams and combines the separate sections at a later beaming stage on to the full-width weaver's beam. As a simple illustration, suppose a warp is required to be made 48 inches wide with 70 ends per inch and having seven cuts each of 80 yards. Assuming the section blocks to be 6 inches wide, then eight sections would be required. The total number of ends in the warp is 48 x 70 or 3,360, so that the number of ends on each section block will be one-eighth of this or 420, which is the number of bobbins or cheeses required in the creel. The length of yarn on each section will be 80 x 7 or 560 yards. When the eight sections are completed they are keyed side by side on a braked shaft and the ends drawn on to a 48-inch wide weaver's beam.

The difficulty with this system is to ensure that each section of a warp is uniform in diameter and density, and contains exactly the same length of yarn and the same number of layers so that all the sections are unwound under the same tension and run out together. Various mechanical devices are attached to the machine to help in meeting these requirements.

The bobbins or cheeses are arranged in the banks of an ordinary vee- or straight creel and the ends drawn singly through a deep reed to be partially condensed prior to passing through a stop motion for detecting broken ends. The stop motion and tension device is shown in Fig. 6.5. A is the condensing reed and B, C, D, E and F are light tin rollers rotating by frictional contact with the yarn. Of these rollers, B, D and F rotate in fixed bearings, while C and E are carried by the sheet of threads and descend to take up the slack in the yarns when the machine is stopped. They also take up the slack when the warp is turned back to tie up a broken end.

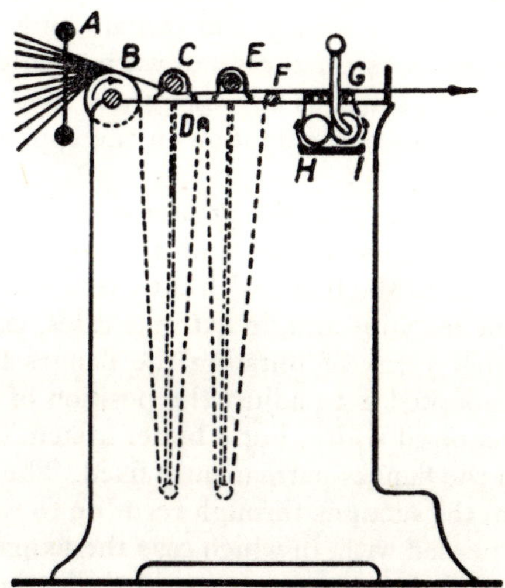

FIG. 6.5. THE STOP MOTION AND TENSION
DEVICE OF A SECTION WARPING MACHINE

Each end supports, in one of the grooves G, a drop pin which, when that particular end breaks, drops into the nip of two heavy rotating rollers H and I. Of these, H rotates in fixed bearings but a dropping pin pushes the roller I away from H and, through a system of levers, operates the strap fork to stop the machine. The sheet of ends then passes consecutively through a second condensing reed, a leasing reed and a vee-shaped reed, over a measuring roller and on to a section block.

In the worsted trade steel flanges are attached to each section block as distinct from usage for cotton, where detachable flanges are used during the building of the sections and removed when the sections are complete. The vee-shaped reed is adjustable to suit different widths of blocks. A pressure roller is applied against the block and is controlled by a system of levers previously set to suit the counts, quality and density of the yarns being warped. The number of revolutions of the section is recorded by suitable gearing from the block shaft. In order to maintain a constant yarn speed during warping, the speed of the block is reduced as its diameter increases, a flange on the block shaft being friction-driven by a small bowl which is moved across the face of the flange as the diameter of the section increases.

In practice, much care is needed to avoid excessive tensions at the various stages. Thus, in the creel, cheeses and warpers' bobbins should not be mixed, particularly when medium and fine counts are being warped. Similarly, the creel should not be stocked initially with all the cheeses or bobbins full size for the tension will decrease as warping continues and the last sections of a warp so wound will contain longer lengths than the first sections. Again, sections for the same warp should not be made before and after a week-end break as any changes in moisture content or relaxation shrinkage can cause an alteration in the apparent length of yarn on the sections.

Care should also be taken that the presser does not bear too heavily on the block at the start of a new section and it is good practice to allow the first half-inch to run on to the block with little tension. Too much tension acts as a brake on the machine and, in extreme cases, can stop it. There is also danger with wool yarns of bursting the flanges from the block. A method sometimes adopted is to adjust the position of the flanges on the blocks to give the required width, but a better system is to keep stocks of various widths with the flanges permanently fixed. The ends of the warp are usually run from the sections through reeds on to weaver's beams but often the reed is dispensed with, in which case the flanges on the weaver's beam should be set a little narrower to avoid slack edges.

BEAM WARPING

This method of warping is essentially similar to section warping, the main differences, in the case of the older machines, being the width of the section beams. In beam warping, the sections are made approximately the full width of the warp at the loom but the number of ends per inch is considerably less and depends on the number of sections used. Thus, if a warp is required to have 3,600 ends over 60 inches, that is 60 ends per inch, and if the creel holds 600 cheeses, then there will be six sections each comprising 600 ends spaced over 60 inches at the rate of 10 ends per inch. Six of these beams are then combined as a separate operation to give the final warp.

This system is chiefly used when the yarn has to be sized, the combination of the sections taking place at the sizing machine. Sizing, however, is not extensively employed in the woollen and worsted industry, being restricted to warps made from fine count yarns, weak single yarns or very fibrous yarns.

In beam warping, the bobbins or cheeses are mounted in an ordinary straight or vee creel. The sheet of ends from the creel are drawn through an open reed, a tension device, a drop-wire stop motion, an adjustable zig-zag reed and ultimately over a measuring roller on to the warper's beam, the operational details being similar to those described for the section warper. The beam is driven by surface contact with a rotating drum which maintains a constant yarn speed throughout each section. In some designs of warper, however, the beams are spindle-driven and here it is necessary to incorporate either mechanical or electrical means of maintaining a constant linear yarn speed during the build-up of the beam. Pressure on the beam is applied hydraulically and the same means are employed to remove full beams from the machine. It is usual for the length of yarn on warper's beams to be sufficient to fill several weaver's beams, making the system particularly suitable for use in connection with bulk production.

A modern beam warping machine employs a magazine creel with a capacity up to 1,000 cheeses or cones, which are usually arranged horizontally with the ends drawn over the nose and then passed through individual tensioning devices to the contracting reed. A reserve cone is creeled alongside each operative cone and the outer end of the reserve cone is tied to a tail made during winding at the beginning of the operative cone so that an automatic change from the empty to the full cone is effected. All the ends are drawn outwards to a series of arms, each containing the individual yarn tensioning devices, before being directed to the reed behind the warping machine. The advantages of cones over the older types of cheeses or bobbins is the more even yarn tension from start to finish of the package and the greater length of yarn that each cone holds.

High-speed warping depends essentially on the magazine creel, on reasonably strong yarns and on large diameter warper's beams. In the Barber-Colman beam warping machine, large diameter cheeses are used. The ends are drawn over the sides of the cheeses and the creel is made in the form of an endless series of vertical bars so that half the creel can be filled while the cheeses on the other half of the creel are being used. With modern high speed warping efficient brakes are needed to stop the machine quickly on the breakage of ends and usually electrically operated stop motions are preferred to the older mechanical types. One such motion allows a drop wire, when released on the breakage of its supporting thread, to block a beam of light which then ceases to excite a photo-electric cell and as a result, suitable relays cause the brakes to be quickly applied.

HORIZONTAL WARPING MILL

This machine is probably one of the most commonly used types at the present time, being adaptable for both plain and fancy warps. The usual section principle is employed but the various sections are arranged method-ically side by side on one swift or mill and, when the total number of ends has been collected, they are run from the mill, under suitable tension, on to the weaver's beam.

The creel is of the usual vee or straight type, the ends being collected and drawn forward through a spacing reed, stop motion, measuring motion and leasing reed, to be secured to a pin underneath one of the bars of a large diameter horizontal reel. These reels or mills are about five yards in circumference and five to six feet wide. At the end of each bar is fixed an incline or wedge as shown at *A* in Fig. 6.6. The width of the first section is *BC* and warping is begun with the side *B* at the bottom of the incline as shown. The reel is rotated and draws the yarn on to itself, while at the same time the reed carriage is made to travel a short distance to the right for each complete revolution of the swift. Thus the complete section is built up on the incline as at *D*.

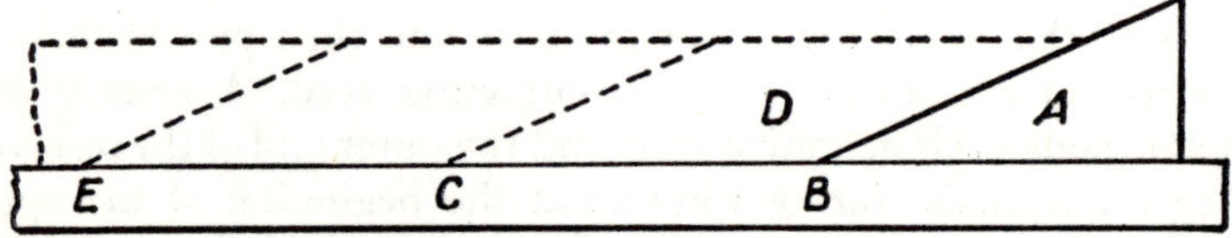

FIG. 6.6.   DIAGRAM ILLUSTRATING THE BUILD UP
OF YARN ON A HORIZONTAL WARPING MILL

When the required length has been obtained, the ends are cut, a new lease made and the ends attached to another peg below one of the bars. The carriage containing the dividing reed is moved a distance to the left equal to the width of a complete section so that warping now starts in the position *CE*. The second section is built up on the incline made by the first section, and the process repeated until the required number of sections has been placed on the mill. All the ends are then drawn from the mill under suitable tension and wound on to a weaver's beam, the beam being moved laterally a short distance after each revolution of the mill so as to keep the flanges in line with the changing edges of the sheet of ends.

Practical points include all those mentioned previously with regard to bobbins, cheeses and cones. The width of the section is varied to suit the details of each warp but is rarely more than nine inches. If a warp were being made with 40 ends per inch, 60 in. wide and the maximum creel capacity was 320, one method would be to make eight sections, each $7\frac{1}{2}$ inches wide, using 300 ends for each section. The incline or wedge can be altered in length and slope to suit different conditions, a steeper slope usually being required for coarser yarns.

WARPING CALCULATIONS

A number of relatively simple calculations is usually encountered during warping, such as to determine weights of warps or weights of component yarns in warps, where two or more different counts, materials, qualities or colours are used. There are also problems concerned with the arrangement of ends in the case of complicated warping plans as well as the calculations giving the width and number of sections and the number of packages in the creel. The last type of problem is straightforward and has been illustrated at the relevant places, but it is proposed to work out one or two examples of the former type by way of general illustration.

Example 1: A warp for a worsted coating fabric is made from 2/36s Botany, is 64 inches wide with 68 ends per inch. The weight of yarn in this warp of seven cuts, each of 70 yards, is calculated as follows: The number of ends in the warp is 68 (ends per inch) x 64 (inches wide) and each end is 7 x 70 yards long. The total length of yarn in the warp is therefore 68 x 64 x 7 x 70 yards. As the count of yarn is 2/36s worsted, there are 18 x 560 yards per pound, so that the weight of the warp is 68 x 64 x 7 x 70 divided by 18 x 560, or $211\frac{1}{2}$ pounds.

Example 2: A striped double plain suiting fabric is made with a navy ground and two different stripe yarns, a blue and navy marl yarn and a white and navy marl yarn. One repeat of the warp pattern is as follows:

2/48 blue/navy marl	...	1			
2/48 white/navy marl	...			1	
2/48 navy	... ...	1	36	1	36
		x4		x4	

The warp has 7,400 ends, including 80 selvedge threads, and it is required to arrange the ends to give a symmetrical pattern across the width of the warp and also to work out the weights of each type of yarn for a 560 yard warp. Allowing for the 80 selvedge threads, there are 7,400—80=7,320 pattern ends in the warp. The repeat of the pattern is on 88 ends, so there will be 7,320 divided by 88, or 83 repeats of the pattern across the warp with 16 extra ends. If the start of the body of the warp at one selvedge is the blue/navy marl and navy stripe, the warp ends would be balanced by adding the corresponding stripe of the 84th repeat at the other end. This will take eight ends, still leaving eight ends to account for. These can now be distributed, four at each side, by following the warping pattern to left and right respectively, giving the following complete warping plan:

Selvedges 40						40	...or 80 ends
2/48 blue/navy marl...	1			1			or 336 ends
2/48 white/navy marl		1					...or 332 ends
2/48 navy	4 1 36	1	36	1	4		...or 6652 ends
	x4	x4		x4			

x 83

Total ... 7400 ends

The weights of each yarn can be calculated as before. If there are 6,652 ends of navy ground each 560 yards long, the total length of yarn will be 6,652 x 560 yards. There are 24 x 560 yards per pound of 2/48s, so that the weight will be 6,652 x 560 divided by 24 x 560, or $277\frac{1}{4}$ pounds. Similarly, the weights of the two stripe yarns can be shown to be 14 pounds each.

GENERAL REMARKS ON WARPING

In the woollen and worsted trades the horizontal warping machine is probably the most popular both in this country and in the U.S.A. The section warper and the beam warper are equally used but are less popular, whilst the upright warping mill is now used only for short or very complicated warping plans. In the U.S.A. there is a tendency for the beam warper to be more used than in this country chiefly because sizing is carried out more for use with automatic looms and because of its adaptability to mass production methods. The traditional horizontal warping machine has also been rearranged for the same purpose[14,15].

One typical modern lay-out is for a number of magazine cone creels to be arranged side by side. In front of them are two lines of rails along which the mill can be moved bodily, either for short distances to allow the start of successive sections to be made, or to a position in front of another creel. These mills are cylindrical and the wedges or inclines of the traditional swift are replaced by a solid brass cone. The same lay-out is adopted for the beam warping system. The size of the weaver's beams is larger than usual, when using these methods. A typical beam would have a 12-inch diameter barrel and 32-inch diameter flanges. Most modern beamers can run up to 800 yards per minute, the limitation being imposed by the yarns in the creel.

WARP SIZING

THE OBJECT OF SIZING is to coat the warp yarns with a substance which will make them smoother, stronger and more compact and thus enable them to withstand better the shedding action in weaving and the abrasion caused by the loom drop wires, healds, reeds and shuttles. In the woollen and worsted industry, sizing is normally carried out only on those warps that would not otherwise weave satisfactorily, such as those made from very fine yarns, weak single yarns or very fibrous yarns. It is also used when the sett and pickage is high, as excessive abrasion often occurs under these conditions. The weave being used also affects the decision to size. Thus many yarns may weave the 2/2 or 3/3 twill unsized but would not weave a plain weave due to the more frequent interlacing of the yarns and the consequent increased amount of chafing.

Experience with automatic systems of weaving suggests that, under those conditions, sizing is advantageous with most yarns as it helps to minimize warp end breakages. Size is normally applied by passing the sheet of warp ends, under tension, through a box containing the size solution. Excess size is removed by roller pressure and the coated yarns are then dried and dressed on to weaver's beams.

The size normally contains an adhesive, an oil to prevent the size from becoming brittle and an antiseptic to prevent mildew. A typical size for woollen warps is made up from 30 to 60 gallons of water, six pounds of "Tragon" and three pounds of glycerine, while the amount applied depends on the nature of the yarn. Thus a light size is used for laying the surface fibres, a medium size is used to give resistance to abrasion, while heavy sizes are used for single woollen and worsted warps to give strength and compactness as well as resistance to abrasion. As the size has to be removed during the finishing of the cloth, it should not contain substances which are not easy to scour out or to remove by desizing agents.

In recent years there has been considerable advancement in the technology of sizing, in the development of sizing equipment and in the adoption of automatic control systems [16,17]. While, therefore, there are various designs of sizing machine, many of which have been adapted from other trades, they all consist of four main sections, a suitable form of creel, a size box with squeeze rollers, drying cylinders or a drying chamber, and suitable dressing and beaming facilities. In the worsted and woollen trades the hot-air drying chamber type is probably the most common but the cotton type of slashing frame is also used. The tendency in the U.S.A. is towards a greater use of the slashing frame owing to the introduction of longer runs and the use of automatic weaving and high-speed preparation machinery. Short-length warps are sometimes sized and dried in ball form, and later dressed at a separate operation on a Yorkshire dressing frame.

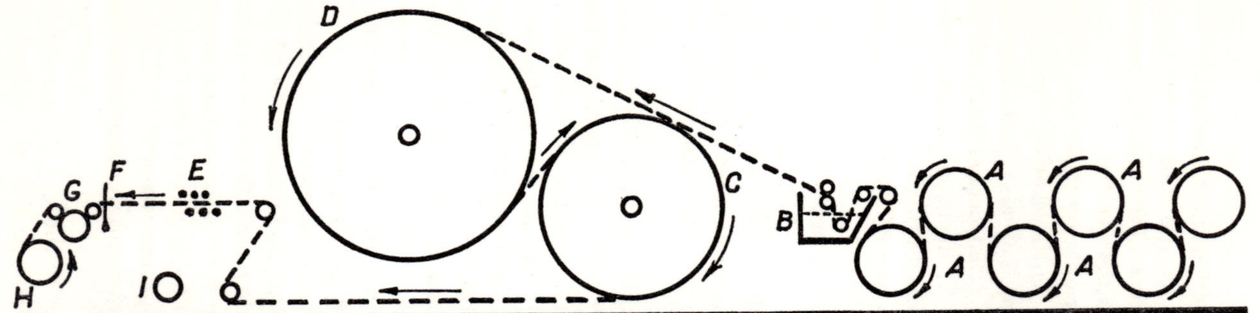

FIG. 6.7.   SCHEMATIC DRAWING OF A SLASHING MACHINE OR TAPE SIZER

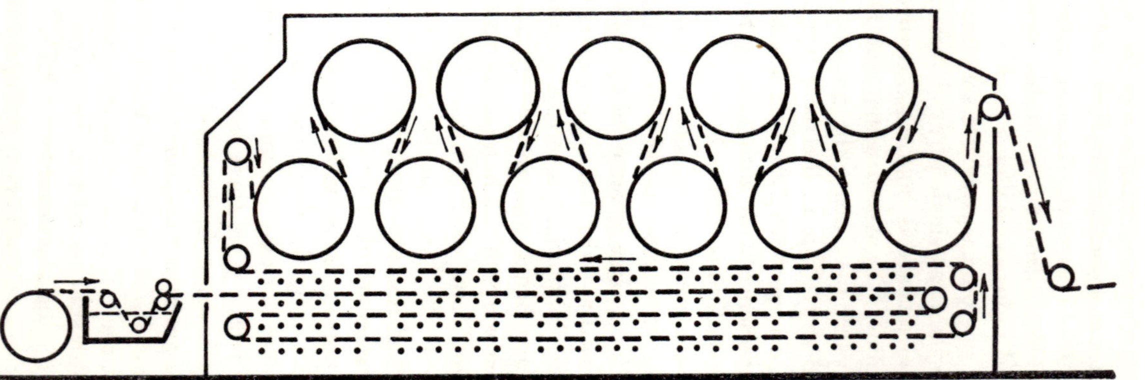

FIG. 6.8.   SCHEMATIC DRAWING OF A SIZING AND HOT-AIR DRYING MACHINE

Figs. 6.7 and 6.8 show respectively the outlines of a slashing machine with steam drying cylinders and the type using a hot-air drying chamber In the former, A is a series of four, six or eight back beams arranged in a two-tier horizontal creel, the total number of ends from which is equivalent to the number required on the weaver's beam. B is a size or sow box, fitted with one or two immersion rollers and one or two pairs of covered squeeze rollers. The size is usually made away from the sizing machine in a large tank from which it is run to small heated storage tanks, being fed from these to the size boxes to maintain a constant level. C and D are two copper drying cylinders, steam heated, around which the warp threads are passed in a wide sheet, while E are split rods, F an expansion comb, G a measuring roller and H the weavers' beam. Fans I are sometimes incorporated after the second drying cylinder to cool the yarn prior to beaming. The purpose of the split rods is to separate threads that have stuck together and the beam is driven at constant linear speed by frictional contact with a positively driven drum.

Care should be taken to avoid stretching the yarn during sizing and to see that it is properly dried. Insufficient drying gives rise to sticky warps with neighbouring ends adhering, while excessive drying causes the size to crack and cause indifferent weaving.

The hot-air drying type of machine at Fig. 6.8 is essentially the same as the slasher with the modified drying arrangement and a modified form of creel. The sheet of sized yarns is passed backwards and forwards, or sometimes upwards and downwards, between banks of steam pipes followed by a passage over a series of small diameter cans or drying cylinders. The object of this system is to secure slower and more even drying and the avoidance of baked yarns. There are no back beams in this system, the creel being suitable for a warper's beam, or for a bank of cheeses or even for ball warps.

There are many different components used for making size and different firms often have their own specific recipes. It was commonly thought that adhesives from protein sources such as glue, gelatine, albumen and casein should be used only on the protein fibres such as wool, while starches and gums should be reserved for the cellulose fibres, such as cotton, and in general this distinction still persists. Glycerol, glycols, oils and waxes are used as softeners while the most common antiseptic is zinc chloride though phenol is also used. Zinc chloride also acts as a deliquescent which prevents the moisture content of the warp yarns from becoming too low. The use of man-made fibres in blends with wool has led to the use of a number of sizes based on such materials as polyvinyl alcohol. The advice of the various man-made fibre producers should be sought, however, to ensure that the sizes are suitable for a particular blend and applied under appropriate conditions.

One of the practical points in sizing is to ensure that the size penetrates the yarn and not merely coats the surface. Wetting agents may be added to the sow box to obtain easier penetration though this should seldom be necessary. The temperature of the drying cylinders or chamber should be maintained within narrow limits, as too high temperatures cause baking of the size, while too low temperatures leave the size sticky, thus causing adjacent ends to stick together. With the vertical steam-heated chamber, the temperature at the top is often higher than at the bottom in order to improve drying conditions. Among new methods of drying which are being used reference should be made to infra-red heating and to the directing of high-velocity air streams on to the surfaces of the yarn sheet. Ball warp sizing is not very common, as it involves separate operations of sizing, drying and dressing or beaming.

SETTING CREPE TWISTED YARNS

Though not connected with sizing, reference may be made here to the setting of crepe twisted yarns. This is usually done by low pressure steam, the yarn on perforated bobbins being pushed into small chambers into which the steam is injected. Modern methods include vacuum steaming chambers and the use of high-frequency currents.

REFERENCES

1   "Winding, Warping and Weaving", W. Barker, Emmott, 1938.
2   *Textile Weekly*, 1962, **62**, 951.
3   Ormerod, A., *Textile Weekly*, 1963, **63**, 830, 868, 929, 975.
4   Snowdon, D. C., *Wool Review*, 1962, March, April, August, October.
5   Brunnschweiler, D., *Textile Mercury*, 1959, **140**, 822, 845.
6   Smith, J. B., *Textile Weekly*, 1961, **61**, 127.
7   *Textile Weekly*, 1962, **62**, 1030.
8   "Modern Developments in Weaving Machinery", Edited by Duxbury and Wray, Chapter 5, Published by Columbine Press, 1962.
9   Campens, F., *Ann. Sci. Text. Belges*, 1962, **3**, Sept. 60.
10 Brierley, M. H., *Textile Weekly*, 1963, **63**, 1065.
11 Deusson, H., *Text Bull*, 1963, **89**, 39.
12 *Textile Recorder*, 1964, **81**, Feb. 78.
13 Van der Veen, A. J., *Textile Weekly*, 1964, **64**, 719.
14 *Whitin Review*, 1950, **17**, No. 6, 29.
15 Thomas, I. H., *Fibres*, 1950, **11**, 122.
16 "The Technology of Warp Sizing", J. B. Smith (editor), Published by Columbine Press, 1964.
17 "Warp Sizing", P. V. Seydel, Published by the W. R. Smith Publishing Company, 1958.

WOOLLEN AND WORSTED WEAVING

ALTHOUGH the main processes concerned in the preparation of warp and weft yarns for weaving have been described in some detail in Section 6, there still remains one operation which is an essential preliminary to weaving, irrespective of the type of loom employed. This operation, to which reference has not yet been made, is generally known as 'looming' and, in view of its fundamental importance, warrants some detailed description.

LOOMING

BRIEFLY STATED, the operation of looming consists of drawing-in the individual ends comprising the warp sheet through mails or eyes attached to the heald shafts – or to the jacquard mechanism – so that they may be lifted for the insertion of the weft in the order and arrangement necessary to produce the particular weave structure required.

The simplest arrangement is obviously one in which only two heald shafts are employed, alternate ends in the warp sheet being inserted through the eyes of one shaft while the intervening ends are threaded through the eyes of the other. This arrangement produces a plain (1 x 1) weave when the shafts are lifted alternately to form a 'shed' for the passage of the shuttle. It will be appreciated that, where more than two shafts are provided, it is possible to raise these in more than one sequence and thus to obtain more than one type of weave. This will be clear from the diagrams shown in Fig. 7.1, where the three horizontal lines in the upper sketches represent shafts and the vertical lines the warp threads, the crosses at the intersections denoting the points where the thread is drawn through a mail. The lower part of sketch *A* shows the intersections of warp (vertical) and weft (horizontal) which occur if the healds are raised singly in the order 1, 2, 3, counting from the front to the back. This weave is known as a 1/2 twill. By lifting two shafts at a time in the order 1, 2; 2, 3; 3, 1, a 2/1 twill is obtained. The upper sketch at *B* shows three shafts with the ends drawn through them in different order. By lifting the shafts singly in the order, 1, 2, 3, a five-end herringbone weave is obtained, as shown in the lower sketch *B*.

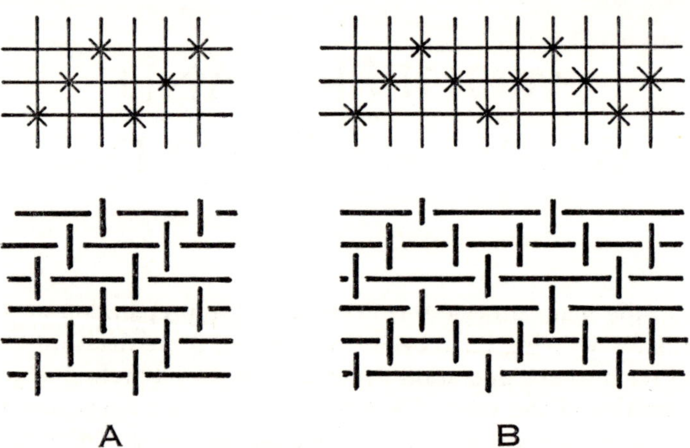

FIG. 7.1.   DRAFTING AND LIFTING ARRANGEMENTS

Incidentally, the weaves referred to above, and elsewhere in this chapter, together with other fundamental and developed weaves, are described in detail and illustrated in Section 8 which deals specifically with woven fabric structures (see page 275 *et seq.*).

WEAVE, DRAFT AND PEGGING PLAN

It will be seen from the above that, when issuing weaving instructions, it is necessary to state (*i*) the number of healds required to produce the desired weave, (*ii*) the order in which the warp ends are to be drawn through the eyes of the several healds (*i.e.*, the draft), and (*iii*) the order in which the shafts must be raised to produce the desired pattern. To indicate this order a 'lifting plan' or 'pegging plan' is produced. Obviously, there must be at least as many shafts as the number of different ways in which the warp ends interlace with the weft. Although all warp ends lifting together can theoretically be controlled from the same shaft, in certain cases it is more convenient to divide them between two or more shafts.

Wherever the design shows warp threads above weft, it is necessary that the heald shaft controlling those threads should rise.

This interdependence of weave, draft and pegging plan is illustrated by Fig. 7.2, which represents the weaving of a 2/2 twill on four shafts with a straight draft. Shafts 1 and 2 are required to be lifted for the first pick and this is shown by the crosses in the appropriate squares of the pegging plan. On the second pick shafts 2 and 3 need to be raised and this is again in-

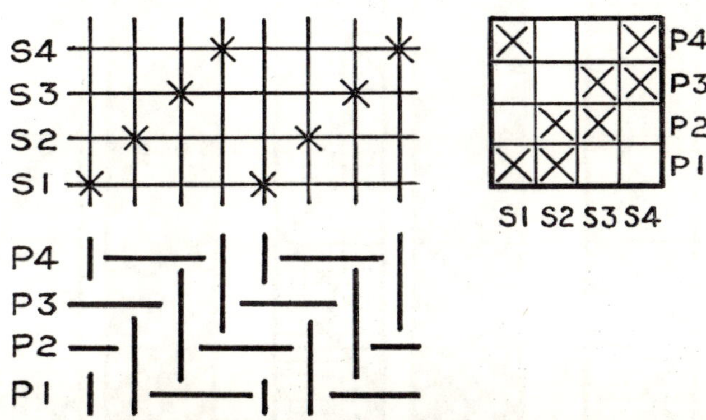

FIG. 7.2.   DIAGRAMS SHOWING INTERDEPENDENCE
OF WEAVE, DRAFT AND PEGGING PLAN

dicated by the crosses in the pegging plan. Pick 3 requires that shafts 3 and 4 be lifted, while pick 4 requires the lifting of shafts 1 and 4. Incidentally, to avoid confusion it is conventional to arrange the design, draft and pegging plan as shown in two simple examples in Fig. 7.3.

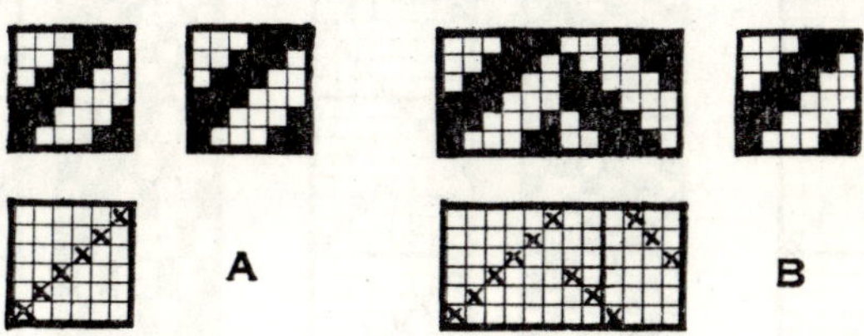

FIG. 7.3.   CONVENTIONAL ARRANGEMENT OF
DESIGN, DRAFT AND PEGGING PLANS

It should perhaps also be pointed out that the designs used in this book for single cloths are based on the generally accepted practice of showing 'warp over weft' by black squares and 'weft over warp' by white squares, horizontal rows of squares representing weft and vertical rows warp. The subject, however, is dealt with in greater detail in Section 8 dealing with woven fabric structures (see page 276).

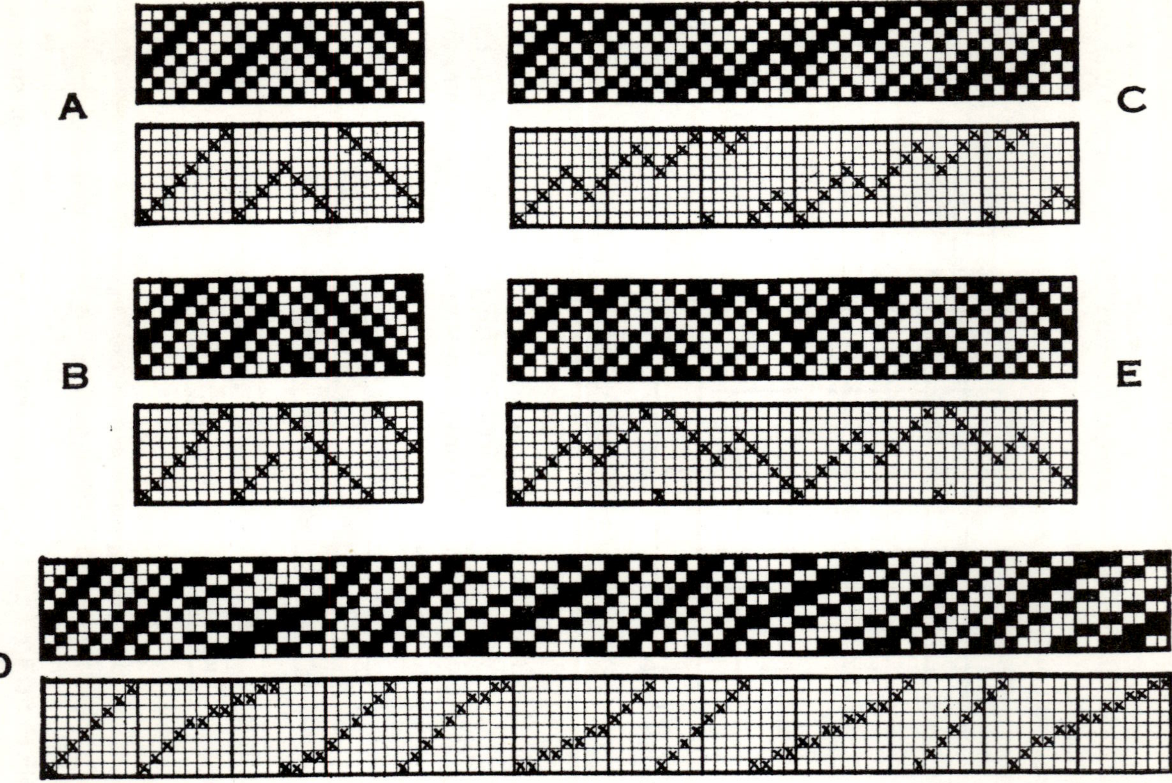

FIG. 7.4. EXAMPLES OF COMPLEX DESIGNS OBTAINABLE BY VARIATION IN THE ORDER OF DRAFTING AND WHICH REQUIRE RELATIVELY FEW HEALD SHAFTS

Other things being equal, patterns that have been woven with the least number of heald shafts are the cheapest, and it is often one of the aims of a designer to produce a complex design requiring few shafts. One method that is used is to vary the order of drafting. Examples of some of the effects which can be obtained in this way are shown in Fig. 7.4. *A* shows the ends drafted straight and reverse – point or 'V'-draft – to give a herringbone effect. Its defect is the long float formed where the weave turns and *B* shows the 'angle' draft method for avoiding this. A 'zig-zag' draft is illustrated at *C* and a 'waved' draft at *D*. *E* uses a combination of angle and waved drafts. Resulting weaves from these examples can be woven on eight shafts and can, therefore, be made on a tappet loom.

There are a number of practical points to bear in mind when determining the draft. The number of shafts to be used is obviously limited by the capacity of the loom on which the warp is to be woven, unless special tappets or other means are available for working an extra one or two shafts.

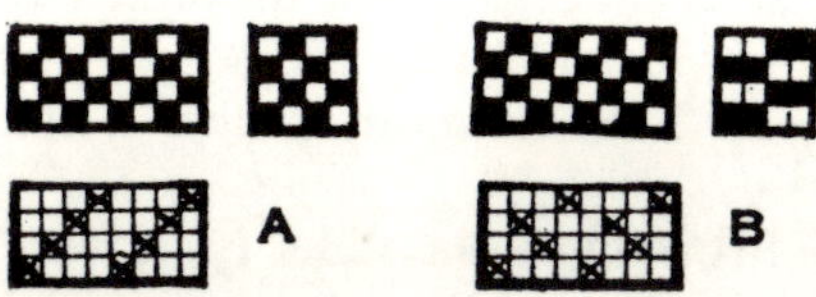

FIG. 7.5.   TWO METHODS OF DRAFTING
A PLAIN FABRIC ON FOUR HEALDS

As a general rule, drafts should be kept as simple as possible, even if this means the use of a few more shafts, for this facilitates looming and eases the work of the weaver when repairing broken ends. It should always be appreciated that an easy draft and a complex pegging plan is much better than a complex draft and a simple pegging plan.

The drafting of twills should be in the same direction as the twill in the cloth, as this eases the work of the weaver in taking up broken ends. The number of ends on each shaft should be equalized as far as possible so as to equalize the load on each lift. If some shafts have to be more heavily sett than others, they should be arranged nearest to the reed, as this again facilitates the weaver's work. If, however, there are two sets of warp threads and one is known to weave less easily than the other, the healds carrying the more difficult ends should be placed to the front of the loom as the lift is less in this position. In extra warp fabrics, the extra ends are usually loomed through slider healds placed at the back. Friction and rubbing of neighbouring heald shafts should be minimized, and for this reason, the draft and pegging plan at *B* in Fig. 7.5 is to be preferred to that shown at *A* in the same illustration.

TYPES OF HEALD

Before discussing the actual drawing-in of the warp ends through the eyes or mails of the appropriate healds, some description of these important items of loom equipment is warranted[1]. In the woollen and worsted industries two main types of heald – one knitted and the other a wire heald – are employed, but there are several modifications of these types in use. Knitted healds are made from gassed worsted or cotton cords and are suspended between two laths or shafts. Worsted cords are much more common than cotton cords. The heald twine supports a steel or brass mail midway between the two shafts and the size of the mail varies with the counts of yarn, an average size being three-eighths of an inch. The depth of the healds depends on the number to be used together, the greater the number, the greater the depth. An average depth for use on tappet looms is 16 inches but up to 20 inches are needed for large capacity dobbies.

The chief disadvantage of knitted healds is their lack of adaptability. They can be used only for the sett or counts for which they have been knitted or for lower setts by casting out unwanted mails. They are, however, much lighter than metal healds and so are preferred when a large number of shafts is used. The maximum spacing of knitted healds is usually 12 per inch.

Wire healds are of two types, the slider type, where two thin wires are twisted to form an eye in the middle and a loop at each end, and the knitted wire heald, which use the same wires as the slider type but which are knitted on to ridge bands. In the slider type, the loops slide along two steel rods so that the wires can be added to or withdrawn to accommodate differently sett warps or they can be stripped from the rods for cleaning or replacing. They can be set more closely than knitted healds.

Flat wire healds are seldom used in the woollen and worsted industries in this country; they are flat strips of wire with holes punched in them to serve the purpose of the loops. In the U.S.A. flat wire healds are mostly used for worsted warps while the slider type is extensively used for the heavier woollen warps.

Great care should be taken when storing sets of healds. Metal healds should be well cleaned after use and any signs of rust should be removed. Bent or damaged wires should be taken out and replaced.

TYING-IN AND DRAWING-IN A NEW WARP

It will be apparent from preceding paragraphs that the looming or drawing-in of the warp ends through the mails or eyes of the appropriate healds so that the fabric may be woven in accordance with the designer's plan, is all-important.[2,3].

In certain cases, all that is required is to replace an almost exhausted warp by a new one in order to continue weaving the same design on the same number of shafts. Here, the procedure usually followed is to mount the new warp behind the loom and to twist by hand or tie by machine each end to the corresponding end of the old warp. When all the ends have been so joined, the new warp is pulled through the healds and reed and attached to the cloth roller ready for weaving. Frequently, this operation is done away from the loom, the thrums (*i.e.*, the ends) of the old warp, reed and heald shafts being first taken out of the loom.

Where a new warp needs to be drafted in a new order, the usual practice is to mount the warp beam and healds in a frame and pass the threads individually through the mails and reed in the required order, one person sitting behind the healds placing each end in turn over the eye of a hook pushed through the mail by a drawer-in seated in front. Reaching-in machines are now available, the drawer-in taking the appropriate threads as selected by this machine. On completion, the warp, shafts and reed are taken from the drawing frame and are ready for gaiting at the loom.

The operation of drawing-in takes up a considerable amount of time and, accordingly, automatic warp tying and twisting machines have been developed[4]. These machines are mounted, either behind the loom or at a separate frame, the old and new warps being positioned relatively to it. Normally the machine itself chooses the ends in correct sequence from an end-and-end lease and corresponding new and old ends are tied or twisted together automatically. Usually, the two ends are cut, both prior to knotting and after the knot has been tied, though there are many modifications of the actual procedure; threads are cut to a definite length in twisting.

In drawing-in a new warp in accordance with a new design, attention has to be given to a number of points, such as the number of shafts to be used, spacing of heddles (or healds) on the shafts, the order of drawing ends through the mails (*i.e.*, the draft) and the order of drawing the ends through the reed. The width and depth of harness will be governed by the loom being used and by the nature of the warp yarn. Cotton or linen twine heddles with metal mails are still extensively used but the all-metal heald is becoming more common.

As previously stated, the minimum number of shafts which can be used for any weave is the number of different ways in which the warp ends interlace with the weft but, in practice, a larger number of shafts are often used, either to simplify the draft or to equalize the load or number of ends drawn on each shaft. There is also a practical limit to the rate at which heddles can be spaced on the shafts for any particular trade; for example, ten per inch for the coating trade. Examples of different types of drafts have already been given and Fig. 7.5 showed how the same weave could be drafted in different ways, illustrating that a simple draft and complicated pegging plan as at *B* is to be preferred to a complicated draft and simple pegging plan as at *A*.

THE SPACING OF HEDDLES

The number of heddles per inch is readily obtained from the draft and the number of ends per inch in the warp. Thus, if there are 64 ends per inch and there are eight shafts, drafted straight, there will be eight ends per inch on each shaft and the heddles will be spaced eight per inch. If the draft is such that there is not the same number of ends on each shaft as in Fig. 7.6, the procedure is similar. In this draft, two ends out of 16 will be on each of the first four shafts; so, again assuming 64 ends per inch in the warp, there will be two-sixteenths of 64 or eight ends per inch on each of these shafts and the heddles will be spaced accordingly.

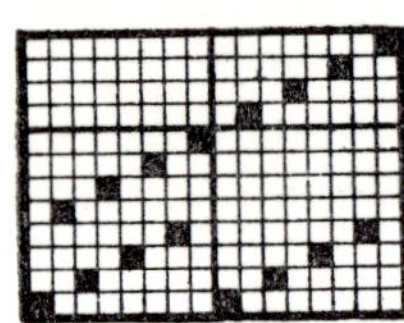

FIG. 7.6.   DRAFT
TO ILLUSTRATE THE
SPACING OF
HEDDLES

On the back eight shafts, however, there is only one end out of 16 on each shaft and, accordingly, the number of ends and the spacing of the heddles on these shafts will be four per inch. Usually, of course, all the shafts would be gaited similarly at the rate of eight heddles per inch, in which case only alternate mails in the back eight shafts would be used. This procedure is known as 'casting-out' and is described more fully in the section on jacquard weaving where it is more extensively employed.

To quote a more complicated healding arrangement, the procedure in the case of a crammed stripe design may be described. The design given at A in Fig. 7.7 represents a weave in which there are 48 ends plain, 24 ends 4/4 warp rib, 36 ends 2/2 warp rib and 24 ends 4/4 warp rib per repeat. The draft for this weave is given at B in Fig. 7.7, from which it will be seen that the first four shafts are used for the plain weave, the second four shafts for the 4/4 warp rib and the third four shafts for the 2/2 warp rib. The denting of this warp in the reed is two ends per dent for the plain weave, four ends per dent for the 4/4 warp rib and three ends per dent for the 2/2 warp rib as shown at C. Assuming the reed to have 24 dents per inch, there would be 24 x 2 or 48 ends per inch for the plain weave, 24 x 4 or 96 ends per inch for the 4/4 warp rib and 24 x 3 or 72 ends per inch for the 2/2 warp rib. The first set of four shafts are thus required to carry 48 ends per inch, equivalent to 12 heddles per inch; the second set of four takes 96 ends per inch, giving 24 heddles per inch, while the third set of four has 72 ends per inch needing 18 heddles per inch. As the largest number of heddles per inch required is 24, the heald knitting machine has to be set up to knit 24 heddles to the inch.

On the first four shafts, only 12 heddles per inch are required and so the knitting machine knits one and misses one twelve times. As the next sections of the design are drawn on the second and third heald sets, and together occupy one inch (48 ends of 4/4 warp rib at 96 ends per inch plus 36 ends of 2/2 warp rib at 72 ends per inch), no heddles are required on the first heald set for this space and the complete heald knitting order becomes knit one, miss one, for twelve times and then miss twenty-four.

The 4/4 warp rib sections are made up of 24 threads drawn in the reed 96 ends per inch. Each section, therefore, occupies ¼-inch and as it is drawn on four shafts, there will be six heddles knitted in ¼-inch at the maximum setting of the machine, 24 per inch. The two 4/4 warp rib sections are separated by ½-inch of 2/2 warp rib so the order of knitting for the second four shafts will be miss 24 where the plain weave section comes on the front four shafts, knit 6, miss 12 where the 2/2 warp rib comes on the last four shafts, and then knit 6. The back four shafts require 18 heddles knitted per inch, and as the machine is set to knit 24 heddles to the

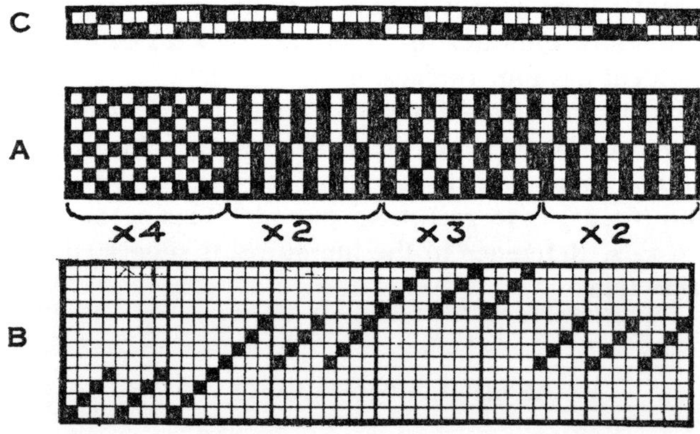

FIG. 7.7.   A CRAMMED STRIPE DESIGN ILLUSTRATING
A MORE COMPLICATED HEALD ARRANGEMENT

inch, the order of knitting will be knit 3 miss 1, giving nine heddles per ½-inch section. The complete knitting order for these shafts will therefore be: miss 30 where the first and second sections occur, knit 3 miss 1 three times, and then miss 6 where the last section occurs.

DRAWING ENDS THROUGH THE REED

The order of drawing ends through the reed is usually straightforward, two or four per dent according to the sett of the warp but care should be exercised in the case of ribs and hopsacks to split adjacent ends that work alike to prevent rolling. Coarse reeds give less abrasion on the warp ends than do fine reeds but finer reeds give better cover. Much depends in practice, however, on such features as the quality of the yarns, the depth of shed and the sett of the warp. All these must be taken into consideration in judging the best system of denting. The construction of various types of reed is described and illustrated on pages 258-260.

REED NUMBERING SYSTEMS

There are various systems of numbering the reeds[5], the best being the Huddersfield and American systems where the sett number is given by the number of dents or splits per inch, that is, a 12's reed has 12 dents per inch. The number of ends per dent is placed after the reed number, e.g., 12/4, where the 4 indicates that there are four ends in each dent giving 48 ends per inch. The other common system of reed and warp numbering in the worsted trade is the Bradford system where the sett of the warp is the number of 'beers', each of 40 ends in a width of 36 inches. Thus, if 40 ends are distributed over 36 inches, the sett number is 1's Bradford, and if 80 ends are spread over 36 inches, 2's Bradford. The standard sley has two ends per dent, so 1's sley Bradford has 20 dents per 36 inches, while a 60's sley Bradford has 60 x 20 dents per 36 inches or $33\frac{1}{3}$ dents per inch. A 60/4 sett Bradford indicates that there are 60 x 20 dents per 36 inches and that each dent has four threads.

It is frequently necessary for the designer to calculate the sett after having determined the ends per inch in the warp. Thus, if a cloth is to be woven with 60 ends per inch, there will be 60 times 36 ends spread over 36 inches and (60 x 36)/40 groups of 40 ends. This is the Bradford sett, equivalent to 54's. Reference to the literature[5] is suggested for other examples of this type.

CLASSIFICATION OF LOOMS

POWER LOOMS are usually divided into three classes according to the type of shedding motion used. Tappet looms are the simplest type and are so called because the heald shafts are actuated by a number of tappets or cams. This class includes the plain, Lancashire or calico loom and the Bradford or Yorkshire loom. The former is usually fitted with two fixed under-tappets and is used extensively in the cotton industry for plain weaves, whereas the Bradford tappet loom is more common in the woollen and worsted trades and has usually eight interchangeable tappets fitted outside the loom framing. The Bradford loom normally runs at a slower speed than the Lancashire type but its figuring capacity is much higher. Many tappet looms are fitted with two or more shuttle boxes at one side of the sley, thus allowing the weft to be mixed or even-picked colour effects to be obtained; boxes at both sides are also used for patterns with single or odd-numbered picks. Compared with other looms this class is cheap, simple and reliable.

Dobby looms are so called because of the dobby mechanism that operates and controls the heald shafts. Up to 48 shafts can be separately controlled but 12, 16, and 24-shaft dobbies are most common. These looms have a much larger figuring capacity than the tappet loom and are often fitted with boxes at both sides of the loom to allow weft patterning.

The third class of loom is the jacquard type which is mounted with a jacquard machine for controlling the lifting of the warp ends. These looms have an almost unlimited figuring capacity and are used for all elaborately figured fabrics such as tapestries, carpets and furnishing fabrics.

Fundamentally the three types of loom referred to above do not differ to any large extent except in respect of the shedding motion and it is logical, therefore, to discuss these three types of mechanism in some detail in the pages which follow before proceeding to other primary and secondary mechanisms, some of which have been the subject of considerable development. This is particularly true of weft insertion systems, not only with regard to the establishment of automatic weft-changing mechanisms, but in respect of the development of a range of unconventional weaving machines designed to use a continuous weft supply and to overcome the limitations of the traditional shuttle-picking systems.

DEVELOPMENTS IN LOOM DESIGN

While the importance of such developments cannot be over emphasized, developments in orthodox loom design should not be overlooked, even if traditional principles remain largely unchanged. Not only loom makers but manufacturers of weaving equipment and ancillary machines continue to introduce new models, often built to finer limits, faster in operation, simpler to operate and easier to maintain. The present trend to locate motions, as far as is possible, outside the loom framing and to control healds from underneath, rather than above the loom, to give it a 'topless' appearance, has the double advantage of assisting illumination and of providing unimpeded access to the work in progress. Many looms are now equipped with pneumatic devices to remove fly, cut ends and extraneous lint, while the adoption of air conditioning in modern installations, in addition to maintaining uniform conditions of temperature and humidity, has had the general effect of keeping the atmosphere clean and more pleasant in which to work.

It is regretted that in the descriptions of the loom mechanisms given in this book, brevity has been essential and reference to many developments has had to be sacrificed for descriptions of traditional motions to illustrate basic principles. For fuller details, reference should be made to such works as those by W. J. Fox[6], W. P. Crankshaw[7], T. Roberts[8], W. Middlebrook[9-11] and to the symposium 'Modern Developments in Weaving Machinery', edited by V. Duxbury and G. R. Wray[12].

SHEDDING MOTIONS

IN DESCRIBING the various types of shedding motion it is logical to deal first with that of the ubiquitous tappet loom, of which there are two main types, the Lancashire calico loom and the Bradford or Yorkshire or cross-rod loom. The former, however, is only occasionally seen in worsted weaving sheds. The Bradford type of tappet loom has eight or twelve interchangeable tappets and is used extensively in the worsted trade for ladies' dress and coating fabrics. For dress fabrics, the looms generally have a reed space of 40 inches and may be fitted with circular or drop-box motions.

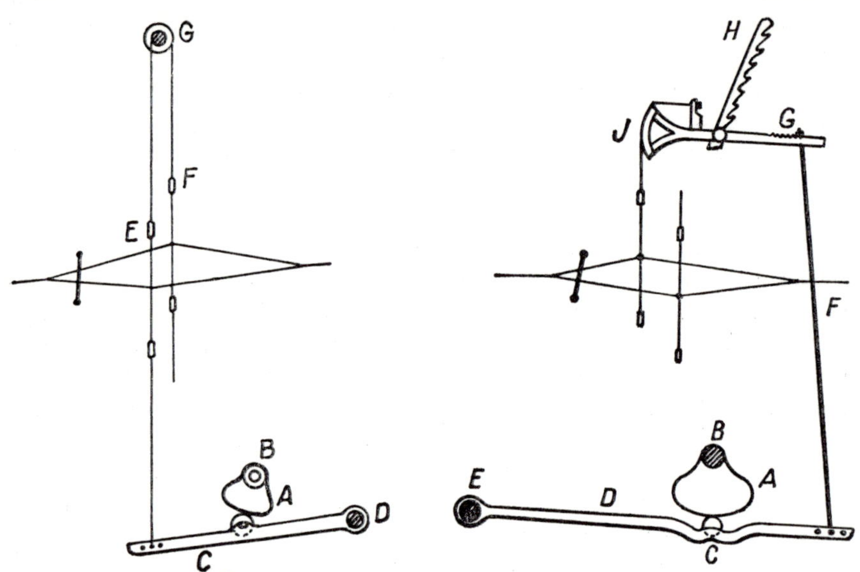

FIG. 7.8.   TAPPET SHEDDING   FIG. 7.9.   TAPPET SHEDDING
FOR A LANCASHIRE LOOM   FOR A BRADFORD LOOM

For coating fabrics, a heavier loom is used with a reed space of about 76 inches and speeds of 100 to 140 picks per minute are possible on these looms. Heavy woollen looms with a reed space of 110 inches have a speed of about 85 picks per minute.

TAPPET SHEDDING MOTIONS

The simplest arrangement of tappet shedding, as used in the Lancashire loom, where two heald shafts receive a reciprocating motion for producing a plain weave, is illustrated in Fig. 7.8. *A* is one of two cams fixed to the shaft *B* which is driven continuously from the crankshaft or main shaft of the loom and at half its speed. The cams operate against bowls in the treadles C which are fulcrummed from the back rail D and extend under the heald shafts E and F. Connections are made to the shafts E and F as shown, the top of the shafts being connected by straps to separate bosses on the short cross-shaft G.

All the threads move a maximum distance to form an 'open' type of shedding, thus putting the maximum stress on the yarns. In rising and falling, the heald shafts should start to move slowly and gradually increase in speed until the centre of the lift is reached. From this point, there should be a gradual decrease in speed until the shed is fully open. The back shaft F has to make a bigger lift than the front shaft E to maintain the proper size of shed and it is also connected slightly more towards the fulcrum of the treadles. Hence a larger tappet is used for controlling the back shaft and a larger boss is necessary on the top shaft G. By suitable modification to the under motion and top roller arrangements the Lancashire shedding motion can be adapted to take three or four shafts.

The essential parts of the shedding motion for the Bradford tappet loom are shown in Fig. 7.9. The tappets A, up to eight and occasionally 12 in number, are keyed outside the loom framing to a sleeve that fits loosely over the bottom shaft B. A wheel is cast with the sleeve and is driven by a train of wheels from the crankshaft. Each tappet is positioned over its own anti-friction bowl C on separate treadles D; each treadle is fulcrummed at E and the outer arm is connected by a streamer rod F to the outer arm of the lever G. This lever is keyed to a square rod carried in brackets H. Two 'half-moon' levers J are also keyed to the square shaft, one at each side of the heald shaft which they carry by means of straps. These connections are repeated for each tappet in the set.

The tappets used on this loom are of several types. For standard weaves, the tappets are sometimes cast together and slipped on to the tappet shaft in one piece. Where the tappets are separate, they may be set as follows: With all the wheels in gear, the loom is turned over until the going part is so far forward that the tongue of the stop-rod or warp protector motion rests gently against the 'frog' on the loom frame. The tappet driving wheel is then secured to the crankshaft and the first tappet on the tappet shaft fixed at a given point. For each subsequent tappet, the loom is turned one complete revolution and the tappet fixed at the same point. Each tappet is fixed directly over the anti-friction bowls of the treadle with which it has to work. In a few cases the individual tappets are built up from small sections.

The outline of the tappet is governed primarily by the weave but is modified to suit particular conditions of timing and shedding. The following points are of interest from the viewpoint of tappet designing: The size of the shed should be as small as possible to prevent unnecessary warp breakages and strains. Too small a shed will result in end breakages and

more force will be needed to drive the shuttle through the shed. Tappets
should be constructed to give an eccentric motion to the heald shafts; that
is, the shafts should move slowly towards the limits of their movement and
quickly when the warp threads are crossing each other.

The dwell or pause of the shafts for shuttle passage should be a minimum, governed by the width and speed of the loom, the yarns being
woven and the cloth 'cover' required. In narrow, fast-running dress-goods
looms a dwell corresponding to one-third of a pick is standard practice
but for wide, slower-running looms a dwell of two-fifths to one-half of a
pick is often employed. The shape of the tappet is modified by the size of
the anti-friction bowl so that a tappet constructed for one size should not
be used with other bowl sizes. The Bradford loom has an 'open' type of
shed so that when a shaft requires to be up or down for more than one
pick, the dwell is carried forward to the next pick and the shaft remains
stationary for as many consecutive picks as required.

It is instructive to draw the outline of a tappet and, as an illustration,
Fig. 7.10 has been prepared for a 2/2 twill tappet with a three-inch diameter boss, three-inch stroke, three-inch diameter anti-friction bowl and
one-third of a pick dwell using the following stages:

Stage 1 : Draw the outline of the boss, three-inches in diameter.

Stage 2 : Draw two circles with centre O to represent the innermost
and outermost paths of the centre of the anti-friction bowl,
the former having a radius of $1\frac{1}{2}$-inch plus $1\frac{1}{2}$-inch or three
inches and the latter $1\frac{1}{2}$-inch plus $1\frac{1}{2}$-inch plus three inch
stroke or six inches.

Stage 3 : Divide the space into four equal segments, this being the
number of picks in a repeat of the 2/2 twill. For a 2/1 twill
tappet, each segment would be 120 degrees and for a plain
weave 180 degrees.

Stage 4 : Draw in each segment lines at OB and OC where angles
AOB, BOC and COD are 30 degrees, or one-third of the size
of the segments. The dwell for picking takes place when the
part of the tappet within angle BOC is against the bowl; the
two outer angles, each of 30 degrees, are for the changes in
the position of the shaft.

Stage 5 : With centre J draw a semi-circle, $1\frac{1}{2}$-inch radius and divide
the circumference into six equal parts. Drop perpendicular
lines from each point on to the line AOK. With centre O,
make six sectors in each segment where shaft changes are
taking place as shown.

Stage 6: With compasses set 1½-inches as the radius of the anti-friction bowl, draw arcs with centres 1, 2, 3, 4, 5, 6 and 7 and with corresponding points for the other change.

Stage 7: Draw the envelope to the arcs and complete the outline of the tappet by *EF* and *GH* which respectively represents the periods when the shafts remain up and down.

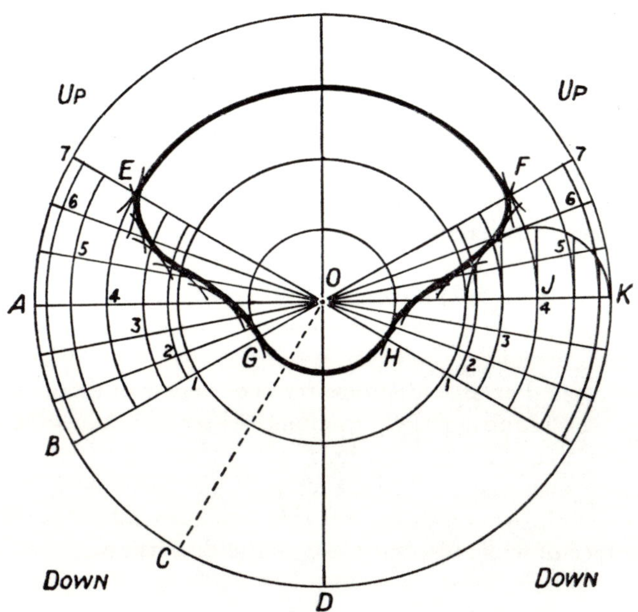

FIG. 7.10.   METHOD OF DESIGNING A SHEDDING TAPPET

The connections between the treadles and the shafts can be altered to suit different conditions. The size of the shed can be modified by altering the position of the streamer rods on either the treadle or jack lever. The lowest central position of each shaft can be obtained by turning the winged nut at the top of *F* (Fig. 7.9). Simple changes in pattern can be produced by changing the order of the connection between streamer rods and jack levers. Thus, a 2/2 twill can be changed to a broken twill or Devon weave by altering the connections from 1, 2, 3, 4 to 1, 3, 2, 4.

The normal timing for ordinary warps is for the shafts to begin to change when the crank is between back and top centres. This is modified to suit the type of cloth and the nature of the yarns being used. Thus, early shedding is given for fibrous and hairy warps to allow the surface fibre to be fully separated when the shuttle enters the shed and also for weaves such as corkscrews or Venetian to avoid stitching. Early shedding puts extra stress on the warp yarns because the reed has to beat up each pick of weft after the shafts have crossed. This tends to lock the last weft pick at the beat-up. There is no tendency for the pick of weft to roll back when the pressure of the reed is removed and hence it is useful to employ early shedding when a heavily picked cloth is being woven. On the other hand, later timing is employed for weak warps to avoid too much friction between the warp and weft yarns when the pick is being beaten up to the cloth fell. Late timing can give rise to cracks weftways when the weaver stops the loom to change the shuttle due to the last pick rolling away from the fell. Late shedding is also often used with cloths that contract excessively weftways. Alteration in the timing of the shedding can be effected by moving the tappets slightly forwards or backwards on their sleeve. The going part should be turned over until the crank arm is midway between the top and front centres. At this position the tappets are loosened, the going part moved to the required new position and the tappets re-fixed to the sleeve.

The tappets depress the treadles and so lift the shafts; depression is effected by springs attached to the bottom of the shafts, by stocks and bowls or, more usually, by special undermotions. Shedding motions requiring a reversing arrangement are termed 'negative' motions as distinct from those not requiring such motions, which are known as 'positive' motions. Negative reversing motions can occasionally become inefficient when weaving warp-faced fabrics, such as Venetians, face upwards, due to the heavy work thrown on them. For this reason such fabrics are occasionally woven face downwards, but this has the disadvantage that it prevents the weaver detecting faults.

The tappets are driven from the crankshaft at a speed which accords to the number of picks in the weave. As the shape of each tappet corresponds to the movement of a heald shaft in one complete repeat of the weave, it follows that a tappet must make one revolution while the crankshaft makes as many revolutions as there are picks in the particular weave or pattern. The socket or tappet wheel which has a neck on to which the tappets are fixed, has usually 120 teeth and is driven from the crankshaft wheel through an intermediate wheel. The crankshaft wheel is the change-wheel and its size is obtained by dividing the number of teeth in the tappet wheel by the number of picks in the pattern. Thus for a 2/2 twill, the change-wheel will have 120 divided by 4, or 30 teeth, and for a 2/1 twill, 120 divided by 3 or 40 teeth. A stud is used in place of a simple intermediate wheel when a large number of picks in the pattern are needed or when the number of picks does not divide exactly into 120, such as is the case with seven or nine. In the latter case, the crankshaft needs to rotate nine times to every revolution of the tappets, while a suitable stud combination can be determined from the following formula:

$$\frac{\text{Tappet speed}}{\text{Crankshaft speed}} = \frac{\text{Crankshaft wheel x Small stud wheel}}{\text{Tappet wheel x Large stud wheel}}$$

Thus, in the above case, assuming the crankshaft wheel has 30 teeth and the tappet wheel 120 teeth, then ...

$$\frac{\text{Tappet speed}}{\text{Crankshaft speed}} = \frac{1}{9} = \frac{30 \text{ x Small stud wheel}}{120 \text{ x Large stud wheel}}$$

$$\text{or } \frac{\text{Large stud wheel}}{\text{Small stud wheel}} = \frac{9 \text{ x } 30}{120} = \frac{9}{4}$$

Suitable stud combinations would therefore be 45 and 20, or 54 and 24.

DOBBY SHEDDING MOTIONS

Dobbies are used on looms with the object of increasing the warp figuring capacity and, in general, occupy a place intermediate between the tappet and jacquard looms. They allow control of up to 48 shafts so that the pattern warp-ways can be extended considerably as compared with tappet shedding looms with up to eight shafts. There are several types of dobby mechanism which can be broadly classified into lever and wheel dobbies and there are different capacities of each according to the type of cloth and weave that is to be produced. Thus, most dobbies take 16 to 24 shafts, although for fine woollen and worsted suitings, trouserings and coatings, up to 36 shafts are used while for fancy dress fabrics as many as 48 shafts may be employed. Dobby motions can also be divided into positive and negative types according to whether or not the mechanism depresses the shafts as well as lifts them. The negative dobby[11] is most suitable for light or medium-weight dress goods while the positive type, which both lifts and depresses the shafts, is better suited for weaving the heavier coating fabrics.

THE NEGATIVE LEVER DOBBY

The principle on which the many types of negative lever dobby operate is indicated at Fig. 7.11 which depicts a modern angular or V-dobby. This is bolted to the top rail of the loom on the opposite side to the driving pulleys and is driven from the low shaft of the loom A by a crank arm B and a long shedding rod C. The top of C is connected by a knuckle joint to the outer arm of a T-lever DE fulcrummed on a horizontal shaft F which passes through the dobby frame. A simple lever with two arms corresponding to D and E is keyed to the opposite end of shaft F and two connected draw knives G and H are free to move in slots in the dobby frame. The knives are connected by rods and studs to the outer arms D and E.

Two rows of catches I and J are fixed in the hollow ends of a series of baulk levers K, two hooks to each baulk lever as shown. Each baulk lever has a hole in the middle which fits on a stud L cast on one side of each jack lever M. These levers are fulcrummed on a shaft N and are connected by hooked streamer rods O and O^1 to two supplementary levers P and P^1 from which a heald shaft is suspended. The series of catches I and J are supported by feelers Q placed side by side and fulcrummed on a rod R. The odd-numbered feelers support the lower hooks but the upper hooks are supported from the even-numbered feelers by needles S. The feelers are made with heavy outer ends so that normally they hold the hooks clear of the draw knives.

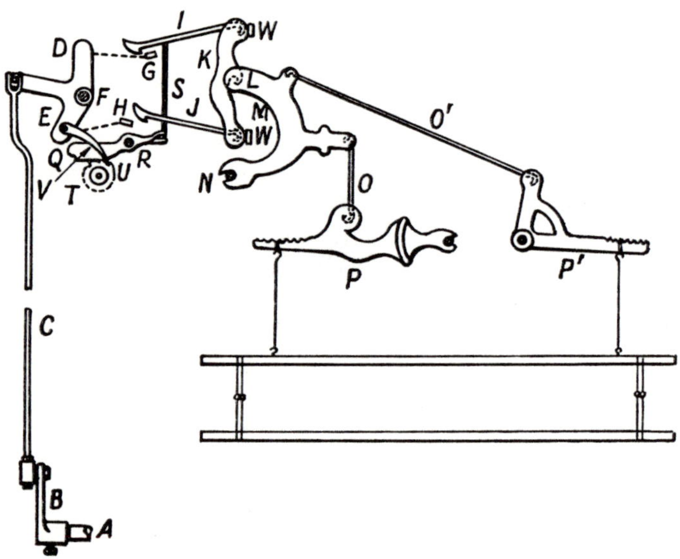

FIG. 7.11.   PRINCIPAL FEATURES OF A NEGATIVE LEVER DOBBY

A lag cylinder T positioned below the heavy ends of the feelers, is provided with eight grooves, each the same size and shape as a lag so that, as the cylinder rotates, the lags in the form of a chain are brought one by one under the feelers. Each lag has two rows of holes and they are set so that short wooden pegs placed in the holes of the front row can lift the odd-numbered feelers whereas pegs in the back row operate the even-numbered feelers. A ratchet wheel U is screwed to the lag cylinder shaft and is rotated intermittently by a long finger V from the arm E.

The action of the dobby is as follows: The low shaft of the loom rotates at half the speed of the crankshaft so that each draw knife moves once inwards and once outwards for each two picks. Assuming that the upper draw knife G is at its innermost limit as in Fig. 7.11, the pegs in the back row of holes of the operative lag will have lifted the outer ends of the feelers Q and caused the corresponding hooks to be dropped on to the draw knife. When the knife moves outwards on the next pick, the dropped hooks are caught and pulled forwards together with their baulk levers and jack levers so lifting the corresponding heald shafts. The lower ends of the baulk levers are prevented from moving backwards by fixed baulk rests W. When the upper knife moves outwards, the lower knife moves inwards so that on the next pick the same sequence occurs with the lower knife.

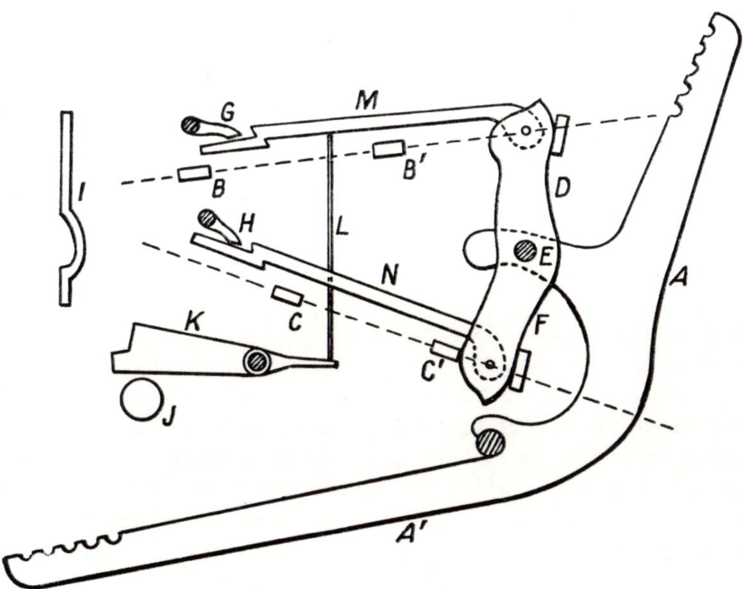

FIG. 7.12.   MECHANISM OF A POSITIVE LEVER DOBBY

The lag cylinder remains stationary for two picks and is then moved forwards to present the next lag by the inward movement of the lever E.

This dobby mechanism lifts the shafts but does not depress them; it is, therefore, of the negative shedding type. The front heald shaft is connected to the notches of P and P^1 nearest to the fulcrum while succeeding shafts are connected farther away, thus allowing the necessary progressive increase in the lifts of the heald shafts.

The timing and setting of both negative and positive dobbies are discussed on page 228.

THE POSITIVE LEVER DOBBY

This type of dobby is illustrated at Fig. 7.12 and differs in detail from the preceding type. The jack levers are extended at A^1 to allow connections to be made at the bottom of the heald shafts while the draw knives B and C are duplicated at B^1 and C^1, these acting upon the ends of the baulk levers DEF thus reversing the action of B and C. The draw hooks M and N are made with a sneck both at the top and bottom; retaining bars G and H can fit into the upper recess when the draw hooks are lifted clear of the draw knives. The needles are shaped as shown separately at I and support both hooks. Each pick requires its own lag so that the lag cylinder $\mathcal{J}$ needs to be turned after each pick.

The action of the dobby is as follows: When a peg is in the lag, the heavy end of the tumbler lever K is raised and the needle L allowed to drop together with hooks M and N. In Fig. 7.12, hook N will drop over the draw knife C as the latter moves outwards. F, E and A will be drawn outwards and thus raise the shaft. If, on the next lag there is a blank, the needle L will rise and lift the hooks. The retaining bar G will engage with M and hold it in its innermost position while the push bar C^1 will push back the end F of the baulk lever and so reverse the action of the jack lever and depress the shaft. The retaining bars G and H will then keep the shaft depressed until a peg appears in the lag chain.

TIMING AND SETTING THE LEVER DOBBIES

The timing of the negative lever dobby, Fig. 7.11, can be modified by altering the position of the crank arm and shedding rod in relation to the low shaft of the loom. For an average setting, the shedding rod C should be vertical when the crankshaft of the loom is about half-way between bottom and back centres, this allowing the shed to be fully open when the shuttle enters. Most positive lever dobby looms, however, employ pick-at-will motions so that the low shaft makes only one revolution per pick. In such cases, the dobby is double-acting. It is driven from the low shaft or sometimes from the crankshaft through two gears, the driving wheel having half the number of teeth of the driven wheel. These gears are made slightly elliptical to give a longer dwell to the heald shafts when the shed is open. The shedding rod is connected by a pin to a plate fastened across the centre of the driven wheel and this plate can be moved round the face of this wheel, within small limits, to allow for earlier or later shedding. Larger changes can be made by setting the gears one or more teeth forwards as required.

With negative dobbies the traverse of the draw knives and consequently, the size of the shed can be altered by sliding the connection of the shedding rod, C, Fig. 7.11, along the slot in the crank arm B. A larger shed is obtained by increasing the effective length of the crank arm. In the same way, the connecting pin on the driven wheel of the positive dobby can be moved towards the periphery of the wheel to give a larger shed. The pattern cylinder should be set with the lag pegs vertical and each peg should be exactly in line with its own feeler. Each draw knife should be pushed inwards a quarter of an inch beyond the snecks on the outer ends of the hooks, thus allowing sufficient space for the dropping of the hooks.

THE WHEEL DOBBY

This type of dobby is similar in principle to the lever dobbies but wheel gearing is substituted for the system of levers. The essential parts are shown at Fig. 7.13. *AB* is one of a series of jack levers fulcrummed on the rod *C*; the upper part *A* is connected by wires and straps to the top of the heald shaft while the lower part *B* is connected to the bottom of the shafts by streamer rods and underjacks. The shafts are thus controlled positively. A pin *D* cast on the jack lever supports the hooked end of a

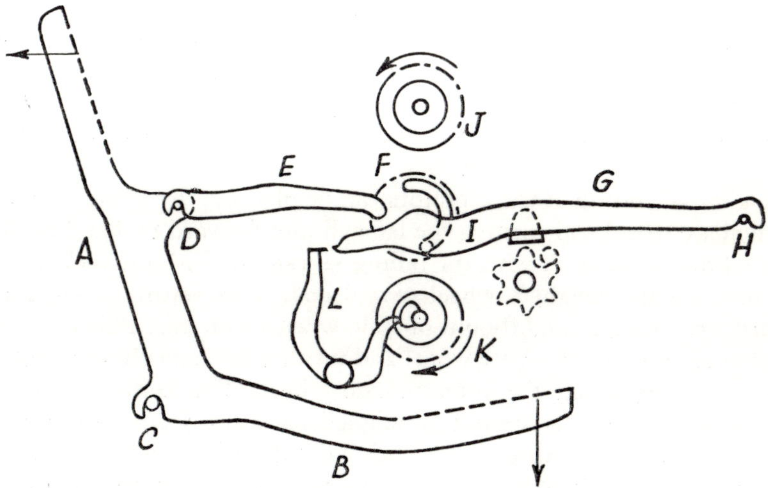

FIG. 7.13.   ESSENTIAL FEATURES OF A WHEEL DOBBY

connector *E*, the opposite end being opened to admit a thin disc *F* known as the vibrator. *G* is the vibrator lever, fulcrummed at *H* and carrying the vibrator *F*. It is supported in position by the bowls or bushes in the pattern chain. The vibrator *F* has teeth cut round its edge thus: 17 teeth, a space equivalent to one tooth, 17 teeth and a second space equivalent to four teeth; it also has a curved slot cut from the body of the wheel to allow the engagement of a pin *I* on the vibrator lever. *J* and *K* are semi-fluted cylinders or 'chills' driven continuously in the direction of the arrows; they have 19 teeth on half the circumference.

The action of the dobby is as follows: Assuming a bowl on the pattern chain moves underneath and raises the vibrator lever; this will cause the vibrator *F* to be lifted sufficiently high for its teeth to engage with those of the top cylinder J. The vibrator is rotated for half a revolution so moving the connector a distance approximately equal to the diameter of the vibrator and thereby lifting the shaft. The space on the vibrator, equivalent to four teeth, is now opposite J so that, as long as the vibrator lever is kept elevated by a succession of bowls on the chain, the shaft will remain raised. The wheel dobby thus produces an open shed.

When the shaft is required down, there will be a bush on the pattern chain. This will cause G and F to fall, the latter dropping far enough to engage with the bottom cylinder K. This will turn the vibrator in the opposite direction to J and thus reverse the movement of the connector, jack and shaft. L is a locking knife to keep the vibrator and cylinder in gear during engagement.

The dobby is driven from the crankshaft through two spur wheels, two bevel wheels, a clutch box and an upright shaft with bevel wheels to the top and bottom cylinders. The clutch is designed to allow the dobby to be disconnected from the crankshaft while the top cylinder bevel wheel is duplicated to allow the cylinders and lag cylinder to be rotated by hand in the reverse direction. The lag cylinder is driven from the upper cylinder through an intermediate wheel.

The initial setting of the vibrators can be obtained by withdrawing the intermediate wheel and turning the lag cylinder forward by hand until the rising vibrators are level with the falling vibrators. With the locking knife fully out, the intermediate wheel is replaced. This setting is correct for forward weaving but slightly out of time when reversing. This is rectified by removing the intermediate wheel and turning the lag cylinder back two teeth before replacing the intermediate wheel. The setting of the lag cylinder is imporant. It should be aligned back and front and at such a height as to allow the vibrators to mesh correctly with the teeth of the top cylinder. As on all dobbies, an escape motion is fitted on the lag cylinder shaft to prevent breakage or damage if a lag jams. Jack missings are due to a number of causes, such as worn parts, too small bowls, too low setting of the lag cylinder or wrong setting of the locking knife. Alteration in the timing of the dobby is made by moving the driving wheel on the crankshaft forward or backward relative to the shaft.

THE LEEMING DOBBY

This is a positive dobby used on many Northrop automatic looms; it has up to 32 shafts for fancy worsteds but usually only 12 shafts for heavy woollen looms, due to the need for more robust construction. A sketch of the essential parts is given at Fig. 7.14. AB is one of a series of jacks fulcrummed at C; the upper end of the jack is connected to the top of the heald shaft and the lower end to the bottom thus giving positive control. There are two sets of cylinders to control the movement of the jacks, the lower set controlling the odd-numbered and the upper set the even-numbered jacks. Fig. 7.14 shows the control of the first shaft only.

The cylinder D is driven continuously one revolution per pick and is the source of power. A toothed segment E is rotated with D and can be moved laterally on an inclined pin F for a distance equal to its own width. G is the jack wheel connected to its jack by the connecting arms H. Normally, the teeth of the segment E do not touch those of the jack wheel G as they are not in the same plane. If, however, the bowl lever I is raised, the segment E is forced laterally along the incline F so that its teeth mesh with those of G and turn it half a revolution. This causes the arm H to push

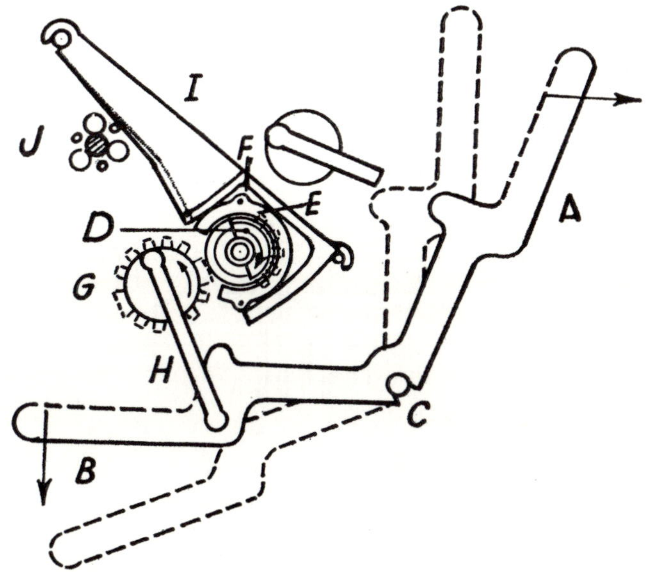

FIG. 7.14. ESSENTIAL PARTS OF A LEEMING DOBBY

down the lower jack arm B and so lift the shaft. Unless I is kept raised, the segment E drops down its incline by its own weight and will stay there, so that its jack will remain raised until I is lifted again.

The movement of the bowl levers is controlled by the bowls and bushes arranged as a chain round the lag cylinder J; a bowl may cause either a lift or a depression, that is, it causes any alteration. Thus the chain for plain weave would consist entirely of bowls, whereas a 2/2 twill would need a pegging plan arranged like plain weave. In practice, a special pegging plan has to be prepared as well as the design. Depending on the type of weave, it is possible to have a pegging plan that repeats on many less picks than the actual design, thus needing fewer lags in the chain than would be required on a normal dobby.

THE JACQUARD SHEDDING MACHINE

Although the weaving design potential of the tappet loom and particularly the dobby loom is considerable, both have their limitations. Thus the tappet loom is limited to designs involving the use of no more than 12 shafts and although the dobby loom can operate as many as 48 shafts, it is impracticable to exceed this number, chiefly because the back shafts would require such excessive lifts as to cause undue strain on the warp

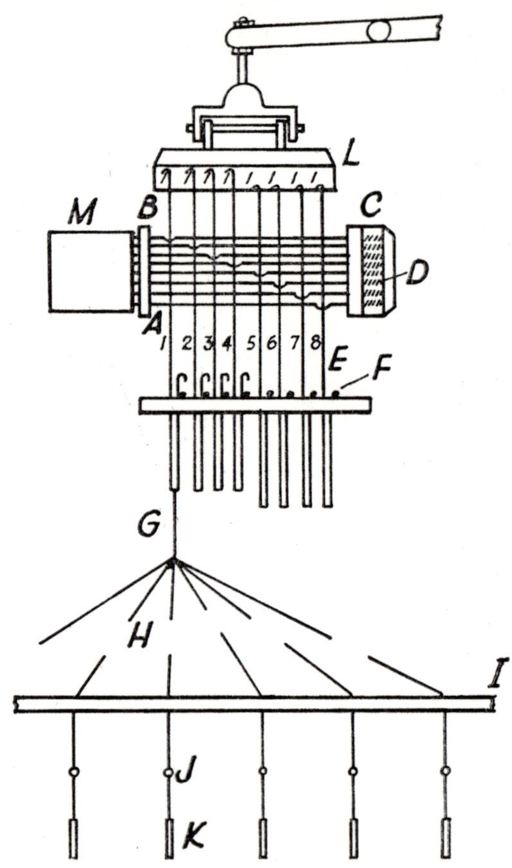

FIG. 7.15.   THREAD SELECTION IN A JACQUARD MACHINE

threads. For designs having more than 48 ends working differently, the jacquard shedding machine which has an almost unlimited figuring capacity, is employed [13-15].

Thread selection in the jacquard machine is illustrated by Fig. 7.15 where A is a set of eight horizontal needles arranged one above the other. They are supported at one end by the needle board B through which they project about half-an-inch, and at the other by horizontal wires in the spring box *C*. The ends of the needles in the spring box are bent so as to press against small spiral springs *D*. *E* is a set of eight vertical hooks, numbered 1 to 8, each being connected to its corresponding needle in the order shown, by passing through a loop or half bend in the needles. The lower ends of the hooks are doubled and pass through a grate; this prevents the hooks turning sideways and also allows the bent ends to rest on one of a series of spindles *F*. Connections are made between the bottom of the hooks and the mails as shown. *G* is a neck cord to which one or more varnished linen harness cords *H* are attached; cords pass separately and in definite sequence through a comber board *I* and carry mails *J* and small heavy weights or lingoes *K*.

The short vertical row of eight needles with corresponding hooks and harness connections is repeated a number of times across the width of the machine so that as many as 408 separate hooks are available. Machines with still larger numbers of hooks are made by having 10 or 12 needles per short row. Each hook is separately controlled and can be lifted independently as required. Thus a 408-hook machine can weave any design repeating on 408 ends or any sub-multiple of 408. The 409-th end will normally lift like the first and so its cord will be attached to the neck cord of the first hook. If there are ten repeats of a design across the width of a fabric, there will be ten cords attached to each neck cord.

The lifting griffe *L* has eight rows of knives; it rises once every pick and so is normally moved by a shedding rod from the crankshaft of the loom. Normally, the hooks are directly over the knives so that, when the griffe moves upwards, the hooks and all the attached cords will be raised and the ends passing through the mails on these cords will be in the top shed line. If a hook is required to be left down, the corresponding needle is moved bodily to the right, so pushing the top of the hook away from the lifting knife. The springs in the spring-box return the displaced needles to their normal position after each pick.

The selection of needles to be left stationary or moved to the right is effected by means of a pattern card on the side of the card cylinder *M* opposite to the needle ends. This cylinder is four-sided and each side is perforated, the holes being of such a size and pitch that the needles will normally enter the cylinder when it moves bodily against them. If, however, a blank card is placed over the perforations, all the needles will be moved to the right and no hooks will be lifted. Thread selection is, therefore, obtained by using one card for each pick, holes being punched in it opposite to the needles, the hooks of which require to be lifted. The cards for successive picks are laced together in correct order and are presented one at a time to the bank of needle ends by the card cylinder moving bodily one quarter of a turn per pick.

The other motions of the jacquard loom, such as picking, letting-off, beating-up are essentially similar to those employed with tappet and dobby looms, and are described later in this section.

In course of time, the jacquard machine has been developed and modified to enable widely different types of complex fabric to be woven. Higher speeds have been realized by double-lift machines while self-twilling, gauze, carpet, split harness and pressure harness jacquards have been specially designed to allow specific types of fabric to be more easily woven[16].

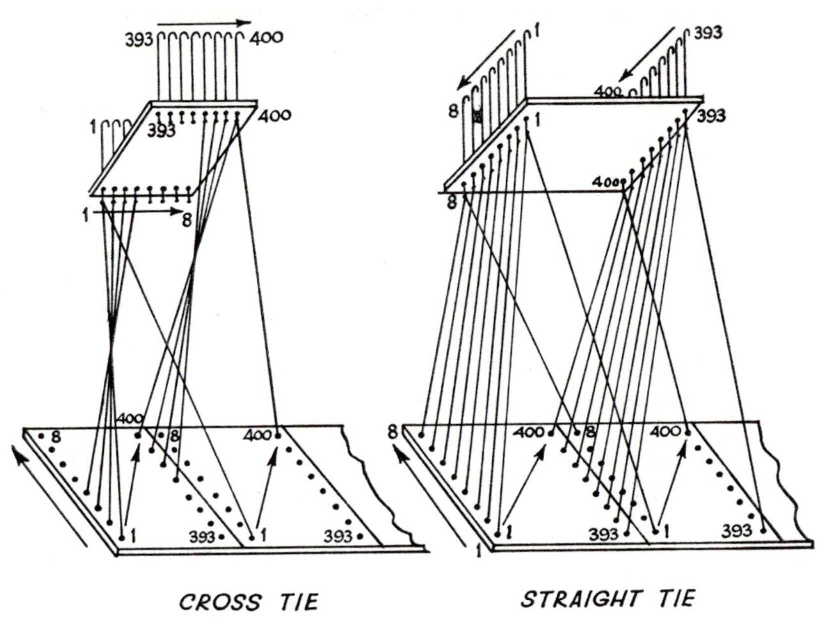

FIG. 7.16. JACQUARD HARNESS MOUNTING AND TIES

In the woollen and worsted industry, jacquard machines are used for figured dress fabrics and for some types of furnishing fabric. The incorporation of yarns other than those made from wool is now extensive, especially for ornamentation. The single-lift and double-lift single cylinder jacquards with hook capacities up to 600 are most commonly used. A minor but important use of the jacquard machine is for pattern weaving, especially for fancy worsteds.

HARNESS MOUNTING AND HARNESS TIES

There are two systems of mounting the jacquard in relation to the comber board, namely, the London or French cross tie and the Norwich straight tie (*see* Fig. 7.16). In the former, the jacquard is placed with the cylinder at right angles to the comber board, giving a quarter twist to the harness. This causes more friction among the harness cords but it is more convenient for the weaver as the cords fall at one side of the loom. In the Norwich system, the jacquard is parallel to the comber board and the cord cylinder works either in front or at the back of the machine. The cords tend to interfere with the light in this system but it is the one most frequently used.

When tying up a harness or when preparing to cut cords, it is important to determine which is the first hook and which the corresponding harness cord. The usual method is shown at Fig. 7.16 while Fig. 7.17 illustrates

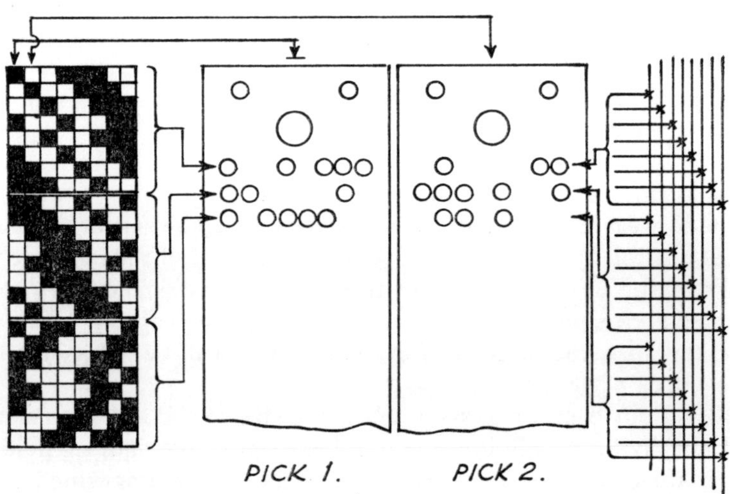

FIG. 7.17.   METHOD OF DRAFTING WARP ENDS THROUGH
THE HARNESS MAILS OF A JACQUARD MACHINE

the method of drafting the warp ends through the harness mails and the relationship between the cords and the design. When the jacquard contains as many hooks as there are figuring ends in the full width of the comber board, the tie is termed a single tie. For most work, a repeating straight tie as shown at Fig. 7.16 is used, each hook having as many cords attached to it as there are divisions across the width of the comber board.

The repeating tie can be modified in many ways to enlarge the figuring capacity of an ordinary jacquard. A centre or point tie is the simplest modification; in the simplest case, the harness cords are tied up straight from the first to the last hook in the first division and then tied up in reverse order for the second. The figure made by the first division is turned over for the second. Mixed ties enable one or more parts of a design to be repeated more or less frequently than other parts. A very common tie is the border tie, where a small number of hooks are reserved for the borders of a fabric, one side reverse tie, while the rest are usually tied straight for the centre or body of the fabric.

CASTING-OUT IN JACQUARDS

The sett of the harness in a jacquard is fixed when it is tied up but the sett of the warp need not be equal to this. In a jacquard with 384 figuring hooks, tied up at the rate of 96 cords per inch, it may be required to weave a warp sett at 64 ends per inch. The number of holes in each short row of the comber board will be eight for such a machine, so that there will be 12 rows per inch. The sett of the warp needs eight rows per inch so that the harness cords of four rows out of 12 will need to be inoperative or will be cast out. The rows cast out should be spaced as evenly as possible across the machine and in this case two rows will be drawn to one cast out. The slightly uneven distribution of the ends in the mails is not important as the cords yield to the draw of the reed.

In the initial selection of a jacquard, it is important to have a machine at least as fine as the finest warp sett that is likely to be used. It is not possible to weave a cloth with a finer setting than the sett of the machine but it is possible to cast cords out to reduce the sett of the machine to suit the sett of the warp. Casting out to equalize harness and warp setts, as illustrated above, will necessarily reduce the figuring capacity of the machine. In this case, the number of available hooks will be reduced from 384 to two-thirds of 384, or 256.

Casting out is also necessary when the size of the design is such that it will not divide exactly into the number of available figuring hooks. Assume, in the case of the above jacquard, that all the 384 figuring hooks can be used and the warp and harness setts are identical. If a design repeats on a number of ends that will divide exactly into 384 such as 192, 128, 96, 64 or 48, cards will be cut each with the necessary number of repeats. If, however, a design does not repeat on such a number and it is not possible to modify the design slightly to accommodate the capacity of the machine, cords will have to be cast out as follows. If the weave repeats on 88 ends, there will be only four full repeats in 384 hooks and the remaining 32 will have to be cast out; that is, four short rows of cords will have to be cast out in every 48 or one out of every 12. The sett of the harness and of the warp would then be different and the overall width of the harness would be greater than the reed.

Occasionally, both the above reasons for casting out occur together as will be seen by the following illustration. A jacquard with 384 figuring hooks is tied up with 96 cords per inch and it is required to weave a design repeating on 56 ends with a warp sett of 80 ends per inch, 60 inches wide The 'cast-out' to accommodate the lower warp rate will be two rows out of every 12 or one in six. This reduces the figuring capacity of the machine to five-sixths of 384, or 320. The design repeats on 56 ends, so the number of repeats on the available hooks would be five with 40 hooks left over. To work with this figure would mean that the harness width would be appreciably greater than the reed width. A better alteration, therefore, is to use six repeats of the design on each section and to reduce the overall width of the harness slightly to less than the reed width. Six repeats, each of 56 ends needs 336 hooks so that 384 minus 336 or 48 need to be cast out, that is six short rows out of 48 or one in eight. This reduces the sett of the harness to seven-eights of 96, or 84 cords per inch. As only 80 ends per inch are needed, the total number of ends will be drawn across 60 times 80 divided by 84, or 57 1/7 inches. Some comber boards are sectional and it is possible to insert narrow pieces of wood between the various sections to equalize harness and reed widths. In the above example, the normal section width is 384 divided by 96, or four inches and the required width is four times 84 divided by 80, or 4 1/5 inches, so that section pieces 1/5-inch wide can be used between the various sections.

TIMING AND SETTING SINGLE AND DOUBLE-LIFT JACQUARDS

The crank for the shedding rod should be arranged to be about 45° behind the crankshaft arm while the card cylinder is timed to press on the face of the needles when the shedding rod is in its uppermost position, which corresponds to the lowest position of the griffe. The shed is a bottom shed in the case of single-lift jacquards and a semi-open shed in the double-lift jacquard. The line of the shed is not clear as all the mails are at the same height; the closer the long rows of holes in the comber board the clearer will be the shed.

The size of the shed can be modified by altering the position of the stud on the double-throw crank and the positions of the studs on the outer and inner ends of the head levers. There should be $\frac{1}{4}$-inch clearance between the hooks and the griffe when the latter is in its lowest position and this needs adjustment after every alteration to the size of the shed. The card cylinder should be carefully adjusted so that the holes in the cards are centred by the needles. One method of testing this is to smear the ends of the needles with black oil or rub them with chalk; lace a card on the cylinder with alternate positions for holes cut and missed and then move the cylinder into contact with the needle board. The impression of the needles on the uncut parts of the card indicates whether the cylinder needs adjustment in either direction.

The jacquard shedding motion is negative acting and because of the heavy weight of the lingoes and lack of counterpoise, high speeds are impossible. The method of driving the griffe tends to pull the loom off the floor although the more balanced arrangement of the double-lift machine allows higher speeds to be attained. For a single-lift jacquard 80 to 90 picks per minute is probably the limit, while 200 picks per minute can be reached with double-lift machines. The closed shed of the single-lift machine produces much less cover than when beating up with the crossed shed of the double-lift. Hooks are made either round or flat; the former produce more vibration but the latter are liable to stick if twisted sideways.

SHUTTLE BOX MOTIONS

FOR A LARGE VOLUME of woven fabric the design is determined solely by the manner in which the warp has been drawn in the healds and by the sequence of heald movements, as described in the previous sections. In such fabrics, using only one type of weft, all that is necessary is that the shuttle should be picked to and fro across the warp shed from a box on one side to one on the other. Even, here, however, it is often advisable – to avoid the formation of bands across the cloth caused by pirns having slightly different characteristics – to employ two shuttles and to change from one to the other after the laying of every double pick. Such weft-mixing looms obviously require two shuttle boxes on one side with some type of reciprocating motion to bring them alternately into the line of the warp. Looms of these type are usually designated "2 x 1'.'

Where the design calls for the use of several different colours or types of weft, multiple boxes are required on one or both sides of the loom and a more complicated mechanism is required to ensure that the correct box is brought into the picking zone in the sequence and at the right time demanded by the weaving design. Such mechanisms are of two main types, the circular box motion and the rising box motion.

THE CIRCULAR BOX MOTION

The circular box motion is widely used in the Bradford worsted dress-goods trade on both dobby and tappet looms. A typical motion is shown in Fig. 7.18, the distinctive feature being the accommodation of the shuttles in a series of six cells arranged in a cylinder A. Shuttle boxes to take seven and, occasionally, twelve shuttles have been used but six is the most usual. Normally, looms are fitted with these multiple boxes at one side only and weft mixing or patterning must, therefore, be in even numbers of picks. The shuttle box A is supported by a spindle at its outer end and a ring at the inner end, the top box being set level with the shuttle race. The control mechanism can turn the box one-sixth of a revolution forwards or backwards as required, thus allowing different shuttles to be used.

On the low shaft of the loom is a cam B which lifts the lever C once every two picks. This lever is fulcrummed at D and, at its outer end, has two slots through which the upright catches E and E^1 pass. The slots are of such a size that if one of the catches is pushed forward, C will lift it when acted upon by cam B. If, however, E or E^1 is not pushed forward, they will pass through the slot and both remain depressed. The lower end of each catch is connected to one end of a lever F or F^1 fulcrummed at P. The front ends of F and F^1 are connected to long draw hooks G and G^1 which are so made that their upper hooked ends can rotate the box A by engaging with one of the six pegs in a disc screwed to the end of the shuttle box. When one of the catches E or E^1 is raised, G or G^1 is depressed and the circular box moved either one box forward or one box backward. A spring-loaded hammer holds the box in correct position.

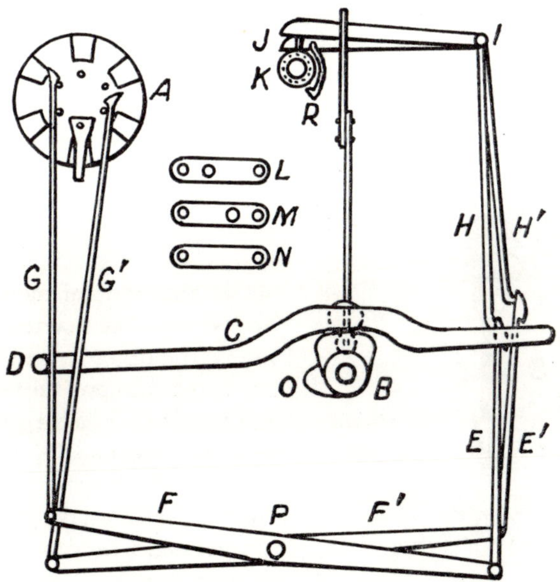

FIG. 7.18. TYPICAL CIRCULAR BOX MOTION

The two crank levers H and H^1 are fulcrummed on a spindle I, the lower arms working against the backs of hooks E and E^1 respectively, while studs J on the upper arms are dropped every two picks on to a card cylinder K. Steel pattern cards as at L, M and N are laced together and pass round K. On every second pick the cam O lifts the upper arms of H and H^1, so lifting the studs above the metal card and moving the lower ends away from the catches E and E^1 while a hook R turns the card cylinder, presenting the next card. If this card is a blank the studs will prevent either H or H^1 falling and the hooks E and E^1 will remain depressed when C rises. A blank card thus represents no box change. If a card is used with a hole opposite the front stud J, lever H will fall pushing catch E on to C and thus turning

A one box forward. Similarly, a hole corresponding to the rear stud *J* will give a movement of one box backwards. Thus by combining the pattern cards in proper sequence, a large variety of wefting plans can be obtained.

The motion illustrated moves the boxes one box forward or one box backward only and thus the weft required for immediately following picks must be in one of the boxes adjoining the operating one. This drawback has been avoided in a skip box mechanism where the circular box is turned by racks instead of levers.

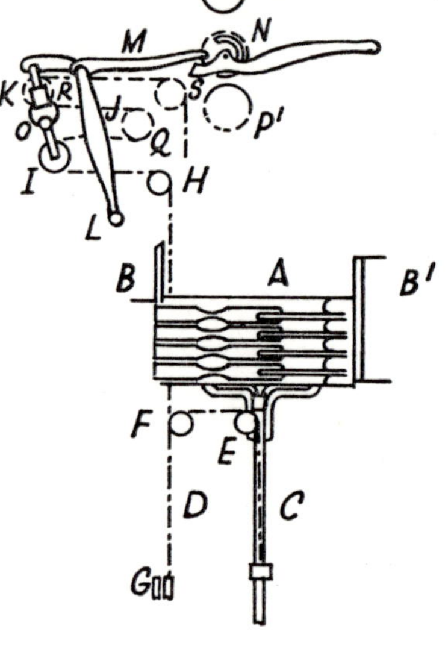

FIG. 7.19.   A COMMON TYPE OF RISING BOX MOTION

Timing and setting of the boxes is very important. The boxes should be half-way turned when the crank is at front centre and the movement of the change should be fully completed shortly after the beat-up of the preceding pick. To prevent mispicks and to minimize shuttle deflection, the box checking arrangements should be kept in good order.

RISING SHUTTLE-BOX MOTIONS

In this type of motion, the boxes are arranged as a series of shelves one above the other; normally, the boxes are lifted into position and allowed to fall by their own weight. Rising box motions are usually placed at both sides of the loom and each has two, four or occasionally six boxes. They are generally used in connection with dobby looms.

One type of rising box motion is illustrated in Fig. 7.19, the boxes *A* being free to slide vertically in the frames *B* and *B*¹. The boxes are supported from the bottom by a rod *C* and the chain *D* which passes round a number of pulleys, *E*, *F*, *G*, *H* and *I*. A system of two levers *J* and *K* arranges for the correct length of chain to be pulled up or paid out to bring the required box to the level of the shuttle race. Lever *J* is fulcrummed at *L* and is moved by the connector *M* and vibrator *N*; lever *K* is fulcrummed at *O* and is controlled by a separate connector and vibrator. *P* and *P*¹ are two semi-toothed cylinders for turning the vibrators, the latter being brought into gear with one or the other of these cylinders by bowls and bushes under the vibrator lever. The series of line diagrams, in Fig. 7.20 illustrate the positions of the levers for top box position, as well as for rises of one, two and three boxes.

The cylinders for the box motion are on the same shaft as those for the dobby shedding motion but are separate from them; the relative position of the two sets of cylinders can be changed to modify the timing. A strong spiral spring on the box rod C serves as an escape motion if the boxes should get jammed.

This particular arrangement is negative in the sense that, although the mechanism raises the boxes, they fall by their own weight. The motion can,

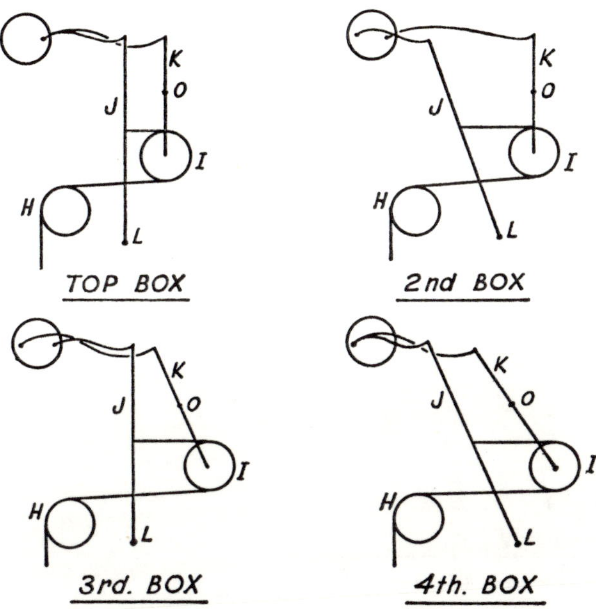

FIG. 7.20.   DIAGRAMS ILLUSTRATING THE POSITION
OF LEVERS FOR VARIOUS BOX POSITIONS

however, be made positive by connecting a second chain at L and passing it round pulleys Q, R and S and other pulleys near the floor to connect it to the bottom of the box rod C. The motion is also available in a modified form to take six shuttle boxes.

Another type of rising box motion is illustrated at Fig. 7.21, where A is one of five rods that can be moved vertically by special lags on an extension of the dobby cylinder shaft. There are two rods to control the boxes at one side of the loom, two rods for the boxes on the opposite side and one for the picking motion. These rods are connected to levers B fulcrummed at C. Wheel D is also on the stud C and gears with wheel E centred on the arm B. Above and below E are the cylinders F and G having teeth on half their circumference and rotating in the direction of the arrows. Connectors H are fastened at one end to the geared vibrators D and at the other to the outer end of a series of levers. Lever I is fulcrummed at J and lever K at

L, L being a stud on the lever *I*. The end of lever *K* is connected with the boxes through the rod *M*, lever *N* and the box rod *O*. When the connector for lever *K* is depressed, the second box is brought level with the race; depression of lever *I* raises the third box while a depression of both connectors brings the bottom box level with the shuttle race. The movement of the boxes is positive in both directions. Springs on the box rod and rod *M* prevent breakage if a box becomes jammed.

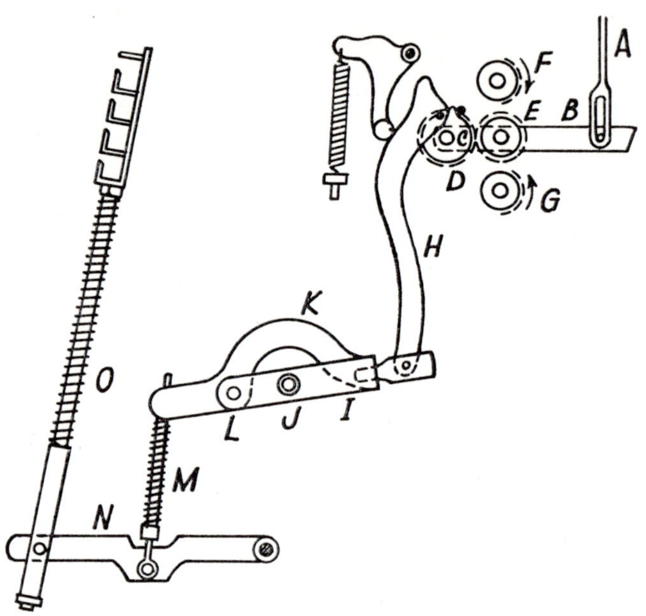

FIG. 7.21.   ANOTHER TYPE OF RISING BOX MOTION

From a practical point of view, the box motion needs much attention. To produce steady running, the timing and setting of the boxes are most important and this is often helped by careful planning of the movement of the boxes. Running boxes should be level with, or slightly higher than, the shuttle race. With the going part at back centre, the nut connecting the chain to the boxes should be turned until the top box is in line with the race; this procedure is then repeated with the other boxes and suitable adjustments made to the chain connections or levers. When all the boxes have been checked once, the procedure should be repeated because the changes needed for levelling one box often affect the position of other boxes. If this has happened, careful readjustments are needed and the sequence repeated until the correct positions have been established.

There are several ways of timing the boxes, one being to turn the loom until a rising box is about a quarter-inch above the shuttle race. The shedding motion is then disconnected from the crankshaft. After removing the shuttles, the going part is then brought forward until the tongue on the fast-reed motion engages with the frog, at which point the shedding motion is re-connected to the crankshaft.

BOX MOVEMENTS AND BOXING PLANS

The movement of the boxes depends upon the order of wefting required as shown by the wefting plan and on a number of practical points

BOX PLAN							
LEFT BOXES				RIGHT BOXES			
1	2	3	4	4	3	2	1
B	A	C					
PICK 1	X					A	
" 2	A					X	
" 3	X					A	
" 4	A					X	
" 5	X				B		
" 6		X				A	
" 7			X				C
" 8		A				X	
" 9		X				A	
" 10	A					X	
" 11	X					A	
" 12	B				X		
" 13		A				X	
" 14			C				X

FIG. 7.22.   BOX PLAN FOR
WEFTING ARRANGEMENT WITH
THREE COLOURS OF WEFT

CHAIN PLAN				
LEFT BOXES		RIGHT BOXES		PICKING
4th.		4th.		
2nd.	3rd.	3rd.	2nd.	
PICK 1	•			•	•
" 2	•			•	
" 3	•			•	•
" 4	•			•	
" 5			•		•
" 6	•			•	•
" 7		•			•
" 8	•			•	
" 9	•			•	•
" 10				•	
" 11				•	•
" 12			•		
" 13	•			•	
" 14		•			

FIG. 7.23.   CHAIN PLAN TO GIVE
THE REQUIRED ORDER OF
WEFT INSERTION

which cannot be summarized as they depend largely on individual conditions. Obvious points are that double and treble drops and lifts should be avoided if possible, the movement of boxes at each side should be balanced as nearly as possible, that is, by having a rising box at one side balanced by a falling box on the other side, and each weft should be brought into sight as often as possible, especially those wefts being used most. To help the weaver, it is useful to try to keep certain boxes associated with certain colours, and to prevent excessive wear the boxing plan should be designed to give the minimum number of movements.

Various devices are adopted to help in obtaining suitable boxing plans, one method being to use a number of cardboard counters to represent shuttles, but boxing plans can also be worked out on paper, as depicted in Fig. 7.22 which shows a boxing plan for the following wefting arrangement:

Colour A, four picks; Colour B, one pick, Colour A, one pick and Colour C, one pick. In this plan eight vertical columns represent the eight boxes, four each on the left-hand and right-hand sides of the loom. The number at the head of each column represents the number of the box, 1 being the top and 4 the bottom box. Each horizontal row represents one pick. The first row shows the initial position of those shuttles containing the three differently coloured wefts A, B, and C. On the first pick, a cross under box 2 on the left-hand side indicates that the shuttle with weft A has been picked and the letter A under box 2 on the right-hand side indicates that the shuttle has been picked into that box. On the second pick, the same shuttle is picked across from the right-hand side to the same box on the left-hand side and this is repeated to insert four picks of colour A. On the fifth pick, the shuttle containing weft B in box 1 on the left-hand side is picked across to the third box on the right-hand side. This has meant a drop of one box on the left-hand side and a lift of one box on the right-hand side, this tending to give smoother running by balancing the power required. The pattern is completed on the seventh pick but, as the shuttles are not in the initial boxes, the boxing plan has to be continued. On the tenth pick shuttle A is run into the top box on the left-hand or weaver's side to allow her to see the weft, while after the fourteenth pick, the shuttles are back in their initial positions. In this plan the weft C is never run into the top box on the weaver's side but it is in the top box on the opposite side for one pick out of fourteen.

The boxing plan shows only the order of running the shuttles and it is necessary to obtain from it the box chain that will give the desired order of wefting. There are five places for pegs or bowls on each lag; one of the outer pegs controls the picking motion and so determines from which side the pick is made. A peg or bowl in the space next to the one that controls the pick lifts one of the second boxes to the level of the race, a peg or bowl in the third space lifts one of the third boxes while a peg or bowl in both positions 2 and 3 lifts the fourth box. The last two spaces on the lag control the opposite set of boxes in a similar way. The actual order of the pegs or bowls in the lag depends on the make of the loom and on the hand of the loom. The plan shown in Fig. 7.23 is for a box-chain to give the previously mentioned wefting arrangement. One horizontal space represents one pick and the five columns represent the five possible positions for lags or bowls.

In this particular example, the first two places on the lag operate the boxes on the left-hand side; the shuttle is required from the second box, so a bowl is placed in the first position and a bush in the second. The second two places control the boxes on the right-hand side; the second box is also needed on this side for the first pick, so a bowl is placed in the fourth position which in this particular case, operates the second box and a bush in the third place. The last place operates the picking. It is required to pick from the left on the first lag, and as a bowl causes a pick from the left and a bush a pick from the right, a bowl is inserted in the fifth place. The complete lag, therefore, reads peg 1, miss 2, peg 2. The same procedure is adopted in pegging the remaining lags. It is often found convenient to make a key or list of all the possible combinations of bushes and bowls.

WEFT INSERTION SYSTEMS

IN ALL CONVENTIONAL TYPE LOOMS, irrespective of whether they are equipped with tappet, dobby or jacquard shedding mechanism or designed with automatic weft-changing motions, as described later, the actual insertion of weft is accomplished by propelling a shuttle housing the weft pirn backwards and forwards through the warp shed. Before discussing the various propelling motions, or picking motions as they are usually termed, a few words on shuttles will not be out of place.

SHUTTLES

Shuttles to house the weft pirn during weaving are made in a variety of sizes to suit different weaving conditions and thus vary with the size of the spool or pirn, the nature of the warp and weft yarns and the width and type of the loom. They are subject to hard treatment and must be made of well seasoned wood, of straight grain, as free from knots as possible and capable of taking a high polish. Boxwood is the most suitable but is too expensive for normal purposes. Cornel is most frequently used, followed by persimmon which is cheaper but less satisfactory. The largest shuttles are often made from beechwood. The ordinary type of shuttle contains a spindle for holding the pirn, a spring clip allowing it to be pulled upwards to permit the replacement of spent pirns, but there are many patented modifications of this part of the shuttle.

New shuttles of the same make may vary slightly in weight, size and in grain and shuttles of different weights need different picking and checking conditions. The size of the shuttle influences the setting of the box front and warp protector motions. It is a good practice to weigh and examine a batch of new shuttles and to try to arrange them in sets for running together; shuttle selection is most important with box looms. Weft brake or tension brushes are usually employed for worsted and woollen yarns and care should be taken to see that each shuttle in a set tensions the weft similarly.

The shuttle boxes, *i.e.*, the boxes from which the shuttles are propelled across the warp shed, and into which they are received, have already been described in preceding paragraphs and it will suffice to reiterate that tappet looms usually have either one box at each side or one box at one side and two or more boxes at the other. In all such looms, picks are inserted alternately from each side and, in multiple box looms, in even numbers from each shuttle.

PICKING MOTIONS

Picking or shuttle-propelling motions are of two main types, the overpick and the underpick type, the difference being that in the former, the picker is actuated from a point above the shuttle box, while in the latter operation is from a point below the box.

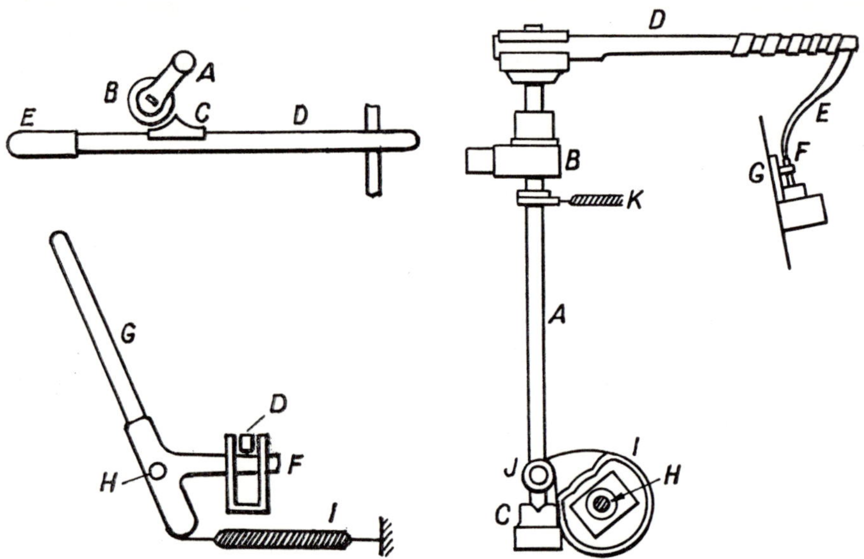

FIG. 7.24.   ESSENTIAL PARTS OF
AN UNDERPICK MOTION

FIG. 7.25.   THE OVERPICK OR
CONE PICKING MOTION

The essential features of the underpick motion are shown in Fig. 7.24. A short arm *A* carrying an adjustable stud and an anti-friction bowl *B* is keyed to the low shaft of the loom. As the shaft rotates, *B* comes into contact with the metal plate *C* bolted to the wooden lever *D* which is fulcrummed at *E* at the back of the loom frame. The outer end of this lever *D* rests upon a short arm *F* projecting from the picking arm *G* which is fulcrummed at *H* in a socket on the rocking rail of the loom. The top part of the picker arm passes through the bottom of the shuttle box and is situated directly behind the picker to which it is connected by a strap. The picker, itself, runs on a spindle behind the box. When the bowl *B* strikes *C*, the lever *D* is depressed, causing the picking arm *G* to move sharply. This movement causes the picker to push the shuttle out of the box and across the loom sley. A spring *I* returns the arm *G* to its normal position.

The underpick motion is clean and simple but requires the parts to be carefully adjusted to avoid frequent breakages of sticks and levers. The intensity of the pick can be altered, to suit the width of loom and strength of weft, by raising or lowering the fulcrum E while the timing may be made sooner or later by sliding the bowl B along a slot in the short arm A. The low shaft of the loom runs at half the speed of the crankshaft so that the two bowls B, one at each side of the loom, are set in an opposite direction, to pick alternately from each side. With wide looms, the low shaft is either driven at both ends to avoid torsion or the shaft is in two halves and each half driven separately.

The chief parts of the overpick or cone picking motion are shown in Fig. 7.25. The upright shaft A is supported in the bearings B and C. A picking stick D is connected to the top of A by clamps and toothed discs while its outer end is connected by a leather strap E to the picker F working along the box spindle G. H is the low shaft of the loom running at half the speed of the crankshaft. A picking tappet I on this shaft makes contact with a bowl J carried on a stud fixed to A, so that as the picking tappet rotates, it strikes the bowl and causes A to turn smartly, thus giving the required impetus to the shuttle through the picking stick D, strap E and picker F. A spring K brings A back to its normal position after each pick.

The picking tappet consists of a boss keyed to H, a shell bolted to the boss and a nose bolted to the shell. This allows easy replacement of a worn nose and also allows the timing of the pick to be adjusted by moving the tappet nearer to or further away from the cone. The horizontal picking arm D is usually set at right angles to the bowl J and its stud and the retaining cap which holds the picking stick in position is fitted with radial teeth so that the position of the stick in relation to the upright may be adjusted as required.

In fixing or adjusting the picking strap, the loom should be turned until the end of the picking stroke is reached. The strap should then be secured to the picker and round the stick so that the picker will be threequarters to one inch away from the buffer. For slow running looms the picking tappet is usually set to start moving the picker at, or a little past, the bottom centre position of the crankshaft; for fast looms, it is usually set a little earlier. With box looms, the timing is often made slightly later to allow more time for the boxes to steady themselves. Small adjustments in timing can be made at the discs that carry the picking sticks, while larger adjustments can be made by taking the driving wheels out of gear and re-setting them one or two teeth forward or backward as required. The strap E can be lengthened or shortened to give less or greater force to the shuttle. The checking of the shuttle should be gradual; the picker should be forward in the box to receive the entering shuttle and the check strap should be long enough to hold the picker away from the end of the box. Any faulty

alignment of reed and box backs and also of the race board and the plates
at the bottom of the shuttle boxes will cause the shuttle to be deviated from
its straight course. The box swell should not be set too far into the box
and should not press too strongly on the shuttle. With strongly sprung
swells, more power is needed to move the shuttle out of the box and they
may cause the shuttle to have a jerky and, possibly, erratic movement.

PICK-AT-WILL MOTIONS

In the weaving of fancy goods in which odd-numbered picks of coloured weft occur, it is essential to be able to pick from either side of the
loom any number of times in succession. This necessitates the low shaft of

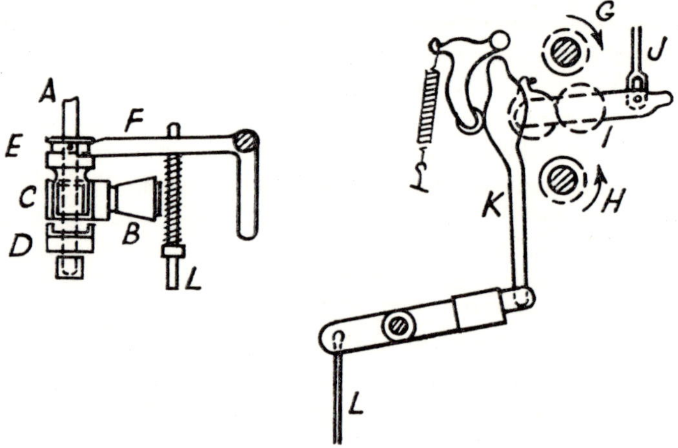

FIG. 7.26.   THE CLUTCH ARRANGEMENT AND THE
MECHANISM FOR CONTROLLING THE CLUTCH IN A
PICK-AT-WILL OVERPICK MOTION.

the loom carrying the picking tappets to be run at the same speed as the
crankshaft; it also requires the application of a clutch arrangement to make
one of the two picking tappets ineffective. Two of the most common types
of pick-at-will motion are described in the following paragraphs.

The Overpick Motion is similar to the standard motion but with the
addition of a clutch motion. In Fig. 7.26, which illustrates the clutch
arrangement, *A* is the upright picking shaft and *B* the picking cone on a
stud fixed to a grooved bracket *C* which is free to turn loosely on *A*. *D* is
a recessed boss keyed to *A* while *E* is a winged bracket which works in the
grooves of *C* and is free to be moved vertically along the shaft *A* by the arm
F. When *E* is moved downwards by *F*, it engages with *D* and connects the
cone and the upright shaft *A* so that, when the cone is struck by the tappet,

picking will take place from that side. If, however, the arm F lifts E out of contact with D, the cone is free and will simply be pushed round A when acted upon by the picking tappet.

The indication to the lever F is also shown by Fig. 7.26. G and H are semi-toothed cylinders while I is a vibrator which can be put into gear with either G or H by means of the rod J controlled by pegs on the box chain. If I is lifted into gear with G, the connector is moved upwards, K is lowered and this causes the rod L to lift the grooves of E out of engagement with D. If the vibrator is dropped to gear with H, E is made to engage with D.

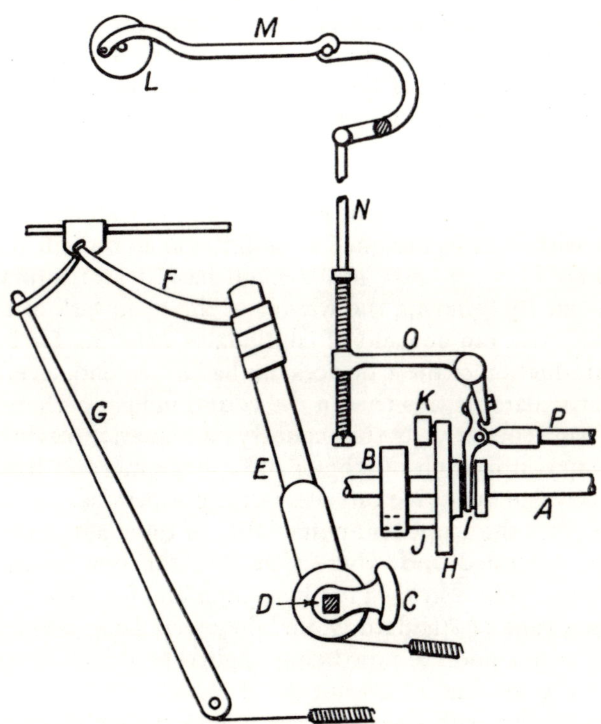

FIG. 7.27. A PICK-AT-WILL UNDERPICK MOTION

A Pick-at-will Underpick Motion is shown at Fig. 7.27 where A is the low shaft of the loom making one revolution per pick, and B is a slotted plate keyed to the low shaft and positioned over the picking shoe C which in turn is keyed to the square cross-shaft D. The picking arm E is connected to the picker by strap F, while G is a jockey stick to bring the picker back to its normal position out of the way of rising or falling boxes. H is a disc having a grooved collar I to move it laterally along A; J is a pin that can be moved in and out of plate B and K is a picking bowl. By pushing the disc H to the left, the pin J engages with the plate and the picking bowl K is brought immediately over the shoe C so that on rotation the shoe is struck and the picker moved sharply to the right. If the disc is kept clear of plate B, it rides loosely on the low shaft. Control is obtained from the vibrator L via the connector M, rod N and crank lever O. P is a rod to control the disc on the right-hand tappet.

In the setting of the underpick motion, the loom is turned over until the picking bowl is immediately under the picking shaft. The shoe is then moved along the square shaft until it is in line with the picking bowl. The picking shoe can be moved closer to, or farther away from, the bowl to alter the strength of the pick; it should be watched for wear at the shoulder and gradually brought nearer the bowl until it needs replacing. The final adjustment in the strength of the pick is made by raising or lowering the strap on the picking stick, a lower connection increasing the pick.

AUTOMATIC WEFT REPLENISHMENT MOTIONS

Automatic weft replenishment motions, first introduced some 70 years ago together with devices designed to stop the loom on failure of the weft or the breakage of warp ends, still remain basic features of the modern automatic loom. By relieving the weaver of the main task of replenishing shuttles as the weft ran out and of continually watching for broken warp ends, the introduction of these devices has had a tremendous effect on productivity. Particularly is this true in the cotton industry where first in the U.S.A. and subsequently in this country, automatic weaving has made possible a better utilization of labour and a large increase in the number of looms which one operative can successfully supervise.

Over the years the scope and potentiality of these automatic looms has steadily been extended and whereas at first the new shuttle or pirn-changing devices were restricted to plain looms and found to be most economical on long runs of standard cloths, they were later developed for use on multi-box looms and are now being applied to almost every variety of loom and for the weaving of every type of cloth.

The original aim with these devices was to reduce running costs and the amount of labour required where labour costs were high. Although these considerations still apply, many other claims are now made for the automatic loom, among which are claims that they produce fewer weaving faults and that they provide cleaner and better conditions for the operative[17-19].

In the woollen and worsted trades in this country new automatic looms have been adopted slowly over the past few years, while in certain cases existing non-automatics are being converted to semi- or fully-automatic types. However, it is still claimed in certain quarters that for the high-quality specialized cloths such as are woven in large volumes in the British woollen and worsted trade, the use of automatic weaving machinery is not economical and accordingly non-automatic looms or only partially automatic looms are often preferred for this section of the trade.

The success of automatic looms depends very largely on adequate preparatory machinery[20] and good yarns. Both warp and weft yarns have to be sufficiently strong to reduce yarn breakages to the minimum and it is for this reason that extra twist is often put into yarns which are to be used on automatic looms. This is also one of the reasons why such looms are more often seen in vertical organizations.

The two essential features of a fully automatic loom arc the warp stop motion (*see* p. 273) and the motion to replace an empty pirn by a full one. The latter motion is usually one of two types, the replacement of the bobbin or pirn in the same shuttle, or the replacement of the running shuttle and emptying pirn by a new shuttle complete with a full pirn. These are known as bobbin-changers and shuttle-changers, respectively. Other motions of the loom have been modified or re-designed to suit the requirements or mechanical details of these two features, automatic warp let-off motions and parallel underpick motions being two such developments.

Bobbin-changing Types: This type of mechanism which replaces an empty pirn by a full one, while retaining the same shuttle, is the most popular type of weft-change unit for woollen and worsted looms. There are many varieties of this mechanism but all depend essentially on a feeler motion to detect the emptying pirn, a battery to hold a number of full pirns suitably prepared for transfer to the shuttle and a plunger to push the full pirn into the shuttle and the empty pirn out at the bottom of the shuttle.

The feeler is usually situated in front of a slot in the shuttle box wall and a corresponding slot in the front wall of the shuttle so that on the forward swing of the sley the feeler enters the slots and presses against the bottom end of the pirn. For use on these looms, the pirn needs to have a metal band at its bottom end, so that when this is uncovered by reason of the yarn exhaustion, either a circuit is completed through the two metal prongs of the feeler or, in another method, the feeler is allowed to slip sideways. The object, in both cases is to bring the changing mechanism into action.

Full pirns are arranged in a circular or vertical magazine situated at the outer end of the loom and in such a position that the bottom pirn is immediately over the shuttle box when the loom is at front centre. Figs 7.28 and 7.29 show the essential parts of a motion using a circular magazine, the first illustrating the parts when in the normal running position and the latter their relative position during transfer.

In this type there is space for 24 pirns in the magazine or battery which is replenished at infrequent intervals by the weaver or an assistant. The pirns *A*, are held by spring pressure between two circular plates and the free ends of the pirns are attached to the spindle of the magazine. *B* is the position of the change-motion shaft which extends across the loom and is rotated slightly by the action of the trip lever; this lever is lifted by a relay controlled by the weft feeler. The movement of *B* causes the battery latch *C* to be lifted into line with the frog or bunter *D* on the sley. As the sley moves into front centre, the bunter pushes the latch backwards which causes the transfer hammer *E*, fulcrummed at F, to rotate smartly and push the full pirn *G* into the shuttle through the guides *H*.

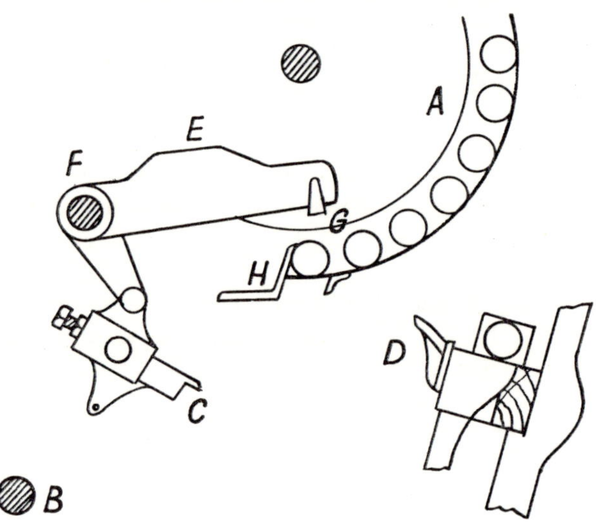

FIG. 7.28. AUTOMATIC BOBBIN-CHANGE MOTION
IN THE NORMAL RUNNING POSITION

In some cases it is possible to replace the magazine or battery by loose, specially designed boxes which are filled automatically during pirn winding, contain many more pirns than do conventional batteries and are so positioned over the loom that pirns can be transferred to the shuttle as and when required. In the usual design, the pirns are released and move by gravity as required through a single opening in the bottom of the box. In other designs the box is divided into a number of vertical compartments which are emptied consecutively by a horizontal shift of the box as required.

The pirn has three metal rings at its base which fit in the jaws of the shuttle and it is important to adjust the picker and check straps so that the shuttle is in the correct position for accurate transfer. On entering the shuttle, the full pirn *G* pushes the empty pirn *I* through the bottom of the shuttle into a container. The transfer takes place at full loom speed an means are provided for automatically cutting the old weft near the selvedge. The new weft is automatically threaded into the eye of the shuttle which is in the form of a zig-zag slot and the trailing end of the new weft is cut near the selvedge. The transfer hammer and battery latch are returned to their normal running positions by a strong spring, while a pawl attached to the hammer moves a ratchet wheel on the battery spindle one tooth, causing the next full pirn to be moved into position for the next transfer.

There are several modifications of this motion, one example being the use of four vertical magazines to allow weft-mixing or weft selection up

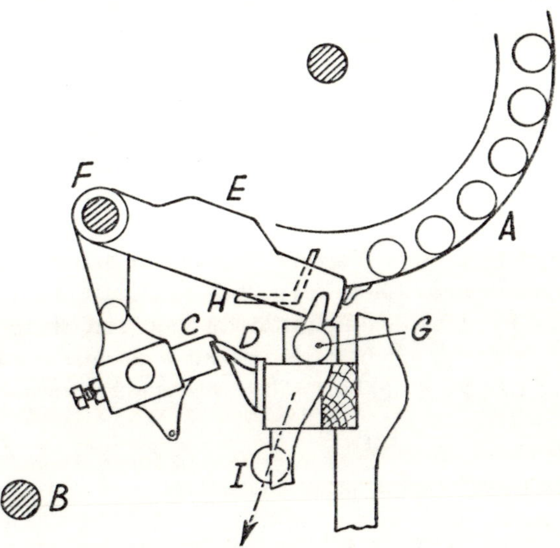

FIG. 7.29. AUTOMATIC BOBBIN-CHANGE MOTION
IN THE BOBBIN TRANSFER POSITION

to four colours. In some looms, control of the change is from the normal weft-fork motion, the change only taking place after the pirn has been completely emptied or when the weft has broken. In such cases the mechanism is simplified but there will be up to two missing or broken picks at each change of pirn. The correct setting and adjustment of the various parts is very important with these mechanisms and with some parts, for example, the transfer hammer and weft feeler, experimentation is necessary to get the best results.

Shuttle-changing Mechanism: Shuttle-changing mechanisms are those in which a shuttle with almost spent weft is replaced by a new shuttle threaded with a full pirn. This type is not used in the woollen and worsted trade to a large extent being originally developed for the silk and rayon industries and for the weaving of delicate and 'lively' weft yarns. The system uses a number of shuttles on the same loom and as they are seldom identical in shape, size, and weight, the setting of such parts as swells, shuttle-boxes and pickers may present serious difficulties.

A weft-feeler motion, usually situated at the back of the box but sometimes at the front, presses against the running pirn every two picks. On contacting the metal band at the bottom of the pirn, the loom is caused to stop at back-centre and the changing mechanism to operate. The change is controlled by a series of cams; one cam causes the picking stick to be moved to its outermost point while a second lifts the front of the shuttle box ready for the removal of the old shuttle and the insertion of the new one. This cam also controls the movement of two rods which push the old shuttle from the back of the box into a padded receptable. Another cam controls the movement of a carrier plate which collects the new shuttle from a magazine, moves into the box with it and returns leaving the new shuttle behind. The box is then dropped by the second cam and a further cam causes the loom to be restarted if all the above motions have been satisfactorily made.

The whole change takes place in four to five seconds, during which time the loom is stopped. There are several modifications in the details of the hinged box-front type of shuttle-changer and there are different methods of effecting the change. For example, in one system, the spent shuttle is picked into a special bottomless box which is raised at the appropriate time to receive it.

UNCONVENTIONAL METHODS OF WEFT INSERTION

With economic trends and conditions continuing to encourage loom developments aimed at the reduction of production costs, it is not surprising that particular attention should have been given to the replacement of the conventional shuttle by a more positive method of weft insertion. Developments in this field have been in progress for many years and, in consequence, there are at the present time several types of 'shuttleless' loom, each representing a practical solution of the problem, though each method has its own limitations, characteristics and effects on other loom features. The principles on which these new looms operate tend to fall into three broad categories, using respectively rapiers, grippers and either air or water jets as the means of weft insertion. Sizeable installations of looms based on these principles are now in existence and increasing shed experience will undoubtedly extend the number and use of these machines.

Despite the essential differences between the three methods of weft insertion referred to above, all these machines have certain technical features in common. Thus, all derive their weft from cone or cheese, usually cleared during winding, and pirn-winding is eliminated. Again, all are capable of high weft-insertion rates, which may be up to 75 per cent higher than those of an equivalent conventional loom operating under the best conditions. In general, the warp shed necessary to accommodate the new weft-insertion systems tends to be smaller than that required for the conventional shuttle and the strain on the warp is thus reduced. Noise and vibration are also reduced appreciably in comparison with conventional looms. On the other hand, looms using some of these new systems occupy slightly more floorspace, while the selvedges they produce tend to be ragged and special devices have to be used during weaving in order to improve them.

Because these new looms have been designed primarily as high-production machines, every other feature of the loom has to be geared to the new and faster method of weft insertion. In particular, great care has to be given to the preparation of the warp and weft yarns, it being essential that yarn breakages and slipping knots should be reduced to a minimum. In the early stages of some of these developments, the versatility of the loom was seriously reduced, but this disadvantage is slowly being overcome.

The various systems of weft insertion employed in these shuttleless looms may be briefly described as follows:

Rapier Systems: In these systems, carriers or nippers mounted on the ends of rigid or flexible steel rods or tapes work in and out of the warp shed to lay the weft. In the Iwer system[21], illustrated schematically at *A* in Fig. 7.30, a single rigid rapier, operating from one side only, crosses the warp shed to grip the end of the weft from the supply cone on the other side, carrying it through the shed on its return journey. The rapier moves with a simple harmonic motion which is reputed to impose minimum stress on the yarn. The Dornier system, shown at *B* in Fig. 7.30, uses two rigid rapiers which enter the warp shed from each side simultaneously and meet in the middle. One rapier carries the weft half-way through the shed, at which point it is transferred to the second rapier which completes the pick on its return journey. In the Draper [22] and Crompton & Knowles versions, shown schematically at *C* in Fig. 7.30, a similar method of laying the weft is employed, but two flexible tape rapiers are used instead of the rigid units of the Dornier system.

Gripper Systems: These systems are of two types. In one, the single gripper system, as employed in the Saurer and Textima looms, a single small gripper-shuttle collects and draws the weft across the warp shed from the left and from the right alternately, there being a supply cone on each side of the loom. This system is shown at *D* in Fig. 7.30.

The multiple gripper type is represented by the now well known Sulzer weaving machine[12,20,22,24,] which employs a number of very small gripper-

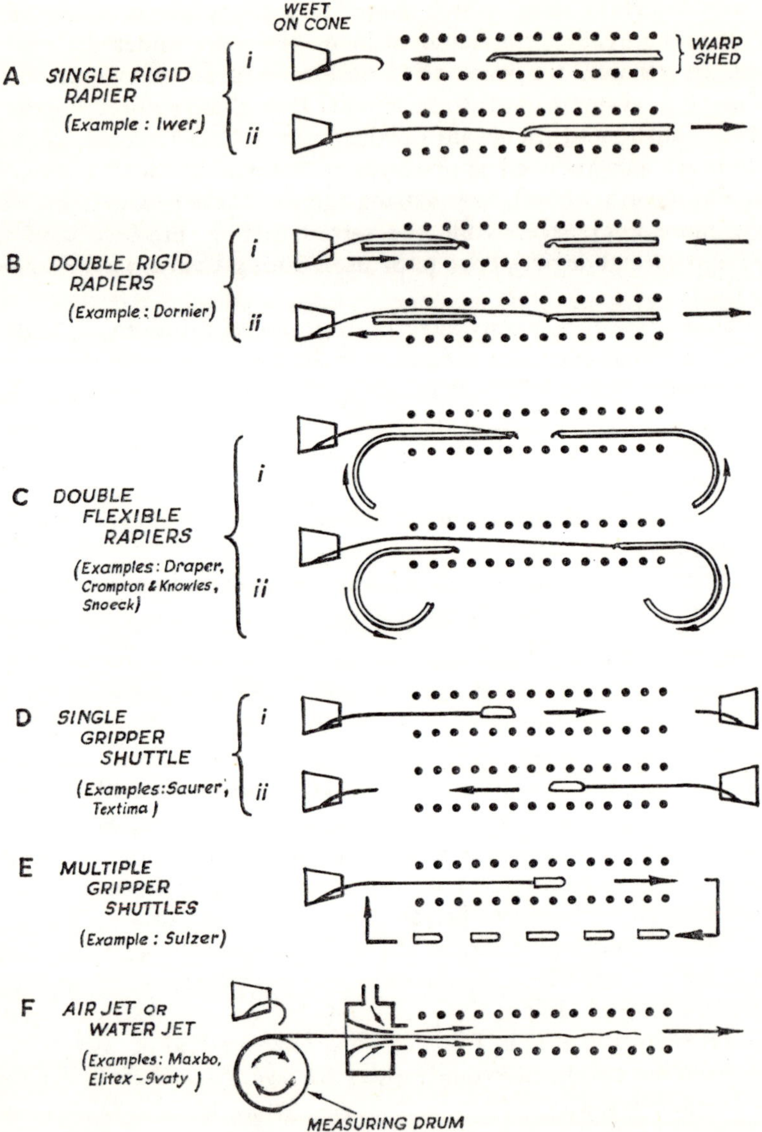

FIG. 7.30. SCHEMATIC DIAGRAMS DEPICTING THE MAIN
TYPES OF UNCONVENTIONAL METHODS OF WEFT INSERTION

shuttles. Each of these, in turn, collects the weft end from a cone supply at one side of the loom and is then propelled by a torsion device across the warp shed, carrying the weft to the far side where the yarn is released. The gripper-shuttles are then returned to the operating side by a conveyor below the warp shed. This system, in which the path of the gripper-shuttle is controlled by guides protruding through the lower half of the warp shed, is shown schematically at *E* in Fig. 7.30.

Air and Water Jet Systems: In these systems [25], a small precision pump directs a jet of air or water from a fine annular nozzle across the warp shed. The end of the weft passes through the centre of this nozzle and is carried across the shed by friction with the stream of air or water, the latter being the more efficient medium in this respect. Both methods originally suffered from the fact that both air and water jets quickly disperse after leaving the jet, so limiting the width of looms operating on this principle, but this disadvantage is being systematically overcome. One interesting feature of these systems is the device whereby the weft is drawn off the cone on to a drum and measured off in lengths equivalent to one pick prior to being fed through the centre of the nozzle for propulsion across the shed.

Apart from the particular weft insertion system employed, all these 'shuttleless' looms have many points in common. In all of them, the picking techniques are carefully synchronized with other motions of the loom and these, though modified in certain respects to meet requirements, mainly follow traditional principles.

On most of these looms the weft cones are duplicated to form a magazine creel, ensuring continuity of supply, while in many cases, a battery of cones and a selection device controlled by a dobby enable up to eight different colours or types of weft to be inserted singly or in succession as required by the fabric design.

The problem of ragged selvedges caused by wefting from one side of the loom has been tackled in several ways, the simplest being to provide a high density warp at each side of the cloth. In the Sulzer system, there is a special tucking device whereby each new weft thread tucks in both loose ends of the previous pick, resulting in a good and firm, but crammed, selvedge. Leno selvedges, using special ends and healds or needles are common, while for light fabrics a tacking thread is sometimes woven into the shed across the width of the selvedge.

Much more, of course, could be written about these interesting developments, but for further details reference must be made to the literature on the subject. In this respect excellent reviews have been given by K. Greenwood[26,27,29,] and by V. Duxbury[28,29]. The economics of production with these machines is a subject in itself and one beyond the scope of this book. Nevertheless, it may be pointed out that, in general, these new looms are precision – and therefore often expensive – machines which therefore demand a high degree of machine utilization. Shift working is almost essential[29]. In addition, long production runs and low yarn breakage rates are essentials in achieving the high productivity of which most of these new machines are capable.

BEATING-UP THE WEFT

BEATING-UP, *i.e.*, the forcing of each pick of weft up to the fell of the cloth, is the third of three primary loom motions. It is performed by the sley which also serves on conventional type looms to provide the race along which the shuttle traverses the warp shed. This double function necessitates a driving mechanism which will provide a quick smart movement to the beat-up or front-centre position, and a slower movement at the back of its stroke when the shuttle is travelling across the sley. An eccentric motion obtained by a crank and connecting rod has been found to give the best conditions and the general arrangement is as shown in Fig. 7.31, where A is one of a pair of sley swords bolted to a rocking shaft B. C is the driving shaft of the loom, D is the crank and E the rod connecting the sword to the crank. One revolution of C causes the sword to swing once backwards and forwards, the degree of eccentricity depending on the relative lengths of crank and connecting rod. Incidentally, attempts have been made to obtain the necessary eccentric motions by means other than the traditional crank and crank arms, but none have been entirely successful. One method utilizes hydraulic cylinders controlled by valves operated by a bank of cams.

The reed F, which consists of a large number of flat wires fastened edgeways between top and bottom baulks, serves several purposes, namely, (*a*) to control the number of warp threads per inch and the width of the warp in the loom, (*b*) to space the threads uniformly across the width of the warp, (*c*) to form a support for the back of the shuttle as it travels across the sley and (*d*) to beat-up each pick of weft. Ideally, the warp threads should be passed through the reed individually. This would allow each end to be 'centred', prevent ends running or rolling together and secure the maximum amount of cover. This is normally not practicable as (*a*) the reed could not be made sufficiently fine, (*b*) fibrous yarns would be difficult to get through a very fine reed, and (*c*) knots would not pass. Two or more ends are normally passed through each dent and care has to be taken to prevent ends working similarly being passed through the same dent.

The construction of a few different types of reed is shown in Fig. 7.32. A represents the standard type and shows how the twine or pitchband separates the wires. B is a double reed, the front set of wires being placed opposite the spaces in the ordinary reed; it is sometimes used for highly sett warps and for weaving hopsacks. C is a false reed, false wires being slung on a long wire or string in front of a standard type of reed. They are placed between the spaces of the ordinary reed and, like *B*, are used for separating the ends of fibrous warps or finely sett warps, and for splitting the ends in fine hopsack weaves. *D* is a reed for making shadow stripes by irregular spacing of the wires, *E* is a zig-zag reed that waves the weft while *F* is a reed that produces ondulé effects by rising or falling about one quarter of its depth for every inch of cloth woven. The reed shown at *G* is a simple gauze reed used for making gauze fabrics, the method of work-

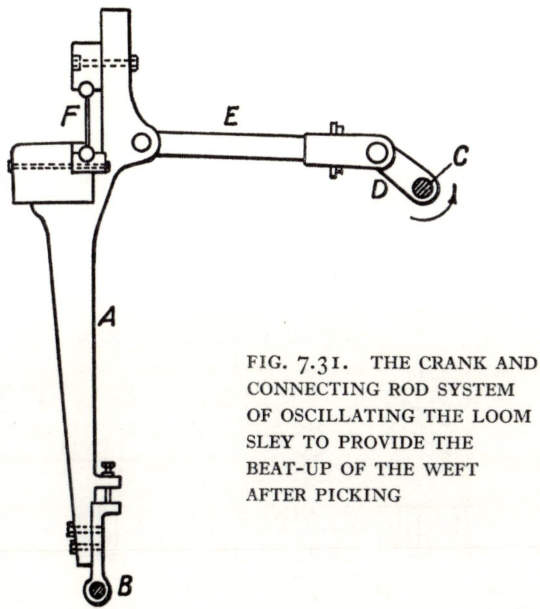

FIG. 7.31.   THE CRANK AND CONNECTING ROD SYSTEM OF OSCILLATING THE LOOM SLEY TO PROVIDE THE BEAT-UP OF THE WEFT AFTER PICKING

ing being illustrated by *H*, *I* and *J*. In this case, the sley moves and causes the crossing threads in the eyes to pass to the opposite side of adjacent stationary warp threads.

CLOTH CONTRACTION AT THE REED

While being woven, almost all cloths tend to contract in width due to the interlacing of the weft yarn with the warp, the degree of contraction depending on the material, the number of intersections in the weave and the counts of warp and weft. If this contraction were allowed to take place immediately following insertion of the weft pick, the outer ends in the warp would tend to be excessively stressed and the outer reed wires would become badly cut, bent or broken. To keep the cloth 'fell' to the full width of the warp in the reed and also to assist in overcoming the drag of the weft on the selvedge threads when the shuttle is passing from one box to the other, temples are employed.

There are several general types of temple from which a choice can be made to suit the weight and nature of the cloth being woven. There are also many patented modifications. A general purpose type in the worsted dress-goods trade is the ring temple consisting of ten or twelve thin brass rings, each having a large number of needle pins projecting outwards from the periphery. These are set on skew-drilled washers sufficiently wide to space the rings along a stud which is bolted to the holder, which in turn is bolted to the loom framing. The pins pierce the cloth and the inclination of the pins

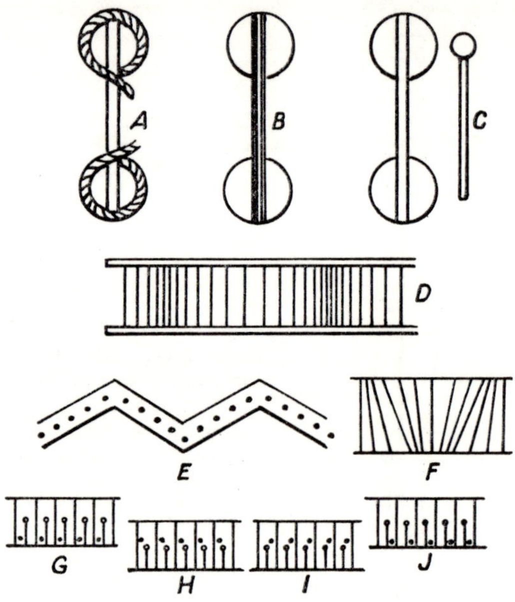

FIG. 7.32.   VARIOUS TYPES OF REED

keeps the cloth distance. As this type of temple is set on top of the cloth, a few inches at the sides of the fabric cannot be seen properly.

The star type of temple employs a pinned disc, supported horizontally below the cloth, the pins piercing the selvedges; it is used for lighter types of fabrics. These temples enable the whole of the fabric to be seen but difficulty is sometimes experienced in pulling back the warp and cloth. Side roller temples are used for the heavier fabrics and consist of two or three spiked rollers set in a suitable frame fixed at each side of the cloth. The lid of the frame is ribbed to ensure that the fabric is pierced by the pins.

Temples should be set as close as possible to the reed and to the shuttle race; they should work freely, care being taken that no broken threads restrict the free rotation of the rollers and that there are no blunt or broken pins.

LET-OFF AND TAKE-UP MOTIONS

OF THE VARIOUS MOTIONS of the loom generally designated 'secondary', two of the most important are the let-off motion, designed to withdraw the warp from the back beam at exactly the rate required for the construction of the cloth, and the take-up motion, a somewhat similar device to withdraw the fabric as it is woven and to wind it on to the take-up roller. To a large extent, the smooth operation of the loom depends on the efficiency of these two motions and much attention has been given in the past to their design. Nevertheless, they can be classified under a limited number of types.

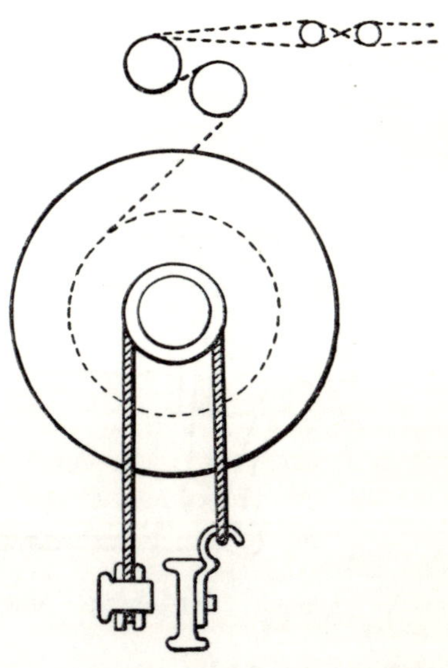

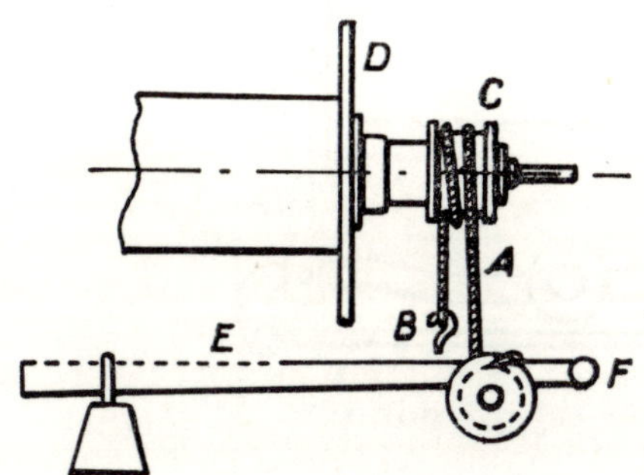

FIG. 7.33.   SIMPLE TYPE OF NEGATIVE
WARP LET-OFF MOTION

FIG. 7.34.   USE OF DOUBLE
BACK ROLLERS WITH HEAVY
FABRICS

NEGATIVE WARP LET-OFF MOTIONS

The most suitable type of let-off motion for lightweight worsted fabrics is the negative let-off motion illustrated in Fig. 7.33. It is a simple mechanism, the warp beam being braked just sufficiently to allow the warp to be withdrawn at the required rate. A rope or chain A is attached to the loom frame at B, passes a number of times round the beam collar C and is then connected to a weighted lever E fulcrummed at F. The amount of tension on the warp depends on the size of the weights, their position on the levers, and the nature and size of the friction surfaces. The advantages of this motion are simplicity, low initial cost and upkeep and the fact that the weights can rise slightly as the shed opens. Drawbacks include adjustment of weights as the girth of the warp diminishes and the necessity of lifting heavy weights. Trouble may also be caused by dirt and other extraneous matter getting on the ropes and collar, thereby causing a jerky let-off and thick and thin places in the cloth. Occasionally the collars are covered with suitable friction linings.

With heavier cloths the tension on the warp is considerable and double back bearers are frequently used as shown in Fig. 7.34. The second roller helps to tension the warp and absorb much of the shock of the beat-up.

Briggs' motion, shown in Fig. 7.35, is now widely used. In this motion a small weight and a system of levers are used to give necessary tension to the warp yarns. The beam collars A rest on a fixed chair B, the inner ends of which extend upwards, while hooks at the top form the fulcrums for the pressing plates C. Connections D are arranged with a system of levers as shown, and the handle E is lowered to relieve the weight on the beam.

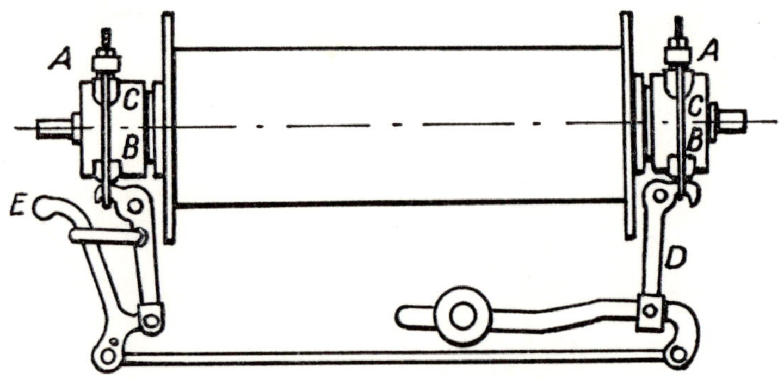

FIG. 7.35.   BRIGGS' WARP LET-OFF MOTION

Care should be taken to see that the collars or ruffles are sufficiently smooth to allow ropes or chains to slip evenly and regularly. French chalk or carbon black may help to give a smoother and more even let-off. New ropes give a more effective brake than do old ones, while chains are often preferred to ropes due to their freedom from stretching, smoother action and smaller upkeep cost. Correct weighting of the warp is important. If the warp is overtensioned, difficulties may be experienced in obtaining a clear shed and irregularity in beat-up may result. An inadequate amount of tension will cause ridges in the fabric or the slackness of the warp will permit the beat-up to drive succeeding picks to overlap each other. The tension on the warp also affects slightly the number of picks per inch inserted and the length of the fabric piece for a given length of warp.

POSITIVE LET-OFF MOTIONS

These motions differ from those previously described in that the warp beam is moved mechanically. The principle is to govern the rate of letting off by having a sensitive back rest which will respond to the tension on the warp.

One type of motion is illustrated by Fig. 7.36. The worm wheel *A* is keyed to the end of the warp beam and gears with a worm *B* on a short cross-shaft. *C* is a ratchet wheel also secured to this shaft and is actuated by the pawls *D* and D^1, the former being set half-a-tooth in advance of D^1. The pawls are supported by two toothed quadrants *E* and E^1 one on each side of the ratchet wheel. These quadrants are in gear with a double quadrant lever *F* which is oscillated by the rod *G* from the sley sword.

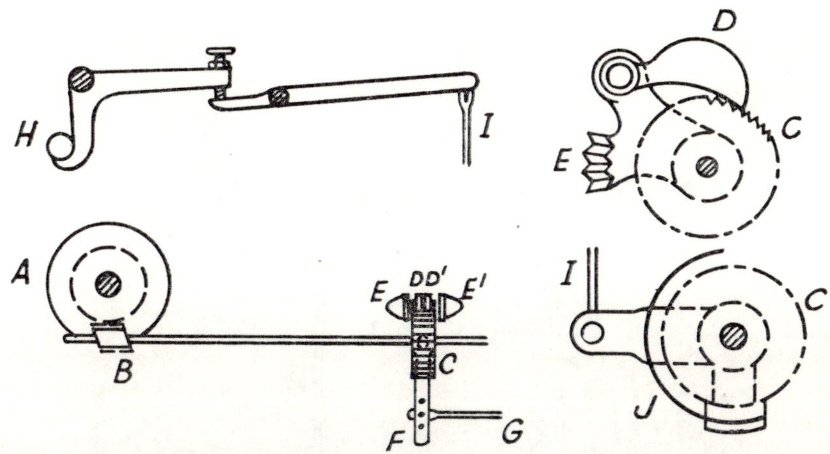

FIG. 7.36.   A COMMON TYPE OF POSITIVE LET-OFF MOTION

The catches are thus caused to move backwards and forwards over the ratchet wheel and normally would cause the cross-shaft to rotate at a uniform speed. Variation in this movement is obtained from the back rest *H*. If the warp tension is increased, the back rest is drawn inwards causing the rod *I* to descend. Normally, about half the teeth of the ratchet wheel *C* are covered by a shield *J*, which is connected to rod *I*. When the latter falls, more teeth are uncovered allowing the pawls to move more teeth each time; when *I* rises due to a slackening warp, the shield covers more teeth and prevents the same number being moved by the pawls.

Another type of positive let-off motion is illustrated at Fig. 7.37, where *A* is the bottom of the sley sword working on the rocking shaft *B*. *C* is a pushing plate screwed to *A*, its smooth outer surface working against the bowl D. This bowl is positioned in a slot of the bowl lever E fulcrummed at *F*. The upper end of *E* is connected to the lifting lever G fulcrummed at *H* and carrying a stud *I*. This stud is immediately below the lever *J* which is raised slightly each pick by the action of the pusher *C* on the two levers. Lever *J* carries a long rod *K*, the bottom of which is secured to a catch lever L carrying two pawls M. These move the ratchet wheel N and consequently the let-off shaft O, the worm P and the beam at Q.

Provision is made for modifying this regular let-off in accordance with the tension on the warp. The lever J is continued backwards beyond its fulcrum and carries an adjustable set screw R. Movement of this screw regulates the amount of warp let-off each pick, by controlling the pull of the rod K. The warp from the beam passes over the back rail S which is carried by lever T fulcrummed at U. The forward part of T is in contact with the screw R and also carries a rod W which is connected at the bottom to another similar rod and weighted. If the let-off is not sufficient, the

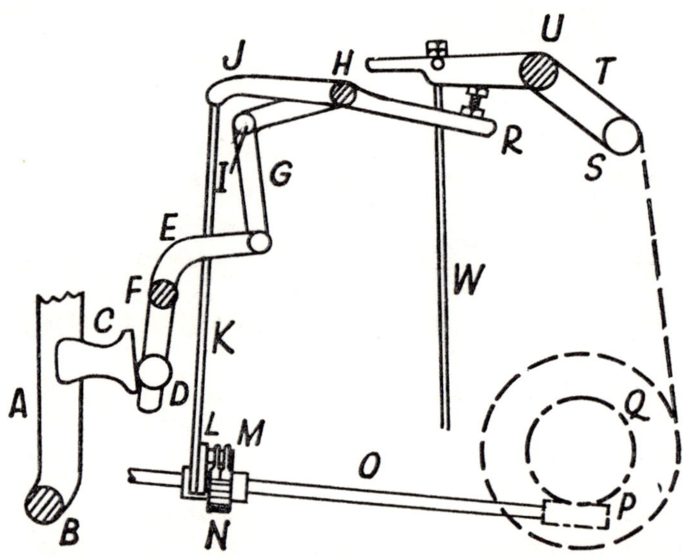

FIG. 7.37. A SECOND TYPE OF POSITIVE LET-OFF MOTION

warp tightens and the swing lever is drawn inwards against the weight on W. This allows the lever J to drop farther for each pick, thus engaging with more teeth of N.

These motions let off the warp but do not take it up when picking back. Let-off motions are available in which provision is made for turning the warp back on to the beam when unpicking, the beam being reversed by connections from the positive take-up motion.

The positive let-off motion is normally applied only to the heavier makes of loom as the motion is largely controlled by the force of the beat-up which is usually insufficient in the case of light fast-running looms. For fabrics having an excessive number of picks per inch it is often necessary to dispense with the positive motion by fixing the swing rail and letting off the warp as in the negative motion. In the motion shown at Fig. 7.37, the bowl *D* can be lowered to give less let-off when highly picked cloths are being woven.

AUTOMATIC LET-OFF MOTIONS

On automatic looms, means are provided to dispense with the manual movement of weights along the warp beam levers as the girth of the warp diminishes. There are many types, but all depend partly or wholly on the

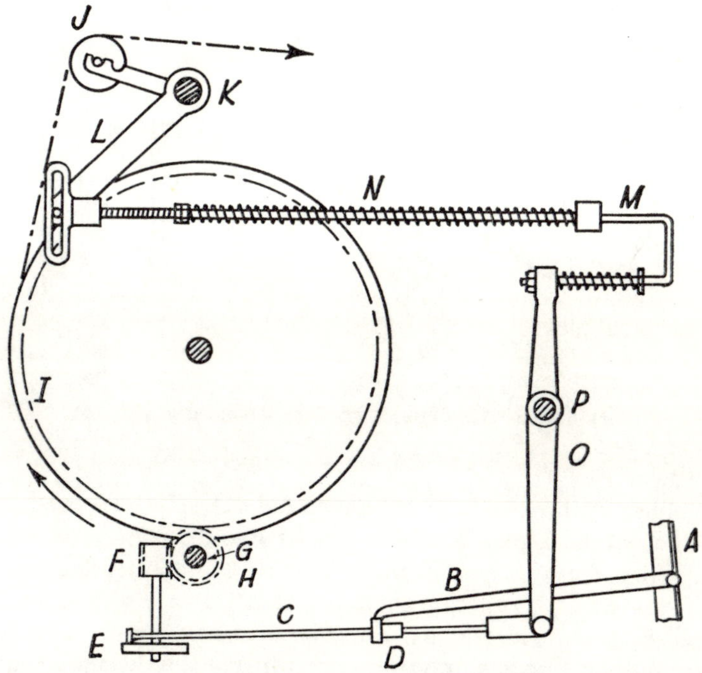

FIG. 7.38. LET-OFF MOTION FOR HEAVY WOOLLEN LOOMS

use of a sensitive back rest. A typical type for use on heavy woollen looms is illustrated by the line drawing at Fig. 7.38 where *A* is one of the sley swords to which the draw lever *B* is attached. The swing of the sword oscillates the draw lever and with it the connecting rod *C*, if the collar *D* is sufficiently near to the head of the draw lever. *E* is a ratchet wheel, rotated by a pawl moved by *C* and the motion of *E* is transmitted to the warp beam through the worm *F*, worm wheel *G*, beam pinion *H* and beam wheel *I*.

This movement is governed by the warp tension, transmitted to the back rest *J*, fulcrummed at *K*. *L* is a lever fixed to *K*, the movement of which moves the horizontal rod *M* against the spring *N*. This movement is passed to the pendulum lever O, fulcrummed at P, the outer end of which is connected to the rod C. A movement of the pendulum lever O will alter the relative positions of the collar D and the head of the draw lever B and, consequently, will alter the number of teeth of the ratchet wheel pushed over.

In practice, when the warp is slack, the collar is set to touch the head of the draw lever when the sley is at front-centre and the pendulum lever is vertical, so that no movement of the beam results from the swing of the sley. Movement of the beam is caused by the gradually increasing warp tension which moves the rod C with its collar towards the back of the loom.

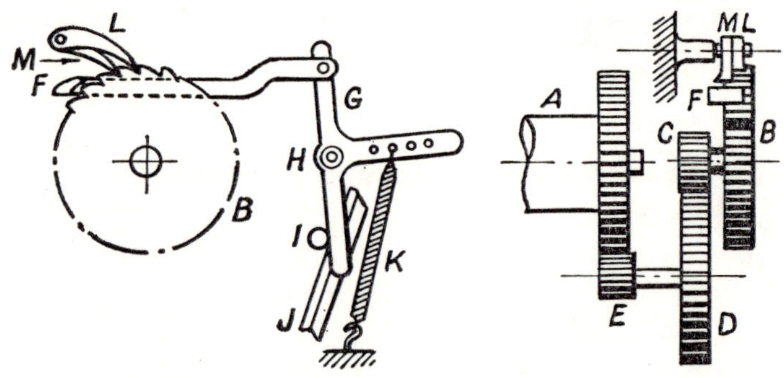

FIG. 7.39.   ONE TYPE OF NEGATIVE TAKE-UP MOTION

TAKE-UP MOTIONS

The object of the take-up motion is to draw the cloth forward a definite distance each time a pick has been inserted so as to preserve a uniform texture. When the weft is uniform in thickness and a definite pick rate is required, the take-up roller is made to move forward a definite distance after each pick. In some looms the take-up roller rotates continuously, while in others it operates intermittently. In the low woollen trade, weft yarns which are not particularly uniform are often used and a barry piece would be obtained if one of the above motions were employed. In such cases, a negative motion, which allows of the cloth being pushed forward by the reed, is more suitable.

One type of negative take-up motion is illustrated in Fig. 7.39, where A is the cloth roller which, in the case of negative motions, also serves as the taking-up roller. It is suitably positioned in the loom frame and can be rotated from the ratchet wheel B through wheels C, D and E which are not change points. The ratchet wheel itself is actuated by the pawl F connected to the upper arm of a three-armed lever G, fulcrummed at H. I is a stud bolted to the sley sword J. When the sley is moving backwards, the stud moves the three-armed lever so that the pawl F is pushed loosely over

the teeth of B against the tension of the spiral spring K. Pawls L and M
prevent the ratchet wheel from slipping backwards. When the going part
is moving forwards, the stud I leaves the lower arm of G and the spring K
is free to pull the pawl back against the tension on the cloth. This it is able
to do as soon as the reed momentarily relieves the tension at the beat-up.
As the effective diameter of the cloth roller increases, more force is required to move the pulling pawl F so the spring K is moved away from
the fulcrum H as weaving proceeds. In some motions of this type weights
are substituted for springs and several attempts have been made to regu-
late the movement of the weights automatically.

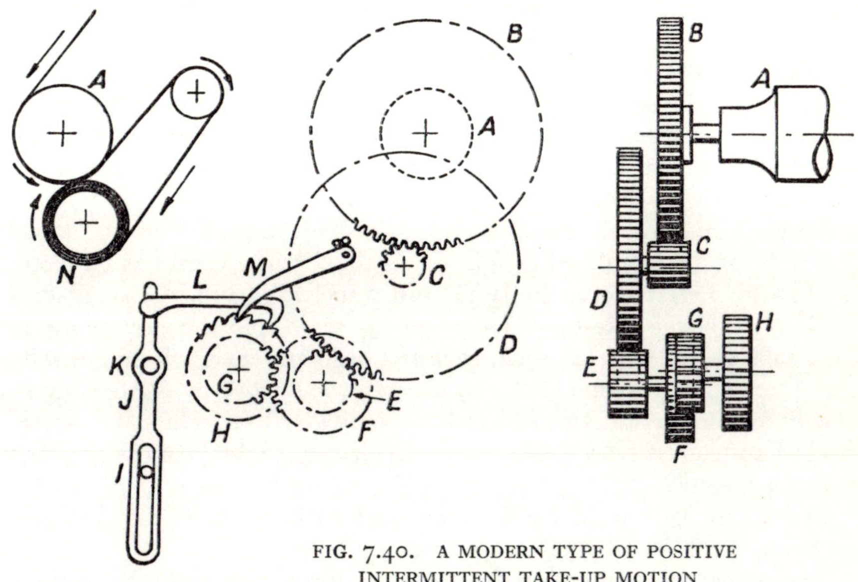

FIG. 7.40.   A MODERN TYPE OF POSITIVE
INTERMITTENT TAKE-UP MOTION

A modern type of positive intermittent take-up motion of the kind
usually applied to tappet looms, is shown at Fig. 7.40. The take-up roller
A is driven through wheels B, C, D, E, F and G from the ratchet wheel H.
The ratchet wheel itself is moved each time the going part swings forwards; a stud I on one of the sley swords works in the slot of the swing
lever J fulcrummed at K. J carries a pawl L which actuates the ratchet
wheel, while a locking pawl M prevents the ratchet wheel from slipping
back when L is moved loosely over the teeth of H.

The position of the stud I is adjustable; the lower it is in the slot, the
less is the distance traversed by L. The stud is usually set to move one
tooth of the ratchet wheel for each pick but, by higher setting, two teeth
can be moved per pick. Wheel F is the change wheel and the number of

teeth in the wheel G is usually so arranged that the number of teeth in the change wheel F is equal to the picks per inch in the cloth.

As an example, let it be assumed that the circumference of the take-up roller is 15·05 inches and therefore must move through 1/15·05th of a revolution to draw on to itself one inch of cloth. If wheel B has 90 teeth, C 15 teeth, D 89 teeth, E 24 teeth and H 24 teeth, then the wheel G must have the number of teeth (x) determined by the following equation for the change wheel F to have the same number of teeth as the picks per inch in the cloth:

$$x = \frac{90 \times 89 \times 101\cdot5 \times 24}{15\cdot05 \times 15 \times 24 \times 100} = 36 \text{ teeth}$$

The cloth usually contracts in length when moved from the loom and the $1\frac{1}{2}$ per cent in the equation is an allowance for this. The wheel G is interchangeable; but if replaced by a wheel of 27 teeth, the change wheel F will give the number of picks per $\frac{3}{4}$ inch, while if replaced by a wheel of 18 teeth, the change wheel will give picks per $\frac{1}{2}$ inch.

An older five-wheel motion is still extensively used, the change wheel for which can be calculated as follows. If the ratchet wheel has 60 teeth, the change wheel x teeth, the large stud wheel 125 teeth, the small stud wheel 19 teeth, the take-up roller wheel 125 teeth, and the circumference of the take-up roller is $14\frac{1}{4}$ inch, then the picks per inch will be given by $1/14\frac{1}{4} \times 125 \times 125 \times 60$ divided by 19×2, or 3,460 divided by x. Allowing $1\frac{1}{2}$ per cent for contraction, this becomes 3,580 divided by x, Thus, if a change wheel of 50 teeth is being used, 3,580 divided by 50, or 72 picks per inch are being inserted.

Conversely, if 50 picks per inch are needed, the required change wheel will be 3,580 divided by 50, or 72 teeth.

The actual allowance for cloth contraction varies with the type of material and weave used but is usually between $1\frac{1}{2}$ per cent and 4 per cent. In the five-wheel motion, the larger the number of teeth in the change wheel, the smaller the number of picks being inserted per inch of cloth, whereas in the seven-wheel motion, the larger the number of teeth in the change wheel, the more picks per inch in the cloth.

In both the seven and the five-wheel motions, the cloth is wound on to a separate cloth roller N (Fig. 7.40). The take-up roller A is covered with a material to give sufficient grip on the cloth to draw it forward without damage. Perforated tin of various fineness is extensively used for woollens and worsteds, while corrugated rubber or emery paper is used for the more delicate fabrics. The cloth roller N is held against the take-up roller by springs or weighted levers or chains. As the cloth roller increases in diameter, it slides down suitable slots or guides.

POSITIVE CONTINUOUS TAKE-UP MOTIONS

This type of take-up motion is usually fitted to dobby looms, its chief feature being the continuous movement of the take-up roller during weaving. One type of motion is shown in Fig. 7.41, where the take-up roller A is driven from the cross-shaft B through the worm C and worm wheel D while B itself receives its motion from the top cylinder of the dobby through a driving star-wheel, chain E, driven star wheel F and wheels G, H, I and J. It is usually arranged so that the number of teeth in the change wheel H equals the picks per inch but both the driving and driven star-wheels can be changed for convenience of operation. Thus, if 40 picks per inch are needed, a change wheel of 40 teeth is used, providing the two stars

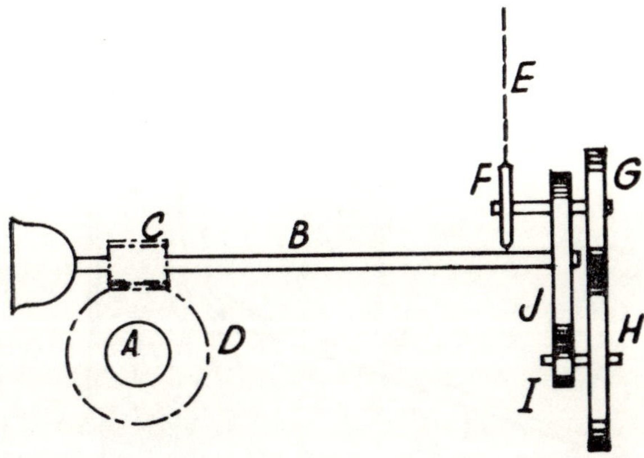

FIG. 7.41. A POSITIVE CONTINUOUS TAKE-UP MOTION

each have eight teeth. By changing the driving star wheel to 16 teeth, the take-up roller would rotate twice as quickly and only 20 picks per inch would be inserted, whereas by having a driving star-wheel of eight teeth and a driven wheel of 16 teeth, 80 picks per inch would be inserted.

As the take-up shaft is driven from the reversing shaft of the dobby, the take-up roller is reversed whenever the dobby is reversed. Arrangement is made, however, to disconnect the worm from the cross-shaft so that the take-up motion can be rotated independently of the dobby.

AUTOMATIC STOP MOTIONS

REFERENCE has been made earlier in this Section to the important part which mechanisms designed automatically to stop the loom on the breakage of warp or weft have played in the automation of weaving, although many of them are equally useful and are applied to looms without auto-

matic weft replenishment motions. One of the earliest of such stop motions
to be introduced was the weft stop motion which stops the loom automatically when the weft runs out or breaks. There are two types, the side weft
fork motion and the centre weft fork motion, the former feeling the weft
at the side of the reed and the latter in the middle. The centre weft fork
motion feels for the weft at every pick, whereas the side weft fork which
is used on most tappet looms, works on alternate picks.

THE SIDE WEFT FORK MOTION

The arrangement of the side weft fork mechanism is shown in Fig. 7.42,
where A is the weft fork, fulcrummed on the rod B. At one end of the fork

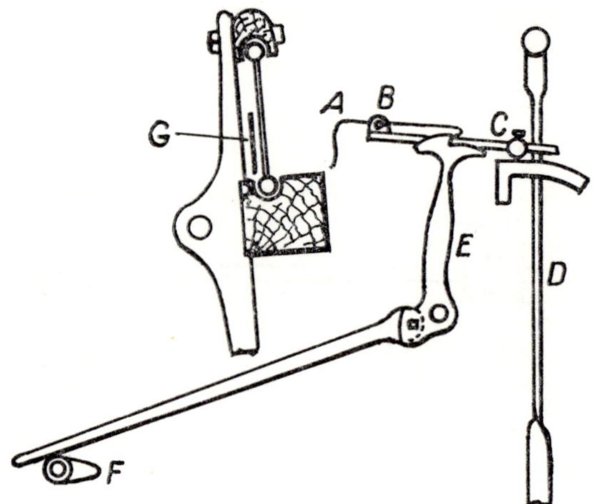

FIG. 7.42. TYPICAL SIDE WEFT FORK MECHANISM

are three right-angled prongs and at the other a hook. The rod B is connected to the outer end of a lever C so that movement of B will result in
the starting handle D being knocked out of its recess and so stopping the
loom. The hooked end of A is weighted and normally rests on top of the weft
fork hammer E, the lower end of which extends over the low shaft of the
loom as shown. A tumbler or cam F on this shaft lifts the lower end of E
once every two picks and, in doing so, throws back the hammer on alternate
picks. If the fork is in its normal position, the step of the hammer engages
with the hook of the fork and moves the hook bodily forward, so knocking
the starting handle from its recess and stopping the loom. Secured to the
end of the box plate and set slightly behind the reed and directly in front
of the prongs of the weft fork is a grid G. With the forward movement of
the going part, the prongs of the fork will pass slightly through the grid
but if there is a weft thread laid across the grate, the fork will be tilted and

its hooked end lifted out of the way of the hammer as the latter moves forwards. The efficiency of this motion depends very largely on the timing
and setting of the various parts and on keeping them in good condition.
Thus the cam F must be timed to lift the lever E when the sley is at front
centre at which time the fork will be tilted if weft is present. The prongs
of the fork must be free to enter the grid without touching the bars while
the tension of the weft in the shuttle must be such that the yarn is not too
slack to fail to tilt the fork.

THE CENTRE WEFT FORK MOTION

Whereas the side weft fork motion, described above, functions on every
second pick, the centre weft fork motion works at the centre of the sley,
'feels' for every pick and is essential on pick-and-pick looms and in other

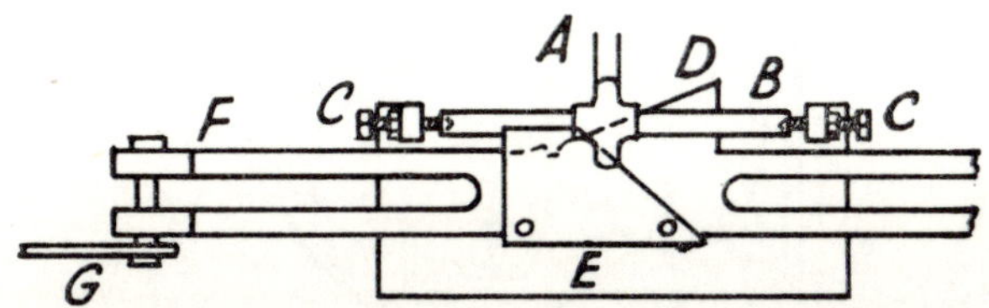

FIG. 7.43.   EXAMPLE OF A CENTRE WEFT FORK MOTION

cases where broken or missing picks in the cloth are not permissible. One
such motion is shown in Fig. 7.43. Weft feelers A are attached to a winged
bracket B which is supported by screws C to the front of the sleys. D and
E are inclined planes fixed to the bracket F which normally slides laterally
to and fro by having its outer arm G connected to the breast beam of the
loom. As incline D controls the inner part of the feeler and incline E the
outer part, the weft feelers are depressed to a mean position by incline E
when the sley is moving towards front-centre and are raised above the
mean position by incline D when moving towards back-centre.

The feelers are positioned opposite to a groove cut in the race and, in
the absence of weft, would fall into this groove when free from the control
of the inclined planes. If this should happen, one wing of the feeler would
drop into a notch in incline D and so prevent the lateral movement of
bracket F, allowing a projection on F to push the starting handle from its
recess and stop the loom. If weft is present, however, the feelers are prevented from falling below the level of the race and the wing is kept clear of
the notch in D. The two set-screws C are pointed and fit into the recess
at the end of B. They should be set to allow the prongs to enter the groove
in the sley centrally and to allow free movement of the prongs without side
play.

WARP PROTECTOR MOTIONS

If a shuttle fails to reach a shuttle box, owing to a mispick or to some other cause, it becomes trapped in the warp shed and, at the beat-up, will be forced through the warp, breaking down a large number of ends and causing a serious blemish in the cloth. Warp protector motions are designed to prevent the warp from being damaged whenever a shuttle becomes trapped. There are two types, known as 'loose reed' and 'fast reed' motions, respectively, the former being used, in general, on narrow fast-running looms and the latter on wide and heavy looms.

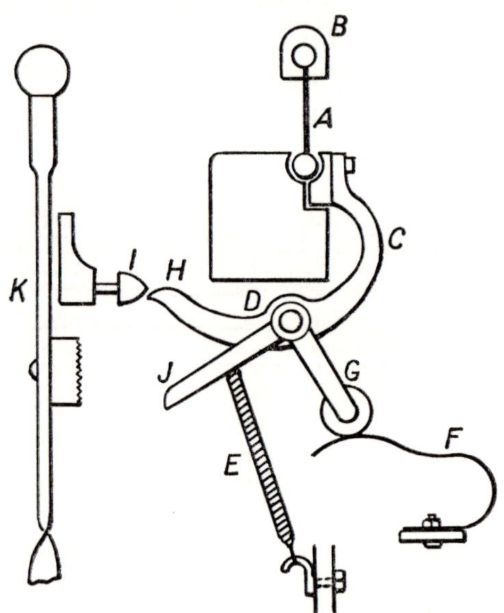

FIG. 7.44. LOOSE REED WARP PROTECTOR MOTION

In the 'loose reed' type shown in Fig. 7.44, the top rib of the reed A is slid into a groove cut in the handrail B while the lower part of the reed is free to swing backwards. This is normally prevented by the pressure of an angle plate held by arms C fixed to the rod D. The necessary pressure to C is given by various parts. Two springs E hold the reed in position when the shuttle is not crossing but during picking additional support is given to the reed by the flat springs F acting on the lever G.

As the going part swings forward for the beat-up, the beater H approaches the frog I bolted to the loom frame. If the shuttle is clear of the shed, H passes underneath the frog and gives the necessary rigidity to allow the reed to beat up the pick. If the shuttle is trapped in the shed, its pressure pushes the reed back against the spring E before H meets I; H

is tilted sufficiently to cause it to pass on the upper side of I so that no support is given to the reed. When beating up takes place, the trapped shuttle pushes back the reed to allow itself sufficient space between the reed and the cloth fell. When the rod D is turned clockwise by reason of the shuttle being trapped, the arm J is raised to meet the buffer on the starting handle K, so stopping the loom.

The chief features of the 'fast reed' motion are shown in Fig. 7.45, where A is the shuttle box, at the back of which is a spring or swell B. This swell is connected by fingers to the tongue C, fulcrummed on the rod

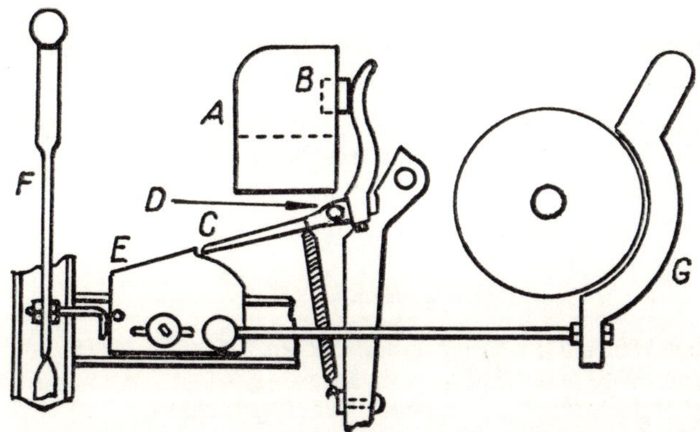

FIG. 7.45.   FAST REED WARP PROTECTOR MOTION

D, E is a 'frog' bolted to the loom framing but allowed a little play against a strong spring; it is connected to the starting handle F and the brake G on the crankshaft. When the shuttle enters the box, the swell is forced backwards, the tongue C is lifted and, as the sley moves forward, passes over the 'frog'. If the shuttle fails to enter the box properly, the swell B is not moved. C remains depressed and in line with the notch in the frog. The sley is thus brought to an abrupt stop, the starting handle is knocked from its recess and the brake is applied to the crankshaft. This type of motion requires very strong sley swords and 'frogs' to withstand the shock of 'banging off'. It is used on heavier looms where the required force for beating up cannot be obtained with the loose reed motion.

The success of these motions depends entirely on the correct setting of the various parts; faulty settings cause undue knocking-off and warp smashes. Difficulty is occasionally met in drop-box looms in getting all the swells and shuttles to give the requisite movement to the stop rod fingers and tongue.

There are many varieties of warp stop motion but all depend on the use of droppers or drop wires. These are thin, light metal strips with small holes through which the warp ends are passed individually. One type has closed ends, in which case they need to be threaded during looming; this can be done by specialized machines. Another type of drop wire has open ends and these wires can be slipped over the warp ends at the loom. The droppers are kept suspended by the tension on the warp ends but, when an end breaks, its drop wire falls and this is used in a variety of ways to stop the loom. A mechanical device is for the drop wire to foul oscillating castellated metal strips which extend the width of the warp, while in other methods, the drop wire completes or breaks an electrical circuit or blocks a beam of light directed on to a photo-electric cell.

In the case of warps more heavily sett than about 40 per inch, the drop wires are staggered in a number of separate rows so that they do not support each other by lateral pressure after an end has broken. There is often a tendency for some size and surface fibre to be removed by the edges of the drop wires and care has to be taken to replace damaged wires. In some weaving sheds, the action of the drop wire is also arranged to complete an electric circuit that causes a warning light to be shown.

REFERENCES

1. "Healds for Weaving", I. Laird, Emmott, 1949.
2. Middlebrook, W., *Text. Manfr.*, 1947, **73**, 397, 500.
3. "Practical Warp Gaiting", W. Middlebrook, Emmott, 1949.
4. *Textile Weekly*, 1950, **45**, 1440.
5. "Calculation in Yarn and Fabrics", F. Bradbury, 1906.
6. "The Mechanism of Weaving", T. W. Fox, Macmillan, 1911.
7. "Weaving", W. P. Crankshaw, Pitman, 1925.
8. "Tappet and Dobby Looms", T. Roberts, Emmott, 1912.
9. "Loom Tuning", W. Middlebrook, Emmott, 1912.
10. "Loom Box Changing Motions", W. Middlebrook, Emmott, 1950.
11. "Negative Dobby Shedding Looms", W. Middlebrook, Emmott, 1951.
12. "Modern Developments in Weaving Machinery",
    Edited by V. Duxbury and G. R. Wray, Columbine Press, 1962.
13. "Jacquards and Harness", T. Woodhouse, Macmillan, 1923.
14. Dracup, C. T., *J. Text. Inst.*, 1951, **42**, p.97.
15. *Textile Recorder*, 1961, **78**, January and February.
16. "Advanced Textile Design", W. Watson, Longmans Green, 1947.
17. "Automatic Weaving", W. A. Hanton, Benn, 1929.
18. "Introduction to Automatic Weaving", G. A. Bennett, Harlequin Press, 1948.
19. "Automatic Weaving", The Northrop System, British Northrop Ltd., 1962.
20. "Automatic Weaving", J. B. Aitken, Columbine Press, 1964.
21. Hodgson, N. T., *Text. Weekly*, 1962, **62**, 1153.
22. Pressley, R. B., *Text. World*, 1961, **111**, No. 7, 30.
23. Steiner, M., *Canad. Text. J.*, 1960, **77**, 76.
24. Thomas, I. H., *Text. Recorder*, 1963, **81**, Sept. 95.
25. Svaty, V., *Melliand Textilber*, 1962, **43**, 1049.
26. Greenwood, K., *Text. Inst. & Ind.*, 1963, 1, No. 5, 13.
27. Greenwood, K., *New Scientist*, No. 377, Feb. 6, 1964.
28. Duxbury, V., *Text. Mercury*, 1960, **142**, 111.
29. "Modern Developments in Weaving Machinery" (Ed. by V. Duxbury
    & G. R. Wray), Columbine Press, 1962.

WOVEN FABRIC STRUCTURES AND DESIGNS

THE WIDE RANGE of fabric designs and structures which weaving techniques and mechanisms make possible has already been indicated in the preceding section of the book, and particularly in that part dealing specifically with the subject of looming. It will, therefore, be apparent that not only are the arrangement of warp ends in the heald eyes and the order of lifting the healds to provide a shed for the interlacing of warp and weft independently capable of wide variation, but that permutation of these variables provides for a very large range of woven structures – and this apart from variety resulting from the use of yarns of different types, colours or counts and the manner of their spacing and general arrangement.

Despite the variety which simple manipulation of these basic factors provides, the range of woven fabric designs and structures is capable of still further extension, one simple example being the use of more than one set of warp or weft threads to produce what are known as compound cloths. 'Gauze' or 'leno' fabrics can be produced by arranging for some of the warp threads to cross one another and to be held in the crossed position by the weft, while another modification of the ordinary woven fabric structure is 'plush' or 'pile'. Such fabrics usually consist of a simple foundation cloth together with a series of warp or weft loops standing up from the body of the cloth to form a 'pile'. These projecting loops may be cut to give a fibrous surface, as in velveteens and in Wilton and Axminster carpets[1], or they may be left uncut as in Brussels carpets[1] and in terry towelling[2]. Such woven fabrics as gauze, leno, plush and carpets, however, are known as complex fabrics and, in general, are woven on special types of loom[3]. Finally, reference must be made to the limitless number of figured designs which the jacquard mechanism makes possible and which are extensively employed in furnishing fabrics.

In the face of such variety, a comprehensive survey of woven fabric structures and designs is obviously impossible in a book of this size. However, a very large volume of cloth is woven on the basis of relatively simple or fundamental weaves or on developments of these basic structures and these accordingly warrant some detailed description. At the outset, however, it may be advisable to clear any confusion which may exist between the terms 'weave' and 'design'.

Weaves and Designs: The terms 'weave' and 'design' refer respectively to the manner in which the warp and weft threads interlace and to its representation on point (squared) paper. In a design, the vertical spaces represent warp ends and the horizontal spaces weft picks. In the worsted section of the trade a mark on a square indicates 'warp over weft', while a blank square denotes 'weft over warp'. Fabrics which have much more weft than warp on the surface are, however, more conveniently designed with marks representing 'weft up' while many designers of woollen cloths adopt this technique for all their designs. To avoid ambiguity it is often advisable therefore to add captions to designs to indicate which procedure has been followed. In the following pages, however, marks on all designs of single cloths denote 'warp over weft'.

There is often a great difference between the design as it appears on point paper and the actual appearance of the woven fabric. This is due to such features as the distortion of threads by pressure and the rolling together of neighbouring floats. An experienced designer, however, can visualize the appearance of a cloth from the design and structure. Incidentally, in designing practice, it is usual to give only one repeat of a weave though it is often an advantage to run out several repeats in order more clearly to see the effect of a design.

FUNDAMENTAL WEAVES

As previously stated, a very large volume of cloth is woven with what are termed elementary or fundamental weaves, such as plains, twills and sateens, or with developments of these.

Plain Weave: This weave, shown in plan and section at *A* in Fig. 8.1 is the simplest and one of the most commonly used of all weaves. It has the maximum amount of interlacing, giving maximum firmness and strength to the resulting fabric. If the warp and weft are of the same counts and the ends and picks per inch are equal, there will be equal amounts of warp and weft on the surface.

Twill Weaves: These are the simplest figured weaves, the figure consisting of diagonal lines which, in the case of worsted and woollen fabrics, usually run upwards from left to right. A simple twill design together with the plan and the sections of the first end and the first pick are given at *B* in Fig. 8.1. It will be observed that ends and picks float over two consecu-

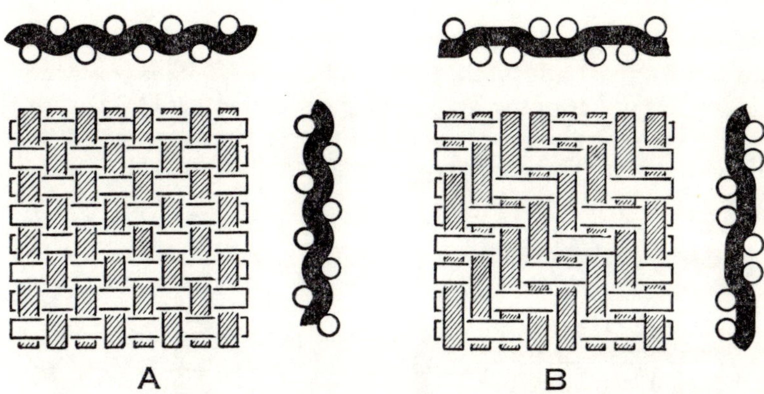

FIG. 8.1. PLAIN AND TWILL WEAVES

tive threads without any interlacing. This reduces the firmness of the resulting cloth. The more frequent the interlacing, the longer has the warp to be for a given length of cloth, while the number of picks per inch which can be put into the cloth is reduced due to the fact that each intersection occupies a space almost equal to the thickness of a thread.

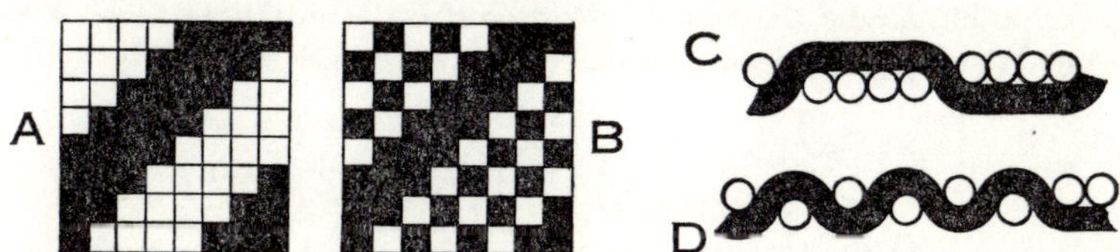

FIG. 8.2. TWO DESIGNS WITH DIFFERENT FREQUENCIES OF INTERLACING

This is illustrated by the sections *C* and *D* of Fig. 8.2 which correspond with the first picks of the designs *A* and *B* respectively. The relative firmness of weaves is sometimes expressed by the average float, this being the number of picks in the design divided by the number of intersections. Thus in Fig. 8.2, the average float of design *A* is 8 divided by 2 equalling 4, while that of *B* is 8 divided by 6, that is, 1·33. Consequently, in the first design, the yarns will be straighter, there will be less contraction of warp and weft, and the fabric will be capable of having either thicker yarns or more threads per inch than *B*. It is extremely important when making a range of patterns across a single warp to have the same average float in all cases so that the correct structure can be maintained. It is also important in fancy weaves to have nearly the same average float for each end. The direction and amount of twist in the warp and weft yarns can be selected to accentuate or reduce the boldness of the twill lines.

Sateen Weaves: These weaves are designed to give the maximum amount of warp or weft on the surface of the cloth. This is accomplished by having all but one of the warp ends in a repeat either lifted or depressed for each weft pick, the former giving a warp-faced sateen and the latter a weft-faced sateen. The intersections of succeeding picks are normally dis-

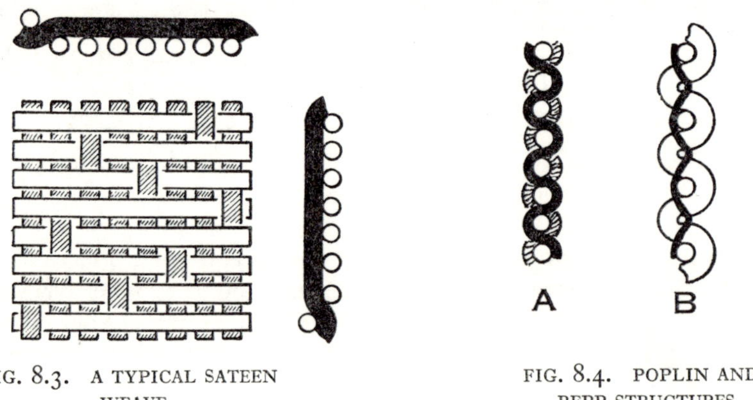

FIG. 8.3.   A TYPICAL SATEEN
WEAVE

FIG. 8.4.   POPLIN AND
REPP STRUCTURES

persed in such a way that they do not make a regular pattern. A typical sateen weave with plan and sections of the first end and first pick is given at Fig. 8.3.

DEVELOPMENT OF THE PLAIN WEAVE

Plain weave fabrics having the same counts and sett in both warp and weft have level surfaces with no distinctive pattern markings. By altering the counts or sett of either warp, weft, or both, a considerable change can be effected in the appearance of the fabric. Thus cords or ribs across the width of a cloth are developed by using a heavily sett fine warp and a small number of coarse weft picks. The thick weft remains straight and the fine warp bends round the weft and hides it completely. This is the structure of the poplin and is illustrated by the section at *A* in Fig. 8.4. Opposite conditions give ribs running warp way. Fine and coarse threads can also be arranged alternately in both warp and weft to accentuate the rib struct-ure as in repp fabrics. This is illustrated by section *B* in Fig. 8.4.

Shadow stripes can be produced by varying the number of threads per inch across the width of the warp, while wavy lines in the cloth can be obtained by causing a specially shaped reed to rise and fall. Tight and slack threads can be combined by using two warp beams differently tensioned, while heavily twisted yarns can be used in either warp or weft to give crêpe **fabrics.**

By the introduction of colour, numerous fancy effects can be obtained with the plain weave. The fabric can be dyed solid or can be printed; by having yarns in the warp and weft which dye differently, cross-dyed effects can be obtained, while warp and weft threads can be coloured and arranged in such an order as to produce check patterns, hairlines or small figure effects. The combination of colour and weave is discussed more fully at a later stage.

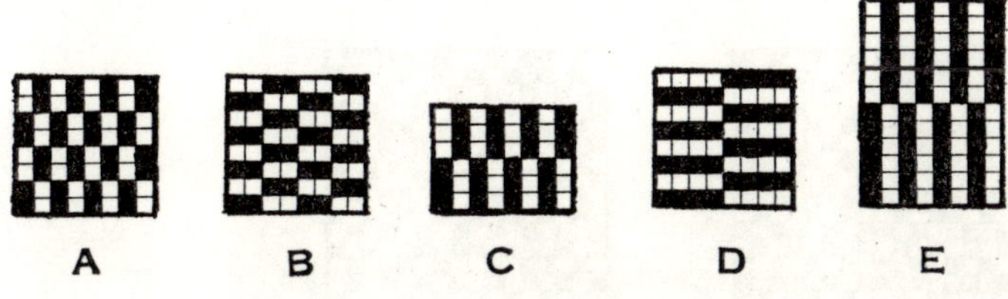

FIG. 8.5.   WARP AND WEFT RIB WEAVES

Warp and Weft Ribs: Weaves of this type are obtained by extending the basic plain weave vertically and horizontally, respectively, as shown at *A* and *B* in Fig. 8.5. In the warp rib type, a series of ribs runs horizontally across the fabric; the weft is almost straight and the warp does all the bending. The warp ends lie close together, both on the face and the back, and cover the weft almost entirely. This is usually enhanced by using thicker weft and a closely sett fine warp. The opposite conditions obtain for the weft rib, though such weaves, by themselves, are usually not practicable due to the high cost of inserting a high number of picks per inch. The length of the floats can be increased as shown at *C* (3/3 warp rib), *D* (4/4 weft rib), and at *E* (6/6 warp rib).

Fancy Ribs: To illustrate this development simple combinations of warp rib weaves are shown at *A*, *B*, *C* and *D* of Fig. 8.6, while *E*, *F*, *G* and *H* illustrate a series of effective weaves combining rib and plain on a plain weave base. In design *E*, areas 1 and 2 are filled with plain weave, while 3 and 4 are occupied by 2/2 warp rib. The result is a twill effect, alternately plain and rib, all signs of check being obliterated. The same plan and weave are used in *F* but the two sets of weaves run in opposite directions to give a correct all-over effect. Designs *G* and *H* are similar weaves on 14 ends and picks. Care has to be taken when making designs in this way to ensure correct joinings and good balancing. Every end must have the same, or very nearly the same, number of intersections so that each takes up to the same extent.

Hopsack Weaves: Regular hopsack or mat weaves have two or more threads working together in the same order to produce an apparently en-

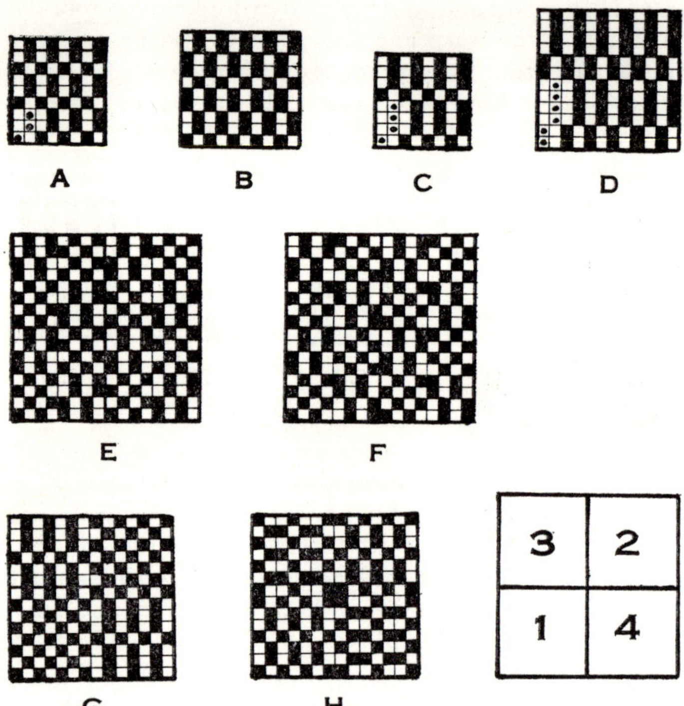

FIG. 8.6.   SIMPLE COMBINATIONS OF WARP RIB WEAVES AND WEAVES COMBINING RIB AND PLAIN ON A PLAIN BASE

larged effect of plain weave. Warp and weft show equally on both sides of the cloth. Designs for 2/2, 3/3 and 4/4 hopsacks are given at *A*, *B* and *C* in Fig. 8.7 while *D* and *E* are irregular hopsacks. On account of the loose way in which the threads interlace, large designs are employed only for fine fabrics. Greater firmness and variety in these weaves can be obtained by stitching. *F* is a simple stitched hopsack, while *G* is an example of a type known as 'barleycorn'.

Fancy effects can be made by combining plain, rib and hopsack. One simple example is shown at *H* in Fig. 8.7, while I and J show the details.

It should be emphasized that the appearance of the cloth is not necessarily similar to the appearance of the design on paper. Due to the large number of intersections, plain weave sections tend to occupy relatively great space, whereas hopsack positions, due to their looseness, roll together to occupy relatively little space. Two more complex examples similar to H are shown at K and L in Fig. 8.7, the method of construction being shown at M and N respectively.

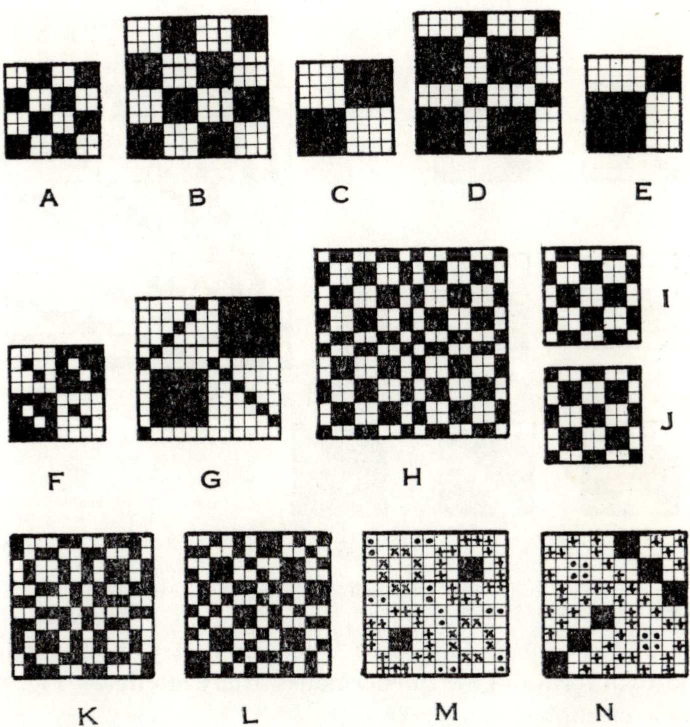

FIG. 8.7.   TYPICAL HOPSACK WEAVES AND FANCY EFFECTS
OBTAINED BY COMBINING PLAIN, RIB AND HOPSACK

DEVELOPMENT OF TWILL WEAVES

In the development of simple twill weaves, a definite system should be adopted so as to obtain the maximum number of results and thus allow the designer to see the possibilities of any particular range. Fig. 8.8 shows the development of simple twills on 8 x 8. D has equal amounts of warp and weft on the surface; A, B and C have a preponderance of weft and are known as weft-faced twills, whereas E, F and G are warp-faced twills. Ordinary small twills, although very popular, are few in number and may be accounted for by the 2/2 twill, the 2/1 twill or the prunella twill, the 3/3 and 4/4 twill, 3/1 twill or swansdown, and the 1/3 twill or crow twill.

The angle of twill produced in the finished cloth depends on the ratio of ends to picks and the move of the twill. If the ends and picks per inch are equal, an ordinary twill with a move of 1 up to 1 on runs at an angle of 45°. A steeper twill is formed when there are more ends than picks, while a flatter twill is obtained when the number of picks exceeds the number of ends. In practice, one normally tries to avoid flat twills by having more ends than picks per inch. *H* in Fig. 8.8 shows how the direction of the twill is altered by different moves.

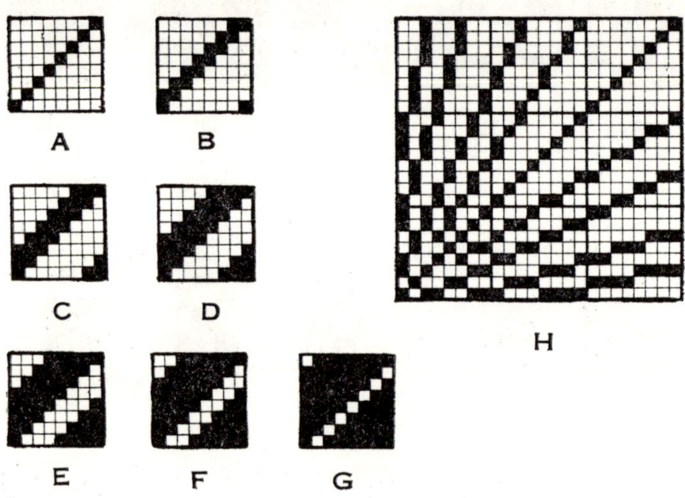

FIG. 8.8.   THE DEVELOPMENT OF TWILL WEAVES

Compound or Fancy Diagonals: The elementary weaves can be arranged in twill form to give an enormous variety of effects. Fig. 8.9 gives four simple examples.

Elongated Twills: These twills are illustrated in Fig. 8.10. The base line of marks required to give the desired angle of twill is set down over the required number of ends and picks. Marks are then added systematically to form new designs. *A, B* and *C* show three weaves based on a move of 2 up to 1 on. *D* moves 3 up to 2 on, and *E*, 3 up to 1 on. In steep twills, the warp should usually show more prominently on the surface whereas the reverse should apply for flat twills. Steep twills that produce distinct twill lines of warp are termed whipcords.

A useful method of producing high or low angled twills is illustrated in Fig. 8.10. *F* is a diagonal on 24 x 24; *G* is obtained from *F* by using only the odd ends and so repeats on 12 x 24. When the third ends of *F* are put together, *H* is obtained which, though not good in itself, is sufficiently suggestive to enable design *I* to be produced. Upright twills can also be made from sateen bases as shown later.

FIG. 8.9.   EXAMPLES OF COMPOUND OR FANCY DIAGONALS

Broken Twills: These are made from simple twills by removing a number of ends in a definite order. *A* of Fig. 8.11 shows the broken 2/2 twill obtained by taking two ends and missing one, the order being 1, 2, 4, 1,

FIG. 8.10.   ELONGATED TWILLS

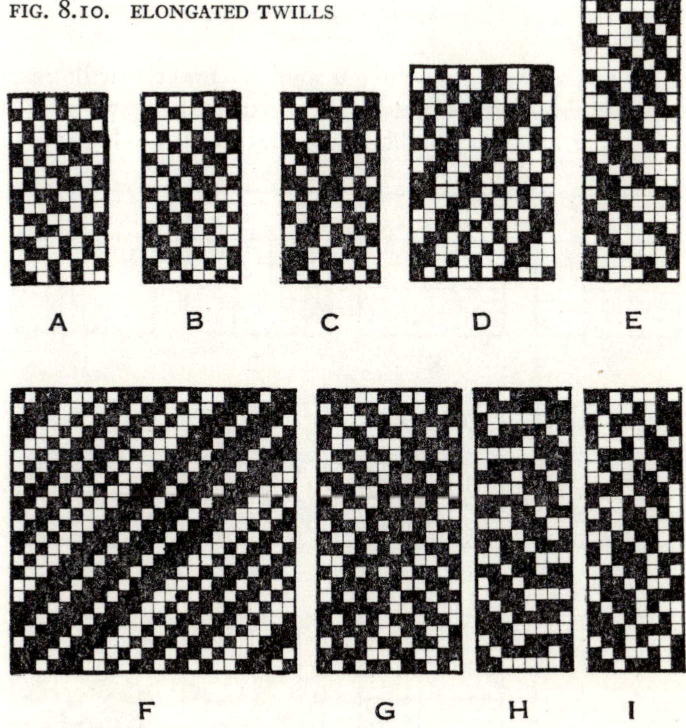

3, 4, 2, 3, as shown by base marks in dots. *B* shows the 3/3 twill taking 3 and missing 2; *C* is the 4/4 twill arranged 4 taken, 3 missed. This type of weave offers considerable scope as a basis for small stripe and check effects,

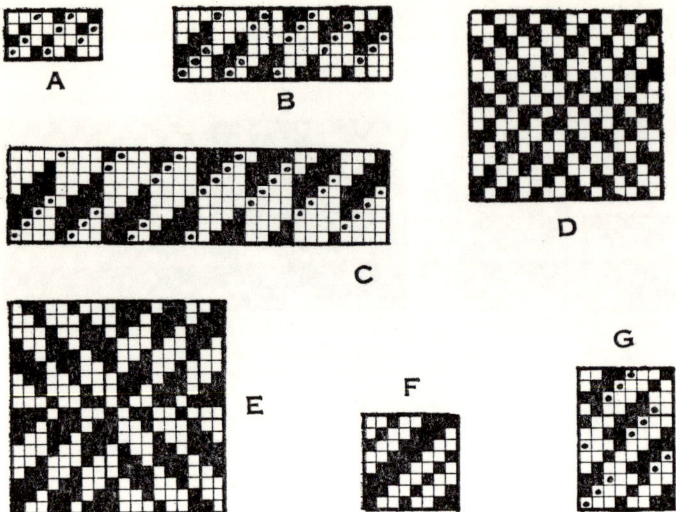

FIG. 8.11.   A SELECTION OF BROKEN TWILL DESIGNS

as seen at *D* and *E*, based on the 2/2 and 3/3 broken twills respectively. Picks can be taken as well as ends as shown at *G*, the standard 8-end diagonal *F* being rearranged by taking three picks and missing three.

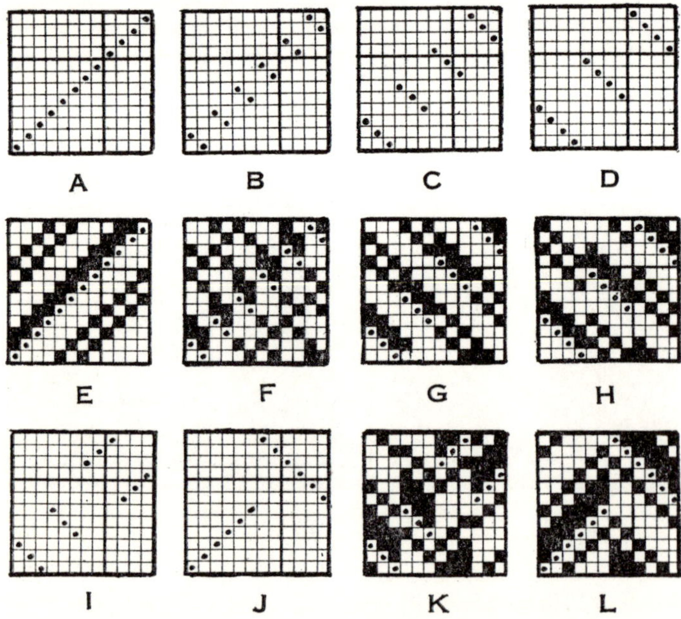

FIG. 8.12.   THE PRODUCTION OF TRANSPOSED TWILL DESIGNS

Transposed Twills: These are weaves obtained by taking the threads of a given weave in groups of two, three or more and reversing the threads of each group. Thus *A* of Fig. 8.12 is the base line of a 12-end diagonal, *B* shows it transposed in groups of two, *C* in groups of three and *D* in groups of four. *E* shows marks added to *A* to make it into a diagonal, while *F*, *G* and *H* are the designs obtained when the threads of *E* are transposed in the orders of *B*, *C* and *D* respectively. Another variation is to arrange the groups of threads in transposed and straight orders alternately, as at *I* and *J*, from which *K* and *L* are produced.

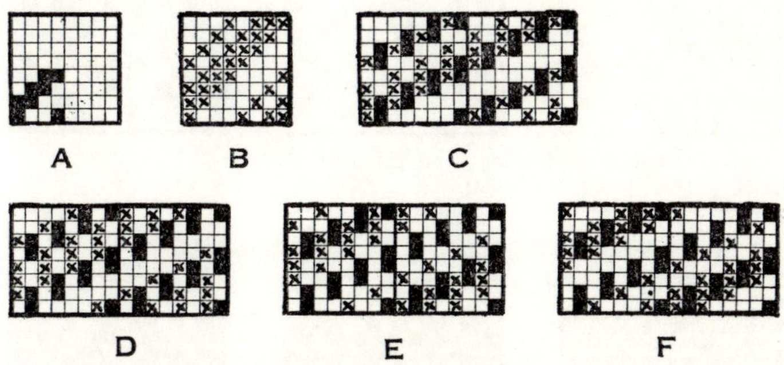

FIG. 8.13.   THE PRODUCTION OF COMBINATION TWILLS

Combination Twills and Diagonals: Combination twills are produced by combining the threads of two other weaves in definite order. Usually, one of the weaves is put on the odd threads of the combined weave and the second weave on the even threads. *A* and *B* of Fig. 8.13 are two weaves to be combined, end and end; *C* is the weave obtained by putting the ends of *B* on the odd ends of *C* and the ends of *A* on the even ends, beginning with the first end of each weave. *D*, *E* and *F* are the effects obtained by starting with the second, third and fourth ends respectively at *B*. Weaves can also be combined, pick and pick.

Interlacing Twills: These can be designed (*a*) from a diamond base, and (*b*) from small twills. In the former, the base marks are first put down over the repeating area, say, 16 x 16, in the form of diamonds as at *A* in Fig. 8.14. This particular base has two diamond spaces, marked 1 and 2 on the design, which can be filled with various small effects; *B* shows 3/3 twill to the right in space 1 and 3/3 twill to the left in space 2. Alternatively, the spaces may be filled and the original base marks removed as is shown in design *C*. *D* shows the diamond spaces subdivided into smaller spaces, numbered 1 to 8; the large diamond spaces are differently divided in the base structures *G* and *J*. Designs *E*, *H* and *K* are built up on the base

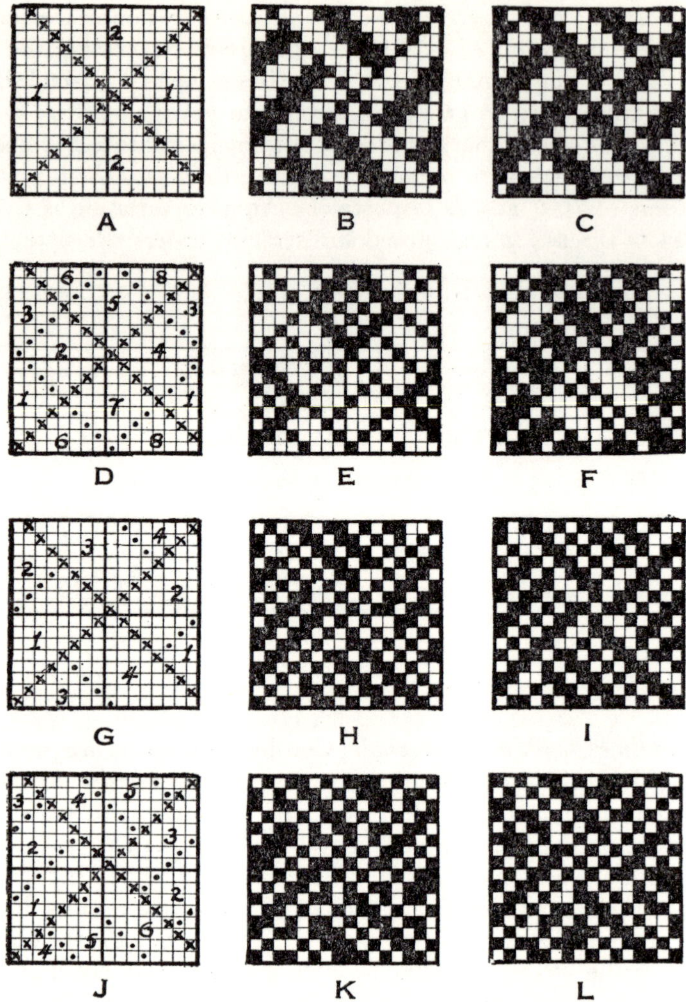

FIG. 8.14.   INTERLACING TWILLS FROM A DIAMOND BASE

marks D, G and $\mathcal{J}$ respectively and designs F, I and L are constructed from
the same corresponding bases with the base lines erased later.

In the second method, a small twill weave is first marked out on the
odd ends over the area of repeat and the marks then joined by new ones
put on the even ends to form the complete design. A systematic method of
construction is shown in Fig. 8.15. A shows 2/2 twill indicated by vertical
strokes on the odd thread spaces over the whole repeating area. In B, lines

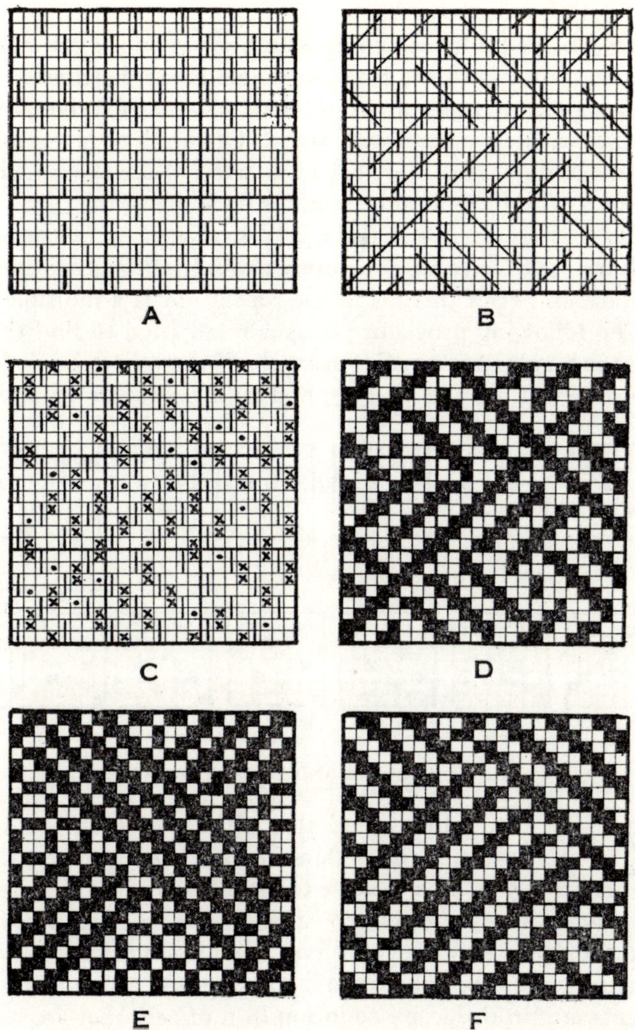

FIG. 8.15.   THE CONSTRUCTION OF INTERLACING
TWILLS FROM A SMALL TWILL BASE

are drawn connecting two or more of the basic weave marks, *C* shows the
key thread marks that have been joined together, connected by crosses,
thus producing 2/2 twill to the right and left. Dots are added to *C* to finish
neatly the warp and weft floats at the top and bottom of the twills. The
complete design is given at *D*. *E* and *F* are two finished designs built up
from key threads working in 2/1 and 2/2 order, respectively.

DEVELOPMENT OF SATEEN WEAVES

Simple twills are built with a move number of one, a distinct twill line resulting as at *A* in Fig. 8.16. *B* shows single floats distributed over eight ends and picks with a move of two, *C* with a move of three, *D* with four, *E* with five, *F* with six and *G* with seven. Of these, *A* is a straight twill, *G* is a reverse twill, *C* and *E* are sateen weaves, while the remainder cannot be woven as there are no intersections on some of the picks.

The only way to distribute the marks so that they fall on a different thread each time is to have a move number which will neither divide evenly into the total number of threads in the repeat nor is a multiple of such a number. The following procedure is usually adopted to find the number of sateens over a given repeat. For example, if the repeat is 8 x 8, the consecutive numbers, 1, 2, 3, 4, 5, 6, 7, 8 should be put down and all num-

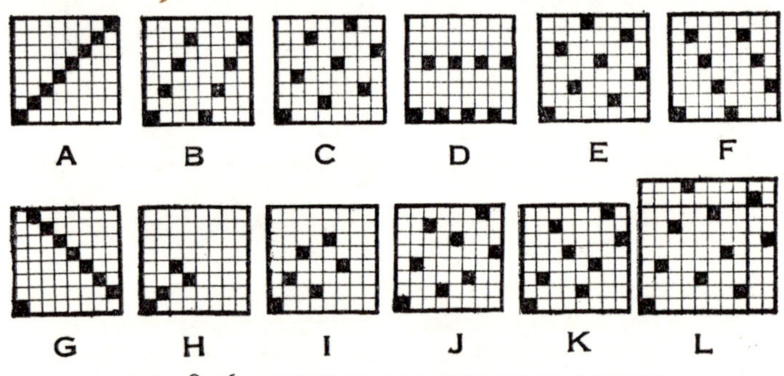

FIG. 8.16.   REGULAR AND IRREGULAR SATEENS

bers which divide evenly into 8 and all multiples of such number should be deleted. In this case 3, 5 and 7 alone remain. As, however, the penultimate number always makes a reverse twill, this too must be deleted. Thus on eight threads, there are only two sateens, one by counting three up to one on and the other by a move of five. It will be noticed, however, that these two sateens are similar but running in opposite directions. In general, similar effects are produced by counting in numbers that are respectively higher and lower than half the number of threads in the repeat. If a weft sateen is required, the marks will represent warp up; marks equalling weft up will give a warp sateen. Warp sateens usually have more ends than picks per inch to emphasize the effect and are, therefore, more common than weft sateens which need a preponderance of weft, involving lower loom productions. The regular sateen weaves mostly used are the five-end and the eight-end.

Irregular Sateens: Although regular sateens cannot be constructed on four or six threads, it is possible to produce irregular sateens as indicated at *H* and *I* of Fig. 8.16. Irregular sateens are entirely free from twill lines, a feature that gives them an advantage over regular sateens. For this reason, sateens are often arranged irregularly on 8, 10, 12 or more threads; *J* and *K* are irregular eight-end sateens, while *L* is one on 10 ends.

Check Effects: Fig. 8.17 shows four weaves built up from warp and weft sateens on a check basis. *A* and *B* are combinations of the four-end weft and warp sateens, *C* uses the five-end and *D* the seven-end sateen.

Sateen Derivatives: Sateens are probably more extensively used as a foundation for other weaves than as weaves in themselves. Thus, *B*, *C*, *D* and *E* of Fig. 8.18 show four designs made by rearranging the threads of the seven-end diagonal given at *A*, in various sateen orders. The dots in *B*, *C*, *D* and *E* are seven-end sateens with moves, of 2 3, 4 and 5 respectively, while the ends of *A* have been rearranged in these new orders to

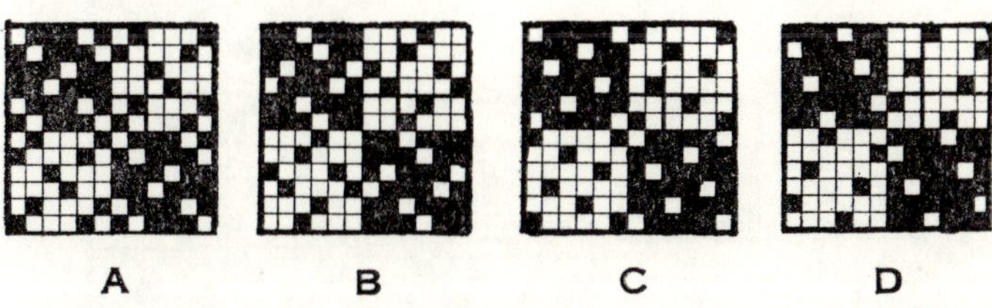

A   B   C   D

FIG. 8.17.   CHECK EFFECTS FROM WARP AND WEFT SATEENS

give the four new weaves. *G* is a rearrangement of the picks of weave F in 10-end sateen order, move 7.

Original designs on sateen bases include all-over effects and twills. In the case of all-over effects, the sateen base is first inserted on the required number of threads and the new design is built up, according to the kind of weave and structure required, by adding marks in the same relative position to each base mark. The six weaves shown in *H* to *M* of Fig. 8.18, are based on the eight-end sateen, move 5, which is shown in dots. A single mark is added in *H* to give the eight-end buckskin weave. More marks are added in designs *I* and *J* producing a firmer weave and a structure of the corkscrew type. *K* is a counterchange effect used considerably in the coating trade with black and white warp and weft. *L* is a tighter weave and *M* is twilled hopsack or the common barathea used in suitings.

A systematic development such as this is essential to exhaust weave possibilities. Twills and diagonals are made by using any sateen weave with a fairly definite twill line and adding one set of marks to one twill and a different set to another line. The twills run at various angles so that both steep and low angled twills can be made; only a few sateens give twill lines of 45°. Design *N* of Fig. 8.18 shows an eight-end sateen, counting 5 put

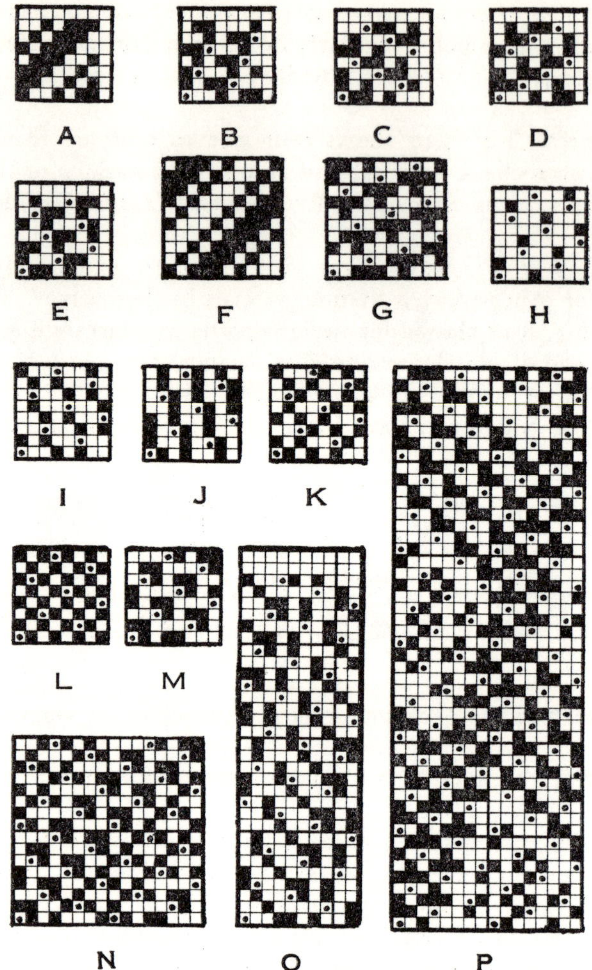

FIG. 8.18.   SATEEN DERIVATIVES

down in dots on 16 x 16, this giving four separate twill lines at an angle of
45°. Two of these lines are made into twilled hopsack and the other two
lines into a fancy weave. Design *O* is based on the 10-end sateen, counting
3, this giving a steep diagonal on 10 x 30; *P* is a more elaborate diagonal
on 16 x 48 based on the eight-end sateen with a move of three.

The marks in a sateen weave can be extended both horizontally and
vertically to give effects which can be used as pure weaves or bases for new
weaves. Horizontal extensions to the marks of the eight-end sateen, move
5, are shown by the heavy marks of *A*, Fig. 8.19, vertical extensions at *B*

and both horizontal and vertical extensions at C and D. Marks can be added systematically to these base marks as shown by the crosses representing the second stage, vertical lines the third stage and the upright crosses the fourth stage. E, F, G and H show the completed designs. I is the preliminary planning of an enlarged sateen on 15 x 15; each base is made into 2/2 hopsack and marks are then added systematically to give the design at J. K is a design on 20 x 20 based on a five-end sateen, L is based on the eight-end sateen, while M and N are both based on 10-end sateens.

WEFT-BACKED AND WARP-BACKED CLOTHS

The preceding designs have been for cloths containing one series of warp and one series of weft threads. It is, however, possible to use more than one series of either warp or weft threads to produce backed cloths, the chief characteristics of which are (*i*) they are heavier than single cloths with an equally fine surface, (*ii*) the extra threads can be used for ornamentation and (*iii*) the extra threads can be of inferior material in order to cheapen the cloth. Cloths containing one series of warp threads and two series of weft threads are known as extra weft or weft-backed fabrics, two warps and one weft as extra warp or warp-backed fabrics, two series of both warp and weft threads are double cloths, while three series of each give treble cloths. The extra threads are held to the face fabric either by special stitching threads which are so designed that they remain hidden in the body of the fabric or by allowing the extra threads to weave loosely with the face fabric.

Weft-backed Cloths: With designs for these fabrics it is convenient to let marks represent weft up. A and B of Fig. 8.20 show the construction of a weft-backed cloth having a 2/2 hopsack face and a 3/1 twill back. The face weave is first run out in pencil over the repeating area or more. The positions of the extra picks are then marked at the side by short ink strokes; in this example, the order of wefting is 1 face, 1 back. Thirdly the 1/3 twill is shown on the design by short ink strokes, care being taken to see that the stitching points are suitably buried. In this case, while the odd backing picks are properly buried between two face floats, the even back picks are not well hidden. The key plan A is now complete and can be expanded to the full design B where the backing picks are represented by shaded squares and the crosses represent backing weft over the common warp. C is the key to a reversible weft-backed design used extensively for motor rugs and dressing gowns. The same design is formed on both the face and the back so that by using differently coloured wefts, similar portions of the weave on face and back are oppositely coloured.

Imitation Weft-backed Cloths: These fabrics are made by using weaves which produce structures resembling weft-backed cloths. If a normal cloth

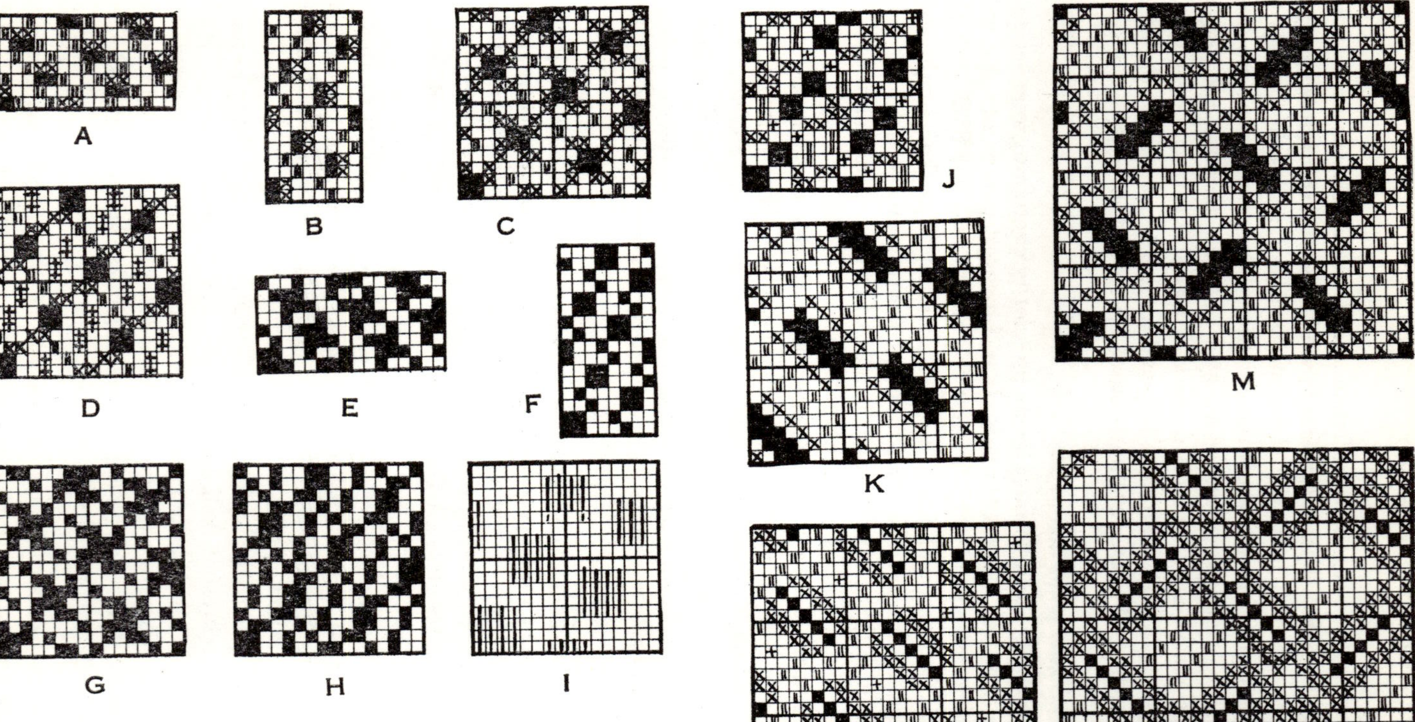

FIG. 8.19.   A FURTHER SELECTION OF DESIGNS
DERIVED FROM SATEEN WEAVES

has 50 ends and picks per inch, then the corresponding imitation weft-backed cloth on the 1-and-1 principle would have 50 ends and 100 picks per inch with the weave modified to enable the extra picks to be crammed in. Design D of Fig. 8.20 shows a 2/2 twill, marks representing weft up. The middle line of twill is put down in E by a line across a space (row 1) while the second line of twill is put on the lines of E to give row 2, the first mark of row 2 being two squares away from the first mark of row 1. These two rows are then run out until a repeat is obtained as at F. The effect pro-

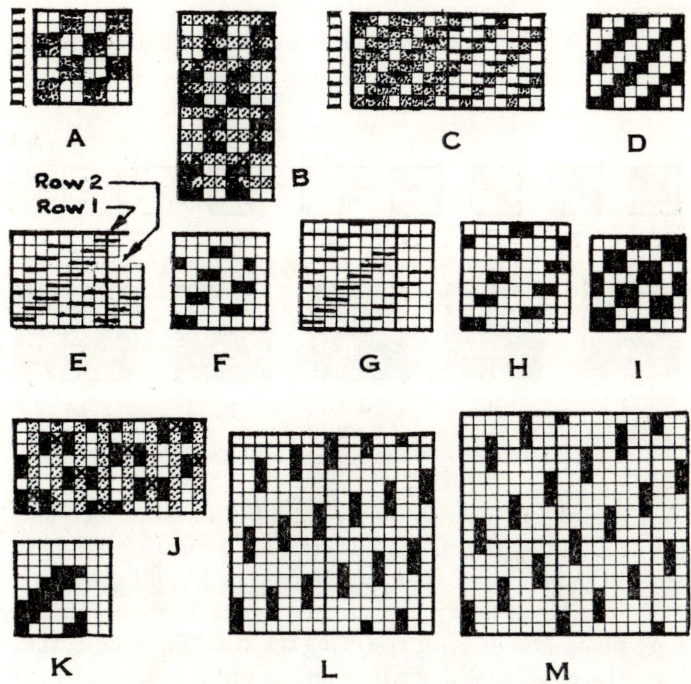

FIG. 8.20.   WEFT-BACKED AND WARP-BACKED CLOTHS

duced is not a true 2/2 twill but a cross between a 2/2 twill and a 2/1 twill. By starting row 2 two squares from the second mark of row 1 as in G, the imitation weft-back H is obtained which is a cross between the 2/2 and 3/2 twills.

Warp-backed Cloths: These are constructed exactly as for weft-backed fabrics, the extra threads being in the warp direction instead of in the weft. J of Fig. 8.20, shows design I backed 1-and-1, whilst designs L and M are imitation warp-backs of the 3/3 twill at K. Marks in these cases represent warp-up.

DOUBLE CLOTHS

A systematic method of constructing double cloth designs can be followed through its several stages by reference to Fig. 8.21. Here, *A*, *B* and *C* show respectively the face weave, the back weave as it would appear from the face side and the order of stitching the face and back. The first stage of construction is to put down the face weave lightly in pencil as indicated by the stipple in *D* of Fig. 8.21. The positions of the backing ends and picks are then indicated respectively above and at the side of the face weave as at *E*. In the third stage, the backing weave is inserted by dots on the intersections of backing warp and weft, as at *F*, and in the fourth stage the position of the stitches are run out, as in *G*. This completes the key plan.

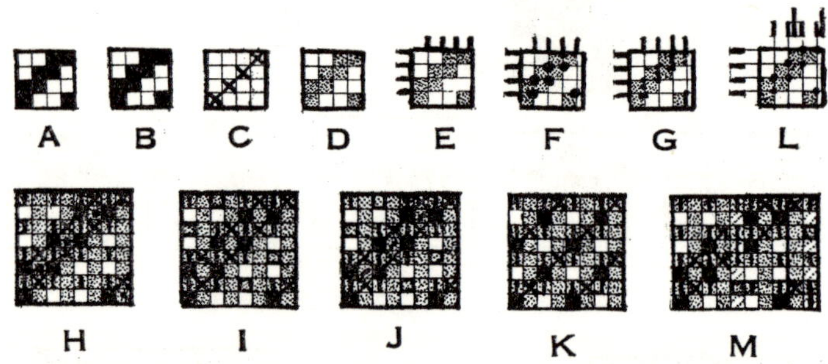

FIG. 8.21.   THE CONSTRUCTION OF DOUBLE CLOTH DESIGNS

The full design is then begun by marking out the face and backing threads, as at *H*, light pencil marks (stipple) indicating backing threads. The details of the key *G* are then transferred to *H*, full squares representing face ends lifted over face picks, crosses representing backing ends lifted over backing picks, and dots representing the stitching points, that is, backing warp over face picks. When a face pick is put into the cloth, all backing ends need to be depressed and when a backing pick is inserted all face ends (except stitching ends) must be lifted. Therefore, on the complete design, all face ends must be lifted above backing picks. These are known as lifters and are represented by vertical strokes.

The above example illustrates the construction of a warp-stitched double cloth, that is one where the warp ends do the binding. An example of a weft-stitched fabric design is shown at *I*, while *J* shows a weave using both warp and weft stitching. In the case of weft-stitched designs, the stitching points are represented by squares to indicate weft up.

Double Plain Cloths: Design *K* in Fig. 8.21 shows the construction of a special type of double cloth made without stitches and having plain weave on both face and back. Variety is obtained by using different orders of coloured ends and picks, and by combining two or more orders. In these cloths, all the ends and picks appear on both face and back.

Centre-stitched Double Cloths: This type of fabric consists of two separate fabrics stitched together by a special stitching thread. By opening the cloth at one corner, the two fabrics can readily be torn apart. The key plan for a typical design is shown at L in Fig. 8.21, ink strokes representing the extra stitching ends. The complete design is given at M, there being a single stitch to both face and back per repeat.

APPLICATION OF COLOUR TO WOVEN FABRICS

Most fabrics contain a certain amount of colour, the dye being applied at one of several stages during manufacture. In woollen cloths the colour is often of more importance that the weave for the latter simply gives the structure and firmness of build and is often completely hidden by milling and raising. Worsted cloths are usually finished clear and colour and weave are, therefore, equally important. The fabric may be required in a single solid shade, in which case the wool is usually dyed in the piece, or occasionally, for woollens, in fibre form. All-wool mixture cloths can be obtained by blending fibres of different colours in the fibre state for woollens and in top form for worsteds, while stripe, check and all-over effects are obtained by dyeing the various threads to the required shade and using them in the correct order during weaving. By the introduction of man-made fibres in blends with wool, mixture effects can be obtained by piece dyeing due to the difference in the dyeing properties of wool and the various man-made fibres. Again, stripes of silk, cotton or man-made fibre are of considerable importance in the suiting trade.

Colour and weave effects are obtained by combining a weave with schemes of warp and weft colouring. Often the colour effect is very different from either the weave or the order of colouring taken separately. These effects can be worked out on point paper, the various stages for a plain weave fabric, warped and picked 1 dark 1 light, being shown at A to E of Fig. 8.22. In the first stage the weave is inserted in pencil over the required area. The warping plan is then placed above the weave and the wefting plan at the left hand side of the weave as shown at A. Marks in the design represent warp up and marks in the colour plans dark ends or picks. In the second stage, each dark end is examined in turn and where there are design marks, that is where the warp is on the surface, the corresponding squares are filled in as at B. The dark picks are then examined and where there are blanks in the weave (i.e., weft over warp) the squares are blocked in as at C. D shows the marks obtained in B and C combined. In the fourth or last stage, the pencil marks are erased, leaving the completed effect at E. This is the appearance of the cloth, woven and coloured as shown. Incidentally, the method is the same if there are more than two colours, this being illustrated by *F* of Fig. 8.22 where the hatched squares represent a medium shade.

There is almost no limit to the range of effects that can be obtained by applying different warping and wefting plans to different weaves. In practice, however, one is restricted to relatively simple weaves and to relatively simple warping and wefting plans, the latter, for example being such that they can be woven on the box motions available. There is much more scope in the warping plan but, as a complicated plan puts excessive strain on the

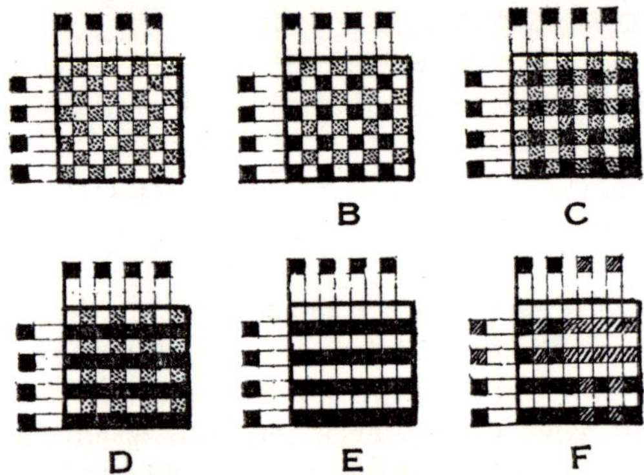

FIG. 8.22.　COLOUR AND WEAVE EFFECTS

operatives during warping, looming and weaving and makes mistakes more frequent, compromise has usually to be effected. The limit to the weave is also governed by the type of loom available. Limited space prevents an adequate discussion of the possibilities here of combining weaves and colour orders but a very valuable treatise is available by W. Watson[4] and many good technical papers have covered different aspects of this subject.

SELVEDGES

Selvedges[5,6] are needed to facilitate several operations during finishing where the cloth has to be held at full width. They also do away with the need for hemming in certain types of textile goods and assist templing during weaving. Selvedges are usually about $\frac{1}{2}$-inch wide and are of different types depending on the nature of the body of the fabric. Piece-dyed woollens and worsteds usually have two or three cotton ends in place of two or three ground ends about $\frac{1}{2}$-inch from each edge while fancy fabrics have solid colour selvedges with or without cotton separation ends. Cloths made from single yarns or those that are delicate, usually have selvedges made from stronger yarns but care has to be taken with the weave and build of the selvedge to allow it to shrink to the same degree as the body of the fabric. To give stability to some types of cloth, selvedges are made with weaves different from the body of the cloth. Skeleton shafts worked from special tappets or spare jack levers in the case of dobbies, are usually used to control the selvedge threads but there are a number of methods of drafting selvedge ends differently from the ground ends on the same shafts, to give different weaves. Thus a 2/2 twill fabric can have a 2/2 hopsack selvedge by drafting those ends that should be on the second and fourth shafts on to the first and third.

THE SETT OF WOVEN FABRICS

THE TWO CHIEF FACTORS in the structure of a woven cloth are the weave and the effective thicknesses of the warp and weft yarns. Theories and formulae have been suggested from time to time to show the interdependence of these two factors and to show how they might be combined to produce cloths of the desired firmness.

The first suggestion was T. R. Ashenhurst's end and intersection theory[7] for square cloths in which the sett was given by $(D \times E)/(E + I)$ where D was the reciprocal of the yarn diameter, E the number of ends in a repeat of the weave, and I the number of intersections in the repeat. He suggested $1/(0 \cdot 9 \sqrt{\text{yards per lb.}})$ as the diameter of worsted yarns. Thus for a 2/2 twill with yarns of 1/100-inch diameter these would need to be $(100 \times 4)/(4 + 2)$, or $66\frac{2}{3}$ ends and picks per inch.

The above calculation was later modified by the angle of curvature theory in which it was assumed that the angle between adjacent threads at an intersection was 30° in well balanced square cloths. Thus, in A and B, Fig. 8.23, if x represents the diameter of the yarns, the distance AB will be $2x$, AC will be x and BC will be $\sqrt{4x^2 - x^2} = 1 \cdot 73 \, x$. BC is equivalent to one diameter plus one intersection, so one intersection is equivalent to $0 \cdot 73 \, x$. Using this, Ashenhurst suggested that the sett should be $(D \times F)/(F + I)$, where D is the reciprocal of the diameter, F the average float and I is $0 \cdot 73$. As an example, assuming yarns of 1/100-inch diameter are again used, the sett for a plain weave fabric would be $(100 \times 1)/(1 + 0 \cdot 73)$ or $57 \cdot 7$ ends and picks per inch.

A series of experiments on the setting of cloths using a variety of weaves was carried out by W. Law. A 2/40's worsted warp and weft were used and the sett was reduced from an abnormally high figure to the optimum value for each of a number of different weaves. A formula was then suggested in each case to fit the experimental values. For plain weaves, the sett was given by $(D \times F)/(F + 1)$ where D was the diameter reciprocal and F the average float. Incidentally, the diameter reciprocal for worsted yarns was given as $\sqrt{500C}$, for woollen yarns $\sqrt{230C}$, and for cotton yarns $\sqrt{800C}$, where C is the count.

The sett for twills was given as $(D \times F)/(F + 1)$ plus 5 per cent per float above two; for hopsacks, $(D \times F)/(F + 1)$ plus 9·5 per cent for each float exceeding two; and for sateens, $(D \times F)/(F + 1)$ plus 5·5 per cent per float above two. To quote an example, the sett for a 4/4 twill would be $(100 \times 4 \times 1 \cdot 10)/(4 + 1)$ or 88 ends and picks per inch. Instead of the term $F/(F + 1)$ plus a percentage in the above formulae, Law calculated a series of weave values or setting ratios.

Similar work was carried out by E. Armitage and S. Brierley. The former devised a formula for twills, $T = \sqrt{6C} \, (F + 4)$ where T is the number of threads and picks per inch, C the counts of worsted yarn, and

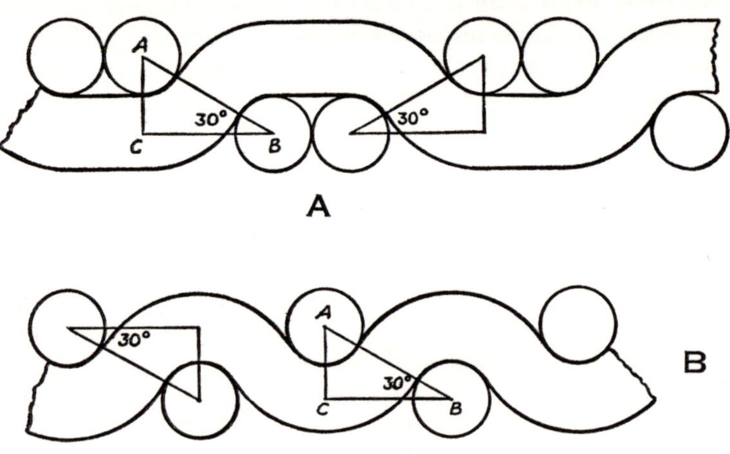

FIG. 8.23.   WARP AND WEFT SETTINGS

F the average float of the weave. For other weaves, Armitage gave a series of setting ratios in place of the term $(F + 4)$. Brierley suggested the following formula: $T = \sqrt{KC} \times F^m$ where T is the sett, K a constant, depending on the quality of yarn and system of counting, C the count, F the average float and m a second constant, depending on the type of weave used.

All the above theories and formulae relate only to square cloths. Law, however, carried out extensive trials on non-square cloths of various types and evolved a series of formulae to give optimum ends and picks per inch. To quote a single example, he found that, for plains and twills, if x were the increase in ends above square, the decrease necessary in the picks would be $1 \cdot 8 \sqrt{x}$. Thus, if a 2/2 twill were made with 66 ends and 66 picks per inch to give a twill line at approximately 45°, a steeper twill could be made with 120 ends per inch, in which case the picks per inch would be 66 $-1 \cdot 8 \sqrt{120-66}$ or 52 picks per inch, for the same degree of firmness. Law's experiments covered almost all the ordinary types of weaves.

Besides giving a guide to the most suitable structure for a new cloth, these formulae are very helpful in practice when it is desired to effect changes in one or more of the various dependent variables. For example, on the basis that in all cases the sett is proportional to the square root of the counts, i.e., sett A/sett $B=\sqrt{\text{counts }A}/\sqrt{\text{counts }B}$, it follows that if a cloth is made with 51 ends and 51 picks per inch of 2/24s worsted, the sett for the same weave and cloth firmness using 2/48s worsted would be $51 \times \sqrt{24}/\sqrt{12}$, or 72 ends and picks per inch.

When it is desired to obtain a similarly built cloth but of different weight, the following formulae are of value:

$$\text{Sett of } A \times \text{weight of } A = \text{sett of } B \times \text{weight of } B$$

$$\text{Weight of } A \times \sqrt{\text{counts of } A} = \text{weight of } B \times \sqrt{\text{counts of } B}$$

As an illustration, let it be assumed that a 2/2 twill is made from 2/12s worsted with 36 ends and picks per inch and weighs 24 oz. per running yard. If a similarly built cloth is required weighing 12 oz., then the new sett can be obtained by the first equation above: $36 \times 24 = x \times 12$, or $x = 72$ ends and picks per inch, while the new counts are obtained by the second equation: $24 \times \sqrt{6} = 12 \times \sqrt{x}$, or $x = 24$ or 2/48s worsted.

Finally, if the weave is also to be changed, the following equations can be used, the first to give new sett and the second the new counts:

$$\text{Set of } A \times \text{weight of } A \times (\text{setting ratio of } B)^2 =$$
$$\text{Sett of } B \times \text{weight of } B \times (\text{setting ratio of } A)^2$$

$$\sqrt{\text{counts of } A} \times \text{weight of } A \times (\text{setting ratio of } B)^2 =$$
$$\sqrt{\text{counts of } B} \times \text{weight of } B \times (\text{setting ratio of } A)^2$$

The setting ratios are $(F + 4)$ if Armitage's theory is used, weave values for Law's theory and F^m values for Brierley's theory. To give one example, a 12 oz. cloth is made with a 2/2 twill weave, 72 ends and picks per inch of 2/48s worsted. It is required to obtain the sett and counts for a 14 oz. cloth made with 3/3 twill weave.

Using Armitage's theory, the formula becomes $72 \times 12 \times 7^2 = x \times 14 \times 6^2$, and x (the sett) equals 84 ends and picks per inch. Similarly the new counts can be determined by the formula $\sqrt{24} \times 12 \times 7 = \sqrt{x} \times 14 \times 6$, and x (the counts) equals 24 or 2/48s worsted.

Using Brierley's work, the formula for the sett becomes $72 \times 12 \times 1\cdot54^2 = x \times 14 \times 1\cdot3^2$, and x (the sett) equals 86·6 ends and picks per inch. For the counts the formula is $\sqrt{24} \times 12 \times 1\cdot54 = \sqrt{x} \times 14 \times 1\cdot3$ and x (the counts) equals 24·7 or 2/49·4s worsted.

Using Law's theory, the sett is calculated by the formula $72 \times 12 \times 0\cdot79^2 = x \times 14 \times 0\cdot66^2$, x (the sett) being $89\cdot7$ ends and picks per inch, whilst for the counts, $\sqrt{24} \times 12 \times 0\cdot79 = \sqrt{x} \times 14 \times 0\cdot66$, x (the counts) being $25\cdot2$ or 2/50·4s worsted.

It will be noted that the various methods give slightly different values.

Considerable work has been carried out by many organizations, chiefly in connection with cotton fabrics, with the object of applying mathematical relationships to various functions of fabric structures and particularly of cloth deformations. These include the shearing and bending forces of the yarns, crimp redistribution, compression of yarns and extension of fibres. Though it is not suggested that the results of such work will allow the designer to construct mathematically correct cloths to suit specific physical requirements, it must undoubtedly lead to a better understanding of certain features and allow improvements in cloth construction to be effected.

COVER

Cover is a term used to denote the spreading of the face threads, usually the warp threads, across the face of the fabric. Thus a slack top shed line tends to spread the warp on the face of the cloth and helps to improve cover and prevent reediness. Reediness or reed marks[8] are caused by having more than one end in each dent and groups of ends running together in the cloth. With wool cloths, the fibrous nature of the yarns tends to reduce reediness and it is usually completely removed by scouring. Good cover tends to make twills more pronounced and it is possible to produce a range of the same fabrics with different appearances due to different degrees of cover. Many fabrics do not need cover, for example, voiles and brilliantines which have a weft face and need opposite conditions. The most common method of increasing the amount of cover is to slacken the top shed by raising the back rail or padding the breast rail. The ratch, or distance between the fell and lease rods can be shortened to give better cover while the draft can often be modified to reduce reed marks.

THE ANALYSIS OF WOVEN CLOTHS

IT MAY occasionally be necessary to determine the structure of a fabric and to illustrate the technique involved in analysing small patterns, parts of an example have been worked out below for a worsted suiting.

If the pattern is small, care should be taken not to destroy any part of it until one is sure that no possible data are being destroyed; for example, part of the repeat of the weave. If the weave is small, a definite area is cut away from the pattern and weighed to give the weight of the cloth. To minimize errors, the greatest possible area should be taken and each edge should be trimmed in turn until it is square. The projecting ends and picks should then be cut away. If a template is employed, particular care should be taken to get the cutting edges square with the ends and picks. From the weight of a sample of known area, the weight of the cloth per running yard of any given width can easily be calculated.

If the weave is small, a number of ends and picks should next be removed from the edges of the pattern and weighed to give the counts of the yarns. The distinction between warp and weft yarns is readily determined by experience and best learned by studying structures of typical cloths.

Owing to bending of the yarns in the cloth, the true length of the threads is greater than the length of the cloth from which the threads are removed. Thus a pattern three inches square may yield warp ends and weft picks 3·4 inches and 3·5 inches long when stretched against a rule. A good practice with woollens and worsteds is to damp the fingers and draw the threads lightly between them to remove most of the weaving crimp. Once the weight of a number of threads of known length is determined, it is quite a simple matter to calculate the yarn counts, *i.e.*, the counts of the yarn as it exists in the finished cloth. The counts of the yarn in the loom state, which is the more important, will be coarser due to the loss of fibre during finishing. It is customary therefore to add to the weight of the yarn, as determined, a figure which experience has shown is sufficient to cover such losses. In general, cotton yarns lose about three per cent, worsted five per cent and woollen up to 10 per cent, depending on the type of finish.

The number of ends and picks per inch in the finished cloth are readily determined with the aid of a piece glass but another good method, especially with heavily sett yarns, is to cut away parts of the fringe left by the removal of threads for weighing until a section exactly one inch, or a multiple of this, remains. This is then cut away and the number of short pieces of yarn counted. A similar technique involves cutting one-inch strips of cloth, both warpways and weftways, while with small weaves, it is possible to count the number of repeats of the weave in a given distance.

For example, if the weave repeats on 24 x 24 and there are 16 repeats warpways in 3·2 inches, the ends per inch will be (24 x 16)/3·2 = 120. The ends and picks per inch in the loom can be calculated from these data, knowing the warp and weft contractions. An approximate reed width can be calculated from the required finished width and the weft contraction. For example, if the finished width is to be 56 inches, the reed width would be (56 x 3·5)/3·0 = 65·3 inches. In practice, this figure is usually slightly low and five per cent. should be added to it. The best method is to refer to past records for similar types of cloth. The calculation to give the total number of ends in the warp and the weights of the component yarns are straightforward.

DETERMINING THE WEAVE

There are many ways of determining the weave, depending on the type of cloth being analysed. With simple weaves or with clear-finished, open structure fabrics, it is often possible to follow the intersections of the warp and weft in the body of the pattern through a piece glass. The most common method is to draw the warp ends, one at a time, into the fringe made at the edge of the pattern and follow their intersections with the weft picks until a repeat is obtained both warpways and weftways.

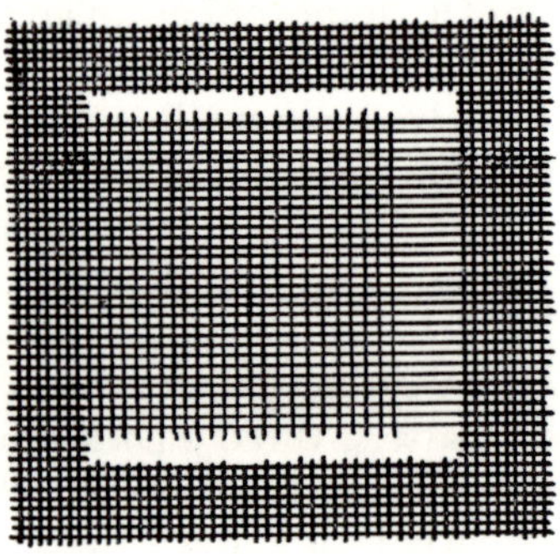

FIG. 8.24.   METHOD OF ANALYSING
A SAMPLE OF CLOTH

This method is often difficult with heavily picked cloths or with crêpe weft or man-made fibre warps and the following technique is recommended. After deciding which is face and back and which set of threads is warp and weft, the pattern is cut at two points as at *AB* and *CD* (Fig. 8.24), the distance between the two incisions being slightly wider than the apparent repeat weftways and the length of the cuts longer than the repeat warpways.

A few of the cut warp ends are then pulled out of the cloth to leave bare a number of weft picks, as shown in the illustration, and into these the remaining cut warp ends can be drawn, one at a time, to follow the intersections for recording on to point paper. The advantage of this method is that the weft picks are kept taut, thus preventing the rolling and crossing of picks and the losing of intersections at the corner which frequently occur when the usual techniques of extracting ends from one side of the pattern are used.

COMMERCIAL WOOLLEN AND WORSTED FABRICS

WOOLLEN AND WORSTED FABRICS cover a wide variety of cloths, ranging from delicate voiles to heavy meltons and beavers. The static physical characteristics of fabrics are functions of a large number of inter-related factors, such as the physical properties of the raw material, the structure and fineness of the yarns, the weave and structure of the cloth and the effects of dyeing and finishing processes. In very general terms, it can be said that worsted fabrics are clear finished and that their appearance and appeal depend on the nature and colour of the yarns and the structure of the cloth. The object of the finisher in these cases is to enhance the work of the spinner and weaver; such cloths are often said to be made in the loom. On the other hand, typical heavy woollen fabrics are milled and raised to provide them with a fibrous cover. Again, using very general terms, it may be said that the object of the woollen spinner in these cases is to provide a thick soft weft which will allow milling and raising to take place most readily and the object of the weaver is to provide a cloth with the simplest and cheapest weave having a float sufficiently long for raising and milling to be most effective. To summarize, typical woollen cloths are made by the finisher, the weaver providing a suitable structure upon which the finisher can work.

There is, of course, a wide field of fabrics where overlapping of the above general features obtains. The monetary intrinsic value of a fabric is proportional to the value of the clean raw material plus the cost of conversion. In very general terms, it can be said that high conversion costs are reserved for the higher priced raw materials. Expensive weaves, such as, for example, those requiring fancy drafts and large capacity dobbies or jacquards, can be used only on those fabrics which will ultimately be sold at a relatively high price. In the same way, the price of a dyestuff used on a fabric is usually proportional to the value of the fabric.

Besides bearing in mind such very important factors as price and the details of the weaving plant on which the cloth is to be woven, the designer builds his cloths with a view to their ultimate end use. In the case of raised fabrics, he must design a looser cloth to allow adequate shrinkage to take place and the structure should be such as to allow raising to be most effective. On the other hand, fancy worsteds or furnishing fabrics need to be built up from elaborate weaves and colourings to give the necessary finished appearance.

Earlier in this Section most of the important principles of fabric structure have been discussed and this will have illustrated the need for a systematic technique in creating new designs. In this connection, it is of interest to study S. A. Shorter's mechanical method of exploiting designs[9,10].

All the designs given or mentioned earlier are not equally important in practice. Many are useful only as simple illustrations of the methods used by designers in building up new designs, while others are more fully employed as scaffoldings or building units in the construction of more suitable and workable designs.

In the following pages, an attempt has been made to classify commercial woollen and worsted fabrics into a number of groups based on special characteristics or on their end or consumer uses and to give the structure and details of certain typical types in each group. The details of cloths given should be considered only as examples; variations will occur in practice depending upon particular circumstances. Similarly, names of cloths vary greatly from one locality to another.

Although this book is primarily concerned with wool and with its products, it will be appreciated that over the past two decades there has been an increasing commercial use of man-made fibres in the woollen and worsted trades. So far as woven fabrics are concerned these fibres are largely used in blends with wool and the blended yarns used in the most appropriate fabrics listed below.

Typical examples are the polyesters and acrylics used for suitings, trouserings and ladies' dresswear. Nylon is used to a lesser degree, while smaller weights of viscose-based fibres are used in selected end-uses. It should also be appreciated that large weights of cotton-spun yarns made from 100 per cent man-made fibres are woven on worsted looms for cheaper and lighter versions of standard wool cloths. Other technical economic and consumer trends are resulting in fewer basic cloths, in the use of lighter and cheaper fabrics – for example, single in place of double cloths – in the larger use of knitted fabrics and in a number of new fabrics based on non-woven, coated or laminated structures.

LADIES' LIGHT-WEIGHT DRESS FABRICS

These cloths comprise a large section of the trade and use both woollen and worsted yarns, but probably a larger proportion of the latter. There is a great variety of types, weights and structures and as there is a continuous change from one type to another, distinctions become difficult. Many dress fabrics use the normal 2/2 twill with different qualities and structures. Thus the alaska is made from blends of cotton and wool, a typical structure being 2/30 w.c. warp and weft with 48 ends per inch and 46 picks per inch. The estamenes, also 2/2 twill fabrics, are made from crossbred wools and are slightly milled and raised to give a blind surface. A typical make for these is 2/36 w.c. warp and weft, 54 ends and 50 picks per inch. The name foulie, is given to a similar cloth but lighter in weight and containing higher quality wools. Anacostas are lighter weight worsted dress fabrics made from single yarns and woven in 2/2 twill with many more picks than ends to give a flat twill line. 1/30 w.c. warp, 60 ends per inch, 1/36 w.c. weft, 100 picks per inch is a typical make.

Two very light worsted cloths are the delaine and the so-called nun's veiling, both woven in plain weave from single yarns. The former is made from approximately 1/36 w.c. warp, 1/30 w.c. weft, 64 ends per inch and 56 picks per inch, while the latter is much lighter, often of the order of three ounces per yard, having 1/48 w.c. warp and weft, with 45 ends and picks per inch.

A number of fabrics are made in the 2/1 weft twill, often with a low twill angle, the most common being the cashmere. These are soft, spongy fabrics using spun silk, wool or cotton warps with botany weft. Many more picks than ends are inserted to keep the twill line low. A typical all-wool cashmere has 1/40 w.c. warp, 1/48 w.c. weft, 50 ends per inch and 108 picks per inch, while a cotton warp cashmere which is the most common, has 2/40 c.c. warp, 68 ends per inch, 1/56 w.c. botany weft, 128 picks per inch. There are many variations of this cloth such as the henrietta and the paramatta.

DRESS FABRICS WITH DISTINCTIVE WEAVES

Many fabrics are distinctive because of the weave employed, a typical example being the honeycomb. This is a fabric in which the weave produces a series of ridges and cavities similar to a honeycomb. A simple honeycomb weave is shown at A in Fig. 8.25, the plain weave parts forming the cavities of the cells and the floats the ridges. A typical make for a worsted honeycomb is 2/36 w.c. warp and weft, 72 ends per inch and 48 picks per inch using the design referred to above.

The Brighton weave is similar to the above, a typical example being shown at B in Fig. 8.25 for which 2/36 w.c. warp and weft, 60 ends per inch and 56 picks per inch would be suitable. The barathea is a fine high quality dress fabric made from spun silk warp on heavily picked botany weft using broken weft rib weaves of the type shown at C in the same illustration. A typical structure is 70/2 spun silk warp, 1/80 w.c. botany weft, 80 ends per inch and 160 picks per inch. Cheaper varieties are made with cotton warps and worsted wefts.

The same name is also given to a heavy worsted military fabric using twilled hopsack, a weave known as the barathea. A typical construction for such a fabric is 2/36 w.c. warp and weft, 72 ends and 68 picks per inch. Similarly, the mayo dress fabric is so-called because of the distinctive mayo twill weave used. This is shown at D in Fig. 8.25, a typical make for which is 2/64 w.c. botany warp, 1/56 w.c. botany weft, 76 ends per inch and 102 picks per inch. The prunella is a woollen fabric using the prunella or 2/1 warp twill weave.

LUSTRE DRESS FABRICS

These are really modifications of the lining cloths described later and include such well-known cloths as brilliantines and sicilians, both plain weave fabrics, the former being lighter than the latter. Typical structures

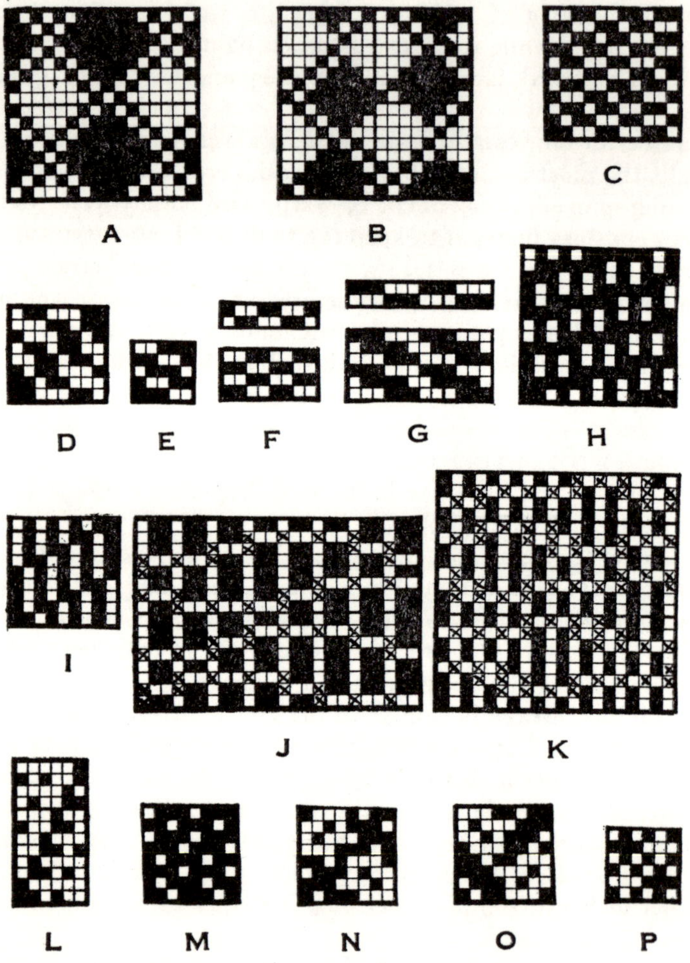

FIG. 8.25.   A VARIETY OF DESIGNS SUITABLE FOR
DRESS CLOTHS

are 2/120 c.c. black cotton warp, 68 ends per inch, 1/28 w.c. alpaca weft, 64 picks per inch, for the brilliantines and 2/80 c.c. black cotton warp, sett 40 ends per inch, 1/12 w.c. alpaca weft, 48 picks per inch for the sicilians. The care required in warping and sleying these cloths is discussed under lining fabrics.

There is also a number of similar fabrics using weaves other than plain to which specific names are given. Thus, the granada uses the weave shown at E in Fig. 8.25 and has a thick mohair weft woven across a black cotton warp. A similar fabric known as the royalette uses the five-end warp sateen. A modification of these fabrics is the so-called Pekin stripe, a fabric having longitudinal shadow effects due to denting the ends irregularly. A typical fabric would have the same structure as the brilliantine above, but the ends might be sleyed 12 ends, two per dent, six ends, one per dent. Another common sleying plan for coarse setts is 12 ends, one per dent, and a number of repeats of one end per dent, one dent missed.

WOOL POPLINS, CORD AND WARP RIB DRESS FABRICS

Poplins are made from most materials but chiefly cotton. They are plain weave and are produced from a fine warp closely sett and a relatively coarse weft to give the typical warp ribbed structures shown at A in Fig. 8.4. A typical structure of a wool poplin would be 2/72 w.c. botany warp, 120 ends per inch, six skeins Saxony weft, 46 picks per inch. A fabric known as the colienne is similar in structure but has a fine silk warp, say 20 denier, sett 100 ends per inch, crossed by a coarser botany weft, 1/24 w.c. to 1/30 w.c., about 48 picks per inch in the case of the 1/30 w.c.

Heavier coating cloths, known as bengalines have more pronounced ribs and a spun silk warp replacing the finer pure silk. A typical make is 40/2 spun silk warp, 72 ends per inch, 1/30 w.c. crêpe twisted weft, 50 picks per inch, woven in plain weave. Similar effects are obtained by using warp rib or modified warp rib weaves with warp and weft yarns approximately the same counts, typical weaves being given at F and G in Fig. 8.25. The order of sleying the warp ends is most important in these structures and suggested orders are shown above the two designs. A typical structure for weave F is 2/56 w.c. botany warp, 72 ends per inch, 1/56 w.c. botany weft, 120 picks per inch. A plain weave fabric, known as cable cord is given a warp rib appearance by sleying a number of consecutive ends through a single dent at regular intervals. Morocains are poplins, with the ribs made wavy in appearance by using spiral weft yarns, a typical make being 2/48 w.c. botany warp, 72 ends per inch and 2/16 w.c. spiral weft, 24 picks per inch.

A light worsted dress fabric having a well-defined warp rib twill is the corkscrew fabric, also used for suitings and lightweight coatings. Typical corkscrew weaves are shown at H and I of Fig. 8.25, one example of such a fabric using weave H having 2/60 w.c. warp, 1/30 w.c. weft, 128 ends per inch and 90 picks per inch. Armures are worsted dress fabrics characterized by an apparent embossed face produced by suitable warp or weft rib weaves, typical ones being shown at J and K of Fig. 8.25. They are made in a variety of structures depending on the weave used but a typical make for weave J has 2/36 w.c. warp, 1/20 w.c. weft, 60 ends and picks per inch. Cotton, mohair and man-made fibres arc now incorporated in many cloths of this type. Whipcords, described later, are made in lighter weights for use as dress fabrics whilst tricotines are similar fabrics, a typical weave being shown at L of Fig. 8.25 and a typical structure 2/48 w.c. botany warp and weft, 80 ends per inch and 68 picks per inch. Ottomans use broken warp rib weaves, a typical design, the Soleil, being shown at M of Fig. 8.25, one make being 1/36 w.c. botany warp, 1/24 w.c. botany weft, 76 ends per inch and 48 picks per inch.

CREPE AND CREPON DRESS FABRICS

There are many varieties of dress fabrics which possess the typical broken crêpe surface but they are essentially of two types, one where the effect is obtained by the use of highly twisted or crêpe yarns with simple weaves and the other where special crêpe weaves are used in combination with ordinary twisted yarns. Silk, man-made fibres, worsted and cotton yarns are used either alone or in combination. A common cloth of the first type, using worsted yarns, is known as estrella and has a silk warp and crêpe twisted botany weft, picked two S twist and two Z twist. The weave is plain. One make has 60 denier warp, 148 ends per inch and 1/48 w.c. weft, 80 picks per inch. All-worsted crêpe-de-chines are also made. Designs N and O of Fig. 8.25 show two typical crêpe weaves for producing the pebbly crêpe surface and a typical construction for weave N is 2/40 w.c. botany warp, 48 ends per inch, 1/20 w.c. botany weft, 48 picks per inch.

A structure resembling the above is found in the crepons or blister cloths. These are fabrics having slack warp ends distributed either in the form of stripes or the form of figures. They are usually obtained by utilizing two warp beams, the slack warp being let off more quickly than the other and by arranging for the two warps to be of materials with different shrinkage properties, so that the blisters or slackness can be developed during finishing.

Other techniques are now available to the trade, including mechanical and chemical methods of preventing some parts of the cloth from normal shrinkage during finishing. A typical make for a figured blister fabric is one end 2/60 w.c. botany, one end 2/40 w.c. mohair warp, 1/30 w.c. botany weft, 72 ends per inch and 40 picks per inch, double plain weave ground.

WORSTED MOCK GAUZE AND LENO

These are open or perforated structures simulating the true gauze and leno fabrics. There are many weaves, the simplest being shown at P of Fig. 8.25. The three-float weft draws three ends together whilst the three-float warp draws three picks together so producing cracks down and across the cloth. The effect is emphasized by denting each group of threads together and further emphasized by missing one dent between consecutive groups. In worsted dress cloths, these weaves are usually combined with other weaves to give added effects.

PIECE-DYED WORSTED SUITINGS AND COATING FABRICS

Very large lengths of these cloths are made, often under the general name of cassimeres. They are made in 2/2 twill, sett firmly, are piece-dyed and are given a clear finish. The actual structure of the cloth depends on the required weight per yard and the nature and scope of the twill line, while the amount of twist in the yarns affects the boldness of the twills. A typical crossbred serge is made from 2/36 w.c. warp and weft, 60 ends per inch and 54 picks per inch, a similar type in botany yarns would use 2/48 w.c. warp and weft, 68 ends per inch and 64 picks per inch while a typical botany coating is made from 2/26 w.c. warp and weft, 52 ends per inch and 56 picks per inch.

SAXONY AND CHEVIOT SUITINGS AND COATINGS

These fabrics form a very large bulk of the woollen weaving trade and are made in a wide variety of weights and structures. The Saxony cloths are normally finished clear or slightly milled, are soft to handle, compact and have a fine, smooth, surface. The Cheviot cloths are of lower quality and therefore cheaper, have a crisper handle and are given a fibrous surface which is not so closely cropped as the Saxony. The fabrics are usually single cloths but backed cloths and double cloths are also made, depending on the weight and type of surface required. The bulk of the single fabrics is made in 2/2 twill.

A typical lightweight Saxony suiting cloth would have about 35 skeins warp and weft, 54 ends per inch and 52 picks per inch, while the heavier types would use about 12 skeins warp and weft with about 30 ends and picks per inch. Cheviot suitings, do not usually use yarns lighter than 20 skeins, when about 40 ends and picks per inch are needed. Ten skeins are about the heaviest count, when approximately 20 ends and picks per inch are inserted.

Many of these suitings and coatings are piece-dyed but a large number is woven from yarns spun from dyed raw material. In the case of tweeds, a type of woollen suiting and coating made from Cheviot-type wools, chiefly in Scotland, the colours are usually distinctive, pronounced checks and colourings often being used. Flannel suitings are usually made of woollen spun yarns of the same structure as the above but the cheaper varieties utilize cotton warps and are semi-milled, while the more expensive types are made from worsted spun warps and wefts. Again, 2/2 twill is the predominant weave.

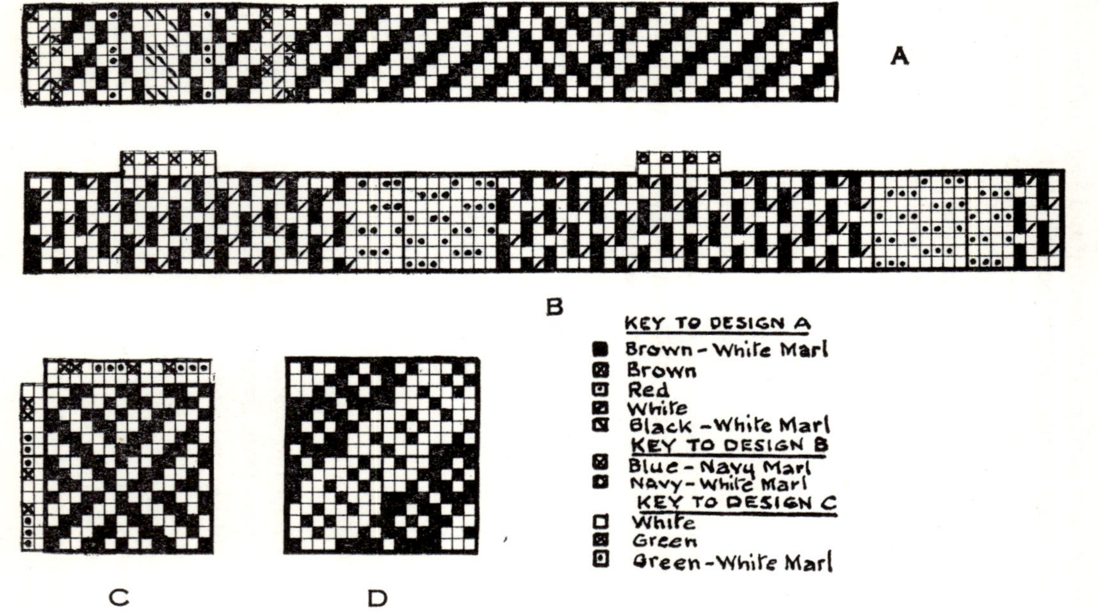

FIG. 8.26.   TYPICAL DESIGNS FOR A LIGHTWEIGHT COATING FABRIC, A FANCY WORSTED SUITING, A SMALL CHECK COSTUME CLOTH AND A FANCY WOOLLEN COATING FABRIC

FANCY WORSTED AND WOOLLEN SUITING AND COATING FABRICS

These are high-quality fabrics, usually made from the best botany wools and are probably the best examples of fabrics that are made in the loom. They are finished clear so that all the details of the yarns, weave and colour are left as distinct and pronounced as possible. The integration of these features probably represents the highest skill of the cloth designer. The designs for fancy worsteds and also for a small number of fancy woollens are usually individual and it is not possible to break them down into a small number of types, each with its own particular characteristics. They are also modified greatly to follow or create changes of fashion and, in the highest class of this trade, many designs are exclusive, assurances being given by the maker that only a certain number of pieces of each design has been woven.

Most of the designs used in this trade repeat on more than eight ends and, consequently, the bulk of the fabrics are woven on dobbies or even small-capacity jacquards. Those fabrics which do use less than eight shafts usually have complex colouring plans, often both warp and weft ways. Design A of Fig. 8.26 shows an example for a lightweight coating fabric, five different colours being used in the warp, the weft being the brown and white twist yarn used for the body of the cloth. The make for this cloth is 2/48 w.c. botany warp and weft, 74 ends per inch and 66 picks per inch.

The design for another typical fancy worsted, shown at B in the same illustration, represents a double plain suiting, the warp ground and the weft being navy and the stripes a navy-blue marl and a navy-white marl. The construction of this fabric is 100 ends per inch 2/48 w.c. warp, 82 picks per inch 1/24 w.c. weft. The design for a small check costume cloth is shown at C of Fig. 8.26. The warp is 2/36 w.c. and the weft 1/18 w.c., with 62 ends per inch and 56 picks per inch. The warping and wefting plan is as follows:

WARPING:

White	..	..	..	1	1		2	:	1	1
Green		..	..	2		1	1	:	2	
Green/White marl		..			3		3	:		10

x 5

WEFTING:

Green/White marl	..	3		3	:	10	
Green	..	..	1	1		2	:	2
White	..	..	2		1	1	:	1	1

x 6

A further example is of a fancy woollen coating made from 2/16 skeins warp, 4½ skein weft, 16 ends and picks per inch. The weave is shown at D of Fig. 8.26, while the warping and wefting plan is given on page 312.

2/16 or 4½ skein dark blue	1	1		1
2/16 or 4½ skein mixture ..	1		1	1
2/16 or 4½ skein fancy yarn		1		1

These examples are given simply to illustrate the type of weave and structure involved in these fabrics, the variations of which are endless. One of the best ways of gaining knowledge of these fabrics is by analysing patterns of typical fabrics.

LINING FABRICS

There is a large number of different types and makes of cloth intended for lining purposes. The aim of the designer is usually to obtain the smoothest surface with the maximum amount of lustre, and the design, material and method of finishing are chosen with these ends in view. One of the oldest of these cloths utilized a single or twofold fine cotton warp, dyed fast black, which was pulled straight during finishing, and an undyed alpaca weft. A large number of weft-faced twills was used, each twill giving the fabric a distinctive name such as Irene for the 2/1 weft twill and Beatrice for the 4/1 weft twill. Makes varied greatly but one typical example using the 4/1 twill was 1/50 c.c. black cotton warp, 84 ends per inch, 1/30 w.c. alpaca weft, 80 picks per inch. A lining cloth, known as 'Italian' uses the five-end weft sateen. It is now extensively made with both warp and weft yarns of cotton but occasionally cotton warp and worsted weft are employed, a typical make for this being 2/80 c.c. black cotton warp, 88 ends per inch, 1/56 w.c. botany weft, 132 picks per inch.

The lustre and smoothness of these fabrics are largely dependent on the even distribution of ends and picks and it is the usual practice either to centre each warp end by reeding one end per dent or, if the sett is too heavy, by reeding two per dent and shedding early. Care is needed during winding and warping to ensure that the warp threads are all as equally tensioned as possible for slight faults or blemishes show abnormally in these fabrics. Rayon weft is now being extensively used in these cloths in place of alpaca while all-rayon cloths are popular.

Hair linings are coarser fabrics used for stiffening certain part of garments to help them to maintain their shape during wear. The most common has a cotton warp and a horsehair weft but the coarser types of camel and goat hair are also used.

WOOL GABARDINES

These fabrics are characterized by a steep twill line, tightly twisted yarns and heavily sett warp and weft. They are mostly shower-proofed for use in raincoats but lighter weights are also used as a dress fabric and coating cloth. Originally made with a worsted warp and a cotton weft, gabardines are now made in many combinations such as cotton warp and cotton weft, cotton warp and worsted weft and cotton and wool twist yarns in both warp and weft to give the speckled gabardine. For the lighter fabrics, a 2/2 twill is used, a 2/1 twill being employed for the heavier. Typical details for the former are 108 ends per inch of 2/64 w.c. botany warp, 80 picks per inch of 2/60 c.c. cotton weft. Gabardines for dress fabrics are usually made from botany warp and weft and, to give a softer handle, singles weft is used. A typical make is 96 ends per inch of 2/48 w.c. botany warp, 60 picks per inch of 1/36 w.c. botany weft in 2/2 twill.

BEDFORD CORDS

These are heavy weight cloths, having well defined, rounded cords running warpways and used chiefly for riding breeches, especially for military

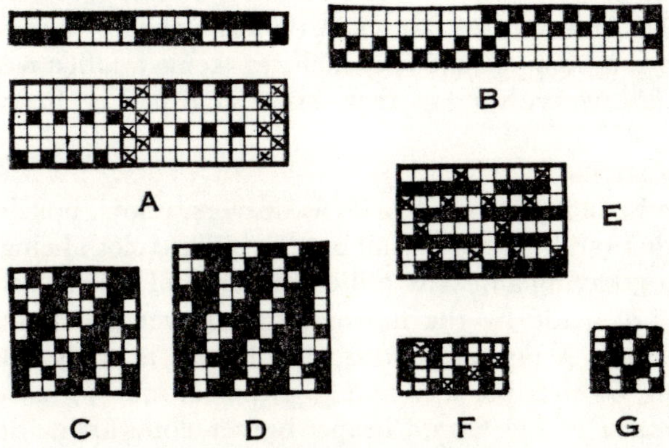

FIG. 8.27. BEDFORD CORD, WHIPCORD AND
DRESS FACED CLOTH DESIGNS

purposes. Lighter weights are used for dress fabrics. The cords are produced by floating some of the weft beneath the points where the cords are required and the indentations are obtained by weaving all the picks in plain weave. The long weft floats cause heavy weft contraction of the order of 30 per cent., so enhancing the cord structure. Increased roundness or prominence of the cords, broader cords or heavier fabrics, can be obtained by padding the cords with thick, loose warp ends.

There are many varieties, weights and weaves in these cloths but a typical military Bedford cord is made from 18 skeins warp and weft with 2/24 c.c. cotton warp for the plain ends in the indentations, 64 ends per inch and 72 picks per inch, using a weave such as that of A of Fig. 8.27. In weaving these fabrics care should be taken to sley the two ends weaving plain in separate dents as shown above the design. A typical Bedford cord fabric suitable for ladies' fabrics is made from 2/60 w.c. botany warp, 1/30 w.c. botany weft, 96 ends per inch, 80 picks per inch with a weave such as is shown at B of Fig. 8.27.

WHIPCORDS

These are fabrics showing steep twill lines in which the warp ends tend to roll together to produce deep cords or ridges. In the heavier weights, they are used for riding breeches and raincoats but they are also made in lighter weights suitable for dress fabrics. The weaves used are elongated twills in a great variety, two typical examples being shown at *C* and *D* in Fig. 8.27. A typical dress fabric would have 2/40 w.c. warp, 1/20 w.c. weft, 80 ends per inch and 56 picks per inch.

CORDUROYS

With a corded velveteen structure in which the extra weft is bound in one continuous warp line, cut to give a dense pile cord, these fabrics are used for riding breeches and workmen's heavy clothing, while lighter varieties are used as ladies' dress fabrics. A typical make for the heavier variety is 2/16 c.c. cotton warp, 52 ends per inch, 30 skeins woollen weft, 160 picks per inch using a weave such as that shown at *E* in Fig. 8.27.

DRESS FACED CLOTHS

These cloths include such fabrics as beavers, pilots, boxcloths, billiard cloths, doeskins and broadcloths, all but the billiard cloth being heavy overcoating fabrics, having a heavily milled surface and a dense, short pile. All these cloths are made by the finisher, the weaver producing a suitable foundation fabric. A typical good quality beaver is made from 20 skeins warp and weft, 60 ends per inch and 40 picks per inch with a warp-backed weave such as at *F* of Fig. 8.27. Cheaper beaver cloths are made with cotton warps, in which case, weft-backed weaves are used, while certain double cloths are often finished as beavers.

The pilot cloth, some qualities of which are used in the Services, is an all-woollen fabric, usually made in 2/2 twill weave or slight modifications of it. A typical make would be 8-skeins warp and weft, 24 ends and picks per inch. The box cloth is another uniform or livery cloth made from woollen yarns in 2/2 twill or broken 2/2 twill weaves. An average construction for a box cloth is 12 skeins warp and weft with 32 ends and picks per inch.

Billiard cloths are usually made in plain weave with about 24 skeins warp and weft, 32 ends per inch and 40 picks per inch. Doeskins have about 24 skeins warp and 14 skeins weft, sett about 48 ends per inch and 30 picks per inch and are usually woven in a five-end warp sateen weave, though double plain doeskins are sometimes made. The twists of the yarns are Z for the weft and S for the warp. Broadcloths are made in plain or 2/1 weft twill, approximately 20 skeins warp and weft, 42 ends per inch and 50 picks per inch. The warp and weft are again of opposite twists to help the pile to be developed in one direction.

MELTONS

The Melton is a heavy woollen overcoating fabric, heavily milled and cropped to give a short, even pile. A typical structure for such cloths is 12 skeins warp and weft, 40 ends and picks per inch with a plain, double plain or 2/2 twill weave, the make referring to a 2/2 twill. Cheaper varieties have cotton warps.

VELOURS

This name is given to an overcoating fabric with a short, dense pile, having a softer handle than the above. It is also made in lighter weights as a costume cloth, often with a worsted spun warp. A typical fabric would be made from approximately 18 skeins warp and weft, 24 ends per inch and 36 picks per inch in the irregular four-end weft sateen weave.

BLANKET CLOTHS

These are heavy woollen fabrics given a fleece finish. A double cloth construction is 16 skeins warp and weft, 50 ends per inch and 52 picks per inch, 2/1 twill face and back, while a typical single cloth is made from 8-skeins warp and weft, 16 ends per inch and 24 picks per inch in 2/2 twill weave. Plain weave is also common in blankets, while cotton yarns or wool and cotton blend yarns are used. Rug blankets are heavier, fleece-finished fabrics made with cotton warps of the order of 2/2 c.c., woollen weft about 8-skeins, 24 ends per inch and 40 picks per inch, using weft face weaves in either small twills or sateens. Travelling rugs are usually fleece-finished, double cloths with bold check styles on face and back. A typical make has 14 skeins warp and weft, 54 ends and picks per inch, 2/2 twill face and back with centre stitching.

VICUNA CLOTHS

These cloths were originally imitations of those made from the soft, downy vicuna hair. Good vicunas have worsted warps and woollen wefts, while low qualities have cotton or woollen warp and woollen weft. The characteristic of the fabric is a slightly raised and milled surface, just sufficient to cover the structure of the fabric. The cloths are usually double with a 2/2 twill face and a plain, 2/2 twill or weft sateen back, often arranged 2 face to 1 back, both warp and weft. A typical structure would be 2/48 w.c. botany, sett 96 ends per inch, two picks 45 skeins face to one pick 20 skeins back, 96 picks per inch.

VENETIANS

These are light, piece-dyed overcoating fabrics, originally made from woollen warp and weft yarns but now made with worsted and cotton yarns. They are warp-faced fabrics having a well-defined steep twill line. A five-end sateen derivative, the venetian weave *G* of Fig. 8.27, is by far the most common weave but slight modifications of it are used to suit different constructions. The woollen venetian is milled and raised to give a dress-face finish but the worsted venetian is cut clear. Covert coatings are similar to venetians except that the warp has a two-colour combination. A typical woollen venetian has a 24 skeins warp and 18 skeins weft with 50 ends and picks per inch.

WORSTED VOILES

These fabrics have a light weight, plain weave, open structure made from highly twisted and gassed warp and weft. A typical construction is 2/40 w.c. warp and weft, 36 ends and 36 picks per inch. Ornamentation is often effected by extra warp or weft figuring or by means of crammed stripes. Owing to the open nature of the structure, the warp ends need to be centred by sleying one end per dent.

TARTAN CLOTHS

The bulk of these cloths is made from woollen and worsted yarns, usually in 2/2 twill with elaborately coloured check designs. There are many different designs, each peculiar to one of the Highland clans. Similar designs are also made in double cloth fabrics for travelling rugs. A typical structure is 20 skeins warp and weft, 36 ends and picks per inch.

LASTINGS

This name is given to a fine, hard fabric made from cotton or wool and used for lining boots, shoes, bags and similar articles. A typical worsted lasting is made from 2/48 w.c. warp 1/22 w.c. weft, 104 ends per inch and 72 picks per inch in five-end warp sateen.

Although the above cloths account for the majority of fabrics produced in the woollen and worsted trade, there is also a small number of specialized cloths which have not been described. Union furnishing fabrics and casements have also been omitted, due to their variation in design and style[11].

REFERENCES

1. "Modern Carpet Manufacture", A. Crossland, Columbine Press, 1956.
2. Pomfret, O., *Text. Manufacturer*, 1944, **70**, 104.
3. "Advanced Txtile Design", W. Watson, Longmans Green, 1947.
4. "Textile Design and Colour", W. Watson, Longmans Green, 1937.
5. *Text. Mercury*, 1945, **113**, 295.
6. *Text. Weekly*, 1941, **28**, 353.
7. Brierley, S., *Text. Manufacturer*, 1931, **57**, 3.
8. Ward, J. A., *Cotton* (U.S.), 1941, **105**, No. 1, 57.
9. Shorter, S. A., *J. Text. Inst.*, 1948, **39**, P113.
10. Shorter, S. A., *J. Text. Inst.*, 1949, **40**, T189.
11. "Technical Terms in the Textile Trade", Vol. 1., E. Midgley, Emmott, 1931.

WOOL IN THE KNITTING INDUSTRY

DESPITE A TREMENDOUS GROWTH in the use of man-made fibre yarns in the knitting industry, there continues to be a strong demand for hosiery, underwear and knitwear composed wholly or largely of yarns spun from the wool fibre. Although wool is not used to the total exclusion of all other fibres in any knitted textures, it is still a most important constituent in the manufacture of single jersey, double jersey and purl or links-links weft knitted fabrics and also finds limited use for special purposes in the warp knitting field.

Included among the single jersey fabrics, in addition to stockinette, are intarsia, tuck, float-stitch, laid-in, accordian, plush, high pile, and lace structures; and among double jersey fabrics are rib, interlock, double piqué, eightlock, jacquard, relief and loop transfer textures. Wool stockinette, in which all loops are intermeshed in the same direction, is used for a wide variety of different purposes, such as tailored knitwear, high-class underwear, fully fashioned and stitch-shaped outer garments. Solid designing in colour is done on a stockinette foundation by intarsia knitting with wool yarns.

When a needle receives new yarn but does not get rid of its old loop, the new yarn is converted into a tuck loop that lies behind the old loop in the same stitch. Due to the fact that tuck loops are hidden behind held loops, figure designs in colour can be obtained and, since tucking gives rise to loop distortion, it is possible to develop fancy stitch effects. When other conditions remain unchanged, the introduction of tuck loops into a fabric gives an increase in weight per unit length and augments the knitting width.

When a needle retains its old loop but does not receive new yarn, the

FIG. 9.1.   STRUCTURE OF LAID-IN FABRIC

new yarn is converted into floating loops which lie on the technical reverse side of the fabric and can be used as units of design. The chief function of selective knitting and missing on one set of needles, however, is the de-

FIG. 9.2.   LAYING-IN WITH BINDING AND FACE
YARNS IN FOUNDATION TEXTURE

velopment of flat figure designs in colour, producing what are known as Fair Isle textures. In modern practice long floating threads are eliminated from these textures by combining tucking with knitting and missing. The tuck loops have an adverse effect on colour definition but tie-in non-knitted threads at pre-determined intervals and thus remove certain restrictions otherwise imposed on patterning possibilities.

Within the range of single jersey weft-knitted fabrics are structures in which a tweed-like appearance is obtainable on a technical reverse side by laying-in weft threads on a stockinette foundation, the weft threads being tied-in where changes take place between tucking and missing. The laid-in threads are usually thicker than the knitted yarn and, if desired, they can be of a fancy character. Astrakhan stockinette is a weft-knitted fabric in which fancy twist loop or curl yarns are laid-in; the stockinette foundation

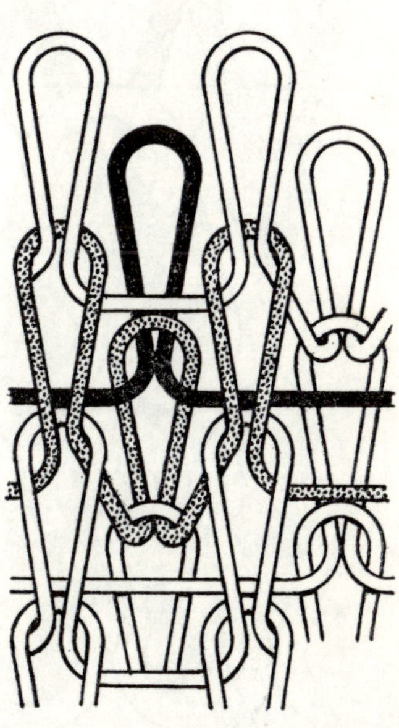

FIG. 9.3. INTERLOCK   FIG. 9.4 SWISS DOUBLE PIQUE

consists of double-loop stitches and, where tying-in takes place, the fancy yarn passes between the two knitted loops.

Wool is extensively used in weft-knitted fabrics of open-mesh construction, particularly those in which the lace effect is obtained by the partial or complete transference of needle loops. The inherent elasticity of the wool fibre assists the loop transferring action and other attributes of the fibre justify its use in the manufacture of high class fabric embodying a relatively slow and delicate knitting operation.

One of the principal uses of wool in the knitting industry at the present time is to make double jersey fabrics for women's and girls' coats and dresses. There is also a growing market for similar cloths to be made up into men's sports coats, golfing jackets, etc. Made chiefly on latch needle cylinder and dial machines with 16 and 18 needles per inch from ends ranging from 1/24s to 1/36s Bradford worsted counts, the double jersey fabrics comprise interlock, single piqué, double piqué, Milano rib, Ponte-di-Roma, Bourrelet, eightlock and other close-knit relatively inelastic stitch constructions that utilize two sets of needles but do not normally entail sub-division of either set into more than two independently controllable groups.

FIG. 9.5. MILANO RIB

Jacquard double jersey fabrics are usually produced by knitting and missing with two sets of needles which are arranged as for making 1/1 rib. It is possible to produce a figure design on both sides of the fabric but, as a rule, the figure design in colour appears on one side only, the other side showing horizontal stripes or a bird's eye effect. As many as six yarns of different colour can be incorporated in each design course but there are seldom more than four and usually only two or three.

The same actions of knitting and missing that characterize rib jacquard fabrics can be employed to make ripple cloth and blister effects. Ripple cloth is produced in self-colour with one set of needles knitting all the time while needles of the other set are selected to knit at predetermined courses, holding old loops where ripples are required to appear on the face side.

The most common blister structure, sometimes known as 'double blister', has a knitting cycle which, when used on circular machines, makes one stitch per six feeders on every dial needle, each cylinder needle meanwhile knitting two, three or four stitches according to how it is selected. A blister yarn is knitted on the same selected cylinder needles at feeders 1 and 2 and floats on the inside of the fabric where cylinder needles are

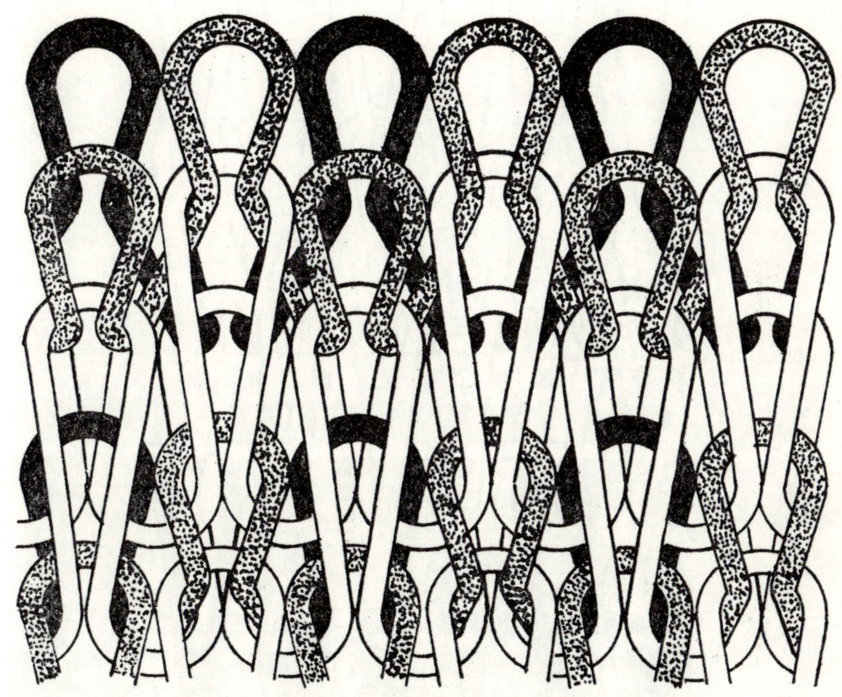

FIG. 9.6. PONTE DI ROMA

not selected to receive it. At feeder 3 a ground yarn is knitted on odd dial needles and on all cylinder needles not in action at feeders 1 and 2. The knitting action at feeders 4 and 5, using the blister yarn, is the same as at feeders 1 and 2, with either the same or a different needle selection. At feeder 6 the ground yarn is knitted on even dial needles and on cylinder needles not in action at feeders 4 and 5.

Many weft-knitted fabrics are composed partly of wool and partly of some other textile material. Use can be made of union yarns in which the different materials are blended together in the fibrous state and cordon yarns in which strands of different kinds are folded together. Almost all types of weft-knitting machines offer scope for horizontal striping and in many instances there are facilities, not only for supplying two different yarns together at the same feeding position, but also for guiding them to cause one to make loops that lie on the face side of the knitted stitches and the other to make loops that lie at the back, thus producing plated fabrics. When plating is carried out in stockinette stitch, one of the two yarns ap-

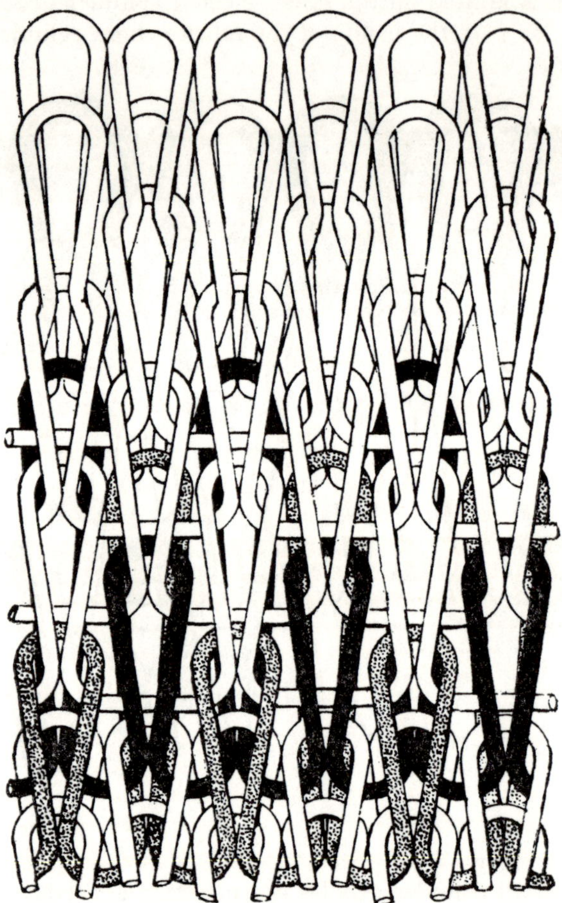

FIG. 9.7. BOURRELET

pear predominantly on the face side and the other at the back. Undergarments may have cotton next to the skin and wool on the outside or wool next to the skin and silk or rayon on the outside.

There is the possibility of plating long and short loops together to produce plush and pile fabrics, including high pile in which the extra long loops are cut. High pile fabrics can also be made by supplying wool fibres and other fibrous materials in lap form to latch needles while stockinette fabric is being knitted. In plated 1/1 rib fabric which is fully contracted widthwise the same yarn is seen at front and back unless some modification takes place in the knitting action, and the same applies in the case of interlock fabric. Tuck plated 1/1 rib and tuck plated interlock show different yarns at front and back.

Yet another method of combining a wool yarn with another yarn in the same fabric is to knit two pieces of stockinette back to back with joining loops at intervals, the wool yarn being used to make one piece and the non-wool yarn to make the other piece.

The characteristic loftiness and soft handle of good wool make it a most suitable substance for the knitting of purl or links-links fabrics, es-

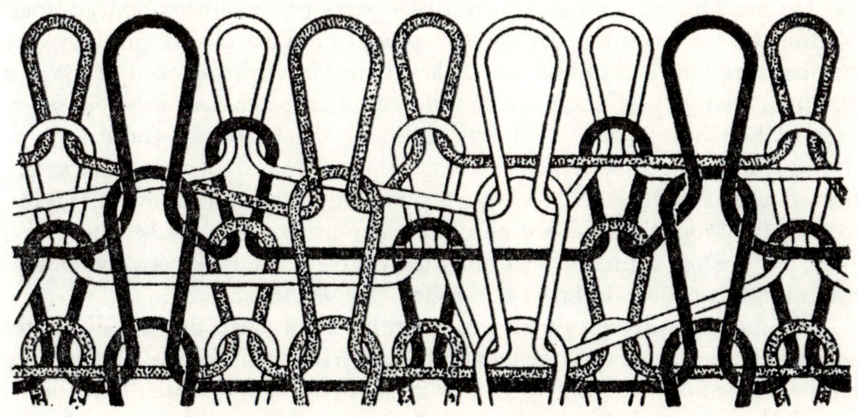

FIG. 9.8. STRUCTURE OF A THREE-COLOUR JACQUARD FABRIC

pecially 1/1 purl in which alternate rows or circuits of loops are intermeshed in opposite directions. This kind of fabric is extensively made up into spencers and lightweight bedjackets, as well as infants' wear. Fancy purl fabrics, comprising loops intermeshed in opposite directions in such a way that the resulting texture is neither rib nor purl also provide an important outlet for wool yarns. They are used in infants' wear and for jumpers, pull-overs, slip-ons, sweaters, half-hose and ankle socks. Many fancy purl fabrics incorporate tuck loops.

The knitting of half and full cardigan stitches and other tuck ribs provides an additional outlet for wool and many attractive fabrics featuring straight and racked wales are producible by combining tucking and racking with an appropriate set out of two sets of needles.

HOSIERY

The term 'hosiery' when used in its broadest sense embraces all knitted wearing apparel, but it is employed here as a comprehensive name for knitted coverings for legs and feet, including stockings and tights for women and girls, men's and boys' hose, three-quarter hose and half-hose, opera and gymnasium hose, children's socks, and ankle socks. Wool stockings for women and girls can be either fully fashioned or circular-knit. If fully fashioned they would normally have either an English foot characterized by seams at the sides or a French foot with diamond point toe and a seam along the middle of the sole. The range covers plain stockings with ribbed top, plain stockings with inturned welt, and ribbed stockings.

Both worsted-spun and woollen-spun all-wool yarns are used for making men's and boys' hosiery. In three-quarter hose there is usually a turn over top and it may be knitted on one machine while leg, heel, foot and toe are knitted on another, the two parts being subsequently joined together by overseaming. In modern practice almost all the products are manufactured on a seamless principle on circular knitting equipment and the great majority of them on double-cylinder machines. Popular fancy lines of half-hose made on double-cylinder machines are those incorporating jacquard, links-links and wale-thread plated designs. Some are knitted with a cushion sole. A large proportion of the well-known 'Argyles' are made of wool; solid coloured diamonds with cross threads are knitted in leg and instep, sometimes automatically but for the most part by manual operation of needles on hand-controlled circular machines.

Among speciality products which utilize wool yarns are three-quarter hose (golf hose) with wale-fashioned tubular rib legs. The wale-fashioning can be carried out by reducing the widths of ribs or by reducing the number of ribs. On a machine with 84 cylinder needles, twenty-one 4 x 1 ribs become twenty-one 3 x 1 ribs or fourteen 6 x 1 ribs become twelve 6 x 1 ribs. In the latter case needle manipulation is such that all the fashion marks lie near the back centre line of the hose and parallel to it. Gymnasium hose, which are also composed of wool, are plain or ribbed stockings with extra long legs and, in some instances, reinforced knees.

Weft-knitted garments for underwear and outerwear are producible by three methods, viz. (a) full-fashioning, (b) stitch-shaping, and (c) cutting and sewing.

Classic full-fashioned garments consist of parts knitted on one set of bearded needles and shaped by wale-fashioning. The number of knitting needles is increased or decreased by moving groups of selvedge loops outwards or inwards, a filling-in action taking place to avoid the formation of holes when the loops are moved outwards. Many garments have ribbed trims, examples being borders, cuffs and collars, which are knitted in rib stitch on machines having two sets of needles. Neck openings can be wale-fashioned, armholes shaped and parts of undergarments reinforced with

additional yarn as and where desired. The full-fashioning method offers
facilities for producing self-front pockets in knitwear, seamless bosom gores
in women's underwear and swimsuits, and crotch pouches for men's briefs.
There is scope for producing fancy effects, not only by tucking and horizontal striping, as in garments made by other methods, but also by intarsia

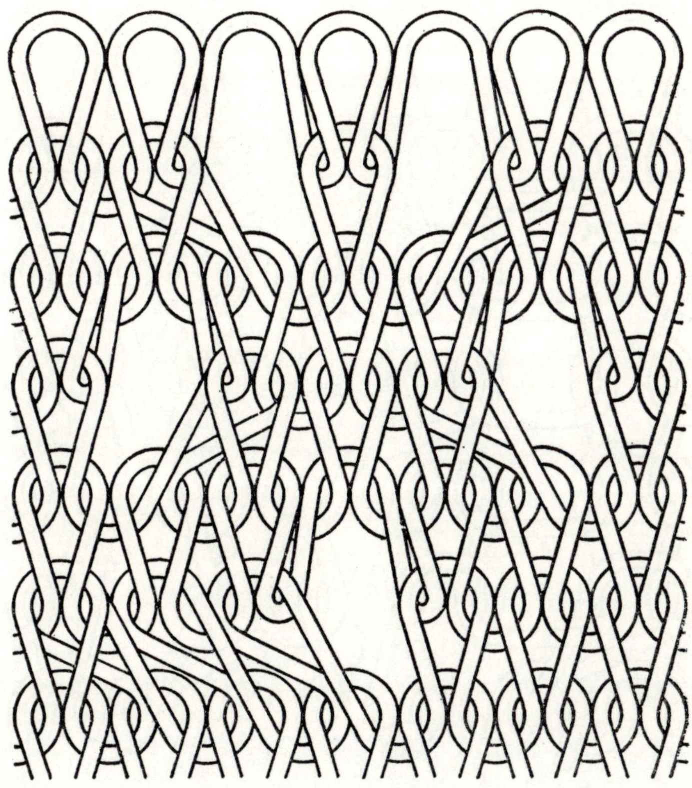

FIG. 9.9. LACE STITCH

knitting, sectional plating and lacing. Besides its other important advantages, the full-fashioning method has the great merit that it reduces to a
minimum the amount of waste made in the process of garment manufacture.

The principle of stitch-shaping is to vary the width of tubular or selvedged fabric by changing the nature of the stitch. In some cases there is
an alteration in the number of knitting needles, as when changing from 1/1
rib to 2/2 rib or vice-versa on cylinder and dial and V-type machines, but
otherwise the width is varied by making an alteration in the nature of the
stitch while keeping the number of knitting needles constant. Stitch-

shaping is done in connection with the manufacture of both undergarments and outergarments but whereas stitch-shaped underwear is exclusive to women, stitch-shaped outerwear is produced for both sexes. With the exception of women's vests having straight opera tops, stitch-shaped garments are almost invariably cut to shape at one place or another. Cutting

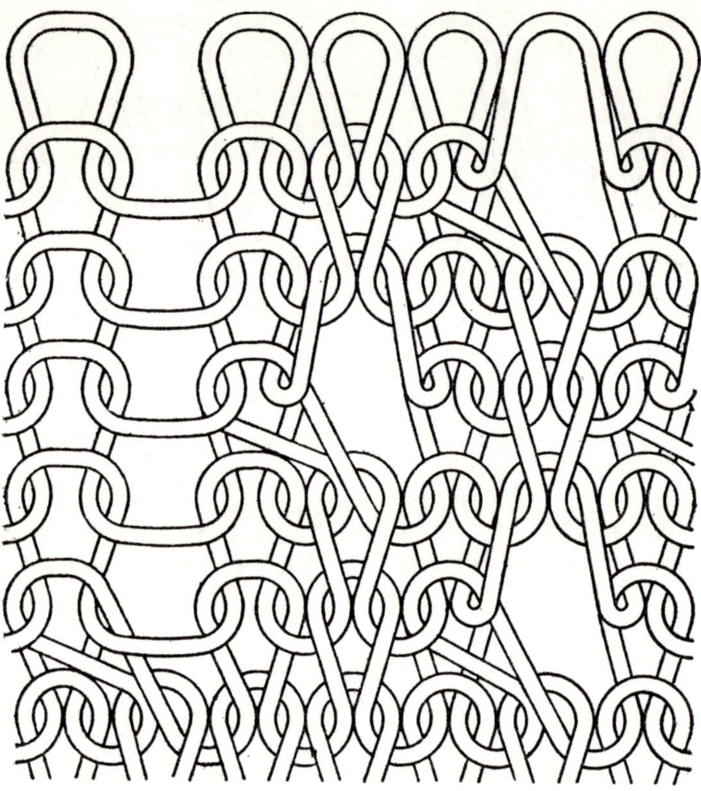

FIG. 9.10. TRANSFER STITCH USED IN STITCH SHAPING

likewise takes place in the making-up of some full-fashioned garments, notably at the neck.

A knitted garment which is made by cutting and sewing differs from one which is stitch-shaped or full-fashioned in that each separate part is cut to shape as in a man's suit. When two or three thicknesses of fabric are cut to shape with shears the garments are said to be 'tailored'. High-class wool goods are not infrequently dealt with in this way. Mass-production methods where several thicknesses of fabric are stacked to make a pile and cutting is done with a band knife or with a rotary knife are widely used, especially for underwear.

LOVES AND BERETS

Wool is the main material used in the manufacture of weft-knitted gloves and berets. Gloves are classified as wrought or seamless according to whether hand and fingers are knitted as flat selvedged pieces or in tubular form. Most gloves are now produced by the seamless method, using an automatic double-cylinder machine for making cuff and hand and a hand-operated V-type flat machine for making fingers and thumb. The way in which the fingers are knitted may be exemplified by giving details for a hand comprising 56 wales.

When the hand lies flat, its uppermost course can provide one loop to each of 28 needles on the front and back beds of the V-type machine. Needles 1-10 inclusive, front and back, are provided with loops for the first or index finger, but before the finger is knitted, loops are made with a draw-thread on front-bed needles 8, 9 and 10. This draw-thread is removed prior to the making of the second finger and six loops are thus released. The hand supplies loops for needles 11-18 and the released loops are placed on needles 8, 9 and 10 in both beds. The second finger is knitted on needles 8-18 after loops have been made with a draw-thread on needles 16, 17 and 18 in the front bed. After released loops have been placed on needles 16, 17, 18, needles 19-24 have received loops from the hand, and loops have been made on needles 22, 23 and 24 in the front bed with a draw-thread, the third finger is knitted. The fourth or little finger is knitted on needles 22-28 in both beds, needles 22, 23, 24 being supplied with loops from the third finger by withdrawal of the draw-thread and needles 25-28 with loops from the hand. The thumb is knitted on the part of the hand where a draw-thread has been inserted automatically on the double-cylinder machine. Fingers and thumb are closed by pulling loops together and securing them with a binding thread.

Coverings for the head include balaclava helmets, children's knitted bonnets and hats, juliet caps, turbans and berets. Some of these are cut to shape, some consist of wale-fashioned pieces of selvedged fabric and others, such as berets, are produced by special methods. The French style of beret is composed of about 24 wedge-shaped pieces of fabric which are knitted together, the first course of each piece being intermeshed with the last course of the previous one. After the whole beret has been knitted in this way, the first course of the first piece is joined to the last course of the last piece by hand-looping or chain-stitching. The machine built expressly for making the French beret has horizontal latch needles and jacquard selecting mechanism. Each wedge-shaped piece is produced by reducing the knitting width progressively; non-knitting needles hold their old loops and are brought back into action to knit one or two courses before the next piece is begun. After its outer edge has been turned outwards and sewn down, the beret is milled, brushed, blocked and, if necessary, sheared.

WEFT-KNITTING MACHINERY

MACHINERY designed for the conversion of woollen and worsted yarns into weft-knitted goods and fabrics may be broadly classified in five main types, namely, (*i*) straight bar machines, (*ii*) circular machines for making piece goods, (*iii*) circular garment-making machines, (*iv*) circular hosiery machines and (*v*) flat bar machines. A brief outline of the characteristics and scope of these various types is given below.

STRAIGHT BAR MACHINES

These machines, evolved from the knitting system patented by William Cotton in 1864, are employed almost exclusively for the manufacture of

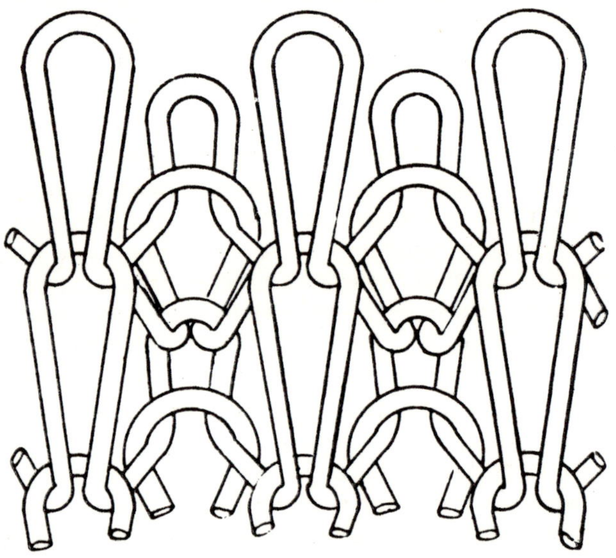

FIG. 9.11.   HALF CARDIGAN

full-fashioned hosiery, underwear and knitwear. There are machines on the market that have both vertical frame needles and horizontal machine needles, as well as those with frame needles only. Although there is still a limited market for full-fashioned wool underwear chief interest in connection with full-fashioned knitting centres on modern machines for making outergarments. These machines are now fully automatic in their action and have turn-round sequences which enable each section to knit the front, back and sleeves of one garment before starting the next. As compared with earlier models their running speeds are very much higher and they incorporate many improvements. Attachments can be fitted to make a wide variety of fancy fabrics. The modern range includes not only machines for knitting rib borders and cuffs but also rib fashioning machines capable of making shaped collars and the wale-fashioned pieces of ribbed garments, including those knitted in half and full cardigan, half welt and racked stitches.

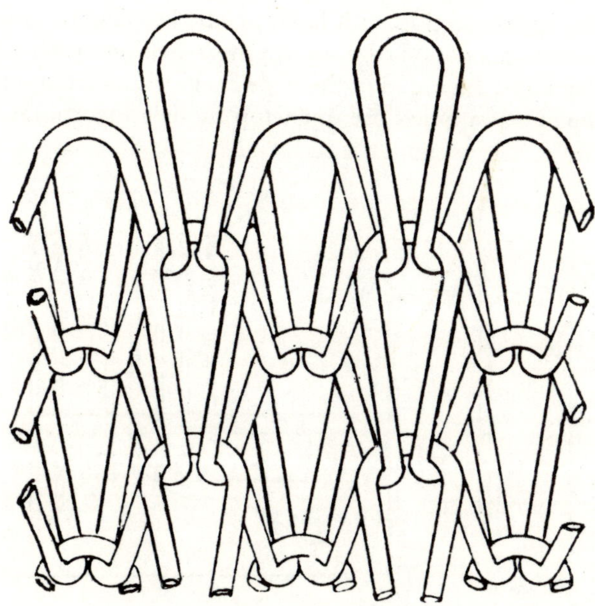

FIG. 9.12. FULL CARDIGAN

CIRCULAR PIECE GOODS MACHINES

Circular machines built to knit continuous lengths of tubular fabric for the cut goods trade embrace both bearded needle and latch needle types, the most important of which are listed below:

The English or American Loop Wheel Type: This type has bearded needles which are held vertically in a revolving needle cylinder. Bladed wheels are used for loop forming and the fabric is drawn off in an upward direction. Its main products are fleecy and laid-in fabrics, including astrakhan stockinette.

The French or German Sinker Wheel Type: Sinker wheel machines are characterized by revolving needle cylinders having horizontal radiating bearded needles and vertical knocking-over sinkers. The loops are formed by means of loop-forming sinkers which are accommodated in tricks in revolving wheels. In addition to high-quality stockinette fabric, sinker wheel machines can make tuck, jersey velour, laid-in, filet lace and other fancy fabrics.

Latch Needle Open Top Machines: For making plain and horizontal striped stockinette, machines of this type with needle cylinders 28 and 30 inches in diameter may have as many as 108 feeders. Much has been done in recent years in connection with latch needle knitting to improve standards of performance, notably by equipping machines with positive yarn feeding mechanisms. Included in the wide range of machinery to which the mechanism has been applied are open-top models incorporating as many

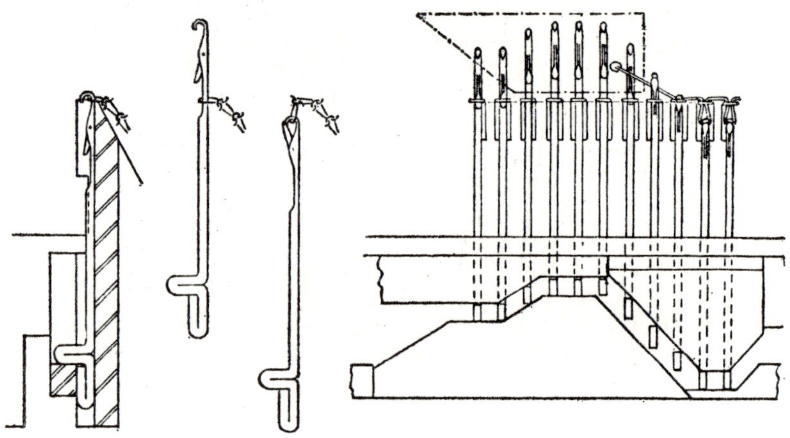

FIG. 9.13. KNITTING ACTION WITH LATCH NEEDLES

as 96 feeders. Machines with up to 40 feeders are not infrequently provided with a four-colour striping unit at each feeder together with a pattern wheel for needle selection. By means of pattern wheels needles can be placed at three different heights to make selective accordian fabrics. The use of pattern wheels for sinker selection enables figured jersey velour to be made.

Latch Needle Cylinder and Dial Machines: Machines under this sub-heading can be very broadly divided into two groups according to whether or not they incorporate mechanism for needle selection. Most of the non-jacquard machines, without selecting mechanism, are either of the inter-lock type with closed double-cam tracks or of the rib type equipped with needle clearing cams which can be repositioned manually to clear, tuck or miss. Machines of the interlock type give higher output than do those of the rib type, but they are less readily adaptable to produce different double-jersey fabrics. Needle selecting mechanisms characterizing jacquard cylinder and dial machines include pattern wheels, multi-step mechanisms, ribbons or films, and punched cards. On machines having up to 16 needles per inch punched cards can select needles individually without any restrictions. With the other mechanisms, however, free scope for designing is confined within specified areas, the dimensions of which vary with circumstances.

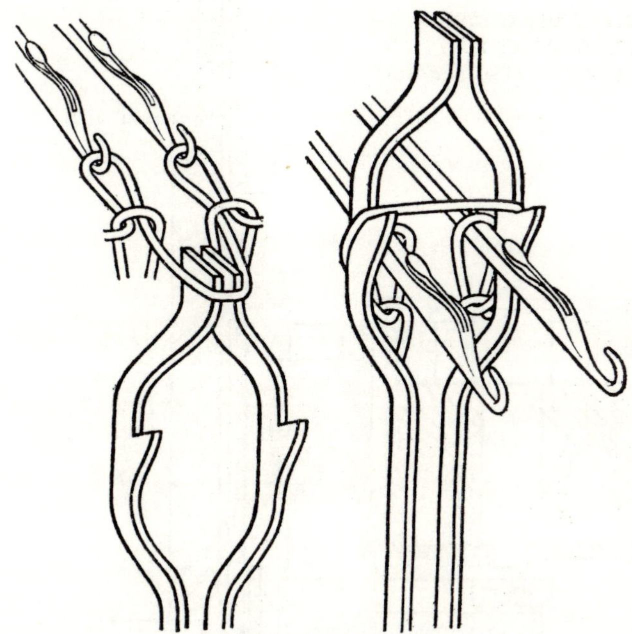

FIG. 9.14. SINKER LOOP TRANSFER IN
ACTION FOR EYELET KNITTING

CIRCULAR GARMENT MAKING MACHINES

These machines can be subdivided according to whether they are built to knit garment pieces for underwear or outerwear. Those unable to make welts, generally unsuitable for outerwear, include tuck rib, rib eyelet and corset machines. Machines using needles with loop-supporting ledges and having a loop transferring system at intervals of every two or three knitting feeders are built in suitable diameters and gauges for both underwear and outerwear. On machines intended for making underwear special provision is made so that every third dial needle can transfer loops to the cylinder, thus facilitating the production of vests with patterned skirt and bust based on 1/1 rib, the waist being knitted in 2/2 rib. On outerwear machines the loop transferring movements are from cylinder to dial only.

Among modern garment-making cylinder and dial machines are some of American origin built expressly to produce interlock sweater strips. With needle cylinders 33 inches in diameter they may have as many as 48

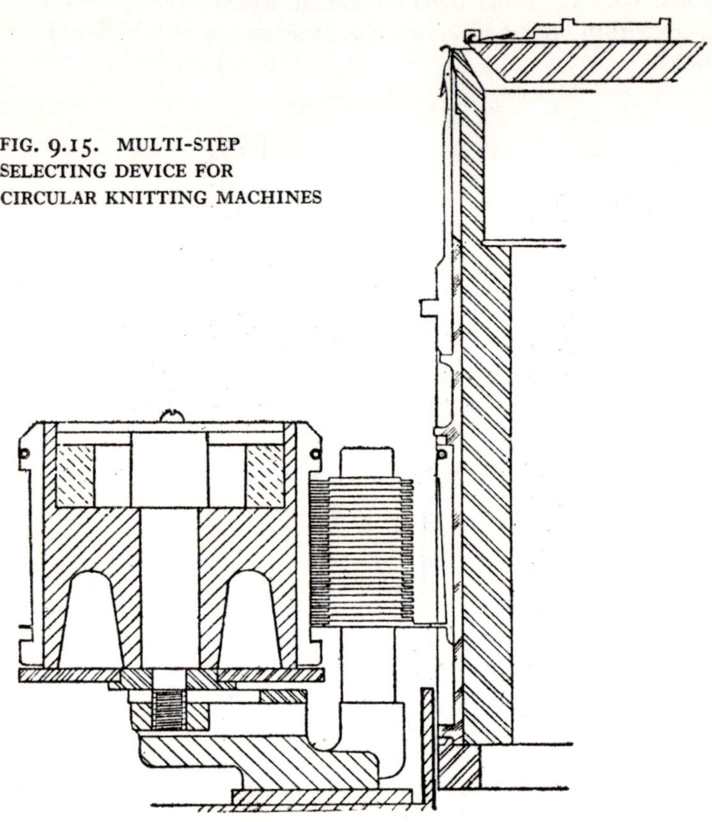

FIG. 9.15. MULTI-STEP
SELECTING DEVICE FOR
CIRCULAR KNITTING MACHINES

feeders. There are machines with 24 feeders which, in addition to offering facilities for making jacquard designs by needle selection, can produce a welt and 1/1 rib border in half-gauge for each garment length. As an alternative to the half-gauge rib border it is possible to knit a deep tubular welt on all needles. Both methods of setting up garment lengths can be preceded by locking courses and a press-off separating course knitted with a draw-thread.

Circular machines for making garment lengths also include double-cylinder models working with double-headed latch needles. There is a slider in both cylinders for each needle and the needle can be transferred from one to the other, knitting a plain loop when transferred downwards and a purl loop when transferred upwards. Needles engaged with their bottom sliders can be selected to tuck in the hook or miss the yarn altogether. Double-cylinder machines can make bodies and sleeves for jumpers, sweaters, pull-overs and other stitch-shaped outergarments, each with welt, rib end, and plain or fancy body.

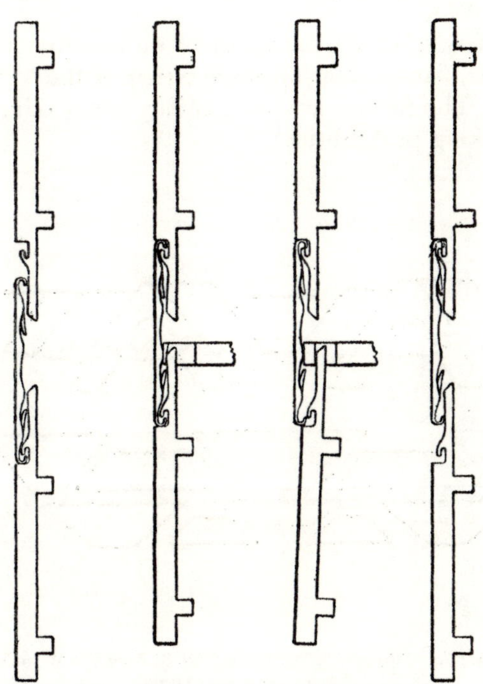

FIG. 9.16.   THE NEEDLE TRANSFER ACTION
OF A DOUBLE-CYLINDER MACHINE

CIRCULAR HOSIERY MACHINES

Where wool is concerned the item of major interest in this field is the small diameter double-cylinder type of machine which is able to knit plain, rib and fancy hose, half-hose and socks. There are machines of this kind now available for producing hosiery in a very wide variety of styles, in gauges extending from $2\frac{1}{2}$ to 25 needles per inch, and in plain, single and broad rib, two-and three-colour jacquard, tuck, links-links and wrap thread plated stitches. Children's socks can be knitted with straight top and welt and also with turn-over top and reverse welt, both kinds showing jacquard designs on the outside of the top and leg when worn.

A few machine builders offer single-cylinder machines with up to six knitting feeders to make half-hose and socks with elastic accordian tops. On these machines designs are producible in multiple colours on a knit-miss basis, selections for knitting and missing being confined to every second needle so that long objectionable floating threads are eliminated. Needles not under control of selecting units knit the yarn at each feeder during every revolution of the machine.

FLAT BAR MACHINES

Excluding a few relatively unimportant models that have either one or three needle beds, flat bar machines are either of the V-type or the horizontal bed type. The former are used chiefly for making rib fabrics and the latter for making purl fabrics.

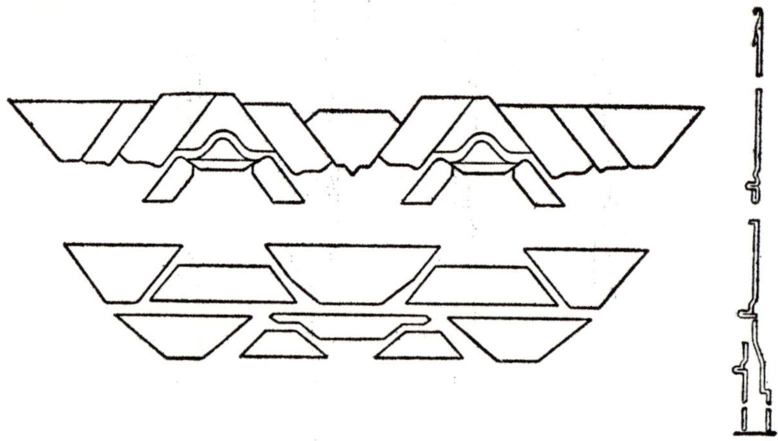

FIG. 9.17.   CAM SYSTEM FOR A DOUBLE-SYSTEM JACQUARD
FLAT BAR MACHINE

V-type Machines: The range of V-type equipment includes hand-controlled and power-assisted machines as well as jacquard and non-jacquard fully automatic machines, most of which are now built in double system. Among new machines are those offering facilities for automatic shaping of rib fabrics by means of loop-transferring points, including a hydraulically-controlled model embodying six knitting heads.

Many jacquard double-system machines can transfer loops from front to back bed when the cam carriage is moving in one direction and from back to front bed when the cam carriage is moving in the opposite direction, and on at least one model it is possible to knit and transfer during the same traverse movements. Among non-jacquard double-system machines there are some incorporating automatic widening attachments and others, the uses of which include the knitting of borders and cuffs for classic fully fashioned garments, can transfer loops from front to back bed, and vice-versa. Hand-operated single-system V-type machines are still widely used for making fully fashioned rib garments, for fingering gloves, and for other special purposes.

Horizontal Bed Machines: These include double-system jacquard models in which needles, when attached to back-bed sliders, can be selected to perform any one of four different operations in either system during each traverse movement of the cam carriage, thus providing scope for the knitting of an almost unlimited variety of fancy effects in stitch and colour.

One of the uses to which both V-type and horizontal bed double system jacquard machines can be applied is the automatic production of cable stitches.

WARP KNITTING

Where wool is concerned, the most important possibilities in warp knitting are (*a*) the construction of dimensionally stable fabrics, (*b*) the production of lightweight textures of exceptional fullness and softness, (*c*) the knitting of nets and other kinds of openwork, (*d*) solid designing in multiple colours, and (*e*) the synthesis of fancy textures featuring novel effects in stitch and colour.

Wool is largely used on Raschel warp-knitting machines with latch needles. These machines have designing scope much greater than that of other types of warp-knitting machine. They can have either one or two needle beds, and several guide bars. The fitting of a solid steel bar, called a fall plate, enables fabrics to be embellished with extra thick and/or fancy yarns which do not enter the needle hooks and are not converted into knitted loops. The latest developments associated with the fall plate promote its much wider use in conjunction with one needle bed and its application to machines with two needle beds. Some Raschel machines have apparatus for inserting straight weft threads to impart greater dimensional stability to fabrics and investigational work is now in progress on Raschel machines having one needle bed and four or five guide bars in an effort to produce warp-knitted material which will challenge the supremacy of woven cloths for men's suits and overcoats.

WARP-KNITTED SHAWL FABRICS

Soft spun worsted yarns are used to make Raschel fabrics for shawls, bed-jackets and infants' wear and the volume of wool yarn that finds its way into warp-knitted fabrics is periodically increased by a vogue among women for dress materials, scarves and stoles made on Raschel machines. The simplest shawl fabrics are knitted on one needle bed, using two guide bars. The guide bars are usually threaded with half-sets of threads, the filled guide eyes being arranged so that they can, when required, work to-gether as the equivalent of one guide bar that is fully threaded. The two half-sets of threads can be used together to knit some courses of single bar fabric while at other times they can be actuated independently to produce openwork. Fabrics for shawl borders often have parallel chains of loops connected by laid-in threads, the latter being extra thick and/or of a fancy character.

The fall plate is employed in the knitting of both shawl and dress fab-rics. It swings backwards and forwards with the guide bars and has an in-dependent up and down movement to take certain overlapped threads be-low the spoons of the open latches of the knitting needles, so that they are cast off when the needle bed descends. At least two guide bars are needed to make fabrics which incorporate fall-plate laps. The use of three or more guide bars enables more elaborate structures to be produced, including those which contain both fall-plate and laid-in laps.

DOUBLE RIB, FANCY RIB AND PLUSH FABRICS

The use within a predetermined knitting width of the full complement of needles in two needle beds, the needles in the two beds lying back-to-back, enables double rib fabrics to be produced. These can be reversible. Fancy rib warp-knitted fabrics which have an appearance closely resemb-ling weft-knitted racked rib are producible by using specially prepared needle beds that give a single rib set-out. Other textures involving the use of two needle beds include cut pile and warp-knitted crêpe. Plush fabric in which the plush threads may be either knitted or laid-in is made by using one bed of latch needles, or a bed of dummy needles or points, and two or more guide bars. Warp-knitted pile fabric for carpets and rugs is made on coarse gauge Raschel machines fitted with one needle bed, one point bar, and three guide bars. The threads constituting the pile are laid-in and cut during the knitting process. The foundation texture comprises knitted chains which are interconnected by laid-in weft threads.

PRODUCTION OF SHELL DESIGNS

Shell designs, made by means of cut pressers on bearded needle warp-knitting machines, are popular for shawls, blouses and bedjackets. A typ-ical shell design is made with a 4 x 4 cut presser working in conjunction with a guide bar that has four guides threaded, the next four empty, and so on, alternately, across the knitting width. The guide bar makes traverse movements and the presser is shogged correspondingly, so that whenever a needle receives a new loop it has its beard closed and casts off its old loop, whereas a needle that does not receive a new loop has its beard left open and does not cast off its old loop. On account of the fact that some needles knit more stitches than others embossed surfaces are developed.

SEWING AND SEAMING

CLOSELY ASSOCIATED with the manufacture of warp and weft knitted fabrics is the making up of these fabrics into garments by the process of sewing and seaming. For this work, in which wool yarns or threads are used as far as circumstances will permit, two systems are available, one being suitable for fully fashioned knitwear, and the other for 'cut and sew' knitted goods.

Insofar as fully fashioned knitwear is concerned, seaming is carried out by means of linking, double-lock chainstitch, cup seamers or over-edge cup seamers, while other machines capable of attaching necks and stollings may also be used. Button-hole, button-stitching and bar-tacking machines are used for the other various making up processes. With 'cut and sew' knitwear most of the seaming is carried out by the use of an overlock machine, although for certain products, the more complex multi-needle flat-seaming machine may be employed. As with fully fashioned production, button-hole, button-stitch and bar-tacking machines will be used.

CHOICE OF STITCH

The choice of stitch used is dependent on many factors. It may be necessary to join a fabric loop to loop, loop to selvedge or selvedge to selvedge. In the first two examples a linking machine would be used, the seam produced being suited to the fabric both in appearance and in performance. Where a selvedge to selvedge joint is required and where each loop does not require to be penetrated, the double-lock chain-stitch cup seamer or the over-edge cup seamer can be used. These seams have a high degree of efficiency when used with the proper type of seaming yarns. Moreover, due to their construction they are not prone to complete breakdown in the event of one stitch being ruptured, as would be the case with the single-chain or lockstitch-type seam.

Where cut goods are being seamed together, the problem is not one of loop to loop or selvedge seaming but that of joining two raw fabric edges together. In the knitted outerwear trade the most popular type of stitch is the 'overlock' stitch. This method of seaming involves the use of three threads, one needle thread and two looper threads. It is usual to have the needle thread of sewing thread quality, while the looper threads (in the case of a worsted knitted garment) can both be yarns similar to those used to produce the garment. This stitch formation is ideal for the seaming of knitted goods as it produces a strong seam with a high degree of elasticity.

In the cut underwear trade the flatlock machine is used to join the garment pieces together. The seam produced in this way comprises nine threads which form four interlocking rows of double-chain stitching with a seam covering yarn and is particularly strong. Due to its appearance, however, this type of stitch is unsuitable for outerwear garments although ideally suited for underwear. The flatlock machine may also be used for attaching elastic waist bands and for many other similar operations. The overlock seam is now being used in the field formerly held by the flatlock seam, but it would seem doubtful whether the overlock will ever completely take over the work done by the flatlock.

In addition to the full range of seaming and making-up machinery, which includes multiple-needle lockstitch and lockstitch machines, flat seaming machines, flatlock machines, seam-covering machines, button-hole, button-stitch machines, elasticating machines and special embroidery machines, two seaming machines particularly suited to the knitwear trade have now appeared on the market. These are the elastic lockstitch machine and the extensible double-lock chain-stitch machine, both of which offer advantages considered to be lacking with the earlier types of lockstitch and double-lock chain-stitch machines.

THE FUNDAMENTALS OF WOOL DYEING

So MANY CHANGES in wool dyeing materials, procedures and techniques have taken place since the first edition of this book was published in 1952 that it has been necessary completely to revise the original subject matter. At the same time it has been considered advisable to divide the subject into two sections, one dealing with the more theoretical aspects of dyeing and the constitution and dyeing behaviour of the various classes of dye now available for wool dyeing, while the other considers wool dyeing in practice and describes the machinery developed for the purpose. Even so, a third section is necessary to cover the dyeing of wool mixtures and blends, a phase which has been completely revolutionized by the development and tremendous growth in the use of man-made fibres in the woollen and worsted industries.

As evidence of the changes which the past fifteen years have brought about, reference may be made to the fact that at least two new classes of dye have appeared. The first of these, comprising the 1:2 metal-complex dyes, has already achieved a position of great importance. The second class, comprising the reactive dyes, is, as yet, of relatively less importance but these dyes may well become important as they prove capable of providing dyeings of particularly high wet-fastness in full depths. The demand for this property and, at the same time, for bright colours is increasing, the ability to machine-wash shrink-resisted articles at high temperatures now being expected by domestic consumers. New auxiliary products, improved dyeing machines, and better control of the dyeing process have led to the successful application of classes of dyes to types of material on which hitherto they have been considered insufficiently level dyeing. Finally, the combined efforts of dyemakers and machinery makers have made the continuous dyeing of loose wool and slubbing a practical proposition.

THE STRUCTURE OF WOOL IN RELATION TO ITS DYEING BEHAVIOUR

As has already been described in Section 2, the wool fibre consists of two main parts, the cuticle (scales) and the cortex which makes up the bulk of the fibre. Coarse wools may contain a third component, a central medulla. This is often discontinuous and usually contains the bulk of any natural colouring matter present in the fibre.

From the point of view of dyeing behaviour[1] the cuticle exerts an influence out of all proportion to its bulk. It is a complex structure surrounded by an outer layer known as the epicuticle. This is some 50-100mμ thick and forms a continuous sheath around a completely intact fibre. It differs from the rest of the fibre in being hydrophobic and thus is penetrated only with difficulty by water-soluble dyes. However, it is readily damaged on exposure to the atmosphere during the growth of the fibre and by physical and chemical processing. The extent to which it has been removed from fibres prior to dyeing largely determines the ease with which they can be dyed.

The cortex forms the bulk of the fibre. It swells considerably in aqueous solutions to give 'pores' in the structure with a diameter of the order of 60 Å. Small dye molecules can thus diffuse slowly into wool fibres at quite low temperatures (30 °C). With increase in temperature there is further increase in swelling and quite large molecules are able to penetrate the amorphous regions of the fibre.

The protein, keratin, of which wool is composed, is a highly complex polypeptide. From the point of view of dyeing behaviour, its most important chemical features are, firstly, that it contains a large proportion of amino ($-NH_2$), carboxyl ($-COOH$), and amide ($-NHCO-$) groups, and secondly, that it contains a large number of disulphide ($-S-S-$) bonds. The former groups are responsible for attracting water molecules and thus promoting the swelling of the fibre in aqueous solutions. The disulphide bonds do not exert a great direct influence on dyeing, except in one or two cases, *e.g.*, when dyeing with chrome dyes, but as they play a large part in determining the strength and other important physical characteristics of the fibre and since they are broken down progressively when wool is treated in hot aqueous solutions under neutral and, especially, alkaline conditions, they play a very important part in determining the effect of dyeing conditions on wool quality.

Variations in the physical and chemical characteristics of wool fibres and of assemblies of them have a considerable influence on practical wool dyeing[2]. Thus within any sample of wool, even though nominally of the same quality, there is considerable variation in fibre diameter, while the variation between fibres of a different quality may be very wide. Fine fibres absorb and desorb dyes more rapidly than do coarse fibres. When both contain the same amount of dye by weight, coarse fibres appear darker than fine fibres because of the greater amount of surface light reflection from the latter.

Rate of dyeing largely depends on the state of the fibre surface. Traces of grease reduce the rate of penetration of the surface by dyes. The degree of continuity of the epicuticle and of the scales affects dye penetration even more. Removal of the epicuticle from the tips of the fibres by 'weathering' during growth and partial removal of the epicuticle and, in severe cases, of the scales during processing leads to marked differences in the dyeing behaviour of different fibres and of different parts of the same fibre. It is such selective behaviour which is the cause of the phenomena known as 'skittery' and 'tippy' dyeing. Complete removal of the scales, as can occur when cloth is abraded, leads to abrasion marks for the same reason[3].

Physical and chemical modification of wool fibres during such processes as carbonizing, bleaching, and shrink-resisting often produces profound changes in dyeing behaviour[4]. In these cases, removal of the epicuticle increases the rate of dye absorption. If, at the same time, chemical modification results in the introduction into the keratin molecule of a sufficient number of new groups, *e.g.*, acidic groups, the final effect may be that the material is less deeply dyed than untreated material. Unevenly treated material may dye unevenly, *e.g.*, light areas appear in unevenly carbonized wool cloth dyed with certain acid dyes.

As will be stressed later, classes of dyes, and individual dyes within a particular class, differ considerably in their response to physical and chemical variations in wool. Thus highly sulphonated acid dyes, *e.g.*, Naphthalene Scarlet 4R (ICI), are very fibre-selective in their dyeing behaviour[5]. The unsulphonated 1:2 metal-complex dyes, on the other hand, are much less influenced by variations within and between fibres.

THE THEORY OF WOOL DYEING

As an introduction to the general theory of wool dyeing[6], it should be pointed out that the object of all coloration processes, except one, is to introduce a coloured compound into the internal structure of the fibre and to ensure that it is retained inside the fibre firmly enough to give a colouring of adequate permanence. The exception is the bonding of pigments to the surface of fibres by means of a thin film of transparent resin, which is formed around the fibres by polymerization, and in which the particles of pigment are embedded. Such resin-bonding techniques are not used with wool.

Every dyeing process is made up of two principal stages. In the first stage the dye is transported to the vicinity of the fibres by bulk liquid flow, and then by diffusion across the liquid boundary layer immobilized at the fibre surface, to give a rapid build-up of dye at the surface of the fibres. In the second stage the dye diffuses into the interior of the fibre and becomes 'fixed' therein by the operation of the various forces of attraction which can operate between dye molecules and fibre molecules and, in certain cases, by a change in the state of the dye inside the fibre, *e.g.*, conversion of a soluble leuco vat dye into the insoluble form, or by union of dye and fibre molecules by chemical reaction, as occurs when reactive dyes are employed.

The two characteristics of a dye of particular practical significance are (*i*) the rate at which it can penetrate the fibre, and (*ii*) the extent to which it is absorbed by the fibre. These are determined by (*a*) the diffusion properties of the dye, (*b*) the substantivity of the dye, and (*c*) the saturation value of the dye.

DIFFUSION PROPERTIES

Diffusion is of major importance. Unless the dye diffuses into the fibre, the dyeings, if such they could be called, would have very poor fastness to dry and wet rubbing, to wet treatments, and also to other agencies. Wherever a significant amount of dye remains on the surface of the material at the conclusion of dyeing, *e.g.*, with chrome blacks on slubbing, it is necessary to scour the dyed material to remove it.

Rate of diffusion depends upon (*i*) the state of the fibre surface, (*ii*) the porosity of the fibre, *i.e.*, the size of the channels or pores in the water-swollen fibre, (*iii*) the molecular characteristics of the dye in the dyebath, *i.e.*, the size and shape of the dye particles, and the extent to which single ions or aggregates are present, and (*iv*) the nature of the dye-fibre absorption process, *i.e.*, the type of forces operating between the dye and the fibre and the magnitude of those forces. Any change in dyebath conditions which affects these properties will affect the rate of diffusion. Thus rise in temperature always increases diffusion rate. Change in pH and addition of electrolytes markedly affect diffusion of dyes in wool. Addition of organic solvents such as benzyl alcohol has the same effect, presumably by reducing the forces of attraction between the dye and the fibre.

SUBSTANTIVITY

A dye is said to be substantive towards a fibre if it is attracted to it and preferentially absorbed by it when dye and fibre come into contact in the dyebath. Substantivity arises through the operation of certain forces of attraction between dye and fibre. These include ionic forces, hydrogen bonds, non-polar van der Waals forces and covalent bonds.

Ionic Forces: These forces operate when both dye and fibre contain groups which can ionize in aqueous solution, *e.g.*, the amino groups in wool keratin and the sulphonic acid groups in acid dyes. It is important to note that the magnitude of such ionic forces depends upon conditions in the dyebath. With wool, as the acidity of the bath falls so does the number of free positively-charged amino groups, until, within the isoelectric region none remain. As the solution becomes progressively alkaline, free negatively-charged carboxyl groups appear and dye anions are repelled. Further, these ionic bonds readily break and reform and thus the sorption process is reversible.

Hydrogen Bonds: These bonds result from the ability of the hydrogen atom to accept a second pair of electrons so that it can form a bridge between, for example, an oxygen atom present in the carbonyl group in the amide linkage in the peptide chain of keratin and the amino group or hydroxyl group in a dye. These bonds, and similar bonds arising from dipole interaction, are weak and the forces between the atoms responsible are very weak. Nevertheless, where a number of such bonds can exist simultaneously between dye and fibre, *e.g.*, with a dye with a linear structure containing a number of groups capable of entering into association with the appropriate groups in the fibre, such multipoint attachment can give rise to strong dye-fibre attraction which is not dependent upon the pH conditions in the dyebath.

Non-polar van der Waals Forces: These forces operate between molecules of similar structure when such molecules are able to come sufficiently close together. They can exist between, for example, the hydrophobic chains in the keratin molecule and the benzene and naphthalene rings in a dye molecule. As with hydrogen bonds, since these forces are weak, multipoint attachment is required to produce strong attraction. Planar molecules of large size are predisposed towards the formation of such bonds, and this type of dye-fibre attraction is also independent of the pH conditions in the dyebath.

Covalent Bonds: In this case atoms unite to form what is, in fact, a new compound, and the dye molecule and the fibre molecule become one entity. Such bonds between dyes and fibres are broken only under certain conditions, *e.g.*, hot, strongly acid, or strongly alkaline conditions, and thus the dyeings and prints obtained have high fastness to wet treatments. As far as wool keratin is concerned, covalent combination between reactive dyes and the fibre molecule takes place readily through amino ($-NH_2$) groups. There is also some evidence that covalent bonds may play a part in the attachment of chrome dyes to wool through the chromium atom in the dye-chromium complex.

Dye-fibre substantivity is essential in all dyeing processes based on preferential absorption of the dye by the fibre. It determines the extent to which the dye is transferred from its external environment to the fibre, and in most cases must be sufficiently high to ensure that exhaustion is good enough to be economic. Even in those cases where the state of the dye in the fibre is altered completely in the later stages of the dyeing process, *e.g.*, when using vat or reactive dyes, dye-fibre substantivity must be high enough in the initial stages to ensure adequate dye absorption.

The term 'affinity' is sometimes used instead of 'substantivity' to describe the behaviour of particular dyeing systems in practical terms. This is to be regretted. The term 'affinity' should be reserved to state mathematically the strength of dye-fibre attraction as measured under precisely defined standard conditions and not employed when considering dye-fibre attraction in general, qualitative terms only.

Substantivity has an obvious influence on diffusion, and hence on rate of dyeing and on the wet fastness of the resultant dyeing. If a dye is highly substantive, *e.g.*, a neutral-dyeing acid dye on wool, under the conditions employed, the rate of absorption in the first few minutes of dyeing (often called the 'strike') will be so high as to be uncontrollable. Diffusion from the surface into the fibre will take place only slowly and little redistribution of dye, arising from dye migration as dyeing proceeds, can be expected. For the same reason, the wet fastness of the dyeing will be high. Any change in the strength of the forces of attraction between the dye and the fibre will result in a change in substantivity. Increase in temperature reduces the attraction between dye and fibre molecules and thus dye-fibre attraction decreases and equilibrium exhaustion falls. In the case of wool the substantivity of, *e.g.*, acid dyes is also profoundly affected by change in the electrolyte content of the dyebath, and in dyebath pH.

Dye-fibre substantivity can also be modified by adding to the dyebath compounds which complex with the dye to form complexes which have very much lower substantivity for the fibre than the dye itself. Such compounds, *e.g.*, Lyogen WD (Sandoz), are widely used when applying highly substantive dyes to wool. The association between the dye molecule and the agent is strong at low temperatures. As the temperature is raised the complex breaks down progressively and the dye molecules become free to be absorbed by the fibre. These products are very useful in controlling dyeing rate but care must be taken to use no more than is required to achieve the necessary control. If too much is added there is likely to be a serious reduction in equilibrium exhaustion.

SATURATION VALUE

Saturation is the term used to describe the condition reached when the fibre will absorb no more dye however much more is added to the dyebath and the dyeing time extended. The practical importance of saturation values is that they indicate whether or not deep colours can be obtained with particular dye-fibre combinations. With wool there is no problem since wool is capable of absorbing large quantities of most types of dye and the deepest colours can be obtained without the saturation limit being reached. With certain dyes on polyamide fibres this is not so and this has repercussions in the selection of, *e.g.*, acid dyes, for dyeing wool-nylon blends.

PRACTICAL IMPLICATIONS OF DYEING THEORY

With anionic dyes, *e.g.*, acid dyes, the more practical implications of dyeing theory are as given below. These also apply with the metal-complex dyes, with the chrome dyes, and with the reactive dyes, in so far as they are anionic in character in aqueous solution. In the case of these dyes, however, the situation is complicated by such additional factors as the formation of dye-chromium complexes within the fibre (with chrome dyes) and covalent dye-fibre bonding (with reactive dyes).

The dyes are absorbed by the water-swollen fibre as the result of the operation of polar forces and non-polar van der Waals forces as shown in much simplified fashion in Fig. 10.1, taken from a paper by Derbyshire[7].

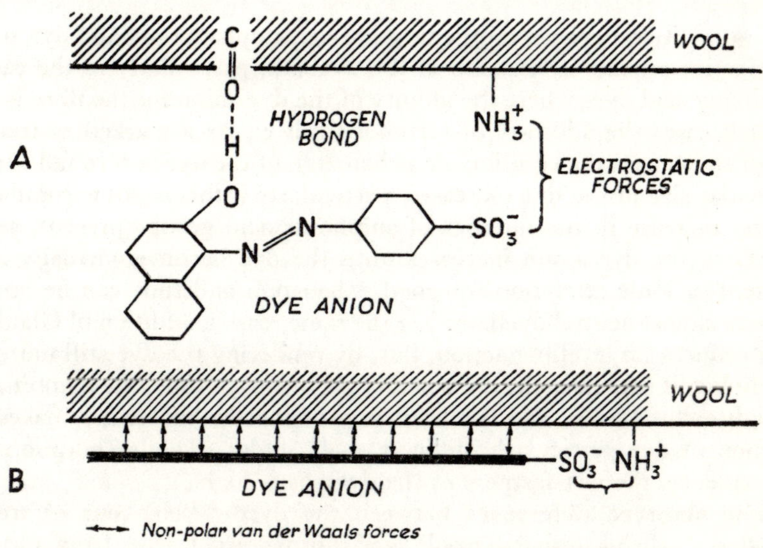

FIG. 10.1 MECHANISM OF ANIONIC DYE ABSORPTION BY
(A) POLAR FORCES AND (B) NON-POLAR VAN DER WAALS FORCES

Under acid conditions the salt-links in the keratin molecule are back-titrated leaving a positive charge on the fibre which is neutralized by the absorption of anions, either inorganic anions, or dye anions. The former are absorbed more rapidly in the initial stages and gradually replaced by the slower diffusing dye anions which have higher affinity, due to the operation of additional forces between the dye molecules and the fibre molecules which come into play as the dye molecules approach the latter sufficiently closely. The whole sequence of changes is represented in the following series of equations.

$$(i) \qquad >\!\!NH_3^+ \quad {}^-OOC\!\!< \; + \; H^+ \; \rightleftharpoons \; >\!\!NH_3^+ \quad HOOC\!\!<$$

$$(ii) \qquad >\!\!NH_3^+ \quad + \quad Cl^- \; \rightleftharpoons \; >\!\!NH_3^+ \quad Cl^-$$

$$(iii) \qquad >\!\!NH_3^+ \quad Cl^- \; + \; D^- \; \rightleftharpoons \; >\!\!NH_3^+ \, D^- \; + \; Cl^-$$

Competition between inorganic ions, *e.g.*, sulphate ions, and dye anions leads to incomplete exhaustion of the dyebath, particularly in the case of equalizing acid dyes where the affinity of the dye anion for the fibre is low. In such cases the addition of Glauber's salt exerts a marked restraining action and causes the equilibrium exhaustion of the dyebath to fall. As the molecular size of the dye increases, particularly if this is not accompanied by any increase in the number of sulphonic acid groups present, so the affinity of the dye anion increases until the dye becomes virtually independent of ionic attraction for good exhaustion and thus can be applied from an almost neutral dyebath. For the same reason, addition of Glauber's salt produces no levelling action, but, by rendering the dye still more hydrophobic, it increases the exhaustion. At the same time, the combination of high anion affinity and the large size of the dye molecules makes desorption of dye particularly difficult, even under alkaline conditions. In consequence, the wet-fastness of the dyeings is high.

The observed differences between the dyeing behaviour of treated wools, *e.g.*, shrink-resisted wool[8], and normal wool arise from physical and chemical changes resulting from the treatment. As has already been pointed out, removal of the epicuticle greatly facilitates the entry of dye molecules into the cortex of the fibre, whereas the introduction of additional acid groups into the keratin molecule makes the entry of dye anions more difficult. Usually, the former effect is much more significant than the latter, *e.g.*, with wool chlorinated with either acidified hypochlorite solution or gaseous chlorine[9], but treatment with some oxidizing agent, such as periodic acid, under severe conditions can cause the absorption of dyes to be strongly repressed. Elimination of basic groups, *e.g.*, by acetylation of wool with acetic anhydride, produces the same effect. Introduction of additional acidic groups and the elimination of basic groups have been used commercially to produce 'resisted' wool, intended for use in conjunction with normal wool to produce multi-coloured effects by one-bath dyeing processes[10].

DYES FOR WOOL

DYES used for the dyeing of wool may be classified as follows: (*i*) acid dyes, (*ii*) metal-complex dyes, (which may be subdivided into 1:1 complexes and 1:2 complexes), (*iii*) chrome (mordant) dyes, (*iv*) vat dyes, including solubilized vat dyes, (*v*) reactive dyes and (*vi*) direct dyes.

With regard to this classification, it should be pointed out that in the second edition of the Colour Index, the group 'acid dyes' includes not only those dyes which have long been described as 'acid dyes' but also the two chemical types of metal-complex dyes, *viz.* the 1:1 and 1:2 complexes, typified by the Neolan (CIBA) and Irgalan (Gy) dyes, respectively. Since these behave in the same general way as the conventional acid dyes, this is reasonable. However, since they are distinctly different in structure, they are often considered separately, and this policy has been followed in the present volume. Again, the classification 'mordant dyes' is used in the Colour Index. As far as wool is concerned, however, chromium compounds are virtually the only mordants employed in the application of these dyes and, in consequence, they are commonly known as chrome dyes.

Of the six groups of dyestuffs referred to above, the acid, metal-complex, and chrome dyes are particularly important. Indigo is the only important vat dye and its use is declining. A few direct dyes are of interest for dyeing wool-cellulosic fibre blends, since they will dye both fibres. The reactive dyes are the most recent addition to the ranges of dyes for wool. Although not yet of major importance, their use is increasing and they are likely to become much more important.

The general chemical structure and dyeing behaviour of each class of dye are considered in turn in the following paragraphs.

ACID DYES

Chemical Structure: The acid dyes are the sodium (very occasionally potassium) salts of sulphonic (occasionally carboxylic) acids of coloured organic compounds. According to the Colour Index, as far as can be ascertained, the bulk of them (65 per cent) are azo compounds. Anthraquinone compounds (15 per cent) and triarylmethane compounds (12 per cent) account for most of the remainder. A few individually important dyes belong to other classes, *e.g.*, azine and xanthene. Azo compounds provide most of the yellows, almost all of the oranges and scarlets, and most of the reds. Some dull blues, including the very important navy blues of the Coomassie Navy Blue type are azo dyes, as are also a few dark greens and dull violets and almost all the blacks.

A typical equalizing acid azo dye is Azo Geranine 2G (ICI)

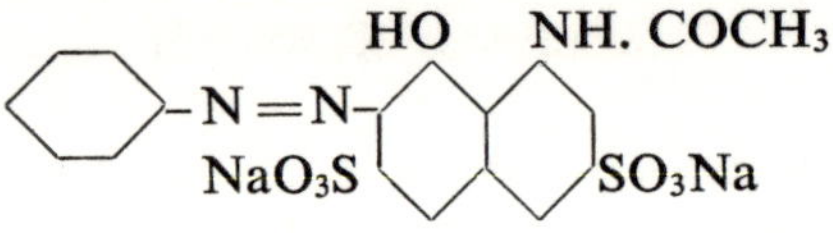

Azo Geranine 2G (ICI)

The introduction of a long alkyl chain ($-C_{12}H_{25}$) into such a structure gives the neutral-dyeing acid dye, Carbolan Crimson B (ICI):

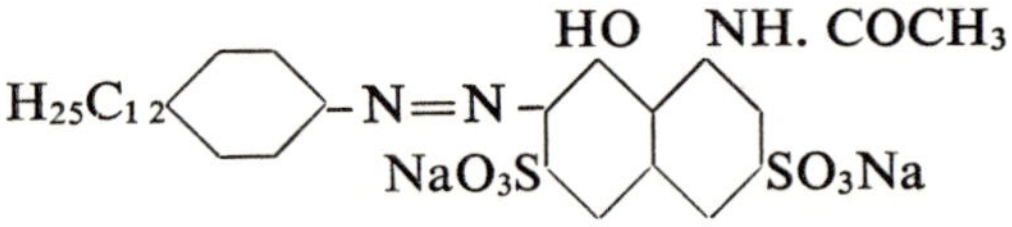

Carbolan Crimson B (ICI)

Coomassie Navy Blue 2RN is a disazo dye:

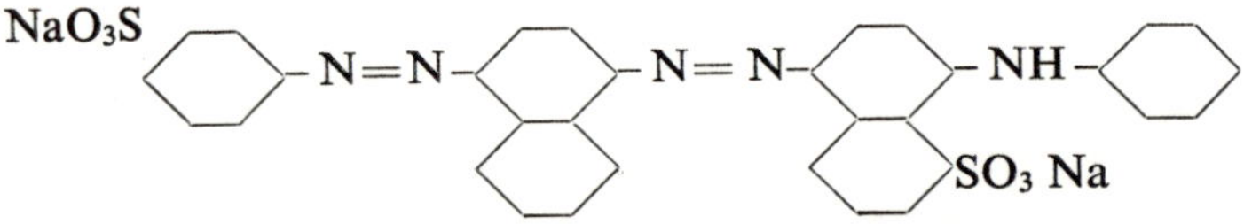

Coomassie Navy Blue 2RN (ICI)

Anthraquinone compounds provide fast-to-light violets, blues, and greens, *e.g.*, the equalizing acid dye, Solway Blue BN (ICI):

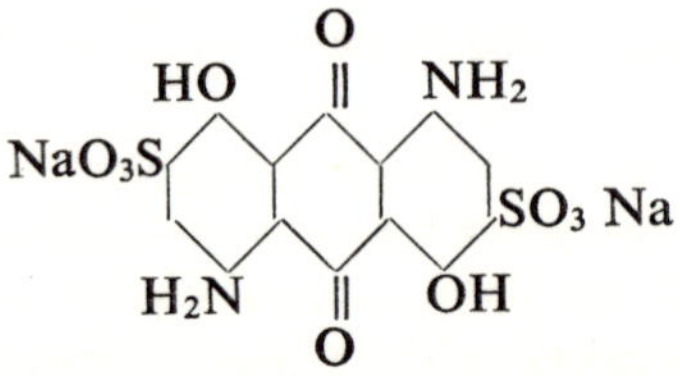

Solway Blue BN (ICI)

The neutral-dyeing Carbolan dyes, Violet 2R, Blue B, and Green G are anthraquinonoid compounds containing alkyl chains similar to that in Carbolan Crimson B (above).

The triarylmethane class provides brilliant violets, blues and greens. Unfortunately, this group of dyes gives dyeings of only moderate fastness to light.

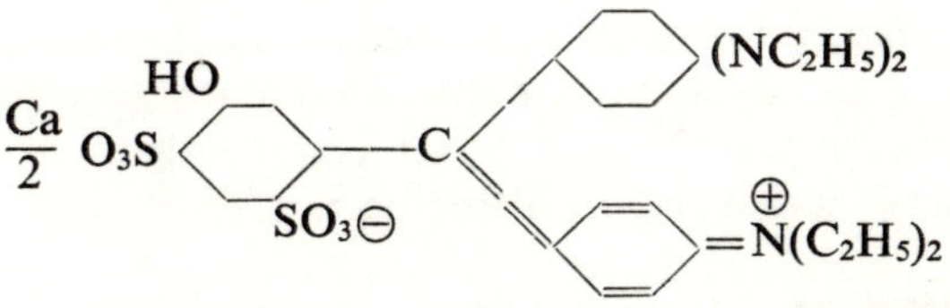

$$\frac{Ca}{2}\ O_3S \quad HO \quad \cdots C \quad (NC_2H_5)_2 \quad SO_3^{\ominus} \quad = \overset{\oplus}{N}(C_2H_5)_2$$

Disulphine Blue VN (ICI)

Important individual dyes belonging to other chemical classes include the xanthene dye, Fast Acid Violet A2R (BASF), and the azine dye, Coomassie Blue BL (ICI).

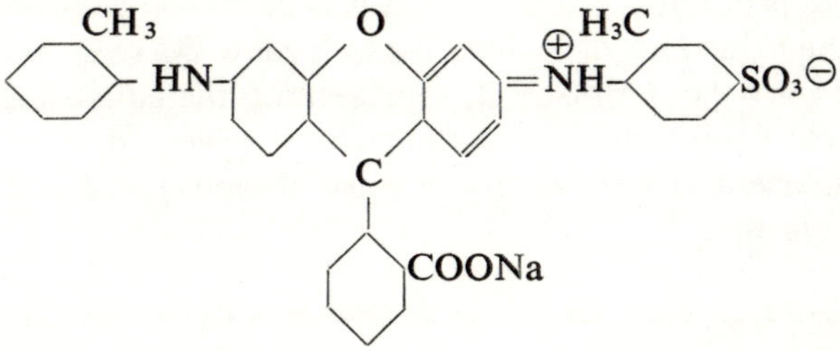

$$CH_3 \quad HN- \quad O \quad \overset{\oplus}{=}NH- \quad H_3C \quad SO_3^{\ominus} \quad C \quad COONa$$

Coomassie Violet 2R (ICI)

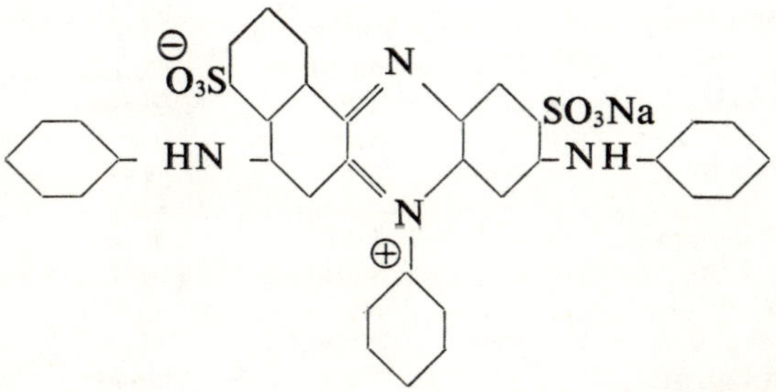

$$O_3S^{\ominus} \quad N \quad SO_3Na \quad HN- \quad -NH- \quad N^{\oplus}|$$

Coomassie Blue BL (ICI)

The brilliance of colour and high chemical stability of the phthalocyanine nucleus has led to the exploitation of phthalocyanines to provide bright blue and blue-green dyes. Coomassie Turquoise Blue 3G is a sulphonated phthalocyanine. It gives bright greenish-blue dyeings, much superior in fastness to light to those obtained using the triarylmethane blues. It cannot compare with the latter in level-dyeing behaviour but dyeings show much better fastness to wet treatments.

Dyeing Behaviour: The acid dyes are directly substantive to wool. The rate and extent of dye uptake is determined by the temperature and time of dyeing and by the pH value and electrolyte content of the dyebath. Surface active compounds also exert a considerable influence on dye absorption and are now widely used as an additional means of control. The effect of the pH of the dyebath is particularly important and forms the basis of the classification of the acid dyes recommended by the Society of Dyers & Colourists[11] as set out in Table 10.1.

TABLE 10.1. DYEING CLASSIFICATION OF ACID DYES

Group	Dyebath Addition	Final pH of Dyebath
1.	Sulphuric acid	2.5-3.0
2.	Formic acid	ca. 4.0
3.	Acetic acid	4.5-5.5
4.	Ammonium salts	6.0-8.5

The dyeing properties of the acid dyes is conveniently summarized by considering the behaviour of Xylene Light Yellow 2G (Sz), Solway Green G (ICI), and Carbolan Crimson B, representing the equalizing acid dyes, the weakly acid-dyeing dyes, and the neutral-dyeing dyes, respectively. The most important characteristics of these three representative dyes are set out in Table 10.2.

TABLE 10.2. TYPICAL PROPERTIES OF DIFFERENT CLASSES OF ACID DYES

	Equalizing	Milling	Neutral-dyeing (Supermilling)
Example	Xylene Light Yellow 2G	Solway Green G	Carbolan Crimson B
State in solution	Molecular	Colloidal	Colloidal
Degree of aggregation	Low	Medium	High
Anion affinity	Low	Medium	High
Approx. pH of dyebath..	3	4-6	6-7
Acid used	Sulphuric	Acetic	None
Levelling effect of sodium sulphate ..	High	Low	None
Rate of dyeing	Rapid	Medium	Slow
Neutral-dyeing ability	Very low	Low	High
Migration	Rapid	Slow	Very slow
Fastness to wet treatment	Poor	Good	Very good

The equalizing acid dyes dye rapidly, but also migrate readily at the boil in the presence of Glauber's salt. Thus, initially they are unlevel dyeing but redistribution (migration) of dye as dyeing proceeds results in dyeings of a high standard of levelness and penetration being obtained. At the other end of the scale, the neutral-dyeing acid dyes dye slowly at temperatures below 70-80°C. Above this temperature rate of dyeing increases rapidly, particularly with increasing acidity of the dyebath. At the same time, these dyes exhibit poor migrating power and thus uniform initial absorption is essential for level dyeing. This means that every effort must be made to establish uniform and optimum pH conditions throughout the material before dyeing proper commences. This done, the rate of dye absorption must be further controlled by controlling the rate of rise of temperature.

The establishment and maintenance of uniform pH conditions should be stressed. Most wool goods contain residual alkali from scouring. The amount of this residual alkali may not be known; its distribution will certainly be uneven. The correct pH is established and its control normally achieved by dyeing in the presence of weak acids, such as formic or acetic acid, or of acid salts, such as ammonium sulphate or acetate. If the need to add further acid to exhaust the dyebath can be avoided, this is an advantage. Distribution of additional acid throughout the material is fairly rapid at high temperatures but is certainly not instantaneous and the unavoidable, high local concentration of acid can lead to uneven absorption of dye[12].

The use of surface-active agents specifically designed to function as retarding agents when dyeing acid dyes (and other classes of wool dyes) has now become established practice. These products are basically non-ionic in character but exhibit cationic characteristics to a degree determined by the molecular structure of the individual compound. They associate with the dye in solution, particularly at low temperatures, and rate of dyeing is thereby slowed down and the equilibrium uptake of dye shifted in favour of more dye remaining in the dyebath. Consequently, distinctly more acid dyeing conditions can safely be employed. Such products include Lyogen WD (Sz), Irgasol SW (Gy), and Dispersol CWL (ICI). The magnitude of the effect that can be produced is shown by Carbolan Yellow 3G applied at pH 5.6. Addition of 3 per cent (o.w.f.) of Dispersol CWL increases the rating for level dyeing from the minimum (1) to the maximum (5)[13].

Such distinctly acid dyebath conditions are easier to establish and to maintain than are more nearly neutral conditions; under such conditions the wool is maintained in better condition and yellowing of the fibre avoided. At the same time, however, since the equilibrium absorption of the dye is shifted in favour of lower exhaustion, use of too much of these products can lead to waste of dye. Thus in the example quoted above the final exhaustion of the dyebath is reduced from 90 per cent to 70 per cent.

METAL-COMPLEX DYES

1:1 *Complexes:* Chemically these dyes are metal chelates produced by reacting, *e.g.*, o-o'-dihydroxyazo compounds with tervalent chromium compounds. An example of such a dye is Palatine Fast Blue GGN (BASF).

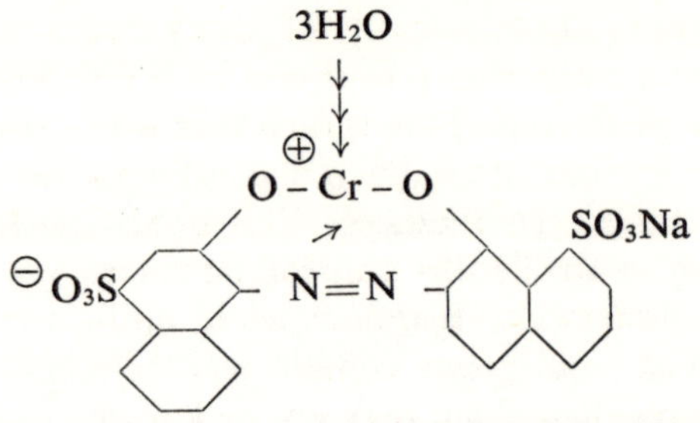

$$3H_2O$$

$$\overset{\oplus}{O} - Cr - O$$

$$^{\ominus}O_3S \quad N=N \quad SO_3Na$$

Palatine Fast Blue GGN (BASF)

This particular dye contains two sulphonic acid groups and the molecule has a net negative charge. The majority of those dyes the structure of which has been disclosed are monosulphonates. One is unsulphonated. They cover the colour range yellow to black but compared with the brightest of the acid dyes they are rather dull, a feature of the majority of metal-complex dyes.

When dyed under strongly acid conditions, pH 1·8 - 2·0, in the presence of 8-10 per cent sulphuric acid, they are characterized by high migrating power. Under progressively less acid conditions equilibrium exhaustion rises to a maximum around pH 3·5 and then falls off again. Migrating power decreases and dyeings become 'skittery'. This behaviour can be explained as follows. With these dyes attraction between the chromium atom in the dye and the imino group in the keratin molecule can occur, except under strongly acid conditions when the imino group becomes positively charged and the dye then behaves like an equalizing acid dye. Under other conditions this additional dye-fibre attraction comes into play with a consequent adverse effect on dye migration but a beneficial effect on the wet fastness of the dyeings[14]. This combination of considerable migrating power when applied under strongly acid condition and relatively high wet fastness is the main attraction of these dyes.

The use of such strongly acid dyebaths has an adverse effect upon the wool and upon the stainless steels used in the construction of dyeing machines and considerable effort has been made to develop modified dyeing methods in which less acid is required. By adding non-ionic surface-active compounds such as Neolan Salt P (CIBA) or Lissapol N (ICI) to the dyebath the amount of acid can be reduced to 5 per cent. Under such conditions the migrating power of the dye is lower but dyeings of an acceptable standard of levelness and freedom from skitteriness can be obtained. Of late the 1:1 metal-complex dyes have declined in importance since improvements in dyeing methods have led dyers to use, *e.g.*, 1:2 metal-complex dyes to obtain the desired wet fastness. For certain specific purposes, such as the dyeing of carbonized or acid-milled materials, they still offer advantages.

1:2 *Complexes:* These are a much more recent introduction, the first appearing in 1949 under the name Polar Grey BL (Gy). Like the 1:1 complexes, they are metal chelates prepared in the main from oo-dihydroxyazo compounds. A few are azamethine derivatives. The metal atom may be either chromium, cobalt, or (in one case at least) nickel. The constitution of individual dyes has so far not been disclosed, with the exception of Irgalan Brown Violet DL which is:

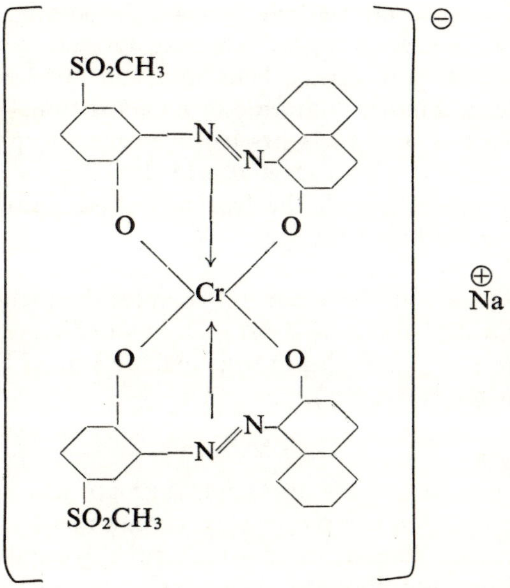

Irgalan Brown Violet DL (Gy)

This dye can be taken as typical of the original, symmetrical, unsulphonated 1:2 complexes. It is devoid of strongly polar (water-solubilizing) groups, water solubility being conferred by the methylsulphone ($-SO_2 CH_3$) groups. In solution the complex carries a negative charge thus making the dye anionic and dye absorption pH-dependent. However, because this negative charge is diffusely distributed and non-polar van der Waals forces play a large part in dye-fibre attraction, the absorption of these dyes is relatively unaffected by variations in fibre characteristics and the dyeings obtained are remarkably free from skitteriness[15].

Quite recently 1:2 metal-complex dyes containing sulphonic acid groups have appeared, *e.g.*, the Lanacron dyes (CIBA). They are fibre-selective in behaviour and thus tend to give skittery dyeings in pale depths. In full depths this is much less of a problem and, as they are cheaper, their main purpose is to provide economical browns, navies, *etc.* Like the 1:1 complexes, the 1:2 complexes give relatively dull colours, browns, greys, navies, and blacks being a feature of the many ranges now available.

Unlike the 1:1 complexes, the 1:2 complexes are 'neutral-dyeing', *i.e.*, they are applied from dyebaths which are, at most, only weakly acid (pH 5·5 to 6·5). Under controlled conditions of temperature and pH they are absorbed slowly to give very level and well-penetrated dyeings. Their migrating power is low, although not as low as that of many of the neutral-dyeing acid dyes. The dyeings have excellent fastness to light and to all except the most severe wet treatments, *e.g.*, potting. Since the individual members of the various ranges have been carefully selected on the basis of their compatibility in dyeing behaviour and fastness characteristics they can be used in mixture with little or no restriction.

Their lack of brightness has led dyemakers to provide small, supplementary ranges of neutral-dyeing acid dyes for use in conjunction with them. Such ranges include the Irganol S (Gy), Cibalan Brilliant (CIBA) and Lanasyn Brilliant (Sz) dyes.

As is the case with the other acid dyes, retarding agents have been developed for use with the 1:2 metal-complex dyes whereby dyeing may be further controlled and carried out under more distinctly acid dyebath conditions (pH 4.5-5.5). Such products include Irgasol SW, already referred to, and Lyogen SMK (Sz).

CHROME DYES

The molecules of these dyes contain groups which enable them to form stable co-ordination complexes with certain metals. The application of a chrome dye thus consists in introducing the dye and a suitable chromium compound into the fibre and then causing them to react together within the fibre to form the dye-chromium complex[16].

Chemical Structure: Most chrome dyes are azo compounds, the following examples being representative.

Eriochrome Black T (Gy)

The oo'-dihydroxyazo structure is responsible for formation of the chromium complex. In other dyes an o-amino-o'- hydroxyazo structure or an o-hydroxy-o'-carboxyazo structure confers chelating power on the dye.

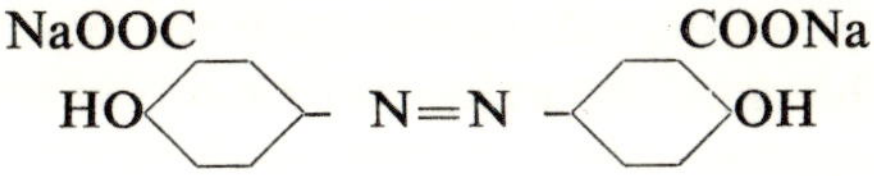

NaOOC   COONa
HO—⬡— N=N —⬡—OH

Eriochrome Flavine A (Gy)

In this case it is the salicylic acid residues which confer chelating power. In a few dyes formation of the required metal complex within the fibre is preceded by oxidation of the dye molecule to a quinone, *e.g.*

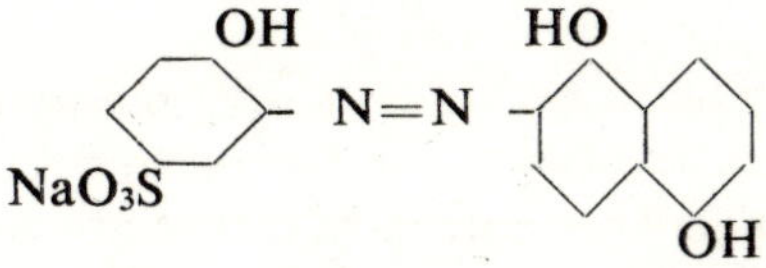

Diamond Black PV (FBy)

Without prior oxidation a valueless dull purple is obtained. Solochrome Blue FB (ICI) is another example. In this case the dye cannot behave as a chrome dye until it has been oxidized. Since, unlike normal chrome dyes, it is not sensitive to alkali it is also used as a red acid dye under the name Carmoisine W (ICI).

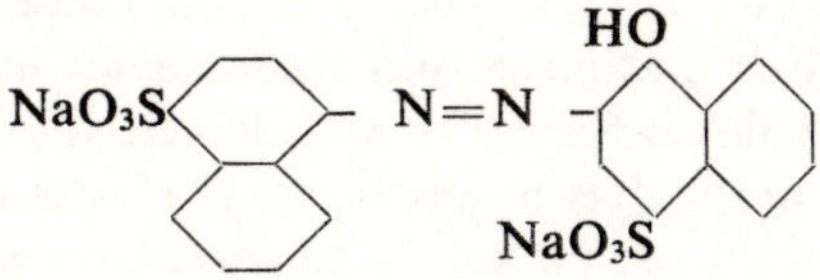

Carmoisine W (ICI)
Omega Chrome Blue FB (Sz)

Triarylmethane compounds account for some 10 per cent of chrome dyes, including some violets and the brightest blues, *e.g.*

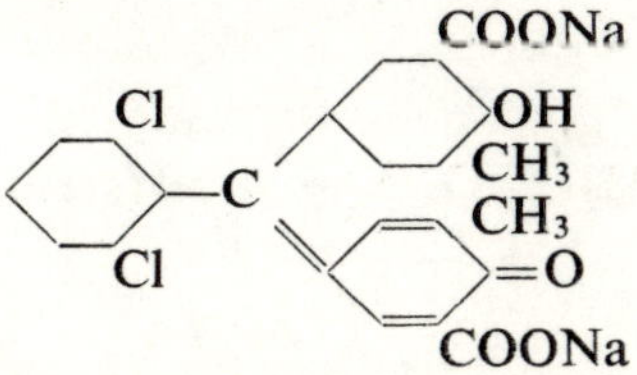

Eriochrome Azurol B (Gy)

Like the triarylmethane acid dyes, the chrome dyes in this group give dyeings of only moderate fastness to light.

Anthraquinone compounds account for 6 per cent of chrome dyes. They include Alizarin which as the natural dye, madder, has been known from the earliest times. The most important chrome dye of this class is Solway Blue Black B (ICI).

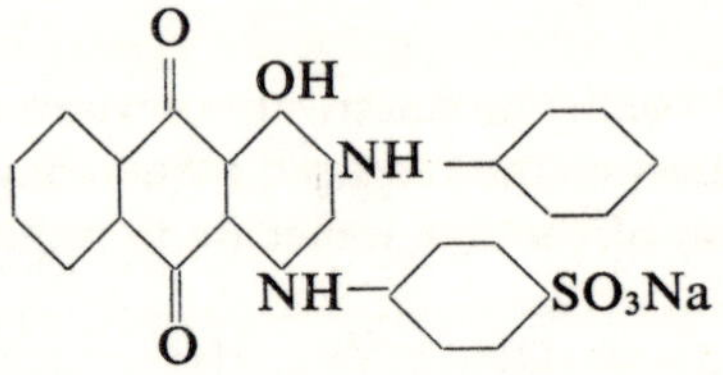

Solway Blue Black B (ICI)

Almost all the chrome dyes currently in use are sodium salts of sulphonic or carboxylic acids. As such they are soluble in water and anionic in character. Consequently they are absorbed by wool in the same manner as acid dyes although (except in the case of such dyes as Solochrome Blue FB) the sensitivity of the dyeings to alkali precludes their use as acid dyes. A few, such as Alizarin, are only slightly soluble in water. In consequence they can be applied only to wool already containing the necessary mordant.

Dyeing Behaviour: As has already been stated, chromium compounds are virtually the only mordants used when applying chrome dyes to wool. This is due largely to their cheapness and convenience in use and to the high stability of the complexes they give and, hence, the high fastness to light and wet treatments of the dyeings obtained. For batchwise, exhaustion dyeing, sexivalent chromium compounds, *e.g.*, chromates and dichromates, are used. For melange (Vigoureux) printing and for continuous dyeing, tervalent chromium salts, such as chromium fluoride and chromium acetate, are generally employed.

When wool is treated in a hot solution of a chromate or a dichromate, a complicated series of reactions occurs which may be represented in simplified fashion, thus:

$$(i) \quad \overset{+}{-NH_3}\ \overset{-}{OOC-} + H_2 CrO_4 \longrightarrow \overset{+}{-NH_3}\ \overset{-}{HCrO_4}\ HOOC-$$

Absorption of chromate ions is pH-dependent and is promoted by adding acid or acid-forming salts to the solution.

$$(ii) \quad Cr\ (VI) \longrightarrow Cr\ (III)$$

The absorbed chromate ions are progressively converted to a tervalent chromium compound which is firmly bound to the fibre. On wool this conversion proceeds very rapidly at temperatures above 70–80 °C. This is in contrast to the behaviour of, *e.g.*, polyamide fibres which also absorb chromate ions but on which conversion to the tervalent form takes place much more closely. The conversion of the loosely held sexivalent chromate ions into the firmly bound tervalent chromium compound related to Cr (OH)$_3$ is vitally important since it is only with chromium atoms in the tervalent state that the dye can co-ordinate. The ease with which it occurs determines the facility with which chrome dyes can be applied to wool[17].

Three methods are available for applying chrome dyes to wool, *viz.*, the on-chrome, afterchrome, and single-bath (metachrome, chromate, or monochrome) methods.

In the first stage of the on-chrome process the material is treated in a boiling solution of sodium, or potassium, dichromate to which may be added a reducing acid (formic acid) or acid salt (cream of tartar), or sulphuric acid. The mordant produced using dichromate alone is known as a 'sweet-chrome' mordant, that with added reducing agent as a 'reduced-chrome' mordant, and that with sulphuric acid as a 'sour-chrome' mordant. The reduced-chrome mordant is primarily intended for use with dyes which are susceptible to oxidation by Cr (VI) remaining in the fibre at the commencement of dyeing, *e.g.*, Eriochrome Red B. The mordanted material is thoroughly rinsed and then dyed in a fresh bath in the presence of a small amount of acetic acid. The temperature of the dyebath is raised slowly to boiling point and dyeing continued at the boil for one-and-a-half hours.

In the afterchrome process [18] the dye is applied first. The dyebath is set with acetic acid or with formic acid or, occasionally, with ammonium acetate. Addition of Glauber's salt is sometimes advocated. The dyeing procedure is the same as for an acid dye of the weakly acid-dyeing type and restraining agents can be used to give further control of dye absorption. The second stage of the process is conversion of the dye on the fibre into the chromium complex by treating the 'dyed' material in a solution of dichromate. Provided the dyebath is almost completely exhausted at the end of the dyeing stage, it is not necessary to use a fresh bath for the chroming stage. The dyebath is cooled to about 70 °C, 0·5-2·0 per cent dichromate added, the temperature raised rapidly to boiling point and chroming continued at the boil for 30 to 45 minutes. Cooling down before adding the dichromate is strongly recommended since failure to do so can result in uneven absorption of chromate ions with consequent local desorption of dye and an uneven final dyeing.

In the single-bath method [19] application of the dye and of the mordant proceeds simultaneously but formation of the dye-chromium complex occurs only on the fibre. The method is applicable to many chrome dyes but not to all of them. The dye is applied in the presence of a mordant which may be sodium (or potassium) chromate plus ammonium sulphate, di-chromate plus ammonia, or similar mixtures. As the temperature approaches boiling point, the absorbed chromate ions are rapidly converted into terv-alent chromium compounds. These combine equally rapidly with the dye already present in the fibre to form the non-diffusing dye-chromium com-plex. Consequently, particular care must be taken to ensure initial uniform dye absorption.

Since many chrome dyes are applicable by all three methods, choice of method is important. The great disadvantage of the on-chrome method is that it is a particularly lengthy two-stage process. A few dyes, *e.g.*, Alizarin, must be dyed on previously mordanted material. The natural mordant dye, Logwood, is almost always dyed this way. Among the advantages of the on-chrome process are regular build-up of the final colour and ease of matching.

The afterchrome method is the most widely used. It is much quicker than the on-chrome method and almost as quick as the single-bath method and permits full advantage to be taken of the migrating power of the dye during the first, acid-dyeing, stage to obtain maximum levelness and pene-tration. Matching is not easy, since chroming normally produces a marked change in the colour of the material. Traces of foreign metal ions in the dyebath, *e.g.*, iron or copper, can cause permanent dulling of the colour due to formation of the unwanted iron or copper complex of the dye. This can be prevented by adding to the dyebath a sequestering agent, *e.g.*, Irgalon BT (Gy), an ethylenediaminetetracetate, which forms very stable co-ordination compounds with these metal ions and thus prevents them from interfering.

The great advantage of the single-bath process is that it is a single-stage process. It is also the quickest of the three, although the difference between it and the afterchrome process in this respect may be smaller than anticip-ated because of the time required to ensure that dye absorption is uniform in the initial stages. As has already been stated, not all chrome dyes can be applied by this method and deep dyeings are likely to be slightly less fast to, *e.g.*, milling, potting and rubbing.

A new development in chrome dyes is their marketing as free acids, *i.e.*, in a form in which they are almost insoluble in cold water but give disper-sions of such fineness that they can be circulated though wool materials without being filtered out. The Francolane (CFMC) dyes are of this type. They are applied by the afterchrome process in the presence of acetic acid in the normal manner to give very level, well-penetrated dyeings. Their excellent level-dyeing properties are considered to be due to the fact that, as dyeing is commenced at a relatively low temperature, only a small frac-tion of the dye is in solution and thus available for absorption by the fibre.

As the temperature rises, more dye dissolves and thus by controlling the rate of rise of temperature the rate of dye uptake can readily be adjusted to the conditions. Further advantages claimed include relative insensitivity to pH, electrolytes, and hard water[20]. A range of dyes of the same type, the Crinolanes (CFMC), has also been introduced for melange printing and for continuous dyeing. These contain, in addition, a chromium compound which functions as the mordant and it is claimed that they are particularly convenient to use and are readily fixed on the fibre.

VAT AND SOLUBILIZED VAT DYES

The chief application characteristics of a vat dye are that before it can be applied to a fibre it must be converted into a soluble substantive (leuco) form and that in the final stage of the dyeing process the absorbed leuco compound is converted into insoluble particles inside the fibre. It is the size of these particles and their insolubility in most of the liquids with which the dyed materials come into contact during further processing and during use that determines the high wet fastness of the dyeings obtained. Conversion of the dye into the substantive leuco form is brought about by treating it with alkali and a reducing agent (vatting) and the material is then dyed in this alkaline solution, after which the original dye is reformed inside the fibre by exposing the dyed material to air or treating it in a dilute solution of an oxidizing agent.

The only vat dye used to any extent on wool is indigo, although selected indigoid, thioindigoid, and other sulphurized vat dyes are offered, *e.g.*, the Helindon (Hoechst) range. Indigo is one of the oldest dyes known. The natural product was used up to the end of the 19th century but from then on has been superseded by synthetic indigo. The application of indigo to wool is a separate branch of wool dyeing, based on procedures which are quite distinct in character. It is described in detail in *Theory & Practice of Wool Dyeing*, and only an outline is given here[21].

The general method of dyeing indigo is as follows. A dyevat is prepared containing leuco-indigo, sodium hydrosulphite, and ammonia. The leuco-indigo itself is prepared by treating indigo powder with Hydros (Associated Chemicals) (sodium dithionite) and sodium hydroxide solution at 50 to 60°C. It is common practice for the dyer to save himself trouble by using pre-reduced indigo, *i.e.*, a concentrated solution of leuco-indigo in caustic soda solution, *e.g.*, Indigo Vat I (ICI). The cloth to be dyed is treated in open width in the indigo dyevat for 20 to 60 minutes at 50 to 55°C, taking care to keep the material below the surface of the liquor. It is then squeezed and exposed to air which converts the greenish-yellow leuco-indigo to the blue parent dye. Since the substantivity of leuco-indigo is low, dark blues and navies are produced by re-introducing the cloth into the dyevat and re-peating the dyeing and oxidation process several times. In this way very deep colours can be obtained. The dye vat is replenished with more leuco-indigo, and alkali and reducing agent as required, and is used repeatedly until the accumulation in it of oxidation products and other material necessitates the preparation of a new bath. Since a considerable amount of loosely attached indigo remains on the surface of the cloth after the final oxidation, a thorough scouring (earthing) in a dolly scouring machine, using fuller's earth or a synthetic detergent, is essential. The sequence of chemical changes which occur when dyeing indigo can be represented:

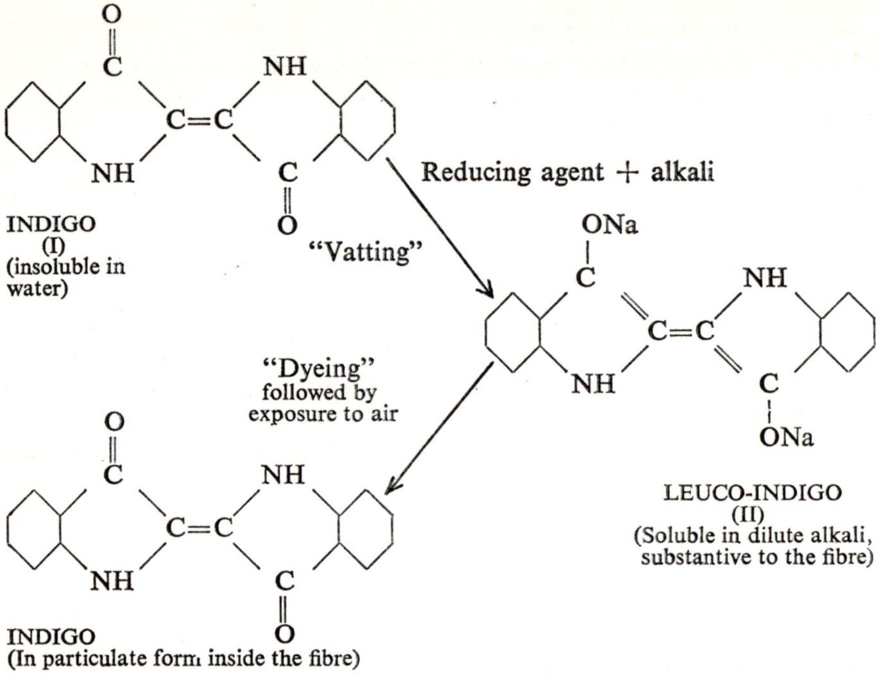

INDIGO
(I)
(insoluble in water)

"Vatting"

Reducing agent + alkali

LEUCO-INDIGO
(II)
(Soluble in dilute alkali, substantive to the fibre)

"Dyeing"
followed by
exposure to air

INDIGO
(In particulate form inside the fibre)

Indigo, today, is seldom used alone. Indigo-dyed material is usually 'topped', *i.e.*, overdyed, with either chrome dye or with acid dyes.

Solubilized vat dyes are the sodium salts of the sulphuric acid esters of the leuco-compounds of vat dyes. Among the ranges of such dyes are the Indigosols (Durand & Huguenin) and the Soledons (ICI). Thus the solubilized counterpart of indigo is:

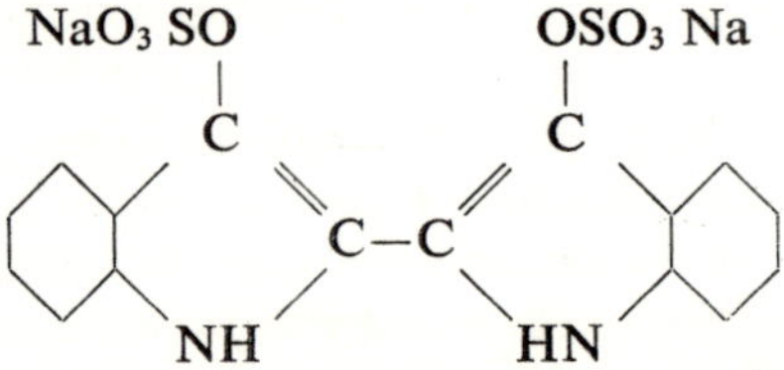

Soledon Indigo LL (ICI)

These dyes are water-soluble and anionic. They behave like fast-to-milling acid dyes as far as their absorption by wool is concerned and are normally applied under weakly acid conditions in the first stage of the dyeing process. 'Dyeing' is followed by regeneration of the parent insoluble colouring matter inside the fibre. This is done by treating the material in a strongly acid solution of ammonium persulphate, or dichromate, or – in the case of Soledon Indigo LL – sodium nitrite. The difficulty of ensuring complete development, the adverse effect on the fibre of the severe oxidative conditions which have to be used, and the skitter-dyeing behaviour of these dyes has severely restricted their use. Soledon Indigo LL is used as a useful alternative to using indigo itself[22].

REACTIVE DYES

The characteristic feature of a reactive dye[23] is that during the coloration process a covalent linkage is formed between the chromophore and the fibre by chemical reaction. The stability of this linkage and the presence within the dyed material of as little dye as possible – preferably none – not chemically bound to the fibre determines the fastness of the dyeing to wet treatments.

Wool keratin contains an abundance of groups, particularly amino groups, with which a fibre-reactive dye can react, either by an addition mechanism or by a substitution mechanism. Thus it seems surprising that the development of reactive dyes specifically for use on wool has lagged behind the development of this type of dye for cellulosic fibres. It is interesting to note that the first commercial reactive dye, Supramine Orange R (IG), a chloroacetyl dye, was produced for use on wool, but at that time it was not realized that dye-fibre combination occurred or, indeed, that such combination was of technical importance. Some of the Cibalan Brilliant dyes, and the Remalan (Hoechst) dyes, which appeared in the early 1950s, are also now stated to be capable of reacting with wool but their reactivity passed unnoticed at the time. Fibre-reactive dyes came into their own with the appearance of the Procion (ICI) dyes for cellulosic fibres in 1956 and have made astonishing progress on these fibres in a very short time.

The main reasons for the slow progress as far as wool is concerned are, firstly, the ability of existing classes of dye to meet most of the requirements of the wool dyeing trade, and secondly, the difficulty of producing on wool dyeings of reactive dyes having the fastness to wet treatments which theoretical considerations, and the performance of reactive dyes on cellulose, suggest is possible. For maximum fastness to wet treatments, the dyed material should contain as little dye not chemically combined with the wool as possible. The presence in a full-depth dyeing of an amount of uncombined dye equal to no more than 5 per cent of the total dye present

on the fibre can cause serious reduction in wet fastness, particularly as
far as staining of adjacent material is concerned. Such a high level of dye-
fibre combination is very difficult to achieve and complete removal of uncombined dye from the dyed material during the final stage of the dyeing
process is equally difficult. A further problem with existing ranges of reactive dyes is their tendency to give 'tippy' and 'skittery' dyeings, since
once the dye molecule has reacted with the fibre molecule it is incapable
of further diffusion and initial unevenness remains.

Chemical Types: A reactive dye consists essentially of a chromophore
to which is attached a grouping which can react with the fibre molecule by
substitution or by addition. The chromophore also carries one, or more,
sulphonic groups, and thus the dye also behaves as an acid dye. Reactive
groups found in reactive dyes suitable for dyeing wool include the following:

(1) *Chloro-s-triazinyl*: The Procion M- and H-dyes (ICI) contain this
group; the H-dyes contain only one reactive chlorine atom.

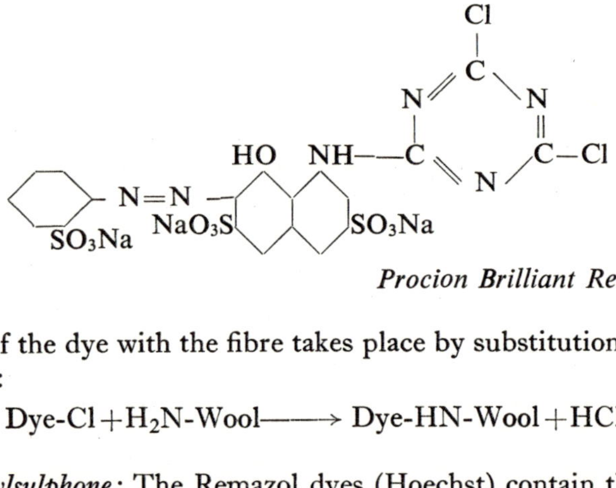

Procion Brilliant Red M-2B (ICI)

Reaction of the dye with the fibre takes place by substitution of a chlorine
atom thus:

$$\text{Dye-Cl} + \text{H}_2\text{N-Wool} \longrightarrow \text{Dye-HN-Wool} + \text{HCl}$$

(2) *Vinylsulphone:* The Remazol dyes (Hoechst) contain this group.
Reaction is by addition thus:

$$\text{Dye-SO}_2.\text{CH}_2.\text{CH}_2.\text{O}.\text{SO}_3\text{Na} \longrightarrow \text{Dye-SO}_2.\text{CH:CH}_2 \qquad (i)$$
(commercial dye)   (active vinylsulphone form)

$$\text{Dye-SO}_3.\text{CH:CH}_2 + \text{H}_2\text{N-Wool} \longrightarrow \text{Dye-SO}_2.\text{CH}_2.\text{CH}_2.\text{HN-Wool}$$

(3) *Acrylamido (or substituted acrylamido):* The Procilan dyes (ICI
are believed to contain this type of group.
$$\text{Dye-NH.OC.CH:CH}_2.$$

The chromophores present in reactive dyes are the same as those used in other types of dye, *e.g.*, azo, anthraquinone, and, for bright greenish blues, phthalocyanine. The Procilans are based on a sulphonated, 1:2 metal-complex structure.

Dyeing Behaviour: The essential stages in the dyeing process are (*i*) diffusion of the dye molecules into the fibre, (*ii*) absorption of the dye molecules at sites within the fibre, and (*iii*) reaction of the dye molecules with specific groups in the fibre molecule.

Diffusion into the fibre and absorption within it are essential prerequisites for dye-fibre combination. All reactive dyes for wool are anionic and thus their absorption is pH-dependent. Uniform absorption is vitally important, since, as has already been pointed out, once the dye has combined with the fibre no redistribution is possible. The risk of obtaining uneven, poorly penetrated, and skittery dyeings is considerable. Careful control of the dyeing conditions is very important. The use of surface-active agents specially developed for the purpose, *e.g.*, Procilan Salt L (ICI), Albegal B (CIBA), *etc.*, is considered essential for a satisfactory dyeing to be obtained.

The reactivity of the dye is also of primary importance, not only its reactivity with the fibre but also its reactivity with water. If reactivity with water is high, than a considerable proportion of the dye will be inactivated as dyeing proceeds. Further, this hydrolyzed dye will behave as a normal acid dye and be absorbed by the fibre. Since this dye is less firmly bound to the fibre than dye that has become covalently bound, the wet fastness of the dyeing will be reduced to an extent dependent upon the amount of hydrolyzed dye absorbed and its substantivity towards the fibre. In the same way, absorbed dye which remains unreacted with the fibre at the conclusion of dyeing is equally undesirable, although, in this case, some of it at least can be made to combine by extending or modifying the dyeing process.

The application of the Procion M and H dyes to wool illustrates the difficulty encountered with the more reactive type of dye. They are applied from a neutral or weakly acid bath (pH 7 to 5·5) in presence of Lissolamine A (a cationic compound) and Lubrol W (a non-ionic compound), the purpose of which is to promote level dyeing. Even when these products are used there is still a tendency to skittery dyeing, particularly in pale depths. This, and poor compatibility in mixtures, appears to have restricted their use to loose wool, slubbing, and, in a few cases, to yarn.

The Procilan (ICI) and Lanasol (CIBA) dyes are examples of ranges of reactive dyes specially developed for wool in the light of the particular problems associated with this fibre. The Procilan dyes are a logical development, based on dye-fibre reactivity and the use of a chromophore – in this case a 1:2 metal-complex – of high intrinsic substantivity. When applied at the boil at pH 6 to 6·5 for one hour, 60 to 70 per cent of the dye present on the fibre is claimed to combine chemically with it. The dye not chemically combined corresponds to, at most, a medium-depth dyeing of a conventional non-reactive, 1:2 metal-complex dye and thus the wet fastness of the dyeing is considerably higher than that of a dyeing of the same depth of a normal 1:2 complex dye. Further, this type of dye does not hydrolyze to any significant extent in the dyebath under the recommended dyeing conditions and thus dye on the fibre but not chemically combined with it is still capable of doing so. Thus by modifying the dyeing process further dye-fibre reaction can be brought about, with consequent increase in wet fastness. Recommended modifications include (*i*) extension of time of dyeing at the boil, (*ii*) increase in the maximum temperature of dyeing to 105°C, and (*iii*) addition of alkali, *e.g.*, ammonia, to the dyebath towards the end of the dyeing time to raise the pH to 8 to 8.5, dyeing being continued for a further 15 to 30 minutes at the boil under these conditions. The Procilans give dull colours, as do metal-complex dyes in general. The first Procilan Brilliant dye, Yellow 4G has been introduced (1967) to meet this difficulty. It is not metallized but fibre-reactive, being compatible in dyeing behaviour and in fastness properties with the Procilan range.

The Lanasol dyes include a yellow, an orange, two reds, and a blue, all giving bright dyeings of very good fastness to light and to wet treatments. An essential ingredient of the dyebath is Albegal B, the function of which is two-fold. Like other products it promotes level dyeing but, unlike them, it is highly substantive to the fibre and increases rate of dyeing by functioning as a 'carrier'. Addition of sodium sulphate to the dyebath is essential to ensure the maximum effectiveness of the Albegal B. The precise nature of the reactive group present in these dyes has not been disclosed but it is stated that they combine with the fibre by an addition reaction and are highly fibre-reactive, but do not hydrolyze in the dyebath under the recommended conditions of dyeing. Only a small proportion of the dye on the fibre at the end of the dyeing remains uncombined, Nevertheless, with dyeings deeper than 1/1 standard depth, or where very high fastness to wet treatments is demanded, it is recommended that as much as possible of this uncombined dye is removed by raising the pH towards the end of the dyeing process by adding ammonia and treating the material at pH 8 to 8·5 for 10 to 15 minutes at 70 to 80°C.

With dyes which are only weakly fibre-reactive, *e.g.*, the Drimarenes (Sz) which contain a chloropyrimidine group as the reactive group, slow rate of reaction assists level-dyeing but too much dye remains uncombined after dyeing at the boil for, say, 90 minutes. Lister has suggested a method of overcoming this by adding 5 to 10 per cent (o.w.f.) of ammonium thioglycollate to the dyebath. This converts cystine links into thiol (–SH) groups with which the dye reacts much more rapidly and 90 per cent dye-fibre reaction can readily be achieved. One problem is that the fission of many disulphide bonds can produce permanent adverse modification of the fibre but this is avoided by reconversion of the bulk of the thiol groups into disulphide bonds during controlled drying after dyeing. Another, quite different, problem is the additional dyeing cost arising from the use of ammonium thioglycollate.

A method has been developed for applying highly reactive dyes of the Procion M type to shrink-resisted wool slubbing under low-temperature, alkaline (pH 10·5) conditions, using a pad-batch process[24]. Dyeings of very good fastness to severe wet treatments are obtained; much better, in fact, than can be achieved by dyeing at the boil under weakly acid conditions. This is due, presumably, to the fact that under these conditions little, if any, hydrolyzed dye is absorbed by the wool. This low-temperature, alkaline dyeing process cannot be used with normal wool. In this case the rate of dye absorption is particularly low and very skittery dyeings are obtained. With shrink-resisted wool, produced by chemical treatment, the epicuticle has been removed almost completely during the process and, provided the treatment has been uniform, dye absorption at low temperature is much more rapid and even.

In addition to these more or less complete ranges of fibre-reactive dyes, a number of other dyes have been introduced recently which either are claimed to be fibre-reactive or can be assumed to be so because of the very high wet fastness of the dyeings obtained. These include the Neopolar and Irgalan Brilliant dyes of Geigy and the Drimalans of Sandoz.

DIRECT DYES

As has already been stated, the only important use of direct dyes in wool dyeing is for dyeing the wool component of wool-cellulosic fibre blends in addition to the cellulosic fibre present, thus making a single-bath dyeing process possible. The vast majority of them show very little substantivity towards wool under weakly acid or neutral conditions. This is not surprising since they are highly sulphonated. Durazol Brilliant Red B (ICI) which is of this type contains no fewer than six sulphonic acid groups and is a tetrakisazo dye.

Chrysophenine G (ICI) and Durazol Red 2B are typical of the few dyes of interest on wool. Both are disulphonated disazo dyes and are indistinguishable in dyeing behaviour and wet fastness properties from fast-to-milling acid dyes.

DEVELOPMENTS IN DYEING TECHNIQUES

IN ADDITION to the work which has greatly extended the range and effective-ness of dyes suitable for the dyeing of wool, considerable attention has been given to the possibility of developing dyeing techniques which will accelerate the process and/or bring it more into line with modern produc-tion flow methods. Such developments have taken various forms, the most promising of which are (*i*) continuous dyeing, with its obvious potential for increasing productivity, (*ii*) high-temperature dyeing in which advant-age can be taken of increased rates of dye absorption and desorption to shorten dyeing time, and (*iii*) the achievement of a similar result at lower temperatures less likely to impair the properties of the wool fibre by the adoption of solvent-assisted processes or methods involving the use of non-ionic surface-active agents.

These techniques are discussed in some detail in the following para-graphs.

CONTINUOUS DYEING

Although the bulk of wool goods is dyed using batchwise, exhaustion dyeing processes, the possibility of dyeing certain types of material con-tinuously has attracted increasing attention in the last ten years and loose wool and slubbing are now being dyed in this way. The continuous dyeing of cellulosic materials has long been established practice in the U.S.A. and certain blends of cellulosic fibres, *e.g.*, with polyester fibres, are being pro-cessed in this way. With cellulosic fibre cloths the reasons for the adoption, and the success, of continuous dyeing are (*i*) the availability of a wide range of dyes which can be fixed in a very short time, (*ii*) the high absorbency of well-prepared cloth, and (*iii*) the demand for sufficiently large amounts of material dyed to a particular colour to justify the necessary capital ex-penditure on machinery. With wool, however, the situation is markedly different and these considerations are much less compelling. It has there-fore still to be shown that continuous dyeing offers overwhelming advan-tages over highly organized batchwise dyeing based on the latest develop-ments in machinery design and automatic process control. Nevertheless the principles and practice of continuous dyeing are certain to be developed further.

Although much initial development work was carried out on cloth, the continuous dyeing of wool materials in bulk is at present confined to loose wool and slubbing. Some continuous dyeing of carpeting is also being carried out. The main technical problems to be overcome were the uniform impregnation of the material with the dye liquor and the provision of suit-able equipment for fixing the dye. The relatively hydrophobic character of the surface of the wool fibre makes it difficult to distribute an aqueous solution uniformly through a mass of wool by impregnation and squeezing. Concentration of the liquid in the middle of the mass occurs, giving rise to the so-called 'sandwich effect'. This can be overcome by adding to the pad-liquor surface-active compounds specifically designed to eliminate the water-repellency of the fibre surface. At the same time padding and steaming equipment suitable for slubbing and loose wool has been developed.

The Cibaphasol (CIBA)[25] and Irgapadol (Gy)[26] systems can be taken as typical. In the Cibaphasol process the material is impregnated with a pad liquor which contains dye and dyeing assistants and also 40-50 grams per litre of Cibaphasol AS, a product which converts the pad-liquor into a 'coacervate' in the form of an emulsion in which the dye and the bulk of the Cibaphasol is contained in the disperse phase and the other ingredients in the continuous phase. When the wool is impregnated with this liquor each fibre is covered with a film of the dye-containing phase, regardless of the surface characteristics of the fibre. No accumulation of dye in the centre of the mass of material occurs and the sandwich effect is avoided. During subsequent steaming the dye diffuses from the surface film into that part of the fibre adjacent to it. There is no opportunity for the dye to transfer itself to any point at a distance and thus, if initial distribution of pad liquor has been uniform, a uniform dyeing is obtained. Irgapadol P, the essential additive in the Irgapadol process, achieves the same end although it does not give a two-phase pad-liquor. One particular feature of this product is that it causes the fibres to 'balloon' apart when the impregnated slubbing or loose wool first comes into contact with the steam during fixation. The effect lasts for a few seconds only but is considered to be particularly valuable in promoting the essential rapid diffusion of dye into the fibre in the initial stage of steaming. Lyogen V (Sz) and Levalin VK and VKC (Bayer) are products offered for the same purpose.

Suitable dyes include acid, 1:2 metal-complex, and chrome dyes. Chrome dyes can be applied by a single-stage process, the necessary mordant being incorporated in the pad liquor. There is some limitation as far as chrome blacks are concerned. Thus the Chrome Fast Black CAT type is not suitable for application by a single-stage process but can be applied by a two-step method in which the dyed slubbing is padded with a chromium salt and then steamed and backwashed for a second time. The more expensive Chrome Fast Black BCP (a special form of Chrome Fast Black A) can be applied in a one-stage process.

Dye fixation is achieved by steaming. Using saturated steam at atmospheric pressure at 100-102°C, steaming times of 15 to 45 minutes are required depending upon depth of colour and type of dye. Using steam under pressure, fixation can be achieved in a much shorter time, *e.g.*, 10 to 25 minutes at 108-110°C. Several steamers have been developed which are suitable for steaming slubbing or loose wool. The construction and use of such steamers is described later in the section on dyeing machinery.

HIGH-TEMPERATURE DYEING

The rate of absorption and desorption of a dye by a fibre increases with the dyeing temperature and the time required to obtain a level, well penetrated dyeing is reduced[27]. The magnitude of the increase in diffusion rate depends upon the activation energy of the particular dye-fibre system. Where activation energy is low, *e.g.* with Class A direct dyes on cellulosic fibres, little is gained by raising the temperature much above 95°C and, in fact, the reduction in equilibrium exhaustion which occurs may offset the advantage of more rapid dyeing. The activation energy of dyeing wool with fast-to-milling acid, 1:2 metal-complex, and certain chrome dyes is high enough for high-temperature dyeing to be of interest. Stability of the dye and of the fibre under the dyeing conditions employed is essential. Some dyes are not sufficiently stable but many can be applied at temperatures well above 100°C without fear of decomposition.

A much more serious matter is the progressive breakdown of wool keratin when wool is treated in hot aqueous solutions at pH values from 7 upwards, and below pH 3. Consequently, it is recommended that the maximum dyeing temperature should not exceed 105-107°C, the maximum time at this temperature should not exceed 60 minutes, and the pH value should be within the range 3.5 – 6.5. Such conditions are normally more than adequate to attain equilibrium absorption.

Dyeing machines capable of operating at this temperature are readily available for dyeing loose stock, slubbing, and yarn. Pressurized winches are also available for dyeing cloth. Pressurized beam-dyeing machines for dyeing synthetic fibre cloths are becoming very common but these are not yet used for dyeing wool cloths, presumably because of the effect on the handle of the material of treating it under tension and compression at such temperatures. Totally enclosed machines can be used to advantage for dyeing at 100°C, since, operating as they do under slight pressure, this temperature can be achieved without cavitation due to steam in the pump and consequent poor liquor circulation. With open machines the maximum temperature attainable without serious loss of efficiency from this cause is about 90°C.

LOW-TEMPERATURE DYEING

A feature of development in wool dyeing in recent years has been the introduction of methods for reducing the maximum dyeing temperature. Evidence has been accumulated which suggests that significant improvement in various physical properties of the dyed material results if dyeing is carried out at temperatures not exceeding 8c-90°C. The strength, elasticity, and abrasion resistance of fibres are higher and this is reflected in better spinning yields and better wearing properties. If, however, the maximum dyeing temperature is lowered without any further modification of the dyeing process, the standard of levelness and penetration decreases progressively and the fastness of the dyeing to wet treatments is reduced until the quality of the dyeing becomes unacceptable. A variety of modifications to the dyeing process has been suggested, all of which claim that the desired lowering of the dyeing temperature can be achieved, with its attendant advantages, without any loss in dyeing quality.

The first of these was the so-called 'solvent-assisted' dyeing process based on the observation by Peters and Stevens in 1956[28,29] that addition of certain sparingly water-soluble alcohols, etc., to conventional dyebaths produced a marked increase in the rate of uptake of certain fast-to-milling acid, 1:2 metal-complex, and chrome dyes, with the result that dyeings of the same order of wet fastness could be obtained at temperatures considerably below 100°C. Arising out of these observations, Geigy (U.K.) Ltd. introduced its Irga-Solvent processes for dyeing loose stock, slubbing, and yarn. The essential features of these processes are that dyeing is carried out for 30 to 45 minutes at 80-90°C in the presence of the requisite amount of acid and from 0.7 per cent to 2 per cent of benzyl alcohol (calculated on the volume of the dyebath), the lower the temperature the higher being the concentration of benzyl alcohol required.

This procedure is certainly highly effective technically, but the obvious drawback is the cost of adding such an amount of a relatively expensive additive to the dyebath. By re-using the exhausted dyebath, after replenishing it with an amount of benzyl alcohol to replace that lost during removal of the previous load – approximately 0.3 per cent of benzyl alcohol (by volume) when using a liquor:material ratio of 20:1 – for a number of times, it is possible to offset this additional cost. Re-use of the dye bath in this way is perfectly feasible but requires care when the series of dyeings is to different colours. The additional cost of the solvent is much less significant when dyeing expensive fibres which are very easily damaged, *e.g.* cashmere.

In contrast to the relatively large amounts of solvents such as benzyl alcohol needed to produce the desired effect, it has been claimed[30] that addition to the dyebath of 0.5-2.0 per cent (calculated on weight of material) of certain non-ionic polyethylene oxide condensation products enables satisfactory dyeings to be obtained using a dyebath of pH 3.6-4.2 and dyeing at a maximum of 90°C for 20 to 30 minutes. The bulk of the work on this development has been carried out by the C.S.I.R.O. which examined a large number of polyethylene oxide condensation products based on octyl- and nonyl-phenol and containing 15 to 45 ethylene oxide residues per molecule of the phenol. It was found that condensates of nonylphenol and 6 to 10 ethylene oxide residues gave the best results as far as penetration and dyebath exhaustion were concerned, excellent dyeings of the complete range of 1 : 2 metal-complex dyes being obtained under the conditions given above. One disadvantage is that washing fastness is slightly lower (less than half-a-point on a 1 – 5 scale) than that of dyeings produced by dyeing at pH 5 – 7 for one hour at the boil.

The general effect on dyeing behaviour of adding the recommended type of non-ionic product is to reduce rate of absorption, although not to the same extent as occurs when non-ionic products having longer ethylene oxide chains are used. No final conclusions have been reached as to the way in which these products function, but as they are absorbed by the fibre under the conditions employed, it is suggested that they act in the same way as solvents such as benzyl alcohol, *i.e.* by increasing the rate of diffusion of the dye through the fibre surface, and increasing the mobility of the dye molecules inside the fibre by reducing the forces of attraction between them and the sites for dye absorption. Since this type of product is relatively cheap and the amount required to be used is small, the major drawback to the solvent-assisted process is overcome.

Solvent-assisted dyeing, and dyeing in the presence of non-ionic surface active agents of the type described, are commercial propositions. Two other suggestions recently put forward are dyeing in the presence of formic acid and dyeing in the presence of urea, but so far the processes are only in the development stage.

In 1959, Harrap reported a considerable increase in the rate of absorption of a wide range of dyes by wool when concentrated (70 per cent or higher solutions of formic acid were used instead of the normal aqueous dyebaths. Subsequent investigations by Milligan showed that dyeings as fast to washing as conventional dyeings could be obtained in as little as two minutes, using selected acid and metal-complex dyes and a dyebath containing 90 per cent formic acid[31]. Continuous dyeing of slubbing has been carried out on a pilot plant scale using an azeotropic mixture of formic acid and water containing approximately 77 per cent of acid and dyeing at 50°C. It is claimed that there is no detectable damage to the wool and that the dyeings are brighter than those produced conventionally at the boil. The equipment must be proof against attack by formic acid of this concentration and special precautions must be taken in handling the dye liquor. More important still, it is essential to recover the formic acid. This necessitates distillation. A more likely application of this idea is in melange (vigoureux) printing and direct printing of wool using a paste containing dye, thickener, and formic acid. Excellent prints are claimed without a need for steaming to promote dye transfer and fixation.

In 1964, Angliss and Delmenico suggested that concentrated solutions of urea might provide a less expensive alternative to formic acid[32]. They found that extremely rapid fixation of dyes could be achieved in 10 minutes at room temperature or in 30 to 120 seconds by steaming at 100°C. Such steaming times are considered to be sufficiently short for realistic continuous pad-dyeing and printing processes. Preliminary tests indicated that the wet fastness of the dyeings was the same as that of conventional dyeings.

In 1968 Lewis and Seltzer[35] described a process for producing fast, bright dyeings on wool cloth using a pad-batch (cold) process. The cloth is padded with a liquor containing a reactive dye (preferably of the highly reactive type), urea (300g. per litre), wetting agent and acetic acid. Batching for up to 24 hours at room temperature under mildly acidic conditions is claimed to give virtually 100 per cent dye-fibre fixation. Yellowing of the wool does not occur and consequently dyeings of a brightness and fastness that cannot be achieved using conventional dyeing methods are obtained.

COLOUR FASTNESS

IT IS A FUNDAMENTAL REQUIREMENT of dyed or printed textiles that, as far as their colour is concerned, they should withstand the conditions encountered during any subsequent processing and during use. In consequence, frequent reference has been made to colour fastness in describing and discussing the behaviour and merits of the various classes of dye used for dyeing wool.

Currently, a good deal of attention is being paid to standards of performance in respect of colour fastness as well as of other properties of textile materials. Textile articles today are often accompanied by a variety of labels, many of which have implications as far as colour fastness is concerned[33]. These labels are sponsored not only by textile manufacturers, wholesalers and retailers, but also by makers of dyes, fibres, detergents and washing appliances, dyers and printers, national standards authorities, retail organizations, and magazines. A national labelling scheme which includes textiles has been announced by the Consumer Council. As far as wool is concerned, one important development in this direction is the setting up of the 'Woolmark' by the International Wool Secretariat.

It is not proposed to include here a detailed account of the determination of colour fastness. Suffice it to say that colour fastness testing has now reached an advanced stage of organization on an international scale through the activity of the International Standards Organisation based on the work of national bodies such as the Society of Dyers & Colourists, operating through its Fastness Tests Co-ordinating Committee. Definitive tests covering a wide range of agencies have been approved and published and the reader is referred to the third edition of *Standard Methods for the Determination of the Colour Fastness of Textiles* and the supplement thereto[34], published by the Society of Dyers & Colourists. It should be noted that developments in colour fastness testing continue and care should be taken to see that testing is carried out according to the latest recommendations.

When coloured textiles are exposed to any particular agency – light, washing, bleaching, etc. – one, or both, of the following effects may occur, As far as the coloured material itself is concerned, there may be an alteration in the depth of colour, in hue, in brightness or in any combination of them. Thus, for example, a red material may become paler, yellower, and duller. At the same time, particularly under the influence of such agencies as washing, perspiration, etc., adjacent white or coloured materials may acquire new colour due to transfer of dye under the conditions employed, such changes being described as 'staining' or 'marking-off'.

The colour fastness of a textile material is therefore defined as its resistance to these changes when subjected to a particular agency, and is specified in terms of the magnitude of the changes which occur. The determination of colour fastness requires that this be assessed as objectively and precisely as the circumstances demand. For a fastness test and fastness rating to be of value, certain requirements must be met. Firstly, the test conditions must correspond as closely as possible to the conditions encountered in practice, and yet be readily reproducible. Secondly, the method of assessing the change in colour and staining consequent upon exposure must be as objective as possible, otherwise the results are of value only to the person obtaining them and likely to be of no more than temporary value to him. Thirdly, the time required to carry out the test and to make the assessments must be as short as possible, consistent with accuracy and reliability, since further progress in manufacture or in marketing often has to await the results of the test.

Fastness ratings in respect of change in colour of the pattern and of staining of adjacent material (where this is measured) are expressed numerically on a 1 to 5 scale (1 to 8 in the case of fastness to light) where 1 represents the lowest and 5 (or 8) the highest fastness. The numerical rating is supplemented by verbal description – weaker, redder, duller, etc. – as required. The ratings are arrived at by comparing the tested sample (or the accompanying white material) with the original coloured material (or the original white) and determining the contrast between them using either the Grey Scale for Assessing Change in Colour (for the pair of coloured samples) or the Grey Scale for Assessing Staining (for the pair consisting of the original white sample and the stained sample). The fastness rating is the number of the Grey Scale contrast judged to be nearest to the contrast observed between the pairs of samples. The use of the Grey Scale thus provides an objective standard of reference as well as a measure of the change.

The determination of fastness to light is an exception. In this case the standard of reference is a series of eight blue dyeings on wool cloth which are exposed to light (daylight or xenon arc) together with the sample under test. The light fastness of the sample is the number of the reference dyeing which is the nearest in its fading behaviour to the sample. The Grey Scale for Assessing Change in Colour is used to determine the extent to which the pattern must fade before the assessment is made.

The fastness of a dyeing depends upon the amount of dye present on the fibre, *i.e.* upon the depth of the dyeing. Fastness to light increases with increasing depth; fastness to washing and to wet treatments decreases with increasing depth, primarily because of the greater possiblity of staining of adjacent material. Dyemakers are well aware of this and for each dye provide fastness ratings for a range of dyeings, known as Standard Depths.

It should be emphasized that the purpose of a fastness test is to provide an indication of the way in which a particular coloured textile material is likely to perform in use and its ability to do so depends upon the factors considered above. It has nothing to do with fitness for use. This requires that many other factors be taken into account and entails a subjective judgment in the last resort. The linking of objective, quantitiatve assessments of colour fastness, *e.g.*, light fastness, to the end-use of coloured textiles in order to provide a minimum performance standard is considered by many to be highly desirable. Indeed, it has been suggested that the extension of the British Standards Institution procedure of establishing minimum performance standards is the only method of ensuring adequate consumer satisfaction in respect of colour fastness, other than to washing, dry-cleaning, and ironing, which conscientious care-labelling should cover.

REFERENCES

1. International Wool Secretariat. *Wool Science Review*, 1966, No. 30, p. 1.
2. Speakman and Smith, *J. Soc. Dyers & Col.*, 1936, **52**, 121; Royer, Millson and Stearns, *Amer. Dyestuff Rep.*, 1943, **32**, 285; Brommelsiek, von Bergen and Millson, *ibid.*, 1955, **44**, (3), 73.
3. Hadfield and Lemin, *J. Soc. Dyers & Col.*, 1961, **77**, 715.
4. Peel, *ibid.*, 1943, **59**, 2; Cookson, Hine and McPhee, *ibid.*, 1964, **80**, 196.
5. Townend, *ibid.*, 1945, **61**, 144; Hadfield and Lemin, *ibid.*, 1961, **77**, 97.
6. Turner, *ibid.*, **71**, 29, 96; Peters, *ibididem.*, 174, 724; Bird, *ibid.*, 1956, **72**, 343; Giles, *J. Soc. Chem. Ind.*, 1966, **92**, 137; Zollinger, *J. Soc. Dyers & Col.*, 1965, **81**, 345; International Wool Secretariat. *Wool Science Review*, 1967, No. 31, p. 32.
7. Derbyshire, *Hexagon Digest*, 1955, No. 21, 12.
8. Stevens, *Wool Science Review*, 1956, No. 16, p. 15.
9. Barritt and Elsworth, *J. Soc. Dyers & Col.*, 1948, **64**, 19; Stevens, Whewell and Bradley, *ibid.*, 1950, **66**, 435.
10. Stevens, *Wool Science Review*, 1956, No. 15, p. 14.
11. S.D.C. Committee on Dyeing Properties of Wool Dyes, *J. Soc. Dyers & Col.*, 1950, **66**, 213.
12. Lister, *ibid.*, 1949, **65**, 97; Lemin and Rattee, *ibididem.*, 217; Hannay and Major, *ibid.*, 1953, **69**, 195; Peryman, *ibid.*, 1948, **64**, 283; 1954, **70**, 83; 1955, **71**, 165; 1957, **73**, 455.
13. Technical Information (Dyehouse) No. 771, I.C.I. Dyestuffs Division.
14. Rattee, *J. Soc. Dyers & Col.*, 1953, **69**, 288; see also ref. 5. Hadfield and Lemin, and ref. 12. Lemin and Rattee.

15. Schetty, *ibid.*, 1955, **71**, 705.
16. Gaunt, *ibid.*, 1954, **70**, 46; 1951, **67**, 570.
17. Carlene, Rowe and Speakman, *ibid.*, 1946, **62**, 372.
18. Gaunt, *ibid.*, 1949, **65**, 429; *Technical Information (Dyehouse)*, 1959, No. 512 and 516. I.C.I. Dyestuffs Division.
19. Stevens, Rowe and Speakman, *J. Soc. Dyers & Col.*, 1943, **59**, 165; Lister, *ibid.*, 1952, **68**, 49; Hannay, Major and Pickin, *ibid.*, 1952, **68**, 373.
20. Stevens, 'Survey of Developments in Dyeing and Finishing', *Wool Record*, April, 1967, p. 11.
21. Bird, C. L., 'Theory and Practice of Wool Dyeing', (*3rd Edition*). Society of Dyers & Colourists. Bradford, 1963.
22. *Technical Information (Dyehouse)*, 1959, No. 507. I.C.I. Dyestuffs Division; Luttringhaus, *Amer. Dyestuffs Rep.*, 1949, **38**, 172.
23. Hadfield and Lemin, *J. Text. Inst.*, 1960, **51**, T1351; Lewis, Rattee and Stevens, 3rd Wool Textile Research Conf. (CIRTEL), Paris, 1965, p. 305; Derbyshire and Tristram, *J. Soc. Dyers & Col.*, 1965, **81**, 584.
24. Stevenson and Stevenson, *J. Text. Inst.*, 1962, **53**, P649.
25. Casty, *CIBA Review*, 1961, No. 6, p. 26; *idem.*, *Textil-Rund.*, 1963, **18**, 538.
26. Beal, *J. Soc. Dyers & Col.*, 1967, **83**, 3.
27. Iannarone, Clapham and Thomas, *Amer. Dyestuff Rep.*, 1943, **42**, P666; Coutie, Lemin and Sagar, *J. Soc. Dyers & Col.*, 1955, **71**, 433; *Technical Information (Dyehouse)*, 1963, No. 681. I.C.I. Dyestuffs Division.
28. Peters, Stevens et al., *J. Soc. Dyers & Col.*, 1960, **76**, 543.
29. Beal, Dickinson and Bellhouse, *ibid.*, 1960, **76**, 333.
30. Hine and McPhee, *International Dyer*, 1964, **132**, 523; *Idem.* 3rd Wool Textile Research Conf. (CIRTEL), Paris, 1965, p. 261.
31. Harrap, *J. Soc. Dyers & Col.*, 1959, **75**, 106; Milligan, *ibid.*, 1961, **77**, 106.
32. Angliss and Delmenico, *ibid.*, 1964, **80**, 543.
33. McLaren, *ibid.*, 1965, **81**, 522.
34. Society of Dyers & Colourists, Bradford. 'Standard Methods for the Determination of the Colour Fastness of Textiles', (3rd Edition), 1962; Supplement, 1966.
35. Lewis and Seltzer, *J. Soc. Dyers & Col.*, 1968, **84**, 501.

PRACTICAL WOOL DYEING

THE DYER of any type of fibrous material has three general responsibilities. First, he must dye the material to match the colour required, and, at the same time, produce a dyeing having a satisfactory standard of levelness and penetration, and sufficiently permanent ('fast') to withstand conditions encountered during subsequent processing and use. Second, he must preserve, as far as possible, the characteristic properties of the material, in particular its strength, elasticity, abrasion resistance, dimensional characteristics, and 'handle' – that property which is so hard to define and so important to the merchant and to his customer. Third, he must hold the cost of dyeing at a satisfactory level in relation to the price obtainable for the dyed goods. Current practice and new developments must continually be evaluated by reference to these requirements. Their relative importance in any particular instance will differ, but the third is always of major importance and often the most important factor.

Dyeing is but one stage in the conversion of wool from its original state to the finished material and the particular dyeing process used depends entirely upon the type of final product required by the manufacturer. Thus, before the dyer can decide upon what dyes to apply and what dyeing methods to use, he must know something of the processes through which the material has still to pass and the intended use of the finished goods. Further, some knowledge of the processes to which the material has already been subjected is desirable, since processing prior to dyeing can produce considerable modification of the dyeing behaviour of wool.

Wool is converted into yarn on either the woollen or the worsted system and the points at which dyeing can be carried out are shown on the abridged flow charts of Figs. 11.1 and 11.2. Not all the processes are shown, nor all the possible variations in procedure. Further, and obviously, dyeing is carried out at one stage only.

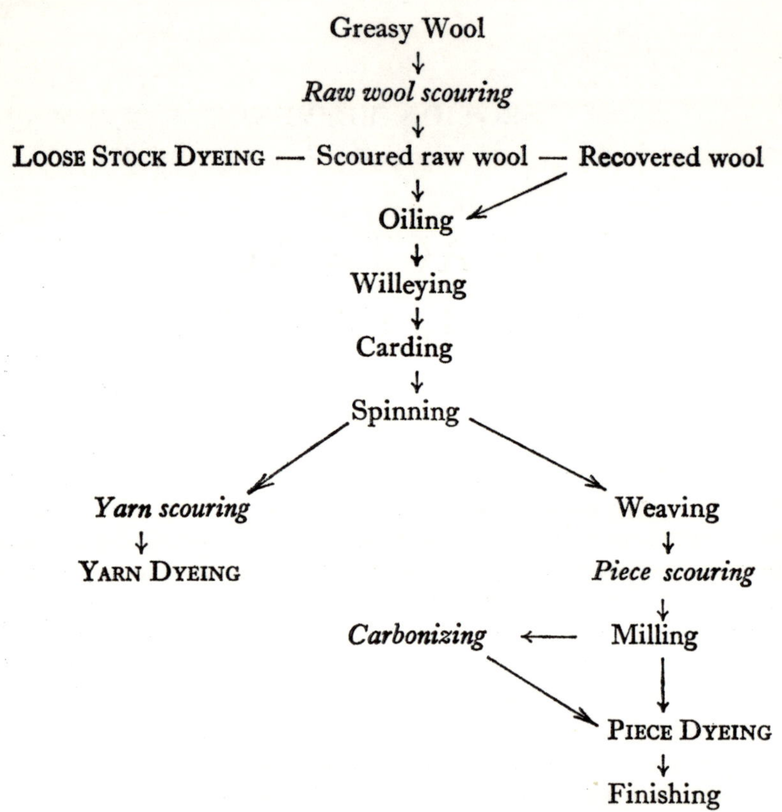

FIG. 11.1 PROCESSING ON THE WOOLLEN SYSTEM

N.B.—Wet processes are italicized; dyeing operations are indicated in capitals.

There are many variants within each of the two main classes of wool materials and a very great number of wool textures. Consequently, the dyeing of wool is not dealt with here under the headings, woollen and worsted, but according to the form in which the material is dyed. These forms include (i) loose wool, (ii) slubbing, (iii) yarn (iv) cloth, (a) woven and (b) knitted, and (v) made-up or partly made-up articles.

Before considering wool dyeing practice, some comment on the effect on dyeing of processing prior to dyeing, and on the importance of controlling such processing, is necessary. It is no exaggeration to say that a large proportion of the troubles experienced by the wool dyer is attributable to some technical fault in the earlier processes. It is imperative to the production of a satisfactory dyeing that every care should be taken to see that

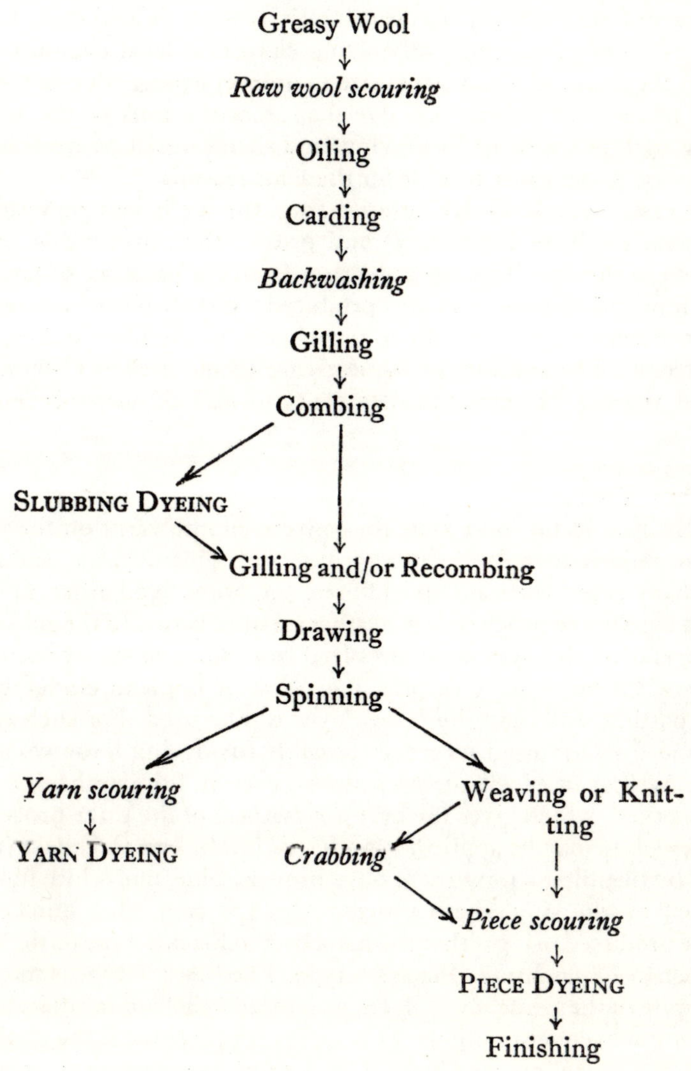

FIG. 11.2 PROCESSING ON THE WORSTED SYSTEM

N.B.—Wet processes are italicized; dyeing operations are indicated in capitals.

preparatory processes such as scouring, carbonizing and milling, should be carried out in such a way that the material delivered to the dyer is as uniform in its dyeing behaviour as possible and does not contain any residual substances which could cause breakdown of the dyes in the dyebath.

Thus, inadequate control of the pH value during scouring may lead to damage to the wool by alkali, either general or local, and confer on the wool in the damaged areas an increased substantivity towards acid dyes. Careless handling of woollens during carbonizing can cause local chemical modification of the material which gives rise to unlevel dyeings due to the acid-damaged material absorbing less dye than does the bulk of the material. Bleaching with peroxide or by stoving, and shrink-resist treatments using chemical means, can cause trouble for the same reasons.

Many cases of unlevel dyeing arise from the inefficient removal of oil (*e.g.* mineral oil from machinery) and grease, thus preventing uniform penetration of the dye. Trouble also arises from the presence of fatty acids or of calcium and magnesium soaps produced when soap has been used as a detergent. Such compounds adhere tenaciously to the fibre and can cause uneven dyeing. The addition of sequestering agents such as Calgon to the water and the use of synthetic detergents instead of soap prevents this trouble.

LOOSE WOOL DYEING

Wool is dyed in the loose state for conversion into yarns on the woollen system, for mixing with dyed cotton or viscose for blend yarns, and for felt hats. In many cases white and dyed fibres, and fibres dyed different colours are mixed together to produce, *e.g.* heather mixture yarns. In the subsequent milling operation the dyes must not bleed from some of the fibres or yarns onto others. Certain woollen cloths, *e.g.* West of England cloths, have to undergo potting, and only the fastest dyes can be used. For such reasons, the chrome dyes are used wherever possible for dyeing loose wool, since they give dyeings of excellent wet fastness, even in full depths. The after-chrome method, which gives the best wet fastness of the three processes by which these dyes may be applied, is preferred but brown and khaki (usually obtained by blending a mixture of olive browns, blue, and white fibres) are often dyed by the single-bath process which is somewhat quicker. The blacks are produced using either the Eriochrome Black T type or the slightly more expensive Solochrome Black PV type. The Black T type is most often used, in spite of the tendency of dyeings to bleed yellow onto adjacent white wool during subsequent milling. This defect is prevented if the cloth is not left lying in an alkaline condition. The natural dye, Logwood, is particularly suitable for dyeing loose wool, giving a good black of excellent fastness to milling. Navies are produced with, *e.g.*, Solochrome Dark Blue B, shaded as required with Eriochrome Azurol B to brighten the colour.

Neutral-dyeing 1:2 metal-complex dyes are suitable for dyeing loose wool for carpets, particularly fawns, browns, olives, and greys. Dyes of the unsulphonated type are particularly useful because they cover tippy wool very well and do not show fibre selectivity when a blend of different types of wool is being dyed.

Although the chrome dyes provide the cheapest and most convenient way of obtaining dyeings of high all-round fastness, they are not particularly bright and, in general, the brightest members do not exhibit the best fastness properties. There is no bright chrome green, the bright chrome blues and violets have rather poor fastness to light, and the range of chrome reds is limited. The same problem of lack of brightness is encountered with the metal-complex dyes which are of no use where bright pastel colours are required.

To meet these deficiencies, acid dyes are used, either alone or in mixture with chrome dyes. In the latter case it is essential to choose dyes which are not affected by chromates and dichromates in the dyebath, *e.g.* the anthraquinone acid dyes such as Solway Green G. The Carbolan range of acid dyes (ICI) containing a long alkyl chain give bright dyeings of very good fastness to wet treatments, being in some cases almost the equal of the chrome dyes in this aspect.

The dyeing of carbonized rags can be regarded as a branch of loose wool dyeing. Fastness to milling is almost always essential as the resulting woollen cloth is generally milled. Good penetration into the rags is also essential to avoid a 'heathery' appearance when the rags are pulled up. Since the rags are always coloured, even if they have been stripped, it is usually necessary to use bright dyes to obtain the required colour. Finally, the dyes must be cheap since the price commanded by the finished cloth it not high. The type of dye commonly used is represented by the Wool Fast Blues, the Brilliant Wool Blues, and the Milling Scarlets. Where the colour will permit, the most level dyeing and tinctorially strong chrome dyes are used. Logwood is largely used, one of its advantages being a 5 per cent increase in weight of the material after dyeing. With gas-carbonized rags there is the possibility of traces of iron remaining in the material after carbonizing and it may be advisable to add a sequestering agent, *e.g.* Irgalon BT, when using iron-sensitive chrome dyes.

SLUBBING DYEING

In the case of worsted materials, slubbing dyeing[1] takes the place of loose wool dyeing. It is used for producing solid-colour yarns as well as blended yarns, *e.g.* greys, for weaving and knitting. Even though dyeing in slubbing form impairs to some extent the spinning properties of the fibres and the coloured waste produced after combing is less valuable, it is often necessary, or desirable, when using dyes of high wet fastness, to dye as slubbing so as to obtain the highest standard of levelness and penetration in the final yarn and cloth. The highest quality coloured yarns are produced in this way.

The processes which dyed slubbing has to undergo are usually less severe than are those applied to dyed loose wool. Thus milling, if carried out, is generally light. However, it is not safe to generalize, because there is a wide variation in the severity of the treatments applied and the slubbing dyer must choose his dyes accordingly.

All the dyes mentioned as suitable for dyeing loose wool, with the exception of Logwood, are suitable for dyeing slubbing, The solubility of the dye is an important factor when dyeing slubbing in top form, *i.e.* in the form of cross-wound balls, and the dye liquor is pumped through the closely packed stationary material. Good solubility at a relatively high temperature, *e.g.* 70°C, is desirable, dyeing often being commenced at this temperature, the pH of the dyebath being adjusted to prevent too rapid initial absorption of dye. The Black PV type of chrome black is particularly suitable for top dyeing because of its good solubility and penetrating power. The newer free-acid forms of chrome dye, *e.g.* the Francolanes (C.F.M.C.), are also very suitable for top dyeing.

The 1:2 metal-complex dyes are particularly suitable for dyeing slubbing to give pale to medium depth dyeings within the colour range which they provide. For deep colours, *e.g.* navies and browns, the more fibre-selective sulphonated types may be employed on the grounds of economy.

Acid dyes are used to give bright colours, both for solid and mixture yarns, *e.g.* greys produced by mixing bright green and violet fibres to give an effect which is unobtainable when all the fibres are dyed the same colour.

All the dye makers produce special ranges of fast-to-milling acid dyes which are particularly suitable for dyeing slubbing, either when used alone, or to brighten 1:2 metal-complex dyes. Such ranges include the Polar and Neopolar dyes and the Irganol S dyes (Geigy), the Lanasyn Brilliant dyes, and the Cibalan Brilliant dyes (CIBA). Acid dyes are also suitable for shading chrome dyes provided they have the necessary stability towards chrome in the dyebath. As has already been stated, in general the fastness requirements for slubbing are less stringent than those for loose wool. Thus worsted cloths are not often milled to any great extent and fastness to light milling is all that is required. Excellent fastness to perspiration and to light is, however, often demanded. The fastness requirements for knitting yarns depend upon the type of garment to be produced and the dyer must select the dyes for slubbing accordingly, The continuing demand for better wet fastness, especially with shrink-resisted materials, emphasizes the need for new dyes capable of meeting this requirement as far as bright, deep colours are concerned and underlies current interest in reactive dyes, *e.g.* the Lanasols (CIBA).

YARN DYEING

Yarns are produced for a variety of specific purposes. The most important types are (*i*) hosiery yarns for hand- and machine-knitting, (*ii*) yarns for carpets and other pile fabrics, and (*iii*) yarns for weaving into worsted cloths. The diverse characteristics of these yarns, and of the conditions of processing and use to which the materials constructed from them are subjected, make it necessary to consider the dyeing of each type separately.

An overriding demand in yarn dyeing is that the dyeing should be very level. This is particularly the case when the knitted or woven material is to be constructed from one coloured yarn only, or, if from two or more different coloured yarns, the resulting fabric contains large areas of one colour. Any unlevelness becomes apparent as highly undesirable bars or zig-zag patterns in the cloth. Consequently, dyes with high migrating power *e.g.* the equalizing acid dyes, have long been favoured, since they offer the best chance of achieving the standard demanded. Where good fastness to wet treatments and the highest degree of levelness are necessary, it used to be customary to dye as slubbing (or as loose wool) and take advantage of blending prior to spinning to produce the required result. Improvement in dyeing technique, particularly in pH control, the use of restraining agents, and the development of more efficient dyeing machines, has resulted in much more use being made of fast-to-milling acid dyes and of 1:2 metal-complex dyes for dyeing yarns of all types and the need for dyeing in the form of slubbing has been reduced. Dyeing in slubbing form or as loose stock is still practised where large weights of material have to be dyed to one colour and a high degree of uniformity is required.

Hosiery Yarns: With these yarns[2], in addition to a high standard of levelness, good fastness to light, perspiration, and washing is required. The usual standard of washing fastness is I.S.O. Washing Test No. 2 (S.D.C. Washing Test No. 2) which is based on treating a composite sample in a solution containing 5g. per litre of soap at 50°C for 45 minutes. The fastness rating in respect of change in colour of the original dyeing and the rating for staining of adjacent white materials are assessed a on 1 to 5 scale (5 represents maximum fastness) using the appropriate Grey Scale. In the case of a dyeing which passes the test, both change in colour and staining are negligible.

Emphasis has already been laid on the increasing demand for a higher standard of washing fastness. It has been suggested that the more severe I.S.O. Washing Test No. 3 (treatment in a solution containing 5g. per litre of soap and 2g. per litre of anhydrous sodium carbonate at 60°C for 30 minutes) should be used for determining suitability. Fastness to wet treatments decreases with increasing depth of shade and thus the deeper the colour required the less likely it is that equalizing acid dyes will be satisfactory. Thus the Xylene Fast P (Sandoz) dyes may pass I.S.O. Washing Test No. 2 in depths up to 0.5 per cent but for deeper colours fast-to-milling acid dyes are essential. For pale colours such as fawns, beige, greys etc., the 1:2 metal-complex dyes are particularly suitable.

The production of bright greens and turquoise blues of adequate fastness to light is a long standing problem. The triarylmethane dyes, *e.g.* Lissamine Green V, Disulphine Blue V, are bright enough and level-dyeing, but the dyeings obtained are of poor fastness to light. The introduction of phthalocyanine dyes, *e.g.* Coomassie Turquoise 3G, enables dyeing of much better light fastness and wet fastness to be obtained but they are difficult to apply to yarn owing to their skittery dyeing behaviour and much poorer migrating power.

For the so-called 'baby' pinks and blues it is also necessary to use very bright dyes and the Sulpho Rhodamines and Lissamine Ultra Sky R are commonly used. Bleaching, *e.g.* by sulphur stoving or with peroxide, prior to dyeing is often carried out to give brighter results. Mention may also be made here of the use of such additives to the dyebath as Product LF (Sandoz) (hydroxylamine sulphate) and Erioclarite B (Geigy). These act as mild bleaching agents during the dyeing process.

Carpet and Pile Fabric Yarns[3]: Provided the amount of yarn required is large enough, dyeing as loose stock is preferred for plain carpets, but great quantities of carpet yarn are dyed as such. The primary demands are very good levelness and penetration, and fastness to light. Penetration is especially important, since it is the cut ends of the pile which are seen and carpet yarns are, in consequence, matched on the cut. With deeper dyeings particular consideration must be given to fastness to water and to rubbing. The increasing tendency for carpets to be shampooed is causing an increase in the demand for better wet fastness.

For many years, combinations of equalizing acid dyes, *e.g.* Xylene Light Yellow 2G, Lissamine Fast Red B, and Solway Blue BN, have been used wherever possible. Such combinations are very level-dyeing and give dyeings of good fastness to light. In consequence, they are particularly suitable for producing the very wide range of colours required, particularly in pale to medium depth. Where rather better fastness to salt water and to animal urine is required the Solway Blue PFN type should be used as the blue component. For medium to deep colours less expensive dyes which give dyeings of adequate light fastness at such depths may be used. Light fastness is proportional to the depth of a dyeing, not inversely proportional to it as is the case with fastness to most wet treatments. For blacks the Black T type of chrome dye is suitable. The dyed yarn is usually dried without rinsing, the residual acid improving the fastness to water and to wet rubbing and assisting in the maintenance of the stiffness of the pile.

Where good wet fastness to water and to shampooing is demanded the whole gamut of fast-to-milling acid dyes and 1:2 metal-complex dyes are used, applied with the aid of restraining agents, *e.g.* Irgasol SW. Fibre-reactive dyes are also recommended by the dyemakers for certain deep, bright colours.

The use of blends of wool with other fibres for carpet yarns has increased greatly in recent years, particularly 80:20 blends of wool and nylon and blends containing wool, nylon, and special staple fibre viscose rayons, *e.g.* Evlan (Courtaulds). The dyeing of these is discussed in Section 12 which deals with 'Union Dyeing'.

Yarns for upholstery and furnishing fabrics are usually spun on the worsted system but the general requirements are the same as for carpet yarns. The same pattern of development is to be seen in this field also, *viz.* a move towards the use of dyes which will give dyeings of better fastness to water, wet rubbing, and wet treatments generally. This is particularly the case with yarns to be used for coverings which have to withstand hard use, *e.g.* upholstery cloths for the seats in public service vehicles.

Worsted Yarns: These yarns are intended primarily for striped suiting cloths. Because they are used in narrow stripes maximum levelness is not essential but wet fastness requirements are the same as for yarns produced from dyed slubbing. In fact, yarn dyeing in this instance is an alternative to slubbing dyeing and the same classes of dyes are employed, and dyeing is commonly carried out in cheese form.

PIECE DYEING

The most important types of cloth which are dyed in piece-form[4] are (*i*) worsted coatings, (*ii*) woollen dress materials, (*iii*) heavy woollens, including blankets, (*iv*) lightweight worsteds, and (*v*) knitted material.

Worsted Coatings: These are dyed mainly with chrome dyes to give browns, greys, navies and blacks. Anthraquinonoid acid dyes may be used for shading. For navies, fast-to-milling acid dyes of the Coomassie Navy Blue type are used, alone or on an indigo bottom, for uniform cloths as a less fast alternative to chrome navies.

Woollen Dress Materials: These fabrics have to be dyed to a very wide range of colours, ranging from pastels to full, bright reds, blues, etc. Good fastness to light is required and also a very high standard of levelness, but fastness to wet treatments is not important. Mixtures of yellow, red, and blue equalizing acid dyes are widely used. Since such cloths are usually carbonized before dyeing, dyes which show good level-dyeing characteristics on unevenly carbonized material are preferred, *e.g.* a mixture of Propolan

Yellow 3G, Propolan Red 3G, and Solway Blue 2G (ICI). Since accurate matching to shade is normally required, only dyes with very good migrating power should be used for shading purposes.

Heavy Woollens: These contain a high proportion of recovered wool and are thus often coloured. If they are white or a pale colour, equalizing acid dyes of the type used for dress goods may be employed. If they are dark-coloured, as in the case of low woollens, the dyer may have no option but to use very bright dyes to obtain the desired colour, in spite of the inferior fastness to light of the dyeing produced.

Structurally, blanket cloths are of the heavy woollen type although all-wool blankets are very much a quality product. They may been have carbonized; they will have been acid-milled and thus will enter the dyehouse in a strongly acid condition. Good fastness to washing is a normal requirement. It is not an easy matter to neutralize or partly neutralize acid-treated cloth uniformly and one convenient way of avoiding the need to do so is to use the strongly acid-dyeing 1:1 metal-complex dyes which show good level-dyeing properties and satisfactory fastness to washing.

Lightweight Worsted Cloths: Cloths of the type used for tropical suitings are normally dyed to pale colours. The same high standard of levelness and penetration is required as on woollen dress materials with the additional need for good fastness to perspiration. A red, yellow, blue combination such as Azo Rubinole 3GP, Xylene Fast Yellow 2GP, and Alizarine Light Blue 4GL is often used. These acid dyes are applied from an acetic acid/formic acid dyebath. They give dyeings of rather better wet fastness than do the most level-dyeing equalizing acid dyes and are satisfactory in this respect, as well as being sufficiently level-dyeing for this purpose. Still better wet fastness can be obtained by using the strongly acid-dyeing metal-complex dyes.

Knitted Materials: These are widely used for ladies' dresses and twin-sets. Dyes of good fastness to light and perspiration are required. Good fastness to washing may be demanded, particularly if the material is shrink-resisted. Equalizing acid dyes are preferred on the score of their ability to give very level dyeings but fast-to-milling acid dyes, or 1:2 metal-complex dyes may have to be used to meet wet fastness demands, with consequent need for additional care in controlling dye absorption to give a level dyeing.

DYEING MADE-UP OR PARTLY MADE-UP ARTICLES

Included in this category are wool hose, certain types of garment and garment panels, berets, and felt hats, and the requirements as far as dyes are concerned are as diverse as the types of goods. Wool socks require to be dyed fast to perspiration and to repeated washing. Some form of shrink-resist treatment is normally given, either before or after dyeing. If given after dyeing, the dyeing must withstand the treatment. In the majority of cases, shrink-resist treatment tends to reduce the wet fastness of the dyed goods. Thus the requirements are similar to those for hosiery yarns and the same classes of dyes are employed, *viz.* chrome dyes for dark colours, fast-to-milling acid dyes for bright colours, and neutral-dyeing metal-complex dyes for fawns, light greys, *etc.* White or coloured effect threads must not be stained. The nylon yarn generally used to strengthen heels and toes must be dyed to the same colour as the wool. This is no great problem, except in very deep colours where it may not be possible to dye the nylon deep enough. In such cases it is better to use pre-dyed nylon yarn. Good penetration of the seams is essential. This calls for careful control of dye absorption and, preferably, the use of dyes with good migrating power at the boil.

Wool felt hats are dyed in the form of hoods, *i.e.* when almost fully formed into hats[5]. They usually contain 2-3 per cent (o.w.f.) of sulphuric acid from planking (acid-milling). Equalizing acid dyes of good fastness to light, water, and, if possible, perspiration are used. To assist in obtaining the best possible penetration, dyeing is usually commenced without adding any acid, but further acid may be added to promote dye bath exhaustion after adequate penetration has been achieved. The strongly acid-dyeing 1:1 metal-complex dyes are of value on such materials where particularly good fastness to wet treatments is demanded.

DYEING MACHINERY

THE FUNCTION OF A DYEING MACHINE is to bring the dye solution and the fibre together in such a manner that uniform dyeing is achieved as rapidly as possible. Wool dyeing is normally a batchwise process, based on the progressive absorption of dye by the fibre from a relatively large volume of dye liquor. The essential continuous movement of dye liquor over the surface of the fibres is achieved in one of three ways, *viz.* (*i*) by circulation of the liquor through the stationary material, (*ii*) by movement of the material through the liquor, or (*iii*) by movement of material and liquor. Since wool is required to be dyed in so wide a variety of forms, machines suitable for dyeing each form are required. From the point of view of technical efficiency a machine designed to dye one type of material is likely to be superior to a multi-purpose machine but versatility is often an overriding advantage, especially to the commission dyer who is called upon to deal with a variety of types of material and a wide range of batch sizes.

Preservation of the physical properties of the material during dyeing is important. Water has a profound effect upon the mechanical properties of fibres, particularly at elevated temperatures and when fibres are assembled in the form of yarn and cloth there is the added complication that the strains which are present as a result of the tensions applied during spinning and weaving are likely to be released during wet processing. In certain cases stabilization of the yarn or cloth by, *e.g.* crabbing is an essential prerequisite.

Under hot, wet conditions fibres are generally quite easily deformed by quite small forces and tend to remain so. Consequently, the less the stress applied and the shorter the time it is applied, the less the risk of permanent deformation occuring. Wool materials pose less problems in this respect than do, *e.g.* acrylic fibres which require to be handled with great care because of their low wet modulus. The considerable improvements in the design of dyeing machinery directed towards reducing the risk of mechanical damage, and maintaining the material in good condition have been due largely to the relative ease with which such fibres can be adversely affected, but it is being increasingly realized that the preservation of wool goods in the best possible physical condition is also highly desirable[6].

It is also becoming increasingly important to consider the dyeing machine in its overall setting. The size, shape and ease of loading of machines, and their suitability for automatic control are becoming more important as the demand for increased output per man-hour grows and maximum machine utilization is demanded. All these are reflected in developments in the design of machines and in the co-ordination of machines into a pattern of operation based increasingly upon the use of automatic and automated control instead of manual operation.

In a survey of this size, it is not possible to enumerate, let alone to describe, all the machines used for dyeing wool goods, and a short selection of machines considered typical of their kind, together with a brief comment on features common to all machines and on automatic controls must suffice. Finally, although batchwise processing is the rule, equipment for dyeing wool continuously must be considered, if only in outline.

Stainless steel is now used for all the component parts of dyeing machines, including pumps and pipes, as well as for the dye vessel and for the carrier for the material[7]. Heating is by steam, through either open, or preferably, closed pipes[8]. It is normal practice to fit all types of machine with lids to conserve heat and to improve working conditions in the dyehouse. In the case of machines designed to operate at temperatures above 100°C, the lid must be pressure-tight and the whole machine constructed to withstand the internal pressure necessary to maintain the temperature at the required maximum. Electric motors are used to drive propellers and pumps and to rotate winches and paddles.

The production of a satisfactory dyeing in the shortest possible time and the repetition of the result as often as required depend upon the standard of control of the functioning of the machine that can be achieved. For a long time now, automatic control of time and temperature of dyeing, and of direction of liquor flow has been possible, thus eliminating the far less accurate manual control which is often incapable of providing the standard of quality and of reproducibility of dyeing now often demanded.

From comparatively elementary beginnings, the stage has now been reached where the whole of the dyeing cycle can be carried through without human intervention[9]. This has been made possible by the development of instruments to detect the variations in the dyeing conditions which affect the dyeing process, the coupling of such instruments to control systems whereby the conditions can be maintained at the required optimum value, the application of controls which cause the operation of the machine to follow a predetermined programme, and the development of machines specifically designed to be operated by these systems and of intrinsically high efficiency.

An example of a modern programmed automatic dye-cycle control system is that operated by the 'Celcon I' (Courtaulds Engineering) controller. With this instrument, information relating to temperature, time, and direction of liquor flow is programmed on a patch board which serves as a 'memory'. All the other information is carried on a punched plastic card. Sensing of this card triggers off electrical impulses which, in turn, are transmitted through relays and solenoid-operated valves to pneumatically-operated valves on the dyeing machine. The most advanced model enables not only the basic operations to be controlled automatically but also the metering of prepared solutions to auxiliary tanks and the addition of measured dye solutions into the dye liquor preparation tank and hence into the dye vessel itself. In fact, there is no part of the whole operation that cannot be controlled, thus relieving not only the operator's hand but also his memory. The programme cards are small, inexpensive, virtually indestructible and readily adaptable to a filing system. An annunciator on the control panel gives constant information on the progress of the dyeing cycle and an alarm system gives immediate warning of a fault in the machine or the process on the 'fail-safe' principle. The Celcon I controller is illustrated by Plate 44.

LOOSE WOOL DYEING MACHINES

Loose wool (and rags) is dyed as a stationary pack of material held in a container fitting into the dye vessel. The Longclose conical pan machine, shown in Fig. 11.3, is typical of those specifically designed for this purpose. The pan A containing the material (500-600lb.) has a perforated base B and a detachable, perforated lid C. The pan fits into a conical seating D in the dye vessel E and the dye liquor is circulated through the mass of material by means of a centrifugal pump F, and reversing valve G, so fitted that a positive flow of liquor is achieved in either direction without the need to alter the direction of flow through the pump.

For loading and unloading the pan is lifted out of the vessel and placed in a tilting frame. By fitting a pressure-tight lid on the dye vessel it is possible to dye at temperatures up to 130°C, *e.g.* when dyeing polyester fibre. Such high temperatures cannot be used when dyeing wool but dyeing at 100–102°C offers advantages. This type of machine is of fixed capacity, but others are available which are capable of accommodating loads of different size. Such types are of particular interest to commission dyers. By using additional conical pans it is possible to be loading a fresh batch and unloading a dyed batch while a third batch is being dyed, thus enabling a very high output to be achieved.

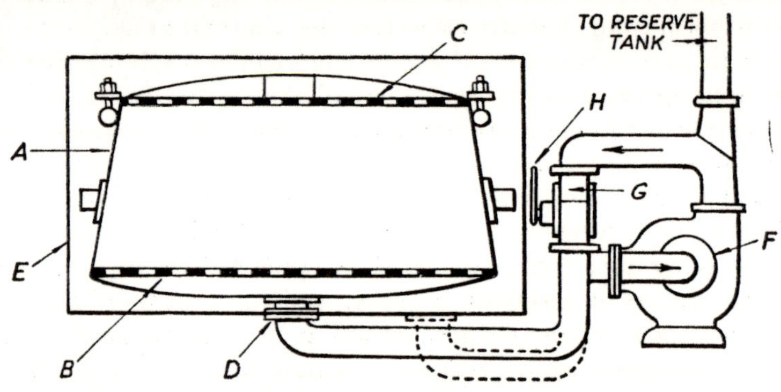

FIG. 11.3 LONGCLOSE CONICAL PAN DYEING MACHINE

A. Pan. *B*—Perforated base. *C*—Perforated lid.
D—Conical seating. *E*—Outer vat. *F*—Centrifugal pump.
G—Reversing valve. *H*—Handle controlling reversing valve.

Loose wool can also be dyed in circulating-liquor machines designed primarily to dye wound packages of material. In this case the carrier for the packages is replaced by a carrier consisting of two concentric, perforated cylinders forming a cage in which the loose material (or hanked yarn, or slubbing in bags) is packed.

MACHINES FOR SLUBBING DYEING

Slubbing dyeing[10] refers to the dyeing of combed sliver, either when wound into flattened balls (tops) or in hank form. Tops are dyed either in can machines or in radial-flow spindle machines, the latter being of more recent introduction and increasingly employed. In these machines (see Plate 43), the tops are mounted on perforated spindles which are fixed into a hollow base which connects with an outlet in the bottom of the dye vessel. To prevent disturbance of the outer layers of sliver, each column of tops is protected by a removable perforated outer cage which is slipped over it. The dye liquor is circulated through the perforated spindles radially through the tops, the direction of flow being reversible at will. Pressurized versions of this machine are produced and a recent development has been the introduction of machines designed to take specially large packages, ancillary equipment being provided for loading the tops on to the spindles.

In the can type of machine the tops are placed one upon the other in pairs in individual cans seated in a rectangular dye vessel and connected to a common circulation system. Movement of dye liquor is slower and relatively gentle.

It is argued by some that dyeing in top form results in loss of loftiness in the resulting yarn, due to compression of the sliver during dyeing. The low liquid pressures used in modern machines are claimed to reduce this. Short-fibred sliver must be dyed in top form.

Slubbing in hank form can be dyed in machines designed for dyeing yarn in this form but this method is not widely used. On the other hand, hanked slubbing in net bags is dyed by packing it into the containers used for holding loose wool in package dyeing machines.

YARN DYEING MACHINES

Yarn may be dyed either in hank form or in wound packages, *e.g.* on cheese or on cone. Thick woollen yarns spun from relatively coarse wools *e.g.* carpet yarns, are largely dyed in hank form. Fine worsted yarns are dyed in package form. However, improvements in hank-dyeing machines have made it possible to dye quite fine yarns in hank form without risk of damage due to entanglement. On the other hand, the advantages of dyeing in package form, particularly large packages, has led to the dyeing of more coarse yarns in this form.

For many years, the standard machine for dyeing yarn in hank form was the Hussong and variants of this type of machine are still widely used. Some for dyeing carpet yarn are of enormous size, taking loads of 4,000 lb., or even more. Further, two, or even four, such machines may be coupled together through a common distributor for the dye liquor, to provide the means of dyeing as much yarn as possible in what is essentially one dyebath and to produce the required amount of yarn dyed to one colour[11].

The Hussong machine consists essentially of a rectangular dye vessel containing a removable frame carrying the hanks of yarn, the dye liquor being circulated either up or down through the hanks by a propeller. The essential features of the machine are illustrated in Fig. 11.4. Largely under the influence of the necessity to handle acrylic yarns more gently, much more sophisticated machines are now available. One such is the Pegg GSH hank dyeing machine which is particularly suitable for dyeing fine wool and wool-mixture yarns. One important feature of this machine is that the hanks are mounted on perforated hollow tubes projecting horizontally from a distributor as shown in the illustration on Plate 41. The dye liquor is drawn from the bath, forced out through the perforations, and passes down through the mass of yarn, the hanks being lifted slightly from the tubes as it does so. A lower row of thin, solid rods passing through the lower part of the hanks prevents undue movement and entanglement.

Yarn packages, *e.g.* cheeses or cones, are dyed by circulating the dye liquor radially through the package mounted on a perforated spindle, in the same manner as is used when dyeing tops in the so-called spindle machine.

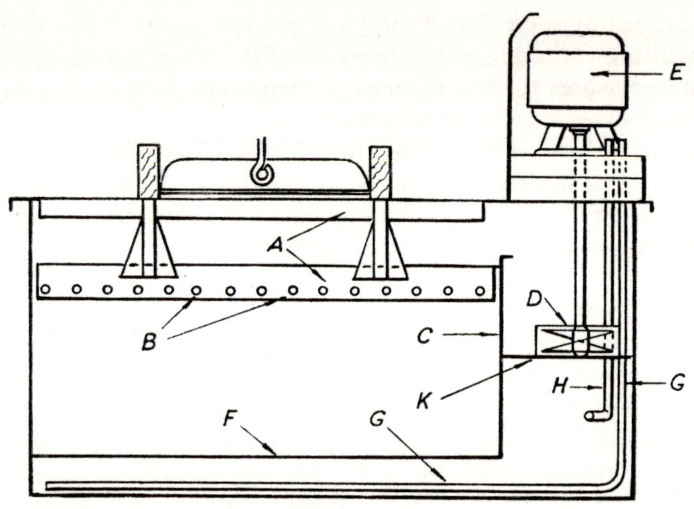

FIG. 11.4   CROSS-SECTION OF HUSSONG-TYPE MACHINE

A—Hank frame.   *B*—Dye sticks.   *C*—Partition plate.   *D*—Reversible.
propeller.   *E*—Electric motor.   *F*—Perforated false bottom.
G—Steam pipe.   *H*—Auxiliary steam pipe.   *K*—shelf carrying
duct in which propellor revolves.

Under these conditions there is no movement of the yarns during dyeing. This means that fine yarns can be handled without risk of damage and high-twist yarns do not need to be set before dyeing. The excellent condition of the dyed yarn makes it much easier to wind. Claims have been made, *e.g.* for yarn dyed on 'rockets', that it is possible to knit directly from the dyed package.

As far as the dyeing operation is concerned consistent size of package and correct and uniform package density are essential[12]. The dye liquor must be completely free from suspended matter and the 'strike' of the dye must be controlled to avoid too rapid build-up of dye on either the outside or the inside of the package, since it is generally impossible to redistribute the dye uniformly by prolonging dyeing time. Foam in the dyebath is un-desirable in any case, since it can reduce the liquor flow catastrophically. It is particularly undesirable in package and pack dyeing and the use of anti-foaming agents to prevent foam formation is strongly recommended[13].

A wide variety of machines is available, the majority being totally enclosed so that positive pressure is obtainable in both directions of flow. Some are pressurized and can be operated at temperatures above 100 °C. The Longclose H.T. package dyeing machine is illustrated in Plate 42. As with hank-dyeing machines, the modern counterparts of the earlier open

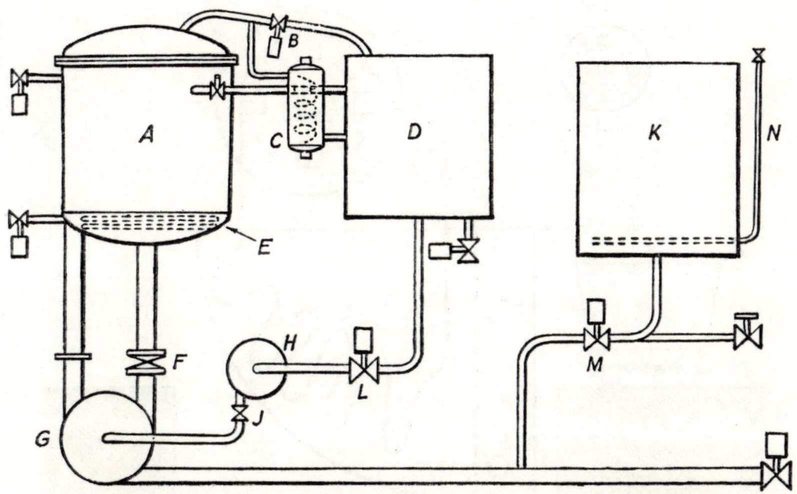

FIG. 11.5 PEGG HIGH-TEMPERATURE PRESSURE-DYEING MACHINE (HTU)

A—Dyeing vessel. *B*—Air release valve. *C*—Condenser. *D*—Expansion tank. *E*—Heating coil. *F*—Butterfly valve. *G*—Main pump. *H*—Secondary pump. *J*—Non-return valve. *K*—Stock tank. *L* and *M*—Isolating valves. *N*—Steam pipe.

machines are highly sophisticated. One such is the Pegg Type HTU machine shown in Plate 45 and Fig. 11.5. This is designed to operate under pressure. The main flow pump is based on a clever combination of centrifugal and axial principles which permit infinitely variable flow control and very simple flow reversal. The expansion tank is open, liquor being bled into it through a reducing valve and pumped from it back into the main vessel by a secondary pump, which also supplies the static pressure.

Machines of this type can be used not only for cheeses and cones but also for loose material, slubbing, tow, and even beams, by using the appropriate type of carrier. Packages are awkward to handle as far as drying after dyeing is concerned and package dryers are available which accommodate the assembly of packages on the dyeing frame and dry them by blowing air through them. Means for re-circulating the air is provided in certain types.

CLOTH DYEING MACHINES

By far the commonest way of dyeing cloth, either woven or knitted, is to use the winch, the fundamentals of which can be clearly seen in Fig. 11.6. The cloth is moved continuously up and over the winch and down through the liquor. Developments in winch dyeing machines have taken the form of refinements but the general principles remain unchanged. The majority of machines are now enclosed, which helps to maintain a higher, and a more

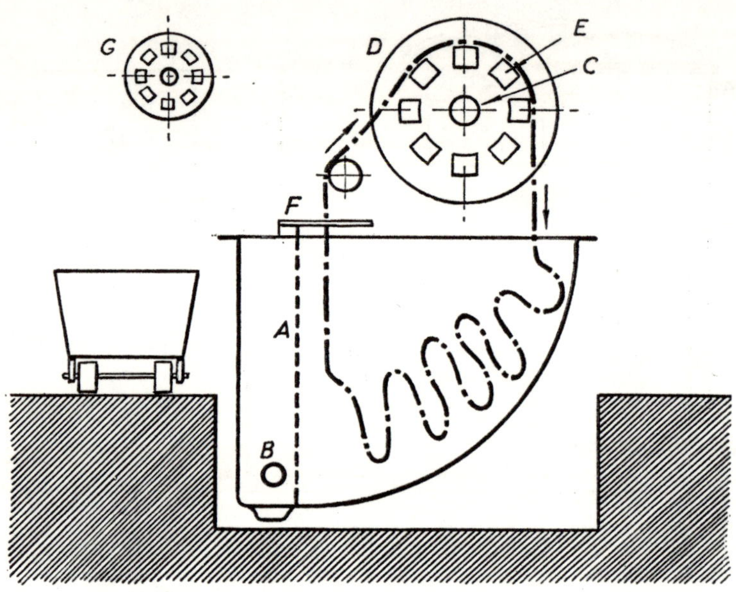

FIG. 11.6.   WINCH DYEING MACHINE

A—Perforated partition.   B—Perforated steam pipe.   C—Shafting.
D—Circular end-plate or winch shield.   E—Bars fitted to end-plates.
F—Projecting bars or guide fingers.   G—Take-off roller.

uniform temperature, and to prevent escape of steam into the dyehouse. By modifying the size and shape of the winch and the dye vessel it is possible to produce a machine more suitable for particular types of material, *e.g.* knitted fabrics. Since the circulation of the dye liquor may leave something to be desired, additional movement may be provided by a pump. With winches used for dyeing carpeting in open width the provision of a pump is essential.

Care must be taken to avoid curling of the selvedges and permanent creasing of the cloth as it passes through the dye liquor, normally in rope form. Some cloths may require to be bagged, *i.e.* their selvedges sewn together to form a tube with the face of the cloth inside.

Interest in dyeing wool cloths on the beam is increasing. This follows the widespread adoption of beam-dyeing machines for dyeing synthetic fibre cloths The material is wound onto a perforated hollow cylinder which is inserted into the dye vessel. Dye liquor is circulated by a pump through the cloth, the general principle of the machine, illustrated in Fig. 11.7, being similar to that of a package machine. As with the latter, by pressurizing the machine it is possible to dye at temperatures above 100°C. The obvious advantage of dyeing cloth in this way is that no creasing of the material

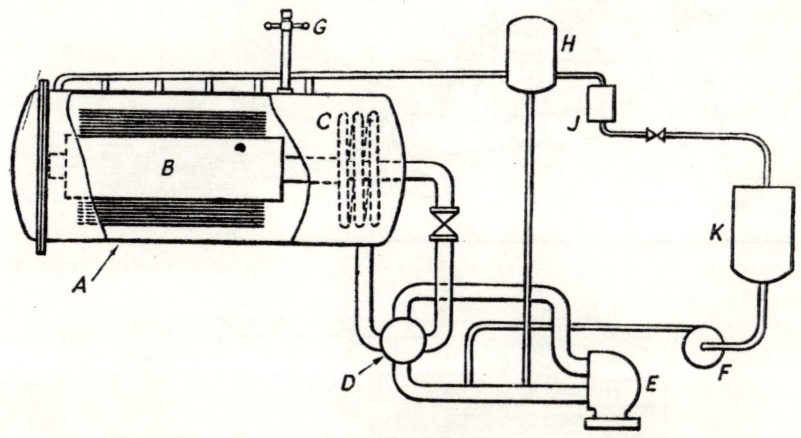

FIG. 11.7. HIGH TEMPERATURE BEAM DYEING MACHINE

A—Dyeing vessel. *B*—Beam carrying roll of cloth. *C*—Heating coil.
D—Reversal device. *E*—Main pump. *F*—Auxiliary pump.
G—Sampling unit. *H*—Expansion tank. *J*—Bleed cooler.
K—Side tank.

can occur. Further, this dyeing procedure is basically more efficient. On the other hand, the subjection of the material to high temperatures in the wet state under tension and compression produces a certain amount of setting which alters the handle of the material considerably. This precludes the universal adoption of beam dyeing and its use is likely to be restricted to dyeing materials for which a firm handle is required. Although not yet used for all-wool materials, it is particularly suitable for dyeing wool-polyester fibre cloths[14] at temperatures up to 107°C.

MACHINERY FOR DYEING WOOL CONTINUOUSLY

As has already been pointed out, the continuous dyeing of loose wool and slubbing is attracting increasing attention and a number of machinery makers, in collaboration with various dye makers, have produced suitable equipment.

For loose wool, the Smith loose stock unit, based on the piston steamer and shown diagrammatically in Fig. 11.8, is perhaps the best known. The blended loose stock is sprayed with pad liquor, squeezed through nip rollers to distribute the liquor, and then charged into one end of a tubular steamer where it is compressed and pushed forward by a piston through the steaming tube where it is steamed with saturated steam at atmospheric pressure

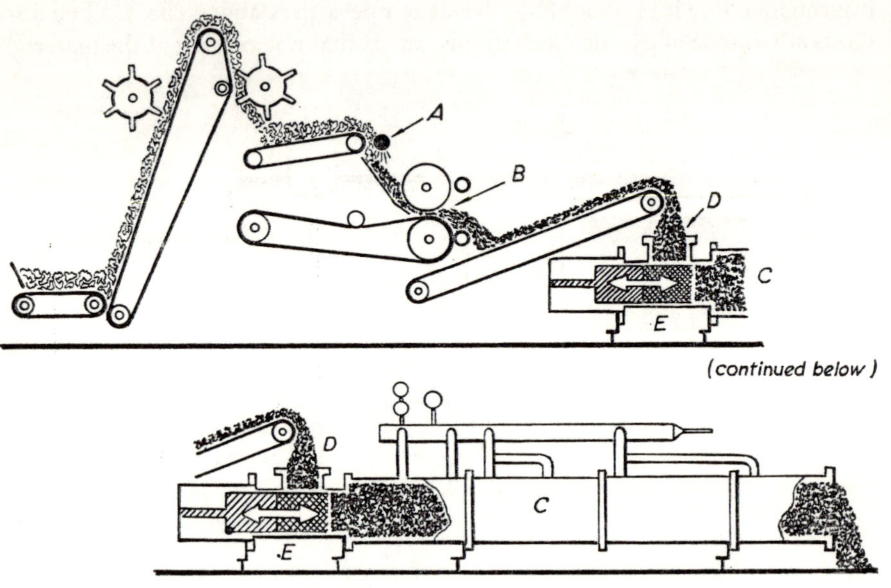

FIG. 11.8. SMITH CONTINUOUS DYEING MACHINE FOR LOOSE STOCK

A—Spraying to apply liquor. *B*—Squeezing of the loose stock.
C—Steamer. *D*—Filling mouth. *E*—Piston for moving the material
through the steamer.

at 100–102°C. for 20–40 minutes. The emerging steamed material then passes forward to a conventional scouring set. The particular claims made for this method of dyeing are vastly superior levelness, even of the most tippy wool and of, *e.g.* wool-nylon mixtures (without the need to use restraining agents) and a better quality fibre.

CONTINUOUS DYEING OF SLUBBING

For slubbing, a variety of machines is available. In one, the ILMA machine, illustrated diagrammatically in Fig. 11.9, the slubbing (20–40 ends) is padded with dye liquor using a horizontal pad fitted with large soft bowls. The padded material passes straight downwards into a small tubular steamer where it first encounters live steam which causes rapid heating up and 'ballooning' of the fibres. It then drops onto a slowly moving horizontal brattice which carries it forward through a cabinet steamer and then into a back washer and dryer, all the operations being synchronized. The steaming temperature is 100–102°C, the steaming time 15–45 minutes, and the pad is automatically supplied with liquor at 60°C from a jacketed pan. As in the case of loose stock, it is claimed that very level dyeings and excellent coverage of the material are obtained and that physical quality of the slub-

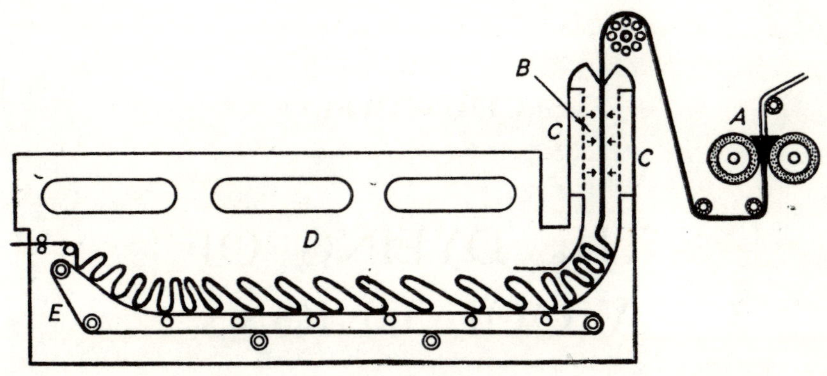

FIG. 11.9. ILMA MACHINE FOR CONTINUOUS DYEING OF SLUBBING

A—Padding of the sliver. *B*—Pre-fixation chamber. *C*—Steam entry.
D—Reaction chamber. *E*—Endless brattice conveyor.

bing is excellent. Obviously the capital cost of the equipment necessitates maximum utilization and this is likely to result in the use of this type of machinery being confined to the production of very large weights of slubbing dyed to standard colours.

REFERENCES

1. Beal, *J. Soc. Dyers & Col.*, 1960, **76**, 78; Gaunt, *ibid.*, 1954, **70**, 46; 1951, **67**, 570.
2. Gaunt, *ibid.*, 1958, **74**, 569.
3. Gaunt and Robinson, *ibid.*, 1953, **69**, 155; Beal, *ibid.*, 1958, **74**, 677; 1967, **83**, 3.
4. Technical Information (Dyehouse) No. 745, I.C.I. Dyestuffs Division; Peel, *J. Soc Dyers & Col.*, 1943, **59**, 2.
5. Haigh, *J. Soc. Dyers & Col.*, 1954, **70**, 539.
6. Brown, Stevens and Whewell, *CIBA Review*, 1962, No. 6, p. 2.
7. Skelly, *J. Soc. Dyers & Col.*, 1960, **76**, 469.
8. Marsh, *ibid.*, 1954, **70**, 105.
9. Bunting, *ibid.*, 1968, **84**, 66.
10. Isles, *ibid.*, 1937, **53**, 417; Gaunt, *ibid.*, 1954, **70**, 46; 1951, **67**, 570.
11. Robinson and Jagger, *ibid.*, 1951, **67**, 557.
12. Whittaker, *ibid.*, 1961, **77**, 690.
13. Hadfield and Lemin, *ibid.*, 1961, **77**, 198.
14. Limbert, *ibid.*, 1966, **82**, 97.

THE DYEING OF WOOL UNIONS

THE COLORATION of union materials[1,2] does not necessarily entail dyeing a mixture of two or more fibres; many two-colour and multi-colour effects are obtained by mixing two or more different fibres dyed separately in the form of yarn or as loose material. Frequently, however, the dyer is required to process a mixture of fibres, sometimes in the form of loose material or yarn, but more commonly in the piece. This last method is the most economical from the point of view of the manufacturer and merchant, since it enables cloth to be held in the 'grey' or undyed state, thus minimizing the time between order and delivery.

A mixture containing two different fibres may be dyed in one of three ways: (*a*) both fibres may be dyed to the same shade, or to different depths of the same shade; (*b*) one fibre may be dyed while the other is left uncoloured; (*c*) the two fibres may be dyed to different shades. Usually, the same colour is required on both fibres, and it is this type of union dyeing which is described in the present chapter.

Union dyeing covers a very wide field, which continues to expand with the ever-increasing number of new fibres. In this survey, discussion is limited to the following important two-fibre mixtures: (*a*) wool and cotton, (*b*) wool and viscose rayon, (*c*) wool and nylon, (*d*) wool and cellulose acetate, (*e*) wool and Terylene, and (*f*) wool and acrylic fibres. Mixtures of minor importance, *e.g.* wool and silk, and wool and casein fibre, have been excluded from the survey.

WOOL-COTTON MIXTURES

THE DYES used for the wool portion of this union material are normally acid dyes, direct dyes being used for the cotton. Direct dyes, however, are chemically similar to acid dyes. Besides possessing affinity for cellulose, they are all capable of dyeing wool to a greater or less extent, so it is theoretically possible to omit the acid dyes.

THE ONE-BATH PROCESS

A mixture of direct dyes is used to colour both fibres, but acid dyes suitable for application from a neutral bath are also included. Acid dyes are necessary where the direct dyes colour the cotton much darker than the wool, when they are not sufficiently bright, and where they do not provide the same shade on both fibres. In general, dyes do not give identical shades on different fibres, and the need for acid dyes to correct the shade largely accounts for the extensive trade in 'union colours', which are ready-made, suitably shaded mixtures consisting mainly of direct dyes. These mixtures are extensively used for standard colours such as dark brown, navy blue and black, and many dyers use them as the basis for lighter colours.

Apart from the use of union colours, there are two alternative one-bath methods. In the first a direct dye (or mixture of direct dyes) capable of dyeing wool and cotton to approximately the same shade is chosen, neutral dyeing acid dyes being used for shading the wool and direct dyes having little affinity for wool for shading the cotton. In the second method neutral dyeing acid dyes are used for the wool and direct dyes for the cotton, acid and direct dyes being chosen which stain the cotton and wool, respectively, to a minimum extent. Whichever method is adopted, it is desirable that the dyes selected should have good fastness to light and, as far as possible, good fastness to washing. Good fastness to light is particularly important in dyeings of pale to medium depth.

Examples of direct dyes which give almost solid shades on the two fibres are provided by Chrysophenine G (C.I. Direct Yellow 12), Chlorazol Fast Red F (C.I. Direct Red 1), Chlorazol Dark Green PL (C.I. Direct Green 1), and Chlorazol Black E (C.I. Direct Black 38). Suitable direct blues and violets are not available. In general, when separate dyes are to be used for each fibre, at least six dyes must be included in the mixture. Browns, however, can be obtained by using Trisulphon Brown B (C.I. Direct Brown 31) together with Coomassie Brown G (C.I. Acid Brown 22), while for navy blues, the standard combination is Chlorazol Black BH (C.I. Direct Blue 2) and Coomassie Navy Blue 2RN (C.I. Acid Blue 113). It should be noted that a brown, for example, produced with a single neutral dyeing acid dye (suitable shaded) is less likely to be 'skittery' than one produced with a mixture of a yellow, a red and a blue. Neutral dyeing acid dyes which colour cellulosic fibres almost as deeply as wool, *e.g.* Coomassie Red PG (C.I. Acid Red 85), should be avoided if possible.

The one-bath process is fairly straightforward. The scoured material, while still wet, is introduced into a bath at 50°C containing the necessary amount of Glauber's salt or common salt, and 5 per cent of an ammonium salt to neutralize residual alkali and give a pH of 6.5-7.5. After running the machine for 10 to 15 minutes, the dissolved dye is added. The temperature is then raised to 90°C in 30 minutes and kept at 90°C for 30 minutes to one hour. If the cellulosic fibre then appears 'thin' or 'hungry' compared with the wool, this difference can usually be corrected by turning off the steam and allowing the bath to cool to 50° to 60°C, when the cotton will take up more dye. However, if a mixture of direct dyes is present, this procedure may alter the tone of the dyeing, owing to differences in the affinity of individual direct dyes at lower temperatures, as compared with dyeing at 90°C. Actual boiling should be avoided, since this is liable to cause the direct dyes to leave the cotton and transfer to the wool; there is also a risk that the dyes will decompose. An addition of 5 to 40 per cent. of Glauber's salt or common salt is made, either at the start or at intervals during dyeing. A fairly low liquor ratio, *e.g.* 20 to 1 for yarns and 30 to 1 for pieces, should be used, but a higher ratio is suitable for pale colours.

To complete the dyeing, suitable dyes for shading may be added to the cooled dyebath; if the colour on the cotton is too light, more of the original direct dye and more salt are required Finally, the material is washed off, hydro-extracted ,and dried at not too high a temperature. When direct dyes of low affinity have been used, a final rinse in water containing 2 to 3 lb. Glauber's salt per 100 gallons is beneficial in preventing 'swealing', *i.e.*, migration of dye during drying.

THE TWO-BATH PROCESS

In this process the wool is dyed first, with acid dyes, the cotton being filled in subsequently with direct dyes possessing low affinity for the wool. During the filling-in stage, staining of the wool by the direct dyes must be minimized by dyeing at a fairly low temperature and, if necessary, by adding a suitable wool resist. The two-bath process provides rather brighter shades than the one-bath process and the handle of the dyed material is better. It is used, in particular, for dyeing cloths consisting of a shoddy weft and an unbleached cotton warp[3].

The shoddy pieces, when they reach the dyer after scouring and milling, are usually grey, owing to the combined effect of the various coloured rags used to prepare the shoddy. If light shades are to be dyed, it is necessary to remove this colour by stripping. If the desired shade is sufficiently dark, stripping will not be required, but it may be necessary to use vivid dyes. For example, a navy blue can be obtained on a dark grey ground by using Acid Violet 6BN (C.I. Acid Violet 15), and a dark brown by means of an orange acid dye.

The pieces are dyed with equalizing acid dyes in the usual winch machine, 2 to 5 per cent of sulphuric acid and 10 per cent of Glauber's salt being added as assistants. The cloth is entered cold and the temperature raised to the boil in 20 to 30 minutes. A 'bit' is then removed from one of the pieces and examined. Further additions of dye solution are next made at intervals until the desired shade is obtained. The dye liquor is then run away and the pieces are washed off.

Before the cotton warp is dyed, the pieces must be neutralized, otherwise the direct dyes intended for the cotton will be largely taken up by the wool. However, care must be taken to avoid excess alkali, as this removes a considerable amount of dye from the wool, except when milling acid or chrome dyes have been used in place of equalizing acid dyes. Usually, a cold solution containing 2 to 4 per cent of soda ash on the weight of the material is employed for neutralization.

After neutralization, the pieces are removed from the winch and transferred to a dolly scouring machine for filling in the cotton. The filling-in process may be carried out with the aid of either (a) direct dyes which at low temperature dye cotton and do not stain wool badly, or (b) iron tannate. Examples of suitable direct dyes are provided by Chlorazol Fast Pink BK (C.I. Direct Red 75), Chlorazol Sky Blue FF (C.I. Direct Blue 1), and Chlorazol Black BH. Dyeing is carried out in either a cold or a warm (40° to 50°C) liquor, with addition of 10 to 20 per cent of common salt, preferably towards the end of the operation. If the cloth has not been neutralized, 0·5 per cent of soda ash may be added. Since dyeing is slow at low temperatures, concentrated dye liquors, *i.e.* short liquor ratios, are necessary. By using 1 to 6 per cent on the weight of the material of a wool resist, *e.g.* Taninol WR (ICI), a much better reserve can be obtained on the wool. In addition, the temperature of the filling-in bath can be raised, *e.g.* to 60°C, without staining of the wool, and the range of suitable dyes is extended. After filling-in, the pieces are washed off and passed in rope form through rubber-covered squeezing rollers; they are then ready for finishing.

In shoddy pieces the cotton warp is well covered during milling and is scarcely visible; consequently, it need not match the wool, especially in dark shades, and all that is necessary is that it should be stained to an appropriate depth. Hence for pieces that are to be dyed navy blue, dark green, dark brown or black, filling-in with direct dyes is usually replaced by 'burl dyeing' with iron tannate, which imparts a better handle together with a gain in weight; the dyeings also have better fastness and there is less danger of streakiness.

The process of burl dyeing or 'inking' with iron tannate depends on the fact that this compound is grey, becoming darker as more is applied, until finally a black is obtained. The tannin used is myrabolans—either the ground material or the extract—while the iron is in the form of 'nitrate of iron', *i.e.* basic ferric sulphate. The pieces are run in the dolly washer for 90 minutes in the 'myrabs' liquor, which is added to the trough or 'sud box'; iron liquor is then added quickly to the trough and the pieces are run for a further 30 minutes. If the cotton is not sufficiently dark, the operation may be repeated. The pieces are then washed off, squeezed and dried.

WOOL-VISCOSE MIXTURES

LARGE QUANTITIES of viscose rayon staple, *e.g.* Fibro (Courtaulds), are blended with wool. Unions of wool and Fibro behave very similarly to wool-cotton unions and the same dyeing methods are applicable, the single-bath method being the one commonly employed. But the types of material to be dyed are usually different. Whereas wool-cotton unions are usually woollen fabrics (with a cotton warp) and pile cloths, many wool-Fibro unions are of the worsted type and demand better fastness to wet treatments. Most direct dyes, however, unless after-treated, exhibit rather poor fastness to wet treatments. The methods outlined below have therefore been developed to overcome this defect. While they are of general application for wool-cellulosic fibre unions, they are of particular interest for wool-Fibro materials. In general, they are applicable only to selected direct dyes. Allowance may have to be made for change of hue resulting from the after-treatment, and the improvement in fastness to wet treatments is sometimes accompanied by reduced fastness to light.

Method 1: If the direct dye contains lake-forming hydroxyl groups, the dyed material can be after-chromed or after-coppered, following a one-bath dyeing, but the number of suitable dyes is quite small. An alternative is to use Benzo Fast Copper (FBy), Coprantine (CIBA) or Cuprophenyl (Gy) dyes, which provide a limited range of direct dyes whose fastness to wet treatments is greatly improved by after-treatment with copper sulphate, the improvement being much greater than with ordinary direct dyes suitable for after-coppering. The wool and the cellulosic fibre are dyed together, using neutral dyeing acid or 1:2 metal-complex dyes for the wool, the acid dyes chosen being those which are altered in shade as little as possible by the subsequent treatment with copper sulphate and acetic acid. Use of these special ranges of direct dyes gives dyeings of good all-round fastness, except to milling.

Method 2: If the direct dye contains amino or hydroxyl groups in the end component, two molecules of dye are capable of reacting with formaldehyde and becoming linked together. The resulting increase in molecular weight renders the dye less soluble and the fastness to wet treatments is consequently improved. This process is particularly useful for certain black direct dyes, *e.g.*, Chlorazol Black E.

Method 3: The use of direct dyes which can be diazotized and developed on the fibre enables dyeings of better fastness to wet treatments to be obtained. This improvement, again, is due to an increase in the molecular weight of the dye without introduction of strongly polar sulphonic groups. Only a few direct dyes containing terminal primary amino groups are suitable for this purpose. Either of two methods of application may be used, *viz.* (*i*) one-bath union dyeing, using a wool resist to keep the direct dye off the wool and acid dyes which are not affected by diazotizing and developing; or (*ii*), the better method, in which the cellulosic fibre is dyed first at 60°C with diazotizable dyes (in presence of a wool resist) and then diazotized and developed, the wool being dyed subsequently with suitable acid or premetallized dyes. This process is mainly important for navy blues and blacks, where the change in hue caused by the after-treatment does not affect matching to any considerable extent.

Method 4: The previous three methods are suitable only for certain members of the direct range. A more general method, which is widely used for dark shades and for reds, consists of after-treatment with a cationic auxiliary product, *e.g.* Fixanol PN (ICI), to form a very sparingly soluble complex with the direct dye on the fibre. The linkage is not particularly resistant to alkali, so, although fastness to water, acids and perspiration is greatly improved, the improvement in fastness to washing and milling is much smaller. Further, the shade is often altered by the after-treatment, necessitating a careful choice of dyes, and in some cases the fastness to light is reduced. With some cationic products, the latter defect can often be largely overcome by incorporating copper acetate in the after-treatment liquor.

Method 5: The wool is dyed with metachrome dyes, the cellulosic fibre being dyed simultaneously with direct dyes, *e.g.* Benzo Chrome dyes (FBy), which are improved in fastness to wet processing by treatment with dichromate. Dyeing is carried out in a bath containing, as assistants, 3 to 8 per cent of metachrome mordant, 1 to 2 per cent of ammonium sulphate, and 30 to 40 per cent of Glauber's salt. The goods are entered into a warm dyebath which is raised slowly to the boil. After one hour at the boil the cotton or viscose fibre is filled up for 30 minutes to one hour in the cooling bath. Very good fastness, except to milling, is obtainable in this way for a limited range of shades.

Method 6: To obtain a really high degree of fastness to wet treatments on cellulosic material, it is necessary to dispense with water-soluble direct dyes and use either water-insoluble or reactive dyes[4,5]. By careful control, it is possible to apply selected vat and azoic dyes to the cellulosic portion of a wool-cellulose union material without damaging the wool portion to any appreciable extent, thus obtaining dyeings of outstanding fastness to washing. Vat and azoic dyes colour both fibres, but with reactive dyes (applied cold) the wool is only stained and can be dyed subsequently with the usual wool dyes.

By choosing one of these special dyeing methods, a satisfactory degree of all-round fastness can be obtained on wool-Fibro and wool-cotton materials. For the highest degree of fastness, however, it is still preferable to dye the two fibres separately in loose or yarn form, using, for example, chrome dyes for the wool and vat, sulphur or reactive dyes for the cellulosic fibre. Alternatively, mass-coloured Fibro (Fibro-Duracol), which is now available in a range of shades, can be used.

WOOL-NYLON UNIONS

NYLON is a generic name for synthetic linear polyamides, but only two varieties, nylon 6.6 and nylon 6, need be considered. The former is represented by Bri-Nylon (ICI) and the latter by Enkalon (British Enkalon) and Celon (Courtaulds).

Nylon is a strong, tough fibre, and it is possible, by using nylon yarns together with wool yarns, or a yarn consisting of a blend of wool and nylon staple, to produce strong lightweight materials which retain the desirable properties of wool. Thus the inclusion of a nylon reinforcing yarn in the toes and heels of wool socks imparts greatly improved resistance to abrasion during wear. A similar benefit is obtained by incorporating nylon in carpets.

Nylon shows high chemical affinity for acid dyes, which are therefore faster to wet treatments on nylon than they are on wool, while good fastness to light is obtained in most cases. The capacity of nylon for acid dyes, however, is limited, and it quickly becomes saturated with dye, except in the case of pale shades. When a mixture of acid dyes is used, this may result in one component being excluded altogether. For example, if a mixture of a blue dye of high affinity and a yellow dye of low affinity is used to produce a green, the nylon may absorb only the blue component, while the wool absorbs both dyes, an undesired two-tone effect thus being obtained.

With equalizing acid dyes, the nylon portion usually dyes darker than the wool in pale shades, and conversely with heavy shades, but no general pattern is discernible in the case of milling acid dyes. With both types, very careful selection of dyes is essential[6].

Equalizing acid dyes are used for pale shades, a colourless compound possessing high affinity for nylon, *e.g.* Propolan Salt WN (ICI), being added to the dyebath to act as a restraining agent for the nylon and so produce a solid shade. The amount of nylon-blocking agent required varies with different acid dyes and different depths, and in general, nylon 6 requires two or three times as much restraining agent as does nylon 6.6.

The methods used are similar to those employed for wool alone, but sulphuric acid is replaced by formic acid. When medium or dark shades are required, neutral dyeing acid dyes which build up well on nylon are used. These dyes are best applied in presence of a levelling agent such as Univadine W (CIBA), from a bath containing acetic acid and Glauber's salt.

Neutral dyeing premetallized dyes of the Irgalan (Gy) and Cibalan (CIBA) type are very useful for colouring wool-nylon unions. They build up well on nylon, and selected dyes give solid shades, but the colours obtainable are not as bright as those given by acid dyes.

Specially selected chrome dyes may be used for fast heavy shades. A fresh bath, acidified with formic acid, may be required for after-chroming, which takes place with difficulty on the nylon. It is assisted by adding one per cent of sodium thiosulphate (a reducing agent) after chroming for one hour, reduction then being allowed to proceed for 15 minutes in the cooling bath.

At the present time, a popular mixture for carpet yarns consists of wool, Evlan, and nylon 6.6 in the ratio 42.5:42.5:15. Evlan (Courtaulds) is an abrasion-resistant, modified viscose fibre, and the union is most conveniently dyed with ready-made mixtures of milling acid and direct dyes, *e.g.* Multilan dyes (ICI), in presence of a nylon-blocking agent.

WOOL-CELLULOSE ACETATE UNIONS

In this country, cellulose acetate is sold by Courtaulds Ltd. in fibrous form under the names Dicel and Tricel. Dicel consists of 'secondary' cellulose acetate, *i.e.* cellulose in which approximately five out of every six hydroxyl groups have been acetylated, while Tricel is fully acetylated. Neither fibre has any appreciable affinity for direct dyes, and dyeing is carried out with disperse dyes. These dyes are non-ionic and are only sparingly soluble in hot water. They are sold in the form of finely ground powders. When added to a bath containing a suitable dispersing agent, they form a stable suspension from which dyeing takes place through gradual dissolution of dye in the water.

WOOL-DICEL UNIONS

Cellulose acetate fibres for blending with wool, *e.g.* for hand knitting and carpet yarns, are used in the form of staple fibre having dimensions similar to those of wool. To avoid saponification of the Dicel, scouring baths should not be strongly alkaline, and a synthetic detergent is used in preference to soap. Except for the delustred variety, which may be dyed at the boil, Dicel should not be dyed at temperatures above 85°C, to avoid delustring. The wool portion of the union is dyed with neutral dyeing acid or 1:2 metal-complex dyes, in the same bath, although penetration of the wool at 85°C is less satisfactory than at the boil.

The main difficulty arises from staining of the wool by the disperse dyes, especially in full shades. Wool has some affinity for disperse dyes, but the stain produced has poor fastness, particularly to light and rubbing. It is therefore inadvisable to rely on this stain for the coloration of the wool portion of the union. Staining of the wool by the disperse dyes takes place in the early stages of dyeing, but at equilibrium the cellulose acetate, because of its much higher affinity, takes up much more disperse dye than does the wool. Sufficient time must therefore be allowed for the disperse dye initially absorbed by the wool to be transferred to the cellulose acetate.

Use of a two-bath process enables the stain on the wool to be cleared before the wool portion is dyed. In practice, however, a one-bath process is almost always used, owing to the saving in time. The dye liquor is prepared at 40°C with half to one pound of a non-ionic dispersing agent per 100 gallons. Next, the acetate dyes are pasted with a little dispersing agent, diluted with water and added to the dyebath, preferably through a fine sieve, followed by the wool dyes in solution and 5 to 40 per cent of Glauber's salt and, if desired, 2 to 5 per cent of ammonium acetate to bring the pH to 6·5-7. The scoured yarn is then introduced and the temperature raised slowly to 85°C, dyeing being continued at 85°C for one hour.

Careful selection of dyes is important, particularly of disperse dyes to give minimum staining of the wool.

WOOL-TRICEL BLENDS

Blends containing 40 per cent of wool and 60 per cent of Tricel are widely used for the production of permanently pleated skirts by steam setting. The cloth is first crabbed and then scoured in rope form.

Dyeing[7] is carried out at the boil, as Tricel dyes very slowly at 85°C, but the higher temperature increases the staining of the wool by the disperse dyes. These dyes tend to volatilize during steam setting, so the less volatile disperse dyes must be chosen. Three methods are used: (*i*) a single-bath method for pale shades, followed by clearing; (*ii*) a two-bath method for medium and heavy depths; and (*iii*) a two-bath method for navy blue or black, using a diazotized and developed disperse dye for the Tricel. Dispersol AC (ICI) is a suitable dispersing agent. With the one-bath method (*i*), the clearing treatment requires an 0·2 per cent solution of a non-ionic compound, *e.g.* Lubrol E (ICI), at 50°C. This treatment causes some loss in depth. Apart from these modifications, the one-bath dyeing is as for wool-Dicel. When the two-bath method is used, the Lubrol E is added to the second bath, in which the wool is dyed with selected neutral-dyeing acid or 1:2 metal-complex dyes.

WOOL-TERYLENE UNIONS

THE POLYESTER FIBRE sold as Terylene (ICI), Dacron (Du Pont), etc., is blended with wool to give yarn or cloth of improved resistance to wear. If Terylene is present to the extent of not less than 55 per cent, the cloth can be given a durable crease or pleat. Most cloths of this type are obtained by blending dyed wool slubbing with dyed Terylene slubbing, but union piece dyeing for solid shades is practised to a considerable extent. The blend is also dyed in yarn form, *e.g.* for carpets, and in the form of knitted fabric. Owing to the wide difference in the abrasion resistance of the two fibres the production of cross-dyed effects to give two different colours is not advisable where the garment may be subjected to moderately heavy wear.

Terylene, like cellulose acetate, is dyed with disperse dyes, but Terylene is very hydrophobic and swells very little in the dyebath. Consequently, dyeing is very slow, even at the boil. In mixtures with wool, this difficulty is overcome by using a 'carrier'. Carriers are organic compounds which are absorbed by the Terylene and loosen the tight bonding between the long polymer chains, thus facilitating entry of dye molecules. One widely used carrier is *o*-phenylphenol, which is sold in the form of its water-soluble sodium salt under the name Tumescal OP (ICI). The sodium salt, however, is not a carrier, and acetic acid must be added to the dyebath to liberate the *o*-phenylphenol. Dilatin TC (Sandoz) and Levegal PT (FBy), on the other hand, are sold as neutral emulsions of the actual carriers, namely, chlorobenzene and methyl salicylate, respectively.

Carriers enable wool-Terylene fabrics to be dyed reasonably quickly at the boil in an enclosed winch machine. Beam dyeing machines are also available, enabling dyeing to be carried out at temperatures up to 107°C.

The choice of dyeing procedure depends on the method adopted for removing the cross-staining on the wool component. The degree of staining is influenced by the choice of dispersing agent and carrier, by the properties of the dyes employed, by the pH of the dyebath, and by the presence of any residual combing oil on the yarn. Wool-Terylene yarns and fabrics should always be scoured thoroughly before dyeing, which is preceded by heat setting in the case of woven cloths.

A typical two-bath method for the production of medium or heavy shades is as follows. The bath is set at 40°C with 0·7 g. of Dispersol AC and 4·6 g. of acetic acid (30 per cent) per litre, and the disperse dyes are added.

The goods are then introduced and the temperature is raised to the boil in 30 to 40 minutes and held at the boil for 10 minutes. A solution of Tumescal OP, equivalent to 3·5 g. per litre of dye liquor, is then added in portions over 30 minutes. The pH of the dye liquor is next adjusted to 5·5 to 6·5 and dyeing continued at the boil for at least 90 minutes. When the Terylene component is considered to be on shade, the liquor is run off and the wool is cleared by treating at 50°C for 30 minutes in a fresh liquor containing, per litre, 3 cc. of ammonia (sp. gr. 0·880), 2 g. of sodium hydrosulphite, and 0·5 to 1·0 cc. of Dispersol VL (ICI). The colour of the Terylene is not affected by this treatment. The goods are then rinsed and the wool is dyed as rapidly as possible with milling acid, 1:2 metal-complex, or chrome dyes.

For light and medium shades it is possible to use a one-bath method, removing most of the disperse dye staining the wool by means of an after-treatment with a non-ionic detergent. The bath is set at 40°C with 3 g. of ammonium acetate, 1 g. of Dispersol AC, and 0·5 to 3 cc. of Dilatin TC, per litre. After circulating the liquor for a few minutes, the bath is adjusted to pH 6·0-6.5. The disperse dyes are then added, followed by the wool dyes. The temperature is raised to the boil in 40 to 50 minutes and held at that temperature for at least 90 minutes. If pressurized equipment is available, it is advantageous to raise the temperature to 105° to 107°C. After dyeing, the goods are rinsed, and then cleared at 80°C for 60 minutes in a solution containing 1 to 2 g. of Lubrol W (ICI) per litre. The clearing bath may be acidified with acetic acid to reduce migration of the wool dyes. Finally, the goods are rinsed and dried.

The one-bath method is particularly suitable for dyeing wool-Terylene yarns in the form of cross-wound chesses or cones, and for dyeing cloth on beam dyeing machines.

In choosing dyes for the wool component, it is important to bear in mind that wool-Terylene garments such as pleated skirts are likely to be washed more frequently than most all-wool garments. Disperse dyes should be chosen mainly for light fastness and for low cross-staining on wool when used with the chosen carrier. The choice of dyes is wider when the two-bath process is employed.

One problem encountered with wool-Terylene materials is destruction of some disperse dyes caused by the reducing action of wool. This difficulty can be overcome by careful adjustment of the pH to 5·0-5·5 by means of a mixture of ammonium sulphate and formic acid[8].

WOOL-ACRYLIC FIBRE UNIONS

ACRYLIC FIBRES consist of copolymers containing not less than 85 per cent of polyacrylonitrile. They can be divided into two types according to whether they contain (*a*) acidic groups or (*b*) basic groups. When acidic groups are present the fibre can be dyed with cationic (basic) dyes, while the presence of basic groups enables the fibre to be dyed with acid dyes. Both types have affinity for disperse dyes, but the affinity of the type with acidic groups is rather low. One important feature of the acrylic fibres is their thermoplasticity. In consequence, hot dyebaths should be cooled gradually to about 50°C by running in cold water over a period of 30 minutes before handling the material.

Fibres of the acidic group type are represented by Orlon 42 (Du Pont), Courtelle (Courtaulds), and Acrilan 16 (Monsanto). Mixtures of these fibres with wool are used for knitted garments which are soft and shrink little, dyeing being carried out in yarn form. Cationic dyes are used for the acrylic fibre, special ranges of good all-round fastness, *e.g.* Astrazone (FBy) and Sevron (Du Pont) dyes, having been developed specially for these fibres. Milling acid or 1:2 metal-complex dyes are used for the wool component. It is possible to use a one-bath method, but the cationic and acid dyes tend to combine to form an insoluble complex, and it is necessary to add a non-ionic, aliphatic auxiliary product to avoid precipitation.

The best results, especially with medium and dark shades, are obtained by means of a two-bath process. The cationic dyes are applied first. They dye the wool initially, but on boiling for one to two hours they transfer to the rather impervious acrylic fibre, for which they have greater affinity. A non-ionic auxiliary product, to the extent of 2 g. per litre, and 10 per cent of acetic acid (30 per cent) are added to the dyebath. Any cationic dye remaining on the wool will exhibit very poor fastness properties, so a short clearing treatment at 60°C with a synthetic detergent is next given. Finally, the wool is dyed to match the acrylic fibre from a neutral or slightly acid bath, using either milling acid or 1:2 metal-complex dyes.

Alternatively, a one-bath two-stage process may be used. After dyeing the wool, the bath is cooled to 80°C and acetic acid and cationic dyes are added. The temperature is then raised slowly to the boil and held at the boil for at least $1\frac{1}{2}$ hours.

Acrylic fibres containing basic groups are represented by the fibre now known as Acrilan Type 36 (Monsanto). The basic groups in fibres of this type are only weakly basic, so they ionize only at low pH values and a strongly acid bath is necessary when dyeing with acid dyes. When wool is present as well as the acrylic fibre, the low pH may cause unlevel dyeing, but this difficulty can be overcome by adding a restraining agent of the cationic type, together with a non-ionic agent to prevent precipitation of the acid dye-cationic agent complex.

For solid shades on union cloths containing wool and Acrilan Type 36, selected equalizing acid dyes are used, in the presence of 5 per cent of sulphuric acid, together with, for example, 2 per cent of the cationic Tinegal W (Gy) and 3 per cent of the non-ionic Irgasol PMC (Gy). The temperature is raised to the boil in 45 minutes and held at the boil for one hour. Some of the 1:2 metal-complex dyes may be applied in a similar way for pale or medium depths, but with addition of 3 to 4 per cent of sulphuric acid. Careful selection of dyes is necessary, since some acid dyes exhibit poor fastness to light on Acrilan Type 36, while others produce different depths or different shades on the two fibres. The low pH causes some damage to the wool portion of the material.

REFERENCES

1. Cheetham, R. C., 'Dyeing Fibre Blends' (London: van Nostrand, 1966).
2. Bird, C. L., 'The Theory and Practice of Wool Dyeing', Chapter 8 (Bradford: Soc. Dyers & Col., 3rd edn., 1963).
3. Webster, G., *J. Soc. Dyers & Col.*, 1943, **59**, 54.
4. Lemin, D. R., and Collins, J. K., *J. Soc. Dyers & Col.*, 1959, **75**, 421.
5. Hadfield, H. R., and Lemin, D. R., *J. Textile Inst.*, 1960, **51**, T1351.
6. Beal, W., *J. Soc. Dyers & Col.*, 1967, **83**, 3.
7. I.C.I. Ltd., Dyestuffs Division, Technical Information (Dyehouse) No. 411 (1958).
8. Carbonell, J., and Sanahuja, V., *Textil-Rund.*, 1962, **17**, 529.

THE FINISHING OF WOOLLEN AND WORSTED FABRICS

THE OBJECT OF FINISHING is to improve the cloth as received from the loom thereby rendering it more acceptable to the buyer and more suited to the purpose for which it is intended. In the past, cloth finishing consisted of carrying out some or all of the following well-established operations: scouring, milling, squeezing, hydro-extracting, drying, carbonizing, bleaching, raising, cutting, dewing, damping, pressing, steaming, conditioning, and rigging, cuttling or rolling. While these still remain the basis of finishing, the scope has been extended in recent years by the inclusion of a variety of chemical processes to produce such special effects as water repellency, unshrinkability, resistance to moth attack, etc. The results obtained are largely dependent on the class of fabric and the difference between the loom and finished states varies widely from one type of cloth to another.

PRELIMINARY PROCESSES

WHEN THE CLOTH leaves the loom, a certain amount of work is necessary before true finishing can begin. These preliminary processes comprise weighing, measuring, numbering or labelling, perching, knotting, and mending.

The pieces are first given a reference number, then measured in length and width, and weighed, the details, together with the date on which the cloth was received being entered into a journal or grey piece book. Numbering and labelling may be done in many ways. Each piece may be marked with a clear indication of its origin, style of finish, and reference number, and it is convenient to adopt a fixed rule of numbering, *e.g.*, at the head end of the piece on the face side. The piece may be marked by sewing on a special machine or by a marking instrument filled with ink which is fast to subsequent processing and of such a colour that it will be clearly visible after dyeing. In some factories a card system is operated, in which a ticket accompanies the cloth through the finishing routine. Direct reading scales and automatic measuring devices are useful for weighing and measuring pieces.

Perching, knotting, and mending are purely corrective but take up considerable time. In certain branches of the trade one burler and one mender are required for every three weavers engaged on two looms, and consequently burling and mending costs may be quite appreciable. The thoroughness with which these operations are carried out depends largely, however, on the type of cloth. It is greatest with fine worsteds and cloths with a clear finish and least in the case of woollens of low qualities with a milled or raised finish.

PERCHING

This operation consists in examining the cloth and marking faults and defects. Faults which cannot be mended are marked with string at the edge of the list, while those to be dealt with in the mending room are indicated by chalk which may subsequently be washed out. Special care should be taken, however, in marking goods which have to be bleached, as some chalks contain iron and traces of this element left in the piece may cause defects during treatment with peroxide.

In most factories the cloth is pulled over two bars by the percher and an assistant, but mechanical perches are favoured in others. All perches should be well illuminated and, where there is difficulty in obtaining satisfactory natural light, it is now possible to produce efficient artificial daylight by the use of discharge tubes. The perch is usually placed in front of a window giving a north light, and the percher examines the cloth as it passes in front of him. Thin cloths are often 'looked through', *i.e.*, the percher stands behind the cloth and facing the window, and is thus able to see irregularities which might otherwise be missed. A good percher is able to decide correctly which faults should be mended and which may be allowed to pass without adversely affecting the quality of the finished cloth.

COMMON DEFECTS

The following defects may be observed at the grey perch or during examination on a table:

Broken warp or weft threads: A special case of this defect is cracked stripes which often arise as a result of the different elastic properties of the yarns composing the ground and the striping threads.

Faulty interlacings arising from trailed-in threads, wrong lifting of harness, bent reeds or wrongly sleyed ends.

Thick threads arising from uneven slubbing, bad piecing, or defective spinning.

Slack threads: When occuring in the warp, these are often due to careless piecing or loose beaming; in the weft they are due to yarn running too loosely from the spool, to shuttles rebounding, or to uneven delivery of yarn.

Tight threads: These occur in the warp as a result of careless warping, the joining of a broken thread without the insertion of an extra piece of yarn or by threads being caught in the eyes of healds. In the weft they are due to uneven winding or threads catching in the shuttle.

Warp stripiness arising from uneven yarns, defective warping, sizing or beaming, unevenly spaced harness, or defective reeds.

Stripes in the direction of the weft are caused by uneven or wrong yarn, faulty let-off or take-up motions, unequal distribution of moisture in weft yarns, wrong picking of weft, or, in the case of fine worsted cloths, by allowing looms to stand idle for too long.

Faults near the edges of pieces: These arise from bad warping, defective temples, bad selvedge construction, or rough treatment resulting in tears and holes.

Streaks due to dirty carding.

Marks in the direction of the warp due to dirty or rusty reeds.

Damage to cloth due to shuttle traps.

Holes arising from a variety of causes.

Stains: Oil (from careless oiling), iron, mildew.

KNOTTING

The piece is drawn over the sloping top of a knotter's table by the operative, who, sitting in front of the table, examines the piece both visually and by passing her hands over the surface to locate knots. The surface of the table must therefore be smooth and even. Fabrics are always drawn over face downwards, so that the knots may be pulled on to the back of the cloth by burling irons or tweezers, but the precise treatment depends on the character of the cloth. In many cases the knots are cut, care being taken not to cause a hole. Slubs are thinned out by the knotter.

MENDING

Defects such as warp and weft bars cannot be dealt with, but menders can effectively correct those due to missing threads, wrong interlacings, wrong yarns, tight and slack threads, and holes. The thoroughness with which cloths are mended depends on the type and quality. Plain and fancy cloths with clear cut finishes are mended thoroughly, special attention being paid to the coloured threads. In milled cloths, only serious faults are dealt with, and milled and raised fabrics do not, in general, require detailed mending. West of England cloths of high quality, such as superfines and doeskins, however, are mended carefully so as to maintain the high standard associated with this section of the industry. Pieces are usually mended in the grey state, as the closing up of the structure during scouring minimizes the possibility of mends being detected.

Mending is done by women who pull the piece over a sloping knotting table, and work with the cloth across the lap. Breakages in weft or warp threads and missing picks are corrected by sewing in new pieces of appropriate yarn, following the interlacings of the cloth and adjusting the tension as nearly as possible to that of the yarn in the rest of the piece. Mending needles used for this purpose are blunt-ended and flexible, and should not be too thick, otherwise unnecessary thread displacement will result. The four ends of yarn remaining after mending a fault of this type (two from the sewn-in piece of yarn and one from each extremity of the broken thread) should be about half-an-inch long and left on the back of the cloth.

Faults arising from wrong yarn are mended similarly, with the additional operation of removing the wrongly inserted thread. In the case of threads which are too thick or of the wrong type, but which have the correct interlacing, a piece of the correct yarn is attached to the faulty thread which is then pulled out, drawing the new one into its place. Tight picks are broken, the cloth is pulled out at the selvedges and worked so as to adjust the tension, the gap so created being mended as above. Holes and bad places are mended so that the repair does not appear lumpy.

BURLING OR PICKING

This operation is often carried out in the mending room and consists of removing burrs, straws, cotton, etc., from the cloth. It is often done after the cloth has been piece-dyed, for it is only then that much of the cellulosic material becomes visible. If there is too much impurity, the piece has to be burl dyed or carbonized.

DESIGN OF MENDING ROOMS

Mending rooms should be well lighted, from both natural and artificial sources, and the mending tables should be placed near the windows. Tables for knotting or burling only can be placed in the centre of the room. There should also be ample space for scrays on which to store cloths before and after mending. The room should be kept clean, and it is therefore desirable for it to be decorated in a pleasing, well-chosen colour scheme.

SETTING PROCESSES

CERTAIN TYPES OF FABRIC must be set before being submitted to wet treatments such as scouring and dyeing. For example, many dress fabrics as received from the loom would cockle hopelessly during dyeing and become quite useless if they were not set. Similarly, crossbred goods would not be satisfactorily finished and many plain weave or hopsack cloths would develop a diaper appearance. The object of setting therefore is to fix the threads of the cloth in position, the degree of permanence required depending upon the treatment which the cloth has to undergo. A cloth which is to be scoured only need not be set so drastically as one which is to be dyed at the boil. It must always be remembered, however, that most fabrics are Hoffman-pressed during making up into garments, and must therefore be stabilized so that they are not unduly distorted or cockled by this operation.

CRABBING AND WET BLOWING

These processes are usually employed to set fabrics and so prevent distortion during finishing. Most dress fabrics are crabbed, as are those of crossbred quality, while it is also advisable to treat Botany goods in plain and hopsack weaves. Whenever the structure of yarn or cloth is such that it tends to slip or distort during finishing and so produce an unattractive material, it is necessary to crab. The modern crabbing machine consists essentially of a perforated roller, capable of being rotated while half-immersed in a trough of hot liquid, together with equipment for winding the cloth on to the roller, and for applying pressure to the cloth by means of a heavy top roller. In practice, the cloth, free from creases, is wound on to the roller, run in the warm liquor for about five minutes and then removed from the roller. It is then treated again in exactly the same manner, except that the end which was originally outside is placed on the inside. This double treatment ensures that both ends of the piece are treated alike.

It is customary to cover the crabbing roller with a cotton wrapper and to attach lengths of cotton (15 yards) to the ends of the piece to be crabbed. The liquor used in crabbing is usually water, but alkaline solutions of borax have been recommended. Although these are more effective as a setting medium, they tend to weaken the cloth unduly, and it is probably unwise to exceed a value of pH 7 in the crabbing bowl. The addition of detergents, such as Lissapol C paste or Melioran, facilitates wetting and may cause a certain amount of cleansing. The temperature of the crabbing liquor should always exceed any temperature to which the material is likely to be subjected during subsequent processing, and cloths to be dyed and those of crossbred quality should always be set at the boil.

In modern crabbing machines, the diameter of the rollers is generally about 24 inches, and it is customary to employ a unit consisting of three bowls, the first two containing boiling water and the third cold water. The cloth to be treated is crabbed in the first bowl and then wound round from the crabbing roller of the first bowl to that of the second bowl, where it is again crabbed. It is finally wound on to the roller of the third bowl and run in cold water for a time.

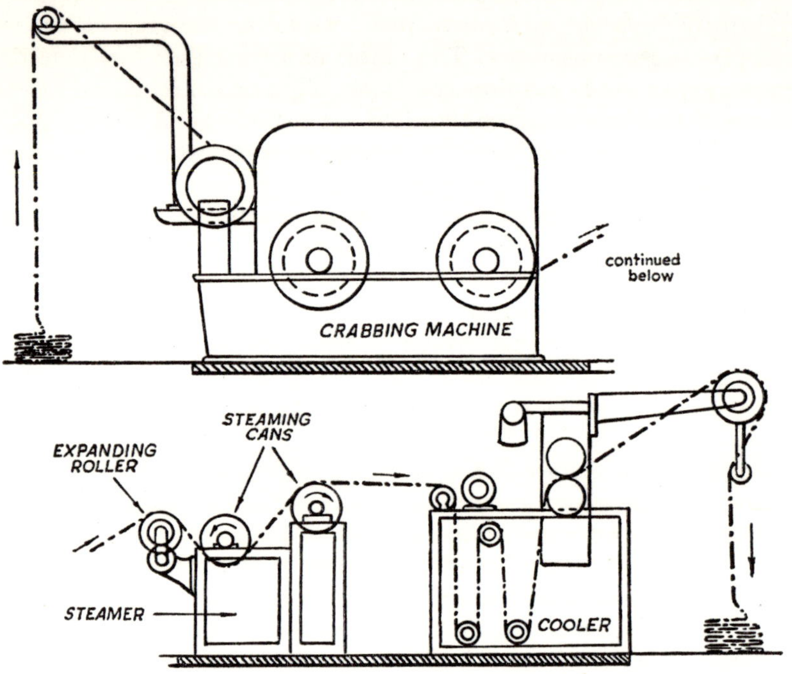

FIG. 13.1.   OUTLINE OF A MODERN SETTING UNIT

An alternative method of setting fabrics is by the operation known as wet blowing—a process which often follows crabbing, if a specially high degree of permanence is required. In this method, the cloth, fitted with end pieces, is wetted out, or is received direct from a crabbing bowl, and is wound on to a perforated metal roller. Steam is blown through the fabric until it is dry and then it is cooled by sucking air through or by passing it through a trough containing cold water. The machine is similar to that employed for the finishing operation of dry blowing. The process is then repeated on a similar roller to avoid ending. By this means, a high degree of permanent set is realised. A modern setting unit often comprises a two-bowl crab, a steaming machine and a cold water trough, on the lines of that shown schematically in Fig. 13.1.

DRY BLOWING AND HEAT SETTING

Many fabrics are dry blown on a conventional blowing or semi-decating machine. The process gives a limited amount of set but there is little risk of colour bleeding. It is widely used to process wool-Terylene blended fabrics. Although setting is best carried out as the first operation, there is some risk of spinning oils being made more difficult to remove. Many finishers therefore scour the fabric before setting it by crabbing or wet blowing.

With wool-Terylene fabrics another method is possible, *viz.* heat-setting. The cloth is scoured and dried before being heat set, a process in which the cloth is passed through a single layer stenter at 170°-180°C, the time of treatment being 25 seconds. The temperature must be lowered if there is any danger of dye sublimation.

DEFECTS PRODUCED IN SETTING OPERATIONS

The chief defects produced in setting operations may be listed as follows:

Inadequate setting due to the use of too low a temperature.

Listing: The pieces dye darker along the lists.

Tendering due to the use of excessive tension or strongly alkaline setting liquors.

SCOURING

WHEN WOOL FABRICS have been numbered, perched, knotted, mended and, where necessary, set, as outlined in the previous paragraphs, they are in a suitable condition for finishing. In most cases, the first operation is scouring, the main object of which is to clean the fabric and so to prepare it for other mechanical and chemical processes. The release during scouring of most of the temporary stresses in the cloth causes it to contract, and hence there is a closing up of the structure. The slight felting which occurs also helps to give the cloth an attractive handle and appearance. Scouring should be carried out so as to obtain maximum cleanliness with minimum damage or adverse modification of the cloth.

Impurities present in greasy cloth include oils and lubricants applied to facilitate yarn manufacture and weaving, size applied to warps before weaving, and dirt deposited on the cloth during manufacture.

The amount of dirt is comparatively small, and only a few warps are sized, but oil is present on practically every piece as it comes to the finisher. The nature of the oil varies with the cloth. Worsteds usually contain about three per cent of neutral oil—olive oil, arachis oil, or modified mineral oil. Woollens of good quality are made from yarns oiled with about 10 per cent of oleine (a mixture of liquid fatty acids) but low woollens may contain 20-30 per cent of oils applied, not only during blending before carding, but also during rag grinding. These oils contain varying proportions of oleines and mineral oils.

Neutral oils are generally removed by a process of emulsification with soap or synthetic detergents, while oleines are scoured out by what is termed saponification, *i.e.*, the cloth is treated with an alkali (sodium carbonate) which reacts with the fatty acid present to form a soap, and this emulsifies the dirt and non-saponifiable material present on the cloth.

The principal reagents employed in scouring are (*i*) emulsifying agents, of which soap is the most important although the use of synthetic detergents is increasing, (*ii*) alkalis, (*iii*) solvents and auxiliaries, and (*iv*) water.

EMULSIFYING AGENTS

Soaps are the metallic salts of fatty acids but, so far as scouring is concerned, the term is often restricted to the potassium and sodium salts. Soaps vary widely in their properties but, for scouring, they should have good cleansing power and should be soluble, so that they can easily be removed from the cloth when scouring is completed.

They should be derived from fatty acids which do not oxidize or become rancid unduly rapidly; otherwise any soap left on the piece will cause it to smell after a period of storage. Although potassium soaps are more soluble than are sodium soaps, the latter are used more frequently because they are cheaper.

Soap scouring is best carried out at about pH 10.7, and hence it is customary to add alkali to soap solutions. This not only increases the efficiency of the scouring but also prevents the formation of acid soaps on the cloth. Moreover, the alkali reacts with any free fatty acid present in the 'neutral' oil.

Soaps cannot be used for washing, however, where hard water is employed, as under such conditions they are precipitated as calcium or magnesium salts. Not only does this reduce the efficiency of the scouring solution, but the scum of insoluble soaps is deposited on the cloth and is difficult to remove. Where the water supply is hard, it is customary to soften it by the lime-soda or zeolite process, or to add a reagent such as Calgon (sodium hexametaphosphate), which reacts in such a way that calcium and magnesium ions are incorporated in the complex phosphate molecule in an unionized form and do not then react with soap.

A second disadvantage of the use of soap arises from the fact that it is precipitated as fatty acid in the presence of mineral acid. Even if insufficient acid is present to convert all the soap into fatty acid, insoluble acid soaps may be formed, and the deposition of these on the cloth leads to faults which are difficult to rectify. Again, soap cannot be used in sea water or in solutions of high salt concentration. Moreover, the best pH value for scouring with soap is about 10.5 and at this value there is some possibility of wool being adversely modified. When cloth has already received severe chemical treatment, or is about to undergo a drastic chemical operation, it is desirable to scour at about pH 7, at which value the detergent action of soap is poor.

Synthetic Detergents: Because of the disadvantages attached to the use of soap, many synthetic detergents have been developed and, although none has replaced soap as the principal scouring agent, they are extremely useful as additions to scouring baths in special circumstances, *e.g.*, to effect a certain amount of scouring during dyeing. Many of the auxiliaries developed during the search for synthetic detergents find use in operations other than scouring, for some are excellent wetting agents while others are softening agents.

Examples of these synthetic detergents are provided by the Teepols (Shell Chemicals), a recent formulation comprising a mixture of alkyl aryl sulphonates, *e.g.*

$$C_{12}H_{25} - \langle\!\!\!\bigcirc\!\!\!\rangle - SO_3\,Na$$

with secondary alkyl sulphates, *e.g.*

$$\begin{array}{c} H \\ | \\ R - C - CH_2 - CH_3 \\ | \\ OSO_3H \end{array}$$

and by non-ionics of the Lissapol N (I.C.I.) type, *e.g.*,

$$R - \langle\!\!\!\bigcirc\!\!\!\rangle - O\,(CH - CH_2 - O)_n H$$

The difficulty of mixing the concentrated form (Lissapol NX) with water is claimed to be overcome with the readily diluted Lissapol NXP. Attention is also being given to the problem of biodegradability, of increasing importance in view of river pollution legislation; the straight chain anionic detergents can be degraded and give no problems in effluent disposal.

Alkalis are used to remove oleines by a saponification process, and to increase the efficiency of soap solutions. Sodium carbonate, the compound of greatest importance, is supplied as light alkali (I.C.I.) in a high state of purity. Ammonia is occasionally used to give an increased brightness to a cloth, and is added during washing off.

Solvents are employed to facilitate the removal of mineral oil, and along with soap as spotting agents. The most frequently used compounds are carbon tetrachloride, paraffins, methylcyclohexanol (Sextol), tetra- and deca-hydronaphthalenes (Tetralin and Decalin), and various chlorinated compounds.

Water in good supply is essential for satisfactory wet finishing. Waters of more than 7 degrees of hardness (100 p.p.m.) are unsuitable: a supply of 3 to 4 degrees is desirable. The water should not contain iron and hard water should be softened.

MECHANISM OF OIL REMOVAL BY EMULSIFICATION

In the first stage of the removal of oil from fibres, the oil, originally uniformly distributed over the fibres, collects together in globules of about 50 microns diameter. As this involves displacement of the oil by the detergent solution, the adhesion between the oil and the fibre is of great importance, its exact magnitude being a function both of the oil and the fibre. The oil globules so formed are removed from the fibres by the mechanical agitation which is an essential feature of all scouring methods. The detergent is adsorbed on these droplets which thus acquire an electrical charge and form an emulsion. During scouring, the wool adsorbs a considerable amount of soap or synthetic detergent, which is firmly held, and the cloth must be washed-off to remove it. Care must be taken not to dilute the emulsion too rapidly or the oil phase will be re-deposited on the cloth.

REMOVAL OF MINERAL OIL FROM WOOL FABRICS

Mineral oil is more difficult to remove from wool than are other neutral oils and hence its use as a wool oil has not been regarded favourably in the past. The war-time shortage of animal fats, however, necessitated further consideration being given to the possibility of using mineral oil, for it is a satisfactory lubricant which does not oxidize on storage and of which an adequate supply is available. The sole difficulty is that of its removal from the woven fabric.

According to J. B. Speakman and N. H. Chamberlain[1], this arises from the high interfacial tension between the oil and detergent solution and the high adhesion between wool and mineral oil. The former is associated with the non-polar character of the mineral oil and it should be possible to reduce this, and thereby improve the ease of removal of the blend, by incorporating a suitable polar compound in the oil. Moreover, it is possible that some of these blends might have a smaller affinity for the wool. Since this principle was first suggested many compounds have been examined of which the following are of greatest commercial interest:

Oleyl Alcohol: Blends of mineral oil containing 7 per cent of oleyl alcohol are comparatively easily removed from wool fabrics by the standard scouring operations.

Mixed Secondary Alcohols: A blend of mineral oil containing about 15 per cent of mixed secondary alcohols can be removed satisfactorily from wool fabrics.

Oleic Acid: In this case it is necessary to add at least 70 per cent of the polar compound (oleic acid) before the standard scouring technique can be applied satisfactorily. This is due to the preferential removal of the oleic acid during the first stages of the scouring. The alkali present in the detergent solution combines with the oleic acid to form soap, leaving the mineral oil still on the fibre. If, however, the soap and soda scour is replaced by a neutral scour, *e.g.*, by using Lissapol, blends of mineral oil and oleic acid which contain as much as 50 per cent of mineral oil may be removed.

Monoglycerides: These compounds may be formed by heating glycerol with fatty acids or other organic acids of high molecular weight; they are buttery solids which are miscible with mineral oil. Blends of this type have been used commercially and are claimed to be satisfactory[2]. Other compounds closely related to the monoglycerides are the diglycerides, glycol mono-oleates, and pentaerithrytol esters derived from fatty acids, and these are also effective in promoting the removal of mineral oil.

Ethylene Oxide Condensation Products and Others: Lissapol NX (I.C.I.) is an example of this type of compound, which can be blended with mineral oils to form a lubricant which is readily removed in scouring. Wool grease derivatives and petroleum sulphonates are also useful additions to mineral oil, and modern modified mineral oils are often carefully formulated mixtures containing several polar compounds and emulsifying agents. Interest is also being shown in lubricants which, though appearing 'oily' are, in fact, completely water soluble; an example is the Oxitex (Shell Chemicals) range – mixed oxyethylene oxypropylene glycols.

$$RO - \left[CH_2 - \underset{\underset{R^1}{|}}{CH} - O \right]_n - R^{11}$$

where $R, R^1 R^{11} = H$ or alkyl.

SCOURING MACHINERY—ROPE WASHERS

Scouring machines are designed to deal with the cloth either in rope form or in open width. The former are more commonly used and consist essentially, as shown in Fig. 13.2, of two squeeze rollers *A*, a trough *H* which contains the detergent solution, a smaller trough *B* through which dirty liquid may be directed away from the machine, suitable guide rollers *C* and *D* and a draft board *G* which separates pieces of cloth which are scoured at the same time. The drawing also illustrates the passage of the cloth through the washer.

In the modern dolly machine, the frame is of iron, and built in two parts to facilitate removal of the rollers, and the wooden parts are constructed of a heavy tongued-and-grooved redwood, pitchpine or cypress. The trough, which may be lined with stainless steel, is fitted with an exit operated by a handle at the front of the machine. The squeeze rollers vary in type and may be of birch or beech (upper roller, 26-30in. diameter; lower roller, 20-24in. diameter), rock maple (both rollers 19·5in. diameter), or rubber (rollers 12in. diameter).

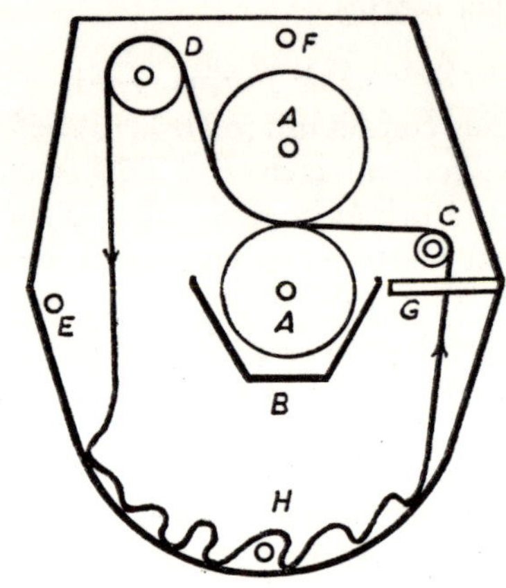

FIG. 13.2   A ROPE WASHER

Pressure is applied either by direct loading, by levers, springs, screws or by hydraulic means. Metal bearings fitted in the framework, or preferably heavy-duty roller-bearings, are employed. The sud box is fitted with openings which can be closed at will, so that liquids may be directed either down a drain or back to the main trough. The draft board has divisions made of wood, glass, resin-coated wood or stainless steel.

Arrangements for water supplies, etc., are usually fixed in front of the machine. Hot water is obtained either by injecting steam into the cold water supply or, preferably, by means of a mixing valve which connects the cold water feed-pipe to a supply of thermostatically controlled hot water. Suitable adjustment of this valve enables water to be produced at any desired temperature between those of the hot and cold supplies. The machines are usually assembled in rows over a drain, towards which the floor on each side of the machines should slope. Each machine or group of machines is fitted with a flock catcher, the purpose of which is to prevent the drains from becoming blocked.

A recent development of the dolly is represented by the Hemmer-Lodge 'Scourmaster', in which a jet box is situated before the squeeze roller, being opened for initial wetting and final washing off. The fabric balloons between the jet and the rollers, after which it falls to a special ridged roller which flings the cloth to the roof of the machine, again opening it out. Speeds of 210-220 yards per minute can be attained with conventional woollen and worsted cloths, and the scouring time can be cut, for example, from $4\frac{1}{2}$ to $2\frac{1}{2}$ hours.

OPEN-WIDTH SCOURING MACHINES

The usual type of machine employs two 12-inch squeeze rollers, either one metal and one rubber covered, or two of rubber, a drawing-off roller, guide rollers, opening and centralizing devices to keep the cloth free from creases and in the centre of the machine, and a fluted roller which operates above the sud box. To improve the efficiency of these machines, some manufacturers increase the number of squeeze rollers and fluted rollers, while others incorporate 'possing' units or suction slots.

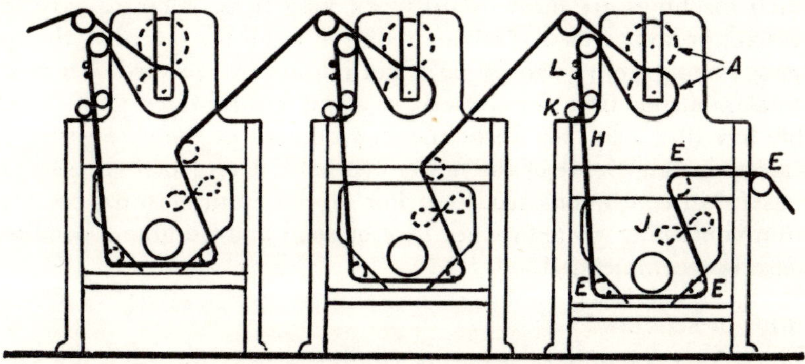

FIG. 13.3.   DIAGRAM SHOWING ARRANGEMENT OF THREE SPOONER SCOURING MACHINES IN SERIES

In the Spooner machine, which is at present used mainly for washing-off and is illustrated diagrammatically in Fig. 13.3, the cloth H is passed between two jets of liquid J formed by forcing water through two parallel pipes with specially shaped slots along their length, the position of the slots with respect to the cloth being carefully arranged to produce maximum effectiveness of the washing operation. Wash liquors which have passed through the cloth are collected in the chamber and after elimination of flock by filtration, are recirculated through the jets by the pump. The machine has squeeze rollers A, guide rollers E, openers K, and a centralizing frame L. In this machine, six pieces may be treated together, After the first passage, the dirty liquor is passed down the drain, and a clean supply admitted from a storage tank which has an outlet of large diameter to facilitate rapid filling. This process is repeated as often as is necessary, and water from the last wash may be used for cleaning a fresh lot of pieces. Three passages through the machine are usually sufficient and, if there is enough work to justify the initial expenditure, it is advantageous to instal three machines in series, the cloth being run continuously from one to the other, and the liquor circulated on a counter-current principle. The Spooner method is claimed to effect a considerable saving of water.

In the United States, Hunter, Riggs and Lombard have introduced ranges which make continuous scouring possible. The whole unit consists of a scouring section and a washing-off section, the former section comprising four scouring machines of the tight strand type. The cloth passes spirally in loop form through each in turn, and arrangements are made to avoid excessive tension being built up in the cloth. The scouring section is followed by six inter-connected bowls through which the cloth passes, each bowl being supplied with hot water. A counter-current system is employed to obtain the greatest economy of water. The cloth is finally washed in cold water in additional bowls.

Such machines are most useful when long runs of fabric have to be processed, for 600 yards of cloth are required to fill the machine, the speed of passage being from 30 to 55 yards per minute. At 40 yards per minute, the total scouring time for a piece is about 20 minutes and therefore soluble low titre soaps are recommended because of the ease with which they are removed. Some of the newer synthetic detergents will also prove very useful in continuous scouring. For fabrics from 8-16 oz. per yard a solution containing 30 grams per litre of soap and 20 grams per litre of soda ash is recommended.

METHODS OF SCOURING

The precise method of scouring employed depends upon the type of cloth and the style of finish required. Cloths shrink during scouring, and it is essential that this shrinkage should be controlled where such cloths as dress fabrics are being processed. In these cases, mechanical action should be reduced to a minimum. Scouring should be carried out so as to clean the cloth effectively without causing too much damage or loss of the essential characteristics of the fabric.

The principal reagents required are soda ash and soap. The latter is conveniently stored as a 2 to 5 per cent solution in a stainless steel or enamelled vessel fitted with a heating coil. Soda ash solutions are piped

TABLE 13.1. RELATIONSHIP BETWEEN DENSITY AND
CONCENTRATION OF SODA ASH SOLUTIONS

Density (°Tw at 15 °C)	Concentration (per cent)	Density (°Tw at 15°C)	Concentration (per cent)
1	0.47	9	4.28
2	0.95	10	4.76
3	1.42	11	5.23
4	1.90	12	5.71
5	2.30	13	6.17
6	2.85	14	6.64
7	3.33	15	7.10
8	3.80		

to the individual machines from a store tank. The concentration of the alkali depends on the class of work in hand, and varies from 3 to 10°Tw. Although it is convenient to express the concentration of alkali in terms of degrees Twaddell, it is preferable to measure actual concentration as determined by titration with standard acid. The relation between concentration and density (degrees Twaddell) is shown in Table 13.1.

PRINCIPLES OF SCOURING

The principles of scouring have been closely investigated by the Wool Industries Research Association, who emphasize the need for carefully calculating the amount of soda ash required[3]. Alkali is used in soap scouring (*i*) to neutralize acid residues from dyeing or carbonizing, (*ii*) to saponify the free fatty acid in the oil, (*iii*) to satisfy the alkali adsorbing capacity of the wool and (*iv*) to act as a soap builder.

SCOURING OF WORSTED FABRICS

About three per cent of oil is usually present in worsted fabrics and this is removed by emulsification, the dolly machine being used, except under very special circumstances. Many fabrics are set before scouring. Four pieces (70 yards) are scoured together using an approximately 2 : 1 liquor: cloth ratio, *i.e.*, 20 gallons of detergent solution for each 100 lb. cloth. Solutions of soda ash for scouring worsteds rarely exceed 4°Tw (1.90 per cent) and the lower the concentration, the less is the possibility of colour bleeding and of loss of handle. Medium weight cloths are run for 10 to 15 minutes in an alkaline solution of 3-4°Tw; sufficient soap is then added to work up a good lather (1 to 2 gallons of five per cent soap per 100 lb. of cloth), and the operation continued for a further 15 minutes. If the liquid after the first alkali wash is very dirty, it is advisable to close the sud box and direct it to the drain. Fresh alkali (20 gallons per 100 lb. of cloth) of 2°Tw strength is then added, together with the appropriate amount of soap, and the scour worked up in the usual way. To wash-off the piece, hot water is added slowly, and the liquor worked up and then eliminated *via* the sud box. This is repeated until the piece is clean, the temperature of the water being gradually reduced. Finally the piece is run in cold water for five minutes.

The scouring of worsted cloths should not be prolonged unduly as they tend to felt. If the colours are liable to bleed, the temperature should be kept as low as possible and, if they appear dull, the addition of ammonia (1 pint 0.880 ammonia) during washing-off is an advantage. The residual oil content of the scoured fabric (measured by extraction with ether) should not exceed 0.5 per cent.

Worsted-Terylene fabrics have been troublesome in that the oil used on the wool migrates to the Terylene during blending and subsequent mechanical processes; it has greater affinity for Terylene and is difficult to remove. One method, as recommended by the Wool Industries Research Association, is to use a special three-bath scour, but they consider it better to blend the tops with addition in the drawing of 0.75-1 per cent of a blend containing, for example, two parts of Lissapol NX (I.C.I.) and one part of Texofor F5 (Glovers Chemicals). Subsequently the fabric can be satisfactorily scoured in a single bath followed by a lather up.

SCOURING OF WOOLLEN FABRICS

The pieces are first run in 5-6°Tw (3-4 per cent) soda ash solution for 15 minutes, using a 2:1 liquor:cloth ratio. Soap is formed by the interaction of the alkali and the oleine. At the end of 15 minutes, if this liquor is dirty, it is drained away and a further addition of alkali at 4-5°Tw is made. The liquor is worked for 20 to 30 minutes, heavier cloths requiring a longer time. If there is difficulty in obtaining a lather, a little soap solution is added. Washing-off is carried out as described for worsted cloths, but for a longer time owing to the greater weight of the fabrics.

SCOURING OF LOW WOOLLEN FABRICS

These fabrics, which often contain considerable amounts of mineral oil, are first run for 20 minutes in 6-8°Tw soda ash solution, but stronger solutions may be used if the pieces are very dirty. The dirty liquors are then sent down the drain, and a further addition of alkali (4-5°Tw) and soap (1-2 gallons of five per cent solution) is made, scouring being continued for a further 15 minutes. The working up of a lather and the elimination of dirty liquor are repeated alternately until the cloth is clean. Additions of solvents (Sextol, carbon tetrachloride) to the extent of about one pint per 20 gallons of liquor help to remove unsaponifiable mineral oil. The cloths are washed-off as described for worsted fabrics.

USE OF SYNTHETIC DETERGENTS IN SCOURING

In view of the increasing use of synthetic detergents, the following information, taken from a manufacturer's circular, relating to scouring with Lissapol N (I.C.I.) is of interest. Worsted cloths are scoured at 50°C with one to two pounds per 100 gallons of Lissapol N and sufficient alkali only to give a non-acidic liquor; the detergent action is improved by adding 10 pounds per 100 gallons of common salt. With woollens the usual additions of soda ash are still necessary, but instead of soap, half to one pound of Lissapol N per 100 pounds of fabric is recommended. Similar procedures are available with other synthetic detergents, *e.g.*, Teepol (Shell Chemicals).

Detergents of this type are particularly useful where the water supply is hard, or when the cloth contains limey wool, as insoluble lime soaps are not formed. If, however, lime soaps are already there and have to be dispersed, Lissapol LS should be used rather than Lissapol N.

WASHING-OFF

It is essential that cloths should be well washed-off after milling to remove soap because, if this is left in, the pieces will smell after storage and will have an unpleasant handle. The operation may be done simply by running the cloth in a dolly or a single Spooner unit containing sodium carbonate solution and then rinsing thoroughly, first with hot and then with cold water. There is a tendency, however, to make this process continuous, especially in the medium and low end of the trade, so that the cloth can pass straight from the milling machine, through a scutcher and a washer, over a suction slot and into a drying machine. Several washing machines have been devised for this continuous type of processing. J. C. Scholefield[4] has developed an effective unit consisting of several troughs each fitted with squeeze rollers capable of exerting high pressure; the cloth is passed through the machine at width. Three or more Spooner units may be arranged in series together with a counter-current flow system for washing liquors.

DEFECTS IN SCOURING

Oil Stains may arise from careless oiling of machines and shafting. If the stain is caused merely by oil, spotting with Sextol or Astol A (I.C.I.), and subsequently re-scouring either the whole piece or the affected part by hand will be sufficient. Stains of this type, however, generally contain depositions of metallic compounds carried in suspension by the oil and are therefore only removed completely by the additional use of acids or cyanides (to remove copper).

Dirty pieces may be caused by incomplete removal of oil (mineral or oxidized oils), soap, or size, or by deposition of insoluble metal (calcium or magnesium) soaps. Often they may be corrected by re-scouring in the presence of solvents and Calgon, or at higher temperatures. The addition of synthetic detergents which have the property of dispersing calcium soaps is often an advantage.

Loss of handle and colour bleeding are caused by scouring at too high a temperature or in too great a concentration of alkali and it is almost impossible to correct them. To avoid these defects, it may be necessary in certain cases to scour with synthetic detergents at pH 7.

Washer marks are due to the cloth running in the same folds. They can be minimized by opening pieces during scouring, by cross drafting, or by bagging the pieces, *i.e.*, sewing the lists of the fabric together.

Cockled Pieces: The distortion of design and structure resulting in cockles in scoured fabrics is usually due to inadequate setting. The piece should be tentered and re-crabbed, but in most cases the fault cannot be rectified.

Excessive shrinking is due to excessive mechanical treatment. When scouring pieces of a type liable to shrink easily, the time of treatment should be reduced, an open washer used, or soap replaced by synthetic detergents.

Faults caused by allowing wet pieces to lie about: Two main defects may result, *viz*, modification of dye affinity and staining. It has been found that alkali migrates in a wet piece which is alkaline, so that selected portions of the cloth, *e.g.*, folds, acquire a high alkalinity. As the piece dries out, the concentration of alkali increases further and the permanent fission of the -S-S-linkages in the wool fibres which results modifies the dye affinity. Another cause of modified dye affinity and of stains is 'mildew', the growth of moulds and bacteria on the cloth. When the cloth contains only a little more moisture than usual, moulds, or vegetable growths, especially those of the species *penicillium* which are green, and *aspergillus* which are usually black, flourish, but when it is really wet, bacteria such as *B. mesentericus*, *B. subtilis*, and *B. mycoides*, and certain *actinomycites* attack fibre, resulting in degradation to cortical cells. Variously coloured stains which are difficult to remove are produced by both these agencies, and the damage which accompanies staining results in a modification of dye affinity. Bacterial degradation can be minimized by adding a little sulphuric or acetic acid to the washing-off liquors.

Longitudinal creases may result from sewing the ends of pieces with too large a stitch.

Curled Lists: The only satisfactory method of avoiding this defect is to re-design the list, but curling can be minimized by bagging the piece.

Holes in pieces are caused by foreign bodies (*e.g.*, nails, wood, *etc.*), which accidentally get into the machine or by the use of excessive pressure on the scouring rollers; this causes chafing and finally results in a hole. Holes can be avoided by careful work.

Wood stains usually occur with new wood or when rollers in the scouring machine begin to rot. They are difficult to remove and should be avoided by careful periodic examination of rollers which should be skimmed up when necessary. Localized rot should be repaired, but if the roller is generally bad, it should be replaced.

Other stains may be caused by the use of indelible pencils, by deposition of flocks or sud from the ends of the scouring rollers, or by water from iron piping dripping on to the cloth.

MAINTENANCE OF SCOURING ROOMS

The following points regarding the maintenance of scouring rooms should be strictly observed. Floors should be frequently swilled and all machines and shafting periodically examined. The rooms should be distempered or emulsion-painted at frequent intervals so that they look clean; a tradition of cleanliness which will result in improved work by the operatives, and consequently fewer faults, should be established. Old alkali bags, dirty flocks, and sud should be removed and carts kept in good condition.

MILLING

THE OBJECT OF MILLING is to shrink the fabric to the required degree, to thicken it and to give it the desired appearance and handle. As a consequence, the weave structure becomes less distinct. These changes arise from the ability of wool fibres to felt, *i.e.*, to form a solid mass from which it becomes difficult to extract single fibres without breaking them. This unique property of wool fibres is attributed to their scaly surfaces which cause each fibre to have different frictional properties in the two directions —tip to root, and root to tip. This differential friction effect (D.F.E.) causes a fibre to move in the direction of the root end when rubbed between two surfaces, as for example, between the thumb and finger—a property of great importance in determining the milling characteristics. The mechanism of felting and of milling shrinkage has been the subject of much research and speculation, many theories being advanced which went some, but never the entire, way towards explaining the phenomenon. Four factors are believed to be of importance in determining the milling shrinkage resulting from the application of a fixed amount of mechanical work. These factors are (*i*) the magnitude of the D.F.E. of the fibres, (*ii*) the ease with which the fibres extend, (*iii*) their power of recovery from extension, and (*iv*) freedom of movement of the fibres.

In a recent comprehensive survey[5] some of the more important theories are compared, and it is concluded that different mechanisms may operate under different conditions of structure, load and lubrication. For example, when fibres are spun they are partially straightened and then twisted into helices, a re-arrangement which is partly fixed by cohesive set. Subsequent wetting enables them to untwist and curl if they are free to do so, and even in a fabric some short portions will have the necessary freedom. As a result, the helices shorten and widen and the fabric shrinks and thickens. Although this may explain the consolidation of fabrics under relatively gentle action (*e.g.*, scouring) it may not be applicable to 'ordinary' felting; one suggestion postulates that a fibre may pass through adjacent zones of criss-crossing fibres, one zone holding it tightly and the other less tightly. Mechanical stress forces these zones nearer together, and the fibre slips rootwards through the less rigid zone which is thus permanently held closer to the rigid zone because the fibre cannot slip back. This sequence of events is repeated many times during the felting process and results in consolidation and shrinkage.

MILLING MACHINERY

Milling machines are of two types, stocks and rotary machines. The former, which are at present used very little except in the felt and hosiery trades, consist of a receptacle for holding the cloth, and heavy hammers or feet made from wood which pound the cloth. The shapes of the container for the cloth and of the hammers are so chosen that the cloth is turned over during the milling operation and so is evenly treated. Stocks may be of the gravity or positive types. In the former the pressure exerted by the hammers is determined only by their weight and the height from which they fall, but in the latter they are connected directly to a crankshaft and exert a constant pressure independent of the amount of cloth in the machine.

The essential parts of a typical rotary milling machine, illustrated in Fig. 13.4, are a pair of weighted squeeze rollers, a spout with a fixed base and a movable lid connected to the top squeeze roller and capable of being weighted by W, a draft board, a guide roller G, a throat H, and the main trough T. The squeeze rollers may be made of green heart oak, or of special composition and are geared together. The machines are driven direct from a line shaft, and the two rollers are connected together, preferably by a chain but occasionally by gears or belts.

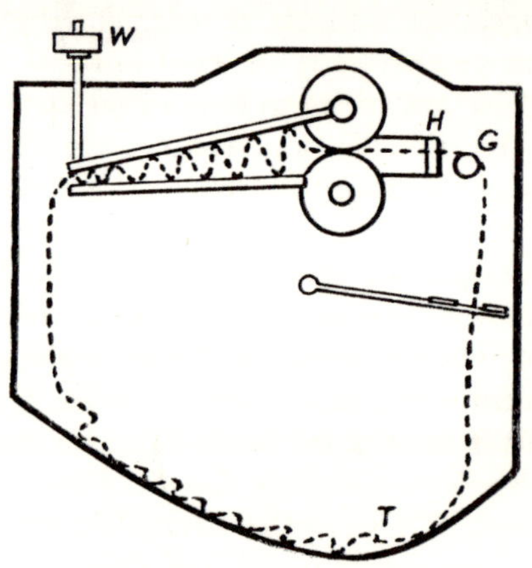

FIG. 13.4.   PRINCIPLE OF THE ROTARY MILLING MACHINE

In modern machines the pressures between the milling rollers can be altered, either by a lever-weight system or by a pneumatic device. Machines for heavy work are often built with a lower flanged roller. It is desirable to be able to control the weight applied to the spout, and this is best done by a lever-weight principle. The draft board, which also serves as a stop motion to knock off the machine should the cloth become fast, should be fitted with non-corrodible divisions. On some machines the guide roller G is replaced by a pair of rollers, to prevent the cloth from rising in the machine. The throat was originally made of porcelain, and different throats were required for different types of cloth. There is an increasing tendency, however, to replace the fixed throat by a pair of vertical rollers, capable of being adjusted at various distances apart by turning a hand-wheel. Machines should be lined with stainless steel, especially if they are to be used for acid milling.

In the past 50 years many modifications in milling machine draft boards, spouts, milling rollers and throats have been made, but many of them have been scrapped, largely because the added advantages failed to compensate for increased complexity. There is however considerable scope for plastic rollers which are easily replaced. One of the most interesting advances has been in the design of combined milling and scouring machines. There have been numerous examples of this type, both modified dollies, *e.g.*, with a row of throats inserted before the nip of the rollers, and modified milling machines. The most satisfactory for general work has been the Williams-Peace model, which is a modified milling machine. The differences between this and a controlled milling machine are the reduced length of the spout and the general shape which more closely resembles a dolly. The spout is about 18 inches long, and the base can be fixed in two positions, the higher one for milling and the lower one for scouring. The rollers and the spout are loaded by a lever system and both top and bottom rollers are driven. It is customary to scour the cloth first with the spout base lowered and then to increase the weight on the rollers so that the excess liquor is squeezed out while the cloth is run at a slower speed. After this, the cloth is soaped up and milled with the spout base raised and with the necessary pressure on the rollers. Subsequent washing-off is carried out with the adjustments as for scouring.

The saving in time by the adoption of this technique of carrying out the operations of scouring, rinsing, soaping, milling and washing off without removing the cloth from the machine is considerable.

FACTORS INFLUENCING MILLING SHRINKAGE

The shrinkage which occurs when wool fabrics and fabrics containing wool are milled for a definite time is determined by (*a*) the raw materials from which the cloth is made, (*b*) the structure of the yarns, (*c*) the structure of the cloth, (*d*) the previous history of the cloth, and (*e*) the conditions under which the milling is carried out, *e.g.*, temperature, milling agent.

EFFECT OF RAW MATERIAL ON MILLING

Fabrics made from fine wools mill more rapidly than do corresponding ones made from coarser wools. For example, merino wool mills better than does crossbred and 60s quality better than 50s of the same breed. As a first approximation, the more scaly a wool is (*i.e.*, the greater its D.F.E.), the better does it mill, but crimpiness, fibre length, yarn and cloth structure also affect the results. As far as blends with other fibres are concerned, most blended cloths containing wool shrink to an extent depending on the proportion of the wool; cotton and man-made fibres in general inhibit milling if present to an extent greater than 20 per cent. Fabrics containing Fibro and wool shrink less than all-wool cloths, the reduction being much more marked in woollen than in worsted fabrics. Wool fibres also tend to collect in balls on the surface of the fabric; these stand out on subsequent piece dyeing and can have a very detrimental effect on appearance. Structural adjustments may have to be made to prevent this.

Blended fabrics containing more than 30 per cent of nylon, Terylene, Orlon, Courtelle, Rilsan, Vinyon, Fibrolane BC or Celafibre shrink less than 100 per cent wool fabrics, and the shrinkage of three-component cloths follows similar trends.

EFFECT OF YARN AND CLOTH STRUCTURE ON MILLING

Fabrics containing woollen-spun yarns generally shrink faster than those containing worsted-spun yarns of the same count and twist. Increasing the twist in yarns reduces the rate of milling shrinkage of cloths made from them due to a reduction in the freedom of movement of the fibres. When cloths of the same weave and containing the same yarns but having various number of ends and picks are milled, the shrinkage in width is greatest when the number of ends per inch is least. In other words, a reduction of ends per inch results in an increase in weft shrinkage due to a reduction in obstruction of the shrinking weft yarn. If the number of ends is greater than the number of picks, the shrinkage warpways will be the greater. As a result of examining a number of fabrics made from the same yarn but of various structures, it has been shown that of the fabrics prepared, plain weave cloths have the smallest actual shrinkage and the lowest rate of shrinkage. Long floats favour shrinkage. In low sets a 4/4 twill is inferior in limiting shrinkage to a 4/4 hopsack, but in normal settings the reverse is true [6].

EFFECT OF CLOTH'S PREVIOUS HISTORY ON MILLING

Treatment with most chemical reagents modifies the milling properties of wool fabrics, and is utilized to produce non-shrink fabrics (*see* p. 465). The normal processes of bleaching, carbonizing, and dyeing have comparatively little effect on milling properties, but excessive bleaching, the use of high alkali concentrations in scouring, and drastic treatment in stripping or carbonizing reduce the shrinking power, and it is well known that slipe and limed wools and wastes (especially extract) are inferior to virgin wool in felting capacity. Unless carried out with undue severity, crabbing and blowing do not affect the milling shrinkage of fabrics.

EFFECT OF MILLING CONDITIONS

Soap and acids are usually employed to facilitate milling. High titre (tallow) soaps are preferred to the more liquid and soluble soaps used for scouring. Soap is more effective than an alkaline solution of the same pH value, but increasing alkalinity from pH 7 to 10.5 does increase milling shrinkage. Further increases cause a fall in shrinkage[7].

Acids promote milling but when they are used it is necessary to mill in machinery protected from the corrosive action. Acid milling is faster than soap milling and the cloth produced is stronger. Some finishers, however, are of the opinion that the handle of acid-milled pieces is inferior to that of soap-milled pieces. It may be improved however, by the addition of synthetic detergents to the acid milling liquor. The optimum temperature for soap milling is 37°C, but the effectiveness of acid milling increases with rising temperature. Acids facilitate milling by increasing the scaliness and ease of extension of the fibres without, at the same time, reducing the power of recovery.

MILLING PRACTICE

Cloths must be finished to a given width and weight, and hence it is possible only to vary the length shrinkage. For this purpose, two marks at a distance of, say one yard apart, are sewn on the list of the piece and measurements are made between them as milling proceeds, until the appropriate amount of shrinkage has been obtained. Alternatively, the two marks are inserted in such positions that when the milling is complete the distance between them will be one yard. The amount of shrinkage required for any type of cloth can be calculated from the following expression, provided that the percentage loss in finishing (mainly scouring) is known:

$$Wf = \frac{(100\text{-}L)\,Wg}{(100\text{-}S)} \quad i.e., \quad S = \frac{100(Wf\text{-}Wg) + Wg.L}{Wf}$$

where Wf = wt. per yard (finished).
Wg = wt. per yard (greasy).
L = percentage loss in weight on finishing.
S = percentage shrinkage in length.

The cloth is placed in the machine in one, two, or three drafts according to the amount of milling and the type of finish required, the drafts being arranged to be approximately equal in length. The machine is started and five per cent soap solution added very slowly from a watering can so that it is uniformly distributed. Sufficient should be added so that, on pressing the cloth between the thumb and fingers, a small amount of white foam is produced. The cloth is then milled for the appropriate time, additional soap being added if necessary. When the milling is prolonged, washer marks may be prevented by removing the cloth at intervals and shaking it. Machines should not be filled too full. If there is a tendency for the cloth to rig, or for the lists to curl, the cloth should be bagged. Shrinkage in length is mainly controlled by the weights placed on the spout, while width shrinkage is governed by the pressure on the milling rollers and the size of the throat. It is advisable to arrange the milling so that the desired width and length shrinkages are affected at the same time. The cloth is subsequently washed off with warm water in a dolly or a Spooner machine.

Grease Milling: Fabrics oiled with good quality oleines may be milled in the grease by passing the cloth through a lecker containing 8-10°Tw soda ash, and squeezing heavily before placing in the milling machine. The alkali reacts with the oleine and soap is formed in situ. A little soap may be added during milling if there is difficulty with the process. It is not desirable to grease mill fabrics which are very dirty but the process has great possibilities for there is a considerable saving of labour and the results can be very good.

Acid Milling: The cloth is impregnated with acid by running it in a scouring machine in water containing the appropriate amount of acid. It is important, however, that the cloth should be washed free from soap before acid impregnation. For impregnation with acetic acid, a 2-5 per cent solution (calculated on the weight of the cloth) is recommended, while 2-3 per cent solutions of sulphuric acid are adequate. The cloth is then hydro-extracted or passed between squeeze rollers, and then milled. Water is added at intervals during milling if the cloth becomes dry. After milling, the piece is washed-off in the usual manner, and may be given a rinse in 2°Tw soda ash before being finally washed clean.

In all methods of milling the amount of moisture present should be carefully regulated, for excess moisture causes the milled cloth to be soft and spongy and the milling to be slow. If, on the other hand, the cloth is dry, the surface is poor and there is excessive waste as flocks. The precise conditions adopted are determined by the finish required.

DEFECTS IN CLOTH MILLING

Mill rigs are streaks running lengthways in the piece, but not, in general, parallel to each other. They are caused by the cloth becoming permanently creased, promoting localized milling in the folds. Creases may arise from excessive pressure on the milling rollers or from over-filling the machine. Owing to their particular design, certain cloths are more liable to rig than others and, if this cannot be prevented by bagging or by frequently opening and shaking the cloth, it is advisable to re-design the fabric. Once formed, mill rigs are difficult to deal with; the appearance of the cloth might by improved by tentering and then dry-raising lightly on a gig before milling again in the stocks.

Chafing marks are caused by the cloth being trapped between the inside of a flange roller and the outside of the top roller, or by the use of excessive pressure and rollers slipping over the cloth.

Dyeing defects are caused by blowing steam directly on to the cloth when endeavouring to maintain a high temperature during milling.

Uneven milling is due to uneven distribution of milling liquor.

Fibres from one piece being milled into another: This results from pieces of widely different character being milled together. The same defect arises with double cloths, when fibres from the back tend to travel to the face, and so spoil the appearance of the cloth.

Failure to obtain adequate shrinkage in grease milling: The piece should be washed-off, re-soaped, and then milled.

Colour bleeding: Fast to milling colours should be used in all cases, but acid milling minimizes colour bleeding.

Cockled pieces arise from the presence of wrong yarns. Yarns of different composition, twist or count have different shrinking powers and will give rise to irregularities.

Curling lists are due to wrong construction of selvedges or to excessive milling. Pieces having a tendency to curl at the lists should be bagged.

Stains arise from alkali migration, mildew, iron, etc., as in scouring.

REMOVAL OF WATER FROM FABRICS

At several stages of the finishing routine it is necessary to remove water from the cloths. This may be done by squeezing, by hydro-extracting or by hydro-exhausting, or by drying, the last named being by far the most expensive.

Squeezing Machines are usually designed to handle cloth in rope form and their use is confined to fairly heavy fabrics. A typical machine has a pair of wood rollers, about 12 inches in diameter and 14 inches wide. Pressure is applied to the rollers, either by springs or levers, and the lower roller is driven. In recent years open-width mangles which are satisfactory for removing water from a wider range of fabrics have attracted considerable interest.

Hydro-extractors consist of a perforated cage mounted on a vertical spindle and enclosed within an outer case, which leaves the top portion of the cage open. Wet pieces are placed in the cage and are revolved at high speed, the motive force being provided, generally by an electric motor, but occasionally by a belt connected with a main shaft. The outer cases are made of mild steel and, if the machine is to be used for removing acids from cloth, lined with sheet lead. Cages are made of galvanized mild steel with holes drilled into them but in special cases they may be made of stainless steel, Monel metal, aluminium alloy, or mild steel lined with vulcanite. Vulcanite-lined cages should not be subjected to high temperatures.

The usual type of machine is 72 inches wide although smaller machines (*see* Fig. 13.5) are now being used in increasing numbers. Modern machines have safety covers which are linked to the starting mechanism so that the machine cannot be started unless the lid is down. They are also fitted with an automatic time switch which cuts out the current after an appropriate time and stops the machine by applying an electrically controlled brake. Hydro-extractors are run at about 600 r.p.m. for a 72 in. machine and up to 1,500 r.p.m. for a 36 in. machine.

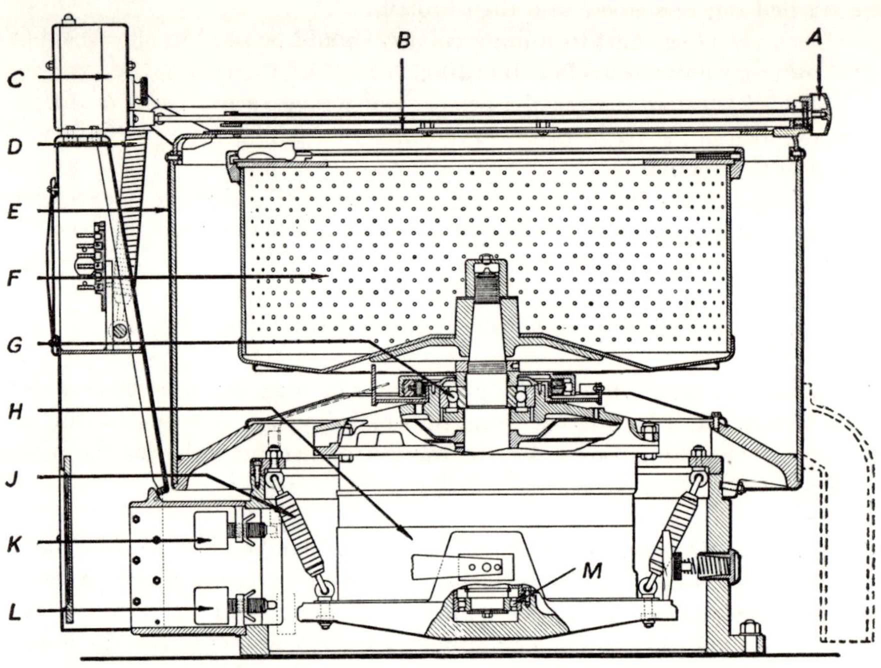

FIG. 13.5.   GENERAL ARRANGEMENT OF A BROADBENT 36 INCH
EXTRACTOR CAPABLE OF DRYING 315 LB. WOOL YARN PER HOUR

A—Starting knob: *B*—Interlocked safety cover: *C*—Time clock: *D*—Self-balancing spring: *E*—Steel shell: *F*—Perforated basket: *G*—Ball bearing: *H*—High torque motor: *J*—Suspension spring: *K*—Reverse direction switch: *L*—out of balance limiter: *M*—Roller bearing.

The material is packed uniformly into the cage and the load arranged evenly. A piece of cotton cloth is placed over the charge and the machine started. Extraction is continued for about $7\frac{1}{2}$ minutes, when the moisture content is reduced to about 40 per cent.

Hydro-Exhaustion in which the cloth is passed at full width over a suction slot has much in its favour. The width of the suction slot is adjusted by two pieces of rubber which are fitted, one on each side of the cloth, these being pushed in position so that the gap of the uncovered slot is as small as possible. Two suction slots arranged in series, are often placed in front of a drying machine.

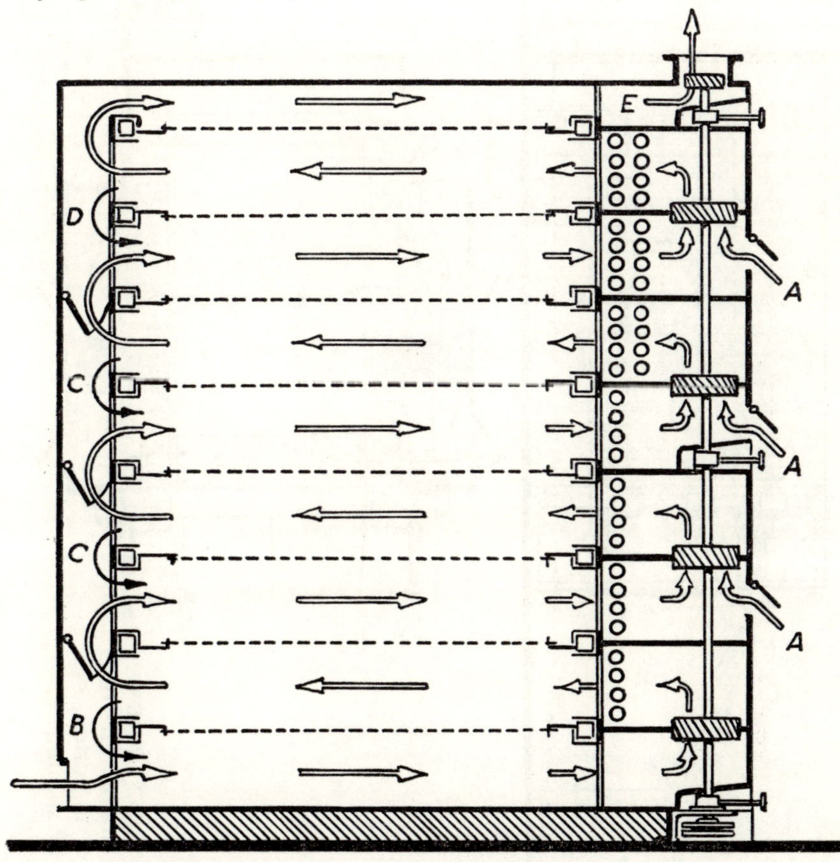

FIG. 13.6.   AIR CIRCULATION SYSTEM OF THE KRANTZ
HIGH-EFFECT PATENT CLOTH TENTERING MACHINE

A—Cool and fresh air: *B*—Cool and dry air: *C*—Warm and moist air:
D—Hot and moist air: *E*—Hot air cooled by a large amount of moisture.

DRYING AFTER CENTRIFUGING

It is necessary to dry cloths after centrifuging and, in the wool trade, it is customary to stretch them a little at the same time to remove creases. The can dryer used in cotton finishing relies upon conduction of heat for its effectiveness but this machine is seldom used for all-wool cloths. Most machines are combinations of convection dryers and radiation dryers. The cloth is attached to two parallel chains fitted with pins, the lists being

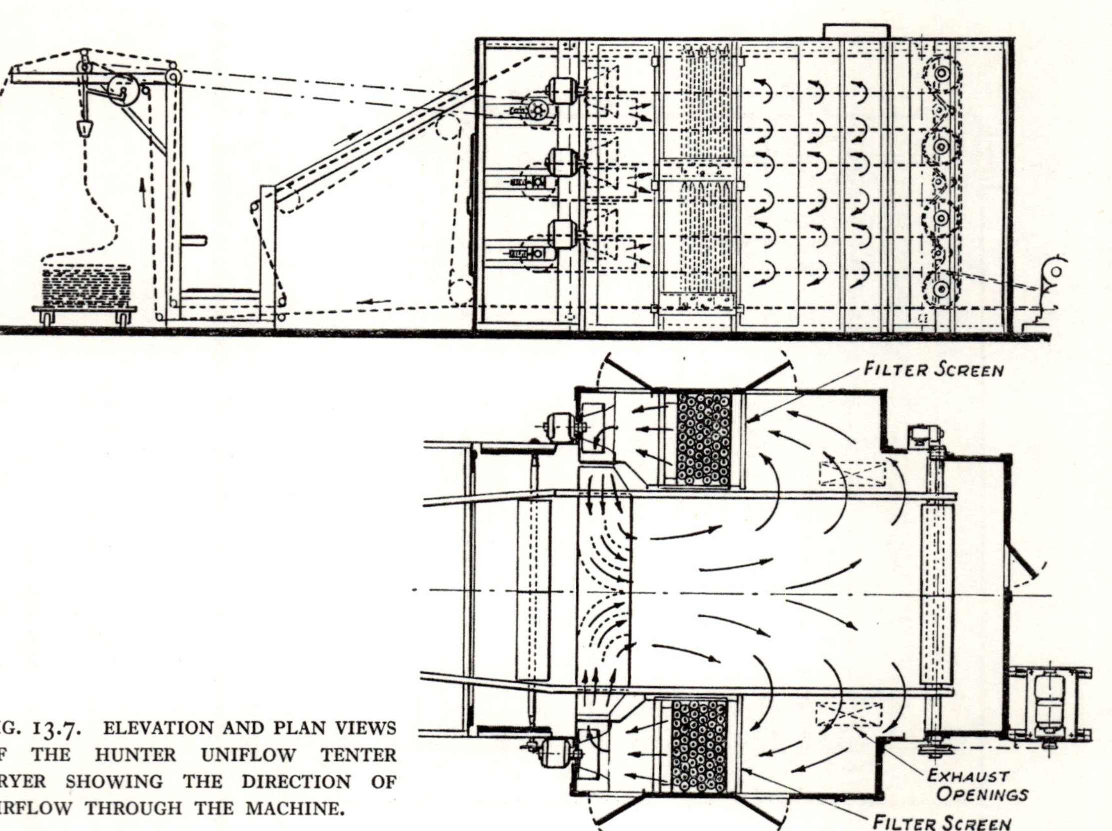

FIG. 13.7. ELEVATION AND PLAN VIEWS OF THE HUNTER UNIFLOW TENTER DRYER SHOWING THE DIRECTION OF AIRFLOW THROUGH THE MACHINE.

pushed on to the pins by a revolving brush. During the passage of the cloth through the first part of the machine the distance between the tenter chains gradually increases so that creases in the cloth are removed and its appearance when dry is improved. By the time the cloth has passed through the machine it should be thoroughly dry.

Drying machines differ largely in the method used to supply the heat. In the Charlesworth-Whiteley machine, and the E. Gordon Whiteley machine, the drying system is a combination of radiation and air-circulation. The drying chamber which is divided into layers is fitted with horizontal rows of steam-heated piping and the cloth is arranged to pass over and under each layer. Circulating fans are installed at such positions that air is drawn from the two bottom layers into the next two, and circulated warp

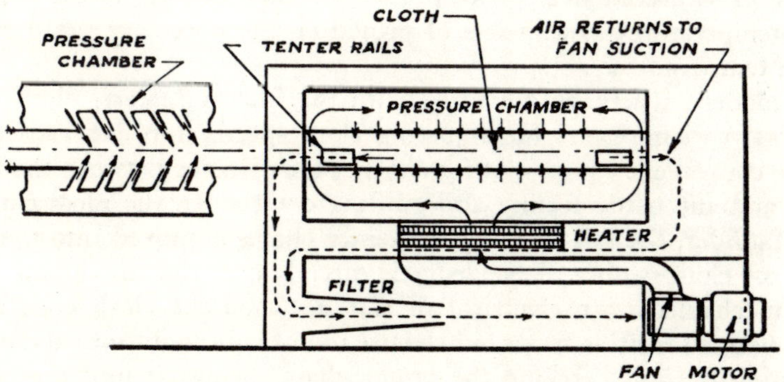

FIG. 13.8.   THE SPOONER AIR CIRCULATION SYSTEM

ways. The moisture-laden air is then removed through an air tube. By such an arrangement, the hottest air is distributed in the upper layers where the cloth is wettest, the temperature of the air gradually falling until it is practically at room temperature when the cloth leaves the machine. The new fresh air enters in this lower layer.

The Krantz machine has its heating units outside the part of the machine which carries the cloth, the air used for drying being first heated by passing over these units and then blown over the cloth from list to list (Fig. 13.6). This machine is, therefore, an air-circulating machine, all advantages of radiant heating being neglected. The position of the heating units is such that the in-going air is hottest at the top of the machine, where the cloth is wet, and coldest in the lower layers.

The Hunter machine (*see* Fig. 13.7) also has forced air circulation, appropriate amounts of fresh air being admitted in all layers.

The Spooner machine is also of the air-circulation type (Fig. 13.8) but differs from other forms in that hot air is directed on to the cloth at a comparatively high velocity, thus promoting rapid evaporation and the removal of the boundary layer of moisture covering the cloth surface. Filtered air is forced by a fan through a built-in heating unit, composed of steam-heated pipes specially designed to form a large surface area, into pressure chambers. On one surface of each chamber is a bank of narrow slots, correctly spaced and accurately formed. The heated air, passing through these nozzles impinges at high velocity on the wet cloth. Spent air is returned to the suction side of the fan to be recirculated after being filtered and heated. A small amount of fresh air is admitted continuously to the closed circuit of drying air by means of auxiliary ports in the fan casing.

The comprehensive range of tenters now available includes a high-speed heat-setting system which utilizes superheated steam (provided by injection of saturated steam with immediate superheating to the required setting temperature) as a means of providing the necessary rapid raising of cloth temperature.

All modern machines are fitted with dial thermometers, cloth speed indicators, variable gears for adjusting cloth speed, stop and start push-buttons, convenient equipment for altering the distance between the tenter chains, and automatic feeling and guiding devices. In the most common types of guider, the rail carrying the tenter chains is moved into the position of the cloth so that the selvedge is directly over the tenter pins. Most of the mechanisms are electrical in action; when the cloth edge makes contact with a sensitive feeler, an electric motor is brought into action and, by rotating the rail carrying the tenter chain, brings it into the correct position. Pneumatic, photo-electric and hydraulic guiders have also been designed. Certain tentering machines are fitted with devices which enable the cloth to be delivered at a constant moisture content.

All the machines described above dry the fabric under tension, but there are occasions when tensionless dryers are necessary. The Spooner type of machine has been adapted for this purpose, as have Dalglish Multi-pass Airlay dryers. In these latter machines the material is carried through on a conveyor equipped with cork-faced supporting slats, which travel up wards and downwards in a series of 'U's' (*see* Fig. 13.9). During its passage through the drying chamber the cloth is held against the conveyor by directed air streams, for the air serves not only to dry the cloth but also to hold it in position.

A considerable amount of attention has been directed to the radiation method of heating known as infra-red drying. Machines of this type consist essentially of rows of special electric bulbs or gas-heated radiators, the cloth passing between two banks of heating units or over one bank.

It is probable that in the drying of textiles the units will find their greatest use as preliminary heaters for wet cloth, or as auxiliary apparatus for use when a specially high temperature is required. Since the number of textile finishing processes which require high temperatures is increasing, it is advisable when overhauling drying equipment to ensure that plant is available for treating cloth at a temperature of at least 130°C. The machine should be fitted with thermo-regulators.

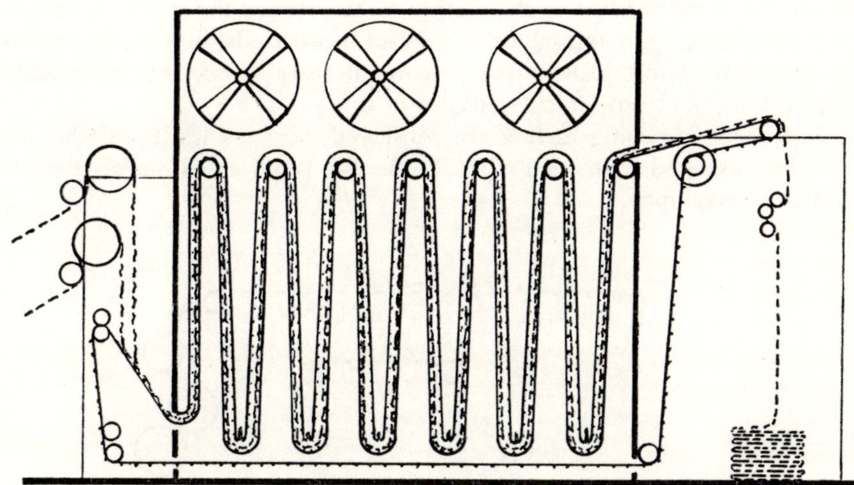

FIG. 13.9. PRINCIPLE OF THE DALGLISH MULTI-PASS AIRLAY DRYER IN WHICH THE FABRIC IS CARRIED ON A CONVEYOR WITH CORK SUPPORTING SLATS AND HELD IN POSITION BY DIRECTED AIR STREAMS

DEFECTS IN DRYING

Baking of the cloth resulting in loss of handle and possibly in yellowing.

Damaged cloth due to the piece coming off the pins during tentering and then becoming caught in the machine.

Marks from tenter pins. It is advisable to use stainless steel pins, of the least size compatible with sufficient strength to handle the cloth.

Scorch marks due to the application of insufficient tension and to the sagging cloth coming in contact with the heating units.

Torn lists due to excessive stretching of the cloth.

RAISING

THE OBJECTS OF RAISING, a process carried out by drawing a rough surface over the face and/or back of a cloth so as to lift the threads, may be enumerated as (*i*) to develop a nap or pile on the cloth to make it more attractive and in some cases to increase its heat retaining properties, (*ii*) to develop certain structural features in the cloth, (*iii*) to prepare the cloth for subsequent processes, *e.g.*, napping, or in the case of worsteds, for cutting, (*iv*) to give the cloth a soft handle, (*v*) to conceal threadiness, (*vi*) to subdue colours, and (*vii*) to soften the outlines of design.

Two types of raising surface are employed, *viz.*, teazles (thistle heads) and rollers covered with card wire. These two types are discussed in the following paragraphs.

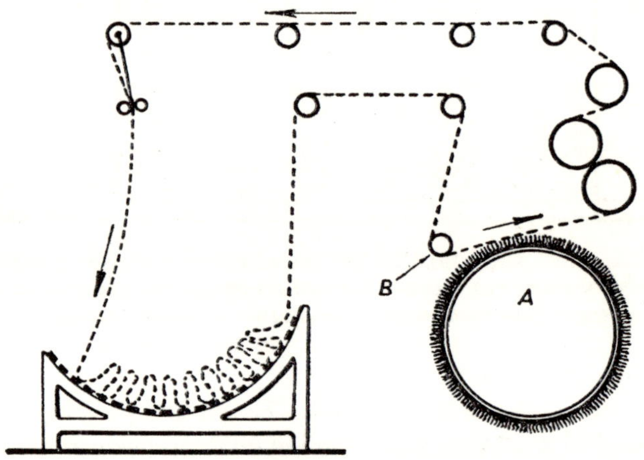

FIG. 13.10.   GENERAL ARRANGEMENT OF A
TEAZLE RAISING GIG

RAISING MACHINES—TEAZLE GIGS

These machines have been developed from the old method of hand raising in which the cloth was placed over a nelly and raised by teazles mounted in a frame which was held in the hand. In the West of England gig teazles are mounted on a cylinder which is rotated, the cloth passing in front of it, in contact with the teazles. The cloth is attached to winding rollers, and is wound from one to the other, and its direction then reversed.

The more usual type of gig—the Yorkshire gig—shown in Fig. 13.10 consists of a cylinder *A* (up to 4 feet in diameter but usually 40 inches) carrying firmly fixed rods or frames filled with teazles. Above the cylinder is an expanding roller *B* the position of which can be varied so as to increase or decrease the severity of the raising by altering the arc of contact made by the cloth with the cylinder. The machine is fitted with draw rollers, guide rollers, and a cuttling device. The cylinder is driven direct from the main shaft at 150-160 r.p.m. and motion is given to the drawing-off rollers by means of gears.

Modifications of this type of machine include multiple contact gigs in which the cloth is brought into contact with the cylinder at two or four points instead of one, and multi-cylinder gigs in which two or more cylinders are employed and guide rollers are so arranged that both back and face may be raised together or that all the raising takes place on the face. Occasionally, a roller covered with card wire is inserted in these larger machines to act as an additional raising surface.

The type of teazle used in the machines varies with the class of material to be raised. Teazles vary in quality and size but are divided into three classes: (a) 'Kings' or 'Scrubs' which are $3\frac{1}{2}$ to 4 inches long and suited only for heavy woollen fabrics requiring considerable raising; (b) 'Mediums' which are softer and more flexible and are $1\frac{1}{2}$ to $2\frac{1}{2}$ inches long; and (c) 'Buttons' which are 1 to $1\frac{1}{2}$ inches long and are used to fill up gaps between larger teazles.

It is customary to wet teazles thoroughly with hot water before placing them in the frame as this softens them and enables them to be set more closely together. They must be arranged in the frame so that they present a level surface to the cloth during raising. They are set either as singles (in the case of 'king' teazles) or 'two-height,' the lower row being 'mediums' and the upper row 'buttons'. Care should be taken to cover the supporting bars of the teazle frame so as to avoid unraised stripes on the surface of the raised cloth.

Because of the short life of the teazles, many attempts have been made to replace them by mechanical devices, but it is only comparatively recently that successful 'synthetic teazles' have been produced. These consist of cylinders about four-inches long and one-inch in diameter which are covered with special card-wire fillet. These units are mounted on the surface of a cylinder thereby producing an effective raising action. Typical machines of this type are made by Scholaert of Tourcoing, France, and by Tomlinsons of Rochdale, England; on a later Tomlinson machine the angle of attack of the teazles can be varied.

CARD WIRE RAISING MACHINES

Card wire machines commonly used in wool finishing are of either the single- or double-action type. The principle of the former is shown in Fig. 13.11. It consists of a number of card wire covered rollers *B* mounted on a cylinder *C*, and capable of rotating about their own axis as well as being revolved as a whole about the centre of the cylinder *C*. The machine is fitted with drawing-off rollers, guide rollers, tension rails, and a cuttling device. The cylinder is driven direct from the main shaft and the raising rollers receive their motion from belts which pass over journals at the ends of the rollers. The belts and the cylinder as a whole are made to rotate, so that the raising rollers rotate about their axes, and, by means of gears and cone pulleys, the speed of rotation can be varied between fairly wide limits.

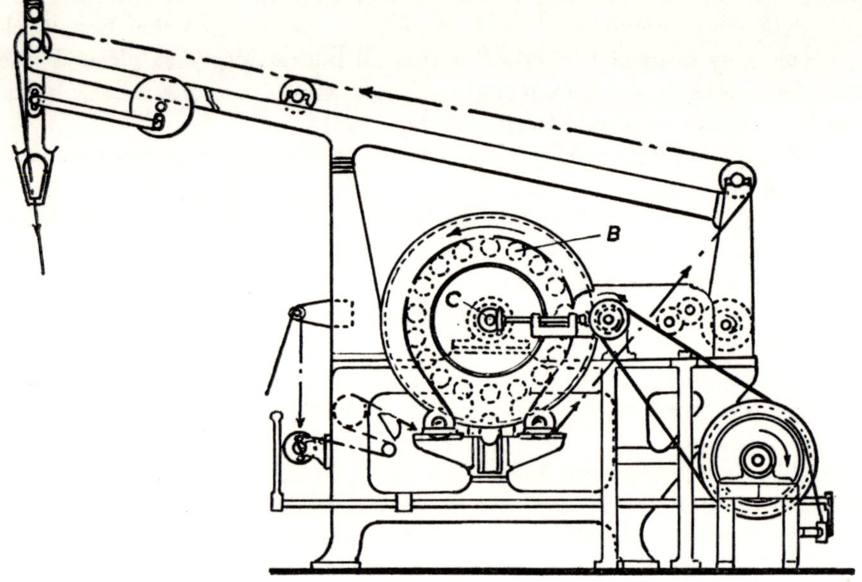

FIG. 13.11.   THE TOMLINSON 'Q-VEE' RAISING MACHINE

It is clear that this driving system is not positive as there is a possibility of slip between the raising rollers and the belts, and also of the belt on cone pulleys. To overcome this, the Tomlinson 'Q-Vee' machine was designed with Vee ropes instead of belts and a P.I.V. gearbox in place of the cone pulleys.

The card clothing used for these machines is in the form of inch-wide fillet and must be wrapped on the roller to give an even raising surface. The foundation is made of three layers of fabric cemented together and covered by a thin layer of vulcanized rubber to minimize the effects of moisture. The back is covered with another piece of fabric. Steel pins are generally used, although teeth made from alloys or brass have been recommended for wet raising A flat or oval wire is preferred, the long side of the wire being placed in the direction of raising. A common clothing for raising machines has 164 points per sq inch, although some finishers use one with 246 points per sq. inch.

THE TOMLINSON 'Q-VEE' SINGLE-ACTION RAISING MACHINE

In the Tomlinson 'Q-Vee' single-action raising machine, the main shaft A (Fig. 13.12) has two discs keyed to it, one at each end, each of these discs carrying 18 bearings arranged every 20° around its circumference.

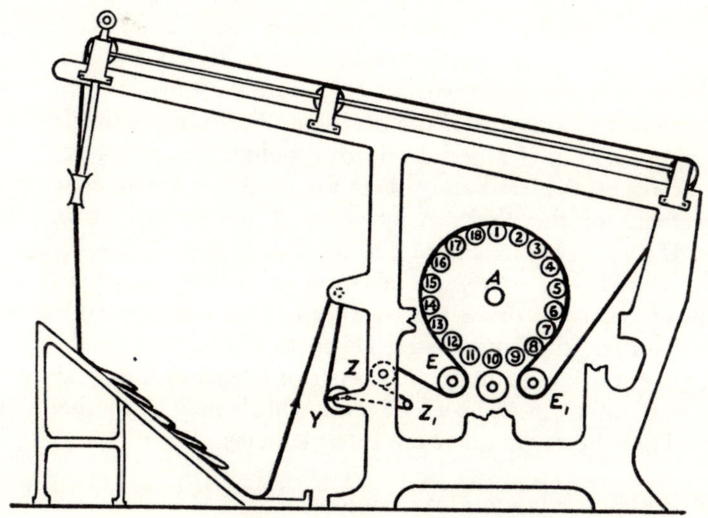

FIG. 13.12. PASSAGE OF THE CLOTH THROUGH A SINGLE-ACTION RAISING MACHINE

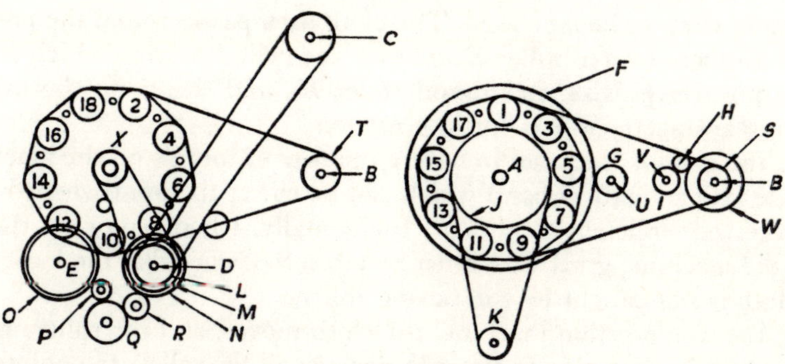

FIG. 13.13. DRIVING ARRANGEMENTS OF A SINGLE ACTION RAISING MACHINE

Mounted in each of these bearings is a pile roller (1-18), each of which is fitted with a four-groove vee-belt pulley; on the odd-numbered rollers, this pulley is attached to the right-hand end of the shaft, whereas on the even-numbered pulleys, it is attached to the left-hand end. These two sets of pulleys are driven by four link-type Vee-belts; in each case three of the four belts are driven by a pulley (S at one end and T at the other) keyed to a shaft *B* situated at the back of the machine, while the fourth belt in each set of pulleys is employed to ensure continuity of drive to those rollers not driven by the other three belts (Fig. 13.13).

The cylinder is driven through the gear wheel *F*, keyed to the main shaft *A*, by the pinion *G* which is keyed to shaft *U* driven by a vee-belt from an 8-10 h.p. motor. In addition the shaft *U* also connects with a P.I.V gearbox, which allows the back-shaft and the pulleys *S* and *T* to be driven at variable speeds *via* the gear train *I*, *H*, and *W*. There is only one other drive on the right-hand side of the machine, *viz.* to the cylindrical cleaning brush and consisting of a belt drive from pulley *J* to pulley *K*.

The drives on the left-hand side of the machines are all concerned with the movement of the cloth. A sprocket *X* on the main-shaft drives a sprocket *M* by means of a chain. The shaft *D* to which *M* is keyed, carries the cloth drawing-off rollers, in addition to driving sprocket *L* and gear *N* which respectively drive the overhead cloth carrying rollers and the cloth feed rollers, the latter being keyed to *E* and operated via the gear train *R*, *Q*, *P*, *O*. Incidentally, *O* consists of a bank of four gears with 100, 102, 104 and 106 teeth and each of these wheels may be meshed with gear wheel *P*. The wheels *Q* and *R* are intermediates.

PASSAGE OF CLOTH THROUGH THE MACHINE

In operation, the cloth to be raised is threaded (*see* Fig. 13.12) through the tension bars *Y*, the position of which can be varied, and round the rollers *Z* and Z_1, one of which is provided with a friction brake to allow the tension of cloth to be increased. The cloth then passes round the positively driven rubber-covered roller *E* and over the cylinder, from which it passes to the positively driven taking-off roller E_1, and thence to the overhead carrying arrangement and cuttling motion.

If the cloth is intended to have a number of rounds on the machine, it is made into an endless band which can be cut at the joint when the cloth has received sufficient treatment. Incidentally, when removing the piece from the machine, great care must be taken to ensure that the loose end of the cloth is not caught by the raising rollers.

In the single-action machine, the cloth moves, and the rollers revolve, in the opposite direction to the cylinder. On all the rollers the points of the wires are arranged forward to the direction of revolution. The amount of raising depends upon the relative speeds of the cloth and the rollers, and for effective raising the surface speed of the rollers must be greater than that of the cloth. Increasing the speed of the rollers increases the intensity of the raising. It is important that the variations in relative speeds of cylinder, cloth and rasising rollers, and the effect of such variations, should be appreciated, as it is upon these factors that the efficiency and utility of the machine depends.

DOUBLE-ACTION CARD WIRE RAISING MACHINES

Unlike the single-action machine in which the cloth revolves in the opposite direction to the cylinder, the double-action machine, also used for raising wool fabrics and especially blankets, is so designed that the cloth passes through the machine in the same direction as the cylinder revolves, while the rollers turn in the opposite direction. Two sets of rollers arranged alternately are, however, employed. In one set, termed 'pile' rollers, the card teeth point in the direction of revolution, while in the other set, termed 'counter-pile', the teeth point the other way (Fig. 13.14). The maximum amount of raising is obtained when the pile rollers run as slowly as possible and the counter-pile rollers at maximum speed.

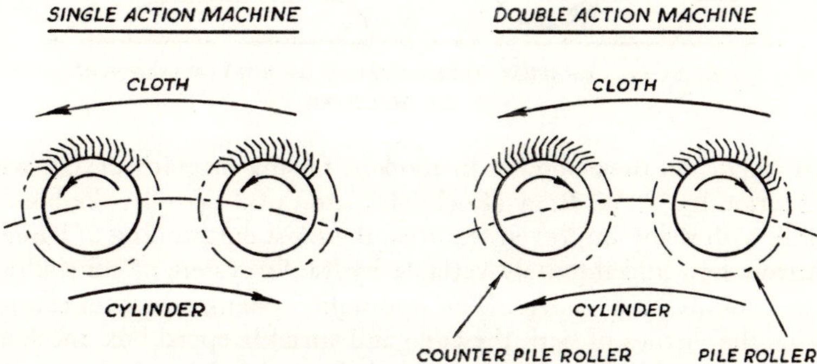

FIG. 13.14. DIRECTION OF ROTATION OF CYLINDERS AND ROLLERS IN SINGLE- AND DOUBLE-ACTION RAISING MACHINES

In the older machines, both sets of rollers received their motion through belts and were controlled by cone pulleys but, as in the case of single-action machines, these have now been replaced by vee-ropes and P.I.V. gearboxes. The general principle of a double-action machine is illustrated in Fig. 13.15. It will be noted that it is equipped with 36 raising rollers, 18 of which are pile and 18 counter-pile. The driving arrangements are such that the speed of the pile and counter-pile rollers can be varied independently of each other. Other models have fewer rollers.

In the Tomlinson 'Electro-Zero' machine it is possible to know when the cloth just begins to raise, thus providing a convenient reference point for subsequent machine settings. In this machine the effects of friction and inertia in the rollers and drivers are compensated so that the rollers adjust themselves to exactly the correct speeds. A working torque is then maintained throughout the operating cycle and is independent of speed variations, control being by way of electro-magnetic eddy current couplings associated with constant-running A.C. motors.

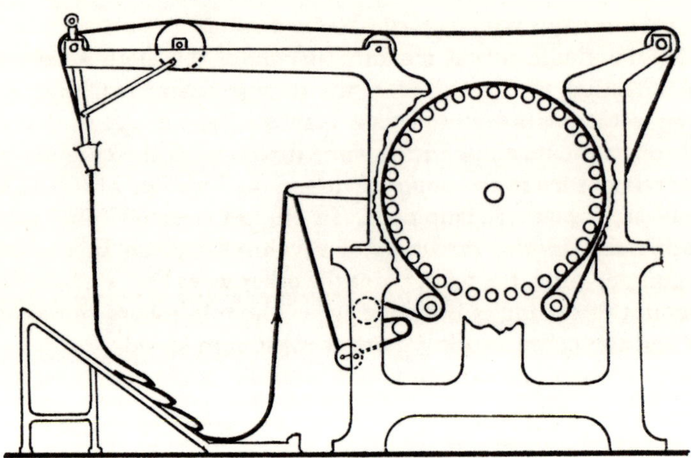

FIG. 13.15.   GENERAL ARRANGEMENT OF A DOUBLE-ACTION
RAISING MACHINE

An important development in modern raising machine design was the introduction by T. W. Riley (Rochdale) Ltd., of a 24-roller double-action machine with many improved features, the most outstanding of which was an entirely new and infinitely variable hydraulic system of controlling the pile and counter-pile rollers. The hydraulic system, which is claimed to combine the virtues of both the cone and variable speed box mechanisms incorporates three units, one of which, chain-driven from the main cylinder shaft, acts as a rotary pump and provides a flow of oil to drive the rotors of the other two units which thus act in the capacity of motors. One of these motors operates the pile rollers and the other the counter-pile, in each case the power being transmitted through a chain drive to the pinion which drives the 'big wheel' to which is attached the studs securing the belt driving the appropriate group of raising rollers.

The hydraulic system employs a completely closed circuit in which the supply tank is slung on the back top frame stay. The oil is pumped by the first unit to a flow control valve and thence to the counter-pile motor, the speed of which is controlled by a valve equipped with a graduated control knob. The excess of oil over and above that required by the counter-pile motor passes into the main supply to the second flow control valve and thence to the pile motor which has its own speed control valve. The fluid then returns to the supply tank and so completes the circuit.

Not only does the hydraulic transmission system allow of great flexibility but control is simplified. In addition the system has the advantage that it allows of the resetting of pile and counter-pile controls without stopping the machine.

The Whiteley-Gessner 'Hi-Torc' double-action machine incorporates a hydraulic pressure drive combined with gear-driven worker rolls; cloth speed and tension, and pile and counter-pile energy are all independently controlled and accurately indicated, previous settings thus being capable of exact reproduction.

OTHER RAISING MACHINES

Tiger raising machines consist of a single roller covered with card wire and carried in a headstock similar to that of a cutting machine. The cloth to be raised passes over a bed reminiscent of a cutting bed, and the rotating wire-covered roller is lowered so that it lifts pile from the cloth. It has a very drastic action but, when operated carefully, is suitable for raising fabrics such as camel hair coatings. It is useful as a setting-up machine for lifting pile before cutting.

Other types of raising machines include horizontal raising machines for blankets, cross raising machines, and sueding machines in which the raising surface is a roller covered with emery cloth.

THE PRACTICE OF RAISING

The effects produced during raising depend upon the composition and structure of the fabric, and the conditions under which the raising is carried out. In general, the looser the fabric, the more easily is it raised, although ease of raising must frequently be sacrificed to obtain a particular effect. For example, slow raising on a closely prepared milled ground is necessary in the production of West of England face cloths. Cloths made from merino wools of short staple give a short dense pile, while coarser wools give a more hairy appearance. Hard spun yarns tend to restrict the raising action and two-fold yarns are less easily raised than single. Since raising results in a considerable loss of strength in the weft direction, care has to be taken to design the cloth so that the desired effect is produced without undue weakening of the fabric. As raising proceeds and the cloth becomes thicker, the weaker are the weft yarns. The relation between thickness and tensile strength of the fabric weft-ways is approximately linear.

Cloths may be raised wet or dry. Wet raising which produces a silky laid pile of the silk hat variety is usually done on the teazle gig and is more effective in acid or soap solutions than in water. To produce the finished characteristic of beavers, billiard cloths, certain overcoatings, etc., the cloth is first thoroughly wetted out and then filled into the machine. Raising is done gradually, the breast roller being lowered by small amounts at intervals. The cloth must be kept wet the whole time and should be turned frequently so that the pile is formed from both sides of the weft threads equally. The fabric is washed-off thoroughly after raising.

Dry raising is usually carried out on the card wire machine, and is employed in the production of velours and blankets. It is also used to soften a cloth, when it is usual to raise the back, leaving the face clear. A special case of dry raising, referred to as raw thread raising, is to raise the greasy material with the object of improving its milling properties. In dry beating, the cloth is first steamed and then raised dry on a teazle gig. This serves to lift the pile and to prepare the cloth for cutting.

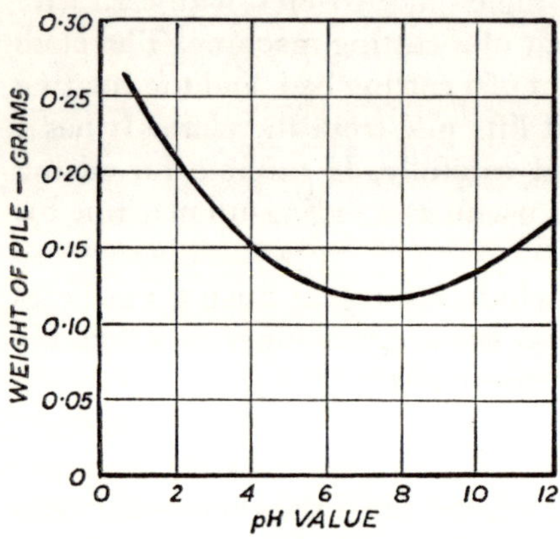

FIG. 13.16.   CURVE SHOWING EFFECT OF ACIDITY AND ALKALINITY ON THE EASE OF RAISING

FIG. 13.17.   DIAGRAM SHOWING THE SHRINKAGE OF A COTTON-NYLON FABRIC DURING RAISING

Although raising is one of the oldest of textile finishing operations, it has not been possible previously to express quantitatively the results of investigations on this process. Recently, however, the amount of pile on raised fabrics has been measured by a method involving the use of an accurately set cutting machine. It was shown[8] that wet cloths raised more easily than dry and that both acid and alkaline fabrics are raised more easily than are corresponding neutral fabrics. This is shown by Fig. 13.16, in which the amount of pile produced by raising fabrics of various pH values is plotted against the pH value of the fabric, all the patterns being raised together on the teazle machine.

TABLE 13.2. EFFECT OF LUBRICANTS ON
RAISING EFFICIENCY

Lubricant	Thickness of Raised Fabric (arbitrary units)
Untreated fabric	109
Quarternary ammonium compound	111
Soap	113
Dipsanil U (I.C.I.)	122
Velan PF	122
Thickness of unraised cloth	31

To facilitate raising, lubricants are particularly useful; for example wax emulsions and polyethylene emulsions. Comparative values of raising efficiency are shown in Table 13.2. Acids and sulphur dioxide are also conducive to good raising but difficulties are sometimes experienced in raising blankets bleached with hydrogen peroxide, probably because these are more or less neutral.

Some interesting effects can be produced by raising fabrics made from synthetic fibres and excellent velour finishes are possible on suitable cloths. The fabric should be milled to yield a dense and blind surface and then raised damp on a teazle gig, after which it takes on a subdued lustre similar to that obtained on the best quality of doeskin or superfine. During the raising of a cloth made from a cotton warp and a nylon weft the fabric gradually shrinks in width as shown by Fig. 13.17, in which the shrinkage is plotted against the number of passages through the raising machine. No significant extension in length accompanies this contraction and the phenomenon is evident on cloths of widely different designs. The fabric so produced is dense and heavy, while the cold handle usually associated with nylon disappears completely. Moreover, it is possible by using this type of construction to shrink cloths made wholly from non-felting fibres and so obtain finished materials having the thickness and handle of milled and raised wool fabrics.

DEFECTS IN RAISING

Streaks are caused by uneven tension in warp or weft threads, this producing surfaces of different raising susceptibilities. Streaks may also be due to bad teazle setting.

Damaged lists are often due to curling or to a badly designed selvedge.

Uneven raising is due to unequal distribution of moisture, or to dirt which alters the raising powers of the various parts of the fabric.

Over-raised and under-raised portions are due to creasing.

Weak cloth is due to over-treatment.

Uneven pile is obtained by raising too rapidly.

NAPPING AND LUSTRING

The napping process is applied to fabrics which have been raised and whose dense pile has been cut level. It consists of rubbing the cloth between two surfaces, the lower one (plush-covered) remaining fixed, while the upper one (rubber-covered and heavily weighted) moves with a reciprocating or rotary motion according to the type of finish required. The former produces a wavy effect while the latter transforms the pile into a mass of balled-up fibres. By suitable choice of the amplitude of vibration it is possible to obtain naps or balls of various sizes.

Certain types of pile are made considerably more attractive by increasing their lustre. With the 'Pol Rotor' device (Heinz Unger) or the 'Electr o finisher' (Turbo Machines Ltd.) the cloth passes over a positively driven felt blanket which holds it against a revolving heated ridged roller which 'polishes' the fibres.

CUTTING

THE OBJECT OF CUTTING FABRICS is to improve their appearance by removing fibrous material from the surface.

CUTTING MACHINERY

Cutting machines consist essentially of a cutting cylinder and ledger blade carried in a headstock, a bed over which the cloth passes, drawing rollers which pull the cloth through the machine, a setting-up roller to prepare the surface of the cloth for cutting, and numerous guide rollers and tension rails. The headstock can be raised or lowered by a foot pedal and the cylinder may be adjusted in relation to the blade by screws, and the blade and cylinder in relation to the bed by a stud resting on a box plate (*see* Fig. 13.18). Details of the cutting parts are shown in Fig. 13.19, and various types of cutting bed available are shown in Fig. 13.20.

For fine worsteds a solid cutting bed has many advantages, especially if a very close cut is required, but there is always a danger of making holes where there are knots or other projections on the back of the cloth. Hollow, roller, spring, rubber and vacuum beds are made to accommodate the needs of other cloths which require different degrees of cutting, ranging from close to 'hair ending', *i.e.*, merely removing the tips of long projecting fibres. Sliding beds are useful where special care has to be taken with selvedges or lists, while special beds, *e.g.*, built from discs or in the form of a rotating engraved roller, may be used to produce cut patterns on velour type cloths. The cloth is presented to the cutting parts only where it is pushed up by the bed and by this means pattern effects are produced. The cylinder is mounted with from six to ten spiral blades which are fixed at the end by screws and subsequently ground. It is made to rotate by means of a belt passing over pulleys connected with a shaft driven from a motor, the arrangement being such that the cylinder can be lifted from the bed while it is still rotating. Machines are often fitted with a beater which removes foreign material from the back of the cloth. The cutting flocks are removed by a vacuum suction system.

It is essential that the cylinder should be exactly parallel to the bed, or the surface of one edge of the cloth will be cut lower than the other. In older machines, the distance between the cylinder and bed was adjusted by inserting pieces of metal or card on the plate carrying a stud, but

automatic cut adjusters are fitted in modern machines. In the Sellers'
machine, the adjuster is of the direct lift type, the base carrying the screw
of the headstock being raised or lowered by a cam device. The Whiteley
mechanism is of a different type, the base carrying the screw being built
in the shape of a wedge; by moving this so that the screw occupies different
positions on the wedge surface, the distance between the cutting bed and
the cylinder may be altered. Both ends of the machine are fitted with these

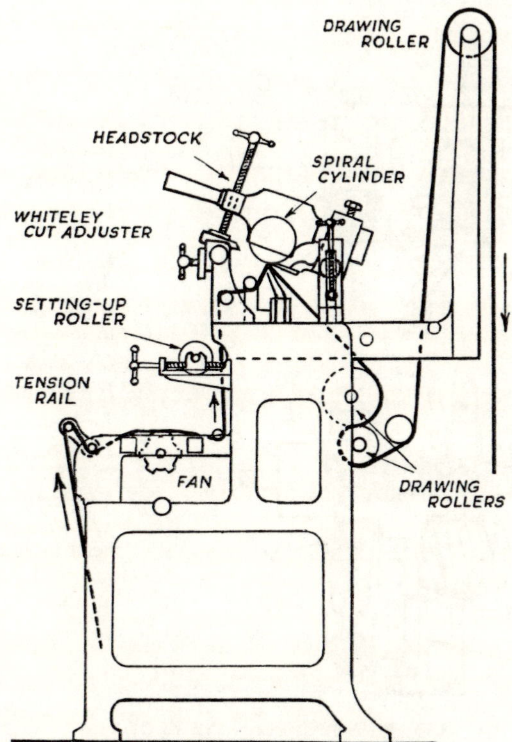

FIG. 13.18.   PASSAGE OF CLOTH THROUGH
A CUTTING MACHINE

wedges which are connected together and operate as one so that a setting
made at one end of the machine is automatically transferred to the other.
The wedges are moved by a handle connected through suitable gears
which engage with the ratchets on the underside of one wedge, the amount
of movement being indicated on a dial.

Cutting machines may also be fitted with selvedge openers which are
useful when dealing with curled lists or curling cloths.

In order to comply with Factory Act requirements, machines must be
fitted with satisfactory guards, so that it is impossible to start the machine

unless the guard is in position. The guard may be lifted and the machine turned by hand, but immediately the operating lever moves on to the fast pulley the guard must close and lock automatically.

MULTIPLE CUTTERS

The modern trend is towards greater use of multiple shearing machines which ensure greater production. These are essentially a number of single cutters connected together (excepting that only one set of draw rollers is

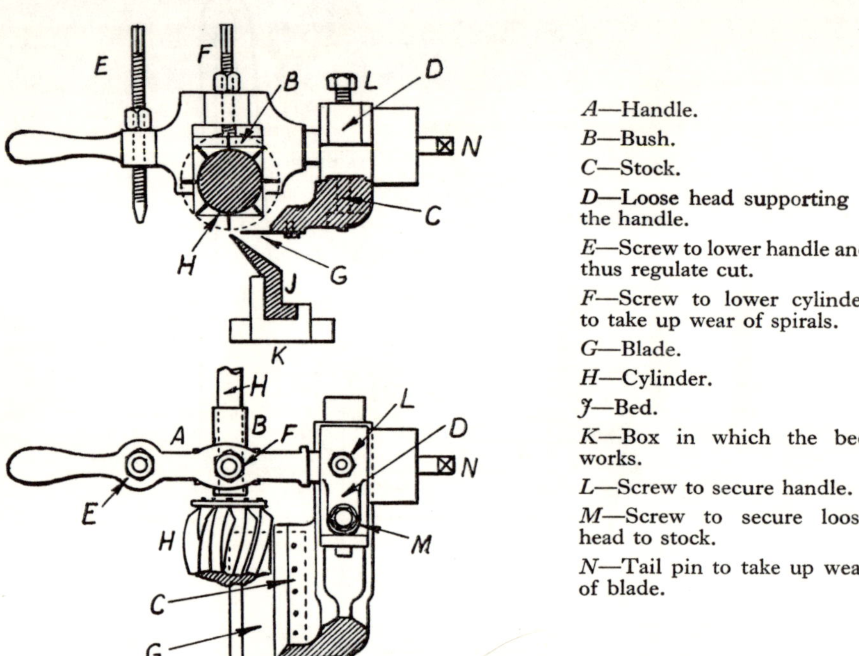

FIG. 13.19.   ELEVATION AND PLAN VIEWS OF THE CUTTING PART
OF A SELLERS' SHEARING MACHINE

provided) and they may be designed to give one cut on the back and two on the face, two on both back and face, one on the back and four on the face, or any other combination which may be desired. Each headstock may be raised or lowered by levers of the signal box type placed in front of the machine. Each set of cutting parts is fitted with automatic cut adjusters and most modern features are incorporated. The difficulty of seeing and inspecting the work as it leaves the blades is minimized by good lighting and, in some machines, the cutting operation is simplified by a device which automatically lifts the headstock from the bed when a thick place or a sewing passes through. When a sewing passes sensitive feelers, fitted a short distance before the cloth passes over the bed, an electric current is sent through a solenoid which actuates a mechanism for lifting the headstock free from the bed. Immediately afterwards, the headstock returns to its original position, its descent being controlled to prevent a sudden fall. Electrical appliances are sometimes fitted to detect the presence of metal pins, etc., in the cloth and to stop the machine before these can damage the cutting parts.

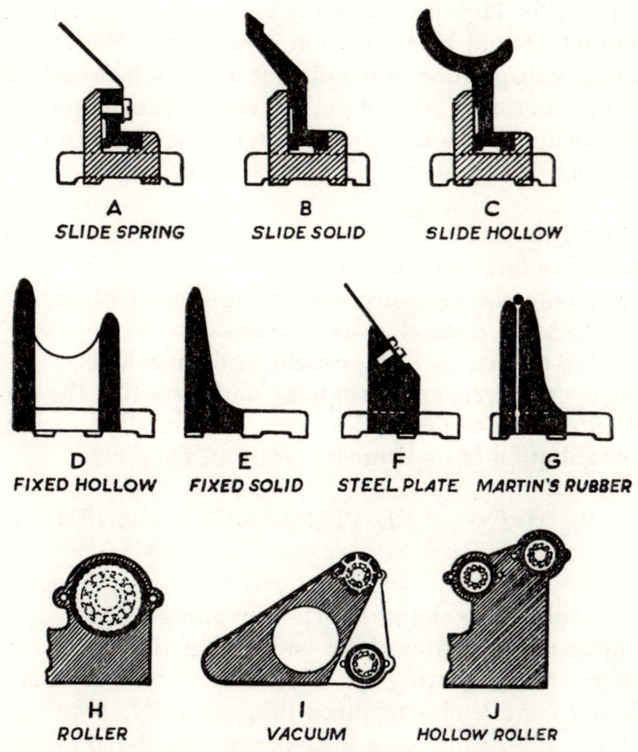

FIG. 13.20. VARIOUS TYPES OF CUTTING BED

THE PRACTICE OF CUTTING

After being examined to ensure that knots are pushed to the back, the fabric is steamed and brushed before being cut. It is placed in the machine so that the back is cut once to remove knots. The face is then cut to match a standard pattern. By this means, the formation of holes by knots lifting the cloth from the bed is minimized. Cloths should be cut sufficiently close to emphasize attractive features of design and colour, but not excessively, as this results in loss of handle. This is especially so with flannels, although these fabrics must be cut sufficiently close to prevent 'pilling' during wear.

It is good practice, when possible, to pass the cloth through the machine several times, removing a little fibre each time, as this avoids any uneven appearance which might result from taking too deep a cut. To cut heavy raised fabrics, it is essential to have good setting-up of the pile, setting-up rollers covered with card wire or special setting-up machines being preferred. The cutting parts should be kept in good condition by frequent grinding, care being taken to grind the blade in a manner suited for the class of work in hand. Although cloths are generally steamed and brushed before being cut, for high production it has been recommended[9] that the cutting operation should be carried out immediately the cloth leaves the dryer. By suitable disposition of the plant it is possible to make drying and cutting into one continuous operation, thereby increasing production. The several pieces being processed should be sewn together with a 'butt-end' sewing machine.

DEFECTS IN CUTTING

Lean cloths due to excessive cutting.

Poor appearance due to inadequate setting-up or cutting.

Holes due to knots or thick places in the cloth.

Damages due to sewings being caught in the machine.

Marks across the piece due to stopping and restarting the machine.

Uneven cutting due to taking deep cuts, to using dull cutting parts, or to uneven distribution of moisture or grease in the piece.

BLOWING AND PERMANENT FINISHING

THE PROCESS OF BLOWING, usually referred to as dry blowing or semi-decating, is applied to cloths which are almost completely finished, with the object of imparting lustre and giving the fabric firmness and solidity. There is some setting action although under normal conditions the cloth is not completely stabilized dimensionally. Blowing may with advantage replace pressing as a final process in the finishing of many fabrics.

The process consists essentially in winding the cloth to be treated, along with a smooth cotton wrapper, on to a perforated roller and blowing steam through the roll of fabric so formed. After blowing for the appropriate time, the steam supply is cut off and air is sucked through the roll by a pump. The cloth is then removed from the roller and may be reblown so that more uniform results are obtained. It is clear that, if the diameter of the roller is small, the end of the cloth on the inside of the roll will be blown under different conditions from that of the other end of the fabric. The second blowing, being carried out with the fabric wound on in the reverse direction, is therefore intended to minimize this difference.

A blowing machine consists of two perforated iron rollers, fitted with steamtight joints and capable of being rotated. Dry steam may be blown through the rollers, and both rollers are connected to a vacuum pump. Small brass tubes of the same diameter as the perforations in the roller are often fitted behind each hole to prevent condensed water from being blown on to the cloth. Between the two blowing rollers is a freely rotating guide roller which supports the wrapper as it passes from one roller to another. Arrangements are made for the rollers to be rotated in either direction.

There is a trend in modern blowing machine design towards the use of large diameter blowing rollers. These have many advantages, the most important being the minimizing of differences in the blowing treatment received by the two ends of pieces. The smaller the diameter of the blowing rollers, the greater is the number of times the cloth has to be wrapped on to them, and the greater is the possibility of 'ending'. Rollers of 20 to 24 inches diameter are common and machines with these large rollers give excellent results.

Two blowing rollers are normally employed, cloth being wound off from one while another piece is being wound on to the second. There are, however, units made with only one blowing roller and these are very useful when the amount of work to be done is small. These machines are fitted with an auxiliary roller to carry the blowing wrapper. In either type of machine it is still desirable to blow twice, reversing the piece between the operations, especially if dyeing is to follow. If blowing is simply to provide a flattening and a consolidating of the cloth, this is not quite so necessary.

Other features incorporated in modern machines are rotary vacuum pumps, temperature and tension controls, and safety appliances to prevent operatives' hands being caught in the machine. An adequate steam supply (usually 60-80 lb. per sq. in.) is necessary and care should be taken to avoid water drops in the steam used for blowing. If the traps used are efficient, there should be little difficulty in ensuring this, but it is not advisable to install a blowing machine at the end of the steam line and steam should be blown off for a time before blowing begins.

BLOWING PRACTICE

Whatever blowing machine is employed, it is customary to wrap about 12 yards of coarse cotton wrapper on each blowing roller to cover the holes through which the steam is blown. The wrapper employed for the actual blowing is smooth on both sides (a typical structure is: Warp: 2/20s, 60 ends/inch. Weft: 1/40s, 220 picks/inch).

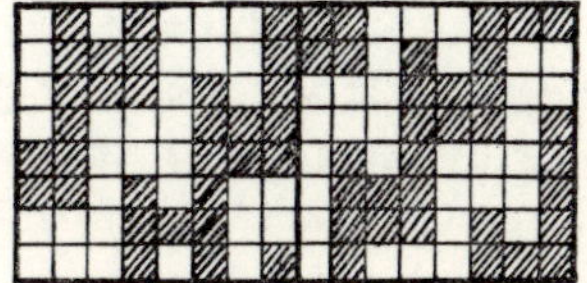

FIG. 13.21. A TYPICAL WEAVE FOR A COTTON WRAPPER FOR BLOWING ROLLERS

A few yards of this wrapper are first wound on one roller of the machine and then the piece to be processed is wound along with it, the tension at which the roll is built up being contıolled by the adjustment of the twitch rails in front of the roller. The tension of the wrapper is governed by the position of collar brakes which operate on the two blowing rollers. When the piece has been wound on to the roller, a further 15 yards of wrapper are wound on and steam is then blown through the roll.

As previously stated, it is good practice to blow off the steam before allowing it to pass through the roll of cloth if there is any possibility of its being wet. Blowing is continued for one to two minutes after the steam appears at the surface of the cloth.

The time of treatment may, of course, be varied and, if the main object of the treatment is to give the cloth a permanent set, the time of blowing must be increased. Completely dry steam is not desirable for blowing but it is essential that it should not be sufficiently wet to form drops, or the cloth will be water-marked, a defect which is very difficult to rectify. When the blowing operation on the first roller has been completed, the steam is cut off and the suction pump is applied to draw air through the roll. This is continued for as long as is necessary, after which the cloth is given a similar blowing and cooling on the other blowing roller, where this is deemed necessary.

CHEMICAL SETTING

The advent of easy-care fabrics for use in shirtings and dress fabrics, and the introduction of permanent creases and pleats by utilizing thermoplastic fibres such as Terylene in blends with wool, has stimulated interest in achieving such effects with all-wool cloths. It has long been realized that the setting effects of hot water on single fibres are greatly enhanced by reducing agents, and modern permanent finishes such as creasing and flat-setting are based on such reagents. In the 'Si-Ro-Set' process fabric was treated along the crease with a 2 per cent aqueous solution of ammonium thioglycollate to give 40 per cent uptake, followed by steaming for 30-40 seconds. This method was unpopular in some quarters and has been largely superseded by the use of monoethanolamine bisulphite (MEAS) applied in a similar manner as a 3 per cent solution. A different approach is to presensitize the cloth by applying the reducing agent to the entire fabric before tentering at as low a temperature as possible. Subsequently the garment maker needs only to apply a water spray before creasing the presensitized material.

As first developed, flat setting entailed treating with a one per cent solution of sodium bisulphite, hydroextracting to 50 per cent retention, and steam blowing in the damp condition for five minutes. The procedure may also be employed with MEAS. One drawback is the deterioration of blowing wrappers, which have to be treated with particular care and regularly dried out.

PRESSURE BLOWING

There are various other methods of obtaining permanent effects on cloth, the most effective being 'pressure blowing' or full decating, in which the cloth is wound on to a perforated roller along with a wrapper and the roller and fabric placed inside a large cylinder which is subsequently sealed. The blowing procedure consists in heating up the outer shell of the machine so as to prevent condensation of water on the fabric, passing in steam and building up the necessary pressure, maintaining the pressure for the requisite time, pumping out the steam, and finally removing the roll to be cooled. Many novel and permanent effects may be obtained by the use of machines of this type and the Sanderson machine which may be evacuated before the blowing is begun makes the process more easily controlled.

In some finishing machines the roll of cloth is run in hot water which is sucked through the roll. In full decating machines such as the Whiteley-Gessner, the K.D. machine (Biella) and the Gladstone-Sellers, the cloth is rolled on to a perforated roller along with a cotton wrapper and then placed inside a steaming cylinder, where it is steamed from the outside in and from the inside out. The roll is then removed and placed in the cooling frame.

DEFECTS IN BLOWING

Most defects which occur in blowing are permanent and therefore should be avoided if possible. The main faults arise from the use of wet steam and from uneven treatment. Long pieces should be treated twice to avoid ending. Insufficient tension on the fabric will give poor setting, a poor lustre and a wavy appearance, while excessive tension will give the cloth a papery handle. Use of short wrappers gives rise to uneven results due to local escape of steam and excessive local action. Metal stains are quite common, and often arise from the interaction of metal compounds and sulphur compounds formed during the blowing.

NOVELTY EFFECTS PRODUCED IN BLOWING

Although blowing is generally carried out to flatten the cloth and give it a lustre it is possible to obtain novelty effects on suitably prepared fabrics. One method is to use specially designed wrappers, *e.g.*, a cotton wrapper on which is sewn coarse string to form the required design. It is advisable to keep the design as simple as possible and effects should be confined to large motifs. The prepared wrapper is wound on to the blowing rollers along with the cloth to be treated and then steam is blown through for a longer period than usual. Pressure machines may be used with advantage in this type of work. The pattern of the wrapper is thereby embossed on to the fabric and the effect is permanent. This technique has been used successfully on cheap pile fabrics.

CLOTH BOILING

The production of a lustrous surface, usually by boiling, is essential for several wet raised cloths such as beavers. With cheaper fabrics, however, boiling is too expensive and blowing is then substituted. The fabric—usually one which has been dressed or wet raised—is wound on to a wooden roller and covered with a few yards of cotton wrapper, the surface of the roller also being wrapped with cotton. It is essential that the roll should be well-prepared, the edges being carefully built up. The roll is then placed in a boiling cistern which is a tank 6 or 7 feet deep and fitted with steam pipes and means of filling the vessel with water and emptying it. The cistern is filled with water containing a little acetic acid (one part of acid to 500 of water) and is maintained at about 160°F. Treatment is usually carried out for 12 hours, after which the fabric is removed and allowed to cool.

High-class fabrics may be boiled five or six times, but the number of treatments is determined by the quality of the fabric, the fastness of the dyes, and the degree of lustre required. In some mills, the cloth is blown before boiling as this reduces the number of boilings necessary. Many face cloths are dressed between the separate boilings.

PRESSING AND CLOTH CONDITIONING

THE OBJECT OF PRESSING is to flatten the fabric and to give it an attractive lustre. A high sheen or glaze is undesirable. According to the finish required, pressing is done hot or cold, and the pressure is also adjusted.

Many firms still use a hydraulic press which is filled by hand. The apparatus consists of four stout iron columns carrying a fixed top plate and a lower plate which can be raised by means of a hydraulic pump. The fabric, after rigging (folding so that the two lists are together), is placed in the press by cuttling along with stout cardboard press papers, and pressure is applied. When pressing suitings, paper is placed between the folds of the cloth so that no two pieces of fabric are in contact, but with dress fabrics, where a clothy handle is desired, alternate cloth-cloth and cloth-paper contacts are employed.

It is customary to repeat the pressing after having altered the position of the papers in the cloth. This presses the unpressed portions of the cloth at the edges of the papers. Originally, the presses were heated by placing hot iron plates at suitable intervals throughout the pile of cloth, but now special press papers with heating elements inside them are used. These are distributed at intervals and when the press has been filled, they are connected to an electrical supply and thereby heat the mass of cloth. Steam heated presses have been designed but are not popular.

The hydraulic press is still used for many of the best fabrics, but except when pressing certain cloths (*e.g.*, face cloths), or when production is very

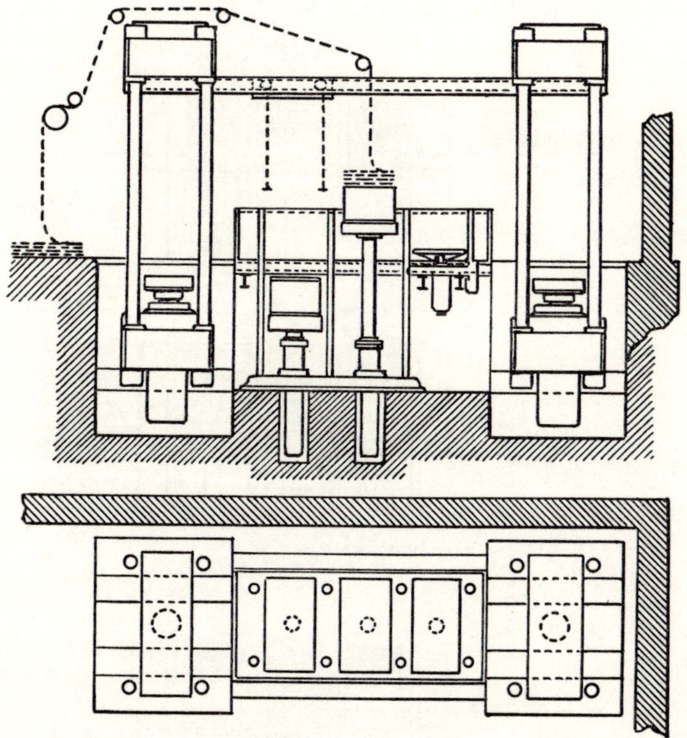

FIG. 13.22. HYDRAULIC PRESS INSTALLATION WITH PAPERING LIFTS

small, papering is now automatic. A typical modern press with papering lifts is shown in Fig. 13.22, the method of papering, turning and de-papering being indicated at *A*, *B* and *C* in Fig. 13.23. The pieces to be pressed are drawn from a pile by means of a variable-speed conveying device, and then over guide rollers on to the table of the middle lift. The other two lifts are loaded with press papers and an appropriate number of heating papers, sufficiently large to press the cloth at full-width.

As cloth is delivered on to the middle lift, the operators slip the papers into the folds. As the pile of papered pieces increases and the piles of papers on adjacent lifts decrease, the three piles can be brought to a convenient level by means of a press-button control, all the lifts being raised and lowered by electric motors. When the guide on the middle lift indicates that the load is sufficiently high to fill half or one of the presses (10 to 11 pieces), the level of the lift is adjusted so that the load is taken up by an overhead railway and transferred to the press. A further 10 pieces are then papered in the same manner and carried to the press.

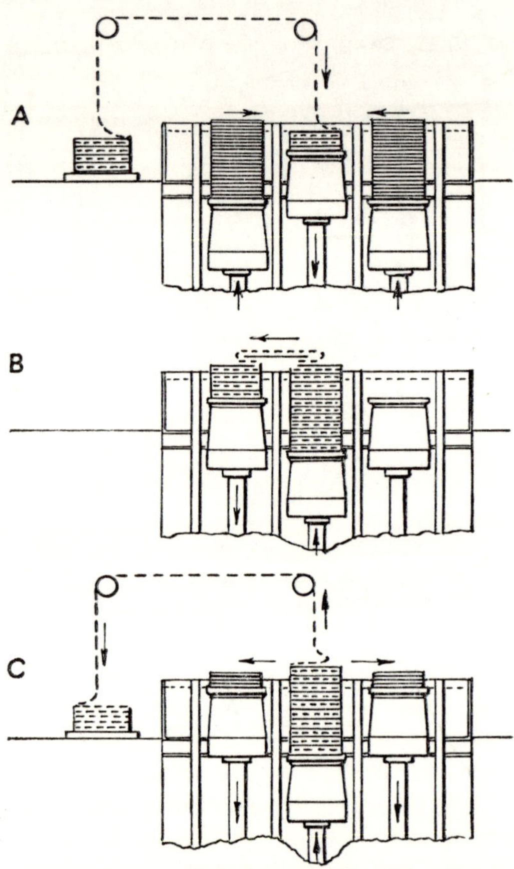

FIG. 13.23. DIAGRAM ILLUSTRATING THE OPERATIONS OF (A) PAPERING; (B) TURNING AND (C) DE-PAPERING

To obviate any possibility of over-heating when the heating papers are connected to the electrical supply, some modern plants are fitted with special heating units in which the papers are heated before being inserted between the layers of cloth. When the first pressing operation is completed, each half-load of pieces is returned to the No. 2 lift and transferred to No. 1 lift by sliding the papers across, care being taken that the unpressed part of the fabric comes in the middle of the paper. The pieces are then returned to the press for a final pressing and are then de-papered as shown at *C* in Fig. 13.23.

In certain designs of pressing plant, production can be increased by de-papering one load while another is being papered and made ready for the press. This also effects economy in heating, for the warm papers from the de-papered piece are transferred directly to a new piece. There is also a machine in which a papering device is built into the press itself.

The Hattersley-Pickard press has been designed with the object of continuous production, for in this case the papers are fixed and the cloth moves (*see* Fig. 13.24). It consists essentially of a fixed top plate, an intermediate plate and a bed, but the number of intermediate plates may be

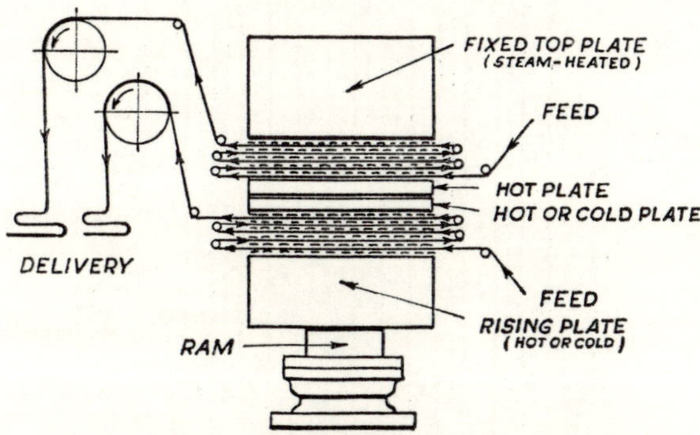

FIG. 13.24.   DIAGRAM SHOWING THE PRINCIPLE
OF THE HATTERSELY-PICKARD PRESS

increased to give an increased number of nips. The papers—usually six between each pair of plates—are fixed. The cloths (two pieces) are threaded as shown, and the lower bed is lifted by a small hydraulic ram in order to raise the middle plate and the cloth so that pressure can be exerted against the top plate. The full pressure is then exerted by a large ram acting on the lower bed. To complete the cycle of operations, the pressure is released, the two lower plates allowed to descend and the cloth moved on to press the next portion. The whole machine is automatic in action and gives good results on a wide range of cloths. By arranging that some of the plates are heated and others cooled by circulating cold water, it is possible to use the machine for hot and cold pressing in one operation.

ROTARY PRESSES

Where a high rate of production is required, there is considerable scope for the rotary press, the modern type of which has been used successfully, especially on cheaper cloths. It consists of a large diameter (21 inches) steam-heated pressing roller, providing a fairly large arc of

contact (14 inches) between the roller and bed, and so enabling the machine
to be operated at very much smaller pressures than was the case with many
of the older machines. Pressure is applied by four large-diameter hydraulic
rams each controlled independently. The pressure is controlled by a special
accumulator pump, which maintains a constant pressure even when the
thicknesses of the cloths vary.

Since this method of pressing reduces the moisture content of the
cloth, it is desirable that the cloth should be permitted to condition before
it leaves the factory. As it is not always possible to store the cloth in
conditioning rooms, many finishers pass it through a conditioning unit—

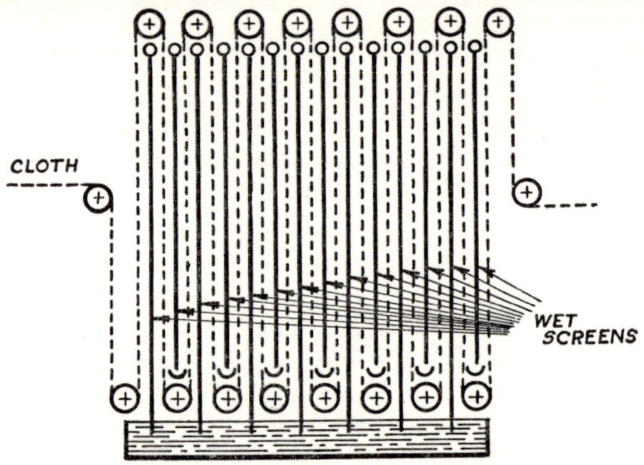

FIG. 13.25.   CONDITIONING UNIT FOR USE
AFTER PRESSING

a chamber containing wet linen aprons arranged vertically—the cloth
passing up and down at a distance of about $\frac{3}{8}$ in. from these. It is claimed
that this treatment gives a great improvement in handle. The principle of
the conditioning unit is illustrated in Fig. 13.25.

In addition to these standard methods of pressing, mention should be
made of the practice of using a blowing machine for obtaining the pressed
finish. This is very efficient for costume and dress fabrics, both handle and
appearance being satisfactory.

Cloths should be brushed and steamed before pressing, and given a
light steaming-off after pressing. This reduces undesirable glaze. Worsted
suitings are pressed warm and given a flat finish, but homespun tweeds are
merely placed between papers under very light pressures. Other fabrics
receive intermediate treatments, the precise nature of which is determined
by the cloth and the market into which it is being sold. For example,
merchants often require a higher standard of pressing than do most of the
wholesale clothing manufacturers.

CLOTH CONDITIONING

Since the physical properties of cloth and the behaviour of the material in many finishing operations are greatly affected by the moisture content of the material, it is frequently necessary to alter the 'condition' of the cloth during the finishing routine. This is the object of processes such as conditioning, dewing, damping and steaming.

When processing the best type of cloth, it is desirable that the material should be allowed to regain its natural moisture content between the several operations. One method is to store the cloth in cool cellars for several days in order to improve the handle and to increase the weight of the cloth. Such a procedure is, however, time-consuming and more rapid techniques have accordingly been developed.

One method is to pass the cloth through a conditioning unit (Fig. 13.25). In its passage through this machine, moisture is absorbed by the fabric and the handle of the material thereby improved. This is particularly noticeable on cloths which have been pressed by the rotary method.

DEWING AND DAMPING

Larger amounts of moisture are applied to cloth in the processes of dewing and damping. Incidentally, the description of these processes arises from the old practice of laying pieces in the fields to be damped by the dew. Machines used in more modern practice include the air-nozzle type and the brush type. In the former, the cloth is passed over a row of jets through which water rises, and is blown on to the cloth by compressed air. Although this process is satisfactory for many purposes, there is a tendency for water distribution to be streaky due to choked delivery nozzles and inadequate air supply.

In brush dewing machines, the cloth is drawn over an open trough containing water, the trough being a few inches wider than the width of the cloth. Dipping into the trough is a rotating brush which whips the water into a fine spray. The atmosphere immediately above the open trough is thus filled with fine droplets of water and, as the cloth passes through this, it becomes evenly damped. It is usual to fit baffle plates inside the trough to concentrate the droplets.

In the Williams-Peace machine cloth is passed between two rollers, the lower one of which dips into a water trough and is accurately machined, thus ensuring even application of liquid.

An alternative method of damping is to fold the cloth along with a previously wetted cotton wrapper and then to allow the fabrics to lie together. Again, it is possible to obtain good results by passing the fabric between two accurately turned squeeze rollers, the lower one of which runs in a trough of water containing a wetting agent. With well-turned rollers, this method is most efficient. A more recent method, however, consists in obtaining an atmosphere of atomized water droplets by directing jets of water against an inclined glass plate. The impact results in the formation of small drops, the size of which can be varied by varying the speed of the water jets. Whatever method of damping is adopted, however, it is advisable to allow the fabric to lie in cuttle for a time in order to allow the water to penetrate into the cloth.

BRUSHING AND STEAMING

This process, which should not be confused with any setting or permanent finishing process, has for its object the removal of glaze from cloth after pressing or the preparation of cloth for cutting and other processes. The standard unit is a box or trough in which is a perforated pipe connected to a low pressure steam supply. The trough is fitted with two sliding lids, one at each end, and these may be adjusted so that the opening between them is just a little greater than the width of the cloth to be processed. After passing over this steam box the cloth is usually brushed by one or two horizontally mounted rotating brushes, the severity of the brushing action being capable of adjustment by means of rollers which support the cloth. When the rollers are in their lowest position, the cloth rests on the brushes and receives maximum treatment. By adjusting these rollers, however, brushing of any desired severity may be carried out. The cloth is pulled through the machine by a pair of drawing rollers and a cuttling device is usually incorporated. It is customary to sew the two ends of the cloth together and to pass it round the machine until the desired effect is obtained.

RIGGING, CUTTLING AND CRAMPING

Rigging, cuttling and cramping are the last operations in the finishing routine. The cuttling and rigging machine folds the material down the middle, with the face inside, this operation being known as rigging, and also cuttles or folds the piece into a neat compact form. The cuttled piece, after being taken from the machine, has one end of the fabric doubly lapped round the piece for convenience in handling and packing in the warehouse.

Cramping has for its object the pressing of the cloth into the least thickness of piled cloth, without affecting the finish that has been produced. For this purpose the separately cuttled pieces of cloth are piled one upon another in a cramp and mildly pressed by sheets of lead or by a hydraulic ram. After about three to five hours the pressure is released and the goods taken to the warehouse. Cramping, or as it is sometimes termed cold flatting, gives a much firmer handle to the cloth and seems to prevent the air from altering the finish or condition that has been given to the fabric.

RENDERING WOOL FABRICS UNSHRINKABLE

FINISHED WOOL CLOTHS may shrink when they are wetted with water, when they are steamed and pressed as in garment making, and when they are washed, either domestically or at the laundry. In all instances this shrinkage is undesirable and should be prevented.

Two types of shrinkage should be distinguished, namely, 'relaxation shrinkage', which arises from the release of strains inserted in the cloth during processing, and 'felting shrinkage', which is due to the felting of the wool fibres. In so far as the former is concerned, it will be appreciated that during the whole of the finishing process the cloth is pulled lengthways and that any excessive tension will lead to an extension in the direction of the warp. Particularly is this likely to occur in the last operation of pressing, especially when carried out on a rotary machine.

Again, if a particular cloth shrinks rather too much during scouring and milling or during dyeing, it is customary to adjust the width by stretching when the cloth is dried on the tenter. Some slight stretching weftways is also necessary to take out creases, but the width of the cloth on the tenter should not be more than $1\frac{1}{2}$ inches greater than the required finished width.

Cloth subjected to excessive warp or weft stretching is given a temporary set and, unless given some further treatment designed to eliminate the strains, it will shrink during garment pressing. Processes such as blowing could be used to stabilize the material, although in practice it is not customary to carry out this process for a sufficiently long time to bring about satisfactory fixation of the cloth. For many fabrics, however, it would be an advantage to adopt blowing as the last treatment and so eliminate rotary pressing. The finish produced by this process is not, however, so acceptable to merchants although the cloth may be more stable dimensionally. It is possible that in much cloth processing too much time is spent on pressing, for much of the cloth finish is removed when the tailor presses the fabric, either by hand or on a Hoffman machine.

LONDON SHRINKING

The best method of removing strains inserted in the cloth is by the process known as 'London Shrinking', which consists essentially of wetting the material and then allowing it to dry in the absence of tension. Wetting may be done either (a) by folding the piece along with a damp or wet cotton wrapper and allowing the pile of cloth so formed to stand a while, (b) by spraying water on the cloth, or (c) by passing the cloth between squeezing rollers, the lower one of which dips into a trough of water. After dissipating strains by hanging the cloth over bars to dry, the cloth is re-pressed in a flat paper press without introducing further strains.

The shrinkage which takes place during the London shrinking process is determined by several factors, of which temperature is particularly important. This is illustrated by the figures given in Table 13.3 which records the shrinkage of a cloth on immersion in water at various temperatures for five minutes.

TABLE 13.3. RELATIONSHIP BETWEEN TEMPERATURE
AND CLOTH SHRINKAGE IN LONDON SHRINKING

Temperature (°F)			60	85	110	140	170	185
Shrinkage (per cent)	..	..	4.3	4.5	4.8	6.0	6.9	7.8

It is also important to note that relaxation may not be complete after the first shrinking and consequently some cloths are double-shrunk or even treble-shrunk. Clearly the need for a second shrinking operation is dependent on the conditions under which the first process is carried out, but when cloths are simply left between damp wrappers, repeated treatments often result in greater shrinkage. In one particular instance, the shrinkages after the first, second, and third shrinkings were 1.8 per cent, 2.8 per cent, and 3.7 per cent, respectively. In practice, the damp wrapper method is widely used, presumably because of the small alteration in the finish of the cloth, but squeezing methods and continuous processes are increasing in popularity.

So far as garment-making is concerned, the shrinkage takes place during Hoffman pressing. In a well-shrunk cloth most of the shrinkage will take place on the first pressing and two more will release all the strains. On badly shrunk cloth six or seven pressings may be necessary before complete shrinkage is attained.

More modern and efficient methods of stabilizing cloth include the flat setting technique discussed previously. It must be mentioned, however, that even these treated cloths show the phenomenon of hygral expansion, *i.e.*, there is an alteration in cloth dimensions with changes in relative humidity.

PREVENTION OF FELTING

Wool fibres are able to felt together and this causes wool fabrics to shrink during washing, even though relaxation shrinkage has been eliminated. The felting of wool arises from the scaliness and the elastic properties of wool fibres and it has been found that, if these characteristics are altered, there are corresponding changes in the felting and shrinking capacity of fabrics made from these fibres. Any method which destroys the scaliness or D.F.E. of wool fibres or which decreases the ease of extension or the power of recovery of the fibres will be effective in reducing the shrinkage of wool fabrics on washing. The problem of preventing felting shrinkage attains greater significance in the case of knitted fabrics, but woven cloths are now being treated and there is an ever-increasing scope for the application of newly developed non-shrink processes.

A satisfactory process should render the wool non-felting without affecting unduly the desirable properties of the fibres. There should be no discoloration of the material and the loss in weight accompanying application of the process should be as small as possible. The process should be cheap and easy to apply. Clearly, non-shrink processes may be applied at several stages in cloth production, *e.g.*, to raw wool, scoured wool, tops, yarn, or pieces. The most popular method is to treat pieces or knitted articles, but there is a great deal to be said for treating tops, and a considerable amount of material is treated as yarn in the preparation of hand-knitting wools. Many processes have been developed but the one commonly used is chlorination.

CHLORINATION PROCESSES TO PREVENT FELTING

Although wet chlorination has many defects and is far from being an ideal process, it is cheap and is still employed by many finishers who find that, provided careful control is exercised, it is possible to obtain commercially acceptable results. Moreover, some of the modern developments of the old wet chlorination techniques are extremely satisfactory.

In the usual practice of chlorination the fabric is treated with a mixture of sodium or calcium hypochlorite and acid, about 3 per cent of available chlorine (calculated on the weight of the wool) being applied. It is customary to process pieces in a dolly machine or in a winch. The cloth is first wetted out thoroughly in water containing a wetting agent [Calsolene Oil (I.C.I.), Teepol (Shell)] and then the appropriate amount of acid is added. Sodium hypochlorite is then added very gradually so that the chlorine which is liberated by the action of the acid on the hypochlorite is adsorbed evenly by the cloth. Control of pH value is essential, as is evident from the figures given in Table 13.4 which indicates the amount of chlorine adsorbed by wool from hypochlorite solutions of various pH values.

TABLE 13.4. ADSORPTION OF CHLORINE BY WOOL FROM HYPOCHLORITE SOLUTION

Initial pH value			Chlorine adsorbed	Initial pH value			Chlorine adsorbed
1.86	..	..	83.2 per cent	6.96	..	..	88.6 per cent
3.02	..	..	86.0 per cent	7.70	..	..	80.5 per cent
3.93	..	..	87.0 per cent	9.04	..	..	35.0 per cent
4.90	..	..	87.0 per cent	9.96	..	..	13.0 per cent
5.72	..	..	90.0 per cent	10.76	..	..	9.1 per cent

The mixture should be maintained acid throughout the treatment to avoid the cloth becoming yellow and to obtain the maximum degree of unshrinkability; and it is generally accepted that pH 3 to 4 is the most satisfactory range for chlorination.

When sodium hypochlorite is mixed with strong acids, both chlorine and hypochlorous acid are formed. As the former is claimed to be the more destructive so far as the wool is concerned, many workers recommend substituting weak acids such as boric or acetic for acids like hypochloric or sulphuric. Additions of phenol to mixtures of hypochlorite and boric acid have also been suggested to ensure that any free chlorine which is formed is adsorbed and prevented from attacking the wool. In the Negafel process, formic acid is used, and the patentees advocate treating unscoured rather than scoured fabric. After all wet chlorination processes the cloth is rinsed in a solution of sodium sulphite or bisulphite to remove unreacted chlorine.

The disadvantages of older forms of wet chlorination have led to the development of other chlorination techniques. It is believed that the reason for the uneven results frequently obtained in the older methods lay in the great affinity of wool for chlorine, with the result that fibres on the outside of the yarn were over-treated while those inside were not treated. Consequently processes were developed in which the active reagents liberated chlorine slowly, among these being 'Aktivin' and 1 : 3-dichloro-5 : 5'-dimethylhydantoin. In other methods, hypochlorites were applied in conjunction with other reagents, conditions being adjusted so that both reactions were controllable. Thus, in a process developed by the Greenwood Dyeing Company the cloth is first treated with hypochlorite at pH 4 and then with alkaline peroxide, while Stevenson's method entails treating the cloth with a mixture of sodium hypochlorite and potassium permanganate, the pH value being carefully controlled slightly on the alkaline side. The fabric is then 'cleared' by adding sodium bisulphite. In the Melafix (CBA) process the adsorption of chlorine is controlled by adding a small amount of Melafix CH, which serves as a buffer. The Wool Industries Research Association has devised a process in which wool is treated with a mixture of peracetic acid and sodium hypochlorite.

An alternative method of controlling the chlorination process is to restrict the action of the chlorine to the surface of the fibres by carrying out the reaction in the presence of an organic solvent which cannot penetrate into the fibres and good results have been obtained by treating wool conditioned to contain about 10 per cent of moisture with a solution of chlorine gas in carbon tetrachloride.

The action of chlorine is probably best controlled by using the technique, developed by the Wool Industries Research Association, in which conditioned wool is treated with dry chlorine gas. The wool is dried so that it contains about 8 per cent of moisture and is then placed in a vulcanite-lined autoclave to which is connected a supply of chlorine and a means of reducing the pressure in the system by vacuum pumps. The air is first removed from the system by the pumps and then about 1 per cent of chlorine (on the weight of the wool) is admitted slowly. When the gas has been adsorbed, the necessary adjustments in pressure are made, and the material is removed from the autoclave. It may be treated with a solution of sodium bisulphite after chlorination but this operation is often eliminated. The process is particularly successful when applied to tops and to socks.

NON-CHLORINATION PROCESSES OF PREVENTING FELTING

Because of the limitation of chlorination techniques, a considerable amount of work has been carried out with the object of obtaining non-shrink finishes with reagents other than chlorine. As would be expected, other halogens, fluorine and bromine, reduce the felting powers of wool. Iodine, however, does not and only bromine offers commercial possibilities. Some of the more important non-chlorine processes are summarized below.

In the 'Dri-sol' process, wool is treated for one hour at room temperature with a 1.5 to 2 per cent solution of sulphuryl chloride in white spirit, after which it is hydroextracted, washed with water and thoroughly neutralized with warm dilute alkali.

In the Freney-Lipson process, wool is treated in a solution of caustic soda or caustic potash in methylated spirits or industrial alcohol, after which it is squeezed and passed into a solution of sulphuric acid in spirit or water. It is then washed and dried.

The Tootal process also uses alkalis and the following example from the patent specification (*B.P.* 538,396; 538,428) illustrates the procedure. Wool socks weighing 8.5 lb. are scoured and lightly milled before washing, drying and conditioning to contain 12.5 per cent of moisture. They are then steeped for one hour in 6.7 gallons of liquor initially at 17.5°C, the liquor being prepared by adding 6 gallons of kerosene to 0.7 gallons of a solution of caustic soda in normal butyl alcohol prepared by dissolving 6 lb. of caustic soda in 10 gallons of butyl alcohol. When the reaction is complete, the socks are neutralized by plunging them into 8 gallons of cold water containing 0.2 gallons of concentrated sulphuric acid, after which they are rinsed in water and dried.

Other methods employ enzymes. Here the wool is treated with a protease solution, *e.g.*, a solution of papain or trypsin in the presence of accelerators. This is the basis of the W.I.R.A. papain process. A typical procedure is to treat 100 parts of scoured wool fabric for 45 minutes at 65°C with a solution of 0.325 parts of commercial papain in 1,250 parts of water with the addition of 125 parts of sodium bisulphite and 2.1 parts of sodium hydroxide. The pH value of this solution is 6.7. The fabric is then rinsed in running water and dried. Attractive effects are obtained on peroxide bleached wool and on dry chlorinated wool, the products so produced being termed 'Perzymed wool' and 'Chlorzymed wood', respectively.

In the Dylan process a combination of oxidizing agent followed by a reducing agent is found to be effective. The cloth is first treated with permonosulphuric acid and then with sodium bisulphite; this appears not to be merely a 'clearing' bath as the reducing treatment is essential in producing the shrinkproofing action.

The C.S.I.R.O. laboratories, Australia, recommend the use of potassium permanganate in a saturated (30 per cent) salt solution, followed by acidified sodium bisulphite, the function of which is to remove the imparted brown colour.

A reagent which has recently become commercially available is dichloroisocyanuric acid, *e.g.*, Basolan D.C. (B.A.S.F.). This shows signs of becoming a most important shrink-resisting chemical and may be employed in continuous or batch processes; a bisulphite treatment is again necessary to remove excess reagent.

DEVELOPMENTS IN THE PREVENTION OF FELTING

All the processes described above owe their effectiveness to the fact that the reagents are capable of degrading the wool fibre so that the scales are rendered ineffective. This, of course, makes the fibres less resistant to abrasion. It would appear that it should be possible to eliminate the effectiveness of the scales by coating them with a thin layer of resistant material.

Of particular interest in this connection are polymers derived from a wide range of starting materials. Thus wool treated for six hours at 50°C with 5 per cent of anhydrocarboxyglycine, dissolved in ethyl acetate to which 2 per cent (by volume) of water has been added, is made unshrinkable by the deposition of a thin film of polymer which masks the surface scales of the fibres. This surface film also increases the resistance to wear. Surface films may also be obtained by polymers derived from silicon derivatives and isocyanates.

Interesting results may also be obtained by synthesizing polymers inside the fibres instead of depositing films on the surface. Often fabrics treated in this way are made unshrinkable, no doubt as a result of modification of the elastic properties. Thus cloth is made unshrinkable by immersing in 0.2 per cent ferrous sulphate solution, squeezing, drying and treating with an aqueous solution of methyl methacrylate containing hydrogen peroxide for one to two hours at 95 to 100°C. Impregnation with non-polymerized alkylated melamine formaldehyde resins followed by baking also reduces the shrinkage of wool fabrics. In the 'Lanaset' process, a fabric is impregnated with a solution of methylated methylol-melamine and an acid catalyst, squeezed, dried, and baked at 140°C and the 10 per cent of polymer which is thereby deposited within the fibres gives a high degree of unshrinkability.

A new idea which has now reached the stage of full scale production is that of interfacial polymerization. In the Wurlan process (the name is derived from Western Utilization Research and Development Division, and *lana*) wool is immersed successively in a solution of a diamine and a diacid chloride to form an ultra-thin resin film. No drying or heat curing is required and excellent shrink stability is achieved with a very low resin uptake. For example, the first bath may contain a one per cent aqueous solution of hexamethylene diamine together with the equivalent of inorganic base. A very efficient squeeze gives a 40-50 per cent wet pick-up after which the fabric passes to a second bath containing 3 per cent of sebacoyl chloride in a hydrocarbon solvent. This bath is kept dry and at minimum volume and a pick-up of 15-20 per cent is desirable. Speeds of 15-25 yards per minute can be attained, and the only after-treatment is a wash in warm running water followed by a 20-minute scour in a non-ionic detergent.

Deposits of ready-formed polymers can be useful provided the surface properties of the polymers permit them to spread and form films on the surface of the fibre. An uptake of about 3 per cent of soft polyacrylates is claimed to give greatly improved abrasion resistance and an increase in tensile strength of about 10 per cent; if the wool is first given a light acid chlorination, true machine washability is attained.

CARBONIZING

THE OBJECT OF CARBONIZING PIECE-GOODS is to remove cellulosic material which may be present in the form of burrs or cellulosic fibres (cotton, rayon). Very small amounts of vegetable matter may be removed by picking or burling, *i.e.*, by the use of tweezers (burling irons). In other cases, it is possible to burl dye the fabric with a direct cotton dye. Dark blue and black fabrics are often burl dyed by mordanting the fabric with tannin (20 per cent of ground myrabolans or the equivalent of extract) and then running in a solution of copperas (25 per cent on the weight of the cloth). The black tannate stains the cellulosic fibres and burrs. These dyeing procedures are satisfactory only for poorer fabrics, and are most used when cotton is the impurity. Burl dyed cloth containing burrs still feels prickly and unpleasant, and it is more satisfactory to remove vegetable impurities completely by treatment with acid (sulphuric or hydrochloric) or a reagent (magnesium and aluminium chlorides), which produces acid when heated.

Opinions differ as to the best position of carbonizing in the finishing routine. The operation is best effected after scouring and before milling and dyeing, but certain finishers believe that carbonizing adversely affects milling properties and that any uneven treatment will be reflected in uneven dyeing. If, however, the process is carried out after milling and dyeing, the cloth is more difficult to impregnate and even carbonizing is made more difficult. It is necessary also to use dyes which are fast to carbonizing. Certain firms prefer to stock carbonized pieces in order that they may produce ranges of fashionable shades from a stock of white fabric at very short notice.

OPERATIONS ESSENTIAL TO CARBONIZING

The operations essential to carbonizing are cleansing of the cloth, saturation with the carbonizing reagent, whizzing to remove excess reagent, drying and baking, dry milling, and neutralizing and rinsing. It is customary to use a winch or dolly machine for impregnating the cloth in rope form, and an ebonite-lined hydro-extractor for whizzing, the cloth being squeezed before whizzing. Drying is done in a simple machine heated with steam pipes, the fabric passing through the machine in a tensionless state—it is not customary to carry it on tenter chains. The first stage of drying is carried out at 60°C, while the baking should be completed at a higher temperature (90°C for sulphuric acid carbonizing, and higher temperatures for aluminium chloride and magnesium chloride processes). Care has to be taken to remove the moist air from the machine, to prevent condensation of liquid which might drop on to the cloth. After drying—before it has been able to regain its normal amount of moisture—the cloth is placed in a milling machine fitted with flanged rollers and the degraded vegetable matter is beaten out. Subsequent neutralization and rinsing may be carried out in a dolly machine.

There is an increasing tendency to make the sequence of operations continuous, and ranges comprising open-width impregnators, open-width squeezers, vacuum extractors, a horizontal or vertical dryer, and a continuous dry milling or beating machine have been built. They are usually fitted with two-speed gears, the speeds of the cloth being six yards per minute and 35 yards per minute, respectively.

CONDITIONS OF CARBONIZING

The most common reagent used is an aqueous solution of sulphuric acid of density 4 to 8°Tw, the higher concentration being used for burr removal and the lower for cotton. Wetting agents of the Leonil type may also be added. An aluminium chloride solution of 9 to 12°Tw or a magnesium chloride solution of 12 to 13°Tw may also be used but with these more expensive reagents it is important to collect all the liquor squeezed or sucked from the cloth after impregnation. Their effectiveness is dependent on the liberation of hydrochloric acid during baking. Aluminium chloride is used principally on high-class materials.

After carbonizing, the fabrics are neutralized by running in water and then, in the case of acid or aluminium chloride carbonizing, in soda ash of 1 to 2°Tw or, in the case of carbonizing with magnesium chloride, in dilute sulphuric acid.

FAULTS IN CARBONIZING

Ineffective carbonizing due to uneven impregnation. This often arises from inadequate scouring or from the presence of lime soaps.

Uneven dyeing due to local drying and concentration of acid resulting in preferential damage by the acid.

Unlevel dyeing due to the prolonged exposure of carbonized pieces to light while they are still acid.

Metal stains, spots and holes.

Poor handle due to the use of too high temperatures in drying.

BLEACHING OF WOOL

THE OBJECT OF THE BLEACHING OPERATION is to eliminate the yellow or cream colour of wool to produce white fabrics or to prepare material for subsequent dyeing in pastel or very bright shades. The reagents most commonly employed are sulphur dioxide and hydrogen peroxide, although other reducing and oxidizing agents have been suggested.

PREPARATION OF CLOTH FOR BLEACHING

The greasy cloth is perched and mended and stains are removed by spotting agents, *e.g.*, Astol A. It is then scoured and again examined. Stains on the fabric should now be few and these must be removed by repeated treatment with the appropriate chemicals, *e.g.*, oil stains with solvents, iron stains with saturated oxalic acid solution or five per cent aqueous hydrochloric acid, and copper stains with aqueous potassium cyanide. Some fabrics are partially finished before bleaching, and this may involve milling and cutting.

REDUCING BLEACHES

The oldest method is to hang the moist cloth in a room and then to burn sulphur, about six pounds of sulphur being used for each 100 pounds of cloth. As this method, known as sulphur stoving, tends to produce uneven results, due largely to uneven distribution of moisture and sulphur dioxide, continuous stoves were devised in which cloth carried on bars is passed slowly through an enclosed chamber containing sulphur dioxide. A cylinder of sulphur dioxide may replace burning sulphur, the gas being admitted gradually.

Precautions must be taken to avoid overtreatment and to prevent condensation of moisture on the cloth. Cloth may also be bleached in a closed dolly machine using a solution of sulphur dioxide in water. The reagent is added in small amounts and it is possible to obtain even results in about 30 minutes. For very high whites the treatment should be repeated once or twice.

In a second method, 100 pounds of fabric are treated in a dolly with 500 gallons of water containing 2½ gallons of 70°Tw sodium bisulphite and four pounds of sulphuric acid. Alternatively, the material is soaked in 2°Tw sodium bisulphite solution for six to 10 hours, and then treated with dilute sulphuric acid for 20 minutes and rinsed in water. The whole of the process may be done in a winch or on a jigger.

In a neutral bleach, the reagent used is a mixture of sodium bisulphite and sodium sulphite in the ratio of two parts of $NaHSO_3$ to one part of Na_2SO_3. For normal bleaching, the concentration of the reagent is two per cent SO_2, and its pH 6.8, bromophenol blue being used as an indicator. Treatment for 24 hours in the cold, or for two hours at 120°F produces a good white.

OXIDIZING BLEACHES

Oxidizing agents give more permanent results than those produced by stoving, but the process is more expensive. Oxidizing agents are also capable of bleaching natural black pigments in hair, which are unaffected by most reducing agents.

Commercial hydrogen peroxide is acidic, and for bleaching it must therefore be made alkaline (usually to phenol phthalein) by the addition of alkalis, such as ammonia or sodium silicate, or of specially prepared buffering agents, *e.g.*, Stabilizer C (Laporte). Bleaching may be carried out either by an aging or a steeping method, the latter being more common. Typical procedures are as follows:

In the aging method, a liquor is prepared by mixing 96 gallons of water at 120°F with four gallons of 100 vol. hydrogen peroxide*, and adding concentrated sodium silicate solution (about 1 lb. 10 oz. of 78°Tw solution) until the mixture is alkaline to phenol phthalein. The fabric, *e.g.*, blankets, is thoroughly wetted out in the liquor, then removed and squeezed, the excess liquor being returned to the bleaching bath. After standing for 24 hours, the fabric is dried.

Typical reagents for use in the steeping method are prepared as follows: In one, 100 gallons of water are mixed with two to three gallons of 100 vol. hydrogen peroxide, sufficient sodium silicate then being added to make the mixture alkaline to phenol phthalein. In another, 98 gallons of water are mixed with two gallons of 100 vol. hydrogen peroxide, four pounds Stabilizer C then being added.

A wool to liquor ratio of 1 to 10 is usual, and both liquors are heated to 120°F before the goods are immersed in them. After standing in the

---

*The volume strength of a hydrogen peroxide solution is defined as the volume in ml. of the oxygen which is liberated from 1 ml. of the hydrogen peroxide. Thus, 1 ml. of 10 volume hydrogen peroxide (which is 3 per cent), yields 10 ml. of oxygen. The reagent is normally supplied as a 100 volume solution.

liquor overnight, during which time the temperature of the liquor falls to about 90°F, the goods are removed, rinsed and dried.

The bleach with Stabilizer C is superior to that with sodium silicate. If the wool has been acid-treated, it should be neutralized before bleaching by soaking in a liquor containing $\frac{1}{2}$ lb. of soda ash in 100 gallons of water. Peroxide baths gradually become exhausted, and should be replenished by adding 100 vol. peroxide and sodium silicate or Stabilizer C, so that the liquor is just alkaline to phenol phthalein and the concentration of peroxide is two to three volumes, as required. Peroxide bleaching may also be carried out under acid conditions with the assistance of Stabilizer NP; this is a fluoride which not only acts as a buffer but also leads to some degree of mothproofing.

Whatever the method of bleaching adopted, many white fabrics are afterwards blued with a dilute solution of methyl violet, methylene blue, or a patent blue. This enhances the whiteness, but is removed by the first wash.

FLUORESCENT BRIGHTENING AGENTS

Fluorescent brightening agents are essentially colourless compounds which absorb ultra-violet radiation and re-emit it as visible light at the blue end of the spectrum. Since daylight contains a significant amount of u.v. radiation, textile materials treated with such agents appear considerably whiter when viewed under such conditions. The whitening effect is additive and is thus superior to that obtained with conventional blueing agents. Examples are Uvitex WS (CIBA) and Blancol TW (LBH) which are applied as for acid dyes. Such substances can be used on their own to improve the natural yellow colour of wool or in conjunction with conventional bleaches to give a still better white. Unfortunately the stability to light of these compounds on bleached wool is only moderate, and it appears that the natural yellowing of wool on exposure to light is accelerated catalytically by the brightening agent itself.

REQUIREMENTS FOR GOOD BLEACHING

A good supply of soft water free from iron is essential. Bleaching vats should be of stainless steel. Monel metal is unsatisfactory, but earthenware is useful for storage tanks, etc. Care must be taken to avoid staining and the use of iron, copper or lead should not be allowed. Lead paints are also undesirable.

Fabrics should be covered during storage with white cotton fabrics, and carts should be lined with sheet stainless steel or Lancaster cloth. All machines should be kept clean and designed with bearings placed outside the machines, which should not be fixed directly under shafting.

The dry finishing room should be kept very clean and used only for white fabrics. Open windows should be kept covered with muslin to keep out dirt and the management should encourage employees to regard cleanliness as a necessity by providing white overalls, and decorating the sheds in a pleasing colour scheme. The wet finishing room should be cleaned and swilled down at regular intervals and accumulation of soap suds and any form of dirt forbidden.

All woods are not suitable for use in bleacheries. Beech and sycamore are probably the most satisfactory; some oaks tend to stain fabrics, and resins may be extracted from pine and deal.

Tentering machines should have stainless steel pins, and vats should be lined with this material. Heating coils should also be made of stainless steel.

DEFECTS IN BLEACHING

Holes due to the presence of iron or copper. These metals catalyse the degradation of wool by hydrogen peroxide, and intense local action results.

Stains due to metals. Copper salts give a blue or brown stain, but black copper sulphide may be formed after sulphur bleaching. Iron gives brown or black stains, and lead black stains.

Weak cloth due to excessive treatment.

Uneven results due to inadequate mechanical movement, resulting in uneven distribution of the reagent.

PROOFING

UNDER THE HEADING 'PROOFING' may be included mothproofing, rot-proofing and showerproofing. Since wool burns only with difficulty, it is not customary to fireproof wool fabrics. In fact, certain types of wool materials are used primarily on account of their fireproof characteristics. This does not, of course, imply that wool cannot be burned, but rather that it is not easily ignited and, when ignited, the speed with which the flame travels is comparatively slow.

MOTHPROOFING

To make fabrics mothproof, treatment with reagents such as Mitin FF (Geigy), Eulan WA new (Bayer) or Dieldrin (Shell) is effective. Mitin FF and Eulan WA are applied as for acid dyes to give an uptake of 1-1.5 per cent on the weight of wool. Dieldrin is applied from solvent or emulsion (the emulsion application being more effective) to give an uptake of 0.05 per cent. Good results are also obtained by the application of Catophrene (Catomance Ltd.) processes and as these do not in general require that the material should be boiled, they find a number of special applications.

ROTPROOFING

Wool is attacked by both moulds or fungi and by bacteria. To protect wool during processing and for comparatively short periods some well established antiseptics are effective. The reagents are applied as dilute solutions. An 0.1 per cent solution of Shirlan NA (I.C.I.) gives good protection against mould attack as does an 0.1 per cent solution of Santobrite (Monsanto) (sodium pentachlorophenate). In Mystox (Catomance, Ltd.) pentachlorophenol is associated in a degraded protein complex and padding cloth with a solution of this product yields more permanent results than does the simple application of pentachlorophenol.

Proofing agents which protect wool during use even in the tropics include 0.25 per cent *p*-nitrophenol in conjunction with either dinitro-*a*-naphthol (0.25 per cent) or dinitro-*o*-cresol (0.25 per cent). The material is coloured yellow but the process finds application when colour is not an important consideration. Pentachlorophenol may be used in certain cases as it is fast to dry cleaning but not to wet alkaline treatments. Copper salts are particularly effective when 0.5-1.0 per cent of copper is present. Copper and chromium compounds together give greater protection. One method of applying such a proof is illustrated by the following details of a laboratory trial.

To a solution of 3 g. copper sulphate crystals in 300 ml. of water at room temperature are added successively sufficient ammonia to redissolve the precipitated cupric hydroxide, 3.5 g. potassium chromate in 200 ml. of water, and 3 g. Perminal PW (I.C.I.) in 400 ml. of water, the total volume being adjusted to one litre. The sample of wool (30 g.) is worked in this solution for five minutes, removed, squeezed, and immediately plunged into water, washing then being continued in running water for five minutes. The material is then dried at less than 60°C.

SHOWERPROOFING

To obtain the highest degree of showerproofing it is necessary to apply a good proofing agent to a suitable fabric. Cloths of the gaberdine type are the most favoured because of their tight construction, although modern showerproofing agents are often put on milled cloths, *e.g.*, heavy overcoatings for military purposes, with excellent results.

The oldest method of showerproofing is to treat the fabric with aluminium acetate solution, usually prepared by mixing equal volumes of 5 per cent solutions of lead acetate and aluminium sulphate. The mixture is allowed to stand for a time so that the precipitated lead sulphate may be removed by decantation. The fabric is then impregnated with the clear solution, squeezed and dried. The proof is not very fast but may be improved by soaping and rinsing in dilute (7°Tw.) aluminium sulphate solution.

Waxes are well established showerproofing agents, being most effective when used along with aluminium acetate. Older reagents were wax emulsions which were cracked when aluminium was added; the showerproofing process was therefore a two-bath technique—impregnation first with a wax emulsion and then with aluminium acetate. Later, wax emulsions were prepared which did not break down immediately aluminium acetate was added and it became possible to showerproof with these reagents by mixing the emulsion and aluminium acetate solution immediately before use, and then impregnating the cloths with the mixture.

With advances in the manufacture of emulsifying agents, showerproofing agents which are stable wax emulsion containing aluminium compounds have been prepared and these enable showerproofing to be carried out as a single-bath process. Many brands of these reagents are on the market and the method of application is illustrated by the following instructions for using Dipsanil V (I.C.I.).

An appropriate amount of reagent is diluted with four parts of water at 40-50°C and the mixture is added to the correct amount of water at 50-60°C contained in the trough of a padding mangle. Usually 5 per cent of Dipsanil V (on the weight of the fabric) is applied. If the treatment is carried out using a mangle of 70 per cent expression then a proofing bath containing seven pounds of Dipsanil per 10 gallons of water will give five per cent on the material. After being impregnated, the cloth is dried at not less than 70°C.

Excellent results may be obtained on both wool cloth and blended cloths by the use of three per cent of Mystolene XP (Catomance, Ltd.), which is applied along with aluminium formate solution. The two reagents are mixed and placed in a dolly along with an appropriate amount of water, and the fabric is run in the liquid until the reagents have been adsorbed. It is then hydroextracted and dried.

A reagent which gives good results which are fast to dry cleaning is Velan PF—a compound closely allied to stearamido-methyl pyridinium chloride. The method of applying this product is shown by the following example. Three to six pounds of Velan PF (depending on the degree of proofing required) and five ounces of sodium acetate crystals per pound of Velan PF are dispersed in 10 gallons of water and the cloth to be proofed is impregnated with the liquid at 30-40°C. It is then hydroextracted and quickly dried before being heated at 100-130°C. The time of heating is determined by the temperature, five minutes being required at 100°C and three minutes at 120°C. Thicker cloths will require longer times of heating than thin cloths. The finish obtained has not only excellent showerproofing characteristics but is also soft.

There are now several truly permanent showerproofing finishes, the only bar to their universal application being that of expense. Silicones have achieved great promise in this field. Originally applied to non-wool fabrics by padding and high-temperature baking, they are now also supplied in a form suitable for exhaustion methods. With Silicone Finish MS 2207 (Midland Silicones) sufficient emulsion (together with appropriate catalyst) is used to give a two per cent solids uptake on the fibre. The time of treatment is about 20 minutes, with a 20 : 1 liquor ratio and a pH value of between 4 and 6. The cloth is hydro-extracted without rinsing and the proof is enhanced by storing the fabric for a few days.

Certain chromium complexes of the type indicated by the following formula have a strong affinity for fibres, though there seems to be some

$$\left[\begin{array}{c} O \rightarrow Cr \\ C_{17}H_{35}.C \diagup \diagdown OH \\ O - Cr \end{array} \right]^{4+} 4Cl^{-}$$

doubt of the precise structures of the products themselves and of the subsequent deposit on the fibre. Quintolan W (I.C.I.) has been developed primarily for use on wool and synthetic fibres; the main drawback is that it imparts a greenish tinge to undyed and pale fabrics. It can be applied either by padding or exhaustion techniques.

Fluorochemical finishes, for example, the Scotchgard process (Minnesota Mining and Manufacturing Co), include compounds such as chromium complexes of perfluoromonocarboxylic acids. The presence on fibres of extremely low-energy fluorinated groups results in both oil and water repellency.

EASY-CARE WOOL FABRICS

The concept of 'easy-care' fabrics has followed the introduction of thermoplastic man-made fibres which are used in garments requiring the minimum of ironing and which have permanent pleats. This development was followed by processes conferring similar properties on fabrics made of cotton and regenerated cellulosic fibres and this, in turn, led to the investigation of ways and means whereby the same label could be attached to wool materials. Finishes are now well established which go some way towards this desirable end. Shrinkproofing, mothproofing and showerproofing all may be said to have eliminated some of the care and caution necessary to maintain a garment in good condition, but perhaps the real breakthrough lies in the more recent development of flat-setting, using either chemicals or high temperature steam, to give a permanent finish. It remains to be seen how effective a combination of these treatments will be in conferring true 'easy care' properties.

FINISHING ROUTINES

FINISHING ROUTINES for woollen and worsted fabrics vary with the type of cloth, the processing to which it has been previously subjected and the style of finish required. It is appropriate therefore to conclude this section on fabric finishing with brief details of recognized routines applicable to a number of typical woollen and worsted fabrics.

HOMESPUNS AND IMITATION HOMESPUNS

For these fabrics the finishing routine is (*i*) perch, measure, weigh and number; (*ii*) knot and mend—the knots should be pushed to the back; (*iii*) scour with alkali, but avoid undue milling, and wash-off; (*iv*) hydro-extract; (*v*) tenter, using sufficient tension to remove creases formed in scouring; (*vi*) steam and brush lightly to raise the surface fibres; (*vii*) pass through cutting machine to remove the longer projecting fibres—hair-ending—care being taken not to cut too closely; (*viii*) damp and allow to stand overnight; (*ix*) press lightly; and (*x*) steam-off to remove glaze and excessive flatness.

FANCY TWEEDS OR FANCY SAXONY WOOLLENS

For fancy tweeds or fancy Saxony woollens, the routine is as follows: (*i*) perch, measure, weigh and number; (*ii*) knot and mend carefully; (*iii*) scour with alkali and a little soap; wash-off well to remove all traces of soap; the pieces must not be left to lie about in an alkaline state or there will be a tendency to colour bleeding; milling should not be excessive, or the cloth will become stiff and too much cover will be developed; a Williams-Peace machine may be used to advantage; (*iv*) hydro-extract; (*v*) tenter; (*vi*) damp and allow to lie overnight; (*vii*) steam well, brush and cut to pattern; (*viii*) blow twice to avoid ending; if lustre is required, the pieces should be pressed before blowing; (*ix*) damp and allow to stand overnight; (*x*) press warm; (*xi*) steam; and (*xii*) cold flat.

LOWER GRADE FANCY TWEEDS

These fabrics are made to imitate the better quality goods in appearance and handle. The following modifications of routine are often adopted: (*i*) grease milling (not excessive) with or without preliminary raising; (*ii*) to reduce the cost of finishing, steam and cold press after blowing, and press on the rotary press.

FANCY CHEVIOT WOOLLENS

The procedure is as for Saxony tweeds, but with certain modifications *e.g.*: (*i*) blowing is generally omitted as it tends to make the cloth stiff; (*ii*) cut the cloth carefully, but not too closely as the handle may be impoverished; (*iii*) steam and brush lightly; (*iv*) damp and allow to lie overnight; (*v*) press warm; and (*vi*) steam slightly on the face.

LOW CHEVIOT WOOLLENS

The routine is as above, but particular care should be taken in cutting, or there will be a loss of handle and appearance. If the cloth has been roller pressed, the steaming on the face should be well done to improve the handle.

FLANNEL SUITINGS AND TENNIS CLOTHS

The procedure for these fabrics is (*i*) perch, measure, weigh and number; (*ii*) mend and knot—the knots being pushed to the back and cut off, care being taken not to cut too closely; (*iii*) scour with alkali and a little soap either in a dolly or a Williams-Peace machine; if the latter machine is used, the requisite amount of milling can be done at this stage; low qualities are lightly raised before scouring, as this aids the production of cover; (*iv*) after scouring in dolly, mill to width; (*v*) wash-off well; (*vi*) hydro-extract; (*vii*) tenter; (*viii*) brush and steam, afterwards laying aside to allow the moisture to permeate; (*ix*) cut carefully and fairly closely to avoid rubbing-up in use, (*x*) blow twice; (*xi*) steam and brush; (*xii*) damp and allow to stand overnight; (*xiii*) press warm; (*xiv*) steam well on both sides; and (*xv*) cold press lightly.

PIECE-DYED WOOLLEN COATINGS

For piece-dyed woollen coatings the routine is (*i*) perch, measure, weigh and number; (*ii*) knot and mend; if the cloth is to be given a blind finish, the mending need not be so thorough as in the case of the semi-milled cloth; (*iii*) scour with alkali and a little soap; (*iv*) mill to pattern; the amount of cover can be increased if the cloth is raised previous to milling, and this procedure is often applied to low qualities; it is advisable to cut the raised cloth level before milling; (*v*) wash-off well, hydro-extract and tenter; (*vi*) blow twice; (*vii*) dye; (*viii*) wash off; (*ix*) run through hot water, wind on to a wooden roller and leave overnight; (*x*) tenter; (*xi*) steam and brush; (*xii*) cut to pattern; (*xiii*) blow twice; (*xiv*)* run in cold water in a washer and wind on to a roller; stand overnight; (*xv*)* tenter; (*xvi*) steam and brush; (*xvii*) press warm; (*xviii*) steam; and (*xix*) cold press.

MELTON CLOTHS

The routine for high-class wool-dyed Melton is as follows: (*i*) perch, measure, weigh and number; (*ii*) knot, and mend the serious faults; knots should be removed or hard places will be formed during milling; (*iii*) scour in alkali and a little soap if necessary—hydro-extract; (*iv*) mill to a limited

*Omitted in all except the best qualities.

extent with hard soap, reversing the cloth frequently; the cloth should not be milled to the finished width at this stage; (*v*) wash-off well; this process is difficult with heavy cloths, and a Spooner machine may be used with advantage; (*vi*) wind cloths on to a roller after passing through a trough of hot water, and allow to stand for a time to remove marks formed in scouring and milling; (*vii*) tenter; (*viii*) steam and brush; (*ix*) cut the pile level on back and face; (*x*) mill in soap to width—the previous cutting gives a better surface; (*xi*) wash-off; (*xii*) hydro-extract and tenter; (*xiii*) press; (*xiv*) boil twice, opposite ends inside, at 160° to 180°F; (*xv*) tenter; (*xvi*) steam and brush; (*xvii*) cut to pattern; (*xviii*) blow twice; (*xix*) damp and allow to lie overnight; (*xx*) press warm; and (*xxi*) steam and cold press.

For high-quality piece-dyed Meltons the routine is as outlined above, but often the fabric is partly dyed when partially milled, and stocked to be sent for final milling when required. Then wash-off well, wind on to a roller, and allow to stand for a time to remove creases; dye to shade, wash-off, hydro-extract, tenter and press; then continue the routine as from stage *xiii*.

A simplified routine for medium qualities is as follows: (*i*) knot and mend after perching, etc; (*ii*) scour, wash-off and hydro-extract; (*iii*) mill to width; (*iv*) wash-off and hydro-extract; (*v*) dye and wash-off; (*vi*) tenter; (*vii*) brush and steam; (*viii*) cut level (one, back; three, face); (*ix*) brush and steam; (*x*) blow twice; (*xi*) press hot; (*xii*) steam-off; and (*xiii*) cold flat.

For low-quality Meltons and army greatcoats the routine is: (*i*) perch, measure, weigh and number; (*ii*) knot and mend; (*iii*) mill in grease—if any difficulty is experienced, the cloth may be raised slightly before milling; if the milling stops, it is advisable to wash the cloth well, soap-up and continue the operation; (*iv*) wash-off well; (*v*) hydro-extract; (*vi*) tenter; (*vii*) cut to pattern; and (*viii*) press.

It should be noted that greatcoats are often acid milled, but in this case the material must be well scoured first. Acetic or sulphuric acid may be used for milling, and the cloth should be rinsed-off after milling. Many army greatcoats must be waterproofed by running in a suitable reagent and drying. The operation is best carried out immediately after or during milling.

VELOUR CLOTHS

When finishing velours, (*i*) perch, measure, weigh and number; (*ii*) knot and mend—generally the bad faults only; (*iii*) scour with alkali and a little soap; hydro-extract; (*iv*) mill to produce necessary cover and density; lower quality goods may be raised slightly on back and face before milling, as this helps to produce good cover; (*v*) wash-off; (*vi*) hydro-extract; (*vii*) tenter—brushing before tentering is useful; (*viii*) steam, brush and cut level; (*ix*) dye; (*x*) wash-off thoroughly and dry; (*xi*) raise on a card wire machine, raising from both ends to produce a deep pile; excessive raising should be avoided as it results in a loss of wear resistance*; (*xii*) steam and brush; (*xiii*) cut level—fancy cut patterns can be obtained at this stage by using special cutting beds; (*xiv*) steam and allow to stand overnight; (*xv*) cuttle and fold—a very light press may be given but this tends to reduce the loftiness of the cloth.

WOOLLEN OVERCOATINGS: CHECK BACKS, ETC

These fabrics are of varied character and it is impossible to give general instructions for their finishing routine. The effects produced are dependent upon milling and raising, together with napping in certain cases. The following routine is an example of one type only.

(*i*) Perch, measure, weigh and number; (*ii*) knot and mend the severe faults; (*iii*) scour with alkali and a little soap; (*iv*) hydro-extract; (*v*) mill; (*vi*) wash-off; (*vii*) hydro-extract; (*viii*) raise wet on teazle gig; (*ix*) tenter; (*x*) dry beat; (*xi*) steam, brush and cut a little; (*xii*) repeat the raising and cutting until the required pile has been obtained; (*xiii*) damp and allow to stand overnight; and (*xiv*) allow to stand between warm papers.

The following additional operations may be performed to produce special effects: (*i*) the cloths are blown or boiled to produce a slight lustre, the blowing in this case being carried out on a perforated roller; the cloth is wound-on, steam is blown through it and it is then allowed to stand overnight; still milder lustring is done by passing the cloth through warm water and winding on to a roller; (*ii*) cloths are napped by passing through a napping machine; the pile is prepared as above, cut level, and the cloth then napped; (*iii*) to increase the loftiness of the pile, the fabrics are beaten before tentering; and (*iv*) Whitneys are produced in a napping machine fitted with a reciprocating motion.

DRESSED FACE-FINISHED CLOTHS

Examples of these cloths are superfines, beavers, billiard cloths, doeskins, pilots, etc. All these cloths are milled and raised wet, the pile being laid in one direction. They are made in light and heavy weights. Although generally of good quality, imitation cloths can be made using cotton warps.

The routine for wool-dyed beavers is as follows: (*i*) perch, measure, weigh and number; (*ii*) knot and mend on both sides; (*iii*) scour in alkali and a little soap; (*iv*) hydro-extract; (*v*) mill; (*vi*) wash-off well; (*vii*) dress wet on teazle gig to get a full, dense pile; (*viii*) wash-off; (*ix*) tenter; (*x*) dry beat; (*xi*) cut level; (*xii*) wet out and dress one way on gig; (*xiii*) tenter;

---

*Dress face velours can be obtained by raising wet on the teazle gig; otherwise, the routine is as given above.

(*xiv*) dry beat, raise and cut several times until the desired effect is produced; (*xv*) press; (*xvi*) 'boil' four or six times at 160° to 180°F, dressing on the gig between each 'boil'; (*xvii*) dry and tenter; (*xviii*) steam and brush—cut, if necessary; (*xix*) damp and allow to lie overnight; (*xx*) press warm; and (*xxi*) cold press. It should be noted that the cloths are often allowed to lie in a cool place between the dry finishing operations, and they are always well conditioned before being despatched.

For piece-dyed beavers, the routine is as above up to operation (*ix*), then: (*i*) 'boil' three times or blow, depending upon quality; (*ii*) dye and wash-off; (*iii*) complete routine as for wool-dyed cloth.

RUGS

These vary considerably in quality and construction, but all should have a full and lofty handle. The routine is as follows: (*i*) perch, measure, weigh and number; (*ii*) knot and mend—prepare fringes; (*iii*) scour in alkali and soap, taking care to avoid colour bleeding; (*iv*) mill slightly—preliminary raising helps to give a lofty handle; (*v*) wash-off and tenter; (*vi*) raise well on card-wire machine—the drier the cloth, the more open will be the pile; the greater the amount of moisture, the more will the pile be laid; (*vii*) brush and steam; (*viii*) cut level; and (*ix*) cuttle and cramp.

PIECE-DYED WORSTED FABRICS

The typical worsted fabric is finished clear to emphasize the sharpness and clearness of the design, but this may be modified by light milling. The fabrics are used for coatings, suitings and ladies' wear.

To produce a clear finish on goods of botany quality, the routine is as follows: (*i*) perch, measure, weigh and number; (*ii*) knot and mend carefully; (*iii*) if necessary, crab or blow to prevent subsequent distortions—this is essential with plain weaves and hopsacks; (*iv*) scour with soap and a little soda; (*v*) wash-off thoroughly; (*vi*) hydro-extract; (*vii*) tenter; (*viii*) if not already set, the fabrics should now be blown or boiled, generally the former; (*ix*) dye to shade and wash-off thoroughly; (*x*) pass through hot water, wind on to a wooden roller and allow to stand overnight; (*xi*) tenter and dry; (*xii*) damp and allow to stand overnight; (*xiii*) perch; (*xiv*) steam and brush; (*xv*) cut to pattern; (*xvi*) burl, if necessary; (*xvii*) blow twice—additional operations, such as boiling and running through hot or cold water followed by winding on to rollers, may also be carried out; (*xviii*) perch; (*xix*) dew or damp and allow to stand overnight; (*xx*) press warm; (*xxi*) steam-off; and (*xxii*) cold flat and cuttle. High-class goods are generally London shrunk.

The procedure where a semi-milled finish is required is the same as that for clear cut fabrics but, after scouring, the goods are milled to obtain the desired surface. If there is difficulty in milling, preliminary raising and cutting may be necessary. The Williams-Peace combined scouring and milling machine is useful for this type of cloth. After milling, the goods should be washed-off well, tentered and dyed, the routine given above being subsequently followed.

For goods of crossbred quality where a clear finish is required, the procedure is as follows: (*i*) perch, measure, weigh and number; (*ii*) knot and mend carefully; (*iii*) crab—this is essential for this class of goods; (*iv*) scour and wash-off—in lower quality fabrics this may be omitted as crabbing carried out in an alkaline bath is capable of effecting a certain amount of cleaning; (*v*) hydro-extract; (*vi*) dye to shade and wash-off; (*vii*) wind on to a wooden roller through hot water; (*viii*) tenter, damp and allow to stand overnight; (*ix*) perch; (*x*) steam and brush; (*xi*) cut to pattern; (*xii*) burl if necessary; (*xiii*) blow twice; (*xiv*) perch; (*xv*) damp and leave overnight; (*xvi*) press warm; (*xvii*) steam-off; and (*xviii*) cold flat, cuttle and cramp. Goods of this quality may also be given a semi-milled finish.

FANCY WORSTED FABRICS

These fabrics are used for suitings, trouserings, dress goods and, in the semi-milled finish, for the production of worsted flannel. The wool is dyed in hank or top form and stripes of silk or mercerized cotton are often introduced. In the highest qualities these fabrics demand the greatest care in finishing.

For goods of botany quality, where a clear finish is required, the routine is (*i*) perch, measure, weigh and number; (*ii*) knot and mend very carefully; (*iii*) crab or blow, if necessary; (*iv*) scour and wash-off; (*v*) hydro-extract; (*vi*) tenter, care being taken to maintain squares square and stripes straight; (*vii*) damp and allow to stand overnight; (*viii*) steam and brush; (*ix*) cut to pattern; (*x*) burl, if necessary; (*xi*) blow twice; (*xii*) perch; (*xiii*) damp and allow to lie overnight; (*xiv*) press warm; (*xv*) steam-off; and (*xvi*) cold flat, cuttle and cramp. The fabrics are generally London shrunk.

The procedure where a milled finish is required is the same as that for clear cut fabrics except that, after scouring, the goods are milled to obtain the desired cover. After washing-off, the routine is as above. The Williams-Peace machine is used for finishing this type of fabric. The fabrics are often London shrunk.

For goods of crossbred quality, where a clear finish is required, the routine is (*i*) perch, measure, weigh and number; (*ii*) knot and mark carefully; (*iii*) crab and blow—this is essential; (*iv*) scour; (*v*) hydro-extract; (*vi*) tenter; (*vii*) damp and allow to stand overnight; (*viii*) steam and brush; (*ix*) cut to pattern—do not cut too closely; (*x*) burl; (*xi*) blow; (*xii*) perch; (*xiii*) damp and allow to stand overnight; (*xiv*) press warm; (*xv*) steam-off; and (*xvi*) cold flat, cuttle and cramp.

DRESS FABRICS

Dress fabrics are generally light in weight and, on this account, require careful handling. Good crabbing is the most essential part of the routine and manipulation in open width is often preferred to rope form.

For worsted voiles, the procedure is (*i*) perch, measure, weigh and number; (*ii*) knot and mend carefully; (*iii*) crab well; (*iv*) scour with soap and a little alkali; (*v*) hydro-extract or hydro-exhaust; (*vi*) dye and wash-off; (*vii*) tenter; (*viii*) cut after brushing and steaming; (*ix*) steam; (*x*) press hot; and (*xi*) cuttle and cramp.

For gaberdines, (*i*) crab, using both bowls and steam—a considerable amount of top weight can be employed; (*ii*) scour in open width avoiding all milling; (*iii*) bleach and dye—bleaching may be omitted; (*iv*) wash-off and hydro-exhaust; (*v*) tenter; (*vi*) steam and brush; (*vii*) cut closely; (*viii*) perch; (*ix*) blow twice; (*x*) steam; and (*xi*) press hot.

For botany dress fabrics, (*i*) perch, measure, weigh and number; (*ii*) knot and mend; (*iii*) crab; (*iv*) scour; (*v*) hydro-extract; (*vi*) dye; (*vii*) hydro-extract; (*viii*) tenter and dry; (*ix*) cut after brushing and steaming; (*x*) tenter; (*xi*) press; and (*xii*) cuttle.

REFERENCES

1. Speakman and Chamberlain, *Trans. Faraday Society*, 1933, **79**, 358.
2. Goodings and Marshall, *Canadian Text. J.*, 1945, Nov. 44.
3. Moxon, *J. Huddersfield Textile Soc.*, 1950-51, 139.
4. Scholefield, *J. Soc. Dyers and Col.*, 1945, **61**, 90.
5. *Wool Science Review* , 1964, **24**, 34.
6. Johnson, *J. Text. Inst.*, 1938, **29**, T7.
7. Speakman, Stott and Chang, *J. Text. Inst.*, 1933, **24**, T273.
8. Whewell, *J. Soc. Dyers and Col.*, 1955, **71**, 902.
9. Seddon, *J. Soc. Dyers and Col.*, 1945, **61**, 93.

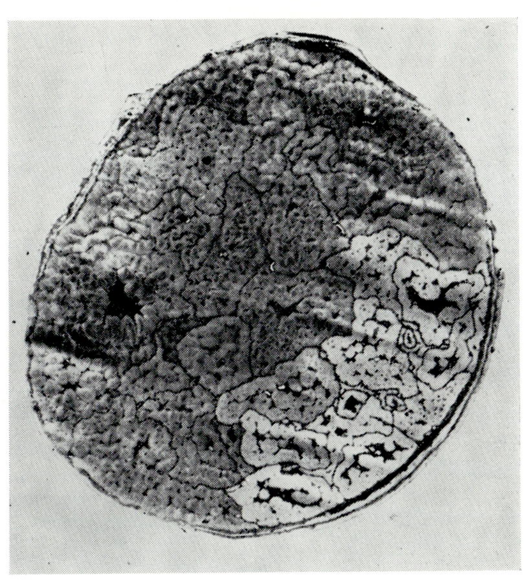

PLATE I.   TRANSVERSE SECTION OF LAMB'S WOOL
SHOWING ORTHO- AND PARACORTICAL SEGMENTS

(Electron micrograph by Dr. Ruth M. Bones)

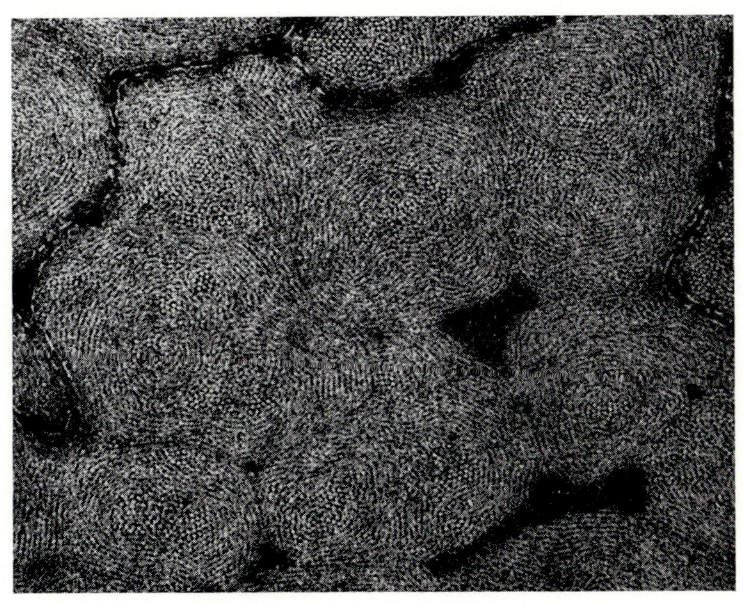

PLATE 2.   TRANSVERSE SECTION OF A LINCOLN WOOL FIBRE
SET IN WATER : 25 PER CENT SET RETAINED

(Electron micrograph by Dr. J. Sikorski)

489

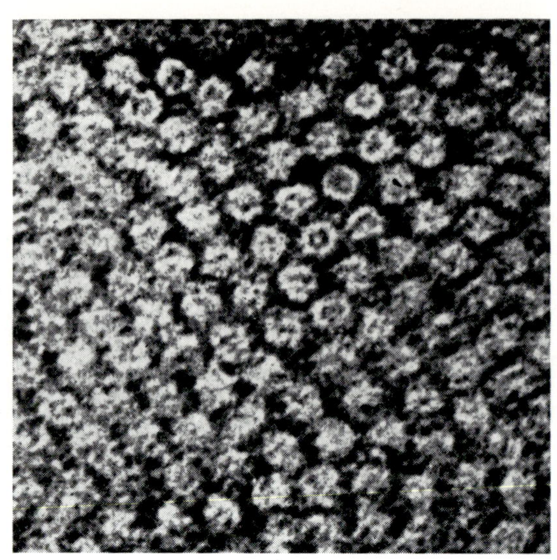

PLATE 3.   TRANSVERSE SECTION OF α-KERATIN
SHOWING THE MICROFIBRIL - MATRIX STRUCTURE

(Electron micrograph by Dr. D. J. Johnson)

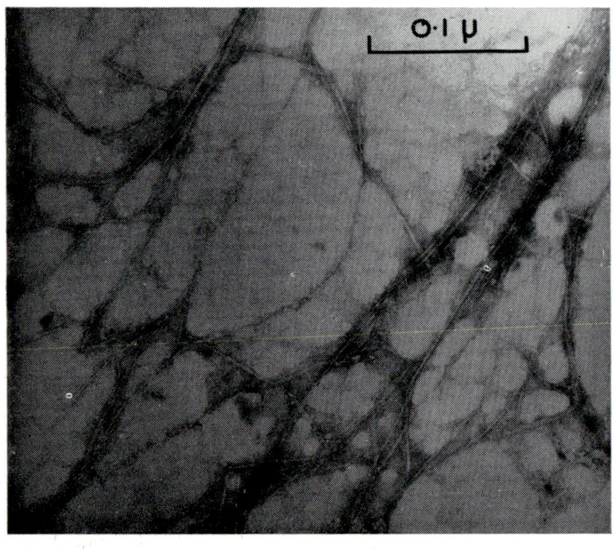

PLATE 4.   PROTOFIBRILS OF MERINO WOOL

(Electron micrograph by Dr. M. G. Dobb)

PLATE 5.   AQUEOUS JET SCOURING MACHINE

(By courtesy of Petrie & McNaught Ltd.)

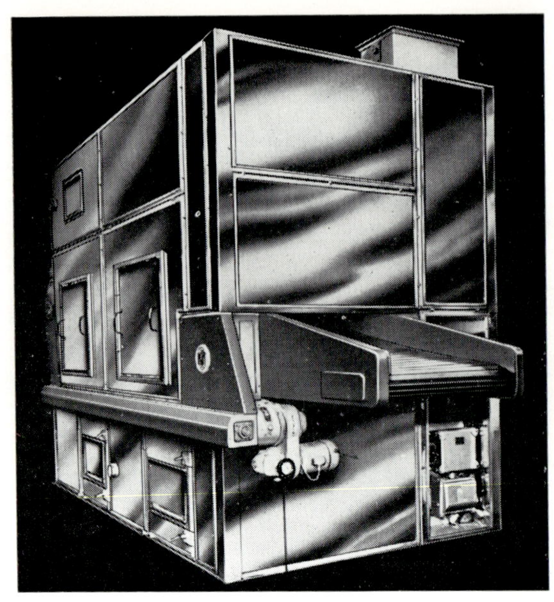

PLATE 6. SUCTION DRUM DRYER

(By courtesy of Petrie & McNaught Ltd.)

PLATE 7. BACKWASH AND DRYER

(By courtesy of Prince-Smith & Stells Ltd.)

PLATE 8.   AUTOLEVELLER GILL BOX

(By courtesy of Prince-Smith & Stells Ltd.)

PLATE 9.   BI-COILER DRAWBOX FOR UNIFLEX DRAWING SET

(*By courtesy of Prince-Smith & Stells Ltd.*)

PLATE 10. SPEED-O-GILL UNIT WITH AUTOMATIC CAN-DOFFING
AND AUTOLEVELLER UNITS

(By courtesy of Prince-Smith & Stells Ltd.)

PLATE 11. NOBLE COMB

(By courtesy of Prince-Smith & Stells Ltd.)

PLATE 12. RECTILINEAR COMB

(By courtesy of Schlumberger et Cie)

PLATE 13. AUTOLEVELLER SPINDLE DRAWBOX

(By courtesy of Prince-Smith & Stells Ltd.)

PLATE 14.   UNIFLEX RING SPINNER

(*By courtesy of Prince-Smith & Stells Ltd.*)

PLATE 15.   MULTI-FIBRE CARDING UNIT (MK. VIII). SEMI-WORSTED SYSTEM

(*By courtesy of James Mackie & Sons Ltd.*)

PLATE 16.   SLIVER TO YARN RING SPINNER.   SEMI-WORSTED SYSTEM

(By courtesy of James Mackie & Sons Ltd.)

PLATE 17.   BATCH BLENDING SYSTEM WITH CIRCULAR BLENDING
BINS AND DUST-REMOVAL CYCLONES

(By courtesy of Spencer & Halstead Ltd.)

PLATE 18.   DOUBLE HOPPER FEED

(By courtesy of John Haigh Ltd.)

PLATE 19.   SCOTCH FEED

(By courtesy of William Tatham Ltd.)

PLATE 20.   TAPE CONDENSER WITH TANDEM CREEL FRONT

(By courtesy of Chadwick Machine Co. Ltd.)

PLATE 21.   WOOLLEN RING SPINNER

(By courtesy of Prince-Smith & Stells Ltd.)

PLATE 22. GENERAL VIEW OF THE SPINNING
POSITION ON THE WOOLLEN RING SPINNER

(By courtesy of Prince-Smith & Stells Ltd.)

PLATE 23.   BARBER & COLMAN SPOOLER WINDING SUPPLY PACKAGES
FOR HIGH-SPEED WARPING MACHINES

(By courtesy of Barber and Colman Ltd.)

PLATE 24.   SCHLAFHORST CONE WINDER

(By courtesy of W. Schlafhorst & Co.)

PLATE 25.   LEESONA 340 (ABBOTT) CONE WINDER

(By courtesy of Leesona Ltd.)

PLATE 26.   BENNINGER WARPING MACHINE

(By courtesy of Benninger Engineering Co. Ltd.)

PLATE 27. UNIFIL LOOM WINDER

(By courtesy of Leesona Ltd.)

PLATE 28.   WARP DRAWING-IN MACHINE

(By courtesy of Barber and Colman Ltd.)

PLATE 29.   HATTERSLEY WORSTED LOOM, 382 MODEL,
SHOWN HERE IN 4 × 1 BOX CONFIGURATION

(By courtesy of G. Hattersley & Sons Ltd.)

PLATE 30.   HUTCHINSON & HOLLINGWORTH 'LOWLINE' HIGH
SPEED WOOLLEN AND WORSTED LOOM

(By courtesy of Hutchinson, Hollingworth & Co. Ltd.)

PLATE 31.   NORTHROP 'HI-SPEED' MULTI-SHUTTLE LOOM

(By courtesy of British Northrop Ltd.)

PLATE 32.   SAURER WORSTED LOOM

(By courtesy of Crowther Ltd.)

PLATE 33.   SAURER DOBBY

(By courtesy of Crowther Ltd.)

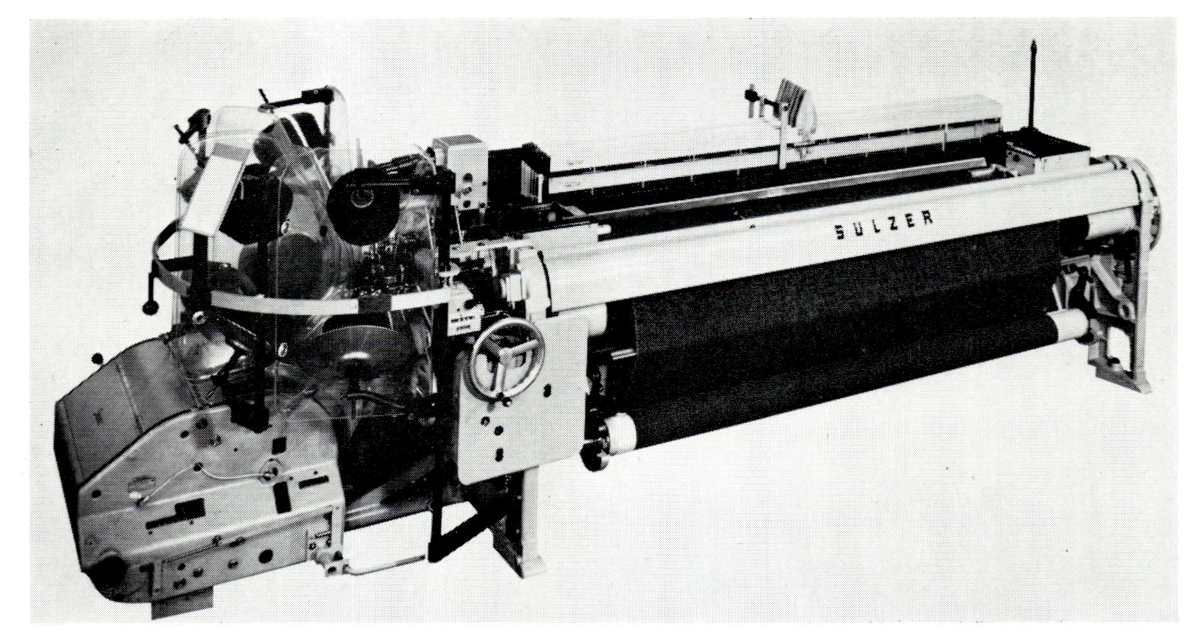

PLATE 34.   SULZER FOUR-COLOUR WEAVING MACHINE OF 85 IN. REED SPACE

(*By courtesy of Sulzer Bros. Ltd.*)

PLATE 35. SULZER
PICKING MECHANISM

The picking motion is derived from the rotation of a camshaft which, by means of a tappet (8) and bowl (7), a toggle (5), link (4) and lever (3) builds up energy in a torsion bar (2) which is held at its far end by an adjustable plate (1). This energy, when suddenly released, is transmitted through the picking arm (9) and shoe (10) to the gripper shuttle (11) which thus enters the shed at high velocity. A hydraulic buffer (6) absorbs the residual energy.

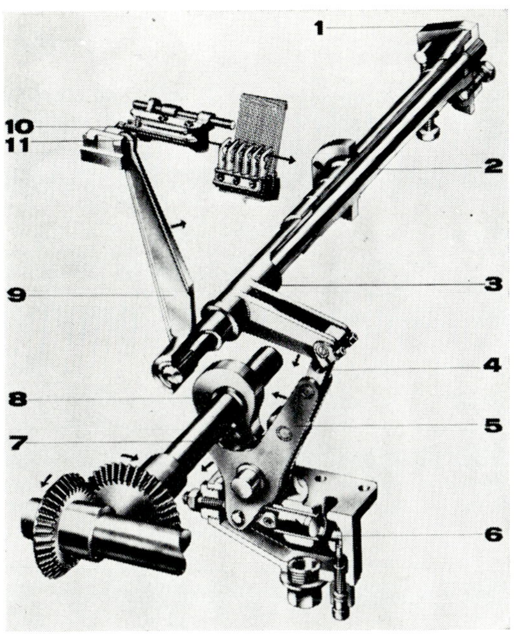

(By courtesy of Sulzer Bros. Ltd.)

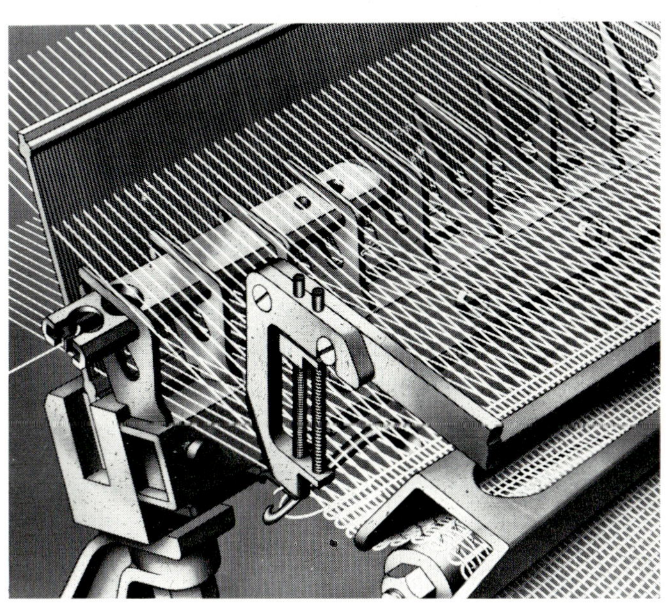

PLATE 36.   SULZER WEFT-INSERTION SYSTEM

(By courtesy of Sulzer Bros. Ltd.)

PLATE 37.   BENTLEY-COTTON AEF FULL-FASHIONED GARMENT KNITTING MACHINE

(By courtesy of the Bentley Engineering Co. Ltd.)

PLATE 38.   BENTLEY STANDARD TC
THREE-FEED FOOTWEAR MACHINE
WITH JACQUARD LINKS-LINKS
PATTERNING

*(By courtesy of Bentley
Engineering Co. Ltd.)*

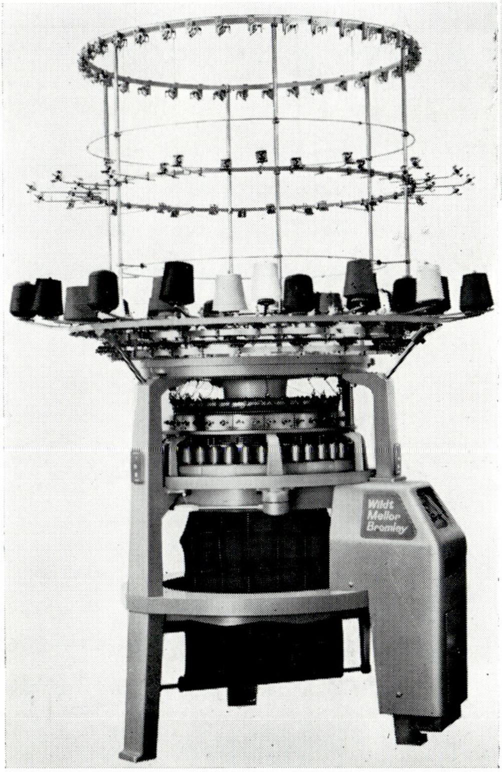

PLATE 39.   WILDT MELLOR
BROMLEY JACQUARD JERSEY
MACHINE

*(By courtesy of Wildt
Mellor Bromley Ltd.)*

PLATE 40.   RASCHEL LATCH-NEEDLE MACHINE
SPECIALLY DESIGNED TO KNIT FABRICS FOR MEN'S SUITINGS

(By courtesy of Karl Mayer
Textilmaschinenfabrik GmbH)

PLATE 41.   PEGG G.S.H. HANK-DYEING MACHINES

(By courtesy of Samuel Pegg & Son Ltd.)

PLATE 42.   LONGCLOSE H.T. PACKAGE-DYEING MACHINES

(By courtesy of Longclose Engineering Co. Ltd.)

PLATE 43.   LONGCLOSE H.T. TOP-DYEING MACHINES

(By courtesy of Longclose Engineering Co. Ltd.)

PLATE 44.   CELCON I CONTROLLER INSTALLED IN A DYEHOUSE

(By courtesy of Courtaulds Ltd.)

PLATE 45.   PEGG HIGH-TEMPERATURE
PRESSURE-DYEING MACHINE, H.T.U.

*(By courtesy of
Samuel Pegg & Son Ltd.)*

PLATE 46.   PEGG WINCH DYEING MACHINE

(By courtesy of Samuel Pegg & Son Ltd.)

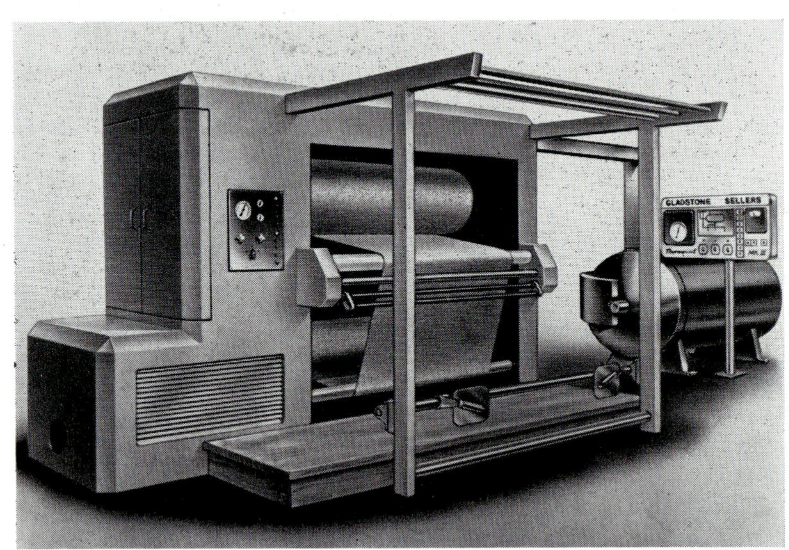

PLATE 47.   GLADSTONE-SELLERS AUTOMATIC THERMOSET
DECATIZING MACHINE

(By courtesy of Sellers & Co. (Huddersfield) Ltd.).

PLATE 48. GORDON WHITELEY TENTER

(By courtesy of E. Gordon Whiteley Ltd.)

PLATE 49. SMITH'S EXPRESS WASHING MACHINE

(By courtesy of F. Smith & Co. (Whitworth) Ltd.)

PLATE 50.   INSTALLATION OF TOMLINSON 'ELECTRO-ZERO' AUTOMATIC
RAISING (NAPPING) MACHINES IN A CANADIAN FACTORY

(*By courtesy of Dominion Dyeing and Printing Co., Drummondville, Quebec.
One of the Viyella International Group of Companies.*)

INDEX